A TASTE FOR PURITY

COLUMBIA STUDIES IN INTERNATIONAL AND GLOBAL HISTORY

COLUMBIA STUDIES IN INTERNATIONAL AND GLOBAL HISTORY

Cemil Aydin, Timothy Nunan, and Dominic Sachsenmaier, Series Editors

This series presents some of the finest and most innovative work coming out of the current landscapes of international and global historical scholarship. Grounded in empirical research, these titles transcend the usual area boundaries and address how history can help us understand contemporary problems, including poverty, inequality, power, political violence, and accountability beyond the nation-state. The series covers processes of flows, exchanges, and entanglements—and moments of blockage, friction, and fracture—not only between "the West" and "the Rest" but also among parts of what has variously been dubbed the "Third World" or the "Global South." Scholarship in international and global history remains indispensable for a better sense of current complex regional and global economic transformations. Such approaches are vital in understanding the making of our present world.

Hayrettin Yücesoy, *Disenchanting the Caliphate: A History of Secular Political Thought in the Early Abbasid Empire*

Anne Irfan, *Refuge and Resistance: Palestinians and the International Refugee System*

Michael Francis Laffan, *Under Empire: Muslim Lives and Loyalties Across the Indian Ocean World, 1775–1945*

Eva-Maria Muschik, *Building States: The United Nations, Development, and Decolonization, 1945–1965*

Jessica Namakkal, *Unsettling Utopia: The Making and Unmaking of French India*

Michael Christopher Low, *Imperial Mecca: Ottoman Arabia and the Indian Ocean Hajj*

Nicole CuUnjieng Aboitiz, *Asian Place, Filipino Nation: A Global Intellectual History of the Philippine Revolution, 1887–1912*

Mona L. Siegel, *Peace on Our Terms: The Global Battle for Women's Rights After the First World War*

Raja Adal, *Beauty in the Age of Empire: Japan, Egypt, and the Global History of Aesthetic Education*

Ulbe Bosma, *The Making of a Periphery: How Island Southeast Asia Became a Mass Exporter of Labor*

Perrin Selcer, *The UN and the Postwar Origins of the Global Environment: From World Community to Spaceship Earth*

Dominic Sachsenmaier, *Global Entanglements of a Man Who Never Traveled: A Seventeenth-Century Chinese Christian and His Conflicted Worlds*

Perin E. Gürel, *The Limits of Westernization: A Cultural History of America in Turkey*

Will Hanley, *Identifying with Nationality: Europeans, Ottomans, and Egyptians in Alexandria*

Simone M. Müller, *Wiring the World: The Social and Cultural Creation of Global Telegraph Networks*

For a complete list of books in the series, please see the Columbia University Press website.

# A Taste for Purity

AN ENTANGLED HISTORY OF VEGETARIANISM

## Julia Hauser

Columbia University Press
*New York*

Columbia University Press
*Publishers Since 1893*
New York   Chichester, West Sussex
cup.columbia.edu
Copyright © 2024 Columbia University Press
All rights reserved

Library of Congress Cataloging-in-Publication Data
Names: Hauser, Julia, author.
Title: A taste for purity : an entangled history of vegetarianism / Julia Hauser.
Description: New York : Columbia University Press, [2023] | Series: Columbia studies in international and global history | Includes bibliographical references and index.
Identifiers: LCCN 2023020389 (print) | LCCN 2023020390 (ebook) |
ISBN 9780231207522 (hardback) | ISBN 9780231207539 (trade paperback) |
ISBN 9780231557009 (ebook)
Subjects: LCSH: Vegetarianism—History.
Classification: LCC TX392 .H353 2023  (print) | LCC TX392 (ebook) |
DDC 613.2/6209—dc23/eng/20230607
LC record available at https://lccn.loc.gov/2023020389
LC ebook record available at https://lccn.loc.gov/2023020390


Cover design: Julia Kushnirsky
Cover image: Heinrich Berghaus, "Nahrungsweise/Volksdichtigkeit,"
from *Physikalischer Atlas*, vol. 7 (Gotha: Perthes, 1848). Photo courtesy of Research Library Gotha.

# CONTENTS

*Introduction*   1

*Chapter One*
In Search of Purity: European Vegetarians and
Their Spheres of Projection   15

*Chapter Two*
Evolution, Cows, and Communalism: Vegetarianism and
the Colonial Encounter in India, ca. 1880–1912   38

*Chapter Three*
The Chicago Effect: Internationalizing Vegetarianism   72

*Chapter Four*
Between Buddha, Gandhi, Sufism, and Militant
Masculinity: Relating to South Asia in Interwar
German and Swiss Vegetarianism   99

*Chapter Five*
Race, Nation, and Peace: (Re-)Internationalizing
Vegetarianism After the Second World War   134

Epilogue    163

ACKNOWLEDGMENTS    173

NOTES    177

BIBLIOGRAPHY    279

INDEX    349

A TASTE FOR PURITY

INTRODUCTION

In 1897, Ravi Varma Press in Ghatkopar, near Bombay, published a print titled "The Cow with 84 Deities." It showed a cow carrying deities in its body, threatened by a huge, dark-skinned monster—part human, part pig, part crocodile—raising a saber menacingly. The monster, dressed in a red loincloth and wearing lots of jewelry, embodies the age of the bloodthirsty goddess Kali. A Brahmin standing immediately in front of the cow begs the monster not to slaughter it, exclaiming that it is "the source of life for everyone." Below the cow, six men seated in four groups receive the cow's milk: three Brahmins, a Parsi, a European, and a Muslim, recognizable by his green stole. The person serving the milk, with noticeably darker skin than the others, wears just a loincloth and red turban. Behind the cow, a semi-nude male figure with long hair raises two verses from the Vedas that extol the virtues of the cow into the sky.

The print is a central source of the cow protection movement that emerged in colonial India in the late nineteenth century, when Muslims began to be characterized as enemies of a desired Hindu nation. The monster, missing from later versions of the print because of British censorship, references Muslims: its jewelry recalls the sumptuous attire of the Mughals, India's Muslim rulers and, from a Hindu nationalist perspective, the subcontinent's first violent colonizers. The saber characterizes it as a meat

FIGURE 0.1. Ravi Varma: "The Cow with Eighty-Four Deities."

FIGURE 0.2. Ludwig Ankenbrand and his fellow travelers, from Walter Hammer, *Dokumente des Vegetarismus* (Leipzig: Vollrath, 1912), n.p.

eater and slaughterer, and its dark skin implies its foreignness. The print was distributed at meetings of cow protection societies that mobilized against cow slaughter and for vegetarianism and that sought supporters among Hindus and sympathizers in other groups—including those Europeans in India who developed an avid interest in vegetarianism in the nineteenth and twentieth centuries.[1]

It was not only Europeans in India who sympathized with vegetarianism in the subcontinent. Members of vegetarian associations in Germany and Britain likewise developed an interest in such practices of abstention in India, with some of them eager to obtain firsthand knowledge. In early 1912, three young heterosexual couples, all vegetarians, set off from Leipzig, intending to travel around the world on foot. A photographer captured them just before their departure. The swastika on the tunic of Ludwig Ankenbrand, the man in the center, reveals the group's spiritual and spatial orientation. The swastika was known at the time as a central symbol of Buddhism but was already used by adherents of the *völkisch* and life reform movements to signify Germanic/Aryan identity.[2] The group planned to visit, inter alia, South Asia and Ceylon, home to a vibrant Buddhist reform movement whose protagonists they hoped to meet in person. Ludwig Ankenbrand was a prominent adherent of the life reform movement in Germany, which tried to address the ills of industrialization, was antivivisection, and focused on natural healing, naturism, teetotalism, vegetarianism, and animal welfare. Ankenbrand characterized Buddhism as the religion most conducive to this agenda. He also considered it the most "Aryan" of religions. Christianity, on the other hand, appeared to him as a "Semitic" religion entangled with materialism and the cruelty that was embodied by meat consumption.[3]

These images capture two facets of what being vegetarian meant in the nineteenth and twentieth centuries. Although Hindu nationalism and Western vegetarian movements may seem like entirely different projects, they were brought closer by a selective yet dynamic knowledge exchange. This book considers these entangled debates on vegetarianism, focusing mainly on the circulation of knowledge between Britain, Germany, South Asia, and the United States. It starts with the beginnings of organized vegetarianism in Europe and the United States in the mid-nineteenth century and goes up to 1957, when the congress of the International Vegetarian Union took place in India for the first time. I show how vegetarianism was connected to seemingly contradictory concerns, including colonialism, race, masculinity, nationalism, internationalism, and anticolonialism—issues related to the ties between humans, not those between humans and animals. This is not to say that vegetarianism in this period was disinterested in animal welfare. This study, however, pays particular attention to the visions for humanity, or specific branches of it, that vegetarians harbored, arguing that their common denominator was a taste for purity.

## SUBJECT AND SCOPE

Along with the expansion of European colonial rule in the second half of the nineteenth century, or so Chris Otter has shown, meat became centrally important to diets worldwide as a signifier of masculinity, strength, good health, and wealth. Agriculture began relying more on exploiting nature and humans on the colonial periphery.[4] New agricultural technologies, including livestock keeping, transport, infrastructure, preservation, and packaging made meat more available and affordable in many parts of the world, with Chicago becoming a major global hub for meatpacking. Yet there were also downsides to these prolonged production chains: livestock diseases, food adulteration, and contamination, as well as abysmal conditions for humans and animals in livestock keeping and meatpacking.[5] As meat became increasingly popular, European and North American workers began to consider regular meat consumption a symbol of wealth worth striving for, and a marker of white racial superiority and masculinity, especially vis-à-vis Chinese migrants who allegedly mainly ate rice.[6] Medicine and the new science of nutrition promoted meat's purported benefits.[7] Nationalists in Japan, where beef consumption was banned until 1872, began touting meat as the food that would give men the strength to defend their nations against colonial powers, pointing out that beef-eating Britain had colonized "vegetarian" India.[8]

But not everyone agreed. From the middle of the nineteenth century onward, an organized vegetarian movement, largely dominated by middle-class white people, emerged in Europe and the United States. They warned of the moral and health risks and the ethical problems of consuming animals. While vegetarian associations were later founded in France or Russia,[9] British and German associations began the movement in Europe and spearheaded it.[10] From the beginning, British vegetarians were in close dialogue with U.S. vegetarians. Their publications took a vivid interest in alimentary cultures in other continents, appropriating and reinterpreting knowledge about alleged dietary patterns elsewhere and arguing that the majority of the world's population ate a vegetarian diet already.[11]

One common reference was the Indian subcontinent. However, Indian society was by no means as uniformly vegetarian as observers in Europe and the United States believed. Those lower in the caste system or outside it, along with Muslims and Christians—collectively a significant part of India's population—often consumed meat. For that reason, orthodox Hindus considered them impure. Some upper-caste Hindus, on the other hand, came to consider eating beef a signifier of modernity.[12] From the late nineteenth century onward, there were heated discussions about the benefits or harmfulness of meat. Some of these debaters—those who wrote and published in English—began using the term "vegetarianism" and citing Western publications on the subject.[13] Many of them were sympathetic to anticolonialism. In order to protect *gau mata* (Mother Cow), the symbol of the nation-to-be, they hoped to rid India of its beef-eating colonizers; not just the British, but also the Muslims, the alleged descendants of the Mughals who had ruled large parts of the subcontinent from the sixteenth century on.[14]

Food in general and vegetarianism in particular are not new fields of research in the humanities and social sciences. From Claude Lévi-Strauss to Mary Douglas and Pierre Bourdieu, anthropologists and sociologists have focused on food as a means of self-fashioning and identity, or as a vehicle of othering, issues that during the past two decades have given rise to the interdisciplinary field of food studies.[15] In food studies and human-animal studies, vegetarianism is often researched from a present-day perspective as a way of alleviating the climate crisis and eradicating hierarchies of species and gender.[16] At times, such studies equate Hinduism with nonviolence, idealizing it as a model for the West—a problematic perspective, as I will show.[17]

Meat abstention and related forms of renunciation in Europe and the United States, on one hand, and those in Asia, on the other, have long been examined separately, thus creating, in the words of Jakob Klein, the impression of "a dichotomy between a 'voluntary' and 'modern' form of vegetarianism located in the West and an 'involuntary' and 'traditional' form of vegetarianism found elsewhere."[18]

Indeed, some works on food in India confirm this view of its alimentary cultures as unchanging.[19] And yet there is a growing body of research on culinary habits under colonial rule in India that emphasizes the alimentary changes brought about by colonialism.[20] Utsa Ray argues that at least for a certain time, members of the Bengali upper class took to meat to underline their modernity.[21] Mrinalini Sinha has shown how the British used the trope of the vegetarian and therefore "effeminate" Bengali to justify colonial rule.[22] Joseph Alter, Parama Roy, and Nico Slate, by contrast, demonstrate that Gandhi used the opposite argument—that vegetarianism could strengthen bodies for the anticolonial struggle.[23] Gandhi is also the only advocate of vegetarianism in India whose contacts with Western vegetarians have been analyzed. Yet in his unconditional support of nonviolence, Gandhi was not necessarily a typical figure. Thus, there needs to be more research on other encounters. Moreover, studies need to focus not only on exchange, but also on what was withheld in these encounters: knowledge that was not communicated, perhaps out of concern that one would lose one's Western allies.

Vegetarianism in the West is largely looked at on the national level.[24] There are numerous studies on vegetarianism in Germany and Switzerland, Britain, and, to a lesser extent, the United States.[25] For Germany, vegetarianism is often examined in the context of the so-called life reform movement (*Lebensreform*), which aimed to comprehensively reform society, starting with the individual.[26] Historians tend to see *Lebensreform* as a movement unique and restricted to Germany and Switzerland, although German and German-speaking protagonists were in close contact with like-minded actors in other European countries as well as overseas, and similar movements existed elsewhere. Most existing studies explore vegetarians' social background; political, medical, and moral motives; and religious outlook,[27] while overlooking their global entanglements. A few studies on the religious aspects of German life reform discuss Asia,[28] but scholars are only beginning to approach this issue in terms of an entangled history.[29]

This book, by contrast, shows that vegetarians in India, Europe, and North America entered into a dynamic exchange of knowledge beginning in the mid-nineteenth century. Vegetarians in the West read and wrote about what appeared to them as age-old and universal vegetarian traditions in South Asia, building new rationales for vegetarianism based on this knowledge. Protagonists from India, on the other hand, employed scientific knowledge produced on vegetarianism in Europe and North America to win back Hindus and others to vegetarianism at a time when colonialism seemed to threaten it. Actors from all sides also engaged in direct contact. Despite these manifold instances of exchange, however, not all knowledge on vegetarianism was communicated, and vegetarianism continued to be embedded in different local contexts.

As this book will point out, motives for vegetarianism differed from those employed today. Vegetarians did not just turn away from meat and other animal foods in recognition of the universal right to life. Beyond this, they often hoped to elevate humankind biologically, intellectually, and morally, a debate that also involved a critical reassessment of masculinity, intimately associated with meat consumption during the nineteenth and twentieth centuries. Many believed that a diet consisting of unprocessed foods and free from meat, fish, and other harmful substances, a diet they deemed natural, would make humans—and particularly men—less hungry for alcohol, sex, and violence, which were seen as leading to biological and moral degeneration. Vegetarians argued that avoiding meat would stifle what they referred to as the "animal within," a shorthand for sexual desire, which they saw as contributing to the degeneration of humankind.[30] While vegetarians were often concerned with animal welfare, many of them had a deeply ambivalent notion of "the animal," as we will see repeatedly in the first four chapters of this book. As an adjective, "animal" signified everything to them that appeared undesirable in humans: lack of reason, cruelty, impulsiveness, and the predominance of sexual desire.

Among Western vegetarians, this kind of hierarchical thinking was reinforced by the encounter with Hindu notions of vegetarianism, which considered meat consumption to lead to impurity and to promote "animal" impulses within humans. Hierarchy was also at the heart of the caste system, where lower-caste individuals, associated with meat consumption, were considered permanently impure, which in turn justified their social exclusion. Whereas studies by Nico Slate or Leela Gandhi have claimed that, for protagonists like Mohandas Karamchand Gandhi, vegetarianism was all about equality, I argue that vegetarians were much preoccupied with hierarchies.

It was not just vegetarians in Europe and North America who were influenced by vegetarianism in India. Influences also went in the other direction. Western rationales for vegetarianism had a major influence on Hindu nationalism, or Hindutva. Previous studies by historians like Kenneth Jones, C. S. Adcock, and others have depicted Hindutva as a self-contained movement, but as my research shows, Hindu nationalists were much inspired by the way vegetarianism was framed in Europe and the United States.[31] At a time when vegetarianism seemed to be on the wane in India, they tried to win back meat-eating Hindus to vegetarianism by drawing on Western scientific arguments for vegetarianism and entering into personal contact with vegetarians from Europe and the United States. Many adherents of Hindutva argued that meat eaters should be fought, if need be with violence. Vegetarians in the West to whom the figure of "the merciful Hindu" (John Oswald) was an epitome of peace often did not realize or understand the actual agendas of their interlocutors in India. They also rarely realized that vegetarianism was an elite phenomenon in India, that foodways in the subcontinent were far more diverse than the habits of upper-caste Hindus might suggest, and that its religious landscape was far more heterogeneous.

As this book will demonstrate, purity was at the heart of vegetarian discourse in India as much as in Europe and the United States. In India, vegetarianism had long been associated with purity, although these traditions were less linear than Western vegetarians believed.[32] Europe and North America, on the other hand, saw the emergence of new religious movements in the nineteenth century, some of them inspired by Asian religions, with many of them characterizing the body as the locus of salvation.[33] In both India and the West, vegetarian bodies were imagined as morally and physically pure, whereas meat eaters were considered to be degenerate. Individual conversions to vegetarianism were imagined as benchmarks on the path toward a new, purer nation, race, or even humankind. Vegetarianism was thus bound up intimately not only with nationalism, but often with eugenics and racism as well. Whereas in India, Muslims were racialized and made the primary targets of such discourse, Jews and other communities imagined as "races" took their place in the West.

This book analyzes the development of vegetarianism by following actors and debates in countries and regions—mainly Germany, Britain, India, and the United States—linked to each other. It looks above all at vegetarians who saw their diet as a means of improving humankind. While it touches upon their ambivalent notion of the animal, it does not delve into the connections between the vegetarian and animal welfare movements. The book also largely leaves out well-researched figures like Gandhi. Finally, socialist and anarchist vegetarianisms do not play a prominent part in this book, as few of the vegetarians examined here were part of these networks. Those branches of the movement merit further research, as their conceptions of humanity might well have been more inclusive and more equal than the ones discussed here.

## APPROACH

This book does not claim to be an exhaustive organizational history of vegetarianism in Germany, Switzerland, Britain, the United States, and South Asia. Instead, it follows the movement of individual actors and organizations involved in entanglements and the knowledge they produced, highlighting mutual influences, but also the fact that knowledge exchange did not necessarily lead to aligned perspectives. In doing so, it takes inspiration from the approach of entangled history, which looks at historical encounters from a perspective that pays attention to all sides involved in such contexts. Rather than assuming that just one side was impacted by such encounters, scholars researching entangled history assume that all of them were impacted and transformed by encounters to such an extent that it is no longer helpful to look at such contexts in terms of binary oppositions or separate national histories.[34] Entangled histories, as Sebastian Conrad and Shalini Randeria underline, are not necessarily comprehensive; in fact, they are often sketchy and incomplete.[35]

Over the past two decades, global history has been acknowledged as a valuable tool for coming to terms with processes that did not just transcend one nation or region but involved actors on different continents.[36] Not all historians championing such approaches employ the term "global," preferring to speak of entangled, connected, or trans-local histories, because the phenomena they study did not necessarily span the whole world.[37] Others have warned that global history could amount to a new colonialism if scholars focus on sources and research in English and only employ European categories.[38] Jean Paul Ghobrial has criticized what he considers global historians' obsessions with "flows" and movement, arguing that actors need to be considered in their respective local contexts.[39] Jeffrey Adelman stresses that global history, when focusing exclusively on movement, risks losing sight of the majority of historical actors: not everyone, after all, was privileged enough to travel.[40] Recently, therefore, global history has also started to study disconnections.[41]

Researching entanglements, after all, does not mean focusing only on congruence or exchange: it also means looking for knowledge that was not shared. To stress "the ambivalences of a history of exchange and interactions," Shalini Randeria coined the concept of *geteilte Geschichten*. Translated into English, *geteilt* means both "shared" and "divided." Randeria and Sebastian Conrad maintain that increased global interactions from the nineteenth century on led not only to shared experiences, but also to an increased desire for distinction, dichotomies, and particularities. A case in point are nationalisms, which emerged parallel, and in response, to economic globalization, global migration, and colonialism. More specifically, Conrad and Randeria apply the shared-divided histories dichotomy to conflictual historical encounters, such as the Herero/Nama genocide perpetrated by German colonial troops, that brought together and at the same time divided the parties involved, creating markedly different perspectives and collective memories of the same event.[42]

The history of vegetarianism can be considered a shared one in that certain bodies of knowledge as well as certain terms—most notably the term "vegetarianism," which was employed not just by Europeans and Americans, but also by English-speaking South Asians—were shared by protagonists in Europe, South Asia, and the United States, some of whom also met in person in and beyond institutionalized contexts. At the same time, as this book will show, it was divided, as vegetarianism continued to carry different social and cultural meanings in each of these contexts, and local actors pursued different political agendas. Partners in a given encounter did not always fully communicate their aims and presumptions. The resulting history is thus also characterized by misunderstanding, ignorance, and friction.[43] In order to highlight these dynamics, I focus not just on knowledge and networks, but also on individual actors, tying this book to research on cultural intermediaries, colonial and non-colonial global lives, as well as men who "never travelled."[44]

Even though the networks I look at, including the Theosophical Society and, later, the International Vegetarian Union, connected actors on three continents and served as important hubs of global debate, the knowledge produced in these contexts was still used to address different issues. Perhaps more importantly, it took on different meanings after traveling across the ocean. Knowledge thus did not have a single center—instead, it was shaped by the place it was formed, the horizons and aspirations of those who formed it, and the places it migrated to.[45]

## SOURCES

This study is based on an extensive array of primary sources, many of them rare and novel. Written in German and English, and to a lesser extent Hindi/Urdu, Arabic, Esperanto, and Persian, these sources were found in archives and libraries in Britain, India, Germany, Austria, the United States, and Lebanon. I also consulted sources from archives and libraries in Switzerland and the Netherlands.

These sources include nineteenth- and twentieth-century treatises on vegetarianism and journals issued by vegetarian societies in Germany, Britain, and the United States, sources from the British colonial administration kept at the British Library, from the National Archives and other archives in India, as well as from the Joseph Regenstein Library at the University of Chicago. I also draw on British and German travelogues to South and West Asia and North Africa, sources related to the World's Columbian Exposition and from Mazdaznan, a cult founded by a German migrant to early twentieth-century Chicago that drew on a variety of religious traditions. Other parts of the book are based on sources relating to new religious movements, including neo-Buddhism, Ahmadiyya Islam and Sufism, texts by German, Swiss, and Persian life reformers, animal welfare activists, Nazi nutritionists, and members of the Esperanto movement. They are complemented by journals from the archives of the Vegetarierunion Deutschlands and its precursor, kept at the archiv für alternatives schrifttum, Duisburg, and the library of Justus Liebig University Gießen. For West Asia, I draw on Arabic sources on Christian Orthodox fasting from the Bibliothèque Orientale, Beirut, and the library of St. John's Theological Institute at the University of Balamand, Lebanon.

Food history, particularly that pertaining to vegetarianism, has long been deemed a trivial subject, a fact that is still mirrored in the jocular bordering on pejorative tone many studies take when considering the subject.[46] Perhaps for this reason, many key sources were not preserved. Moreover, vegetarian organizations generally developed from private initiatives, so their documents rarely found their way into state archives. Most importantly, however, many individuals and organizations were highly reluctant to share their sources. Part of this reluctance, I suspect, might be founded in the uneasy relationship these organizations and individuals have with the problematic tendencies of the vegetarian movement, particularly with regard to racism and colonialism.

## CHAPTER OUTLINE

This book looks at the history of vegetarianism from its beginning as an organized movement in Germany and Britain in the mid-nineteenth century up to the point when India turned from a sphere of projection into an active part of the international community in the 1950s.

In chapter 1, I argue that nineteenth-century Western vegetarians conceived of their national cultures as in decline due to industrialization, urbanization, and the consumption of meat. In their search for purity, they took regions outside industrializing Europe as models. For Britain, it was India, while German vegetarians tended to look toward West Asia and North Africa. British vegetarians extolled the virtues of the "merciful Hindoo," conflating India with Hindu, or more specifically Brahmin, dietary norms, and sometimes approving of the notion of caste. In the German states, vegetarians were fascinated by the trope of the "frugal Oriental," which they saw as a model for Europeans, particularly the working class, to emulate. These alimentary geographies shared a preoccupation with race and the exotic and an ignorance of the connections between vegetarian diets and social inequality.

In chapter 2, I examine how South Asians, Europeans, and occasionally Americans in South Asia in the late 1880s to early 1890s collectively framed vegetarianism. Actors selectively employed Western knowledge to win members of various communities for vegetarianism when it was increasingly questioned as weakening Hindu bodies and as an expression of Brahmin orthodoxy. A shared notion of common "Aryan" descent, and a concomitant sense of racial and cultural superiority, brought Europeans and South Asians closer. This same period saw the emergence of a nationalist, anti-Muslim and anti-British cow protection movement that sought to purify the nation-to-be of its non-Brahmin, meat-eating subjects. Indian protagonists stayed silent on the violent aspects of the cow protection movement in order to keep the sympathies of their European and

INTRODUCTION

American partners, who perceived the subcontinent as the peaceful cradle of vegetarianism.

Chapter 3 looks at the circulation of knowledge about vegetarianism from India to the United States in the context of the World's Columbian Exposition in Chicago. I show that the exposition had a lasting influence on the alternative religious landscape in the United States. It helped yoga, intimately associated with vegetarianism in the minds of many Americans, become popular in the United States; yoga then influenced Mazdaznan, a religious community that tied vegetarianism to racial theory and would soon become influential among vegetarians in Europe. While Mazdaznan appropriated Hindu knowledge extensively, it admitted only a debt to a vaguely defined Orient, as Hindus did not fit into its notions of purity and white supremacy. When Mazdaznan opened a branch in Leipzig in 1907, the knowledge created in the aftermath of the World's Columbian Exposition was further transformed. With the foundation of the International Vegetarian Union in the same city, Leipzig became a center of international organized vegetarianism, albeit initially a Eurocentric one.

In chapter 4, I consider how vegetarianism and the role of all things South Asian changed in interwar Germany and Switzerland by following the trajectories of four actors: Ludwig Ankenbrand, an anti-Semite and adherent of reformist Buddhism; Hossein Kazemzadeh, a Berlin-based Persian Shia Muslim who connected vegetarianism and Sufism while sympathizing with Mazdaznan; Werner Zimmermann from Switzerland, a passionate promoter of Gandhi who nonetheless opposed his restrictive views on sexuality; and Magnus Schwantje, an antiracist, animal welfare activist, and pacifist in contact with a radical Hindu nationalist of whose anti-Muslim ideology Schwantje was unaware. The trajectories of these protagonists illustrate the importance of South Asia in interwar German-speaking vegetarianism and show that while German vegetarians were not interested in Hinduism, they did equate India with nonviolence.

Chapter 5 examines the tensions between nationalism/racism and internationalism in organized vegetarianism after the Second World War. It starts by investigating the activities of Gloria Gasque, the future president of the International Vegetarian Union, in wartime Bombay, where she gained Parsi supporters because of her advocacy of race science and eugenics. The chapter then considers West German vegetarians' attempts to reorganize and re-internationalize German vegetarianism, with race and nation continuing to play a dominant role. Finally, I examine the Fifteenth World Vegetarian Congress, held in India in 1957, as another of vegetarianism's tension points between nationalism and internationalism. Indian protagonists used the conference as a backdrop against which to showcase their country's transition from a sphere of projection for Western vegetarians to an active member of the International Vegetarian Union and a force for peace in the Cold War. At the same time, they were conscious of national goals, defining independent India as an unmistakably Hindu state in which upper-caste norms represented the values to which Muslims, Christians, and lower-caste people had to submit. Even after the formal end of colonial rule in India, and of Nazi rule in Germany, vegetarians were torn between internationalism, on the one hand, and racism and nationalism, on the other. They continued to have, in other words, a taste for purity.

Chapter One

# IN SEARCH OF PURITY

European Vegetarians and Their
Spheres of Projection

Between 1845 and 1848, Heinrich Berghaus, a German geographer, published a comprehensive "physical atlas" with the renowned geography publisher Perthes. Addressing an academic audience, the atlas introduced readers to the world's meteorology, hydrology, geology, botanical and zoological geography, and eventually anthropogeography. A map in the anthropogeographical section (figure 1.1) related population density to foodways.

The map divided the globe into four sections. The sparsely inhabited northern polar regions and the upper parts of the North American and Asian continents were classified as zones whose inhabitants lived solely on meat. The next region had the greatest population density, and its inhabitants supposedly preferred a mixed diet. It encompassed most of the United States of America, Europe, Russia, North Africa, Iran, the northern part of the Arabian Peninsula, South Asia, and Japan. The inhabitants of half of Central and South America, most of the African continent, the southern part of South Asia, Polynesia, and the northern Australia, collectively the second most densely populated regions of the planet, were ascribed a plant-based diet. Chile, Argentina, Tierra del Fuego, South Africa, most of Australia, and New Zealand, low in population density, were referred to as regions whose inhabitants ate a mixed diet.[1] According to this map, therefore,

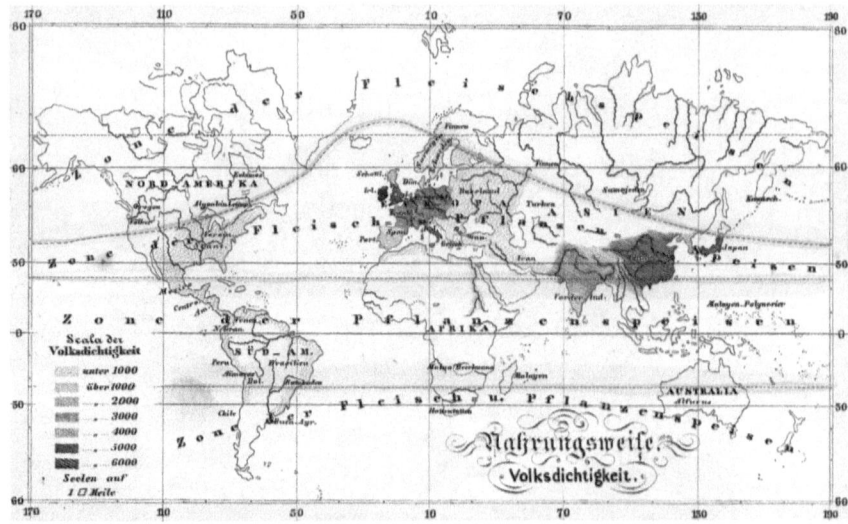

FIGURE 1.1. Heinrich Berghaus, "Nahrungsweise/Volksdichtigkeit." From *Physikalischer Atlas*, vol. 7 (Gotha: Perthes, 1848), n.p. Photo courtesy of Research Library Gotha.

plant-based dishes were consumed in three-quarters of the planet, but exclusively in only one-quarter of it.

Classifying the regions of the world according to the diet allegedly embraced by their respective populations had been a staple element of travelogues since early modern times.[2] Enlightenment philosophers like Montesquieu linked food to climate, bodily constitution, and character.[3] Ethnographic travelers typically inquired into food regimes and agriculture in order to position civilizations on the ladder of progress.[4] A classification of populations according to their alleged foodways had been central to colonial discourse since Europeans arrived in the Americas.[5] And since the late eighteenth century, when the health and growth of a country's population began to be considered a source of power, governments and experts had become increasingly interested in optimizing subjects' diet.[6]

From a present-day perspective, classifying the world by foodways may seem like an oddly static approach as dietary patterns do not just vary within societies, but are in constant change throughout history, and this was especially true in the nineteenth century. After all, it was precisely at this time that the length of food chains increased.[7] More and more foods were traded globally, often because colonies supplied metropoles with food.[8] In conjunction with grain speculation, environmental crises, and economic exploitation, the prolongation of food chains and agricultural transformations often led to scarcity and malnutrition for large parts of the population in colonies.[9]

Yet despite the increasing importance of global trade, the nineteenth century also saw the assertion of distinct national cuisines and hence of the connection between food and identity.[10] Governments and employers increasingly attempted to optimize workers' diets to increase their work capacity. While in the metropole, these concerns translated to attempts at amelioration,[11] they had less benevolent overtones in the colonies, where administrators calculated how much (or rather how little) workers could consume to keep metropolitan budgets low.[12]

Disregarding the inequalities caused by European expansionism, many contemporary observers saw a connection between diet, race, and progress. They put Europeans, whom they judged to be mentally, morally, and physically superior by virtue of their diets, at the apex of this civilizational ladder.[13] This superiority seemed to result from their consumption of meat.[14]

Approaching the world in terms of alimentary geography was also a central aspect of nineteenth-century European vegetarian discourse. But vegetarians were less convinced of Europeans' dietetic superiority. They saw meat's prominence on European menus as a sign of degeneration. Many treatises on vegetarianism contained passages on the world's foodways, and the major journals published by vegetarian associations regularly included articles on this topic. But authors who favored vegetarianism divided the world up quite differently than Berghaus had: from their perspective, the majority of the world's inhabitants already lived on a plant-based diet, and so should the European middle classes, if they wanted to avert their decline. This discourse has generally been overlooked in existing research on vegetarianism. This chapter explores why alimentary geographies took such pride of place in European vegetarian discourse and which regions featured most prominently in them. This will help elucidate why vegetarians began to establish contacts with seemingly like-minded protagonists, for instance in South Asia, which will be looked at more closely in the next chapter.

To understand why alimentary geographies came to play an important role in European vegetarian discourse, it is instructive to consider when, why, and in which social context organized vegetarianism emerged in

Europe. After this brief overview, the chapter looks at the most important points of reference—India, the Ottoman Empire, and Egypt—with the dual aim of understanding why these regions mattered so much to European vegetarians and shedding light on the lacunae in Europeans' perceptions of these societies.

## BEGINNINGS OF ORGANIZED VEGETARIANISM IN BRITAIN AND PRUSSIA

Abstention from meat was debated in Europe well before the nineteenth century. As shown by Tristram Stuart, since the seventeenth century Protestant religious dissenters and philosophers had discussed vegetarianism, referring to ancient Greece and India, as a means of disciplining mind and body.[15] In medicine, its merits had been extolled by Enlightenment physicians such as Christoph Wilhelm Hufeland, whose concept of macrobiotics owed much to his readings of ancient Greek medicine. Eighteenth-century French physicians had considered supposedly vegetarian "primitive people" as reflecting the natural state of humankind. British physicians in India at the end of the eighteenth century had advocated the rejection of meat for the sake of health and longevity. Meat, they all concluded, inflamed the passions, gave rise to harmful processes of putrefaction that weakened the body, and generally rendered humans morally and physically impure.[16]

But although vegetarianism had earlier advocates, it was only in the nineteenth century that it became an organized movement. Industrialization, socioeconomic changes, transformations in human-animal relations, and, finally, the emergence of evangelicalism and its specific approach to alleviating poverty were intimately related to this process.

With the invention of the steam engine, the mechanization of textile production, and the expansion of the mining and metal industries, a development long referred to as the "Industrial Revolution" took off. As Gurminder Bhambra and others have argued, the systematic exploitation of workers and material resources in South Asia, the Caribbean, and Africa and the destruction of previously existing local industries were central to this development.[17] In Britain, factories drew thousands of men, women, and children who worked up to sixteen hours a day. This left them little time for what came to be considered the hallmarks of middle-class existence—family life, education, and church attendance.[18] Low salaries forced workers to live in poor conditions, with whole families sharing one single room and often renting out their only bed to further roommates.[19]

Already dismal, living conditions in the growing industrial regions of Britain and other European countries were aggravated by a series of agrarian crises in the second half of the 1840s. The Irish Potato Famine, possibly caused by manure imported from South America, claimed over a million lives in a country whose poorer inhabits relied almost exclusively on the potato, a tuber brought to Europe in the wake of the Spanish conquest of South America and hailed as a nourishing food for the people during the eighteenth century.[20] The German states, too, saw an agrarian crisis in 1847, one of the factors leading to the revolution of 1848.[21] These agrarian crises made the question of what the lower classes—and indeed the lower middle classes—were to eat more urgent. They may well have been a reason for the growing British interest in vegetarianism in the 1840s. While there was no similar immediate effect in the German states, where the first vegetarian association was founded in 1867, several founders of the German movement had earlier participated in or sympathized with the 1848 revolution.[22]

Soon, workers' living conditions became the object of middle-class concern as self-declared social reformers ventured into the working-class quarters of the city, likening these excursions to expeditions into "darkest Africa."[23] Indeed, race was central to reformers' perception of the poor. Most social reformers argued that it was not economic inequality but immorality that caused working-class misery: workers, at least those classified among the "undeserving poor," were believed to be prone to alcoholism, smoking, and licentiousness.[24] Workers' alleged lifestyle, reformers agreed, damaged not just their own bodies, but those of their children. Vegetarians concurred with these views, but they ascribed workers' low morality not to their inherent proclivities, but rather to the wrong kind of nutrition.[25] Staving off "degeneration" became central to solving the "social question" from the middle of the nineteenth century on.[26] Vegetarians' contribution to this discourse was a diet free of meat, fish, alcohol, tobacco, coffee, and tea, which, they said, would halt racial deterioration.[27]

Industrialization and the wider transformations it entailed did not just affect human lives. Beginning in the nineteenth century, relations in Europe between human beings and animals underwent a number of changes.[28] Meat became more affordable and easier to consume as a result of innovations in agriculture and then in transport and slaughter.[29] In the second half of the century, large-scale abattoirs were established in urban peripheries.[30] Animals from Asia and Africa became objects of curiosity and entertainment for a mass audience in zoos and circuses.[31] Certain kinds of animals became objects of affection,[32] with pets assuming the status almost of family members in many middle-class households.[33] Newly founded associations dedicated themselves to animal welfare.[34] Vegetarianism, at once a symptom of a growing distance between humans and animals and an attempt to bridge this divide, clearly addressed these concerns.[35]

Interactions between protagonists in Britain and the United States suggest that organized vegetarianism emerged around the middle of the nineteenth century. Manchester, where the first vegetarian association was founded, in 1847, was a hub of the Industrial Revolution in a growing empire, a city characterized by impressive warehouses but also abject poverty and squalor, a place where, according to Friedrich Engels, "one may live . . . for years, and go in and out daily without coming into contact with a working people's quarter or even with workers."[36] The Manchester Vegetarian Society was the most influential British voice on vegetarianism well into the late 1880s. After a slump in membership in the late 1860s, member numbers increased steadily, reaching 2,070 in the early 1880s. By the turn of the century, it had almost 6,000 members, including, from the 1850s on, some from India.[37] Soon other British cities had similar societies.

While books on vegetarianism had previously been published in German-speaking regions, with the German democrat Gustav Struve celebrating the abstention from meat in his India-inspired epistolary novel *Mandaras Wanderungen* (Mandara's journeys, published in 1843), it was not until twenty years after vegetarianism's emergence in Britain that it assumed an organized character in Prussia. The impetus came from Eduard Baltzer, pastor of a nonconformist parish in Nordhausen, Thuringia, and a sympathizer with the 1848 revolution, who founded the Verein für Freunde der natürlichen Lebensweise (Association of Friends of Natural Living) in 1867.[38] From 106 members in 1868, its membership rose to 1,572 in 1884; by 1898, it had 1,039 members and associates.[39]

Although vegetarian associations were later founded in many other countries, including France and Russia, Prussia and Britain—two Protestant strongholds—were the most important bases of organized vegetarianism in Europe well into the twentieth century.[40] In both countries, evangelical and other nonconformist communities played prominent roles in vegetarianism's emergence.[41] Conceiving of the social and political crises of the late eighteenth and early nineteenth centuries as essentially moral ones brought on by the abandonment of religion, these communities emphasized individual responsibility. Self-induced personal transformation was imagined as heralding the evolution of society and eventually humankind.

While the theme of social reform through diet was prominent among vegetarians in both German and British contexts, Eva Barlösius argues that German vegetarians from the late 1860s onward were also obsessed with fears of their own downward social and economic mobility. Vegetarianism, which was seen as costing less than a meat-based diet, seemed to offer a solution to the tightening budgets of the middle class while also disciplining those middle-class minds and bodies, an argument also advanced by British vegetarians.[42] While Barlösius is correct to point out the centrality of the economic argument, she ignores vegetarians' ethical and political motives, which they themselves saw as central.

As Corinna Treitel stresses, vegetarianism cannot be pinned down to one political tendency.[43] Nonetheless, most vegetarians subscribed to two aims. Many shared the idea of a "universal brotherhood," as the Manchester Vegetarian Society put it in its bylaws.[44] What precisely was meant by this "universal brotherhood," however, was rarely spelled out explicitly or even coherently. Some included nonhuman animals, others only humans. The brotherhood had the potential to bridge boundaries of gender, class, religions, race, and species. Vegetarianism would free women from long hours in the kitchen, since vegetarian dishes—or so European vegetarians believed—took less time to prepare.[45] Rejecting meat and lavish preparations would make cuisine more frugal, more natural, and purer, thus leveling class-based differences while enabling members of the lower class to spend less on food and invest more in education.[46] Since meat was believed to arouse harmful passions, including a propensity for violence, abstaining from it would end war and violent conquest.[47] Some even argued it would improve Christianity, making it more congruent with religions that apparently did not differentiate between the killing of humans and animals.[48] Notable eighteenth- and nineteenth-century vegetarians in Europe such as John Oswald, Percy Bysshe Shelley, Gustav Struve, or Eduard Baltzer were, therefore, not just nonconformists, but sympathetic to democracy or even socialism, to women's rights, animal welfare, and pacifism, and opposed to monarchy, capitalism, and colonialism.

Whereas the element of equality was a prominent aspect of vegetarian discourse from the outset, there was a second one that counteracted it. Advocates of vegetarianism often argued that abstinence from meat, fish, alcohol, and tobacco would stop meat-induced moral and physical degeneration: abstaining from animal food would make humans purer. Contending that "the human" and "the animal" were opposite categories, the former driven by reason, the latter by instinct, and that the food humans ate had a transformative effect on them, vegetarians underlined that consuming animals unleashed the "animal within" and made humans hungry for sex, violence, and other transgressions.[49] Rejecting meat would thus help individuals—and later, societies—advance to a higher level of civilization, leaving those who still clung to meat consumption on a lower plane.[50] Seeing humans and animals as opposites undermined the idea of a universal brotherhood, or at least qualified it in an important respect: brotherhood, in this context, did not mean equality but rather hierarchy. It also implied a hierarchy between allegedly superior plant eaters and supposedly inferior meat eaters.

Although early vegetarians supported the abolition or mitigation of social hierarchies, their ambivalent attitude toward animals/the animal, and thus their understanding of humans/the human as mentally and morally superior, meant that there was always a political ambiguity in their rationale. By the turn of the twentieth century, as we will see, some vegetarians maintained a hierarchical perspective not just on human-animal relations but on humanity itself, thus turning vegetarianism into an instrument of racial improvement. In India, it helped justify calls for purification in the name of an emerging anticolonial nationalism, triggering violence against allegedly less human communities of meat eaters.

From the beginning, vegetarian journals and periodicals featured articles and digressions on foodways in other parts of the world. Periodicals like the *Vegetarian Messenger* of the Manchester Vegetarian Society and the *Vereins-Blatt für Freunde natürlicher Lebensweise*, the journal of Baltzer's association, reported on the purported diet of the inhabitants of Central and South Africa,[51] of Japan (where beef was indeed prohibited until 1872),[52] Chinese foodways,[53] ancient Greek and Roman diets,[54] contemporary

Mexico and the Andes.⁵⁵ These examples were drawn from a range of sources: encyclopedias, travelogues, but also personal contacts, most often association members who had lived or traveled abroad. Some of these articles discussed the possibilities of founding vegetarian colonies in South America or the Caribbean, which were imagined to be better equipped for growing vegetables than cold and rainy northern Europe.

That slave labor would be part of these utopias was tacitly accepted, or at least not openly criticized. To the contrary, some authors, like Anna Kingsford, a champion of women's rights and animal welfare, praised the strength of enslaved Africans, which, cynically enough, she attributed to their frugal diet.⁵⁶ Vegetarian discourse, therefore, was entangled with racist discourse from the beginning. Though at times critical of the brutality of colonialism, many vegetarians continued to consider race a viable category of distinction and accepted racial divisions of labor. Emerging in Manchester, one of the centers of capitalist industrialization, British vegetarianism was a product not only of industrialization but of what Kris Manjapra, echoing Cedric J. Robinson, terms "racial capitalism"—the racialized division of labor that turned Britain into the world's leading industrial power.⁵⁷

While vegetarians often described supposedly preindustrial societies, their analyses were strangely insensitive to class, never asking why the "frugal" people they praised consumed meat so rarely and focusing on their supposed strength rather than on the illnesses and despair brought on by poverty. In Britain and Germany, vegetarian journals focused on two regions in particular: India, on one hand, and the Ottoman Empire and Egypt, on the other. We will see why vegetarians focused on these regions as emblems of purity and why they characterized them the way they did.

## INDIA IN THE BRITISH VEGETARIAN IMAGINATION

British advocates of a plant-based diet had looked to India as a model since the seventeenth century. From the late eighteenth century on, however, as the East India Company expanded its influence on the subcontinent, these references increased considerably.⁵⁸

Since antiquity, India had been misperceived as a country whose inhabitants abstained from meat. Greek and Roman authors like Porphyry (223–301/304 CE) and Palladius (fourth century CE) had written about the "naked philosophers" or "gymnosophists" of India, ascetics and hereditary priests who rejected meat as part of their habitus. Porphyry and Palladius used the gymnosophists to make a case for vegetarianism, stressing that killing animals for one's physical well-being was morally wrong, physically corrupting, and greedy.[59] Neither author looked at eating habits outside the Brahmin elite.

From the early modern era on, Europeans traveled to India and wrote about it. While, as Tristram Stuart shows, they were more ambivalent than their ancient predecessors, they also focused almost exclusively on Brahmins, whom they identified as non–meat eaters.[60] Europeans praised this rejection of meat even as they condemned Brahmin veneration of animals.[61] Only Jesuit missionaries, here as elsewhere trying to embrace local cultural techniques to increase their chances of converting members of local elites, attempted to understand the logic of local elite foodways, sometimes rejecting meat themselves in order to render themselves acceptable to locals.[62]

When the first anti-meat-consumption treatises appeared in seventeenth- and eighteenth-century Britain, some referenced India directly. As Tristram Stuart argues, many early vegetarians were either political radicals questioning the monarchy, religious nonconformists, or both. Starting in the late eighteenth century, some observers, oblivious to the way vegetarianism reflected social hierarchies on the subcontinent, misread Indian society as more socially equal than European ones.[63]

One of the first British authors to write extensively about vegetarianism in India was Thomas Tryon (1634–1703), an Anabaptist adhering to the teachings of the German Protestant mystic Jakob Böhme.[64] A wealthy merchant of humble origins, Tryon embraced an austere lifestyle. A sojourn in Barbados turned him into a critic of slavery, albeit, as Timothy Morton shows, partly for economic reasons.[65] At the age of twenty-three, Tryon turned to the study of "the art of Medicine improperly called Physick, for Physick implies the whole study of Nature." This study gave him insight into the "Method of God's Government in Nature, and Administration of the World," and convinced him to reject meat, fish, and alcohol, and, sometimes, all animal products and cooked foods.[66]

As other parts of his work suggest, Tryon learned of this diet from books on Arab medicine and ancient Greek philosophy. In his treatise *Averroeana* (1695), the philosopher Ibn Rushd (whom Europeans called Averroës) corresponded about food consumption and ethics with a follower of the Greek philosopher Pythagoras. Both rejected meat, but while Ibn Rushd did so on health grounds, Pythagoras's disciple emphasized ethics, introducing his interlocutor to the teachings of the "Indian Brachmans," who he said stressed the connections among humans, animals, and the universe.[67] This allowed Tryon to claim that these teachings came to India through Pythagoras.[68] By purging this genealogy of non-Christian religion and placing Greek influences as the origin of these arguments, Tryon rendered India far less foreign—an effect augmented by his calling Brahmins, in an echo of ancient Greek authors, "philosophers."[69]

Tryon's writings inspired others, including Benjamin Franklin and Percy Bysshe Shelley, to experiment with vegetarianism. However, it is unclear how much influence he had during his lifetime.[70] A document attached to his autobiography, the rules of a "Society of Clean and Innocent Livers," suggests that Tryon attempted to establish a community of abstainers who eschewed defiling substances, including meat, fish, tobacco, and alcohol, and avoided dining with, sharing dishes with, living with, or marrying "those that eat Flesh or Fish."[71] These prescriptions, which were more extreme than those instituted by the first vegetarian societies, clearly reflected Hindu caste taboos against marrying and dining with those who consumed meat and other foods deemed nonvegetarian.[72]

Whereas Tryon himself had never been to India, the first British author of a treatise on behalf of the rights of animals, John Oswald, served on the subcontinent as a member of the armed forces from 1780 on. He returned to the United Kingdom in 1784, and began writing on political subjects.[73] In 1790, he moved to France, then at the height of the revolution, attending sessions of the National Assembly, editing a monthly journal, and speaking in the Jacobin Club.[74] In 1791, he published *The Cry of Nature, or, An Appeal to Mercy and to Justice on Behalf of the Persecuted Animals*.[75] Arguing that animals had the same right to life as human beings, Oswald's treatise complemented his revolutionary convictions.

The tract framed mercy toward animals as a moral duty exercised through alimentary choices: if human beings abstained from meat and fish, animal suffering would be greatly reduced. Oswald also made economic, physiological, and medical arguments. He described meat as expensive and hence largely unavailable to most European peasants,[76] and said humans were poorly equipped to digest it, as their teeth were too dull and their intestines too sensitive.[77] But his argument was primarily ethical. Consuming meat, or so he warned, "clogs the functions of the soul, and renders the mind material and gross."[78] Moreover, when humans killed animals for food, they were murdering their closest relatives. To support this argument, Oswald pointed to Hindus' supposed treatment of animals—even though his citations included no works on India.

Unlike Tryon, Oswald did not speak of Brahmins, but of a generalized "merciful Hindoo" who supposedly saw "in every creature, a kinsman" and believed that "of all creatures the essence is the same." In Oswald's version of Hinduism, every animal was sacred, as all deities metamorphosed into animals.[79] This supposedly made it impossible for Hindus to accept the Western habit of eating meat: "From our tables turns with abhorrence the tender-hearted Hindoo." To make these views appear less foreign, Oswald added that "Hindus" relied on "arguments independent of mythology" when trying to convert nonvegetarians to vegetarianism. He sometimes drew on Greek mythology to render Hindu concepts intelligible to his European audience: "To [the Hindu] our feasts are the nefarious repasts of Polyphemus."[80]

In order to bolster his argument that these views were not culturally specific, Oswald reminded his audience that butchers were considered to be of "the lowest class of men" in every country.[81] They certainly were in India, where slaughter was usually performed by people of lower caste or non-Hindus—with one notable exception: animal sacrifice, which was generally performed by Brahmins. Oswald, however, skipped over the problem of animal sacrifice, and despite his revolutionary credentials, he took an uncritical view of Hindu hierarchies that assigned those who handled dead animals to the very bottom of society.

In *The Cry of Nature*, former soldier Oswald criticized Europeans' consumption of beef in general, arguing that "from the practice of slaughtering an innocent animal, to the murder of man, the steps are neither many nor remote."[82] A critique of British colonialism in India could be read between the lines, but was not made explicit: Oswald instead turned against the larger ill of human violence in general.

By contrast, George Nicholson, a British printer who also embraced the values of the French Revolution, directly attacked British colonialism in his book *On the Conduct of Man to Inferior Animals*.[83] Published seven years after Oswald's treatise, it was more than just indebted to it: especially in the second edition (1819), Nicholson plagiarized considerable parts of Oswald's text.[84] In passages that he wrote himself, Nicholson praised India as "the only public theatre of tenderness to brutes."[85] He claimed that "the religion of the Hindoos is the most extensive and ancient of all religions now existing," but that conditions in India meant that anything that could be learned about India and Hinduism in Britain came "through very polluted channels."[86] Hindus, he claimed, were doubly oppressed: "The followers of Brama are, for the most part, meek and patient sufferers under savage and bigoted Mahometans; who, in their turn, are oppressed by cruel, tho' not bigoted Christians"—that is, the British.[87] Both oppressors were morally inferior, their cruelty manifest in their consumption of meat.[88] Although Nicholson elsewhere lauded Muslims' gentle treatment of animals, here he focused on their alleged cruelty, quoting a polemical source already cited by Oswald.[89] This ambivalent characterization was consistent with images of Muslims and Islam in British early nineteenth-century radicalism.[90] Nicholson was the first British author writing on vegetarianism who contrasted Brahmins and Muslims as the epitome, respectively, of clemency and cruelty—but by the end of the nineteenth century, this argument was central to the writings of Hindu nationalists.

In the decades to come, Oswald and Nicholson were quoted only sporadically in vegetarian treatises and journals, but their depictions of "the merciful Hindoo" and of India as "the only theatre of tenderness to brutes" were highly influential among British vegetarians. Overall, the violent Muslim disappeared from vegetarian texts, while the "meek Hindu" remained, becoming, in some cases, also strong, energetic, and industrious. Because of their vegetarian nutrition, or so the argument went, Hindus were not just "mild," but singularly hardy and hardworking.

Accordingly, William Alcott, a Connecticut-based physician whose writings had considerable influence on the development of organized vegetarianism in Britain, stressed that India, because of its vegetarianism, could have "outstrip[ped] the other nations of the world in manufactures, and in the arts and sciences," if only the Indian government—presumably Alcott was alluding here to the Mughals, the immediate predecessors of the British—had been less despotic and the Hindu priesthood "more enlightened."[91]

The *Vegetarian Messenger*, the journal of the Manchester Vegetarian Society, continued to refer to Hindus as meek and merciful.[92] In line with the increasing emphasis on efficiency in vegetarian perceptions of India from the 1830s on, it also took up the argument of industry. Characterizing

India as the "land of vegetarianism"[93] with a supposedly unbroken tradition of eschewing meat,[94] the *Messenger* stated that its inhabitants possessed unequalled physical strength.[95] Only rarely did articles or letters to the editor question the idea of homogeneous foodways in India.[96] Authors published in the *Vegetarian Messenger* occasionally intimated that their observations were limited to "the higher caste," but they did not elaborate on the alimentary relevance of caste. When monographs on vegetarianism mentioned caste as a relevant aspect, it was always with approval.

John Smith, author of a vegetarian cookbook and a general treatise on vegetarianism, likewise stressed the physical energy of the "Hindoos," referring to them as "well nourished, athletic, and active."[97] He admitted, however, that this was not true for all Hindus, but merely the upper three of the four "distinct orders or classes" into which they were separated. Those of the fourth "class," or so Smith stated, could eat all kinds of meat except beef, while those below the four groups were not subject to any restrictions. Smith characterized these "lowest classes" as "the most miserable, ill-formed, and indolent portion of the native inhabitants of India," and thus as a stark contrast to their upper-caste compatriots, who were "intelligent, temperament, and virtuous."[98]

Anna Kingsford, a prominent vegetarian, antivivisectionist, and Theosophist, repeated Smith's views in the early 1880s in her treatise *The Perfect Way in Diet*, stating that the three upper castes of Brahmins, Kshatriyas, and Vaishyas abstained from meat for religious reasons. In embracing this argument, Kingsford neglected both internal heterogeneity—among the Kshatriyas, the warrior caste, meat consumption was widespread[99]—and historical change, as will be seen in the next chapter.[100] However, she surpassed Smith's argument, claiming that Buddhists also adhered to strict vegetarianism.[101] Like Oswald and Smith, Kingsford accepted the logic of the caste system, likening the "pariahs" who were outside the system to butchers in Europe, "persons notorious for brutality, coarseness, or love of bloodshed."[102]

Whereas late eighteenth- and early nineteenth-century sources stressed Hindus' allegedly mild and merciful attitude, from the 1830s on authors focused on how vegetarianism gave its adherents greater energy—even if their diets consisted solely of rice. In stressing Hindus' supposed agility, authors may have been reacting to contemporary colonial discourse that justified British rule over India by emphasizing Hindus' supposed inability to defend themselves because of the weakening effects of their rice-based vegetarian diet.¹⁰³

But these vegetarian writers cannot be called anticolonial, as their focus on diet and capacity for physical exertion also emanated from a colonial perspective, measuring humans by their potential for exploitation and doing so based on race.¹⁰⁴ Admittedly, British vegetarians increasingly tried to optimize their own endurance through diet as well, but the dietary suggestions in British vegetarian journals and cookbooks went beyond a diet centered on rice, proposing a varied menu and sometimes rather rich dishes. Even if vegetarian journals criticized the violence of colonialism, they still applied different standards to British and South Asian bodies. While some nineteenth-century vegetarians might have considered themselves universalists, they continued to differentiate along the lines of race.

The image of India presented in British vegetarian sources was a selective one. Most authors did not examine how vegetarianism functioned as a means of social distinction and hierarchy, and those who did approved. But British vegetarians' idealization of India facilitated dialogue between protagonists in the two countries. Many on the Indian side were Brahmins or people embracing Brahmin dietary precepts. This further cemented the dominant image of India in British vegetarian sources, which continued characterizing the country as wholly vegetarian and "the Hindu" as the epitome of mildness.

## A FRUGAL CRESCENT: THE OTTOMAN EMPIRE AND EGYPT IN GERMAN VEGETARIAN DISCOURSE

German authors turned to vegetarianism considerably later than their British peers. While Christoph Martin Hufeland, an Enlightenment physician and dietician, had suggested that a meat-free regime was beneficial at the end of the eighteenth century,¹⁰⁵ the first major German-language work on ethical vegetarianism appeared in the tumultuous period of the early to mid-1840s (*Vormärz*), when German radicals began to call for a unified German nation and for reform if not abolition of the monarchy.¹⁰⁶

Gustav Struve, a radical democrat, lawyer, and writer was a key actor in the 1848 revolution in Baden. Born into a noble family from Livonia, he married Amalie Dusar, a teacher and illegitimate daughter of a military officer. During the revolution, when Struve fought and wrote for democracy and a unified German nation, Amalie supported him while campaigning for women's rights, eventually accompanying him into exile in Switzerland, Britain, and finally the United States.[107] In 1843, Struve published a novel, *Mandaras Wanderungen*, in which he suggested that equality, the key principle of the German nation-to-be, ought to be applied not just across boundaries of class and gender but those of species as well. This novel, largely overlooked by researchers so far, was a major contribution to emerging vegetarian discourse in Germany, and it featured the fascination with Asia that had been present in Europe since the Enlightenment.[108]

*Mandaras Wanderungen* presented an argument for vegetarianism motivated by compassion for nonhuman animals, centering a protagonist from India—an India that conspicuously resembled Germany. Indeed, Struve was the German vegetarian who most stressed this alleged proximity.[109] Well before "Aryanism" was spelled out as the alleged common thread linking high-caste Hindus and Europeans by Indian and European race theorists, Struve, who was interested in phrenology, described his protagonist Mandara as a "tall and slender youth of noble features."[110] Though initially introduced as "exotic-looking," Struve soon described his blue eyes, luscious blond curls, and fair skin.[111] Mandara somehow looks exotic and German at the same time—he even sports the feathered hat that was the symbol of German radical democrats in the *Vormärz*. He travels to Germany on the advice of his future father-in-law in India (a fluent German-speaker) to achieve the maturity required for marriage, but the country brings him death, not marriage.[112] Interned for a lack of papers, Mandara dies in a German prison, having refused the nonvegetarian fare served to him.[113] Before that, he holds up a mirror to German society, which he finds disturbing: people bow to statues of Christ on the cross, punish criminals with the death penalty, and eat the flesh of animals. These customs, or so he tells his interlocutors, are wholly unknown in his native country, India, where no one eats meat,[114] venerates images, or embraces polytheism.[115] When a Jesuit tries to convert him to Christianity, he stresses that he cannot take on a religion that sanctions murder.[116] Animals, according to Mandara, are sentient beings and as such have a right to life. Moreover, human bodies are not equipped to digest the flesh of animals. Even if humans had nothing else to eat, it would be better for them to die than to commit such an injustice.[117]

Struve's book, often dismissed as merely an "entertaining novel" (*Unterhaltungsroman*), has barely been examined by historians.[118] Marc Cluet sees it as bearing the influence of Montesquieu's *Lettres Persanes*, an epistolary novel in which two fictional Persian gentlemen deliver a pungent critique of French society under Louis XV. Cluet argues that Struve might have borrowed the close association between India and Germany from Carl Ritter.[119] Ritter, who was influenced by William Jones's discovery of the common roots of Sanskrit, Greek, and Latin, and the theories of the common descent of Europeans and Indians subsequently put forward by the Schlegel brothers, argued that "Aryans," a term borrowed from the Vedas that initially signified social status rather than linguistic or "racial" identity, invaded Europe from India.[120] Hindu nationalists, through the writings of Max Müller and the members of the Theosophical Society, would soon subscribe to this theory, as Romila Thapar shows. Struve's novel, however, did not meet with any resonance in India.[121]

Struve may also have been indirectly inspired by Hindu reformist discourse, notably the Brahmo Samaj, a religious association founded in Calcutta in 1828, whose publications soon appeared in English. Responding to Christian missionary critiques of Hinduism, the Brahmo Samaj rejected such Hindu traditions as the veneration of images and polytheism while promoting reforms in women's education and the abolition of child marriage and widow immolation (known as sati).[122] Their attitude toward vegetarianism, however, was by no means unanimous. Indeed, one of its founders, Ram Mohun Roy, who, like many Bengali Brahmins, consumed fish, initially argued that the core texts of the Hindu tradition did not mandate strict vegetarianism.[123]

Whether Struve was aware of the Brahmo Samaj's lax attitude toward meat eating or the heterogeneity of what Europeans subsumed under the term "Hinduism" remains unclear.[124] Nonetheless, its stance against the veneration of images and polytheism rendered the Brahmo Samaj close to Protestantism, and hence more sympathetic to Protestant Europeans than less sober Hindu traditions such as bhakti (in which images played a prominent role) or left-handed tantra (in which meat and alcohol were consumed during rituals).[125]

Struve's version of Hinduism was purged of intoxicants, polytheism, and caste. Throughout the book, and much like Oswald, Struve never quoted from Hindu texts such as the Code of Manu, which justified caste hierarchies through diet.[126] Apart from its emphasis on metempsychosis, Struve's Hinduism was a deist religion of reason in which the concept of equality was central.[127] Like Oswald, Struve was a revolutionary who, while ready to take up arms for the cause, considered India the epitome of an equal, nonviolent society. Vegetarianism appeared to both men as the very centerpiece of that peaceful equality.[128]

Struve's eulogy to India, however, was atypical of German vegetarian discourse, which usually focused on the Ottoman Empire and Egypt. In the year *Mandaras Wanderungen* appeared, another radical democrat, Wilhelm Zimmermann, published a utopian vegetarianism treatise, *Die Rückkehr zum Paradies* (The return to paradise), which examined "the chief causes of the physical and moral decline of civilizations, as well as natural remedies to atone for it."[129] Zimmermann was a lawyer and writer who was a member of the short-lived Frankfurt Parliament in 1848. Like Struve, he was inspired by British (as well as French) advocates of vegetarianism.[130]

According to Zimmermann, the decline of civilizations was caused by a change from a plant-based diet to a meat-based one. This unfortunate development had drastic consequences: "The herbivores were destined to preserve the original image of human nature; the carnivores were doomed to decline into animality."[131] To prove the merits of vegetarianism, Zimmermann sought to locate it across the globe. But he did not look for it among urban populations or the German-speaking lower classes: idealization required geographic distance and a "denial of coevalness" (Fabian) as much as a denial of economic inequality.[132] Hence, the ancient Egyptians, the Incas, Hindus, and the inhabitants of the Ottoman Empire and Egypt were his models.[133]

Why did Zimmermann and other contemporary authors use these alimentary geographies? First, and most obviously, they helped to establish a vegetarian diet, a fringe phenomenon in European middle-class society, as the most common dietary regime around the globe. Second, they countered the assault on middle-class habits that vegetarianism represented by resorting to a middle-class value par excellence: education. Finally, they justified an acute critique of European society.

Although Zimmermann's, and other authors', geographical references seemed almost random, certain regions were invoked with particular frequency. Next to India, these were the Ottoman Empire and Egypt.

According to Zimmermann, among the models of vegetarian living were "the Arabs." Clearly referring to Muslim Arabs (and condemning the alleged immoderacy of their Christian neighbors), he argued that Islam's prohibition against alcohol led them to embrace moderate dietary habits as well.[134] Indeed, their important contributions to the cultural heritage of humankind were a direct result of this perceived moderation.[135] In the vegetarian map of the world, the Ottoman Empire and Egypt were perceived as regions where little meat was consumed.

In 1868, the first issue of the periodical published by the Verein für Freunde natürlicher Lebensweise, the first vegetarian association in Prussia, quoted from a paper presented at the local Deutscher Verein by Dr. Wilhelm Reill, a corresponding member of the association and a German physician resident in Cairo. Reill spoke about the foodways embraced by what he referred to as the "common man" of Egypt. After enumerating the various foods and vegetables present on an average Egyptian table—milk, cheese, and butter, eggs, olives, and olive oil—he concluded that "even on this diet people can bear the hardest strains.... The fact that people do not live long is due to other harmful habits."[136]

Even before Reill's report, German clergymen traveling to Ottoman Syria were impressed by the alleged frugality of the region's inhabitants. Boat trips shared with locals offered the pastors the opportunity to see supposedly modest alimentary practices. Theodor Fliedner, a German Protestant clergyman traveling in the 1850s through Greece, the Ottoman Empire, and Egypt, praised "the moderate habits embraced by Turks, Armenians, and lower-class Greeks in dining," saying that during the trip, they "consumed nothing but some raw cucumbers and pumpkins, olives in brine, radish, and particularly ample amounts of leeks, onions, and bread."[137]

The *Vegetarian Messenger* and the *Vereins-Blatt für Freunde natürlicher Lebensweise* regularly reported on the supposedly moderate foodways embraced by the inhabitants of the Ottoman Empire, Greece, and Egypt.[138] A critical look at some of these passages is revealing. None of these observations was made in a domestic setting, and they were limited to lower-class alimentary patterns. These aspects confirm what scholarship on Orientalism and gender has long argued—that Europeans' fantasies about local ways of life largely resulted from the fact that their access to the domestic sphere was limited.[139] Moreover, none of the observers were interested in why the consumption of meat was purportedly lower in these areas than in

Europe. What they emphasized was the supposed effect of meat abstention on physical endurance, gleaned from observations made in public and with a specific social and gendered focus.

## Meat and Meat Abstention in the Ottoman Empire and Egypt

Recent research has tended to question the notion of the Ottoman Empire and Egypt as regions where little meat was consumed. Because of the sources available, much of this research focuses on upper-class cuisine and indeed on pre-Ottoman times. Foodways in Abbasid times, from which date the earliest cookbooks in Arabic, have been amply researched. As these studies emphasize, courtly cuisine did not reject meat; indeed, a meal without meat was not considered a proper one. Meatless fare was for the sick.[140] Ottoman palace cuisine seems to have also valued meat.[141] Meat was of central importance to hospitality, not just in courtly contexts, but also among the Bedouin.[142] Writers like al-Ghazali who were concerned with the ethics of eating enjoined hosts to serve meat to guests.[143]

There is less research on the foodways of the lower classes, but in her recent study of food in medieval Cairo, Paulina Lewicka cautions against considering lower-class cuisine as the precise opposite of courtly fare, suggesting that, despite economic constraints, alimentary norms and ideals embraced by the upper layers of society might have trickled down.[144] The less affluent could buy cheaper cuts of meat in the market, either raw or as part of ready-made dishes.[145] Because lower-class people often lived in crowded conditions and did not necessarily have a kitchen or sufficient fuel at their disposal, the latter might have been an attractive option.[146]

Lower-class diets, then, represented a middle ground, neither strictly vegetarian nor as rich in meat as those of the upper classes. In nineteenth-century Egypt, meat was rarely consumed by the less privileged,[147] and was thus frequently chosen as an item for almsgiving, particularly during Ramadan.[148] In the Ottoman Empire, it was also occasionally served in establishments for the poor.[149] This, however, did not necessarily translate into meat-heavy dishes. Food charities, as Christoph Neumann cautions, seem to have operated on a "hierarchical, generally two-tiered system, with standard fare and luxury fare."[150] Without access to charity, meat might have been less available, particularly in Egypt, where the first half of the nineteenth century was characterized by scarcity caused by a decrease in the animal population.¹⁵¹ A cuisine relying on plant foods was also common for rural regions of the Levant, such as al-Koura, a mountainous region in present-day Lebanon, where inhabitants primarily relied on plant food, including wild plants.¹⁵²

Overall, then, it may be assumed that the cuisine of the less wealthy was not necessarily a meat-free one, but that it featured far less meat than that of the affluent. However, deliberate abstention from meat for ethical reasons was also present. One notable example was Abu al-Ala al-Maarri (973–1057), an agnostic, philosopher, and poet, who rejected not just meat consumption but all animal products—a position on which his contemporaries frequently challenged him.¹⁵³ Meat abstention also played a role in early Sufism. Although the evidence is somewhat ambiguous, and Sufi abstention cannot be equated with the logics of modern-day vegetarianism since its value was spiritual first and foremost, tales about saints like Bishr al-Hāfī and Rabʾia al-ʾAdawīyya mention their reluctance to consume animal fat or meat because of the harm done to fellow creatures and because the substances would interfere with spiritual growth.¹⁵⁴ Meat abstention was also practiced by certain Sufi orders. By the nineteenth century and later, however, Sufi monasteries seem to have abandoned these restrictions.¹⁵⁵

Finally, Orthodox and Coptic Christians, a significant minority in the Ottoman Empire and Egypt, were expected to abstain from meat for part of the year, although there are signs that this practice was on the wane in the second half of the nineteenth century.¹⁵⁶ Fasting, a practice embraced not just in the six weeks preceding Easter but at regular intervals that effectively amounted to half or two-thirds of the year, was based on a reduction of the number of meals, the gradual rejection of animal products (first meat, fish, and butter, then dairy products), oil, and wine, and total fasts on some days.¹⁵⁷

Although probably originally reflecting the limited availability of meat among certain parts of society, the main purpose of fasting was spiritual.¹⁵⁸ Lenten fasting in particular was to bring about *rabīʾ al-nafs*, a "spring of the carnal soul,"¹⁵⁹ as Gerasimos Masarrah, the Greek Orthodox bishop of Beirut, put it poetically in a sermon reproduced in the Greek Orthodox periodical *al-Hadiyya* (published out of Beirut) in 1889.¹⁶⁰ While Protestant missionaries challenged the practice in the late nineteenth century,¹⁶¹ fasting continued to be an aspect of quotidian life and religious practice.¹⁶²

### Reading Foodways in the Middle East

The impact of social status, religious practice, and cultural transformations on the menus of the inhabitants of the Ottoman Empire and Egypt was largely lost on European advocates of vegetarianism. But these views did not just reflect a lack of access to parts of local society—they also served a distinct didactic purpose.

If people able to bear the hardest physical strain could live on a plant-based diet, then surely Europeans could follow their example. European vegetarians characterized this as the ideal diet for all parts of the globe and all classes, particularly the working classes, with whom advocates of vegetarianism were particularly concerned. In their view, the consumption of meat went hand in hand with an increase in thirst, which workers would likely quench with alcohol. Vegetarianism would teach them abstinence and thrift and increase their physical strength, health, and longevity.[163]

In serving as a didactic example to a European middle-class audience able to choose from an increasingly wide range of foods in an age of agricultural and industrial transformation, West Asia and North Africa were not exceptional cases in German- or English-speaking vegetarian periodicals. These journals reported on the foodways embraced in other parts of the globe as well, all in an effort to promote vegetarianism as a healthy choice available to the Western individual, a "technology of the self" that would benefit members of the middle class as well as members of the working class—and thereby regenerate not just individuals, classes, or societies, but European civilization as a whole.

From the beginning, organized vegetarianism embraced a consciously global perspective. Vegetarians were able to assume this perspective because of the knowledge collected in the course of European colonialism, and they used it to make their alimentary choices appear less unusual. Abstaining from meat, after all, was a clear rupture with nineteenth-century middle-class eating habits.

Whereas North Africa and the eastern Mediterranean were prominent in German vegetarian discourse, British vegetarians focused mainly on India or, to be more precise, the figure of the "merciful Hindu," equating Hinduism with Brahmin norms. Nineteenth-century German vegetarian magazines and publications tended to foreground the Ottoman Empire and Egypt rather than India. It is important to note that ideas of alleged racial closeness, which often took the form of the "Aryan myth" (Poliakov), did not play a role in early vegetarian discourse, with the exception of Gustav Struve.[164] Among German vegetarians, India only began to play a more prominent role from the early twentieth century onward, when individual vegetarians traveled to the region or encountered perceptions of it through organizations like the Theosophical Society, and German interest in South Asia increased through figures like Gandhi. Even then, however, as will be seen in chapter 4, German vegetarians focused not on Hinduism but on Buddhism as the allegedly more "Aryan" and more modern religion, idealized by intellectuals like Schopenhauer.

What was conspicuous in both Germany and England was vegetarians' willful blindness to social hierarchies abroad, even as some prominent vegetarians were invested in their abolition in Europe. A rejection of meat in South Asia potentially signified high social status; in the Ottoman Empire and Egypt it reflected the opposite, a difference to which most European vegetarians were oblivious. Others explicitly approved of the fact that vegetarianism in India went along with high social status, whereas the handling of dead animals generally entailed social exclusion.

Vegetarians' stance toward colonialism was also ambivalent. On the one hand, articles on vegetarianism often portrayed European colonial power as cruel and sought to reverse the stereotypes of the weak and effeminate Hindu. On the other, judging bodies by their efficiency reflected a colonial perspective. Even if vegetarians would soon apply the same logic to themselves, they imagined that they would need a more varied and richer diet than that of the prototypical Indian worker, supposedly content with rice alone.

Whereas Western vegetarianism met with little resonance in the eastern Mediterranean and North Africa before the 1920s, it received considerable attention in India—so much so that South Asians began enrolling in the Manchester Vegetarian Society from the late 1850s on. However, these were by no means the only encounters, and they were not just limited to personal contacts. A dynamic exchange of knowledge on vegetarianism started in the 1880s, as we will see in the next chapter.

*Chapter Two*

# EVOLUTION, COWS, AND COMMUNALISM

Vegetarianism and the Colonial Encounter
in India, ca. 1880–1912

In 1893, the National Press of Amritsar published *An Essay on Cows Protection*. Permission to publish the pamphlet had been granted by pandit Jagat Narain, otherwise known as the Go-Savak, or "the servant of the cow." As this epithet suggests, the pandit, the founder of the "Indian Association of Gauraksha Lecturers," agitated on behalf of cow protection as a traveling preacher in Varanasi, Amritsar, and Bihar. He was also associated with the then fairly new Indian National Congress.[1]

Claiming that the essay was by Theo Baness, a Dutch contractor in Amritsar, Narain exhorted "our Mohamedan and Christian friends to peruse impartially and carefully these lines, as they are from the worthy pen of a disinterested and importial [sic] European gentleman."[2] The treatise, in other words, sought to convince its readers of the superiority of Hindu values using the voice of a European author. The author argued that cows provided humans with dairy foods, that cows were crucial to the economy, and, finally, that they were of prime importance in religion. Countering Western notions of hygiene, the author also stressed that cows' dung was a useful building material, fuel, and indeed a purifying agent. Killing cows and eating beef was portrayed not just as harmful to agriculture and an infringement upon religion, but as a danger to human health, as diseases like cholera were allegedly far more frequent among Muslims.[3] The tract made no reference to Western scholarship on and perceptions of cattle.[4]

## EVOLUTION, COWS, AND COMMUNALISM

It is not just the arguments that called into question the pamphlet's supposed European authorship. From the beginning of the British presence in India, if not earlier, Europeans had distinguished themselves by their performative consumption of meat. Colonial authors criticized male Hindus for their supposed lack of masculinity, attributing it to their vegetarian diet. At the same time, more Hindus turned to the consumption of meat to beat the colonizers with their own weapons, or to rebel against religious tradition. Western hotels in India allowed wealthy Hindus to consume meat outside the home.[5] Reacting to these developments, some upper-caste Hindus argued for the virtues of vegetarianism, and some lower-caste Hindus turned to the practice to achieve upward social mobility. Vegetarianism and cow protection became central to an emerging Hindu nationalism, a development that would soon take a militant turn. Finally, late nineteenth-century India became a laboratory for anti-vice movements that were often connected to vegetarianism.

Although it is unlikely that Baness authored the text, given the nature of its arguments, European expatriates and Hindus, Parsis, Jains, and Sikhs repeatedly allied to promote vegetarianism in the subcontinent toward the end of the nineteenth century. They translated or exchanged pertinent literature and sources, formed associations, and lent their expertise to related concerns such as cattle rearing and cow protection.

This chapter examines the cooperation and associations among Europeans and Hindus, Parsis, Jains, and Sikhs that were founded between the beginning of the 1880s and the eve of the First World War in Calcutta, Bombay, and Lahore in an effort to promote vegetarianism. I set out by looking into traditions of abstention in the Indian subcontinent and transformations under colonial rule. I then look at entanglements between the Theosophical Society and the Arya Samaj, two organizations whose members would collaborate in the context of vegetarianism, and the role of Allen Octavian Hume, a British colonial official, in this process. The chapter then moves to an analysis of five self-declared vegetarian organizations in Calcutta, Bombay, Lahore, and Britain, which I situate in emerging debates on the future independent nation and against colonialism. I argue that while most were short-lived, these organizations' concern with vegetarianism tied in with larger debates about cow protection, concepts of the nation, and the legitimacy of colonial rule. The use of scientific arguments for vegetarianism played a crucial role in this context.

These arguments, however, did not replace but rather complemented religious ones.

Cow protection and the ensuing tensions between religious communities in the subcontinent, known as communalism, have long been considered central to the emergence of Hindu nationalism, and are therefore treated as a purely indigenous phenomenon. Kenneth Jones argued that the Arya Samaj, a Hindu revivalist organization, was a driving force in this process.[6] According to Sandria Freitag, the cow served as a sacred symbol that enabled political mobilization against Muslims.[7] Gyanendra Pandey showed that class played a role in communalism, with lower-caste people joining the movement in the hope of achieving upward social mobility.[8] According to Rohit De, cow protection ushered in a new mode of political participation: petitioning.[9]

More recently, the discourse around cow protection has been interpreted as a move toward secularism. Therese O'Toole and Cassie Adcock both contended that cow protection ought not to be seen in terms of religious revival, but rather as evidence of growing secularization.[10] Samiparna Samanta looked at the use of Western knowledge in the context of debates on meat production and consumption, arguing that science came to replace religion as an argument against meat consumption and slaughter.[11] Scholars have only recently questioned this view. Shabnum Tejani, for instance, foregrounds the role of emotions in her analysis of the cow protection movement, showing that religious stereotypes played a central role in political mobilization.[12] Cassie Adcock stresses that scientific arguments were often inseparable from religious ones in debates around cow protection—and that the colonial state supported demands for cow protection by promoting cattle breeding.[13]

In this chapter, I focus on the research on cow protection to argue that in late nineteenth-century India, Europeans and local protagonists engaged in debates on vegetarianism that overlapped with calls for cow protection and the violence connected to it. The sources I examine show that these new debates on vegetarianism and cow protection were not secular in the sense of calling for a total absence of religion. Religious stereotypes continued to play a role and were used to mobilize against certain groups, most of all Muslims, although cow protection also had clear anti-British overtones. Nonetheless, the use of Western science likewise played a prominent role in these debates and therefore in Hindu nationalism. Religion and science, then, rather than being considered mutually exclusive, were in fact complementary. South Asians were not the only ones to receive inspiration from these encounters; rather, knowledge flowed in a circular movement between the parties involved. Thus, Western actors were also influenced by Brahmin cosmology, in which the consumption of animal foods was linked to spiritual and moral regression as well as low social status—a rationale that their South Asian partners used against the meat-eating British colonizers and Muslims.

## TRADITIONS OF ABSTENTION AND CHANGING ALIMENTARY LANDSCAPES

Practices of abstention from meat and other substances had a long history in India, although they were embraced only by certain parts of the population, in this case upper-caste Hindus and Jains. Lower-caste and casteless individuals; tribal people; Muslims, Christians, Jews, and Parsis of all classes; members of the warrior and ruling castes (Rajas and Kshatriyas), and the Kayastha (scribal) caste rarely rejected meat. And even for those who were vegetarians, vegetarianism was "a matter of considerable contestation and of historical and regional variation," as Parama Roy puts it.[14]

In the Vedas (1700–800 BCE), a number of animals were named as legitimate for sacrifice and human consumption, with cow sacrifice accorded an important function.[15] Epics such as the Mahabharata and the Ramayana likewise testify to the prevalence of meat consumption.[16] In Ayurvedic compendia, meat was recommended as a strengthening food or medicine for certain illnesses.[17] In normative writings such as the Code of Manu (Manu Smriti, first century CE), the question of meat consumption was treated more ambivalently. On one hand, the code listed conditions under which ingesting meat was acceptable for Brahmins. On the other, avoiding causing harm to living creatures (*ahiṃsa*) was represented as a cardinal virtue.[18]

Already in the third and fourth century BCE, when Buddhism and Jainism had gained influence in India, animal sacrifices and slaughter were increasingly criticized. Meat was discussed as a food that inflamed the passions and that should be avoided. From then on, *ahimsa* became an ideal among Jains, Buddhists, and Hindus.[19] From the rule of Ashoka (268–232 BCE), who converted to Buddhism and proclaimed laws protecting certain species, Brahmins began to replace meat with dairy and plant-based foods in sacrifice.[20]

Members of the Jain religion were supposed to reject not only meat but also fish and vegetables grown under the surface of the earth, which were considered impure. They also abstained from eggs, honey, fruits whose flesh was interspersed with seeds, and unfiltered water, all of which were thought to contain incipient life. Jains were also enjoined to avoid consuming garlic, onions, ginger, turmeric, and other spices believed to be sexual stimulants.[21]

Most Brahmins no longer consumed meat.[22] Beef in particular became increasingly taboo, with cows venerated as holy animals; in contrast, milk, *dahi* (curd), and ghee (clarified butter), as well as cows' excrement, and especially the mixture of these products (*panchgavya*), came to be considered particularly pure and purifying substances.[23] Because of their high status, dairy products were rarely available to lower-caste and casteless people.[24] Asylums for ill and old cows were established.[25] Although meat was often central to Muslim courtly cuisine, Mughal rule in India did not interrupt these customs. Rulers like Akbar even prohibited cow slaughter.[26] Even before the onset of Mughal rule, legendary figures like the Muslim warrior Ghazi Miyan, later venerated as a saint both by Hindus and Muslims, were praised as protectors of cowherds and their flocks.[27]

Vegetarianism was tied closely to an individual's social rank and age. For male individuals during the first and last stages of their lives, as well as widows, it came to be considered mandatory along with sexual abstinence.[28] Warriors and rulers, on the other hand, who did not lead an ascetic lifestyle, were encouraged to consume meat, or at least not criticized for doing so.[29]

Vegetarianism was inextricably connected to notions of purity. Not only were certain foodstuffs, or combinations of them, considered impure; if individuals from high castes ingested them, they risked becoming impure on a lasting basis. Moreover, pure foods could become impure if they came into contact with even the gaze or shadow of a person of low caste.[30] Lower castes, communities outside the caste system, and members of religions that did not prohibit meat consumption were considered permanently physically and morally impure, or *mleccha*, a term that also meant "foreign."[31] Indeed, from the late nineteenth century on, Hindu nationalists often referred to these groups, particularly Muslims, as not being part of the "Aryan race."[32]

## EVOLUTION, COWS, AND COMMUNALISM

According to the Bhagavad Gita and other texts, Brahmins were entitled to the purest foods. They were not only on top of the alimentary hierarchy, but also the ones who determined what those lower in the hierarchy should eat. Food was considered both an agent of and an obstacle to moral and physical purity. Pure foods helped individuals striving for truth and purity (*sattva*) attain their goals; individuals of pure character in turn preferred pure (*sattvic*) nutrition, a diet ideally characterized by an abundance of dairy products and an absence of meat, fish, garlic, onions, hot spices, and alcohol.[33] Foods deemed pure, most of all dairy, were inaccessible to those on the margins of society. "By the kindness of the Brahmin," as the Code of Manu put it, they had to rely on carrion, stale foods, and leftovers, foods rejected by Brahmins as they were considered impure and sources of *tamas* (inertia, immorality, and darkness).[34]

While the Brahmins were at the top of the alimentary hierarchy, lower-caste people were at its bottom, a status at once justified and reinforced by their diet. Brahmins were supposed to leave food for these lowly creatures on the floor, just as they would for "dogs, . . . dog-cookers, persons with evil diseases, crows and worms."[35] While no sources written by lower-caste people survive from before the twentieth century, later Dalit autobiographies often feature scenes in which Dalits received food scraps thrown from windows or fought with dogs for their meals.[36] These practices rendered them ritually unclean and, along with their occupations and even the alleged smell of their bodies, was seen as justifying their social exclusion and spatial segregation.[37] They formed a considerable part of India's population and workforce, performing essential unfree and unpaid labor such as handling the dead bodies of humans and animals, cleaning latrines, and working the fields. Brahmins, by contrast, were elevated by the vegetarian food they consumed—the pure food they denied to others—thereby cementing social and religious hierarchies.

From the late eighteenth century onward, the cultural meaning of diet in India began to undergo changes in the context of colonial rule. Many British in India not only ostentatiously consumed beef, they also justified British military aggression and rule by saying that Hindus were weak because they rejected meat. In the late nineteenth century, some Indian nationalists borrowed this argument, claiming that meat consumption was necessary to end colonial rule: only meat could endow the nation-to-be with sufficient strength to overcome British domination.[38] Some upper-caste

Hindus openly consumed meat to demonstrate their cosmopolitanism and resentment of Brahmin orthodoxy.[39]

Castes interested in upward social mobility, on the other hand, often turned to vegetarianism, a process M. N. Srinivas termed "Sanskritization."[40] Parts of the emerging nationalist movement also advocated a return to vegetarianism as a way to demonstrate moral superiority over the British and Muslims.[41] They argued that only a pure body, one nourished exclusively by plant and dairy foods, had the health and strength required to topple colonial rule. This nationalist notion of vegetarianism could be accompanied by an espousal of cow protection and support for violence toward those suspected of slaughtering cows and consuming beef, above all Muslims and lower-caste people. But nationalist appeals for cow protection and vegetarianism were also directed against the British colonial administration, which, rejecting intervention in religious affairs, refused to outlaw cow slaughter. Meat eating and abstention remained contentious in India well into the twentieth century.

## THE THEOSOPHICAL SOCIETY AND THE SEARCH FOR AN AUTHENTIC HINDUISM

A small number of Europeans in India chose to abstain from meat, for climate and health-related reasons, religious and spiritual motives, or to win the sympathy of Brahmins and other meat-abstaining groups. Many of these Europeans and their local partners were members of the Theosophical Society, an esoteric organization founded in New York City in 1875 by Helena Petrovna Blavatsky, a Russian noblewoman, and Henry Steel Olcott, a former American military officer.[42]

The Theosophical Society aimed to find the shared message among what it called "World Religions" and their esoteric traditions, among which Olcott and Blavatsky counted Buddhism, Hinduism, Jainism, Zoroastrianism, Christianity, and, to a lesser extent, Judaism and Islam.[43] Theosophists also hoped to reconcile this shared message with spiritism and present-day science, above all evolutionary theory.[44]

Seeing India as the place where most of these religious traditions met, Blavatsky and Olcott moved there in 1879,[45] and they soon attracted the interest of Brahmins, Jains, Buddhists, and Parsis, but hardly any Muslims.[46] By 1891, the society's journal, *The Theosophist*, listed 113 branches across the subcontinent, all headed by Indian members.[47] Alongside texts by European and American authors focusing on science, esotericism, and, occasionally, nutrition, *The Theosophist* also published local authors' translations of religious texts and their articles about questions of religious practice and, occasionally, politics.

Existing research on the Theosophical Society overwhelmingly focuses on its European leaders. Indeed, recent scholarship stresses that Indian members were treated as "subaltern acolytes."[48] Despite Europeans' racist attitudes, however, the Theosophical Society had a considerable number of Indian members on whose knowledge Western theosophists depended. At the same time, these Indian members tried to use the organization to their own ends.

Before moving to India, Olcott and Blavatsky had looked for a guru to acquaint them with the teachings of Hinduism. Eventually they came upon Swami Dayananda Saraswati,[49] the founder of the Arya Samaj, a Hindu reformist organization founded in Bombay the same year as the Theosophical Society.[50] While Blavatsky and Olcott were interested in all religions, Dayananda directed his efforts at reforming Hinduism. He wished to see India transformed into an exclusively Hindu country free from Muslim influences. He even rejected the term "Hinduism" on account of its Arabic/Persian—and therefore Muslim—origin. His organization's name, Arya Samaj, recalled the Aryas, the mythical first conquerors of the subcontinent who had subdued the pagan and allegedly darker-skinned Dravidians and spread their religion through the Vedas.[51]

Literally translated, Arya Samaj means "Society of Nobles," which related to the second aspect of Dayananda's desired reforms: abolishing the caste system and emphasizing that anyone who embraced the right faith and moral precepts could be "noble." Dayananda's aim was to lead Hinduism back to its alleged roots while reforming social and cultural practices like polytheism, image worship, arranged child marriage, widow remarriage, the caste system, and the privileged status of Brahmins as interpreters of Hinduism.[52]

The Arya Samaj welcomed people outside and at the bottom of the caste system and Muslims and Christians into the Hindu fold after a ceremony of purification (*shuddhi*). New members had to maintain a pure lifestyle. Some of the group's leaders wished to tie this to a rejection of meat. Other members took a more liberal stance, leading to a controversy that would split the organization in 1893, with the advocates of meat forming a separate section, the more liberal Meat Party.[53] Believing that British colonial education led to cultural alienation among Hindus, the organization emphasized the importance of providing a modern education that included sciences and foreign languages while still respecting Hinduism.[54]

Dayananda claimed that his reforms were based on the Vedas and other texts he deemed central to Hinduism such as the Code of Manu. It was this seeming traditionalism along with a general interest in racial theory that drew the founders of the Theosophical Society to the Arya Samaj.[55] Dayananda initially accepted them as his disciples, not least because aligning with the Theosophical Society offered him advantages. Unlike Indologists such as Max Müller, the Theosophical Society stressed that the "Aryas" had not come from abroad but were indigenous to India, and that their allegedly superior culture had spread from India to Europe.[56] Recognizing that the Theosophical Society offered a forum for furthering his agenda, Dayananda took the opportunity, publishing, for instance, an article on cow protection in *The Theosophist* in 1880.[57]

Existing research suggests that the two organizations cooperated only briefly.[58] Dayananda cut ties with the Theosophical Society in 1882, characterizing its teachings as a fraud during a public talk in Bombay. Olcott and Blavatsky then distanced themselves from him.[59] As I will show in this chapter, however, individual members and branch organizations of the Arya Samaj and the Theosophical Society continued to cooperate for much longer.

## HINDU NATIONALISM, CULTURAL TRANSLATION, AND COW PROTECTION

From the turn of the 1880s onward, the Arya Sama's attention turned to a central political question of the day: cow slaughter. In Hinduism, cows were considered the holiest of animals.[60] While scholars like Wendy Doniger and Dwijendra Narayan Jha stress the ambivalence of early Hindu sources on the slaughter of cows and beef consumption,[61] nineteenth-century texts and prints insisted on the cow's special status as a central tenet of Hinduism.[62] The Arya Samaj was a central actor in this context, initiating the establishment of the first cow protection society (*gorakshini sabha*), which soon established branches in the North-Western Provinces and Maharashtra.

Interestingly, Indian actors seem to have stayed silent on the issue of cow protection in conversation with their Western supporters; cow protection, after all, was observed carefully by the colonial state, which did not want to get involved in religious matters or nourish violence between Hindus and Muslims. Instead, protagonists, while quoting from religious texts every now and then, stressed the dietetic and moral aspects of vegetarianism in order to make their agenda sound similar to that of their Western partners. There was thus a great degree of silence involved in these alliances. Cow protection, however, was crucial to most of these organizations.

Champions of cow protection scapegoated two groups in particular: Indian Muslims and the British. Indeed, beef consumption among the British in India, including in the British Army, was prolific, even if some physicians warned of the risks of ingesting perishable animal products in tropical climates.[63] Muslims were more likely to consume meat than high-caste Hindus and often insisted on the practice of public slaughter during the Muslim Feast of Sacrifice (Id al-Adha), known as Bakr-Id (Cattle Feast) in India.[64]

Environmental factors aggravated the situation. From the late 1860s on, Bengal was repeatedly hit by the Rinderpest, a disease whose spread was exacerbated, in part, by the increasing distances that cattle were transported by rail. In 1869 alone, the Rinderpest killed 90 percent of cattle in Bengal. Since cattle were indispensable in ploughing the fields, their decrease affected harvests, leading to scarcity and famine.[65]

Dayananda Saraswati followed up the article against cow slaughter he published in *The Theosophist* in 1880 with a treatise in Hindi in 1882.[66] This treatise, *Go Karuna Nidhi* (The ocean of mercy to kine), is well-known, but scholars have failed to notice that its arguments for cow protection resembled those put forward by European vegetarians. Dayananda pointed to economy, stressing that cows' milk and the use of cattle in agriculture nourished far more people than beef. He also drew on comparative anatomy to show that humans, whose teeth resembled that of vegetarian animals, were not meant to consume meat.[67] Dayananda may have been introduced to the work of prominent vegetarian Anna Kingsford, a member of the Theosophical Society in Britain, through Blavatsky and Olcott. Kingsford published her book *The Perfect Way in Diet*, in which she elaborated these arguments, in 1881.[68] Dayananda did not read English, but had a secretary from Bengal to help him with the colonizers' language.[69]

As mentioned, the fact that Dayananda relied chiefly on economic and physiological arguments has caused scholars like Therese O'Toole and C. S. Adcock to consider his treatise an example of a turn toward the secular in cow protection discourse.[70] This is questionable, however, since his tract also tied beef consumption to religion. In a chapter featuring a dialogue between a "Destroyer and ... Preserver of Animals," the preserver of animals was recognizably Hindu, and the destroyer recognizably Muslim.[71] Thus, even though Dayananda drew on Western scientific knowledge, his treatise represents a form of hybrid knowledge—and one in which the idea of religious difference continued to play an important role.

Dayananda's treatise met with considerable approval, leading to the establishment of a cow protection society with local branches that drew up petitions and organized collective action against cow slaughter as well as petitioning the British government for abolishing the practice.[72] Cow protection societies organized public events with traveling preachers advocating for its cause. They raised funds by stressing cow protection as a religious duty and treating the failure to donate as a sin tantamount to eating beef. These funds were used for buying cattle from butchers and cattle fairs and establishing cow shelters (*goshalas*). Societies set up lists of offenses and tribunals, establishing a system of justice that competed with the colonial state.[73] They also pressured Muslims to stop buying and slaughtering cattle and consuming their meat by threatening to boycott their businesses, loot their houses, or kill them—and by calling on Hindus to protect the cow, if need be, with force. Violence against Muslims was common, with eighty-six "riots," as these incidents were referred to in British sources, taking place all over India between 1889 and 1893 according to British reports.[74]

## ALLEN OCTAVIAN HUME: COLONIAL AGRARIAN REFORM AND VEGETARIANISM

Most colonial officials did not react to calls for cow protection. One former official who did was Allan Octavian Hume, formerly the secretary to the Department for Revenue, Agriculture, and Commerce and son of a radical member of Parliament who was a longtime Indian Civil Service employee. As secretary, Hume had spoken in favor of wide-reaching agrarian reforms. His appeal was not necessarily disinterested, however: Hume was convinced that the British would increase their revenue by reforming agriculture.[75]

Hume also stressed that "fill[ing] the stomachs of the people" and offering them "a certain degree of material comfort" was the government's duty, and as such was central to maintaining British rule in India.[76] He argued that the British had ruined the land and pointed out that epidemics and bad nutrition had decreased cattle's capacity for fieldwork. Hume recommended improving cattle breeds and feeding them better, thus foreshadowing the alliance of British agrarian politics and cow protection that, according to C. S. Adcock, started in the early twentieth century.[77] Ultimately, his call for reforms and sharp criticism of existing administrative structures led to his dismissal. In this moment of crisis, around 1880, he turned to Theosophy.[78] He also became a vegetarian.

In a letter to *The Pioneer* summarized in the *Times of India*, Hume called upon the British to stop consuming meat, especially "beef, the worst of all flesh." Yet instead of addressing the political aspect, of which he must have been aware, Hume appealed to his compatriots' self-interest, arguing that in India's hot climate, meat would ruin their health. Using the logic of central Hindu religious texts, Hume warned that meat consumption would lead to "bad spirits, bad tempers, and bad passions."[79] A few months later, the *Times of India*, in the same ironic tone in which it had previously discussed the supposedly eccentric ideas of "A. O. Humebogue,"[80] reported that Hume had applied to the Vegetarian Society in Manchester to start a branch in India.[81] While this branch was never founded, Hume remained in contact with the Vegetarian Society, paying an annual subscription and promising to ensure its participation in the Indian and Colonial Exhibition.[82] Hume became vice president of the Vegetarian Society in 1885, the same year he helped found the Indian National Congress.[83]

Hume's commitment to agrarian reform and vegetarianism was evidently driven by apprehensions that the economic situation of the country might threaten British rule in India. As his biographer Wedderburn mentions, Hume was in contact with gurus who warned him that discontent with British rule was on the rise and revolts were imminent.[84] After retiring from public service, he helped establish the Indian National Congress, which became the engine of anticolonial efforts after the First World War.[85] When the Congress met for the second time in, Calcutta in 1888, Hume stressed the need to improve food security in India.[86]

Hume's interest in vegetarianism thus reflected ideas about agricultural reform and colonial rule in India as much as the Theosophical Society's quest for what it deemed an authentic Hinduism. As the example of Swami Dayananda Saraswati and the contributions of less well-known Indian fellows of the Theosophical Society show, local actors allowed European and American Theosophists to imagine a homogeneous and strictly vegetarian "Hindu" tradition. These local supporters in turn availed themselves of the Theosophical Society as a forum for promoting their own agendas, borrowing arguments of European vegetarian discourse along the way. Their use of scientific arguments, however, did not render their texts free from religion. Indeed, they followed a Brahmin logic by characterizing all meat eaters as impure. Their embrace of Aryanism also rendered meat consumers—Muslims and lower-caste/casteless people—as foreign and culturally, biologically, and morally inferior. In this manner, religious, caste, and racial biases merged in the discourse on vegetarianism and cow protection.

By the late 1880s, Europeans and Hindus, Parsis, Jains, and Sikhs started founding associations explicitly devoted to vegetarianism and carrying the term in their names. These initiatives were all connected to the Theosophical Society, although not organized by it. Most of them tried, with varying degrees of success, to establish contact with British organizations. After the World's Columbian Exposition of 1893, some of these associations also tried to contact like-minded bodies in the United States.

When these organizations managed to establish contacts overseas, it was because of their allegedly shared language and arguments. But achieving this apparent overlap required that other aspects potentially less palatable to European and American audiences—like cow protection and the violence connected to it—be obscured. The knowledge provided through Western contacts, and the hybrid knowledge forged, sometimes with the help of Europeans in India, helped justify aggression against Muslims, lower-caste people, and, finally, British rule in India.

## EVOLUTIONARY THEORY MEETS BRAHMIN COSMOLOGY

Calcutta may well have been the Indian city whose inhabitants consumed the most beef. The winter seat of the British colonial administration, it had the greatest number of Western hotels and clubs, including clubs dedicated to the consumption of beef, the British food par excellence since the late eighteenth century. Beef, however, was not just consumed by the British. Some members of "Young Bengal," a group of radical freethinkers who graduated from Calcutta's Hindu College, as well as other wealthy Hindus intent on flaunting their rejection of traditional values, equated beef consumption with modernity.[87]

From the second half of the nineteenth century, Hindus, Parsis, Jains, and Sikhs, on one hand, and Europeans in India, on the other, began discussing cattle as more than just a food source. According to Samiparna Samanta, the Rinderpest that hit Bengal during the 1860s marked an important turning point,[88] increasing fears of contagion but also concerns for cow protection and animal welfare in general.

It was these concerns—animal welfare and public health—that an organization founded in 1861 by British, Hindu, and some Muslim notables, including Peary Chand Mittra, a writer, member of the Young Bengal group, and president of the Bengal Theosophical Society since 1882, sought to address.[89] The Calcutta Society for the Prevention of Cruelty Against Animals (CSPCA) was associated with the Royal Society for the Prevention of Cruelty Against Animals in Britain. It intervened on behalf of working animals and promoted slaughter reform.[90] Only shortly before its founder's death, in 1880, did the CSPCA address the treatment of milk cattle and milk supply, issuing a "Caution to Milkmen, Cowkeepers, and others" that condemned certain milking practices among *goalas* (cowherds and milkmen).[91] Although slaughter reform and criticism of the *goalas* hinted at both Brahmin priorities and the influence of European humanitarianism, the CSPCA did not openly advocate vegetarianism.[92]

In the second half of the 1880s, Bengal became a hot spot of cow protection.[93] It may have been in this context that the Calcutta Vegetarian Society was inaugurated in March 1887. It existed until at least 1894, bringing together Bengalis and Europeans and operating a journal, *Ahar Tattwa* (True principle of food), that, according to the Bengal Library's catalogue of books published in Bengal, published articles, mostly translations from English, "designed for encouraging vegetarianism and to point out the bad effects of eating meat."[94] Some members of the Calcutta Vegetarian Society were also members of the Theosophical Society, including Leopold Salzer, an Austrian homoeopath who spoke at its inauguration.

Instead of justifying vegetarianism merely in terms of health, Salzer attempted to find scientific and occult rationales for a vegetarian diet.[95] In India, Salzer, apparently a convert to Christianity from Judaism, enjoyed success with a homoeopathic cure for cholera. His practice was initially located in Calcutta's Lal Bazaar, the city's red-light district.[96] Theosophy and homoeopathy brought him into contact with upper-caste Bengalis, with whom he frequently socialized.[97] Although his claim to have a medical degree may have been false, he was familiar with contemporary scientific research and appropriated it to support his theory of psychic powers. In his inauguration speech, Salzer argued that since the human body could no longer be perfected through physical evolution, humans could only advance spiritually. Plant-based food, in his view, was of central importance in this process, as meat negatively affected spiritual progress.[98] Indeed, consuming meat could throw humans back to previous evolutionary stages because animals were lower on the ladder of evolution. By eating meat, humans risked ingesting "all the previous instincts of animal life; a life that is far behind your own, had you even been born a savage or a monkey!"[99]

Salzer's argument echoes ideas of rebirth in the Code of Manu, which, evoking the concept of the three *guṇas*—*sattva, rajas, tamas*—found in the Bhagavad Gita, states, "People of lucidity [*sattva*] become gods, people of energy [*rajas*] become humans, and people of darkness [*tamas*] always become animals."[100] In the Bhagavad Gita, the three temperaments were tied to food preferences and caste, with people of *sattva* equated with Brahmins and characterized as pure, and of *tamas* described as preferring dirty and putrid food (e.g., meat), and being associated with those at the bottom of caste hierarchy. Ultimately, Salzer's argument implied hierarchical relations not just between humans and animals, but between humans and other humans, with meat eaters occupying a lower position on the evolutionary ladder.

Whereas Dayananda Saraswati drew on Western science, Salzer, in a way, took the opposite road. Although he did not cite Hindu religious texts, his work merged evolutionary theory with Brahmin cosmology. His case shows, therefore, that it would be simplistic to speak of a trend toward the secular in knowledge production on vegetarianism in late nineteenth-century India. Instead, while South Asian actors were influenced by Western scientific knowledge (while also drawing on religion), Western protagonists were inspired by Brahmin rationales (while also drawing on science). None of them produced a kind of knowledge that was entirely secular or homogeneous.

Salzer was not primarily concerned with cow protection or animal welfare.[101] Instead, he argued that consuming meat kept humans from achieving spiritual perfection. While his argument was compatible with hierarchic notions embraced in classical Hindu texts, Salzer modernized it via evolutionary theory.[102] As seen above, evolutionary theory had credibility even with anticolonial nationalists and champions of cow protection like Swami Dayananda Saraswati.[103] Salzer's theory of vegetarianism not only suggested that meat eaters were less advanced, indeed less human, than vegetarians; it could also be read as implying that Hindus who had been vegetarian since birth were more spiritually advanced than even those few Europeans who had adopted vegetarianism. As a consequence, Salzer would become an attractive partner for Hindu nationalist protagonists.

## PARSI VEGETARIANISM BETWEEN SOCIAL REFORM AND PURITY

In Bombay, similar attempts were made to found a society for alimentary abstention. Bombay was a center of the textile industry, one of the most important port cities in India, and a hub of regional and international trade.[104] Because of the city's centrality to the textile industry and its drastic social inequality, contemporary sources called it the "Manchester of India."[105] Bombay was hit by frequent epidemics, with the poor suffering most. For these reasons, it became a laboratory of social reform and public health in the latter half of the nineteenth century, with leading industrialists often supporting reform because of their desire to maximize workforce efficiency.[106]

Bombay had significant Jain, Parsi, and Muslim communities.[107] Parsis did not necessarily abstain from meat, but some notable Bombay Parsis came to embrace meat abstention toward the end of the nineteenth century in the context of a reform of Zoroastrianism that aimed to make it align more closely with Brahmin norms. At a time when Hindu nationalism emerged and began to focus on those said to be foreign to the subcontinent, they might have felt pressed to adapt.[108] Bombay was also close to Gujarat, a center of cow protection.[109] The region was also home to a large percentage of India's Jain and Parsi communities, the latter having fled to

Gujarat when they were expelled from the Persian Empire. Even though in the nineteenth century most Parsis lived in Bombay, many still had social and economic ties to Gujarat.[110]

Bombay Parsis were prominent in charity, social reform, and the nationalist movement.[111] Byramji Pandey, a Parsi citizen of Bombay, helped found a vegetarian association there around the turn of the 1890s. In 1884, Pandey ordered publications from the Vegetarian Society in Manchester.[112] Two years later, he told the same organization that he planned to found a "Pure Food and Temperance Society" in Bombay, and he put in a request for the two to affiliate. Pandey even suggested that the Vegetarian Society should adopt the same name, a recommendation his British correspondents declined.[113] The Manchester Vegetarian Society also rejected Panday's request for affiliation, arguing that "the Indian Society is not so organized that we can ask them to affiliate."[114]

Pandey was not discouraged. In 1890, he published a vegetarian cookbook in Gujarati with an appendix containing Western medical opinions on vegetarianism.[115] The next year, the Vegetarian and Natural Living Society opened in Bombay. Among the fourteen members of the board were two Hindus and two British, one of whom was president, but the majority were Parsis.

Board members included Behramji Malabari, a writer, journalist, and prominent opponent of child marriage, and Phirozeshah Mehta, founder of the *Bombay Chronicle* and a member of the Indian National Congress and the Bombay Corporation. The British members were architect David Gostling and his wife, Sarah. They were members of the Fabian Society, authors of economic treatises, and advocates of female education, temperance, anti-vaccination, and homoeopathy. All board members were fellows of the Theosophical Society and committed to social reform.[116] Once officially in existence, the society sought in vain to affiliate with the Vegetarian Federal Union, the union of British and American vegetarian societies.[117]

Much of the history of the Vegetarian and Natural Living Society, including how long it survived, is elusive, but its bylaws, published in English by the J. N. Petit Parsi Orphanage Captain Printing Press, are preserved in the records of the Vegetarian Society. At first glance, the bylaws resemble those of the society's British counterparts. It aimed to recruit a diverse membership in terms of class and to keep membership fees on a sliding scale

EVOLUTION, COWS, AND COMMUNALISM

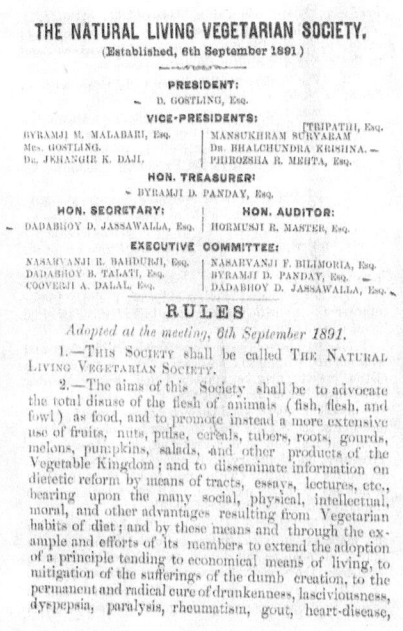

FIGURE 2.1. Frontispiece for *The Natural Living Vegetarian Society (Established, 6th September 1891)* (Bombay: J. N. Petit Parsi Orphanage Captain Printing Press, 1891).

depending on income.[118] Eliminating meat from one's diet, the bylaws suggested, would free up money to spend on educating one's children. Industrialists on the board may also have conceived of vegetarianism, which, as in Britain, entailed rejecting alcohol, as a means of disciplining their lower-caste workforce.[119]

The society's other aims also resembled those of British societies. Members were to "advocate the total disuse of the flesh of animals . . . and to disseminate information on dietetic reform by means of tracts, essays, lectures etc." Vegetarianism was to be propagated as "a principle tending to . . . mitigation of the sufferings of the dumb creation [i.e., animals]," while meat eating was characterized as "barbarous and loathsome."[120] Above all, however, the human body profited from a vegetarian diet, which would "enable . . . the permanent and radical cure of drunkenness, lasciviousness, dyspepsia, paralysis, rheumatism, gout, heart-disease, headache, bowel complaints, hemorrhoids, fevers, epilepsy, and other chronic diseases of the human body and mind."[121] Adopting vegetarianism would contribute "to true civilization, to universal humaneness, and to the increase of human happiness more generally."[122]

While these resembled the health benefits enumerated by vegetarians in Europe, elsewhere in the bylaws there was a slightly different rationale that recommended vegetarianism "because vegetable food is cleaner, purer and more healthful than flesh food, the former being obtainable from first hand, while the latter at best from the second hand, and is often found diseased."[123] This emphasis on touch is reminiscent of Hindu discourses on food purity, a frequent topic in contemporary debates on dairy farming, where authors stressed the supposedly doubtful role of the lower-caste *goalas* (cowherds and milkmen), and their harmful handling of both cows and milk.[124] Uncooked vegetables and grains, on the other hand, were considered foods that could be exchanged over caste boundaries.[125] Linking meat to the spread of disease, however, would have struck a chord with European advocates of public health and social reform.[126] The bylaws of the Natural Living and Vegetarian Society, then, were another example of how secular and religious motives, and Western and South Asian forms of knowledge, were merged in the knowledge produced by the new vegetarian societies.

The Natural Living and Vegetarian Society was founded when members of the Parsi community, like Hindu communities before them, were debating whether their religion needed reform. Perhaps due to Hindu nationalist discussions of cow protection and vegetarianism, animal sacrifice and meat eating came in for criticism.[127] Michael Stausberg argues that these calls for reform often came from Parsis involved with the Theosophical Society, whose Bombay lodge was populated mainly by Parsis.[128] The Vegetarian and Natural Living Society was not the last such Parsi initiative. In 1907, a Parsi Vegetarian and Temperance Society, still in existence today, was established in Bombay.[129] Ervad Phiroze Shahpuri Masani, the cofounder of the society, later described vegetarianism as a core principle of Zoroastrianism.[130] Perhaps subscribing to vegetarianism allowed the Parsi founders of the Vegetarian and Natural Living Society to underscore their alignment with Hindu and European reformist discourse.

The society was founded against the backdrop of a rising mobilization for cow protection and food purity in the city and wider region, as shown by the quarterly catalogues of publications registered in the Bombay Presidency.[131] A cow protection society, whose membership would rise to 1,500 by the early 1890s, was founded in Bombay in 1887. Its president was a Parsi industrialist, Sir Dinshaw Petit. In 1888, a Parsi delegation forwarded a petition to the Government of Bombay, asking it to abolish cow slaughter.[132] At the same time, the group tried to win the support of the Vegetarian Society in Manchester.[133] Another cow protection society, more radical than the first one, was founded in 1893 and petitioned the government in London to expand pastures and stop cow slaughter. Byramji Pandey was involved in one of these cow protection societies.[134] These were not just harmless producers of knowledge. By the very knowledge they produced, they also contributed to an increasingly hostile climate toward nonvegetarian communities. In 1893, this communal violence climaxed, with 70 persons killed, several hundred wounded, and 4 Hindu temples and 2 mosques destroyed. In the wake of these events, cow protection societies disappeared from public view.[135]

## MUSCULAR VEGETARIANISM: THE PUNJAB VEGETARIAN SOCIETY

Paris, August 1930. In his spacious apartment close to the Champs-Elysées, Umrao Singh Sher-Gil of Majithia, dressed only in a dhoti, poses for his camera (figure 2.2). As his note on the image indicates, the photo was taken on the "15th day of fast." Even though he had reduced his weight and was content with the shape of his legs, which "have always been less fat . . . owing to walking exercise, his stomach still "had enough fat for another week's fast at least."[136]

Umrao Singh, sixty years old at the time of his Paris fast, was a Sikh leader from the Punjab.[137] An amateur photographer since his youth, his photos were mainly self-portraits; a practice akin to diary writing, what Foucault calls a "technology of the self."[138] These self-portraits documented his intellectual and physical exertions, but also his self-fashioning across religious, cultural, and possibly gendered boundaries.[139] Umrao Singh, a friend of the poet Muḥammad Iqbal and a scholar of Persian and Arabic as well as Hindu religious texts, was fascinated by physical culture.[140] Well into advanced age, he bicycled and kept in shape with fasting and dietary experiments.[141] An adherent of Tolstoy, he was a strict vegetarian and

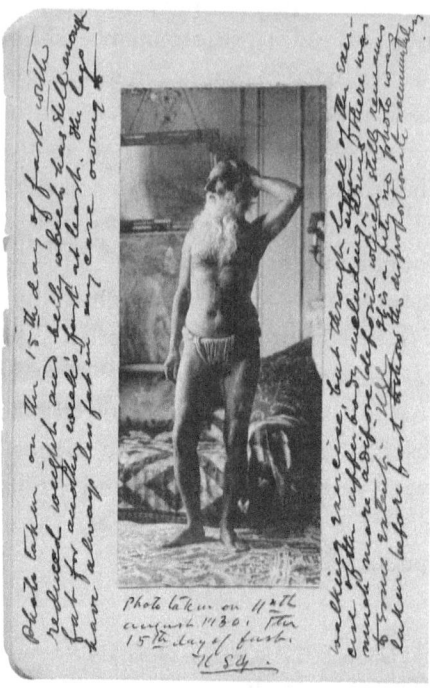

FIGURE 2.2. *After Fifteen Days of Fasting 11*: self-portrait, August 11, 1930, 11 Rue Bassano, Paris, France. Photograph by Umrao Singh Sher-Gil. Photograph courtesy the Estate of Umrao Singh Sher-Gil and PHOTOINK

teetotaler.[142] Umrao Singh was fiercely anti-British, at one time considering membership in the revolutionary Ghadar Party, which aimed to overthrow British rule in India by force.[143] His dietary experiments show the extent to which debates on vegetarianism in an age of growing nationalism in India were entangled with the desire to strengthen the male body, even among the so-called martial races, among whom the British counted the Sikhs first and foremost.[144] As a young man, Umrao Singh was vice president of the Punjab Vegetarian Society, which brought together Western and local dietary conceptions.[145]

The Punjab Vegetarian Society was established in 1889 in Lahore, a city in which the symbols of both British rule and the earlier Mughal reign were tangibly present. Nineteenth-century Lahore, as William Glover put it, was an "urban palimpsest."[146] It had been one of the most magnificent cities of the Mughal Empire, and the British repurposed many important buildings

EVOLUTION, COWS, AND COMMUNALISM

FIGURE 2.3. *Standing with Ankles Crossed*: self-portrait, ca. 1926, place unknown. Photograph by Umrao Singh Sher-Gil. Photograph courtesy the Estate of Umrao Singh Sher-Gil and PHOTOINK

(including Mughal tombs) to use as administrative buildings.[147] Even though Mughal dominance was followed by a brief interlude of Sikh rule, the Mughals and the British shaped the visual aspects of the city—to the chagrin of the burgeoning Hindu nationalist movement.

Durga Prasad, the secretary of the Punjab Vegetarian Society, belonged to the Punjabi middle class. A writer, translator, educator, and Arya Samaj member, he was born into the Kayastha caste, one of the middling castes whose members sought a higher social status during the nineteenth century, a process in which Kayasths came to adopt Brahmin norms like abstention from meat and alcohol.[148] Durga Prasad was also a member, and for some time the president, of the Kayastha Temperance Society, and he became a fellow of the Theosophical Society around 1893.[149]

Established shortly after the Arya Samaj split over the meat question, the Punjab Vegetarian Society's aims included "induc[ing] habits of abstinence

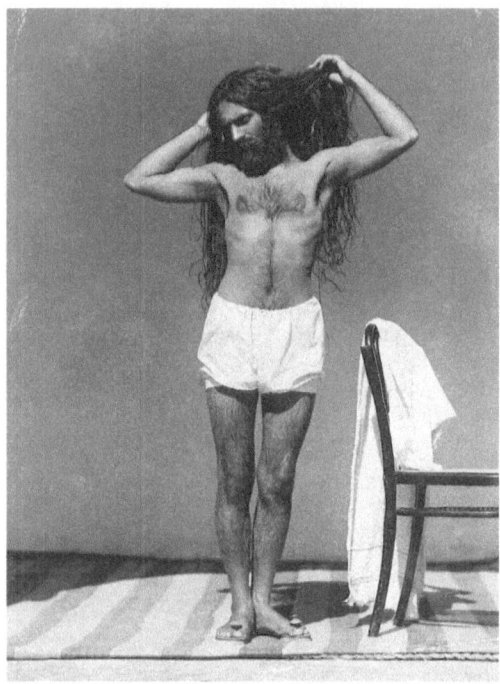

FIGURE 2.4. *After a Bath*: self-portrait, 1904, Lawrence Road house, Lahore, India. Photograph by Umrao Singh Sher-Gil. Photograph courtesy the Estate of Umrao Singh Sher-Gil and PHOTOINK-

from the flesh of animals (fish, flesh, fowl and eggs) as food, . . . promot[ing] the use of fruits, pulse, cereals, vegetables and milk," and advocating "Temperance, Happiness, Longevity, Strength, Humanity, Health, Plenty, Thrift, Peace and Love." Individuals could join the society as subscribers, paying one rupee per year and pledging themselves to a vegetarian diet, or as members, who were obliged to embrace the latter only. Sympathizers, finally, merely encouraged others to abstain from meat without necessarily being fully vegetarian themselves. After a month of abstinence, members received a certificate.[150] The exact number of members remains unknown. At its 1893 anniversary, the society won fifty new subscribers and fifty members who promised to give up meat eating.[151]

The board of the Punjab Vegetarian Society consisted of Arya Samaj members. Most of its presidents and vice presidents, on the other hand, came from outside, reflecting Durga Prasad's extensive correspondence

EVOLUTION, COWS, AND COMMUNALISM

FIGURE 2.5. *Study in a Vase*: self-portrait, February 9, 1892, Lawrence Road house, Lahore, India. Photograph by Umrao Singh Sher-Gil. Photograph courtesy the Estate of Umrao Singh Sher-Gil and PHOTOINK

networks with partners in Britain and the United States. Leopold Salzer, who spoke at the inauguration of the Calcutta Vegetarian Society, was co-opted as president, and Allan Octavian Hume became its vice president. Later, the society added additional vice presidents, including David and Sarah Gostling of the Bombay Vegetarian and Natural Living Society; Henrietta Muller, a British feminist, educator, and fellow of the Theosophical Society; Umrao Singh Sher-Gil; Josiah Oldfield of the London Vegetarian Society; and John Harvey Kellogg, the famous U.S. vegetarian, dietician, and physician.[152] On paper, the Punjab Vegetarian Society was thus far more cosmopolitan than the Bombay Vegetarian and Natural Living Society. In practice, however, it is unclear to what extent these vice presidents were actively involved in the work of the association: most of them were clearly too far away to be of any practical help. Umrao Singh Sher-Gil, however, is mentioned as someone who regularly made generous donations to the society, and who also helped it expand its knowledge of vegetarianism through his dietetic experiments and his "vast" knowledge of vegetarian books.[153]

Most likely, appointing prominent advocates of vegetarianism as vice presidents was intended to increase the renown of the Punjab Vegetarian Society, as well as its financial support. Durga Prasad contacted the Vegetarian Society early on to report on the success of his initiative. He claimed that this success stemmed from the fact that the Punjab Vegetarian Society had borrowed its arguments for vegetarianism from the organization in Manchester.[154] U.S. contacts may have been facilitated through the World's Columbian Exposition of 1893 in Chicago, which built interest in "Indian spirituality," and which was attended by two Arya Samaj members from the Punjab. Kellogg congratulated Durga Prasad for establishing his "little paper," *The Harbinger*, and praised him for "organizing so many vegetarian societies in your country."[155] He encouraged Durga Prasad to collect and publish passages from the Vedas in favor of a vegetarian diet.[156] Oldfield and Kellogg did not just send their own publications to Lahore: they also received copies of *The Harbinger* and reviewed them in their papers.[157]

In *The Harbinger*, which appeared from about 1891 to at least 1900, mostly in English, the Punjab society claimed to advocate "Vegetarianism, Temperance, Female Rights, Hygiene, Philanthropy, Aryan Philosophy, Psychic Development by Yoga System, Commerce, Manufacture, Fine Arts, Scientific Study, Agriculture, Social Reform, Sanskrit Study."[158] The society's publications profited from Durga Prasad's extensive networks and

FIGURE 2.6. Title vignette of *The Harbinger*.

borrowed freely from vegetarian periodicals in Europe and the United States, just as the journal of the Calcutta Vegetarian Society had done. Summarizing and commenting on articles from Western vegetarian and medical magazines helped Durga Prasad give vegetarianism a scientific and thus a modern valence. He presented it as corresponding to the laws of nature rather than an inherited cultural practice to make it more popular among Hindus, particularly members and students of the Arya Samaj.[159]

Nonetheless, *The Harbinger*'s rationale for vegetarianism was neither entirely Western nor secular. Some articles merged Western scientific arguments with religious discourse, as was the case, for instance, in a series of articles by Arya Samaj member Pandit Khunni Lal Shastri titled "Doshkal Charya." Published in both Sanskrit and in English translation under the title "Natural Living,"[160] the articles discussed purity, first taking up water, which Hindu notions of purity saw as one of the most easily polluted substances.[161] Khunni Lal Shastri described how to use herbs, filters, metal, and wood to purify water, concluding by saying that boiling water, as was common in the West, would also purify.[162] From a European or American perspective, the series dealt with public health, though its title, "Natural Living," was couched in the idiom of life reform. From a Hindu perspective, the articles dealt with ritual purity.

*The Harbinger* also featured a regular column called "Sacred Authorities for Vegetarianism" that juxtaposed quotes from the Vedas, the Mahabharata, and the Code of Manu with passages from the Bible and the Zend-Avesta, the Zoroastrian holy book.[163] These passages were brief enough to be easily learned by heart, and they might have been intended to help Punjab Vegetarian Society members publicly promote vegetarianism, as stipulated in the association's bylaws.[164]

Several articles alluded to the special status of the cow in Hinduism, underlining its maltreatment at the hands of Muslims and the British—but they never discussed the militancy of the cow protection movement, which included riots, pressuring of the local Hindu population, and violence against Muslims. Nonetheless, the tone of the articles was noticeably nationalist. Accordingly, Durga Prasad reported on penalties for selling adulterated milk in Britain and suggested similar measures for India.[165] An abstract of an article from the *Animals' Friend* introduced readers to the Duchess of Hamilton, a British animal welfare activist, calling her "a devoted friend of cows" and adding that such kindness toward animals was rare among the British. Commenting on the excerpt, Durga Prasad presented the duchess as a model for Indian women, likening her to Yashodha, Krishna's stepmother, who had trained the "divine hero" as a cowherd.[166] If they took to milking cows, or so the brief article suggested, Indian women would strengthen not just their own body but also that of the (Hindu) nation at large.[167] In this manner, Durga Prasad drew an analogy between the female body, the body of the nation, and the body of the cow as *gau mata* (mother cow), thereby embracing a leitmotif of Hindu nationalist discourse.[168] Brief reports on the sale and slaughter of cows on the Muslim holiday of Id al-Adha, finally, had explicitly anti-Muslim overtones: Muslims appeared as a threat not just to Hindus, but to social peace more generally.[169]

In line with these Hindu nationalist positions and in opposition to British colonial stereotypes of the weak Hindu, the Punjab Vegetarian Society represented vegetarianism as the path to male strength and courage, indeed as something that could be used in the service of nationalism. To celebrate the society's second anniversary, Durga Prasad read a paper by Leopold Salzer, "Vegetarianism, Pure and Simple," which presented Salzer's argument that meat rendered humans spiritually insensitive, thus animalizing them.[170] Another paper challenged the apparent nexus between meat eating and hegemonial masculinity, arguing that vegetarians were as brave as meat eaters.[171] The third anniversary was celebrated with a speech on vegetarianism and physical culture that again addressed the connection between vegetarianism and an alleged lack of masculinity that was so prominent in colonial discourse. It also featured public conversions to vegetarianism. The fourth anniversary was celebrated not just with the usual procession and public discussion, but with a demonstration of Sikh martial arts.[172] On other occasions, the members of the society marched through the central bazaars and streets of Lahore, singing militant "vegetarian hymns" composed specifically for the society, including this one by a Parsi author, Pestonji Sorabji Hormudji:[173]

> In Vegetists' battle
> Will only prevail
> When daily march onward
> We never shall fail

With an eye ever open
A tongue that's not dumb
And a heart that will never
To sorrow, succumb
We'll battle and conquer
Let thousands assail!
We are mighty and strong
So never shall fail![174]

While the hymn did not spell out who the opponent "in vegetists' battle" is, it seems likely that it alluded to British and Muslim populations in India. Quite possibly the members of the society stopped in front of mosques when singing hymns, thus symbolically claiming ownership of Muslim sites of prayer, a strategy that often preceded acts of physical violence and was frequently employed on major Hindu holidays.[175] Even though Durga Prasad stressed that the Punjab Vegetarian Society was not driven by religious bias, asking for donations in order to acquire a location not associated with any religious body and emphasizing that his association was ready to assist "all religions and all other organizations that have the good of God's creatures for their aims and objects," and although the society's vice presidents included Umrao Singh Sher-Gil, who was on friendly terms with Indian Muslim intellectuals, the Punjab Vegetarian Society clearly positioned itself in the Hindu nationalist field.[176] Having written a number of polemical theological treatises, its secretary, Durga Prasad, regularly went on religious tours as a preacher, inter alia on behalf of cow protection.[177] This, at any rate, was the context in which the British police monitored the Punjab Vegetarian Society, according to the available reports.[178] Establishing contacts abroad may thus have been intended not just to increase the society's renown but also to render it less suspicious to British authorities in India.

In Britain, the Punjab Vegetarian Society met with far greater resonance than had its Calcutta or Bombay counterparts, almost certainly because of the energetic campaigning of Durga Prasad. While *The Harbinger* (which the Manchester Vegetarian Society seems to have received) was relatively silent on Hindu-Muslim tensions and violence, its avid use of Western vegetarian discourse suggested a congruence of motives.[179] Around 1896, the Punjab society obtained affiliation with the Vegetarian Federal Union, the British and American union of vegetarian societies.[180]

## DELEGITIMIZING COLONIAL RULE

Around the time he corresponded with Durga Prasad, Josiah Oldfield of the London Vegetarian Society joined another British group advocating vegetarianism: the Order of the Golden Age. Founded in 1896, the group sought exchange with partners in India, influencing the establishment of another new vegetarian association in the subcontinent, the Bombay Humanitarian League (discussed later in this chapter). The order promoted vegetarianism "as the prevention of disease, a practical remedy for physical and moral deterioration, and an efficacious way of lessening human suffering, and the most essential and valuable means of aiding spiritual development."[181] It was chaired by prominent clergymen, physicians, and Oxbridge graduates, including tennis champion Eustace Miles, Sidney H. Beard, a man of private means and a philanthropist, and Oldfield himself.[182]

The Order of the Golden Age published and sold books and leaflets supporting vegetarianism and animal welfare and inveighing against vivisection, as well as self-help books on spirituality and the exigencies of modern urban life.[183] Its journal, the *Herald of the Golden Age and British Health Review*, also addressed these issues.

The order hoped to work toward "a coming Era of peace and happiness, of national and individual health, of systematic physical and spiritual culture, of kindness, unity, and goodwill"—in other words, the golden age its name promised.[184] Members advocated a renewal of Christianity, arguing that the killing of animals could not be reconciled with its claim to be a religion of peace. Since the Church of England was not bothered by this contradiction, this renewal would take place outside the church,[185] thus creating a Christian religion that could win the trust of Buddhist and Hindus, and eventually convert them.[186] The Order of the Golden Age aimed at bringing about a renaissance of Christianity and vegetarianism across the world.

The order's publications frequently represented Hindus as morally and physically superior to meat-eating Europeans. Interestingly, at least some of its members knew that not everyone in India was vegetarian, as evidenced by a publication by John Todd-Ferrier, a member of the order, in which he described the New Man of the future, purified by vegetarianism, as a member of the "Highest Caste, the Spiritual Priesthood, the Oligarchy of God," while depicting meat eaters as the "lowest caste," linked to the body and "animal desires."[187]

India was more than just a distant fantasy to members of the Order of the Golden Age. Oldfield was in contact with both Gandhi and Trimbakrai Desai from Bombay, a former student of medicine in London and, like Gandhi, a member of the London Vegetarian Society.[188] Another board member, Sir William Earnshaw Cooper, had owned a company in Cawnpore and had been a member of the Chamber of Commerce of the North-Western Provinces and the Legislative Council from 1889 to 1900.[189] Already in 1899, the organization claimed to have "representative Members in twenty-two Countries and Colonies." Due to the contacts of the British members of the order, South Asian partners would soon join this list.[190]

Josiah Oldfield went on a lecture tour to India in 1902, visiting Lahore, Ahmedabad, Agra, and Bombay. In Ahmedabad, he gave a talk on "Caste in Relation to Diet"; in Bombay, he addressed the Jain Association.[191] That same year, the *Herald of the Golden Age* made its first explicit mention of its connections to India in the person of a "local councillor," Labshanker Laxmidas, a Brahmin from the Muslim-ruled Princely state of Junagadh, whom it described as "Our Indian Pioneer."[192] Laxmidas gave public presentations on the Order of the Golden Age and had articles about it translated into different local languages, publishing them in the press or as leaflets.[193] N. F. Billimoria, a Parsi notable, and Lalubhai Gulabchand Jhaveri, a Jain jeweler, both from Bombay, were also members of the order. In 1911, Jhaveri ordered and distributed six hundred thousand copies of its *Testimony of Science in Favour of a Natural and Vegetarian Diet*, a collection of statements by prominent scientists and European and American advocates of vegetarianism.[194]

The previous year, Jhaveri, encouraged by Labshankar Laxmidas, had founded an association of his own, the Bombay Humanitarian Fund (later to be named the Bombay Humanitarian League).[195] The fund's first president was Benjamin Guy Horniman, a well-known newspaper editor, colonial critic, and vegetarian; he stepped down in 1919 when he was exiled from India for his criticism of British colonial policy.[196] As its Hindi name implied, the aim of the association, which became a foundation in

1918, was to spread knowledge about how to improve the conditions of living beings.[197] Its bylaws were taken almost verbatim from those of the Order of the Golden Age. Vegetarianism, or rather "a natural and hygienic dietary," was recommended as "preventive of disease," a "practical remedy for physical and moral degeneration," and an "efficacious way of lessening human suffering and sub-human pain," with "sub-human" here referring to animals. Like the Order of the Golden Age, the Bombay Humanitarian Fund had a utopian perspective; its bylaws evoked the "great ideal ... of [a] coming era of peace," "physical and spiritual culture," and "kindness, unity and goodwill." As a third major aim, the bylaws specified "deliver[ing] the animal creation from oppression," by, among other methods, spreading the notion of "universal kinship."[198] More than the Order of the Golden Age or any of the organizations discussed thus far, the Bombay Humanitarian Fund embraced animal welfare and promoted the use of Western humanitarian and (popular) scientific arguments from disciplines such as anthropology, medicine, and the science of nutrition.

Starting in 1912, the association organized regular essay competitions on topics related to animal welfare and vegetarianism. Participants from all over India were provided with publications by the Order of the Golden Age, the London Vegetarian Society, the American Humane Association, and other organizations, including Beard's *Testimony of Science*, and the essays were supposed to refer to these publications.[199]

The essays were judged by a jury composed of Europeans, Americans, and Indians.[200] Entrants—initially only university graduates—belonged to the middle and upper classes, as did jury members.[201] Jurors, awardees, and funders had another trait in common: they were all Jains, Parsis, Hindus, or, occasionally, Christians. What they were not was Muslim.

The prize-winning essays from the 1913 competition were collected and published as *Essays on the Advantages of a Vegetarian Diet*, which offers a glimpse into the perspectives on vegetarianism championed by the Bombay Humanitarian Fund. The essays reflect the influence of European and American vegetarian organizations, including the Order of the Golden Age.[202] Each of the authors (including a former prime minister of a princely state, a pandit, a headmaster, and a female physician) used information from the science of nutrition, talking about calories, proteins, carbohydrates, and lipids.[203] They discussed recent studies on such subjects as daily protein requirements.[204] At the same time, however, they argued that lay knowledge ought to be given the same weight as its scientific counterpart.[205] Some authors distanced themselves from Western scientific ideas about the proper amount of protein, dairy, or legumes in a vegetarian diet,[206] or whether cooking was necessary to safeguard purity. Some vegetarians in Europe had begun stressing the value of raw foods, whereas cooking seemed advisable from a Brahmin perspective to ensure purity.[207]

The authors agreed that meat posed health risks, mentioning cancer, rheumatism, "ovarian disease," and leprosy as possible consequences of eating meat.[208] Moreover, meat caused visible degeneration and shortened human lives.[209] Some authors underlined the alleged inexpensiveness of a plant-based diet, claiming that it could level social hierarchies by allowing the poor to spend more on education, thus increasing their children's cultural and social capital.[210]

Above all, however, the contest winners argued that vegetarian nutrition was "more hygienic," and that animal protein was impure.[211] In doing so, they cited not only Western science but also the Code of Manu and the Bhagavad Gita to show that alimentary choices affected character and social status: "The *tamasas* [ignorant]—low in the grade of civilization—eat such food as is stale, putrid and corrupt—foods which are leavings [of others] and filthy," or, as the Bhagavad Gita put it, "food dear to the dark."[212] Authors associated meat consumption with laziness and lethargy, thereby turning a central argument of the colonizers for their rule over India against them: the colonizers were now on the same level as Indian meat eaters—lower-caste Hindus, Christians, and Muslims.[213] Evolution, or so another author warned, meant that the "ferocious and indolent tribes" would give way to "the more innocent ones."[214] While this author did not explain how this process would unfold, another argued, somewhat paradoxically, that a vegetarian diet bestowed both military prowess and a love of peace.[215]

S. C. Chatterji, a physician from Calcutta who came in first place in the essay-writing contest, was more consistent, emphasizing that meat consumption involved the eater in the killing of members of his own species, implying that meat eating was the main cause of war, and by extension present-day colonialism. The war-like British had reason to be concerned: as soon as a nation entered the path of self-indulgence, its decline was imminent.[216]

Most contributions, though based on a largely congruent body of European and American sources, had an explicitly nationalist perspective. It is worth noting, too, that *Essays on the Advantages of a Vegetarian Diet* was dedicated to the ruler of Baroda, Sayaji Rao Gaekwad III (1863–1939), who was increasingly distancing himself from British authorities and supporting anticolonial actors.[217] By quoting Western sources alongside Hindu religious texts, the prizewinners laid the foundation for a rejection of meat on medical, moral, and religious grounds, for the stereotyping of meat eating, and, eventually, for anticolonialism. By stressing the purported congruence of Islam and Christianity with Brahmin norms by way of a somewhat skewed reading of these religion's central texts, they suggested that these were nonnegotiable norms in the "coming era of peace" and indispensable for its onset. While the nation was not explicitly portrayed as a Hindu polity, India was presented as an imagined community in which Brahmin norms reigned supreme. The consumption of meat, therefore, appeared as the greatest possible deviance, the most drastic threat to peace, and the most tangible manifestation of "physical and moral degeneration." The most radical argument, however, was directed at the colonizers, suggesting that meat eating not only made them cruel and rendered them inferior to the vegetarians they colonized—it would also bring about their downfall.

In late nineteenth-century India, the question of whether to consume meat became highly political. Some Hindus reacted to British colonial stereotypes by adding meat to their diet, while others rejected it, stressing that only pure bodies could successfully challenge colonial rule. Meanwhile, small groups of Europeans, some of them critical of aspects of colonial rule, declared their sympathies with vegetarianism, founding, together with local actors, initiatives that sought to advance the cause of vegetarianism.

As we have seen, it was not just Hindus of different castes who were involved in these initiatives, but also Parsis, Sikhs, and Jains. While the new associations were characterized by cooperation across divisions of caste and religion, they never included Muslims. Indeed, they overlapped with an emerging Hindu nationalism and a cow protection movement that represented beef eaters—which potentially meant both Muslims and British colonizers—as abominable and morally inferior. Ultimately, they aimed to define communal belonging along the lines of purity and dietary preference, excluding those who did not comply, or at least proclaiming the superiority of Brahmin values. The idea of Aryanism played a crucial role in this context, an idea Hindu nationalists shared with Europeans and Americans involved in the Theosophical Society, some of whom were vegetarians.

Connections to European and American vegetarians and vegetarian associations helped undergird this agenda. Europeans, Americans, and their Hindu, Parsi, Sikh, and Jain interlocutors engaged in the creation of "pidgin" knowledge, connecting classical Hindu texts like the Code of Manu and the Bhagavad Gita with evolutionary theory, medicine, and dietetics. Some European authors showed enthusiasm for the caste system, according to which the top place in the social hierarchy was reserved for vegetarians, even if such ideas were often marginalized and ridiculed in Europe. None of them developed empathy toward Indian Muslims or lower-caste and casteless people beyond turning them into objects of social reform. Unlike British authorities in India, who insisted that they were religiously neutral, these vegetarians clearly sympathized with Hinduism, Jainism, and vegetarian tendencies among Parsis and Sikhs. In this manner, Europeans contributed to the deterioration of Hindu-Muslim relations in the subcontinent, thereby encouraging anti-Muslim violence.

Although the organizations analyzed in this chapter seem to have been dominated by South Asians, their use of European rationales for vegetarianism enabled them to establish contact with vegetarian societies in Britain and the United States. This was facilitated by a shared language of purity that obscured differences in motives and the fact that they glossed over their involvement in the cow protection movement in India. With regard to the United States, the World's Columbian Exposition, which helped create an interest in "Indian spirituality" among an American audience, encouraged the internationalization of organized vegetarianism—even if, as we will see in the next chapter, these transnational ties would ultimately prove rather precarious.

*Chapter Three*

## THE CHICAGO EFFECT

Internationalizing Vegetarianism

It was not solely in the context of the colonial encounter that protagonists from India and Europe met and reconfigured knowledge about vegetarianism. From the 1880s on, South Asians also visited the West, giving lectures and publishing papers on vegetarianism. These encounters exerted an influence on the vegetarian scene well beyond the United States.

The World's Columbian Exposition in Chicago in 1893 was a crucial part of this process. Representatives from India visited Chicago as participants in the Parliament of Religions and the International Vegetarian Congress and accompanying exhibition that took place at the exposition. They brought notions of "Hindu spirituality" to the United States, often touring other cities after the World's Columbian Exposition and inspiring a variety of new religions. In doing so, they represented India as a homogeneously Hindu and vegetarian country, thus reaffirming the simplified image of India developed by Western vegetarians and the Theosophical Society. As we will see, their activities created a surge in interest in India that helped inspire the first yoga boom, which soon spilled over to Europe. Vegetarianism was central to this popularization of yoga because U.S. audiences expected the two to be linked.

Yet the influence of images of India on vegetarianism in the United States did not stop here. In the wake of the Parliament of Religions, Chicago also became a hub of new religious communities inspired by Asia. Some of them, such as Mazdaznan, were vegetarian. Mazdaznan's founder, a German migrant by the name of Otto Hanisch, claimed not only that he was indebted to "Oriental" knowledge—he pretended to be "Oriental" himself, thus obliterating his Hindu inspiration. Race, particularly Aryanism, was key to Hanisch's teachings, developed at a time when anti-Black and anti-Asian racism surged both in the United States and in Germany, a budding colonial power. Aryanism, as seen in chapter 2, was also an important point of reference for Hindu nationalists, but Hanisch excluded Hindus from this supposedly elect community of Aryans. I argue that he resorted to this discursive strategy both because of the prominence of the "Orient" in German vegetarian discourse and to make his cult appear more unique within the crowded market of religions in the United States. Furthermore, in obliterating his indebtedness to Hindu influences, Hanisch also ensured that Mazdaznan's Aryanism lost the Islamophobic and anti-British or anticolonial overtones it carried among Hindu nationalists in India. In a few cases, this would render it attractive to Muslim protagonists and those supportive of British colonial rule in India, as we shall see in chapters 4 and 5.

The United States, as a result, was a hub of international organized vegetarianism, a place where different influences met. In this manner, the idea of India as a uniformly Hindu, vegetarian country and a moral model to the rest of the world reached the United States and Europe—societies that had seen themselves as harbingers of a global civilizing mission throughout the nineteenth century, but which were now cast as the targets of precisely such a mission. Nonetheless, it was still Western actors who translated—and often misunderstood or obliterated—these influences, while international umbrella organizations remained Euro-American in practice. Eventually, or so I argue, participants again wrote South Asian protagonists and their knowledge out of the story. Organized vegetarianism remained pronouncedly Western and white.

## THE WORLD'S COLUMBIAN EXPOSITION AND THE BOOM IN "HINDU SPIRITUALITY" IN THE UNITED STATES

From the beginning of May to the end of October 1893, Chicago celebrated the fifth centennial of Christopher Columbus's arrival in the Americas with the World's Columbian Exposition. More than twenty-seven million visitors from across the world saw the exhibition.[1] World expositions had glorified colonialism and progress and measured up nations ever since the Great Exposition in London in 1851.[2] The Chicago fair was the eleventh of these expositions and the first to take place in the United States.[3] It was intended to show participants and exhibitors from all over the world how the United States had advanced from a British colony to an independent, wealthy nation.[4]

Chicago was a fitting emblem of this development. Built on marshy land wrested from Native Americans, it became a larger-scale settlement in the first half of the nineteenth century.[5] After the Civil War and the abolition of slavery, it also became a preferred destination for the Black American community, offering a chance of greater economic prosperity and safety compared to the southern states.[6] The famous fire of 1871, which destroyed most of the city, was a turning point. Chicago recovered from the destruction, becoming one of the most economically potent areas of the United States.[7] Central to Chicago's wealth was meatpacking, for which the city became the largest global hub in the late nineteenth century. Chicago was thus exemplary of the United States' growing ambitions in the world economy.

The main buildings erected for the World's Columbian Exposition, all in splendid white, drew on Greek and Roman antiquity, thus revealing the United States' "desire to play a more substantial role in world trade and world politics," and laying claim to its success as a supposedly free, democratic country.[8] Only a pamphlet edited by Ida B. Wells, one of the most prominent Black journalists and activists of the time, challenged this narrative, referring to the exposition, in Frederick Douglass's words, as a "whited sepulchre." Wells argued that the exposition told a success story about the United States without mentioning that much of this success was due to slavery and the ongoing economic exploitation of Black Americans.[9] After all, in spite of the limited upward social mobility that some Black Americans came to enjoy during the last decades of the nineteenth century, this was also a time when they were disenfranchised and when lynchings were common in the South.[10] The World's Columbian Exposition remained silent on these problems.[11]

Indeed, racism was central to the World's Columbian Exposition. A whole stretch of the exposition grounds, organized by entertainment entrepreneur P. T. Barnum, featured shows like an international dress and costume exhibit, a Japanese bazaar, a street in Cairo, an "Algerian and Tunisian village," a "Moorish palace," and an "East Indian Bazaar."[12] This part of the exposition, called the Midway Plaisance and meant solely for entertainment, was the most visited.[13] Encountering the exotic other helped fairgoers experience themselves as embodiments of progress.[14] This renders futile the question of whether world expositions reflected a tension between "racism and a sense of cultural superiority versus a genuine desire for intercultural awareness."[15] At world expositions, these were not opposite poles but rather two sides of the same coin.[16] There can be no doubt that these "human showcases" led American and European visitors to exoticize and racialize Asian and African participants in other parts of the exposition as well—even though these participants had agendas of their own.[17]

### American Vegetarians Encounter "India"

At the exposition, the intention of showcasing the superiority of American and Western civilization was not limited to the architecture and exhibits. There was a series of congresses aimed at promoting social progress that dealt with religion, social reform, temperance, public health, and women's role in society,[18] with one specifically about vegetarianism.

At first glance, Chicago was an odd place for such a congress. Since the opening of the Union Stock Yards, the city had been the world's largest meatpacking center. At these facilities, animal slaughter was mechanized, and a division of labor made butchering faster and more efficient, lowering both meat prices and workers' salaries. Even the most minute parts of animals were turned into commodities. The invention of the refrigerator car made slaughter, once mainly performed in winter, independent of the seasons. Most importantly, the Union Stock Yards increased the distance between consumers and the act of killing. Eating meat was now an easier, cheaper, and more guilt-free activity than ever.[19]

It was a prominent vegetarian and socialist from Chicago, Upton Sinclair, who, after the meatpackers' strike of 1904, exposed the exploitation of humans and animals at the heart of the Union Stock Yards.[20] Perhaps it was this blatant exploitation of animals and human labor that made Chicago, even before the publication of Sinclair's novel *The Jungle*, one of the centers of vegetarianism in the United States.[21] As in Britain, where Manchester saw the first establishment of a vegetarian society, and Germany, where the booming trading city of Leipzig became a hub of organized vegetarianism, vegetarianism once again took root in urban capitalist societies.

Relative to their British counterparts, U.S. vegetarians had been slow to organize. Since the 1830s, there had been various advocates of vegetarianism in the United States, including Sylvester Graham and William Alcott, the latter the founder of Fruitlands, a short-lived community experiment.[22] The American Vegetarian Society was established in 1850, but only existed for twelve years, which left many American vegetarians with no option but to join the Vegetarian Society in Britain.[23] From the 1880s onwards, John Harvey Kellogg, a member of the Church of Latter-Day Saints, was a vocal advocate of vegetarianism as a means of achieving moral and physical purity who paved the way for vegetarian convenience products and meat substitutes. It was only in the latter half of the 1880s that American vegetarians started organizing again, first in New York, then Chicago. Still, American vegetarians had fewer international contacts than their British peers.[24]

The vegetarian congress at the World's Columbian Exposition was planned precisely to create an international network among vegetarians. To an unprecedented degree, the vegetarian congress, organized in early June 1893, offered delegates and attendees the opportunity to establish personal contacts across national borders. More than 200 delegates from the United States, England and elsewhere in the United Kingdom, Germany, Switzerland, and Australia attended the congress, including Josiah Oldfield, John Harvey Kellogg, and Paul Förster, chairman of the Internationaler Verein zur Bekämpfung der wissenschaftlichen Tierfolter, an antivivisection association based in Dresden, Germany. Already in 1889, this association counted members from Britain, France, and indeed India, including Helena Petrovna Blavatsky and several Bengali Brahmins.[25] Delegates at the Chicago conference included vegetarians with a theosophical and humanist bent, as well as ones with racist and anti-Semitic leanings.

Interestingly, American delegates accepted an invitation to a reception by the Black American community.[26] After a speech by Frederick Douglass, the eminent abolitionist and social reformer, in which he referred to vegetarianism and temperance as integral parts of all social reform movements, the vegetarian delegates were asked to explain "how Vegetarianism might help in mitigating social prejudice."[27] As far as can be judged from the congress reports, however, delegates refrained from discussing vegetarianism as a means of challenging racism once back on the exhibition grounds.

India, meanwhile, was a fairly prominent focus at the vegetarian congress. Before the event, it had not been much of a topic in American vegetarianism. It had played a role in transcendentalism, with Thoreau referring to Hinduism as a model for ascetic, nonviolent living close to nature. The Theosophical Society had likewise done much to bring its notion of India to the American imagination.[28] But the Columbian Exposition and the vegetarian congress made the encounter much more tangible. Several papers given at the event were concerned with India, and there were two Hindu delegates from the subcontinent. This offered American vegetarians contact with supposedly like-minded activists while enabling organizations like the Punjab Vegetarian Society or, later, the Bombay Humanitarian League, to find support in the United States.

While most papers at the congress were concerned with medical and moral aspects, a few discussed vegetarianism in other locales. Among these, a presentation by Alice Bunker Stockham, a member of the Theosophical Society, a vegetarian, and one of the first female gynecologists in the United States, stood out. In her talk "Food of the Orient," she told the audience about a trip to a temple near Coimbatore with five Brahmin companions in 1891. According to Stockham, Hindus of all castes abstained from "animal food." Moreover, they were masters in self-denial, or so she inferred from seeing neither her companions nor the group's servants eat anything during the day. Regardless of their physique, this ability bestowed an enormous physical strength upon them, far beyond that of the average European or American. It did not occur to Stockham that her travel companions and their servants might not have taken any food because of caste restrictions on commensality, meaning that the presence of non-Brahmins, whether Indian or American, would have polluted their food. While she did stress that Hindu motivations for meat abstention differed from those embraced in the West, with disgust of dead bodies the most important motive, her views fit with mainstream vegetarian discourse that equated Hinduism with Brahmins.[29]

The two Indian delegates, Siddhu Ram and Lala Jinda Ram, also talked about vegetarianism in India. Unlike Stockham's talk, however, their paper was not reproduced in official accounts of the vegetarian congress. Both were members of the Arya Samaj, and Lala Jinda Ram was president of a Vedic Temperance Society.[30] Siddhu Ram seems to have been a convert from Islam who had undergone the ceremony of *shuddhi* (purification), invented by the Arya Samaj to win back members of lower castes whose ancestors had converted to Islam to improve their social status.[31] It may have been Siddhu Ram and Lala Jinda Ram who laid the groundwork for Durga Prasad's and the Punjab Vegetarian Society's close contacts with American protagonists of vegetarianism, Theosophy, and social reform. They stayed in the United States until September and participated in the opening of the World's Parliament of Religions.

The vegetarian congress largely focused on Europe and the United States, an emphasis that was reflected in its participants. Nonetheless, India, previously barely a point of reference in U.S. vegetarian discourse, was elevated to a model of purity for European and American vegetarians. The congress reinforced the image of India—antimaterialist, and with a monolithic, vegetarian Hinduism that was essentially Brahmin—that had been developed by British vegetarians. At the World's Columbian Exposition, this image resonated well beyond the vegetarian congress.

### Swami Vivekananda and the Mixed Message of Meat

Another major event at the exposition, the Parliament of Religions, also had an impact on the development of vegetarianism in the West. The parliament echoed the message of the Columbian Exposition, presenting the United States as the apogee of civilization. Although its aim was to bring together all so-called religions and find their shared message, the parliament's organizers intended to show the superiority of Protestant Christianity.

As Richard Seager and others have argued, however, several notable Asian delegates at the parliament turned this message on its head. Arguing that it was not Asia but the West that had to be reformed, the delegates made a case for the superiority of Buddhism and Hinduism.[32] While none of the Asian speakers addressed vegetarianism at length, their contributions led to a surge in interest in Asian religions as a way of reinvigorating Western culture.[33] This gave rise to quasi-missionary movements in the United States and beyond whose proponents argued for a direct connection of religious, moral, alimentary, and bodily reform—contexts in which vegetarianism played a crucial role.

One of the most eloquent speakers about the superiority of Hinduism was Narendranath Datta, known as Swami Vivekananda, a thirty-year-old monk from Bengal who rose to fame in the wake of the World's Columbian Exposition. Addressing his "Sisters and Brothers of America" in Chicago, Vivekananda portrayed India as a place that had given sanctuary to members of persecuted religions, thus making it the country where these religions had been maintained in their purest state. Hinduism, according to him, was not only the most tolerant religion, but also the "mother of religions."[34] It also anticipated modern-day science, most notably evolutionary theory, in its concept of rebirth.[35] Vivekananda, therefore, connected Hinduism with the signature elements of progress,[36] thus reformulating relations between Asia and the West. He claimed that it was not Asia that needed a civilizing mission, but the West.

Vivekananda did not tie the West's spiritual needs to alimentary reform—at least not in Chicago. Indeed, as Parama Roy has shown, he was hardly an advocate of vegetarianism.[37] In his treatise "The East and the West" and elsewhere, he argued that while the West needed to learn from the East spiritually, the East had much to learn from the West about food: Hindus had to consume beef and fish to gain the strength needed to combat colonialism. Indeed, anyone living an active life had to forego vegetarianism.[38] With his tall, heavy frame, he literally embodied this message.

Vivekananda's position on meat consumption owed much to his background: he had been born into a Kayasth family, a caste not traditionally vegetarian.[39] Unlike other Hindu reformers, he had undergone a British education, graduating from Presidency College, Calcutta. After coming into contact with Nava Vidhan, a Hindu reformist organization founded by Keshub Chandra Sen, a notable reformer who had converted to Christianity and then reconverted to Hinduism, he met the man who had encouraged Sen to return to Hinduism: Ramakrishna, a priest at the Kali temple in Dakineshwar.[40] Kali priests were Brahmins, yet worship of the goddess demanded the slaughter of animals for sacrifice, with *prasād* (sacred portions of the offering) distributed to the faithful and consumed by the priests as part of the ritual.[41] As a consequence, Ramakrishna's community was not strictly vegetarian.[42]

At the same time, Vivekananda also stressed the virtues of vegetarianism, though only occasionally and well after the Parliament of Religions had ended.[43] Most likely, he adapted his message to the specific audience he addressed: preaching beef eating in India to strengthen the body politic and advocating vegetarianism in the United States, possibly to live up to the expectations of his American audience, who could not imagine India without vegetarianism.

Vivekananda attracted great attention at the World's Parliament of Religions. His eloquence and popularity with the audience turned him into "a major authority on Indian religions"[44] and allowed him to spend considerable time traveling the United States and Europe after the Columbian Exposition, eventually founding the Ramakrishna Mission, which established centers in London, San Francisco, and New York—a development closely tied to the emergence of yoga in Europe and North America.

As scholars like Dermot Killingley and Lola Williamson have argued, Vivekananda was able to style himself as an authority on yoga authority in the United States, very much gearing his message to the expectations of his audience.[45] Not having been trained in yoga in India, he delved into the practice while in the United States, drawing on Theosophy as well as what were then still obscure Sanskrit texts like Patānjali's *Yoga Sutra*.[46] He was also influenced by the deism of American transcendentalism, social Darwinism, and Keshub Chandra Sen, who wanted to reform Hinduism to make it more like Christianity.[47] He was thus well versed in translating Hinduism for Western audiences, and he presented yoga to American audiences accordingly.

In classical yoga, hardly a uniform set of traditions,[48] the body is a means to an end. Hatha yoga, which aims to preserve the energy believed to be inherent in semen (*bindu*) through a number of bodily practices, emerged centuries after yoga was established as a meditation practice. To some extent the forerunner of modern postural yoga, it required a great degree of training and was mostly performed by wandering ascetics.[49] As Mark Singleton points out, Europeans' perception of yogis was largely pejorative. As people outside the caste system, they were also looked down upon by orthodox Hindus.[50]

In Vivekananda's yoga, the body was not that prominent. Instead, it was the mind through which purity was to be achieved. Claiming that hatha yoga was inferior, Vivekananda drew on the meditative tradition elaborated in Patañjāli's *Yoga Sutra* (fourth century BCE), including a translation of some parts in his treatise on raja yoga.[51] Vivekananda's yoga was limited to sitting upright, controlling one's breath, and eventually one's thoughts. The way Vivekananda interpreted Patañjāli's treatise, however, was decidedly modern. He presented yoga as a scientific method that improved concentration and would eventually complete human evolution.[52] Indeed, he claimed that Patañjāli had already conceptualized evolutionary theory, not in terms of a biological development of *Homo sapiens*, but of the spiritual development of the individual, an interpretation that was doubtlessly informed by theosophical readings of evolutionary theory.[53]

Vivekananda did not just address religious men and women or those ready to take up an ascetic lifestyle. Nor did he ask audiences to embrace Hinduism, instead stressing its shared aspects with New Thought and Christian Science.[54] Broadly speaking, his yoga appealed to anyone interested in improving their powers of concentration. His version of yoga, other than that of the wandering sadhus (ascetics) of Hinduism, was perfectly reconcilable with a capitalist work ethic, even though he warned that overwork threatened spiritual advancement.

Vivekananda's dietary requirements for yoga beginners were equally moderate. The *Yoga Sutra* emphasized that *ahimsa*, and thus a diet free from meat and fish, was indispensable to advancing in yoga, but Vivekanada did not stress these requirements.[55] He recommended that anyone wishing to advance in yoga restrict their diet in the beginning, but said that "when our practice is well advanced, we need not be so careful in this respect."[56] Those who came after him, however, emphasized yoga as a bodily practice and linked it to vegetarianism—in all likelihood because classical texts demanded it, and because audiences in the United States expected it.

Why a Hindu Is (Not) a Vegetarian: A Ramakrishna Missionary
Between American Audiences and Fleshly Temptations

After Vivekananda's speeches in Chicago brought him fame across the United States, he continued touring the country.[57] From 1896 on, he sent disciples of Ramakrishna to Britain and the United States, establishing centers in San Francisco and New York.[58] Vivekananda entrusted the mission to Kaliprasad Chandra, known as Swami Abhedananda, who came to the United States from London in 1895.[59] It was under his leadership that the body, and thereby vegetarianism, again began to assume greater prominence in the new kind of yoga invented for American audiences—albeit to the unease of Abhedananda himself.

## THE CHICAGO EFFECT

Vivekananda told Abhedananda that Western audiences should not be overtaxed with detailed knowledge about Hindu spiritual traditions. Instead, simplification was the way to go.[60] Diet seems to have been one aspect in which Abhedananda followed this advice, albeit with some discomfort. Abhedananda's collected works show that he was not a vegetarian by birth. In the United States, however, he was ordered by the secretary of the Ramakrishna Mission to observe a strict vegetarian diet to "set an example."[61] In a paper given in 1898 before the New York Vegetarian Society, Abhedananda reaffirmed the link between Hinduism and vegetarianism, discussing "Why a Hindu Is a Vegetarian."[62] The talk was published as a book two years later.

While there was a surge in interest in vegetarianism in the West during this period, Abhedananda claimed that vegetarianism in India had much deeper roots. Even Pythagoras had learned of it from "Hindu philosophers

FIGURE 3.1. Swami Abhedananda, from Swami Abhedananda, *Why a Hindu Is a Vegetarian. Delivered Before the Vegetarian Society, New York, March 22, 1898* (New York: Vedanta Society, 1900).

who from prehistoric times had advocated and practiced a strictly vegetarian diet."[63] "Hindu physicians" of old had known that "animals fattened for slaughter are more or less diseased on account of their unnatural mode of living and the unnatural food which they are forced to eat; that the germs of various diseases are introduced into the human system and that parasites come into the human body through the medium of animal flesh." They had also known that meat contained poisonous substances because slaughter trapped products of elimination inside animals' bodies and that meat acted as a stimulant, "ultimately leading to the nervous debility which afflicts many meat eaters."[64]

Essentially, Abhedananda claimed that the understandings of modern science had already been achieved by Hindu sages of "prehistoric times." He also obliterated sectarian differences among Hindus, such as those between the strictly vegetarian Vaishnavism and the less strict Shaktism, the tradition that relied on animal sacrifice, creating a homogeneous vegetarian Hindu religion.[65] In contrast, as Abhedananda pointed out, in the West, religion was an obstacle to vegetarianism because it claimed that "the lower animals have no soul, no mind, no feelings." It was these arguments, not medical ones, as well as "superstition, prejudice and ignorance," that made meat consumption so popular in the United States.[66] Abhedananda thus turned "superstition," a central argument of colonial civilizing discourse, against the West.

Asserting that "the idea that animals were created for food for man is entirely Semitic in its origin" (and thus conflating Christianity, Judaism, and Islam), Abhedananda argued that Hinduism differed from these traditions in recognizing the relatedness of humans and animals. He described the concepts of *atman* and *brahman* in terms of evolutionary theory, claiming that the development of consciousness brought about an "evolution of man from lower animals." Like Theosophists such as Leopold Salzer, Abhedananda argued that humans could also fall back on the ladder of evolution both morally and physically, "degrading themselves to the lowest animal plane," by consuming meat. He added that "most of the murderers in Chicago come from the butcher class."[67]

To advance spiritually, humans had to abstain from meat, like the "greatest men and women Yogis in ancient India" had. As an example of these heroic figures, Abhedananda mentioned the goddess Durga,[68] failing to tell his audience that Durga, the war goddess, did not abstain from meat.

Indeed, in some epochs in regions such as Nepal and Abhedananda's home region of Bengal, Durga was pacified by animal sacrifice, although the custom came under fire in colonial times.[69]

Abhedananda had to make great efforts to justify "Why a Hindu Is a Vegetarian." Apparently, he also experienced difficulties in embracing vegetarianism himself. In his correspondence and diary, Abhedananda stressed the pains he took to comply with his superior's demand to abstain from meat, suggesting that his vegetarian diet was making him ill.[70] Eventually, or so the correspondence preserved in his collected works suggests, Sarada Devi, the female head of the Ramakrishna Order, allowed him to "take good meat instead of [a] purely vegetarian diet" to gain sufficient strength to carry out his work.[71] After seven years of supposedly living as a vegetarian in the United States, Abhedananda received formal orders from Calcutta to "give up the vow of vegetarianism."[72]

Despite his personal failure, Abhedananda continued telling Americans that vegetarianism was indispensable to advancing in hatha yoga.[73] So did other speakers at the centers established by Vivekananda, including some American women who became disciples.[74] Despite Vivekananda's and Abhedananda's ambivalence, therefore, yoga came to be associated with vegetarianism in the United States.

## MAZDAZNAN: A PRODUCT OF THE WORLD'S COLUMBIAN EXPOSITION

As Swami Abhedananda and others were teaching yoga in the United States, borrowings from their notion of yoga appeared in different contexts elsewhere. Chicago saw the emergence of a group that the local papers referred to as a "sun-worshipping cult."[75] Focused on the interplay of mind and body, with teachings on breathing, dietetics, hygiene, self-healing, and eugenics at its heart, the "sun cult" was headed by a man who called himself Otoman Zar Adusht Ha'nish, allegedly born in Tehran to the Russian ambassador and his wife and raised in a Tibetan monastery.[76]

While this biography was entirely fictitious, it points to the genealogy in which this sun cult, otherwise known as Mazdaznan, situated itself. Tibet, according to Kant the birthplace of humankind,[77] and Russian origins recall the autobiography of Helena Petrovna Blavatsky, who claimed to have visited Tibet before founding the Theosophical Society.[78] This genealogy shows Theosophy's central influence on alternative religions in the United States. Hanisch, I argue, created a unique profile by veiling his references to Theosophy, Brahmin spirituality, and an American religious movement known as New Thought (itself influenced by Theosophy) by claiming to be an authentic voice from a vaguely defined "Orient" that stretched from Persia to Egypt. This allowed him to rid the concept of the Aryan, so central to Mazdaznan's notions of purity, of any associations with India—a strategy that would sell well not only among certain vegetarian audiences in the United States but also in Europe, particularly in Germany and Switzerland. Eventually, Gloria Gasque, a high-ranking American Mazdaznan member, would become the first female president of the International Vegetarian Union in the 1950s.

As we saw in chapter 1, the notion of the "Orient" on which Mazdaznan drew was already highly influential in German-speaking vegetarian discourse. U.S. audiences, meanwhile, had their own relationship with the Arab-Islamic world. Since the 1830s, American Christians, looking for financial support for their missions, had painted a dark picture of the region.[79] In esoteric contexts, meanwhile, the "Orient" became an object of fascination that could also be shown in a positive light. The Shriners, a charitable offshoot of freemasonry founded in 1870, dressed in pseudo-Ottoman garb, including the tarboosh, while having a prominent opponent of French colonialism, Abd al-Qadir al-Jazairi (1808–1883), as their patron.[80] In Chicago, Ibrahim Jirjis Khairallah, a Christian from Mount Lebanon, began spreading the Baha'i faith in the 1890s. By the count of a contemporary journalist, the Baha'is were one of at least fifty new religious groups in the city.[81] Chicago's new religious scene, therefore, was densely populated. In order to stand out, newcomers had to forge a distinct profile for themselves while also reacting to local demands for the exotic.

Mazdaznan's "Oriental" references obfuscated its appropriations from Theosophy and yoga. Hanisch interjected Arab elements into his writings, including the (corrupted) greeting "Salem Aleikum."[82] His purported first name, Ottoman, also alluded to "Oriental" origins. Zar Adusht, which Hanisch translated as "prince of peace," pointed to Zoroastrianism, as did the group's name, Mazdaznan, with Mazda being the highest deity in Zoroastrianism.[83] Hanisch never acknowledged his borrowings, instead claiming that his cult represented actual Zoroastrianism, a religion little known in the West, though Nietzsche's *Thus Spoke Zarathustra* had made its founder's name vaguely familiar to educated audiences.[84] It is likely that Hanisch was influenced by Nietzsche's book, which described man's attainment of the status of superman through self-mastery, self-cultivation, self-direction, and self-overcoming, aims central to Mazdaznan teachings and allegedly to be achieved through vegetarianism.[85]

Hanisch could not have been further from being a Zoroastrian, as his astute contemporary Upton Sinclair, himself a vegetarian and temporary member of the Theosophical Society, revealed in a scathing study of Chicago's new religious communities, *The Profits of Religion*. In this book, Sinclair characterized Hanisch as a fraud—a German immigrant by the name of Otto Hanisch whose claims to "Oriental" origins were entirely fictitious.[86] Other sources confirm Sinclair's observations. Hanisch seems to have been one of five children born in Katowice, Silesia, to Protestant parents. In 1878, when Otto was twelve, the Hanisch family left for Rochester, New York. Still an adolescent, Hanisch went to Salt Lake, Utah, where he joined the Church of Latter-day Saints[87] and worked on a sheep farm before apprenticing to a grocer.[88] Later, he was trained as a typesetter, a trade in which he still worked in 1894 in Salt Lake.[89] While Mazdaznan members claim the religion was present in Chicago from 1890, thus predating the World's Parliament of Religions, local papers only mention it in the first and, with increasing frequency, the second decades of the twentieth century.[90] Given the Columbian Exposition's clear role in shaping Mazdaznan, the latter's claim to an earlier presence may be discounted.

At the same time, Mazdaznan was also influenced by a movement known as New Thought, which saw a surge after 1893.[91] New Thought sought to achieve a transformation of society through the conversion of the individual. Its adherents believed that, while the body played a role in conversion, the mind, or consciousness, began the process, which then unfolded through electricity.[92] New Thought replaced belief in God with belief in the self, which was closely associated with material success, although its representatives sought to distance themselves from materialism.[93] New Thought was also open to aspects of various non-Christian religions and sought contacts with protagonists outside Europe.[94] As in Theosophy, women played a special role in the movement, being considered manifestations of the "Divine Feminine."[95] New Thought encouraged women to go beyond the restrictions that nineteenth-century middle-class contexts placed on their sexuality,[96] but without embracing libertinage. Discipline was deemed as important as pleasure, with the two to be kept in an (always precarious) equilibrium. Techniques like fasting, control of one's thoughts, and concentration were key to New Thought self-fashioning. They would also be central to Mazdaznan's teachings.

Focusing on the interplay of mind and body, breathing, dietetics, hygiene, self-healing, and eugenics, Mazdaznan drew most of its ingredients, including vegetarianism, from the new American religious landscape, but combined them in a unique way, as shall be seen in the following sections. It was, therefore, very much a product of the global exchange influenced by the World's Columbian Exposition and its aftermath—and it would shape vegetarianism in Europe, particularly Germany and Switzerland, in the decades to come, before eventually becoming influential in the International Vegetarian Union in the 1950s, as we will see in chapter 5.

### Breathing for Evolution, or Pharaonic Yoga

In the early years of the twentieth century, Hanisch published two books that combined hygienic and dietetic advice with prayer. The first, *Mazdaznan Health and Breath Culture* (1902), established breath as both the foundation of Mazdaznan practice and the key to health and success. The book specifically targeted male readers, although Mazdaznan breathing exercises would soon be performed by both men and women. While *Mazdaznan Health and Breath Culture* was indebted to yoga, and not just Vivekananda's concept of it but also hatha yoga, it did not acknowledge this, instead claiming to be influenced by Ancient Egyptian traditions.

In the book's preface, Hanisch distanced himself from physical culture, which by the late nineteenth century had become the established means of articulating one's ability to engage in self-governance. Physical culture was seen as a Protestant, male, and middle-class domain.[97] According to Hanisch, however, building muscle was obsolete "in an age of brain and nerves."[98] The exercises in his book were designed to train the mind, not the body. Nonetheless, Hanisch embraced the aim of physical culture, stressing that "the first thing you owe to yourself is to tune up the instrument, the body, by such means as will insure immediate results beneficial to your being."[99] Knowing one's body was a prerequisite for starting this process.[100] Hanisch thus inscribed himself into New Thought discourse, claiming that the maintenance of the body, the "Temple of the Living God," should never be entrusted to others.[101]

By referring to the present as the "age of brain and nerve," Hanisch picked up on his era's obsession with nerves, nervousness, and neurasthenia, a disease that seemed to attack primarily young middle-class men, and that, according to historian Julian B. Carter, had by the late nineteenth century become a marker of whiteness.[102] It was not coincidental that *Mazdaznan Health and Breath Culture* addressed men first and foremost. Correct breathing, or so Hanisch assured his readers, would enable them to enter "the Army of Successful Men."

Breathing, according to Hanisch, purified the body, protected against illnesses, and improved intellectual function. Unlike medicines, it was free.[103] Moreover, correct breathing would slow down ageing, if not prevent it altogether, allowing humans to live for four hundred years or more.[104] To breathe properly, Hanisch advised his readers to reject conventional dress and tight shoes.[105]

Without acknowledging it, Hanisch borrowed central aspects and terms from yoga as taught by Vivekananda and his followers: breath as a life-giving force, the *kundalini* as the center of energy, and the *shusumna* as leading to that center,[106] merging these concepts with mesmeric notions of the nervous system as fired by electricity and turning them into a motor of success in a manner reminiscent of New Thought. Arguing that human bodies possessed twelve rather than five senses, Hanisch proposed a set of twelve exercises to direct energy toward each sense.[107] These exercises would not just distribute electric force evenly throughout the body, they would also ensure concentration, the most important mental facility—an essential prerequisite for performing work efficiently, and a key term, as seen above, in Vivekananda's raja yoga.[108] Ultimately, or so Hanisch, echoing Vivekananda, claimed, concentration was a motor of evolution, moving people beyond what he referred to as the inferior animal stage of life. In the illustrations accompanying the text, the exercises were done by male figures in loincloths and headcloths reminiscent of those worn by the pharaohs of ancient Egypt. Hanisch called the exercises Egyptian postures, thus obscuring his borrowings from hatha yoga.[109]

According to *Mazdaznan Health and Breath Culture*, correct breathing was not the only means of ascending the ladder of evolution. Diet also played a part in this process. The consumption of meat, or so Hanisch claimed in a manner reminiscent of theosophical authors like Leopold Salzer, was detrimental to evolution in that "the intelligences of these bodily dead creatures continue to live in you spiritually," carrying on "their work as foreign agencies in your body."[110] Humans consuming a certain kind of meat frequently eventually came to resemble these animals in their habitus.[111] While this critique of meat consumption is at first glance much in line with previous vegetarian discourse, Mazdaznan did not reject sex to the same extent. Thus, while "the animal" in this context did connote the inferior, it was not necessarily identified with sexual urges as much as physical and intellectual inferiority. Indeed, Mazdaznan would soon become an explicit advocate of pleasure—to an extent authorities in the United States and Germany deemed scandalous.

While meat was clearly the most harmful of foods, Mazdaznan adherents were to avoid other foods as well. Most notably, Hanisch, echoing Jain dietary precepts (without direct reference), warned them of vegetables and fruit grown under the earth. Only plants exposed to the sun could be healthy: "if you consume foods produced in darkness you will be kept enchained in the shadows of death."[112] It was a bright food grown aboveground that Hanisch deemed the healthiest one. Wheat in his mind was "the staff of life."[113] Mazdaznan's dietary recommendations, then, were a curious mixture of Brahmin and Jain alimentary norms and British colonial discourse, which had extolled the alleged manliness of the so-called martial races of northern India, purportedly the result of their consumption of wheat rather than rice.[114]

Correct breathing, the allegedly "Egyptian" postures, and a diet free from meat and plants grown under the surface of the earth would promote evolution, with Hanisch's notion of it characterized by a heavy emphasis on race, or more specifically, Aryanism—even though he claimed that Egyptians could not be characterized as such.[115] Hanisch's notion of race was thus characterized by a fusion of Orientalism, white supremacy, Theosophy, and heavy borrowings from the sort of "Indian spirituality" brought to the United States by Vivekananda and his disciples—yet without acknowledging the latter.

### From Hatha Yoga to a Sexualized "Orient"

Hanisch's *Inner Studies* (1902), the second Mazdaznan manual, also drew on yoga.[116] The book was a sex manual for both men and women, and its contents led to legal action against Mazdaznan on the grounds of impropriety, causing Hanisch to move the organization from Chicago first to California and then to Leipzig, Germany, before another lawsuit in Saxony forced his representatives in Germany to move to Switzerland. The scandal the book caused was very much due to its detailed descriptions of human anatomy and sexuality, and its emphasis on women's right to pleasure.[117] Again, the book drew on yoga and, paradoxically, Hindu concepts of male chastity, but did not acknowledge these influences, instead once more foregrounding an alleged indebtedness to the "Orient."

While *Inner Studies* was also concerned with the regulation of breath, digestion, and elimination, sexuality was at its heart. The book presented sex not as duty or danger but as a source of pleasure for both men and women—and something to be engaged in systematically. Mazdaznan was one of the first vegetarian groups to question the negative notion of sexuality many vegetarians had embraced up to that point. Keen to ensure "the efficacy of sexual intercourse," for which both men and women required precise anatomic knowledge,[118] Hanisch included a detailed description of male and female reproductive organs in *Inner Studies*.[119] By efficient sexual intercourse, Hanisch did not mean sex for procreation, indeed not even sex up to the point of ejaculation. He believed that men and women were magnetically attracted to one another, and that sex served to maximize this magnetic attraction and ensure a mutual exchange of energy.[120] Hanisch also questioned a binary notion of gender, arguing that individuals possessed both male and female aspects in varying proportions.[121] "Effective" sex, according to Hanisch, lasted a long time, with men foregoing orgasm in order not to waste semen, considered essential for male longevity and intelligence.[122]

The argument that men needed to avoid ejaculation was plagiarized from Alice Bunker Stockham's famous work *Karezza*, which proposed a new approach to sex that combined female pleasure and birth control: prolonged sexual intercourse without male ejaculation.[123] Whereas Stockham wanted men to avoid orgasm for the sake of birth control, Hanisch also stressed the supposed benefits of withholding ejaculation for male longevity. While this echoed a popular argument against masturbation in Western nineteenth-century medical discourse, Hanisch may have once again been indebted to hatha yoga, in which exercises like the headstand were intended to keep semen inside the body. Yogis believed that semen was produced inside the head, and that the only way of ensuring longevity and maintaining intelligence was to prevent it from trickling down.[124] Both hatha yoga and Stockham's work seem to have informed Hanisch's thinking. As in *Health and Breath Culture*, he did not acknowledge any of his sources, least of all the influence of hatha yoga.

While proponents of yoga addressed Protestant notions of self-restraint, Hanisch, even while taking inspiration from yoga, again foregrounded alleged "Oriental" influences to preach pleasure rather than self-denial. Arguing that "Oriental philosophies" did not "teach asceticism," Hanisch contributed to the Western sexualization of the region that Edward Said describes as a main characteristic of nineteenth-century Orientalism.[125]

Decades before nudism was accepted in the United States, but clearly responding to Orientalist clichés as expressed in art, Hanisch claimed that "Oriental" men and particularly women had long engaged in the practice of going naked, and that, when wearing clothes, they preferred loosely flowing dress, arguing that both were highly conducive to the development of physical beauty and maintenance of reproductive health.[126] He also encouraged his female readers to engage in "pelvic movements," preferably accompanied by music and wearing as little as possible, to "arouse" the "action of the life fluids" and thereby stimulate their reproductive organs.[127] Without stating it explicitly, Hanisch here drew inspiration from various forms of Eastern dance, which were viewed as scandalous by many contemporary Western sources, but which were beginning to exert an influence on dance and physical culture in the West from the early twentieth century onward.[128]

In *Inner Studies*, then, Hanisch placed pleasure rather than self-denial at the center of his teachings, even though he stressed the benefits of occasional fasting.[129] He also gave a prominent role to women, acknowledging their right to pleasure and even their purported intellectual superiority—a strategy that would prove efficient in courting wealthy female supporters such as Chicago socialite and billionaire Gloria Gasque, who would become the first female president of the International Vegetarian Union in the 1950s. Most importantly, Hanisch once more drew on influences from yoga, even if he foregrounded his alleged indebtedness to influences from the Arab-Muslim world.

FIGURE 3.2. Otto Hanisch (Otoman Zar Adusht Ha'nish), from Otoman Zar Adusht Hanish, *Ainyahita in Pearls. From the Original* (Chicago: Mazdaznan, 1913).

Removing Hindus from the "Aryan" Fold

Mazdaznan had appropriated elements of diverse religions from the beginning. Hanisch dressed in gowns reminiscent of the cassocks worn by Catholic clerics (figure 3.2). His books contained what were effectively prayers addressed to a personal male god, although they were referred to as "outbreathings."[130] Nonetheless, Mazdaznan's initial publications were first and foremost about the body, the "Temple of the Living God." It was only in the 1910s that Hanisch published two books of supposedly religious content: *Ainyahita in Pearls* and *Yehoshua Nazir*, a biography of Jesus.[131] This was the first time that Mazdaznan made explicit reference to Zoroastrianism, even if these borrowings were highly selective. Most importantly, both books placed anti-Semitism and white supremacy at the center of Mazdaznan's teachings.

*Yehoshua* and *Ainyahita* were published when Mazdaznan was increasingly becoming the subject of judicial scrutiny, with Hanisch facing trials in Chicago and Los Angeles. The first lawsuit accused Hanisch of practicing medicine without a license.[132] Later court cases focused on Mazdaznan adherents who had died from fasting or committed suicide,[133] abduction of and "immoral conduct" with boys,[134] and the supposedly obscene content of *Inner Studies*.[135] By this time, Hanisch's associate David Ammann had moved to Germany to establish a branch beyond the reach of U.S. authorities.[136] Hanisch's religious publications, aimed at both U.S. and German audiences, can thus be read as a strategy to make the community appear more respectable. Much more than his earlier books, moreover, they pitted the "Orient" against India, Hanisch's notion of Zoroastrianism against Hinduism, and articulated anti-Semitism and white supremacy at a time when segregation in the United States was being reinforced, and anti-Semitism and colonial racism in Germany was surging.[137]

*Yehoshua Nazir* was part of the popular genre of Jesus biographies initiated by Ernest Renan and taken up by authors like Nicolai Aleksandrovitch Notovitch.[138] While Renan argued that Jesus had overcome his Jewishness, Hanisch claimed that "Yehoshua Nazir had never been a Jew nor, more broadly, a Semite."[139] He thus evoked the idea of an Orient without Jews, an idea embraced by Christian missions active in the region.[140] This vision of an Aryan Jesus, which aligned with Houston Stewart Chamberlain's depiction, let Hanisch tie in with the "soteriology of white flesh" (Eric Arden Weed) central to white supremacy.[141] Hanisch further purified Jesus by turning him into a vegetarian. With his stepfather allegedly close to the Essene sect, Yesshu (as the protagonist was referred to everywhere in the book but its title) rejected the consumption of meat. Along with the Essenes, according to Hanisch, Yesshu was inspired by Hinduism and Buddhism and "Egyptian Therapeuti."[142] Like Notovitch, Hanisch claimed that Jesus had visited India and Tibet as a young man and had been deeply inspired by Zoroastrianism.[143] Hanisch concluded that the teachings of Jesus were not superior to Zoroastrianism, but in line with it, and that one could be an adherent of Mazdaznan even while nominally embracing Christianity.

The protagonist of *Ainyahita in Pearls,* a ten-year-old blond, blue-eyed, fair-skinned girl living in the Himalayas as a shepherdess, was loosely inspired by the Zoroastrian goddess Anahita but was also reminiscent of both Mary—a virgin—and Jesus, often likened to a shepherd. Dressed in white, she is described as the epitome of purity,[144] and often cries pearl-like tears when confronted with the sinfulness of the world. Each time, Mazda, the personal (yet invisible) male god who treats her as an elect, offers explanation and comfort. Eventually Ainyahita saves her flock from impending doom. In a key scene of this loosely structured book, Ainyahita learns of the development of humankind, explained to her in terms of the progress of seven distinct races, from the brown race to the most elevated one, the "Race Transparent," as yet undeveloped. Ainyahita, Mazda promises, will live to see its emergence.[145]

Another conversation between Ainyahita and Mazda suggests that the coming of the "Race Transparent" will be tied to fundamental dietary change. Shocked after encountering "a tribe killing kine and sheep" during her wanderings, Ainyahita asks Mazda why humans kill animals for food.[146] He explains that, while humans and animals had originally fed "upon the fruits of the Earth," after a demon created vermin, humans started killing nonhuman life for fear of being overrun by it.[147] With the "white race" having already recognized the sinfulness of this practice, it would subside once "the fair-faced lead a life pure and simple, while the shaded ones are conquered..., eventually turning pure and undefiled even as the Luminary." At this stage, all humans would recognize each other as brothers and sisters.[148]

While vegetarianism in Europe and North America had been tied to the development of humankind and the emergence of New Man, Hanisch was the first to couch this assumed trajectory explicitly in terms of racial progress, possibly reflecting both Brahmin and Theosophist notions. The Bhagavad Gita and the Code of Manu tied moral disposition, temperament, and dietary preferences to (skin) color, arguing that it was the dark and inert (*tamas*) who lusted for meat. Helena Petrovna Blavatsky, on the other hand, developed the idea of the ascent of the Root Races, which assumed a linear development of distinct successor races like the one envisaged by Hanisch.[149]

In 1914, Hanisch's "ambassador" David Ammann, drawing loosely on contemporary concepts of eugenics, further elaborated on Mazdaznan's racial theory.[150] Ammann was then based in Leipzig, where Mazdaznan had just opened its first German branch,[151] but his article was published simultaneously in Germany and the United States and was aimed at both German and American audiences. Claiming to sum up the thoughts of Jesus and Zarathustra, Ammann evoked a contemporary scientific racism that hailed blood as a new category of classification.¹⁵² Ammann claimed that skin color reflected the relative purity of one's blood; white people had the purest composition, while "yellow," "green," "grey," "red," "brown," and "black" ones were inferior. In contrast to *Ainyahita*, where Hanisch had indicated that the "shaded ones" might eventually "turn pure," Ammann envisaged no such future for Black people, who, in his view, possessed no evolutionary potential.¹⁵³ Clearly, such views courted both sympathizers of white supremacy in the United States in an era when Black Americans were striving for equality and Germans supportive of racial segregation in the German colonies.

While both Ammann and Hanisch unabashedly embraced white supremacy, their notion of "whiteness" differed from the mainstream of contemporary science and from popular racism by including people from the Mediterranean, as well as Christians, Muslims, Zoroastrians, and Jews.¹⁵⁴ It also differed from the racial theory of the Theosophical Society, and that of Hindu nationalists, in excluding Hindus, whom members of the Theosophical Society, as well as many Hindu nationalists, classified as Aryan.¹⁵⁵ According to Ammann, "Indians" had both Aryan and Dravidian ancestry, which rendered them inferior to the country's Muslim invaders. Amman claimed that the Zoroastrian Avesta, on the other hand, cautioned against mixing with "the dark."¹⁵⁶ The alleged racial inferiority of "Indians" impacted not just their moral and physical condition, it rendered Hinduism and Buddhism inferior religions unable to "satisfy pure racial Aryans."¹⁵⁷ Zoroastrianism was "the only true Aryan" religion.¹⁵⁸ Once again, Mazdaznan's racial theory gave pride of place to an invented "Orient" while rejecting Hindu and Buddhist elements, thus distancing itself from protagonists in the American religious market who claimed allegiance to both, and adapting to the geographic focus of German vegetarian discourse.

Even though the worldwide conversion to vegetarianism Hanisch assumed in *Ainyahita* was tied to the idea of universal human kinship, the hierarchy at the heart of the concept was clear: vegetarianism would further optimize the alleged superior potential of select members of the "white race." These individuals would evolve into the "Race Transparent" as long as they maintained their "purity" by rejecting contact with other races. This demand was well in line with racial segregation in the United States as it had evolved since the 1870s and with demands for racial segregation in the

German colonies, where marriages between Germans and Black people continued to be prohibited until 1914. In each of these contexts, as scholars like Jane Dailey and Lora Wildenthal have shown, women were frequently addressed as guardians of racial purity.[159]

It was a hierarchy that would sell elsewhere, as Mazdaznan opened branches and became popular with parts of the vegetarian movement in Canada, Britain, Germany, and Switzerland. The community even gained some Parsi contacts in Bombay.[160] Although it remained far from being the global cult its leaders presented to their adherents, and was an object of ridicule among mainstream vegetarians in Germany and Switzerland for its exoticism,[161] Mazdaznan established itself as a transnational organization. It espoused a notion of whiteness that allowed members to set themselves apart from those deemed racially inferior, most of all people of African descent, thus appealing to anti-Black sentiment in the United States and colonial racism in Germany. At a time of growing anti-Asian sentiment in both countries, it also flaunted anti-Asian tendencies in excluding Hindus and Buddhists.[162] At the same time, Mazdaznan texts fostered a sense of solidarity across national boundaries among the supposedly chosen race, thus combining racism with an internationalism that appealed to social and intellectual elites in Europe, North America, and, surprisingly, some Parsis in Bombay.[163] If scholars like Stefan Kühl and Kieran Klaus Patel have argued in recent years that internationalism was not limited to left-wing political actors, and that advocates of racism, and particularly eugenics, were likewise internationally organized, Mazdaznan's peculiar internationalism aligns with these findings.[164]

The participation of Swami Vivekananda, Arya Samajis, and other South Asian protagonists in the World's Columbian Exposition was an indirect consequence of the encounters addressed in chapter 2. In the wake of the exposition, the United States saw a surge in interest in "Indian spirituality," particularly yoga, which came to be considered as inseparable from vegetarianism, even though those who brought yoga to the United States might not have participated in that kind of abstention.

The consequences of the World's Columbian Exposition and the yoga boom went well beyond Vedanta missions. Yoga was also appropriated by new religious communities including Mazdaznan, which, however, veiled its indebtedness to Hindu influences through references to Zoroastrianism and a vaguely defined "Orient." Mazdaznan "de-Hinduized" Aryanism while expanding it further, including Muslims, Jews, and Zoroastrianism in this supposedly elect group. This strategy, a response also to anti-Black and anti-Asian racism in the United States and Germany, helped Mazdaznan distinguish itself from Theosophy and find a niche in the dense market of new religions in the United States.

The World's Columbian Exposition in Chicago was a catalyst for producing hybrid knowledge on yoga and nutrition in and beyond the United States.[165] It was also important in the history of vegetarianism because it promoted vegetarianism as an internationalized and organized movement, albeit a precarious one, as will be seen. This internationalization did not start in Chicago, but it received an impetus from the exposition and the vegetarian congress.

At a congress of German and British vegetarian societies in Cologne in 1889, delegates agreed to organize "a great International Union between all Food Reform, Temperance, and Natural Living Societies."[166] The Vegetarian Federal Union was founded some months later in London. This organization claimed that its work concerned "the whole people, humanity at large," and was "of an international character,"[167] but only British representatives were present at its inaugural meeting. Nonetheless, the Vegetarian Federal Union was "defined as an association of such Vegetarian Societies throughout the world as may be willing to unite together for certain specific purposes hereinafter to be determined."[168]

Its second congress, held in 1890, again in London, included delegates from Britain, the United States, France, Germany, and Italy.[169] A young student of law from India was also at the event: Mohandas Karamchand Gandhi.[170] In 1891, twenty-three societies were affiliated with the Vegetarian Federal Union, and two more were asking to be.[171] Members included Durga Prasad's Punjab Vegetarian Society and some associations from central Europe and the United States. After the World's Columbian Exposition, members of the Vegetarian Federal Union met again in London in 1897 and in Paris in 1900.

The board of the Vegetarian Federal Union took care to lend an international aura to these meetings. At the 1897 meeting, delegates were offered vegetable curries that a British vegetarian journal claimed had been prepared by a "renowned Indian chef."[172] For its fifth congress, held in Paris in 1900,[173] the board received "papers and promises of speeches from Russia, India, Holland, Australia, America."[174] Yet despite these auspicious beginnings, the Vegetarian Federal Union remained dominated by its British and American members.

After its last meeting, in St. Louis in 1904,[175] the Vegetarian Federal Union came to a standstill. Vegetarians then made a new start in Leipzig, where the International Vegetarian Union was formed in 1908. Leipzig was an appropriate place for several reasons. First, it had long been an important center of education, culture, publishing, and trade.[176] Secondly, it was one of the centers of vegetarianism in Germany and the seat of the German Vegetarian Union (Deutscher Vegetarier-Verband), established in 1892 with the merger of Eduard Baltzer's association and the Hamburg Vegetarian Society.[177] Finally, Leipzig was a hub of new religious movements, including Buddhism, Theosophy, and Mazdaznan.[178]

Despite its name, the International Vegetarian Union was mainly European, and remained so for half a century. Before the Second World War, its ten conferences all took place in northern, central, and eastern Europe.[179] The union remained an agglomeration of national associations. It never had a journal of its own, and presidents and vice presidents were only nominated after the Second World War. Prior to the early 1950s, no representatives from outside Europe were mentioned in the meeting reports that appeared in German and British journals.

While events like the World's Columbian Exposition allowed Westerners to meet supposedly like-minded protagonists from India, organized vegetarianism remained centered on Europe and the United States. Asian protagonists enjoyed symbolic value but wielded limited influence. Particularly in Germany and Switzerland, German-speakers translated knowledge from or about Asia, even, in cases like Hanisch's, claiming Asian origin for greater authenticity. Apart from Gandhi, however, few Asian protagonists occupied any space in vegetarian journals for the next fifty decades. In organized vegetarianism, even the supposedly foreign had to be local.

*Chapter Four*

# BETWEEN BUDDHA, GANDHI, SUFISM, AND MILITANT MASCULINITY

Relating to South Asia in Interwar German and Swiss Vegetarianism

During the first decades of the twentieth century, German vegetarians were part of a wide network that connected them to eastern, central, and northern Europe, and, to a lesser extent, western Europe as well as the United States. Some of them were also adherents of the Esperanto movement, which overlapped with pacifism, temperance, and vegetarianism.[1] Readers of German-language vegetarian magazines were regularly informed of the movement's progress in countries such as Hungary, Estonia, or Norway, and of the increasing communication between international youth, in which vegetarianism played an important role.[2] Contributors to these periodicals reviewed works, or translations of works, by prominent authors such as Tolstoy and Gandhi.[3] Until the Nazis' rise to power, these magazines also carried articles on and in Esperanto, and readers published advertisements seeking partners or domestic servants in this most influential of invented languages.[4]

In the wake of the World's Columbian Exposition, India, hardly prominent before, other than in Gustav Struve's writings, likewise came to play a prominent role in German-speaking vegetarianism. In contrast to Britain, however, the figure of the "merciful Hindoo" was hardly present in the German-speaking context. The India created by German-speaking vegetarians was above all a sphere of projection, as Swiss and German vegetarians breathed rhythmically as per Mazdaznan instructions, rubbed their bodies with "Arya Laya Oil," drank "Kundalini Herbal Wines," or sent their children to the Theosophinum boarding school in Jena, where students were fed raw fruits and vegetables only, and whose facade was decorated with a Sanskrit inscription and a font reminiscent of Chinese script.[5]

German-speaking vegetarians' growing interest in India was to some extent connected to the shifting political geographies of the time. As scholars like Kris Manjapra, Harald Fischer-Tiné, Heike Liebau, Razak Khan, and others have pointed out, Germany and Switzerland became important places of exile for South and West Asian nationalists during and after the First World War. Through political cooperation and affective ties, these activists soon came to be connected to German and Swiss nationals.[6] But even German-speaking vegetarians without these links were likely to be fascinated by the man who came to embody the subcontinent in the interwar years for large parts of the German-speaking (or even European) public: Gandhi.

The First World War and the multiple crises that followed added to the sense of threat that drew the middle class to vegetarianism and related life reform movements. The vulnerability of both the body politic and the individual body, particularly the male one, fallen and wounded in the First World War, made calls for a New Man ever more urgent.[7] Alimentary reform appeared to be a way to shape the New Man.[8] The accumulation of crises caused a loss of orientation that led men and women across the political spectrum to look for a strong, ascetic leader. Vegetarianism addressed all these concerns, becoming the symbol of the regenerated, hardworking, controlled individual—indeed, of an exemplary political leader like Gandhi.

Research on German-speaking vegetarianism and life reform, up to Florentine Fritzen's and Corinna Treitel's recent studies, has long been characterized by a strict focus on Germany and Switzerland.[9] But as I will argue in this chapter, encounters with South Asia became an important inspiration to German-speaking vegetarians in the wake of the World's Columbian Exposition and during the interwar era. In this, my research complements existing studies by Suzanne Marchand, Bernd Wedemeyer-Kolwe, Bernadett Bigalke, and others that have shown the influence of South Asia on the German and Swiss life reform movements.[10]

# BETWEEN BUDDHA, GANDHI, SUFISM, AND MASCULINITY

However, it goes beyond these works in stressing that South Asia was not merely a sphere of projection, and that German-speaking vegetarians actually met and formed ties with protagonists from South Asia, whether at home or abroad.[11] Moreover, advocates of vegetarianism from other parts of Asia exiled in Germany likewise drew on the growing enthusiasm for South Asia in shaping their rationales for vegetarianism. These encounters were crucial aspects of the production of new, hybrid knowledge that became central to German vegetarianism—knowledge that could be accommodated to a wide range of political agendas, whether socialist, conservative, or fascist.

Some anti-Semitic vegetarians, or so I show in the first part of the chapter, drew inspiration from reformist Buddhism, whose protagonists gave center stage to Aryanism and anti-Semitism, at times even in South Asia. Merging Sufism and Ahmadiyya Islam with borrowings from Mazdaznan allowed an exiled Persian intellectual, introduced in the second section of the chapter, to become a central figure in German-speaking vegetarianism well into the 1950s. As I show in the third section, German vegetarians of different political convictions became enthused with Gandhi, who appeared as the savior-like ascetic leader crisis-shaken Weimar Germany seemed to need—before another ascetic vegetarian finally took over in 1933.[12] Very much contrary to his own positions, or so I argue in the fourth section, Gandhi also served as a point of reference in vegetarian agendas incorporating nudism and sexual liberation. Finally, I point out that some vegetarians idealized South Asian concepts of nonviolence to such an extent that they overlooked violent Hindu nationalist tendencies.

Many of those currents in German vegetarianism survived Nazism and persisted into the restored internationalism of postwar vegetarianism—which also contradicts the long-espoused argument that organized German-speaking vegetarianism was interrupted during Nazi rule: indeed, only part of it was.[13]

## IN SEARCH OF "ARYAN" HERITAGE IN CEYLON

In early 1912, a group of young vegetarians set off on an adventurous journey: from Leipzig, they would travel around the world on foot, getting to know vegetarian foodways while testing the efficacy of different vegetarian diets and a range of life reform products.[14] Ludwig Ankenbrand, who planned the journey, was a member of the newly founded Bund für Buddhistisches Leben established in Halle, near Leipzig in 1911, and an ardent animal welfare activist and vegetarian.[15]

Buddhism—in fact, a new kind of Buddhism—came to Germany through a series of encounters. Though Ceylon had been under British rule since the early nineteenth century, Buddhism was still the dominant religion on the island, even though it had been targeted by Christian missions. Resistance to these missions and colonialism shaped a new, reformist Buddhism. Central to this development was Don David Hewavitarane, who, as a young man, met the founders of the Theosophical Society in Ceylon. Hewavitarane joined the Theosophical Society, but broke with it in 1891 after it started turning toward Hinduism. He established the Maha Bodhi Society to win back Bodh Gaya, the site of the Buddha's enlightenment, from the Hindus.[16]

The Maha Bodhi Society's Buddhism was heavily influenced by both Theosophy and Protestantism.[17] It rejected caste and the power of the *sangha* (monastic clergy), focusing instead on the personal responsibility of the faithful, whom it called on to embrace a "thisworldly asceticism" that stressed the benefits of hard work, sexual restraint, and service to society. Most importantly in the present context, Hewavitarane claimed that Buddhism had always been unequivocally vegetarian.[18] In 1893, Hewavitarane, now calling himself the Anagarika Dharmapala, loosely translated as the "Dharma Guardian,"[19] participated in the Parliament of Religions at the World's Columbian Exposition. Dharmapala represented Buddhism in a manner reminiscent of Vivekananda's image of Hinduism: it was a philosophy that had anticipated the discoveries of modern-day science, most notably evolutionary theory, by millennia.[20]

Through German protagonists at the parliament, a milieu open to Theosophy, and the Anagarika Dharmapala's extensive travel, knowledge of this new kind of Buddhism spread in Germany. Leipzig saw the foundation of a Buddhist Missionary Society (Buddhistischer Missionsverein) in 1903, whose assemblies were held in a local vegetarian restaurant.[21] Despite the name, the association was founded by German scholars and enthusiasts of Buddhism, men who conceived of Buddhism from a Protestant perspective.[22] This association soon merged with the German Maha Bodhi Central, also in Leipzig, and received enthusiasts like Ankenbrand into their ranks.²³ Parallel to these developments, Anton Floris Gueth, a Catholic violin virtuoso from Wiesbaden, set off for Ceylon to become the first German Buddhist monk. Gueth, now called Nyanatiloka, was consecrated in 1904, founded the Island Hermitage on an island in Ceylon, and received many German novices over the next decades.²⁴ The Island Hermitage was Ankenbrand's and his fellow travelers' ultimate destination.²⁵

These developments were not the first seeds of Buddhism in Germany. In the first half of the nineteenth century, Arthur Schopenhauer had been inspired by Buddhism. He saw the Buddhist notion of nirvana as the highest aim for all, not just Buddhists. Schopenhauer also appreciated Buddhism because of its merciful attitude toward animals. His work introduced later German intellectuals to Buddhism—some, like Richard Wagner and Friedrich Nietzsche, only loosely, others, like Gueth, to the extent that they came to consider themselves Buddhists.²⁶ As Suzanne Marchand argues, therefore, German intellectuals were attracted to Buddhism long before Weimar Germany. Their convictions were also less benign and less free from Orientalism and racism than Marchand maintains, since Neo-Buddhism was deeply entangled with Aryan discourse from the beginning.²⁷ Like Hindu members of the Theosophical Society, Anagarika Dharmapala argued that Buddhist South Asians were Aryans, and in fact, the better Aryans, with Europeans no more than a "lost tribe."²⁸ Buddhism was both the most modern religion and the Aryan religion par excellence.²⁹ Dharmapala disdained Christianity, Judaism, and Islam as "Semitic" religions. Western neo-Buddhists like Ludwig Ankenbrand adopted Dharmapala's interpretation, implying that by embracing Buddhism, Westerners could reverse their cultural decline and even end up superior to South Asian "Aryans."³⁰ They also turned Dharmapala's negative feelings about Semites, which he directed mainly at Muslims, into an anti-Semitism that mainly targeted Jews, thus tying in with older anti-Semitic tropes in Germany.³¹

Aryanism held particular significance for German neo-Buddhists. It let them distance themselves from Christianity, and it helped them claim a common racial ancestry with a geographically remote religion. Wolfgang Bohn, a physician, anti-vivisectionist, and member of the German branch of the Maha Bodhi Society, even asserted that the Buddha's ancestors hailed from Saxony.³² Buddhism's supposed birthplace was conveniently close to that of its ally, vegetarianism. Leipzig, Saxony, where the German branch of the Maha Bodhi Society had its seat, was a stronghold of Theosophy and other alternative religious movements,[33] home to the German Vegetarian Union, and site of the International Vegetarian Union's founding in 1908. Several German Maha Bodhi affiliates were members of the German Vegetarian Union. So was young Ludwig Ankenbrand.

To Ankenbrand, Buddhism connected the seemingly diverse reform movements in turn-of-the-century Germany: life reform, dress reform, vegetarianism, anti-vivisectionism, nature cure, anti-vaccination, temperance, pacifism, and animal welfare. Claiming that Buddhism differed from "Semitic religions of revelation" such as Christianity and Judaism in not relying on priests, Ankenbrand argued that it connected with contemporary religious reform movements like German Catholicism or Monism. Ankenbrand's notion of Buddhism was based on a binary opposition between "Aryanism" and "Semitism." If Germans were to reverse their cultural decline, it was, in Ankenbrand's view, to the most "Aryan" of religions they had to turn.

Ankenbrand's praise of "Aryanism" and indictment of "Semitism" hit a nerve in German vegetarianism. While Eduard Baltzer's association had accepted Jewish members and never polemicized against *shehita*, calling it less painful than other modes of slaughter, there had been undercurrents of anti-Semitism in the movement since the late 1880s.[34] By the end of the decade, Bernhard Förster, one of the most radical anti-Semites of the Wilhelmine era, had commissioned articles in Balzer's and other vegetarian magazines to publicize his plan of founding a vegetarian "Aryan" colony in Paraguay called Nueva Germania.[35] The short-lived project ended when Förster, in 1891, died by suicide in a hotel room in Nueva Baviera, another German colony in Paraguay.[36]

The failure of Nueva Germania, however, did not taint the Förster family's reputation in German vegetarianism. Paul Förster, Bernhard's brother and, like him, a radical anti-Semite, remained a central figure in the German animal welfare and anti-vivisectionist movements.[37] In 1880, he founded the Internationaler Verein zur Bekämpfung der wissenschaftlichen Thierfolter, an organization combatting vivisection.[38] Important figures of the anti-vivisectionist movement, including Helena Petrovna Blavatsky and some Hindu members of the Theosophical Society, were affiliated with it.[39] He and Ankenbrand, despite their difference in age, were close friends, sharing a commitment to animal welfare and anti-Semitic positions.[40]

Ankenbrand had set off to encounter "our brethren from ancient Aryan times," but his journey soon led to disillusionment. Two members left the group midway, while Lisbeth Ankenbrand's sister-in-law, Minna Symanzick, was sent back to Germany after a mental breakdown brought on by rape.[41] Ankenbrand's dog died of thirst.[42] Amid their troubles, the travelers struggled to focus on the dietetic experiments they had envisaged. After a two-year journey, they arrived in Ceylon at Nyanatiloka's community at the Island Hermitage just as the First World War broke out. Within a few months, all Germans and Austrians in Ceylon were interned in a camp with few opportunities to encounter non-German "brethren," except for the Punjabi prison guards. Camp routine posed a further challenge to the vegetarian diets followed by the monks and other members of the group.[43] Frustrated, Ankenbrand, under the pseudonym "Richard Kaisertreu,"[44] started a newspaper for the German-speaking inmates that reported on the progress of the war and activities organized by the prisoners.

More than anything, this newspaper reflected Ankenbrand's embitterment and prejudice. The only person who received emphatic praise in the newspaper was the German emperor, characterized as a man of peace. The only country, apart from Ceylon, that was idealized was the German *Heimat*. Articles included vitriolic attacks on the British, on Jews as the supposed helpmeets of British aggression against Germany, on socialists, Catholics, Polish nationals (though Ankenbrand's wife was of Polish descent), the Punjabi guards, and Hindus in general.[45] Ankenbrand's anti-Semitism remained intact, but his idea of an "Aryan" brotherhood with South Asians was shattered by his war experience. He idealized the Ceylonese—or more precisely, Ceylonese Buddhist Tamils—but saw Ceylonese Hindus as morally corrupt.[46] The Punjabi guards, meanwhile, were reviled for their allegedly uppity behavior rather than acknowledging their supposed Aryan brotherhood with the German camp inmates.[47]

After five years of internment, first in Ceylon, then in Australia, Ludwig and Lisbeth Ankenbrand were finally able to leave for Germany, where he wrote articles for vegetarian and Buddhist periodicals and books. In these writings, Ankenbrand no longer stressed the idea of an "Aryan" brotherhood between South Asian Buddhists and Germans, even though he coauthored a book that claimed that Germans understood Buddhism particularly well and that Buddhists were especially close to reform movements like anti-vivisectionism.[48] The book also praised the Hindu caste system, for "caste means pure, and the higher a caste stands, the purer its origins" and the "paler its skin color (the Indian expression for caste being *varna*, color)."[49] With his "Aryan" convictions waning, Ankenbrand also stopped openly expressing anti-Semitism. Indeed, he no longer saw Buddhism and Christianity as opposites, with the one purely positive, the other wholly negative, instead embracing both Buddhism and Christian nonconformism.[50]

Though Ankenbrand abandoned the idea of an "Aryan" brotherhood, he was not a dissident under the Nazis, publishing on *Heimat*-related issues after joining the Nazi Party in 1937.[51] Lisbeth Ankenbrand published several bestselling books on vegetarian cuisine and the maintenance of female beauty, including one called *The Will to Beauty*.[52] She held on to the idea of an "Aryan" race, but it no longer included South Asians. Even though she occasionally recommended to her readers personal hygiene practices embraced by South Asian women, she stressed that (European) "Aryans" were the superior and most beautiful race.[53]

Ankenbrand continued interacting with South Asians, but his contacts were confined mainly to Muslim exiles in Germany, among them Sheikh Muhammad Abdullah, the imam of the Ahmadiyya mosque in Berlin Wilmersdorf, and H. Mazooruddin Ahmad, a foreign correspondent living in Berlin who sympathized with Subhas Chandra Bose's efforts to use Nazi support to end British rule in India by force.[54] From someone with little sympathy or interest in non-Buddhist South Asia, Ankenbrand turned into someone who loosely sympathized with Indian anticolonial resistance—probably more because of his own anti-British animosities than a genuine opposition to colonialism or concern for non-Buddhist South Asians and a common "Aryan" cause.[55] None of these attitudes, however, caused him trouble under the Nazis.[56] In fact Ludwig Ankenbrand got through the Nazi era largely unscathed, continuing his career as a spokesman for both Buddhism and vegetarianism well into the postwar era, while Lisbeth Ankenbrand continued to be a bestselling author.[57]

As Ankenbrand's case shows, the World's Columbian Exposition also shaped part of vegetarian discourse in Germany by exposing it to reformist Buddhism. Thus, it was in 1910s and 1920s Germany that South Asia received some degree of attention in vegetarian circles, although it was always less than in Britain. Unlike their counterparts in the United Kingdom, German vegetarians were not fascinated with South Asia because of Hinduism; their main interest was Buddhism. Their resentments, moreover, were not directed against Muslims but against Jews. And since their vegetarianism was coupled with an emphasis on a supposed Aryanism, race was central to it.

## FROM MAZDAZNAN TO SUFI VEGETARIANISM

By the time Ankenbrand and his companions set off on their journey, a young intellectual from Tābrīz, in Persia, had arrived in Berlin. Hossein Kazemzadeh, a Shiite, had worked for the Persian embassy in Istanbul before becoming a lecturer in Persian at the University of Cambridge. In 1915, he was invited to join the National Committee for the Liberation of Iran, founded in Berlin. In the course of his stay in the German capital, he came to embrace spirituality and vegetarianism.

Heavily in debt to Western countries and fought over by Russia and Britain, Persia had experienced a revolution and introduced a constitution in 1906 before falling into political instability until the 1920s.[58] Those looking for political change called for demographic renewal, arguing that Persia had become politically weak because of its supposedly small and sickly population. For Persia (or Iran, as modernist intellectuals termed it) to regenerate, it needed women to be educated and participate in political life and a new kind of hegemonic masculinity.[59] Along with calling for Western education and dress, this new masculinity rested on a heteronormative model based on companionate marriage. This type of union, a hallmark of the "global bourgeoisie" (Dejung/Motadel/Osterhammel), would produce healthy new citizens.[60] Kazemzadeh, the son of a doctor specializing in herbal medicine,[61] took up these debates, addressing himself to both German and Persian audiences.

In Berlin, Kazemzadeh became a member of the National Committee for the Liberation of Iran, in which capacity he worked to overthrow the Persian monarchy.[62] Like other nationalist initiatives in South and West Asia, the National Committee was supported by the German Foreign Office, which hoped to weaken British imperial power in Asia.[63] After the committee sent him to Turkey to prepare a revolution in Persia, Kazemzadeh was interned and deported, but was able to return to Berlin due to an intervention by the German Foreign Office. The National Committee then changed its strategy, suggesting that the Foreign Office support the training of fifty Iranian male students from elite families in Germany who would form the avant-garde of a new, politically and culturally regenerated Iran.[64] The Foreign Office consented, placing twenty young men in German families under the tutelage of a committee composed of Germans and exiled Iranians.[65] Kazemzadeh joined the supervisory committee.[66]

At the same time, he was a member of the German Orientalist Society and a cofounder of the German-Persian Society and the Berlin Ahmadiyya community, composed of Muslims and Muslim converts from South and West Asian, German Protestant, and German Jewish backgrounds, in whose journal, *Moslemische Revue*, he published a number of articles.[67] He became friends with Wilhelm Schwaner, one of the exponents of the *völkisch* movement.[68] Until 1921, Kazemzadeh worked for *Kaveh*, a journal funded by the German Foreign Office. After the German Foreign Office stopped supporting the journal, he founded a bookstore, publishing house, and journal called *Iranschähr*, the name of Persia under the Safavids, which he also used as his pen name.[69] Contributors to the journal discussed the ways that Persian society needed to be regenerated.

Apart from discussing literature and history, *Iranschähr* took up women's education and family life.[70] Articles considered how society could be reformed through the body of the individual, and discussed physical education and nutrition, especially the harmful effects of tea, tobacco, and meat.[71] While only advocating it openly later on, Kazemzadeh was clearly sympathetic to vegetarianism.[72] In this context, he introduced his readers—liberal, educated Persian expatriates in Europe—to an eccentric community in the United States and Europe: Mazdaznan.

In a sequence of articles, Kazemzadeh described Otto Hanisch, whom he characterized as "a man of European visions [who] accepts [Zarathustra's] teachings, mixing them with scientific elements and Christian principles, thus reviving the old tenets of Zoroastrianism," and his core teachings.[73] Kazemzadeh approved of the Mazdaznan diet, including its emphasis on eating less, consuming raw foods, and fasting.[74] While acknowledging that Hanisch was controversial, Kazemzadeh praised the "scientific and practical force of this outstanding, superhuman personality."[75] He stopped short, however, of praising Mazdaznan's championing of racial theory.

It is unclear whether Kazemzadeh ever formally joined Mazdaznan.[76] He published a German translation of the Gathas, a core text of Zoroastrianism, in 1930, possibly intended for Germans sympathetic to Mazdaznan.[77]

By the time Kazemzadeh wrote about Mazdaznan, the community had become notorious in Germany. On the one hand, the active support of intellectuals like Bauhaus founding member Johannes Itten, a vegetarian and ardent admirer of Gandhi,[78] shows that it enjoyed a certain prestige among the intellectual elite. Itten integrated Mazdaznan exercises into his preliminary course at the Bauhaus, introduced vegetarian food to the Bauhaus canteen,[79] and wrote articles that connected Mazdaznan racial theory to the history of art, arguing that the allegedly leading role of the "white race" in art was biologically founded.[80]

On the other hand, one of the major German vegetarian journals at the time, the *Vegetarische Warte*, had stopped reporting on Mazdaznan after outing it as a sham in the 1910s (although it continued to feature ads for its mail-order business).[81] German authorities were also critical of the organization. While small Mazdaznan groups continued to exist in larger German cities through the 1920s and 1930s, its superior in Leipzig, David Ammann, was expelled from Germany in 1914 for indecency. Mazdaznan established its European headquarters in Herrliberg, near Zurich.[82] When Johannes Itten left the Bauhaus in 1923, he joined the Herrliberg group, becoming one of its leading figures.[83]

Mazdaznan was still popular in Germany after Ammann's deportation, but its situation became precarious in 1935 when the Nazi Deutsche Gesellschaft für Lebensreform (German Society for Life Reform) was established.[84] A series of articles in *Leib und Leben* (Body and life), the society's official journal, attacked the community over the group's notion of race and its incompatibility with Nazi policies. The importance Mazdaznan attached to wheat and its preference for "the most exotic foreign foods" were incompatible with Nazi food policy, which placed a premium on goods cultivated on German soil, particularly *Schwarzbrot*, whole bread chiefly made from unhusked rye.[85] Mazdaznan's recommendation of spices, onions, and garlic, which Hanisch, according to somewhat misinformed Nazi reviewers, had borrowed from "Brahmanic prescripts," might have been "useful for [Hindu] religious service," but was clearly harmful to German bodies.[86] Most important, however, was Mazdaznan's notion of race and eugenics, which was starkly at odds with Nazi ideas of race, since it assumed that race was not static and determined by heredity, but could be "upgraded" by means of diet.[87] Finally, *Leib und Leben* criticized Mazdaznan's focus on reform through the individual, since it was the national community—the *Volksgemeinschaft*—that had to be the focus of any reform.[88] Nazi experts deemed Mazdaznan an "intellectual plague" that had to be abolished, despite the fact that many leading Nazis were enthusiastic about South Asia–inspired esotericism.[89]

Mazdaznan was first abolished in Saxony, its main center in Germany, then deemed "hostile to the people and the state" (*volks- und staatsfeindlich*) in a decree issued by Wilhelm Frick, minister of the interior, on October 9, 1935.[90] Before the decree, the British branch had sent Hitler a note in August 1935 that stressed German Mazdaznan members' loyalty to the Nazi state, but to no avail.[91] The Swiss branch became more important as a hub for German-speaking Mazdaznan adherents and continued to host international Mazdaznan meetings, even though they were hampered by the German and Swiss members' poor command of English.[92]

How could a Persian intellectual be so appreciative of Mazdaznan, given its dubious intellectual roots and its championing of what it called the "white" or Aryan "race?" It is important to remember that while Mazdaznan was shaped by white supremacist discourses, its idea of Aryanness included Jews, Arabs, and Persians. Gerdien Jonker argues that Kazemzadeh also embraced the concept of an Aryan race,[93] but a closer look at his work suggests a more nuanced interpretation. Kazemzadeh's books focused on humankind, not race. He never mentioned race or religion as criteria of distinction or division, perhaps due to the religious heterogeneity of the Berlin life reform milieu and the interreligious dialogue Kazemzadeh located himself in in Switzerland.

Perhaps what attracted Kazemzadeh was Mazdaznan's notion of the relation between body and soul, an idea that became increasingly important in his own thought. Both argued that the body could alter the spirit and thereby contribute to evolution. For Kazemzadeh, who wanted to regenerate Persians culturally and spiritually, Mazdaznan might have seemed like a valuable approach.

Even if one doubted Mazdaznan's authenticity (and Kazemzadeh's characterization of it does imply some doubt about its religious foundations), the community offered a model of how an individual could establish a spiritual brand—one that centered vegetarianism. While Hanisch's claims to Persianness came under attack, Kazemzadeh's "Orientalness" could hardly be doubted.[94] It might have especially appealed to his audience since German vegetarians had been interested in the "Orient" since the second half of the nineteenth century.

Whatever the reasons for Kazemzadeh's turn from political activities to esotericism, he began establishing his spiritual brand after giving up his journal *Iranschähr* in 1927.[95] After 1927, he wrote mainly in German,[96] reflecting a publishing strategy that now targeted German-speaking readers in search of spiritual guidance.[97] At the same time, he changed outwardly. While continuing to wear impeccable Western suits, he grew a long beard, a fashion also sported by many German life reform "prophets."[98] In 1927, he became master of the Berlin Sufi Lodge established by the late Inayat Khan. He also joined the Theosophical Society.[99]

Sufism, of course, was not a new religious movement, but in the nineteenth and twentieth centuries it became popular in the West, and some of its advocates entered into dialogue with new religious communities, gearing their message to their audiences' tastes. The Sufi Lodge became part of the Ahmadiyya mosque in Berlin Wilmersdorf in 1933. Ahmadiyya Islam, meanwhile, had emerged in Lahore, India, partly in response to the attempts of the Arya Samaj to convert Muslims to Hinduism. It became a missionary movement that established mosques in many countries, including in the United States and Europe. The community assembling in its Berlin mosque united South Asians and Germans, many of whom were also members of various new religious communities in the city. According to Gerdien Jonker, the members of the Berlin Sufi Lodge were mostly wealthy Germans—a clientele similar to the one Mazdaznan appealed to, and possibly overlapping with it.[100] Interestingly, while Inayat Khan remained vague on the issue of meat consumption, arguing that pure nutrition should be based on the three *guṇas* (temperaments), but that meat could be consumed as long as it was halal, thus mixing Hindu and Muslim prescriptions, Kazemzadeh insisted on vegetarianism as a means of achieving spiritual purity.[101]

Like Mazdaznan's publications, Kazemzadeh's treatises drew on interrelated bodies of knowledge, including Sufism, Theosophy, and Mazdaznan. Like Hanisch, Kazemzadeh claimed that the goal of life was cultivating a higher self; he tellingly called the body a "*beast* of burden."[102] Facilitating the higher self required rejecting tobacco, alcohol, and meat, and undertaking regular fasting and abstention from overeating. Overeating and eating the wrong foods nourished what Kazemzadeh called man's "animal" aspect.[103]

Like the Theosophists, but also in line with Sufi authors, Kazemzadeh argued that consuming animal matter turned humans into animals, with sexual desire the most palpable expression of this animality. Eating meat nourished not the body but *nafs hayyawānī*, the carnal animal soul, or so Kazemzadeh explained in a Persian book published in 1926, possibly written for the Persian students in Germany under the tutelage of the National Committee.[104] While Kazemzadeh advocated treating animals gently, animals and the animal were clearly on a lower level than humans.[105]

Yet because of the importance he attached to the birth of New Man, Kazemzadeh did not condemn sexuality completely. Unlike Hanisch, who had appropriated Alice Bunker Stockham's feminist views on sexuality, he never openly supported pleasure, particularly female pleasure, perhaps wary of the scandals Mazdaznan's teachings on sex had caused in Germany in the 1910s.[106] Other than advocating total abstinence, however, he enjoined his followers to maintain their sexuality for the sake of procreation, which he described as a holy act that had to be performed in constant meditation to eliminate all impure thoughts.[107] With regard to sexuality, nutrition, and his view of the aims of life, Kazemzadeh's perspectives resembled those of Mazdaznan, but they were more conservative with regards to sex and less concerned with race.

In the end, no clear statement can be made on whether and how intimately Kazemzadeh was associated with Mazdaznan, although he remained close to it both discursively and geographically.[108] In 1936, a year after the banning of Mazdaznan in Germany, he moved to Degersheim, near the famous St. Gallen monastery in Switzerland, where he founded the Ecole Mystique Esoterique in 1942.[109] He published books and, from 1949 on, a journal called *Weltharmonie* (World harmony).[110] Until his death in 1962, he attended vegetarian conferences frequented by Mazdaznan members and moved in the same milieu of esotericism and religious reform.[111] Kazemzadeh was and remained the only prominent Muslim in German-speaking vegetarianism.

## BETWEEN BUDDHA, GANDHI, SUFISM, AND MASCULINITY

### FROM ASCETIC LEADERSHIP TO VEGETARIAN ARMAMENT

By the time Kazemzadeh moved to Switzerland, German vegetarianism had already been affected by Nazi efforts to control public life (*Gleichschaltung*).[112] After the war, many leading German vegetarians claimed their movement had been banned. While the main vegetarian associations were indeed gradually dissolved, vegetarians were not necessarily silenced during the Nazi era. Staunchly pacifist and socialist vegetarians were indeed persecuted by the regime,[113] but at least two vegetarian journals founded before the Nazis' rise to power continued to appear.[114]

During the 1920s, parts of German vegetarianism developed strong affinities to ideas that would later characterize Nazi rule, including support for strong male leadership and hierarchy. Vegetarians on both the left and the right articulated these tendencies, albeit in different contexts. It was particularly pronounced in the Internationaler Sozialistischer Kampfbund (ISK), which fought Nazism, and the *Vegetarische Presse*, which increasingly supported the Nazi Party. They shared an emphasis on the figure of the ascetic male leader.[115]

The ISK was founded in 1925 by Leonard Nelson, professor of philosophy at the University of Göttingen, and Minna Specht, an educator, as a socialist youth organization that brought together students and workers.[116] It mainly attracted young people from Germany, but also some from other European and Asian countries, many of them Nelson's students.[117] Nelson advocated animal rights and vegetarianism,[118] but the association's main purpose was to fight emerging right-wing tendencies throughout Europe, tendencies that only increased after Nelson's early death in 1927.[119] The ISK issued a declaration in 1932 that warned of the consequences if the Nazis won the general elections of 1933.[120] The ISK objected to the Nazis' economic policy and their anti-Semitism,[121] but was less bothered about their anti-democratic tendencies. Nelson favored a hierarchy topped by a male leader,[122] and despite the decentralized and often creative character of its political operations, the ISK was structured hierarchically.

Required to subordinate their entire lives to the cause, ISK members were not allowed to correspond with anyone outside the organization. They were to donate a major part of their income to the movement, embrace celibacy and vegetarianism, abstain from alcohol and tobacco, and regularly confess their failings to each other—principles Nelson considered central to his concept of *Führererziehung*, education for (male hierarchic) leadership.[123] After the Nazis seized power, ISK members in and out of Germany often used vegetarian restaurants as inconspicuous bases for their planning and operations, even founding them for this purpose.[124] The ISK journal, meanwhile, reflected both the practical and theoretical aspects of vegetarianism. Like most socialist vegetarians, ISK members included animals in their vision of a more equal society.[125] They also rejected colonial rule. But though they supported the Indian freedom struggle, they did not report much about Gandhi's vegetarianism.[126]

The figure of the ascetic leader appealed equally to vegetarians with right-wing leanings. Much has been written about Hitler's vegetarianism,[127] but what is more interesting is how German vegetarians applied the trope of the ascetic leader to both Hitler and Gandhi.[128] We can see this in the *Vegetarische Presse*, the journal of the German Vegetarian Union. Edited by Georg Förster from 1926 to 1941, it was the most important German-language vegetarian journal in this period.[129]

Like the *Vegetarische Warte*, the other main German-language vegetarian journal in the 1920s, the *Vegetarische Presse* turned to a cult of leadership early on. Articles focused on outstanding male figures, usually historical advocates of vegetarianism including philosophers, writers, artists, or (rarely) statesmen or prominent present-day advocates. The *Vegetarische Presse* even introduced a regular column titled "Führer" (Leaders).[130] The importance of leading figures was further highlighted in articles discussing the hopelessness of the times. Förster and his collaborators deplored Germany's defeat in the war, reparations, the occupation of the Rhineland by French colonial troops, and, finally, the world economic crisis.[131] Only a strong leader could help the nation rise again.

To vegetarians like Förster, it was obvious that only those who rejected any kind of addiction, whether to alcohol, tobacco, or meat, had the requisite mental clarity to assume responsibility for society at large. Self-discipline came from mastering one's baser desires. Förster's journal embraced some pacifist ideals around 1926, featuring articles on why there should never be another war, but the masculinity it promoted always centered physical and mental strength and the ability to keep in check one's desires and emotions.

It was in this context that the *Vegetarische Presse* reported on India and Gandhi, taking up the motif of the ascetic vegetarian we have already seen.¹³² In 1926, a brief article with a portrait referred to him not just as a vegetarian and "enemy of tobacco" but as "one of the most important leaders of India."¹³³ A longer article, written in 1930 by Paul Albrecht, extolled Gandhi as one of the "demi-gods of world history," all, or so Albrecht claimed, "genuine vegetarians." To Albrecht, these men, especially Gandhi, were characterized above all by a total absence of weakness. Albrecht emphasized that Gandhi "did not shy away from any consequence, not even from revolution, indeed from combat," preferring "the use of violence . . . over the whole race being enslaved." Albrecht went on to say that this attitude exhibited not just a sense of "noble masculinity" (an interpretation that disregarded entirely Gandhi's fierce critique of masculinity as well as his pacifism), but a capacity to love his nation above all others, since "anyone who tears from their heart the love of their home country, preferring foreign nations to his own fellow nationals suffers from mental degeneration."¹³⁴ So impressed was he by Gandhi that Albrecht warned in another article that his leadership could help "the colored races" prevail over the "white race"—a fate the latter could avert only by embracing Gandhi's ascetic vegetarianism.¹³⁵

Albrecht's article must be read in its historical context. The demands of the Versailles Treaty and the stationing of French colonial troops in the Rhineland were often characterized as signs of the "enslavement" of the German people and nation, no longer a colonial power, by Africans. Socialists and communists were generally seen as antinational by large parts of the middle class.¹³⁶ By connecting a lack of nationalism with mental illness, Albrecht can be read as embracing this perspective, arguing that only a strong, masculine, vegetarian leader could save his people from "enslavement" and, indeed, from mental degeneration.¹³⁷ Georg Förster, in another article on India's struggle for independence and Gandhi's role in it, agreed: "Vegetarianism is the path toward light and all hail."¹³⁸

The *Vegetarische Presse* was sympathetic to the Nazi Party even before its rise to power. In 1929, several authors called for political unity among vegetarians so they could exert greater influence on the German parliament and government.¹³⁹ In 1932, Georg Förster explicitly called upon German vegetarians to vote for the Nazi Party.¹⁴⁰ Although the *Vegetarische Presse* had flirted with pacifism in the 1920s, and there could be no doubt that the Nazi Party espoused rather than rejected violence (something the *Vegetarische Presse* never discussed), Förster saw a vegetarian head of state as a victory for the vegetarian cause. Such a leader would help Germans break free from the curses of alcohol, tobacco, meat, and prostitution, which the *Vegetarische Presse* insisted had worsened, if not actually caused, the world financial crisis.[141] Once Hitler's victory was secured, vegetarians, advocates of natural healing, opponents of vaccination and vivisection had to form a "cartel" and articulate their demands during the next elections.[142]

The paper enthusiastically welcomed Hitler's rise to power, interpreting it as a major step toward a vegetarian world order.[143] Gandhi was no longer a model leader. Instead, in a programmatic article in the December issue of 1933, Hitler was portrayed not just as the prototype of the ascetic leader, but as a Christlike saviour.[144] "We are the first country on earth with a vegetarian leader, and we will become the leading country in life reform for the whole world," or so Förster and his coauthor proclaimed.[145]

Hitler's vegetarianism was also praised abroad, including in India, but German vegetarians soon turned their back on the world after Georg Förster and the presidents of the two other German vegetarian associations decided to exit the International Vegetarian Union. Prior to that, Germany had been an important member,[146] but the *Vegetarische Presse* began publishing attacks on other European vegetarian associations soon after Hitler's rise to power. German vegetarians, as a consequence, felt ostracized within the movement.[147] They did not return to the organization until the early 1950s.[148]

Although the three vegetarian associations did not unite and join the Deutsche Gesellschaft für Lebensreform, the Nazi organization bringing together all branches of life reform, they were unanimous in their appreciation of the regime, even though the Nazi government, as shown by Corinna Treitel and others, never recommended full-fledged vegetarianism to its citizens.[149] While the Nazis, like other fascist regimes, aimed at economic independence, they were unwilling to cause discontent by forcing vegetarianism on their country's meat-loving population.[150] Germans were exhorted to reduce their consumption of meat and animal fat and eat fish and skimmed dairy products. The state researched alternative sources of protein, including soy (first imported from Japanese-occupied Manchuria, then cultivated, with limited success, in Poland, Romania, and Bulgaria) and synthetic protein products derived from yeast. Even with rationing, "Aryan" Germans always had meat, and pig breeding was promoted.[151] Germans were asked to make better use of the nutritional resources at hand, eating vegetable stews the first Sunday of the month, unpeeled fruit and vegetables, and consuming *Vollkornbrot* (whole-grain bread).[152] Thus ideas central to *neuzeitliche Ernährung* (modern nutrition), as nutritionally oriented vegetarians called their way of life, were adopted, but for the sake of economy and "racial health," not ethics.

Since economic independence could not be achieved solely through German resources, the occupation of eastern Europe was supposed to close the gaps. German forces in the East worked to fill "Aryan" bellies by starving those deemed racially inferior. Jews, Polish and Soviet POWs, and those forcefully recruited for labor in eastern Europe had their food allowances radically cut and were deprived of animal products.[153] They were fed surrogates of doubtful quality (such as the infamous Biosyn sausage, an artificial yeast product teeming with bacteria tested in the Dachau concentration camp) while their bodies were pushed to their utmost capacity, putting the nutritional experimentalism and debates on fasting long central to vegetarian discourse to sinister use. The idea was not to save animal lives or improve human vitality, but to impose racial hierarchies and kill by inches.[154]

German vegetarian magazines never discussed the casualties of Nazi vegetarian food politics. Both the *Vegetarische Presse* and *Neuleben*, the other vegetarian journal at the time, aligned themselves with the new regime, embracing an ideal of hard, combative masculinity that accorded with the outright rejection of pacifism in the Deutsche Gesellschaft für Lebensreform.[155] Well before the war, *Leib und Leben* mobilized against pacifism in both text and image, denouncing pacifist vegetarians as traitors. Images such as a lithograph by Erich Sperling of two soldiers shouldering spades for gardening, meanwhile, suggested that German soldiers were fighting for "peace and humanity" and providing Aryan Germans with *Lebensraum* (living space) and food.[156]

As early as 1936, the *Vegetarische Presse* began arguing that there was no contradiction between vegetarianism and joining the army; in fact, it was the duty of vegetarians to defend their home country. During the war, the journal's covers often featured images of Hitler Youth and heroic German soldiers.[157] One lithograph in particular, published in October 1940, embraced German expansion in the East, which Nazi leaders justified by a need for *Lebensraum* and arable land suitable for the cultivation of grain. It showed a German soldier behind a freshly harvested grain field, with a *Vollkornbrot* framed by flowers in the foreground, conveying that it was the courage and hardiness of German soldiers that ensured that "Aryan" Germans received their daily bread.[158]

The journals never mentioned violence against opponents of the regime or Jews. Instead, the *Vegetarische Presse* (which had published articles by and on the German Jewish vegetarian, Esperantist, and artist Nathan Chavkin up to Hitler's rise to power[159]) was openly anti-Semitic. Articles praised the Nazi government's prohibition of ritual slaughter and its restrictive attitude toward vivisection.[160] Even after the abolition of *shehita*, the journal depicted Jews as cruel to animals and humankind.[161]

The cult of the ascetic leader, then, led German vegetarians to abandon some of their core principles—namely, that vegetarianism would create a more peaceful world, and that ending the killing of animals would end human-on-human violence. Articles now discussed how vegetarianism facilitated killing by providing soldiers with greater energy than a meat-based diet could.[162] The cult of the ascetic leader, starting with German enthusiasm for Gandhi, the champion of satyagraha, climaxed in a perfect synthesis of vegetarianism and violence.

While this change in attitude enabled the *Vegetarische Presse* to carry on its work until 1941 (even after Förster disbanded the German Vegetarian Union in 1936),[163] the Nazi regime's interest in vegetarianism was limited. As much as Hitler represented himself, and was represented, as the embodiment of the ascetic vegetarian leader, the *Volksgemeinschaft* was not asked to follow his example.

## A SWISS GANDHI?

At the World Vegetarian Congress in Eden in 1932, the last one held in Germany before German organizations left the International Vegetarian Union, an impassioned man, sinewy, slim, and naked but for a pair of shorts, addressed the audience.[164] Even among German-speaking vegetarians, many of whom encouraged nude sunbathing and supported dress reform, this kind of (non-)attire at a formal gathering was surprising.[165]

The zealous man in shorts, a Swiss vegetarian and naturist named Werner Zimmermann, was officially lecturing on "Vegetarianism as Global Reform and Japanese, Chinese, Indian, and American Perspectives on Vegetarianism." More specifically, he spoke about a person with equally scanty clothing but different objectives: Gandhi.[166] Until well into the late

## BETWEEN BUDDHA, GANDHI, SUFISM, AND MASCULINITY

FIGURE 4.1. Werner Zimmermann at the International Vegetarian Congress, Eden/Oranienburg, Germany, 1932. Photo courtesy Archiv der deutschen Jugendbewegung, Witzenhausen, Germany.

1950s, Zimmermann, one of the most important connectors in the European vegetarian and related movements, toured Germany and Switzerland lecturing on, among other topics, India and the Mahatma—so much so that he became a virtual avatar of Gandhi for German-speaking audiences.[167] Why was Zimmermann so preoccupied with the champion of satyagraha, and how did Gandhi's teachings fit into his own agenda? Although Zimmermann was a central actor in German-speaking vegetarianism and reform education, his India connections are only starting to be explored.[168] Because of his Swiss nationality and the lack of transnational studies on German-speaking life reform and vegetarianism, he has also been left out of research on vegetarianism or nudism.[169]

Zimmermann, the son of a factory worker, was born near Berne in 1893. After training to become a teacher, he traveled to the United States on a shoestring in 1919, hoping not only to "build character" and "satisfy" his "thirst for adventure and the beauty of this earth," but to follow his socialist convictions. He wanted to "witness all kinds of hard labor and the causes of the psychological misery besetting the proletarian."[170] On his trip, he worked as a farmhand, railway worker, and a welder while living on uncooked food, bread, fruit, peanut butter, and water. He pushed his body to its limits on as little food as possible—experiments not unlike those Gandhi pursued throughout his life.[171] After another trip to the United States in 1923, Zimmermann journeyed around the world in 1929, visiting North and South America, Japan, China, India, and the Middle East.[172] Another journey after the Second World War followed much the same route.[173] On both his trips around the world, Zimmermann visited Gandhi's ashram in Sevagram, yet he never met the Mahatma in his home. During his first visit, Gandhi was imprisoned.[174] On Zimmermann's second visit, Gandhi had already been assassinated.[175]

Zimmermann's agenda of shoestring travel to build character and see the world related to the agenda the German-speaking youth movement had held from the fin de siècle on.[176] The Wandervogel (Hiking Bird), an association founded in Steglitz, Berlin, that later expanded throughout German-speaking Europe, advocated hiking as a means of celebrating youth as a time of unique freedom while also strengthening bodies and patriotism.[177] Whereas the Wandervogel addressed mainly middle-class youth, the Naturfreunde (Friends of Nature) targeted a working-class audience with activities that included "social hiking," which let members encounter the rural workers or industrial workers in other regions, all in an effort to foster mutual solidarity—an objective similar to Zimmermann's aim of seeing workers' living conditions.[178]

Yet while the Naturfreunde and the Wandervogel restricted most of their hikes to the immediate environs or the nation, Zimmermann went to other continents. In his travels to far-flung destinations (supposedly alone, but usually with fellow travelers he failed to mention), Zimmermann adopted the heroic explorer persona so popular in the nineteenth and twentieth centuries.[179] From the early 1920s until the mid-1930s, he edited a journal, *Tao-Blätter* (later *Tau-Blätter*), that printed letters he wrote on the road and select letters sent to him by young fans.[180] Readers could follow Zimmermann to his most distant destinations, learning about educational reform in Japan; about the Doukhobors, a vegetarian Russian sect in Canada; or the Indian freedom struggle.[181]

They were also introduced to Zimmermann's notions of Asian spirituality. Despite his enthusiasm for Gandhi, he was uninterested in Hinduism, Jainism, or other religions present in or associated with India.[182] Instead, Zimmermann's journal loosely drew inspiration from his interest in Taoism, as evidenced by his translation of Henri Borel's novella *Wu-Wei* published outside his journal.[183] He saw Taoism as offering an opportunity to discard the "slave[ry] of our imagined deities" and to create "free people only believing in their own (divine) self, ... who do not acknowledge any lord, state, morality, man-made laws or ownership over themselves."[184] To find one's way back to one's Tao, an approach of *Wu-Wei*, or noninterference (as Borel and Zimmermann translated it), was essential.[185] For Zimmermann, only this kind of radical freedom would bring about New Man.[186]

Zimmermann saw noninterference as synonymous with Gandhi's notion of satyagraha (quest for truth), the principle at the heart of his concept of resistance. In reality, though, the two were quite different. Zimmermann and Gandhi both criticized established political power as well as capitalism, but Gandhi would never have subscribed to the degree of individualism and moral laissez-faire that Zimmermann espoused. Gandhi never referred to individual freedom in terms of giving in to pleasure. Instead, he used the term "swaraj," meaning self-rule, to refer to what he considered political and individual freedom: the ability to govern one's urges.[187] Freedom in terms of unrestrained personal liberty was anathema to Gandhi—but at the heart of Zimmermann's agenda.

Zimmermann's notion of Taoism served as a path to an all-encompassing agenda of reform, which he outlined in his journal. The early volumes embraced orthographic reform, a central objective of many German-speaking life reformers.[188] *Tao* also advocated economic reform, including the abolishment of currency and taxes on land; indeed, Zimmermann endorsed giving land to cultivators for free.[189] He opened a settlement of his own, Schatzacker, near Zurich, in 1932 where members exchanged goods without money.[190]

*Tao* was also concerned with dietary reform. Zimmermann and his coauthors agreed that vegetarianism was the key to living better: meat sullied the body and made it prone to illness. *Tao* authors also thought that most people ate far more than they needed, in contrast to wild animals, which allegedly never overate. Articles advocated *Rohkost*, a vegan diet composed of raw fruits, vegetables, and nuts that excluded cereals and dairy products. Eating raw foods allowed the body to better absorb vitamins, but fasting was also required, since only a clean body could absorb nutrients well. As one contributor to *Tao* argued, fasting could be practiced for up to eight weeks, and might help cure even potentially fatal diseases like cancer.[191] Fasting also provided mental clarity and mental strength.[192]

Many advocates of fasting and raw foods also claimed that uncooked fruits and vegetables, or abstention from all kinds of food, curbed sexual appetite. Gandhi, too, made this argument, although his dietary choices were also informed by the wish to live as simply as the average Indian, save time and energy for his political commitment, and liberate women from cooking. More importantly, however, eating, for Gandhi, was a sin that could lead to other kinds of physical gratification. Fasting, in contrast, was a means of penitence.[193]

Gandhi's alimentary choices were also connected to a concern for animal welfare. He was a vocal anti-vivisectionist and opposed vaccines. Throughout his life, Gandhi fought against cow slaughter. At the same time, he underscored that meat eaters should be convinced by arguments, not force.[194] Gandhi considered milk an important food, especially for poor people whose access to it was limited, and he worked to improve Indian cow stock, cooperating with foreign agricultural experts such as Sam Higginbottom to cultivate new breeds.[195] Zimmermann was not interested in this aspect of Gandhi's commitment, rarely discussing animal welfare in *Tao*.[196] Also absent from Zimmerman's writings was the idea of the animal that was so ubiquitous in nineteenth- and twentieth-century vegetarianism: "the animal" as a shorthand for sexual desire.[197]

Zimmermann's and Gandhi's approaches to fasting, therefore, were rather different. This showed especially in their respective attitudes toward sexuality. For his time, Zimmermann was remarkably liberal about sex.[198] He never claimed that fasting and raw foods minimized or even extinguished desire.[199] Well-read in psychoanalysis and sexology, Zimmermann did not see sexuality as an "animal" drive but as something deeply human. Even though he argued that an individual would only reach maturity after overcoming their sexual urges, this process, in his view, was reached through affirmation, not repression.[200] Zimmermann and other authors writing in *Tao* favored abolishing marriage, arguing that lifelong monogamy was untenable. Relationships ought to be based on mutual attraction and should end when the attraction subsided.[201] Sexuality should be freed from economic considerations: women, even if they ought not to be a formal part of the labor market, should be paid for every child they gave birth to. This would let them leave a relationship if they were no longer happy.[202] Unlike well-known life reformers and vegetarians such as John Harvey Kellogg, he did not condemn masturbation.[203] However, Zimmermann's notion of sexuality was limited to cisheterosexual encounters.

For Zimmermann, sexuality was not just for procreation: pleasure was an end in itself. And since having too many children could cause economic difficulties, Zimmermann approved of contraception, though he preferred coitus interruptus to condoms.[204] Thirty years after its first edition, he translated Alice Bunker Stockham's *Karezza* into German.[205]

How would one find an ideal sexual partner? Nudism. If men and women saw each other naked before considering a relationship, unwelcome surprises would be avoided: without clothes, no one could pretend to be more attractive than they were. Besides, clothes prevented the skin from "breathing," and even deformed the body. Zimmermann advocated outside baths in the nude, allowing the body to take in as much sunlight and fresh air as possible and to move without restrictions. Naturism complemented a raw food diet, cleansing and strengthening the body. It also had a strong social aspect: Zimmermann believed that seeing others move without being restrained by clothes created an impulse to do the same.[206] Zimmermann organized naturist trips and events for youths and young people,[207] but unlike many contemporary nudists, he did not pursue overtly eugenic aims.[208]

Gandhi's views differed considerably from Zimmermann's. Gandhi's *Guide to Health* (1921), which was translated into German and reviewed by Zimmermann in *Tao*, shows that Gandhi, while possibly influenced by Indian concepts of nudity like those of Jain asceticism, was also familiar with life reform debates on nudism and sex reform.[209] Referring to Jung and other European authors, Gandhi claimed that nude bodies were more beautiful than dressed ones and more immune to illness, and that regular nudity precluded shame.[210] But shame came back when Gandhi wrote about sex. Gandhi was not an advocate of sexual liberty. Although he had four sons, Gandhi stressed the merits of lifelong *brahmacharya* (abstinence) for both women and men. *Brahmacharya* had been associated with one stage in the male life cycle and was compulsory for longer only for ascetics, but Gandhi extended it to everyone.[211] Sexual union, for him, was permissible only if a married couple wanted to have a child—and even then only once in each case. Pregnancies were to be limited, being a strain on women's energy, but abstention was the only legitimate means of birth control.[212] Desire was something to repress and do penance for (for instance, by fasting).[213] Gandhi agreed with yogic teachings that considered semen the source of life energy, and saw sexuality as an expenditure of this limited resource. Just one ejaculation left a man a "broken vessel" that could not be repaired.[214] Sex emasculated men and defeminized women.[215] *Brahmacharis* and *bramacharinis* were the "true men and women."[216]

Despite their disagreements, Zimmermann championed Gandhi's concept of nonviolent resistance since he felt that living under capitalism in Switzerland was as bad as living under colonial rule in India. Nonviolent resistance, or noninterference, as he called it, appeared to him as the best means of overcoming moral conventions, currencies, and land tax; the best means of freeing oneself from the dire yokes of a mixed diet, conventional dress, and received orthography. Noninterference meant transforming society through love, offering an alternative to both communism and capitalism.[217]

Zimmermann hoped to explain his views on sexuality to Gandhi in person. When Gandhi went to visit his friend, the writer Romain Rolland, in Switzerland on his way to the London Round Table Conference in 1931, Zimmermann took the chance to meet his hero, accompanying him on his train journey to Geneva. On the trip, Gandhi asked Zimmermann to explain his views on sexuality—only to announce, a few moments later, that he was tired and needed sleep.[218] To Zimmermann's great disappointment, this was to be their last encounter. Zimmermann had advertised Gandhi's trip to Europe in *Tao*, and called on vegetarian associations in Germany, Switzerland, and central Europe to invite him for lectures.[219] Yet after five days visiting Rolland, Gandhi, exhausted by his trip, canceled the lecture dates Zimmermann had made for him. For Zimmermann, Gandhi's decision was both a disappointment and an opportunity. Instead of canceling the talks, Zimmermann took Gandhi's place (and his fees).[220] It was thus that he virtually became Gandhi to German audiences—even though some of his views were diametrically opposed to the Mahatma's.

From the mid-1920s on, Zimmermann was the central German authority on Gandhi. German-speaking audiences, particularly young left-wing vegetarians, were attracted to Zimmermann's radical vegetarianism. But

Zimmermann was clearly a less vigorous advocate of nonviolence, and was not pronouncedly antifascist, either. Indeed, as Stefan Rindlisbacher shows, he admired Mussolini for his positive stance on vegetarianism, tried to win the Nazi government over to his notion of a free economy without currency and land ownership, corresponded with Nazi authorities to ensure that his books continued to be published in Germany, and even after the war insisted that there had been genuine life reformers among the Nazis.[221] While his German publisher had to shut down for political reasons in 1937, Zimmermann continued lecturing in Germany during the war, including lectures to strengthen soldiers' morale.[222] Although not as supportive of the Nazi regime as Georg Förster was, he blurred the line between pacifism and militancy enough to remain popular with German-speaking vegetarians during Nazi rule and well into the late 1950s.[223]

## OF MUTUAL MISUNDERSTANDINGS: ANTIRACIST MEETS ARYAN MILITANT

While Werner Zimmermann derived inspiration from Gandhi because of his views on diet, Magnus Schwantje, a notable exponent of animal welfare activism, pacifism, and socialism, was taken with Gandhi because of his espousal of nonviolence. Ultimately, however, Schwantje fell for another Indian hero, Ram Chandra Sharma, a Hindu nationalist activist, drawn by his apparently selfless and untiring campaigning on behalf of animals.[224] Ram Chandra impressed him more than even Gandhi, since his agenda appeared less anthropocentric—and even more nonviolent than the Mahatma's. Yet as we will see, Schwantje was too far from Ram Chandra in both space and ideology to correctly understand him.

In the vegetarian scene of interwar Germany, Schwantje was something of a respected outsider, even though he regularly published in vegetarian magazines. He reproached German vegetarians for framing their movement as a question of diet, as he saw it as an ethical issue. He consistently stressed that vegetarianism was incomplete, indeed useless, if it was not accompanied by a commitment to improving and saving animals' lives. Schwantje connected cruelty to animals with cruelty to humans, urging vegetarians to commit themselves to pacifism, socialism, and gender equality.[225] He supported women's suffrage and democracy and opposed the monarchy. A stern opponent of war and militarism, he regularly participated in and reported on pacifist conferences in and beyond Germany.[226] To Schwantje, all lives were equal: no animal, whether pet, "useful" animal, or insect, counted more than another. No human life, whether European, Asian, or African, was more valuable than another. No nation deserved more respect than another. In his uncompromising rejection of speciesism, racism, and nationalism, Schwantje stood out among German vegetarians and animal welfare activists. After the Second World War, moreover, he worked for Christian-Jewish reconciliation.[227]

In 1907, Schwantje founded the Gesellschaft zur Förderung des Tierschutzes und verwandter Bestrebungen (Society for Promoting Animal Welfare and Related Concerns), later renamed the Bund für radikale Ethik (Union for Radical Ethics). He maintained a wide international network, attending animal welfare congresses in Europe, lecturing in European capitals, corresponding with activists in Britain, France, Denmark, and India.[228] He never married or entered a heterosexual relationship, rejecting relationships in favor of what he termed "active asceticism."[229] Schwantje never wavered in his pacifist and antiracist positions throughout Nazi rule and the war, suffering persecution and exile in Switzerland as a consequence.[230] From 1935 on, his articles were no longer printed in Germany, and he left the country for Switzerland, destroying most of his personal papers before departing. In exile, Schwantje's situation was difficult. He suffered from a lack of funds, and he and his close coworker Ria Scheib experienced illness and depression. Nonetheless, Schwantje maintained his international contacts.[231] Thus it was in 1937 that he learned of Ram Chandra Sharma's campaign to stop animal slaughter in Hindu temples.

Schwantje had been interested in India, particularly Buddhism, since his youth. Most likely, his interest had been kindled by reading Schopenhauer, although Schwantje later criticized Schopenhauer's anti-Semitism.[232] It was only in the interwar era, however, that Schwantje made contact with Indian activists.

At the International Animal Protection Congress in London in 1927, Schwantje met Mohan K. Shah, the secretary of the Bombay Humanitarian League (as the Bombay Humanitarian Fund was by then called).[233] As explained in chapter 2, the Bombay Humanitarian League had established an extensive international network since its 1910 foundation. When communicating with European and American partners, the league represented its work in the idiom of Western humanitarianism, stressing its rejection of violence against both animals and humans. When targeting Indian audiences, it highlighted cow protection, proselytizing among lower-caste Indians, Dalits, and Adivasis and launching anti-Muslim polemics. It also supported research into cattle breeding.[234] Its richly illustrated 1938 publication *The Romance of the Cow* at once worshipped *gau mata* (Mother Cow) as a symbol of the Indian nation to come and explained how she could be made more productive.[235] Finally, the league cheered Hitler's rise to power, hoping it would bring about the worldwide victory of vegetarianism.[236] Aspects such as these would have appeared bizarre, even objectionable, to Schwantje, but, like most of the league's international supporters, he was apparently unaware of this aspect of its activities.

Mohan K. Shah was not Schwantje's sole, or closest, Indian contact. Schwantje also became friends with M. P. T. Acharya, an Indian anticolonial activist. A former resident of the India House in London, Acharya lived in Europe during and after the First World War.[237] In Berlin, he was part of the Indian Independence Committee supported by the German Foreign Office, for which he conducted missions among Muslims in Constantinople during the First World War.[238] Like Schwantje, Acharya considered himself an anarcho-pacifist[239] who was critical of "Bolshevism."[240] His anarchism, therefore, was nonviolent; indeed, even Gandhi was too violent for him since he aimed to provoke a violent response from India's British colonizers.[241] Both Schwantje and Acharya were antiracist. Acharya rejected Aryanism in both Germany and India, stressing that there was no such thing as a pure race without incest; his wife was a Russian Jew.[242] Research on Acharya and Schwantje does not reveal where they met, but their correspondence suggests that both may have attended meetings of the Theosophical Society in Berlin, for Schwantje, although critical of what he considered Theosophy's anthropocentrism, had esoteric leanings, including a belief in telepathy and aura reading.[243]

It may have been through Acharya that Schwantje and his associates developed an interest in the Indian freedom struggle. In 1931, Schwantje's colleague Ria Scheib gave a paper at the Verein vegetarischer Frauen (Vegetarian Women's Association) in Berlin looking at how vegetarianism could be used to "combat violence." Scheib criticized both "occidental religions" and Theosophy and Anthroposophy for not "extending justice and love to

FIGURE 4.2. Portrait of Ram Chandra Sharma in Magnus Schwantje's essay on Sharma's activism. Photograph courtesy archiv für alternatives schrifttum, Duisburg, Germany.

animals," criticizing the latter two because they rejected meat as part of a program for "perfecting the human soul" rather than for the sake of animals.[244] To Scheib, only a vegetarianism allied to animal welfare and pacifism was morally coherent, and Gandhi was the perfect embodiment of this approach. Gandhi, Scheib said, had brought to bear these principles "in the politics of an entire people" as well as in his "vegetarian lifestyle," and he had promoted women's rights in his campaigns for Indian independence.[245]

Around 1936, Schwantje learned of Ram Chandra Sharma's protest against animal sacrifices in Hindu temples in a letter from Acharya. The fact that animals were sacrificed in Hindu temples in the first place was news to Schwantje, as he had equated India with Buddhism, vegetarianism, and respect for animals. Fascinated by Ram Chandra's commitment, he began publishing articles and leaflets about him.[246]

## BETWEEN BUDDHA, GANDHI, SUFISM, AND MASCULINITY

Alerting his readers to the fact that not all Indians were vegetarians and that Buddhism, which, in Schwantje's view, opposed animal slaughter with particular vehemence, was no longer a significant religion in India, Schwantje introduced them to Ram Chandra Sharma's campaigns against "religious animal sacrifice." This "noble youth," as Schwantje referred to the twenty-six-year-old pandit, had founded a "major association for combatting these atrocities," and, after allegedly abolishing animal sacrifice in Kalyan, Bombay Presidency, where twenty-five thousand goats were sacrificed per annum, had also threatened to fast unto death if animal sacrifice was not stopped at Kalighat temple in Calcutta, where the goddess Kali was pacified with the slaughtering of animals. Twenty companions had declared themselves willing to join the hunger strike.[247]

Schwantje and Ram Chandra exchanged five letters between May 1937 and January 1938. Schwantje, despite his evident trouble with English and his constant state of overwork, wrote extensively, whereas Ram Chandra stressed his inability to respond in due time and length because of his ongoing campaigns, presenting himself as far less available.

While Ram Chandra seems to have engaged in the correspondence hoping to win support for his campaigns abroad, Schwantje was emotionally invested. Looking closely at the portrait sent by Ram Chandra, Schwantje compared his "physiognomy... to BEETHOVEN, ... the greatest genius of mankind."[248] When Ram Chandra expressed his "extreme respect" for Schwantje, the latter confessed that "also my love for you ist [sic] 'extreme.' Every day I look with deep emotion at your portrait and speak with you, and often I have the feeling as if you were near me."[249] Ram Chandra, in return, stressed that he held Schwantje, then sixty, in the same high regard as his own father.[250]

It was not just the two men's availability and tone that were incongruent. Neither understood the other's political situation. Ram Chandra did not understand why Schwantje was in exile in Switzerland, and Schwantje explained only in very general terms, without referring to Nazism, possibly fearing censorship.[251] Schwantje, on the other hand, was unaware of the precise structure of colonial rule in India. When he learned that Ram Chandra had been arrested due to a protest in 1937, he asked him whether he had been arrested and mistreated by British or Indian police and prison officers, and tried to organize help from abroad.[252] Most importantly,

Schwantje had no idea of the nature of Ram Chandra's activities, about which the latter was vague.

Born in 1909 in Viratnagar, Rajasthan, Ram Chandra Sharma was married at the age of thirteen. His last name hints at Brahmin status, and he may have attended the Gurukul Kangri, a secondary school established by the Arya Samaj, or otherwise have accepted Swami Shraddhanand, its founder, as his guru.[253] He began devoting himself to anticolonial resistance at a young age. Already eschewing meat, fish, and eggs, he rejected wheat and salt at the age of fourteen to protest British rule. He attended conferences of the Indian National Congress in Calcutta and Lahore and, in 1932, was imprisoned for speeches against British rule. While in prison, his parents agreed on a new marriage for him. Though brief, it gave him a son, who later joined him in his activities.[254] In 1935, he began protesting against animal sacrifice among Hindus in Kalyan, but was stopped by the police.[255] He also fasted against cow slaughter during the 1930s, publishing a treatise titled *Hamari Gomata* (Our mother, the cow) and rallying Hindu youth to the cause.[256] In the course of these activities, Ram Chandra acquired or took on the title "Veer" (hero), which was also used by Vinayak Damodar Savarkar, the founding figure of radical Hindu nationalism (Hindutva).[257]

Ram Chandra seems to have borrowed Gandhi's notion of satyagraha for his campaigns. To Gandhi, satyagraha meant sacrificing one's own life for a larger cause, whether by fasting or other forms of political protests that revealed the lack of humanity in colonial rule.[258] But while Ram Chandra used Gandhi's methods, he had different goals.

In contrast to Gandhi, Ram Chandra vocally opposed Hindu-Muslim cooperation. Like V. D. Savarkar, he considered Muslims foreign elements in India who for centuries had raped Hindu women, destroyed Hindu temples, and killed cows.[259] After Gandhi started his campaign against foreign cloth, Ram Chandra suggested that Muslim merchants had profited while participating Hindu merchants had suffered losses. Ram Chandra implied that Muslims' alleged behavior resembled that ascribed to German Jews—namely, robbing "Aryan" merchants of their capital. For this, the Jews had been rightfully punished by the Nazi government. Ram Chandra argued that the same ought to be done to Muslims.[260] The Congress Party, in contrast, was too pro-Muslim; in its efforts at Hindu-Muslim unity, he saw (much like Nathuram Godse, who eventually killed Gandhi) a Muslim conspiracy against Hindus.²⁶¹ He also rejected Buddhism, the religion Schwantje revered: in a 1943 treatise, Ram Chandra called on Hindus to fight Muslims violently, claiming that the idea of nonviolence, allegedly first developed in Buddhism, had led to India's ruin. India could only recover if Hindus drove out the British and killed all Muslims on Indian soil.²⁶²

Even before Ram Chandra published his explicitly anti-Gandhi and pro-violence treatise, the Mahatma had been irritated by him. Gandhi and other Congress leaders intervened during the Kalighat protests, asking Ram Chandra to stop the fast, to lead a movement against animal sacrifice rather than sacrificing his life for it.²⁶³ In his personal correspondence, Gandhi said he rejected Ram Chandra's campaign because it revealed "ignorance and violence."²⁶⁴

Schwantje never learned of Ram Chandra's involvement in the cow protection movement, his anti-Muslim beliefs, or his anti-Semitic stance. Did Ram Chandra fear British censorship? Did he suspect that a German activist little acquainted with Hinduism would not understand the importance of the cow? Did he think that his commitment to cows would strike Schwantje, who frequently emphasized the equal value of all animals, as unethical? Whatever the reasons for his silence, the correspondence ended in 1938. In 1950, when Schwantje received a letter from M. P. T. Acharya— the first since 1937—he asked after Ram Chandra. Schwantje received information from K. G. Mashruwala, the editor of *Harijan*, the magazine founded by Gandhi. Mashruwala had only met Ram Chandra once, and Gandhi, he told Schwantje, had not been impressed by him as his fasts "appeared to be a technique for getting celebrity." Gandhi felt that he and "the people will after a time lose interest in his fasts."²⁶⁵ Rather than leading Schwantje to doubt Ram Chandra's sincerity, this harsh judgment lessened his respect for the Mahatma. Gandhi, or so he argued, had been "a very honourable man, yet sometimes pronounced wrong judgements."²⁶⁶

Among German-speaking vegetarians in the interwar period, Schwantje had the most extensive contacts with Indian activists. This led him to partially question his previous image of India as a Buddhist and wholly vegetarian country where violence against animals was unknown. At the same time, he was unaware of the violence of the cow protection and Hindu nationalist movements. In the end, however, it was not just his lack of knowledge or his Indian friend's silence on these issues that led him to idealize the "noble youth." It was also his desperate situation in exile.

The first decades of the twentieth century, particularly the interwar era, saw an unprecedented interest in South Asia in German-speaking vegetarianism. This interest translated into an obsession with Buddhism, a fascination with Mazdaznan or Sufism, or a focus on the singular figure of Gandhi.

Some were interested in Asia as a place where allegedly, thousands of years ago, "Aryan" culture had flourished, considering vegetarianism a means of regaining this alleged greatness. Others saw in Gandhi a model of the ascetic leader crisis-shaken Weimar Germany seemed to need. The desire to regain a purported Aryan greatness was often tied to a eugenicist agenda, a position that survived the interwar era and paved the way for women's increased role in international organized vegetarianism after 1945. For the time being, however, German-speaking vegetarianism was dominated by men, as well as a notion of a fit, aggressive, or at least emotionally restrained masculinity.

Not all German vegetarians, however, were taken by Gandhi or by an Aryanism that included South Asia. *Völkisch* vegetarians like Walter Sommer, a vegetarian (in today's terms, a raw vegan) and youth leader based in Hamburg, embraced a concept of Aryanism that traced Germans' origins back to the Teutons, and he sharply criticized German vegetarians' fascination with India.[267] According to Sommer, the Teutons were the chosen people in world history. They had been able to attain hegemony well beyond Europe because they held land in common and used it to cultivate fruits, vegetables, nuts, and grains, thus achieving autarky, and eventually military, moral, and intellectual superiority, without harming animals. Only if Germans returned to their allegedly original diet could the German race recover.[268]

Yet what sounded like an invented tradition that would perfectly suit the Nazis' racism and their desire for food independence did not please the new powers. Even though Hitler presented himself as a vegetarian, the Nazis did not consider vegetarianism a means of pursuing their eugenic policies. They saw race as a stable rather than dynamic category, one that could not be altered by alimentary choices. They had no intention of prohibiting meat consumption, but merely wished to limit it. Furthermore (and despite individual leading Nazis' sympathies for both), esotericism and esoteric vegetarianism were anathema to the Nazi government, which feared the rise of competing soteriologies.

Like pacifist or socialist vegetarians, esoteric ones were also persecuted, albeit to differing degrees. Vegetarian associations were either disbanded or disbanded themselves, but vegetarianism persisted, particularly among those who could accommodate themselves to the Nazis' vision of hard, combative masculinity, as well as the regime's racial views. Georg Förster, Ludwig Ankenbrand, and Werner Zimmermann continued their work well into the postwar era. Others—Schwantje, Kazemzadeh, and Mazdaznan—survived the Nazi era by shifting their activities to Switzerland.

Although Nazi rule forced German vegetarians to focus on national rather than transnational exchange, most notably by leaving the International Vegetarian Union, global references and contacts did not disappear in the interwar era. Indeed, Hindu nationalist activists in India such as the French national and Hitler devotee Maximiani Julia Portas (Savitri Devi) and Labshankar Laxmidas of the Bombay Humanitarian League appreciated the Nazi government as a potential ally in transforming the world along vegetarian lines.[269]

German vegetarians would soon claim otherwise, but National Socialism did not end their movement. Some tendencies that chimed with Nazi rhetoric had been present among vegetarians since the 1920s, and some remained after the war ended. These tendencies shaped the international vegetarian movement after the Second World War—a movement in which India was an active participant rather than a mere sphere of projection.

*Chapter Five*

# RACE, NATION, AND PEACE

(Re-)Internationalizing Vegetarianism
After the Second World War

While international organized vegetarianism had been weakened during the preceding decade, with German organizations leaving the International Vegetarian Union in 1935 and no conferences taking place from 1938 to 1947, it was revived in the late 1940s. German organizations, eager to seek international ties, were readmitted. They were not the only newcomers. For the first time, Indian representatives joined the International Vegetarian Union, soon taking leading offices and organizing the union's first conferences in the newly independent country. Mazdaznan also came to play an unprecedented role in international organized vegetarianism. Finally, women became more prominent than ever in the International Vegetarian Union.

This chapter shows that these developments were closely connected. First and most obviously, this can be observed on the level of personal networks. It was due to the initiative of a leading Mazdaznan member, Gloria Gasque, that the International Vegetarian Union was revived, and German representatives welcomed back. It was also due to the efforts of Gasque and some of her allies in the subcontinent that Indian activists joined the organization, as Gasque had spent much of the Second World War in India, making contacts in the Parsi community and beyond. Finally, it was by her and other female delegates' initiative that women became more visible in the organization, hailed as a force of peace in an age when war seemed more threatening than ever due to nuclear armament.

However, this newly revived internationalism did not prevent various protagonists from conceiving of vegetarianism as a tool of national and racial purity. Indeed, it was precisely the centrality of race and nation to postwar vegetarian discourse, rather than the mere presence of personal networks, that connected the seemingly disparate strands brought together in this chapter: Gasque's sojourn in India, the entry of German and Indian protagonists into the International Vegetarian Union, and the revival of organized international vegetarianism. Gasque met with a certain echo among Bombay Parsis because she advocated vegetarianism and eugenics at a time when Parsis were discussing both as a means of revitalizing the community. Despite the demise of Nazism, German vegetarians conceived of vegetarianism as a means of reviving the "Aryan" race they continued to believe in—a program that led them to rekindle an interest in Mazdaznan, and that pushed them to assume a leading role for German vegetarians in healing the world after the war. Brahmin and other allied protagonists in India had a strong interest in representing India as a Hindu nation at a time when the subcontinent had been divided along religious lines, but Brahmin supremacy was increasingly being questioned. Couching vegetarianism in terms of national heritage allowed them to write meat-eating Muslims, Christians, and lower-caste Hindus out of their country's history while at the same time representing India as the driving force of a global civilizing mission for peace and as a nonaligned power above the divisions of the Cold War.

In stressing the interplay between internationalism, nationalism, and racism, this chapter complements recent research on international organizations.[1] It goes beyond this research, however, in focusing on the International Vegetarian Union, which has thus far been ignored in the history of internationalism, as well as the role of religion and new religions in shaping postwar internationalism.

### TAKING "TRUE ZOROASTRIANISM" TO THE PARSIS

In the autumn of 1939, Maude Gasque, née Meacham, a prominent member of the Mazdaznan community, took a suite in the Taj Mahal Hotel, then and now the most luxurious hotel in Bombay.[2] Born into a rich family in Chicago, Gasque was the widow of Woolworth's financial director in London, Clarence Gasque,[3] who gave her the "Phantom of Love," an extra-lavish

Rolls Royce Phantom I with Louis XVI–inspired furniture, painted wooden panels, and a drinks cabinet, for her birthday in 1926.[4]

After Clarence Gasque's untimely death a year later, Maude, while continuing to receive London's conservative elite at her large estate in Hampstead, focused on furthering the cause of Mazdaznan.[5] "Mother Gloria," as she would soon be called within the organization, participated in Mazdaznan meetings in Britain, the United States, and Switzerland, while also assisting in the organization's attempts to reverse the Nazi government's ban against Mazdaznan in Germany.[6] She also helped the community gain a foothold in the most unlikely of places: India. How this was accomplished has not yet been much researched.[7]

While Hanisch, facing several lawsuits, had tried to obtain contacts in India in the early 1910s, hoping that appreciative letters from prominent Bombay Parsis would restore Mazdaznan's credibility as a neo-Zoroastrian community, he had largely failed.[8] Arthur Fitzroy Gault, one of the five trustees of Mazdaznan and a high-ranking Canadian military official who lived in London in the interwar era,[9] had maintained a regular correspondence with Professor A. S. Wadia of Bombay, who had come into contact with Mazdaznan in Canada during the First World War.[10] At the same time, however, as seen in chapter 3, Hanisch was trying to distance himself from the Hinduphilia that tended to characterize late nineteenth-century esotericism.[11] Establishing a branch on the subcontinent would have contradicted this strategy.

Gasque initially came to India in the context of a planned trip to Persia and Tibet, where she wanted to visit places of alleged biographical significance to Hanisch, who claimed to have been born in Tehran and raised by monks in Tibet.[12] But rather than travel on to these places, she stayed in India.

Her fascination with India was an ambivalent one—at least when it came to food. During her stay at the Taj in Bombay, Gasque was appalled by the food served to her. None of it was reconcilable with Mazdaznan rules, and even more surprisingly, no one in India seemed to abstain from meat. Only in some dubious "Brahmin food shops," as Gasque described them, could one find vegetarian dishes, but these would hardly "solicit European patronage."[13] Realizing that India was not familiar with Mazdaznan principles, Gasque made it her mission to bring it the information it supposedly needed.

With the help of local Parsi contacts and some Swiss Mazdaznan members, Gasque started giving lectures on "pure food," Mazdaznan eugenics, and breathing and exercise, first in Bombay, then in Kashmir, where she spent most of her summers.[14] To her audiences, she taught only the simplest of Mazdaznan breathing exercises, comfortably seated on a chair like Swami Vivekananda facing his American yoga disciples.[15] In 1940, she opened a center in Bombay that was soon moved to a prominent location, the Industrial Assurance Building, opposite the massive neo-Gothic Churchgate Station.[16] From 1941 onward, the center published a journal that focused on dietetics and Mazdaznan texts, particularly eugenics and "raciology."[17] In line with Hanisch's notion of race, Parsis, but not Hindus, were characterized as members of the "white" or "Aryan" race in these texts, which warned of intermarriage between races.[18]

As scholars from Ann-Laura Stoler to Lora Wildenthal and Antoinette Burton have shown, Western women often expanded their agency in colonial contexts by claiming to fulfill a motherly role vis-à-vis the local population, often depicting them as children.[19] "Mother Gloria's" approach to India was very much along these lines. The title of "mother" was conferred on her within the Mazdaznan system, in which leading women, particularly wives of leading male figures, carried this title. But unlike the rest of the Mazdaznan "mothers," Gasque was widowed and had no male superior in India. "Mother" also characterized the way she behaved toward those she considered to be her Indian subordinates: whether they were Parsi priests, "bearers," or "coolies," she referred to herself as their "most royal Mother," in line with colonial tendency to imagine "natives" as children.[20] As a white woman in a colonial context, Gasque expected not just respect but reverence—and sternly opposed Indian initiatives for independence. The inhabitants of the Indian subcontinent, according to Gasque, ought to have "equality of opportunity" rather than of "possession." Disregarding economic inequality and caste barriers, Gasque argued that this would leave the decision to get an education up to individual initiative. Only the "weaklings," or so the passionate eugenicist claimed, "should be taken care of as invalids and made to produce what they can under supervision" by the government.[21]

Gasque's ability to make contacts among Parsis was certainly facilitated by the fact that her audience was already familiar with the Theosophical

Society, which in Bombay had been dominated by Parsis since the 1880s. As pointed out in chapter 3, Mazdaznan had borrowed amply from Theosophy, especially in the areas of racial theory and evolution, although it posited a far more direct causal relationship between the two. Like individual representatives of Theosophy such as Leopold Salzer, Mazdaznan claimed that individuals could influence evolution positively by their lifestyles. While non-white races were described as stagnant, members of the "white" or "Aryan race" could become the "race transparent" if they abstained from meat. Mazdaznan's racial theory was even more elitist than that of the Theosophical Society, and it favored Parsis to an extent no other Western new religion had done previously, yet in language and gesture it was strongly reminiscent of the Theosophical Society.

This was also true of the way Gasque staged herself. Her attempt to reach Tibet evoked the fictive biographies of both Hanisch and Helena Petrovna Blavatsky.[22] Like the female heads of the Theosophical Society, Gasque was an elderly single white woman in charge of an organization that, in India, was staffed mainly by non-white people who, although far more familiar than she was with the religion she claimed to represent, were considered acolytes.[23] Like Blavatsky (who championed Buddhism) and Besant (who espoused Hinduism), she supported and claimed to embrace Zoroastrianism, even though the religious "system" she represented borrowed from a number of religions. But unlike Blavatsky and Besant, she incorporated the aspect of spiritual motherhood into her role, which amplified the imagined hierarchical relationship between her and her target group, Parsis. As it turned out, however, not all Parsis were interested in being mothered by an American parvenu.

Given that Mazdaznan's appropriation of Zoroastrian elements was rather haphazard, and its founder was not himself Zoroastrian, the question arises as to how Gasque found Parsi supporters in the city at all. As mentioned in chapter 2, Parsis had been interested in reform, and indeed in vegetarianism, since the late nineteenth century. They had articulated this message with a view to their role as cultural intermediaries for the British, but they also took cues from emerging Hindu nationalism, which stressed the importance of being born on and having roots in the subcontinent and having values that were compatible with Hindu ones, such as respecting *gau mata* (Mother Cow). While foreign origins were central to their sense of identity, Parsis came to stress the centrality of cow worship in Zoroastrianism and to abstain from animal sacrifice.[24] Parsis already formed a considerable part of the steering committee of the Vegetarian and Natural Living Society founded in 1891, but organizations like the Parsi Vegetarian and Temperance Society, established in 1907, argued that vegetarianism was part of Zoroastrian heritage and necessary for spiritual progress.[25] This was invented: Parsis, apart from the Mazdakites, an early current in Zoroastrianism, had abstained from meat only periodically—at certain times of the year and during mourning.[26] But claiming that vegetarianism was central to Zoroastrianism helped Parsis fit in with Hindu nationalist discourse, and set them apart from the other alleged "foreigners" in India—namely, Muslims.

Although reformist Parsis were never dominant in Bombay, they were nonetheless a significant group, and reformist discourse and organizations, including the Parsi Vegetarian and Temperance Society, were still present in the 1930s and 1940s. By then, however, another concern had emerged. Independence was becoming increasingly likely, and Parsis feared losing the wealth and influence they had acquired under British rule and being caught up in a Hindu-Muslim conflict.[27] They were concerned both about how they would fit into the emerging nation and how they could remain a sizeable and valuable faction within it, considering eugenics as a possible solution.[28]

One prominent eugenicist was Sapur Faredun Desai, a scientist who would soon serve the Bombay Parsi Panchayat as secretary. In his book *Parsis and Eugenics*, which had a foreword by H. H. Laughlin, one of the most vociferous proponents of forced sterilization in the United States (and a model for leading Nazi scientists and lawmakers), Desai warned that the Parsis, scions of "the great Emperors of Iran" and of "Aryan descent like the descendants of the Vedic Hindus," were currently creating a community that would soon contain an appreciable number of the "feeble-minded," "epileptic," and "insane," as well as the "diseased," "demoralized," and "deteriorated."[29] While the wealthy were having too few children, the poor, due to early marriage and women's emancipation, were ignorant of how to limit their offspring.[30] The wealthy needed to be encouraged to have more children while the poor, and especially the "feebleminded," had to be prevented from doing so, if need be, by segregation during their fertile years, sterilization, castration, or removal of the ovaries and uterus—measures that Desai considered in no way harmful to society.[31]

In case "negative eugenics" could not be implemented, however, the population would at least need to be educated—not just about contraception, but also about food, since a deficient diet weakened the body's "power of resistance." The diet of the rich contained too much fat, protein, and carbohydrates, while the diet of the poor was insufficient in every respect. "All the schools including those for boys must have a theoretical course of instruction in values of different foodstuffs, vitamins etc.," argued Desai—a recommendation Mazdaznan soon took up.[32] Only by embracing these measures and following them for at least a thousand years could Parsis regain their "innate intelligence" and ancient grandeur.[33]

Given the enthusiasm for vegetarianism, esotericism, and eugenics among some parts of the community, Mazdaznan's ability to gain adherents in Bombay seems less surprising, especially since some of its leaders had already been in contact with Parsis there. Perhaps the fact that Mazdaznan arrived during the Second World War, when the alimentary situation began to deteriorate, was another point of attraction.

Mazdaznan's initial local supporters included Nanabhoy F. Mama and Dastur Framroze Ardeshir Bode, both devoted to reforming Zoroastrianism. Mama, an advocate and member of the Parsi Vegetarian and Temperance Society, was also a proponent of *ilm-e khshnoom*, Parsi esotericism.[34] Bode, a priest (*dastur*) who was educated in Bombay's Petit Parsi orphanage, and thus perhaps a son of indigent parents, was intent on expanding the fold.[35] He offered seemingly authentic ceremonies to European and American Mazdaznan members, introducing the purifying element of fire so central to Zoroastrian religious practice into their services. Outside Bombay, he offered the Navjote, a ceremony welcoming Zoroastrian children into the community, to orphans of dubious Parsi descent.[36] All of this went against Zoroastrianism's status as a non-proselytizing religion that accepted no converts and admitted no outsiders to its ceremonies. Bode's willingness to overlook these long-standing rules hurt his reputation among more conservative Parsis.[37] When Mazdaznan acquired quarters in the Industrial Assurance Building, Bode became the head of the new center, whose establishment he had lobbied for with the British heads of the organization from 1939 on.[38] Alliances with Bombay Parsis such as Mama and Bode strengthened Mazdaznan's position and lent a community that claimed to be the true Zoroastrian faith (but actually pilfered from Theosophy, yoga, and Christianity) a little more Zoroastrian flavor.

In 1944, with Gasque spending more time in Kashmir, Mazdaznan's activities in India ran into serious difficulties. When its landlords no longer wanted to rent out space to the community, Mazdaznan claimed that it was running a fire temple and that its services were attended by a regular audience of about seven hundred individuals.[39] The building's proprietors were not convinced. Some Parsis also feared that Mazdaznan intended to convert members of their fold to Christianity, opposed Bode's openness toward the community, and resented Gasque's colonial arrogance, something A. S. Wadia had long warned his British contacts about.[40] In the end, Mazdaznan lost the battle for its premises and thereby its foothold in India, and leading Parsi *dasturs* once more confirmed the exclusion of non-Parsis from Parsi ceremonies.[41]

While Gasque occasionally returned to Bombay to lecture on Mazdaznan teachings there, she mainly shifted her activities to California, where the sun shone more favorably on all things esoteric. Since the early 1900s, the Theosophical Society, spiritual teachers like Jiddu Krishnamurti, the Ramakrishna Mission and other yoga gurus, and Mazdaznan had all established themselves there.[42] Gasque's stay in India had helped Mazdaznan acquire more of a Zoroastrian veneer and strengthened her voice in the organization. Still a member of Mazdaznan, she channeled her energy into reviving the dormant American Vegetarian Society and eventually the International Vegetarian Union (IVU). If she could not reform India, she would reform the United States, and, from there, the world.

At the IVU congress in Sigtuna, Sweden, in 1950, Gasque participated as a representative of the American Vegetarian Society, and donated money for the paid position of a secretary.[43] At the union's next congress, held in Paris in 1953, she was elected IVU president, an office she retained until her death in 1959.[44] In that capacity, she appointed Framzoze Ardeshir Bode (who had moved to California with his wife in the meantime) as regional secretary for the Americas.[45] Together, they organized the IVU's 1957 congress, held in India, the alleged heartland of vegetarianism. But first, Gasque helped a lost sheep—West Germany—rejoin the flock.

Even though Gasque's Bombay sojourn was not as successful as she may have hoped, with Mazdaznan remaining a small community, she succeeded in winning local allies with agendas of their own who would support her in taking over the IVU, reviving postwar international vegetarianism, and attracting representatives from India, which thus far had received scant representation in the international organized movement.

## RACE TO INTERNATIONALISM: WEST GERMAN VEGETARIANS REJOIN THE MOVEMENT

### *Völkisch* Roots and a German Gandhi

In 1944, as Mazdaznan was leaving India, German vegetarians were taking their first steps toward reorganization. In May 1944, Adolf Briest, a proponent of raw foods who had worked as a government expert in natural foods in East Hanover, published an appeal to German vegetarians in the Swiss vegetarian journal *Der Wendepunkt* calling for initiating a settlement of "true vegetarians."[46]

Briest had turned to vegetarianism after being wounded in the First World War. In 1932, while running an association of "raw foods teachers" and a publishing house devoted to raw foods in Hamburg, he coauthored a treatise on vegetarianism. According to this book, humankind was on the verge of a "global crisis, which, last but not least, is a crisis of nutrition."[47] Only a turn toward raw fruit and vegetables could make Germany economically autonomous.[48] But a diet of this type was not merely a matter of economy: it helped prevent illnesses,[49] and was uniquely suited to present-day exigencies. Raw plant foods, the authors claimed, echoing Mazdaznan publications, constituted the diet of the "modern man of nerve," who no longer relied on muscle power.[50] Nutrition should be adjusted to an individual's occupation and temperament.[51] Abandoning cooked in favor of raw foods would leave men and women with more time for education, building homes, and working the soil according to the principles of emerging organic farming. Agriculture would no longer involve the keeping of livestock as humans had exploited animals for far too long; it would not even rely on manure. Working the fields would strengthen inhabitants' bodies, allowing women (whom Briest deemed mentally inferior to men) to "develop upwards"—that is, to become closer to healthy men, the pinnacles of civilization, and give birth to healthy children.[52]

Despite his nationalism—and indeed, as we will see, racism—Briest was an ardent admirer of Gandhi because of the latter's combination of vegetarianism and political leadership.[53] A rather sarcastic article on Briest in

*Der Spiegel* reveals that Briest referred to himself as the "German Gandhi."[54] Unlike the Mahatma, however, he was far from being a critic of his government.

Indeed, Briest openly championed the concept of Aryanism. He started his campaign for a vegetarian settlement by writing to the famous painter Fidus to ask him to support the project. Fidus, in addition to being a member of the Nazi Party, had been one of the iconic figures of the life reform movement from the early twentieth century on.[55] Briest told Fidus that his aim was "to collect all Germans striving toward the light, who recognize that we need Nordic Man, Aryans and aristocrats of the soul, or rather, the white race, to regenerate collapsing Europe, and that the final insights and the energy to put this plan into practice can only result from a diet not encumbered by moral wrong." Fidus, or so he hoped, would adorn his circular with one of his masterful drawings.[56] The "white race" was also a frequent topic in Briest's *nordbron* newsletter. The *nordbron* title was a neologism referring to "the Nordic well from which Nordic-Aryan spirit flows into the country," which was the role Briest imagined his future settlement playing.[57] Like Nazi officials, he also differentiated between supposedly valuable and non-valuable life: only healthy men and women likely to produce healthy offspring would be admitted to the settlement.[58] Briest regularly quoted Hitler, referring to him as a harbinger of the new age that the "white race" would enter by embracing a raw plant diet.[59] Finally, religion would be banned from the settlement: he saw vegetarianism as the only true religion and hoped that the future would be happily pagan,[60] thereby helping humankind transition from the "Age of Pisces" to the "Age of Aquarius."[61]

Briest started collecting data from vegetarians interested in establishing settlements in 1944, yet he could not start negotiating for land until war's end, when he solicited West German regional administrators in Hanover and Lüneburg. Although Briest kept the fact that the settlements would be vegetarian quiet, fearing it would brand them as esoteric, administrators he deemed trustworthy were forwarded copies of *nordbron*, in which the group's vegetarian, esoteric, and racist leanings were made clear.[62]

By 1946, Briest was collaborating with vegetarians elsewhere in West Germany, mostly people rooted in the *völkisch* movement, such as Oswald Kiehne from Donnershag.[63] Founded in 1919 by the Deutscher Orden, a pagan *völkisch* organization named after the leading chivalric order in the

Holy Roman Empire, Donnershag aimed at a racial regeneration of Germany. Only "valuable" Germans of "Aryan" descent and "Nordic" types could settle there. To increase the number of offspring, its founders abolished Christian marriage and monogamy, allowing inhabitants, including women, to choose their sexual partners freely and temporarily—a system known as "*Midgard* marriage."[64] The settlement failed well before the onset of Nazism.[65] Another of Briest's collaborators, Heinrich Frantzen from Cologne-Müngersdorf, resided in an institution that was known well into the 1960s as Haus Midgard, a name alluding to the Donnershag concept of marriage and procreation and suggesting, prior to 1945, an agenda of sexual freedom—at least for men—in the name of eugenics and racial purity.[66] Research on the *völkisch* movement has so far concentrated only on the period up to Nazi rule, but as these examples show, the movement was by no means extinct after the Second World War, and may in fact have fed into postwar West German right-wing extremism.

Briest, Kiehne, and Frantzen were leading figures in the early postwar vegetarian movement in West Germany after 1945. As evident from their agenda linking vegetarianism, race, and organic farming in ways that overlapped with the early debates on organic farming recently analyzed by Venus Bivar, the idea of racial revitalization was crucial to German vegetarianism during this period.[67] It shared this centrality of race and eugenics with Mazdaznan, particularly Gasque's activities in India. Indeed, at least Briest was interested in the Mazdaznan community, perhaps even a member of it. This may have helped his organization in rejoining the IVU, where Mazdaznan was becoming prominent.

Yet one aspect of West Germany's admission request posed a problem: the lack of unity among West German vegetarians. Briest had hoped to emerge as the leader of all West German vegetarians, and though he endorsed the formation of regional branches, he had been instrumental in excluding the southwestern branch represented by Helmut Th. K. Rall and Oswald Kiehne at the annual convention in 1946.[68] The branch was now forbidden from carrying the name of Vegetarier Union, but Rall, a publicity expert, continued referring to his organization as Deutsche Vegetarier Union. In 1948, Rall founded a journal called *Vegetarisches Universum*. As we will see, the title was programmatic. Rall wanted not just to surpass Briest in unifying West German vegetarians, but to return them to the international stage, while making vegetarianism appear enjoyable instead of focusing on abstinence.

### Pacifism and Race in a "Vegetarian Universe"

*Vegetarisches Universum* differed from previous vegetarian magazines in its tabloid-like format, its layout, and, occasionally, its content. Its half title featured color, and the cover showed black-and-white photos of famous vegetarians, animals, or young female vegetarians in suggestive poses, in a fashion similar to West German tabloids like *Bild*.[69] Moreover, *Vegetarisches Universum* teemed with ads for newly invented vegetarian foods. As West Germany was taken over by the economic boom of the 1950s and the *Fresswelle* (literally, the "binge-eating wave"), vegetarians rejected the meat and perhaps the alcohol—but not the gustatory pleasures.[70]

In its first issues, however, *Vegetarisches Universum* faced a very different situation, with food in West Germany still scarce.[71] Moreover, as the Cold War began, there was no way of knowing how long peace would last. Finally, West Germans needed to prove they could adapt to democracy and would not do anything to start or consent to another war.

Accordingly, the first issues of *Vegetarisches Universum* discussed how to establish lasting peace across the world. In the early Cold War period, a nuclear war seemed imminent, and many West Germans feared that their divided country might be its epicenter.[72] These fears had a profound impact on vegetarian discourse, which became even more closely associated with pacifism. After the first deployment of the H-bomb, the emphatic connection between vegetarianism and militant masculinity disappeared from West German vegetarian journals.[73] Authors instead stressed the fundamental contribution vegetarianism could make to world peace by outlawing any form of killing.[74]

That said, pacifist utopias in *Vegetarisches Universum* were not limited to matters of dietary ethics. Authors also made more far-reaching suggestions for a new world order that illustrate the extent to which pacifist and internationalist visions in Germany were suffused by Eurocentrism, racism, and colonialism during the early Cold war.

One example was the "Magna Charta Humanitatis" of 1949. Its author, Heinrich Molenaar, was a vegetarian, anti-vaccinationist, and developer of

Universal, a constructed international auxiliary language.[75] At first glance, his agenda evoked a humanist internationalism. He demanded an end to all wars, the global unification of measures, weights, and currencies, and the establishment of absolute freedom of religion. Humanity should embrace vegetarianism and natural cures, he argued; vaccination should be banned. Yet Molenaar's internationalism was underpinned by anti-Semitic and white supremacist assumptions. To ensure lasting peace, he recommended coming up with a "fair, generous, all-encompassing and final solution" of the "Jewish question," and allocating "every nation on earth a piece of land corresponding to its size," with "intermixing of the races to be avoided at all cost." The "white race," Molenaar stressed, should receive the greater part of the earth.[76]

Both Briest and Rall claimed their unions were open to all political views, but they clearly leaned right even while claiming to be "entirely neutral with regards to race." Some authors distanced themselves explicitly from the Nazi era, claiming that Hitler had never been vegetarian, and that vegetarians had been persecuted for their convictions during the Third Reich.[77]

Despite these truth-bending efforts, there were many continuities with Nazism, as shown by an article by Friedrich Vogtherr published in *Vegetarisches Universum* on the *Atlantropa* scheme developed by engineer Hermann Sörgel.[78] In the 1920s, Sörgel had started building hydroelectric dams in the Mediterranean to make the sea level drop. The land gained would ultimately join Europe and Africa into a single continent that Europe could exploit. This would make Germany "self-sufficient" and give it more *Lebensraum* without using military means.[79] The Nazi government, to which Sörgel had offered his plan in the 1930s, was interested, but ultimately deemed it too pacifist. In the early 1950s, however, it met with renewed interest. At a time when colonial empires were crumbling, plans like *Atlantropa* or the Eurafrica scheme seemed to offer a less violent alternative to other forms of colonial exploitation.[80] Vogtherr's description focused on the benefits of the scheme, not its racism: he argued that lowering the sea level would create "densely settled, arable land" that would profit "everyone" in Europe and Africa. Once production reached a surplus, food could even be exported to parts of the world suffering from hunger, such as India and China.[81]

Sörgel's and Molenaar's articles contrasted with those by Hossein Kazemzadeh, who also wrote about peace in the early issues of *Vegetarisches*

*Universum*. In his articles, Kazemzadeh rarely referred to Persia, Sufism, or Islam, though he retained his pen name, "Iranschähr." Instead, he sought to appeal to a Christian audience,[82] arguing that after the Second World War peace could only come about if humanity atoned for its sins; if it did not, it would cause its own extermination via nuclear arms.[83] Unlike Molenaar or Vogtherr, Kazemzadeh did not differentiate along racial lines: all humanity had to atone for the past global conflict, and no branch could claim moral superiority over another.[84] His position coincided with that of authors like Werner Zimmermann, who—after having given talks to German troops during the war—now stressed the necessity of rejecting military expansion and military service.[85]

*Vegetarisches Universum*, then, displayed a degree of ambivalence in its manner of integrating vegetarianism into a vision for global peace. The rejection of meat, fish, and potentially other animal products was now imagined as a force of peace. This represented a marked contrast to mainstream vegetarian positions under Nazism, which had stressed vegetarianism's ability to strengthen soldiers' masculinity. Notions of racial hierarchy, however, continued to undergird some of these pacifist utopian designs. Moreover, some of these texts show the limited extent to which German intellectuals felt guilty about Germany's involvement in the Second World War. Instead, they presented Germany as a force for good that would make the world a peaceful place.

### Provincial Internationalism: Helmut Th. K. Rall's Olympics of Hearts

Publishing pacifist visions was not the only way Rall sought to reintegrate German vegetarians into the international scene. From 1952 on, he also organized annual vegetarian conventions that he presented as international affairs, although they were attended almost exclusively by German and some Swiss and Austrian participants.

German vegetarians had a long tradition of holding annual meetings. But the conventions organized by Rall's union and heavily advertised in *Vegetarisches Universum* were more than that. They took place in what had been one of the heartlands of German pietism, the eighteenth-century Protestant revival whose participants had stressed the necessity of a personal religious awakening and moral conversion.[86] Nonetheless, the meetings organized by Rall amounted to pleasure trips.[87] First organized in Bad

Liebenzell, and then in Freudenstadt in the Black Forest, a popular health resort in Nazi Germany that had sustained heavy bomb damage during the war, these meetings were referred to as the Kongress der Ideale (Congress of Ideals), or, alternatively, the Olympiaden der Herzen (Olympics of Hearts).[88] They were supposed to embody a spirit of love and reconciliation that would help Germany heal after the war. The allusion to the Olympics evoked memories of the Berlin Olympics of 1936, the chief international event in Nazi Germany, suggesting a similarly international and glamorous character as regards both participants and visibility.[89]

Whereas previous vegetarian meetings had been modest, even austere, the Kongress der Ideale did everything to spoil its participants. In the newly built, elegant assembly rooms of the health resort, they were treated to full board with fruits, vegetables, and some of the new vegetarian convenience foods advertised in *Vegetarisches Universum*. In chartered buses that would, in later years, take them as far as Lago Maggiore or even the Mediterranean, the favorite destinations of German postwar tourists,[90] they visited nature food companies like the juice factory founded by Walter Schoenenberger, a former high-ranking Nazi official of Swiss nationality.[91] Between excursions, participants joined Mazdaznan exercise and breathing classes or listened to papers on gender, eugenics, alternative science and esotericism, and the history of vegetarianism. Congresses also featured beauty contests seeking the most beautiful German vegetarian (invariably a young woman, usually blond).[92] The Olympics of Hearts also featured vegetarian stars. Lil Dagover, an actor who had risen to national fame during the Weimar and Nazi periods and who played for German troops in the Second World War, and Elly Ney, a pianist and former ardent Nazi, graced the meetings of Rall's union with their presence, dressed in fake fur coats and signing autographs.[93]

Most importantly, the Kongress der Ideale gave participants a sense that they were connected to the international movement by seemingly inviting guests from all over the world. Whereas speakers at the first convention in 1951 had hailed mainly from the region and other parts of Germany, the following congresses saw a rapid transformation. In 1952 and 1953, about a quarter of speakers joined the Olympics of Hearts from abroad.[94] Gloria Gasque attended the congress in 1953.[95] From 1954 on, nearly half the speakers came from outside Germany—or so it would seem.[96] In fact, information on their origin was vague and sometimes incorrect. The farther away from Germany they hailed, the more likely a speaker's origin was to be indicated just by country—or indeed by continent. Kazemzadeh, who had not set foot on Persian soil for half a century, was announced as "Hossein Kazemzadeh Iranschähr (Persien)."[97] Ernst Ganz, a Swiss Mazdaznan member who lived in Zurich and owned a plantation in Kenya, was listed as "Dr. Ernst Ganz (Afrika)."[98] Rall, a publicity expert, clearly wanted his list of speakers to appear more international than it was. Most of the foreign speakers came from Switzerland, Austria, Scandinavia, and, to a far lesser extent, Britain and the United States, and those from farther away were often of German origin.

Rall's Middle East expert was actually from the region, although he had lived in Germany from the 1950s on. Tadros Megalli, a Copt born in Fayyūm, Egypt, in 1912, became a member of the Esperanto movement during the late 1920s, helping it take root in Egypt during the Second World War.[99] He cooperated with both Muslims and Jews in the Esperanto associations to which he belonged.[100] He also visited Palestine for an Esperanto congress in 1944, where he was impressed by Zionist agricultural settlements.[101] In an interview with the journal *L'avenir*, Megalli, explicitly turning against fascism, referred to Esperanto as "a political language—that of the progressives of all countries."[102] But although he remained active in both Esperanto and pacifist contexts into the 1970s, it was vegetarianism that became the focus of his activities in Germany.[103]

Practicing Copts, like other Orthodox Christians, avoided meat and dairy for a considerable part of the year. But Megalli began rejecting meat in 1939 for health reasons. While becoming a vegetarian had not been a problem in Egypt, he feared running into obstacles on an Esperanto lecture tour in Europe. In fact, he got along fine.[104] Meeting with plenty of interest in his lectures on ancient and modern Egypt and the "Holy Land" (accompanied by slides and Arab music), Megalli, invariably dressed in a dark suit and the tarboosh, signifier of secular Egyptian modernity,[105] decided to make Germany his home, and began advertising for a German wife in *Vegetarisches Uniersum* in 1954.[106] By the same year, he had already given more than four hundred lectures in Germany.[107]

In his articles for *Vegetarisches Universum*, Megallli confirmed existing German stereotypes about "vegetarianism" in Egypt, stressing the fellahin's modest habits and their healthy lives spent working outside in the sun. But he also criticized German alimentary culture (or the lack thereof), and the limited availability and high cost of fresh fruit and vegetables, leaving no doubt as to Egypt's superiority in meatless nutrition. Not only did its soil yield abundant high-quality, affordable fruit and vegetables. Egyptians were so used to consuming a plant-based diet that the country had no need for vegetarian associations.[108]

Megalli only attended Rall's congress twice, and his attempts to find a partner in *Vegetarisches Universum* seem to have met with little response. It was not until 1960 that he finally married and settled down for good in Germany.[109] While he did continue his lecture tours, Megalli—one of the few guests who had the potential to make Rall's congresses truly international events—stopped seeking close contact with German vegetarian associations from 1960 onward.

Rall's events turned out to be a case of provincial internationalism at best. A 1959 documentary broadcast on Südwestdeutscher Rundfunk described it even more harshly. Instead of the muscular, youthful physiques vegetarians claimed, Dieter Ertel's caustic camera captured aging, flabby women and men in loden coats and matching hats. Rather than documenting vegetarians' progressive mindset and their internationalism, he showed their credulousness and narrow-mindedness, and the absurdity of New Age religion. The vegetarians interviewed by his crew spoke a heavy southwestern German dialect and believed in flying saucers and pseudo-Zoroastrianism. From Ertel's perspective, German vegetarianism was an object of ridicule, as provincial as the German rural Southwest—and about to become extinct.[110]

Despite Ertel's critique and the congresses' provincialism, Rall's events testified to German vegetarians' efforts to present themselves as part of the international movement again—yet also to the limits of this endeavor. Continuities with Nazi vegetarianism were manifest, and so was the ongoing attraction of vegetarianism as a means of racial improvement, evident through the regular lectures and exercise and nutrition classes conducted by Mazdaznan members.

## FEMINIZING ORGANIZED VEGETARIANISM

Partly due to Gloria Gasque's patronage, Rall's and Adolf Briest's organizations were both accepted into the IVU in 1950,[111] integrating German vegetarianism more fully into the international movement. In German vegetarian magazines, particularly *Vegetarisches Universum*, the new internationalism found expression in conversations on how vegetarianism could establish lasting world peace, and particularly on women's roles in this context.

In the late 1940s, when Gasque started aiming for a leadership position in the IVU, she connected her ambitions to women's rights around the globe. In 1951, Gasque founded the Mazdaznan Women's Federation, appointing German Mazdaznan member and vegetarian Elisabeth Ecker-Lauer as secretary.[112] Ecker-Lauer became IVU vice secretary when Gasque became IVU president in 1953.[113] While Gasque's presidency strengthened Mazdaznan's position in vegetarianism internationally as well as in Germany, it also led to a shift in the organization's agenda. Women and women's position in society, long of secondary importance among German vegetarians, moved to the center stage in international vegetarianism.[114]

In a number of articles published, inter alia, in *Vegetarisches Universum*, in 1951 and 1954, the leaders of the Mazdaznan Women's Federation, like prominent members of the IVU, argued that women had a core role in society around the world, as the war had shown that men were unable to solve the world's problems on their own. The world, or so Mazdaznan's leading women argued, could only function through two complementary principles. While men were seen as in command of reason and law, women were seen as representing religion, intuition, and love. It was only through the interplay of both principles that the world could progress.[115]

Women were represented first and foremost as educators in the family. Because of their purportedly innate maternal qualities, however, they should also work as teachers as well as in medicine and public health, especially with regards to nutrition, as well as in agri- and horticulture. Whether they worked inside or outside the home, they should receive a salary for their work, either from their employers or from their husbands, which, as Mazdaznan claimed somewhat paradoxically, would ensure their independence from both their families and the state. As "bearers of the human race," women should help it progress through education, proper nutrition, exercise, eugenics, and "prenatal education,"[116] a concept that Mazdaznan had advocated ever since Hanisch's time and that was shared by Mazdaznan's possible associate, Hossein Kazemzadeh.[117]

Seeing society as resting on the interplay of a binary, cis, and heteronormative gender model was hardly revolutionary. Since the late eighteenth century, this very model had been central to middle-class identity in Europe and North America.[118] During the nineteenth century, as research by scholars such as Leonore Davidoff, Catherine Hall, Clare Midgley, and others has shown, women had legitimized their entry into charity, education, social work, and foreign missions with reference to their allegedly innate maternal qualities.[119] What was new about Mazdaznan's agenda was its demand for parity in political representation. Women, or so Gasque and her colleagues argued, should be equally represented in parliaments and the United Nations, where they should participate not just in decision-making, but also in legislation, making sure that laws pertaining to women and children were adequate.

Yet even this demand for equality was undergirded by difference, as were Mazdaznan's views of humanity. Even though the articles stressed the need for an enhanced understanding between nations as a precondition for world peace, and women's role in solving political conflicts on a diplomatic rather than a military level, some nations were deemed "more highly developed than others." Higher development resulted in augmented needs: according to the articles published by the Mazdaznan Women's Federation, those at the top needed "valuable foods like wheat, oil, fruits, vegetables, herbs, spices, nuts"—this list forming a summary of Mazdaznan dietetics. This left little for the allegedly less developed—except the meat and fish that Mazdaznan members did not eat.[120] Associating the "less developed" with the consumption of meat and fish did not just reflect Mazdaznan's combination of dietetics and racism. It was also strongly reminiscent of Hindu notions of caste and purity—and indeed, the IVU greatly intensified its relations with India in the 1950s.

## FROM SPHERE OF PROJECTION TO ACTIVE PARTICIPANT: INDIA ENTERS THE INTERNATIONAL VEGETARIAN UNION

In the same year that Gasque was elected president of the IVU, she appointed two vice secretaries from India, Jayantilal N. Mankar of the Bombay Humanitarian League and Rukmini Devi Arundale, who organized the Fifteenth World Vegetarian Congress, held in 1957 in India (and the first IVU congress to be held outside Europe).[121] This congress took up the message of vegetarianism as a force of peace and indirectly reacted to Gasque's and Mazdaznan's demands for gender parity by granting prominent roles to female politicians from India. But its chief feat was to turn India from a sphere of projection to an active participant in international organized vegetarianism. This newfound prominence allowed Indian actors to present and define their country on the world stage as a newly independent nation that was both progressive and aware of its supposed traditions, to define the Indian nation along the lines of perceived dietary, racial, and religious purity, and to gain international support for national issues.

In late October 1957, journalist P. R. Lele referred to that year's celebrations of Diwali as the "Festival of Famine." Directing readers' attention to the disastrous state of food security in the states of Bihar, Orissa, and Chattisgarh, he commented on a speech by Prime Minister Nehru, in which the latter had declared that "we will starve, if necessary." Lele recommended that "Mr. Nehru ought to take the lead in breakfasting, lunching, and dining every day at home. He ought, as the next step, to compel every Union Minister to follow his lead. All marriage feasts ought to be banned as they were during the war.... UNNECESSARY CONSUMPTION OF FOOD MUST BE FORBIDDEN IN EVERY PART OF THE COUNTRY, IMMEDIATELY AND FOR THREE YEARS."[122]

This crisis happened at a time when India was heavily dependent on foreign food aid, a situation exacerbated by the 1957 famine. While attaining autarky had been at the heart of the independence movement, with the Bengal famine of 1943 the ultimate tipping point, India's food situation deteriorated with independence, as Benjamin Siegel has shown. Due to the partition of the subcontinent, the new state lost much of its most productive land. The new government started campaigns under such slogans as "Grow More Food" and "Miss a Meal," calling upon its citizens to help the country in becoming self-sufficient.[123] Likewise, citizens were asked to rethink their dietary choices, replacing rice and wheat with pulses, tubers, and new substitute foods.[124] To the chagrin of Hindu nationalists, including members of the Congress Party, the government also started marketing meat.[125] Nonetheless, India could not have done without aid from both Russia and the United States. Yet despite this support, famines kept recurring regularly.

Only a week after Lele's article had appeared, however, a major food-centered event took place in India: the Fifteenth World Vegetarian Congress of the IVU. From November 6 to 25, 1957, delegates from seventeen countries, but mainly the United States, western Europe, and the

Commonwealth were taken around the subcontinent and fed lavishly.[126] India was presented to IVU delegates as the heartland of vegetarianism. In Bombay, they were welcomed to a food exhibition organized by Lilavati Munshi, a member of parliament and the wife of the former minister of food and agriculture.[127] They met high-ranking Indian politicians, and the IVU board was invited to tea at Rashtrapati Bhavan, the president's official residence.[128] They also encountered high-caste representatives of religious communities who rejected meat, including Hindus, Namdhari Sikhs, and Jains.[129]

The congress attracted considerable media attention. Participants and Indian members of parliament delivered speeches on All-India Radio. The *Times of India*, the *Free Press Journal*, and the journals of various vegetarian associations reported on the event.[130] At the end, delegates came up with a ten-point agenda that exhorted the governments of the world to prioritize animal welfare and the government of India to stop marketing meat.[131]

### National Heritage as a Global Mission: Indian Perspectives at the IVU Congress

Ten years after independence, Indian representatives at the 1957 congress painted a remarkable picture of the new nation. Ignoring the country's diverse alimentary traditions, Indian representatives constructed vegetarianism and *ahiṃsa* (nonviolence) as national heritage. By doing so, they did not just turn against the agricultural policy pursued by the Indian government. They also conveniently ignored vegetarianism's entanglement with cow protection, violent Indian nationalism, and caste hierarchy. Instead, representing *ahiṃsa* as the central value of India allowed protagonists to represent their country as one in which Brahmin norms ruled supreme while Muslims, lower-caste Hindus, and Christians were rendered invisible. Finally, participants stressed India's importance as a harbinger of peace in the Cold War world.

As the right hand to Gloria Gasque, the IVU's president, Framroze Bode, the Parsi priest from Bombay, had a prominent voice in the congress, writing the preface to the volume published by the IVU to mark the occasion. In this short text, Bode introduced vegetarianism as an age-old tradition in India, referring to *ahiṃsa* as the country's "most ancient and unique heritage." At the same time, he implied that this heritage was under threat: younger generations no longer believed in vegetarianism, and even many older people just held on to it out of a sense of tradition. Western civilization had exerted a harmful influence on India, including on its government officials, who were now marketing meat. World peace and true progress depended on humankind embracing vegetarianism. Only if humans stopped being cruel toward animals, or so Bode argued in a manner reminiscent both of Theosophist and Mazdaznan treatises, could "the full upward movement of the human race" be accomplished. Only then could humans become morally and physically pure, unleashing the "Divine nature which is latent in everyone" and thus bringing about the New Age. Those who clung to the consumption of meat were by implication backward, cruel, and impure.[132]

Rajendra Prasad, the president of India, described both tolerance and *ahiṃsa* as core values of Indian society in his inaugural speech at the congress. Along with vegetarianism, these values, or so Prasad argued, had helped India "survive trials and vicissitudes which few other nations ... have faced as we have had to do in history." They had allowed India to exercise a beneficial influence even on other religions: even "Islam ... became tamed in India." In its allegedly unbroken tradition of *ahiṃsa*, India had a lesson to teach the world, one that was particularly important during the Cold War. Prasad, who had also inaugurated the World Pacifist Meeting in India in 1949,[133] saw vegetarianism, if adhered to by the majority of humankind, as the only way "to escape the hydrogen bomb." Turning a blind eye to the violence of communalism, partition, and the First Kashmir War, Prasad depicted India as above the divisions of the Cold War, a moral superpower that could save the world.[134]

Lilavati Munshi opened the food exhibition that accompanied the congress. It featured vegetarian dishes from different parts of India, partly prepared with Indian Multi-Purpose Food, a plant-based surrogate that had been developed after the Second World War to help India cope with food, particularly protein, shortages.[135] Munshi, a Jain and member of the Indian National Congress, participated in her function as the president of the All-India Women's Food Council, a body instituted during the first grain shortage of the 1950s when her husband, K. M. Munshi, had been minister of food and agriculture. As Benjamin Siegel stresses, Lilavati Munshi's husband had accorded a leading role to women in changing Indian dietary habits. It was in this context that the All-India Women's Food Council was founded. It went on to establish canteens all over India that served dishes based on Indian Multi-Purpose Food. Lilavati Munshi also opened a hotel management and catering college in Bombay, which initially operated along these lines.[136] Munshi argued for vegetarianism on economic and ethical grounds: a diet free from meat could feed more people. Vegetarianism would ensure freedom from hunger and bring peace to the entire world. Bringing together economic considerations and Hindutva values, and ignoring the degree to which vegetarianism still signified the exclusion of most lower-class and casteless people in India, Munshi characterized vegetarianism as a potential "unifying force for all people" in and beyond India.[137]

The resolutions passed at the congress echoed this confidence in the global mission of vegetarianism. Addressing the governments of the world, the resolutions condemned "the exploitation of animals for food," and underlined that "the slaughter of animals is inconsistent with an enlightened way of life," thus implying the necessity of a complete ban on slaughter.[138] They asked "Education Departments . . . of all countries to take steps to include . . . vegetarianism in the curriculum . . . of schools and colleges," exhorted "all Governments to ban the use of atomic powers for destructive purposes," and urged the Indian government to stop marketing meat. The resolutions also took a stand against the export of monkeys from India for use in scientific experiments. Finally, they lent explicit support to "the vegetarian movement in India, a land made illustrious by the great name of Gandhi."[139]

That such support was necessary was implied by one of the main organizers of the congress, Rukmini Devi Arundale, an acclaimed dancer, member of the Theosophical Society, animal welfare activist, and IVU vice secretary. Born into a Brahmin family close to the Theosophical Society in Madurai in 1904, young Rukmini Devi was soon entrusted with an important position in the community, being nominated World Mother by Annie Besant. In 1920, she married George Sydney Arundale, the future president of the society. During a trip to Europe, she had become interested in ballet. Back in India, she learnt *Sadhir*, the dance traditionally practiced by the lower-caste Devadasis, which she merged with elements from ballet to create a new style she called *Bharata Natyam*. Rukmini Devi considered her efforts an attempt to revive Indian traditions that had been interrupted by centuries of "foreign" (i.e., Muslim and British) rule. In the 1950s, she was appointed to the Rajya Sabha (House of States), the second chamber of the

Indian parliament.[140] In her welcome address at the IVU congress, Rukmini Devi agreed with Prasad and Munshi in emphasizing *ahiṃsa*'s centrality to Indian culture, yet argued that this heritage was in danger of being forgotten. Centuries of colonial rule had alienated Indians from their culture and caused them to eat meat. Modern science had encouraged Indians to part with these very ideals, with medicine and even astrophysics crucially relying on animal experiments. Now the country needed "friends from afar . . . to help us rediscover our ancient ideals."[141]

### The IVU Congress: An International Stage for National Issues

In his congress report in *The Vegetarian*, Geoffrey L. Rudd, secretary of the Manchester Vegetarian Society, claimed triumphantly that "we have definitely put vegetarianism on the Indian map."[142] Ignoring both long-standing vernacular practices and (like his Indian hosts) the previous contacts between advocates of meat rejection in Europe and India, Rudd saw "Western vegetarianism" as part of a civilizing mission to India. But while this suggested that vegetarianism lacked support in India, it had a significant lobby in the country during the 1950s—a lobby, however, that considered its influence to be on the wane and that was eager to obtain international support.

The 1950s were a time of heated debate in Indian politics, pitting modernizers against conservatives.[143] The Hindu Code Bill, which, for the first time, placed casteless and lower-caste people on a similar legal footing compared to upper-caste Hindus, was debated for nearly a decade because of Hindu orthodox opposition. Instrumental in the bill's passage into law was the first minister of law and justice in independent India, Bhimrao Ramji Ambedkar. Born into a family deemed untouchable, Ambedkar had become one of the most important and radical activists on behalf of lower-caste and casteless people, for whom he coined the name "Dalits" (broken people) because of their long and systematic oppression.[144]

While Ambedkar's own conversion to Buddhism, a religion that enjoined, though did not require, meat abstention, led many Dalits to make a similar choice, another Dalit activist, Periyar, called upon lower-caste people to embrace self-respect by holding on to their nonvegetarian diet.[145] At the same time, members of the Rashtriya Swayamsevak Sangh, a right-wing youth organization, founded the Bharatiya Jana Sangh, a Hindu nationalist party promoting cow protection.[146] If Brahmin supremacy started at least to be questioned in the 1950s, vegetarianism and meat consumption were at the very center of these topics. Against this, Hindu nationalists asserted their notion of national and racial purity, which excluded Muslims, Dalits, and Christians, or at least required them to submit to Brahmin ethics.

The early independence period was also characterized by heated debates on agriculture and economics. While there had been debates on agricultural modernization well before 1947,[147] they intensified after independence with the launching of two five-year plans, which the government sought to popularize among India's citizens.[148] Because of the shortage of grain, the plans sought to add "protective foods"—namely, those believed to benefit the immune system—to the average Indian diet. Meat was classified as one such food,[149] and to increase its availability the first five-year plan introduced artificial insemination to cattle breeding. It also challenged the *goshalas*, the homes for aged and dry cattle, proposing a new establishment, the *gosadan*, where "useless and inefficient animals" would be "segregated." Instead of honoring aged animals, the *gosadan* judged them by productivity, effectively allowing those deemed to have no productive value to perish.[150]

These aspects of the first five-year plan may have inspired the foundation of a new All-India Animal Welfare Association in 1951. Its constitution strongly resembled that of the Bombay Humanitarian League. Indeed, it was J. N. Mankar, the organization's secretary and the IVU's vice secretary, who launched the All-India Animal Welfare Association. Its honorary patrons included Mankar, Rukmini Devi Arundale, and Rajendra Prasad, who, while willing to criticize *goshalas*, did not approve of *gosadans*.[151] Arundale, Mankar, both Brahmins, and Prasad, although from a Kayastha family,[152] were all staunch vegetarians.[153]

The All-India Animal Welfare Association moved quickly: in 1953, Rukmini Devi, supported by the association, proposed a new Prevention of Cruelty Against Animals Bill in the Council of States. Although an older version of the bill existed, this one went much further, demanding a stop to using animals in performance and religious rituals, including ritual slaughter—an initiative that primarily targeted Muslims. It further prohibited using animals in scientific experiments or exporting them for that use.[154] With this, the bill paralleled debates against vivisection—a topic that British protagonists had long been concerned with, but which was also pushed by the Theosophical Society in India.[155] In its preamble, the bill was justified with the necessity of "bring[ing] the laws of India ... in conformity with the ideals of Asoka and the teachings of Mahatma Gandhi, and with the conclusions of enlightened opinion," the same authorities to which the resolutions of the Fifteenth World Vegetarian Congress had appealed.[156]

Because of opposition from the states and the prime minister, the Council of States referred the bill to a select committee composed of Hindu members of parliament, including Rukmini Devi, but also of Muslim members like the then minister of food and agriculture, Rafi Ahmed Kidwai, who opposed the law.[157] While religious freedom was cited as the most important argument against the bill, it also went against the intended animal husbandry reforms specified in the first two five-year plans—a point, however, that opponents did not make explicitly.

Although the law was finally passed seven years later, it resembled Rukmini Devi's bill only in name. It legalized the export of animals and their use in research, even though it tasked the government with instituting a committee to set up a code of conduct for animal researchers and to sanction any breaches. It also permitted the employment of animals in performances, although their keepers had to register with the government. The new law explicitly permitted ritual slaughter.[158] Modern techniques in animal husbandry and their potential harm to animals were not even mentioned in the text.

Even if Rukmini Devi was a member of the new Animal Welfare Board created by the law,[159] its provisions were hardly in tune with her intentions—possibly because these were found to be irreconcilable with both a modernizing agriculture and an India that included large Muslim, Dalit, and other meat-eating communities. Even after partition, the majority of Indian politicians continued to uphold the country's religious plurality.

As this chapter has shown, the 1940s and 1950s marked both a new phase in the history of vegetarianism and a continuation of existing tendencies. What was new was the increased stress on internationalism and pacifism in view of the threat of nuclear war. The latter also signaled a turn away from a masculinity defined through strength and aggression as the dominant gender focus in vegetarianism. Instead, vegetarianism saw a feminization as leadership functions in the movement came to be filled by women, and the movement's agenda in turn came to focus on women's potential as a force of world peace. What linked the 1940s and 1950s to the past was the interest in race and the nation, which vegetarians had already articulated previously, although the fact that racism and nationalism coincided with pacifism and internationalism lent both a newly ambivalent outlook. It was only fitting that Mazdaznan, a community that embraced both racism and internationalism, moved to center stage in postwar organized vegetarianism, connecting vegetarians in the United States, Germany, India, and beyond.

German vegetarians likewise tried to revive their movement at the end of the Second World War. They still stressed race, with Adolf Briest attempting to collect "true German vegetarians" to start a settlement to restore the "Aryan" race. As soon as the war ended, Briest resumed relations with Mazdaznan and the IVU, but while German vegetarians largely agreed on the importance of both race and internationalism, they were unwilling to unite under one national organization. Instead, they tried to outdo one another in internationalist ambition, even though this internationalism was limited and undergirded by racist and colonialist tendencies.

The copresence of nationalism and internationalism was also palpable in Indian protagonists' politics, as seen at the IVU's Fifteenth World Vegetarian Congress. Hosting this event allowed Indians to highlight their country's new status as a major global player with a civilizing mission.[160] The congress offered Indian protagonists a chance to present their country as progressive, with several prominent speakers being female members of parliament. Secondly, representing *ahiṃsa* and vegetarianism as national heritage let them fashion India as a moral superpower above the divisions of the Cold War—though leading organizers of the congress such as Rukmini Devi Arundale and Lilavati Munshi were members of the Indian Congress for Cultural Freedom, an organization supported by the CIA, and were thus by no means impartial.[161] The Fifteenth World Vegetarian Congress also allowed the high-caste Indians who had brought it to India to represent upper-caste Hindu/Sikh/Jain/Buddhist values as inherently Indian, thus branding as impure all those who did not embrace them.

Although race and purity loomed large among protagonists on both sides, vegetarianism in Germany and India continued to operate in vastly different contexts. Most importantly, vegetarianism in Germany was a small movement with little influence on politics. In India, on the other hand, vegetarianism was pursued by a significant, and socially influential, part of the population. Despite the protestations of Indian delegates at the Fifteenth World Vegetarian Congress, it was too established to even need a movement.

The reemergence of Germany and the emergence of India and the United States as major protagonists in organized vegetarianism made Britain less central. Britain was also no longer the main partner for Indian activists, though some Hindus in Lahore joined the Manchester Vegetarian Society in 1946,[162] and a small number of Hindus living in India, Britain, Nigeria, South Africa, and the United States continued to join the society in the late 1940s and early 1950s.[163]

Meanwhile, vegetarians in Germany and India forged closer ties from the 1950s on. Geo Hiller,[164] Adolf Briest's successor as president of the German Vegetarian Union, published his impressions from the IVU congress in India in the union's magazine in monthly installments in 1957 and 1958.[165] His report was preceded, accompanied, and followed by a surge in articles on India, Hinduism, and related topics.[166] In his rival magazine *Sontraer Gesundheitsbote*, Oswald Kiehne of Donnershag celebrated "German-Indian World Peace" in a regular exchange of correspondence, in German, with D. V. Gokhale, a professor of history in Poona, who had most likely studied in Germany.[167]

What accounts for this sudden interest in India among German vegetarians and the emphasis on a German-Indian connection despite the dramatic differences in context between the German and Indian movements? Hiller was clearly impressed by his trip, but Kiehne never visited India. If one looks elsewhere for (West) German-Indian connections at this time, one finds them in the sphere of economics[168] and, more obviously, in yoga. While only a few vegetarians in the nineteenth and early twentieth centuries invoked a shared Aryan past, Aryanism had a heyday in German yoga magazines during the 1950s, a tendency helped by the fact that some proponents of yoga had served the Nazi government as academic experts.[169] Remarkably, these invocations were accompanied by a profession of Christian values, and, in Kiehne's case, a claim that German-Indian friendship would bring about world peace.[170]

While India had played a subordinate role in German vegetarianism until the early twentieth century, it came to the fore when the failed "Aryans" of postwar Germany sought redemption and spiritual replenishment from the "Aryans" of India. Indian partners in these exchanges, by contrast, may have hoped to garner support for their vision of an Indian state defined along upper-caste Hindu lines that marginalized supposedly meat-eating communities. While 1950s vegetarianism had sought to distance themselves from the legacy of the war, many of its adherents continued to praise nation and race in Germany and beyond—values that they considered in line with, indeed complemented by, internationalism.

# EPILOGUE

### PRESENT-DAY ECHOES

Today in Europe and the United States, vegetarianism is no longer considered eccentric. A diet free of meat and other animal products is widely recommended as a way of slowing down climate change and fighting global hunger, since a plant-based diet is less wasteful than one that needs to feed not only humans but also livestock. Indeed, vegetarianism has itself become outdated with the spread of veganism.[1] Although vegan and vegetarian associations including the International Vegetarian Union still exist, veg(etari)anism and animal welfare are no longer separate concerns. These days, activists and organizations commit themselves to animal rights, stressing that human and nonhuman animals have equal rights to life and happiness.[2] As a range of sexualities in Europe and North America has become, for the most part, more accepted than ever, no vegan today would justify abstaining from animal products to tame their "inner animal." Indeed, some cookbooks characterize vegan food as a libido enhancer.[3]

Yet, there are still traces in the present—some subtle, some less so—of the encounters discussed in this study. Entering a U.S. or German organic or health foods store, one will come across dozens of varieties of Yogi Tea, an allegedly Indian product that no Indian grocery store in the West or on the subcontinent stocks.[4] In German organic food and cosmetic stores

(*Reformhäuser*), one can still find cosmetics by Arya Laya, a brand founded in the early twentieth century and advertised in the pages of German vegetarian magazines in the interwar era whose names alludes to the concept of Aryanism influential in German vegetarianism but also, in a different way, in Hindu nationalist contexts.[5] COVID-19, of course, gave rise to anti-vaccination protests in Germany and elsewhere. Although participants come from many milieus, including the extreme right wing, and not all of them practice nonviolence, flags with Gandhi's portrait were omnipresent at the early protests at Berlin's Brandenburg Gate.[6] While protestors no doubt wanted to underline the allegedly peaceful nature of their protests, Gandhi, in his own time, was also vocally anti-vaccination.[7]

In India, conversely, very little of the encounter between Western vegetarians and their supposedly like-minded partners on the subcontinent is currently tangible. That, however, does not mean that vegetarianism is no longer an issue in the country—it very much is. In the past decade, cow protection has surged, with Dalits and Muslims accused of having maltreated cows, or consumed or traded beef, being lynched.[8] Laws against cow slaughter were imposed in many Indian states.[9] Muslims or other individuals believed to be nonvegetarians face difficulties renting apartments in cities like Mumbai.[10] In April 2022, the sale of meat was prohibited in Delhi bazaars during a holiday marking the god Ram's birthday, and violence broke out over students consuming meat in the canteen of Jawaharlal Nehru University on the holiday.[11] These incidents are accompanied by larger political developments that target Muslims, making them appear, as Kalyani Devaki Menon argues, as "marginal, suspicious, and, in this era of global Islamophobia, dangerous subjects."[12] In present-day India, Gandhi's vision of vegetarianism as nonviolence, along with his politics of tolerance, however problematic in some of its aspects, is largely a thing of the past.

The British press has covered these transformations. German newspapers, by contrast, have been slow to realize their significance. Vegetarian associations, whether British, German, or American, have taken no notice of the violence associated with cow protection. Indeed, some gladly cooperate with Indian partners without taking a deeper look into their political projects: an interest in animal welfare/rights, the more uncompromising the better, is generally all that matters to them. This, too, of course, is reminiscent of the period described in this book.

# EPILOGUE

## SUMMARY

Since this study is concerned with the past rather than the present, however, let me return to its contents and sum them up briefly. While existing research on vegetarianism tends to focus either on the West or on Asia, this study shows that global connections were central to vegetarianism from the "long" nineteenth century on.

When vegetarianism emerged in Europe, or so I argue in chapter 1, vegetarians looked to the non-European world to show that the greater part of humanity already lived without meat. Vegetarians used the East as a moral model for a Europe they perceived as degenerating. Industrialization and urbanization, as well as the working-class lifestyle and middle-class cuisine, were blamed for this decline. As European vegetarians searched for purity, Britons focused on India, where the figure of the "merciful Hindoo" appeared as an embodiment of all the perceived virtues of vegetarianism: meekness, modesty, moral sobriety, and health. What they ignored was that India was neither a wholly Hindu nor a wholly vegetarian country; indeed, they were unable or unwilling to see that vegetarianism was a means of social distinction and exclusion tied inseparably to caste. German vegetarians, with the exception of Gustav Struve, whose novel *Mandara's Wanderungen* drew on the "merciful Hindoo" trope, found their ideal in the "Orient," a vaguely defined Eastern territory that included Greece, Egypt, Turkey, Syria, and sometimes Persia. Whether looking at India or the "Orient," vegetarians either ignored the connections between food and social inequality, or, in some cases, explicitly approved of them, as the comments of some British authors on caste show.

Vegetarians' interest in the world beyond Europe rendered them open to cultural encounters, as I show in chapter 2. These encounters were often facilitated by the networks of the Theosophical Society; through the concept of Aryanism, which implied that Europeans and high-caste Hindus shared common roots; and through seemingly shared notions of purity. Those Hindus (and occasionally Jains, Parsis, and Sikhs) interested in cooperating with Europeans were often nationalists who defined the nation-to-be through values in line with upper-caste Hinduism. These values were bolstered by employing dietetic knowledge developed in the West to render ways of eating that were challenged by colonial discourse, which often linked meat consumption with masculinity, more attractive. Advocates of the new vegetarianism claimed the contrary: rejecting meat, alcohol, tobacco, and other foods would strengthen individual bodies and the body politic by making it more masculine. Many of these protagonists supported the cow protection movement, which often called for violence against supposed consumers of beef—Muslims, lower-caste Hindus, and the British. Others sought to reform lower-caste and casteless people who consumed meat, alcohol, and other substances deemed impure.

Some of the knowledge developed through cultural contacts in India traveled to the United States, where it was further transformed during and after the World's Columbian Exposition in Chicago in 1893, a process examined in chapter 3. An international vegetarian congress at the exposition brought together participants from India, the United States, and Europe, initiating a formal internationalization of the movement organizationally. The World's Parliament of Religions also represented all the religions present in India to a curious American public, thus starting the global yoga boom, a rich field for Hindu cultural brokers, whom Americans expected to be vegetarian. Yoga and vegetarianism came to be considered complementary practices in the West, a symbiosis inspiring many further appropriations, notably that of Mazdaznan. A cult founded by a German migrant in Chicago and sold as the "true Zoroastrianism," Mazdaznan fed notions of vegetarianism and yoga into a white supremacist soteriology that appealed to middle- and upper-class white Americans—and soon to their counterparts in Britain, Germany, and Switzerland. While heavily indebted to yoga and Theosophy, Mazdaznan obscured these influences, claiming to be inspired by a vague Orient. It also "de-Hinduized" the concept of Aryanism, excluding Hindus (but not Persians, Arabs, and Jews) from this supposedly elect community.

In chapter 4, I trace the diverse yet distant contacts—both textual and personal—German and Swiss vegetarians made with South Asia in the interwar period. Surprisingly, Hinduism was rarely an explicit reference in these encounters, as German-speaking vegetarians were not interested in it. Instead, some anti-Semitic vegetarians like Ludwig Ankenbrand were taken with South Asia because of the "Aryan" past it allegedly shared with Germany or its status as the home of Buddhism. Others were inspired by knowledge with ties to South Asia, like Hossein Kazemzadeh, who joined Sufism with *Lebensreform* notions of vegetarianism and at least an

## EPILOGUE

admiration of Mazdaznan. Others were fascinated not with South Asia, but with Gandhi, celebrating him as the embodiment of a strong ascetic male leader—the type of leader Germany, in their view, desperately needed. German vegetarians thus openly welcomed the rise of another seemingly ascetic leader, Adolf Hitler. But not all vegetarians were unambiguous militarists. Both the Swiss reformer Werner Zimmermann (who nevertheless viewed both Mussolini and the Nazi government positively in the beginning and also gave lectures to German troops during the Second World War) and the German animal welfare activist Magnus Schwantje championed the idea of nonviolence they had seen articulated in India. Zimmermann admired Gandhi as someone who transformed society through love, although Gandhi's promotion of sexual abstinence sat uncomfortably with Zimmermann's sexual liberalism. Schwantje was taken with Ram Chandra Sharma, a Brahmin and Hindu nationalist who went on a hunger strike against animal sacrifice, not knowing that Ram Chandra's nationalism included an approval of violence against Muslims and an increasingly critical stance toward nonviolence in general.

In chapter 5, I show the close links between internationalism, nationalism, and race in organized vegetarianism as it began to reconstitute itself after the Second World War. In the chapter's first section, I examine the activities of Gloria Gasque, a high-ranking American Mazdaznan member resident in Britain, and the future president of the International Vegetarian Union, in India, arguing that while her mission of proselytizing to Parsis failed, she met with some resonance because she championed eugenics, a concern among some Parsis during this period, and wished to bolster Zoroastrianism at a time when it seemed to be under threat in India. Indeed, Gasque's Bombay links would be instrumental during her time in office in the International Vegetarian Union. The chapter next considers Germany, where vegetarians started reorganizing toward the end of the war. While they dismissed the links between masculinity, militarism, and vegetarianism espoused by many vegetarians before and during the Nazi era, the concept of race and the notion of Germans as "Aryans" continued to be employed in the postwar era, indeed serving as the foundation of German-Indian vegetarian encounters, as I show in the conclusion of chapter 5. The final section of the chapter offers an analysis of the Fifteenth World Vegetarian Congress, held in India in 1957, the first IVU congress to take place outside Europe. I show how the event allowed Indian protagonists to turn their country from a sphere of projection for Western vegetarians into an active participant in the international movement. At the same time, they also tried to define their nation along unmistakably upper-caste Hindu lines, largely erasing the nonvegetarian alimentary practices of both Muslims and lower-caste and casteless people, and to secure support for more restrictive animal welfare legislation.

## IMPLICATIONS AND QUESTIONS FOR FUTURE RESEARCH

What new insights can this study offer into the history of vegetarianism and global history more generally? I have showed that vegetarianism was not necessarily about nonviolence and tolerance in India or the West. Its adherents were as concerned with relations between humans and visions for humanity as they were for human-animal relations. These visions oscillated between nationalism and internationalism, opposition to and approval of colonialism, equality, and racism. To some extent, therefore, vegetarians around the globe shared a certain discourse. Nonetheless, they were embedded in local contexts that framed vegetarianism differently, even if actors drew on and appropriated other bodies of knowledge. The knowledge produced by vegetarians, then, was at once connected and disconnected.

This is also a point of interest for global history more generally. Over the past two decades historians have stressed the importance of locating entanglements, but while this is important, we should not ignore aspects that were less or unentangled, or that became disentangled in the course of a given encounter. This book seeks to point to both entanglements and aspects that remained less or unentangled. The latter do not devalue or disprove the significance of global processes of exchange, since these processes often continue even if the protagonists participating in them go their separate ways in other contexts. In fact, these shifts and variabilities make the phenomenon of entanglements more complex and therefore an even more important and relevant topic of research.

How can we attend to this other side of entanglements? First of all, as scholars like Margit Pernau caution, it is important not to assume that our categories of investigation carry the same meaning globally. With regards to the subject of this book, this means realizing that vegetarianism did not mean the same thing in Europe and the United States as it did in India (and indeed realizing that, for a time preceding this book's period of

## EPILOGUE

investigation, it is not even a term that protagonists in a Hindu context were familiar with). This helps, secondly, with looking for connotations and practices that did not match those embraced by vegetarians in Europe and were therefore not noticed by or communicated to them. The same attempt at looking for the unfamiliar—in the present context, for that which might have struck Hindu and other South Asian audiences as unfamiliar—should be pursued for all other sides in the encounter. Looking for the place of the unfamiliar, or rather the lack of such a place, in cultural encounters, does not only mean being aware of discontinuities, thus living up to the conditions of effective history as defined by Foucault and Nietzsche.[13] It also means delving into the field of "agnotology" (Proctor and Schiebinger), paying attention to aspects that were unknown, not communicated, even actively silenced, and asking why protagonists opted for such strategies.[14]

In doing so, this book attempts to contribute to a number of regional histories—namely, German, British, U.S., and South Asian history—while at the same time connecting them. As outlined at the beginning of this book, the history of vegetarianism has long been written in terms of national history, with scholars frequently contrasting a seemingly modern, secular European vegetarianism with a seemingly immutable, traditional one in South Asia.[15] This book has shown that this perception is in need of correction. Although there was a much longer history of meat and related forms of abstention in Brahmin, Buddhist, and Jain contexts in South Asia, debates on vegetarianism in India were greatly impacted by emerging scientific knowledge on vegetarianism developed in Europe and the United States. On the other hand, Asian religions were a major inspiration to vegetarians in the West, often themselves members of new religions, who used this kind of knowledge to justify their theory of vegetarianism a tool of human evolution. Scholars of German, British, and North American history, therefore, can learn from this book that intellectual exchange with protagonists from Asia crucially shaped some of the movements central to modernity in the West. A study of global entanglements, therefore, is not something that is marginal to German, British, or North American history. Instead, it enhances our understanding of some of its central aspects, often radically transforming our assumptions. By the same token, this book could show that the vegetarian movement was not necessarily secular or progressive. Religion and new religions were at the heart of international organized vegetarianism, and so was race, with white supremacy, Aryanism, Hindutva, and Islamophobia, but also eugenics, a core concern of many of its protagonists. Just as in the case of religion, these overlapping racisms were often inspired by each other through the dynamic exchange of knowledge on vegetarianism, a means of racial evolution to many of its adherents. The book therefore calls for a more nuanced evaluation of the modern, not just regarding its global entanglement, but also its dark sides. At the same time, it also seeks to contribute to the history of South Asia, pointing to the centrality of food in anticolonial debates, as well as to the seemingly unlikely contribution of Western knowledge, and of circulations of such knowledge between Europe, South Asia, and the United States, to strands of Hindu nationalism. Such exchange, the book argues, fueled debates on vegetarianism and masculinity, but also the scapegoating of nonvegetarian minorities such as Muslims, Christians, and lower-caste Hindus, thereby contributing to growing tendencies toward communalism.

At the same time, there were aspects that this study could only touch upon. First, the networks of the actors in this study were not restricted to Europe, the United States, South Asia, and, to some extent, West Asia and North Africa. Leo Tolstoy, the Russian aristocrat, novelist, pacifist, and correspondence partner of Gandhi, was a towering figure in nineteenth- and twentieth-century vegetarianism, revered by vegetarians well beyond Europe. His example shows that it might be worth incorporating Russia and central Europe, as well as Africa, in future analyses, and to more systematically consider the overlap between pacifism and vegetarianism.

Secondly, it might be interesting to examine more closely the interplay between Islamophobia in Hindu/Parsi/Jain debates on cow protection and anti-Semitism in European vegetarianism. Now that we know that actors in both contexts were in contact, it might be no coincidence that campaigns against Jewish practices of slaughter in European vegetarianism in the 1880s and 1890s began at the very time when Hindu nationalism and cow protection emerged as interrelated movements explicitly targeting Muslims and their methods of slaughter.

Finally, there are connections between vegetarianism and revolutionary movements for equality in the Pan-African/Black American context that require closer scholarly attention. Both Booker T. Washington and later Elijah Muhammad, the founder of the Nation of Islam, were convinced of the revolutionary potential of vegetarianism.[16] It is thus important not to equate

## EPILOGUE

all nineteenth- and twentieth-century vegetarianism with racist and white supremacist notions of purity. While many vegetarians subscribed to these convictions, they were not the only people defining the field.

In the end, emphasizing entanglements and showing how they led to appropriations and reinterpretations of knowledge can only be a first step. What this book could not show is what effect this circulation of knowledge had on those who did not have a prominent role in its making. If some Western actors fascinated with India turned out to be equally intrigued with racial theory, or some Hindu and Jain protagonists flaunted Islamophobia, those influenced by them in turn might not have had the same outlook. They could have been antiracists, pacifists, anti-caste, or critical of exclusive concepts of the nation. They might have been less interested in the question of how vegetarianism could improve humanity and more interested in its benefits for animals.

This book could only look at those who were vociferous—not those who were silent, who listened, and perhaps interpreted what they read or listened to differently. It focused on those who communicated through texts rather than in conversations or through practices, thus necessarily providing an incomplete picture. Like any academic study, it leaves to the scholarly community the task of pointing out other parts of this picture and telling different stories, whether complementary, more complex, or competing.

# ACKNOWLEDGMENTS

Many people were involved in the development of this project on various levels, and listing them here rather concisely and in a certain sequence is not meant to suggest an order of importance.

First of all, I would like to thank my reviewers and the series editors of Columbia Studies in International and Global History, Dominic Sachsenmaier, Cemil Aydin, and Timothy Nunan for accepting me into the series, and Caelyn Cobb, Monique Laban, and Kathryn Jorge at Columbia University Press for their support. Martha Schulman's copyediting considerably improved the text. Ryan Perks at Columbia University Press not only added the last polish and spotted any remaining inaccuracies, but even made the process an enjoyable one.

This book could not have been written without the support of the Max Weber Foundation, which awarded me a Gerald D. Feldman Travel Grant to Britain, India, and the United States, and the Gerda Henkel Foundation, which funded work on the book in 2020 and 2021, and paid travel and copyediting expenses. A grant by the Arab-German Young Academy of Sciences and Humanities (AGYA) allowed me to conduct research in Lebanon. A further grant from AGYA enabled my colleagues Bilal Orfali and Kirill Dmitriev and I to host a conference on food as a cultural signifier, and to subsequently publish the volume *Insatiable Appetite*. Finally, the University of Kassel allowed me to conduct further research in India in 2017,

ACKNOWLEDGMENTS

facilitated by an affiliation with the Centre for Studies in Social Sciences Calcutta.

During those trips, staff at various archives and libraries facilitated my research. Apart from the archives and libraries mentioned in the list of unpublished primary sources, I mainly drew on material from Murhardsche Bibliothek, Kassel; Niedersächische Staats- und Universitätsbibliothek Göttingen; Universitätsbibliothek J. B. Senckenberg, Frankfurt am Main; Staatsbibliothek Preußischer Kulturbesitz, Berlin; British Library, London; Adyar Library of the Theosophical Society, Chennai; New York Public Library; the library of the University of California at Berkeley; Plansprachenarchiv, Österreichische Nationalbibliothek, Vienna; and Deutsche Nationalbibliothek in Leipzig and Frankfurt am Main.

Just as important were discussions with colleagues, inter alia Harald Fischer-Tiné, Hubertus Büschel, Rebekka Habermas, Indra Sengupta, Bernd Wedemeyer-Kolwe, Parama Roy, Gauri Viswanathan, Rebecca Earle, Razak Khan, Maria Framke, Shaheed Tayob, Maria Moritz, Maria-Magdalena Pruss, Jana Tschurenev, Yasmin Amin, Anny Gaul, Charu Gupta, Gerdien Jonker, Souad Slim, Norman Aselmeyer, Veronika Settele, David Motadel, Sebastian Conrad, Ali Usman Qasmi, Hemant Sareen, Teresa Segura-Garcia, Shilpi Rajpal, Lalit Vachani, Sarover Zaidi, Gautam Pemmaraju, Robert Kramm, Mieke Roscher, André Krebber, Jürgen Bacia, Susanne Rappe-Weber, Lalit Vachani, and Srirupa Roy. Discussions with my colleagues in Kassel as well as at conferences and seminars, inter alia at the German Historians' Conference in Munich, the German Historical Institute London, the German Historical Institute Paris, the EHSSC conferences in Valencia and Belfast, the Centre for Studies in Social Sciences Calcutta, the Zentrum Moderner Orient Berlin, the History Department and Centre for Modern Indian Studies, Göttingen, the global history research seminar at the Universities of ETH Zurich, Heidelberg, and Erfurt, and the research seminar in modern history at the University of Kassel, the Archiv der deutschen Jugendbewegung, and Gut Siggen, were likewise important in the writing process.

Rhea Dagher, Khaled al-Boushi, Alaa Kayali, Nandini Roy Chowdhury, Hemant Sareen, Sarover Zaidi, Anne-Marie Brack, Niusha Ramzani, and Stefan Popp helped me with translations of sources. Nadia Vinogradova, Nicola Camillieri, and Ozan Özavcı kindly sent me digitized material from the Bibliothèque nationale de France, Joseph Regenstein Library in Chicago,

## ACKNOWLEDGMENTS

and the library of the International Institute of Social History, Amsterdam. Kai Drewes borrowed and scanned countless books for me from various libraries.

Alexandra Keller, Vivian Donath, Miguel Ohnesorge, Ruth Knüppel, and Annabell Boerger helped me sort my archive photos and feed my always hungry reference manager. I am also indebted to Miguel Ohnesorge for inviting me to a talk at the University of Porto and for many discussions about the project. Classes with my students at the University of Kassel were likewise helpful in developing my research and making it understandable. Jasmin Daam, then my doctoral student, and Petra Klein, my former secretary, as well as my student assistants provided me with a welcoming and warm working atmosphere at the University of Kassel.

During my research trips, my various hosts in India, the United States, Britain, and Lebanon made me feel at home and thus contributed in no small way to making these stays enjoyable and productive.

Finally, I would like to thank my friends and family for discussing the project with me and supporting me throughout the process of writing this book and the uncertainties of an academic career.

# NOTES

## INTRODUCTION

1. On the print, see Christopher Pinney, *Photos of the Gods: The Printed Image and Political Struggle in India* (New Delhi: Oxford University Press, 2004), 106–112.
2. Walter Hammer, ed., *Dokumente des Vegetarismus. Als Privatdruck herausgegeben von Walter Hammer in Elberfeld-Sonnborn*, 6th ed. (Leipzig: Dr. Hugo Vollrath, 1914), 40; "Kreuz," in *Meyers Großes Konversations-Lexikon* (Leipzig: Bibliographisches Institut, 1907), 645–647; Uwe Puschner, Walter Schmitz, and Justus H. Ulbricht, "Vorwort," in *Handbuch zur "Völkischen Bewegung,"* ed. Uwe Puschner (Munich: Saur, 1996), iii; Ulrich Linse, "Völkisch-Rassische Siedlungen der Lebensreform," in Puschner, *Handbuch zur "Völkischen Bewegung,"* 397–410; Walter Schmitz and Uwe Schneider, "Völkische Semantik im George-Kreis," in Puschner, *Handbuch zur "Völkischen Bewegung,"* 711–746.
3. Ludwig Ankenbrand, "Buddhism and the Modern Reform Efforts (Germany, 1911)," in *Religious Dynamics under the Impact of Imperialism and Colonialism*, ed. Björn Bentlage, Marion Eggert, Hans Martin Krämer, and Stefan Reichmuth (Leiden: Brill, 2017), 191–196.
4. Christopher Otter, *Diet for a Large Planet: Industrial Britain, Food Systems, and World Ecology* (Chicago: University of Chicago Press, 2020).
5. Out of a copious and growing body of research, see Otter, *Diet for a Large Planet*; "Planet of Meat: A Biological History," in *Challenging (the) Humanities*, ed. Tony Bennett (Canberra: Australian Academy of the Humanities, 2013), 33–49; "Civilizing Slaughter: The Development of the British Public Abattoir, 1850–1910," *Food and History* 3, no. 2 (2005): 29–51; James Staples, *Sacred Cows and Chicken Manchurian: The Everyday Politics of Eating Meat in India* (Seattle: University of Washington Press, 2020); Thomas David DuBois, "Many Roads from Pasture

INTRODUCTION

to Plate: A Commodity Chain Approach to China's Beef Trade, 1732–1931," *Journal of Global History* 14, no. 1 (2019): 22–43; Joshua Specht, *Red Meat Republic: A Hoof-to-Table History of How Beef Changed America* (Princeton, NJ: Princeton University Press, 2019); Wilson J. Warren, *Meat Makes People Powerful: A Global History of the Modern Era* (Iowa City: University of Iowa Press, 2018); Yves Segers, Jan Bieleman, and Erik Buyst, eds., *Exploring the Food Chain: Food Production and Food Processing in Western Europe, 1850–1990* (Turnhout, BE: Brepols, 2009); Paula Young Lee, ed., *Meat, Modernity, and the Rise of the Slaughterhouse* (Durham: University of New Hampshire Press, 2008); Boris Loheide, "Beef around the World. Die Globalisierung des Rindfleischhandels bis 1914," *Comparativ* 17, no. 3 (2007): 46–67.

6. Massimo Montanari, *Der Hunger und der Überfluß. Kulturgeschichte der Ernährung in Europa* (Munich: Beck, 1993), 186–187; Hans Jürgen Teuteberg, "The Birth of the Modern Consumer Age: Food Innovations from 1800," in *Food: The History of Taste*, ed. Paul H. Freedman (London: Thames & Hudson, 2007), 233–262; Specht, *Red Meat Republic*, 223.

7. William H. Brock, *Justus von Liebig: The Chemical Gatekeeper* (Cambridge: Cambridge University Press, 1997); Mark R. Finlay, "Early Marketing of the Theory of Nutrition: The Science and Culture of Liebig's Extract of Meat," in *The Science and Culture of Nutrition, 1840–1940*, ed. Harmke Kamminga (Amsterdam: Rodopi, 1995), 48–74; Hans Jürgen Teuteberg, *Die Rolle des Fleischextrakts für die Ernährungswissenschaften und den Aufstieg der Suppenindustrie. Kleine Geschichte der Fleischbrühe* (Stuttgart: Steiner, 1990).

8. Tatsuya Mitsuda, "'Vegetarian' Nationalism: Critiques of Meat Eating for Japanese Bodies, 1880–1938," in *Culinary Nationalism in Asia*, ed. Michelle T. King (London: Bloomsbury Academic, 2019), 23–40; Geoffrey Barstow, *Food of Sinful Demons: Meat, Vegetarianism, and the Limits of Buddhism in Tibet* (New York: Columbia University Press, 2017); Hans Martin Krämer, "'Not Befitting Our Divine Country': Eating Meat in Japanese Discourses of Self and Other from the Seventeenth Century to the Present," *Food and Foodways* 16, no. 1 (2008): 33–62; Ayu Majima, "Eating Meat, Seeking Modernity: Food and Imperialism in Late Nineteenth and Early Twentieth Century Japan," in *Critical Readings on Food in East Asia*, ed. Katarzyna J. Cwiertka (Leiden: Brill, 2013), 111–133; Katarzyna J. Cwiertka, *Modern Japanese Cuisine: Food, Power and National Identity* (London: Reaktion Books, 2006).

9. Ceri Crossley, *Consumable Metaphors: Attitudes Towards Animals and Vegetarianism in Nineteenth-Century France* (Oxford: Lang, 2005); Arouna Ouédraogo, "De la secte religieuse à l'utopie philanthropique: Genèse sociale du végétarisme occidental," *Annales. Histoire, Sciences Sociales* 55, no. 4 (2000): 825–843; Peter Brang, *Ein unbekanntes Russland: Kulturgeschichte vegetarischer Lebensweisen von den Anfängen bis zur Gegenwart* (Cologne: Böhlau, 2002).

10. For Britain, see Julia Twigg, "The Vegetarian Movement in England, 1847–1981" (PhD diss., London School of Economics, 1981), 83–88; James Gregory, *Of Victorians and Vegetarians: The Vegetarian Movement in Nineteenth-Century Britain* (London: Tauris Academic Studies, 2007), 30–50. Surprisingly, Manchester's global connections have not yet engendered much resonance among historians. See, however, Alan J. Kidd and Terry Wyke, eds., *Manchester: Making the Modern*

## INTRODUCTION

*City* (Liverpool: Liverpool University Press, 2016). For the German-speaking movement, see, for comparison, Wolfgang R. Krabbe, *Gesellschaftsveränderung durch Lebensreform* (Göttingen: Vandenhoeck und Ruprecht, 1974), 50–77; Eva Barlösius, *Naturgemäße Lebensführung. Zur Geschichte der Lebensreform um die Jahrhundertwende* (Frankfurt/Main: Campus, 1997), 24–25, 36–47; Corinna Treitel, *Eating Nature in Modern Germany: Food, Agriculture, and Environment, c. 1870 to 2000* (Cambridge: Cambridge University Press, 2017), 29–40.

11. Julia Hauser, "Körper, Moral, Gesellschaft: Debatten über Vegetarismus zwischen Europa und Indien, 1850–1914," in *Geschichte des Nicht-Essens: Verzicht, Vermeidung und Verweigerung in der Moderne*, ed. Norman Aselmeyer and Veronika Settele (Munich: Oldenbourg, 2018), 265–294; "A Frugal Crescent: Perceptions of Foodways in the Ottoman Empire and Egypt in Nineteenth-Century Vegetarian Discourse," in *Food as a Cultural Signifier: Perspectives on the Middle East and Beyond*, ed. Kirill Dmitriev and Bilal Orfali (Leiden: Brill, 2020), 292–316. As Alison Bashford argues, the question of food security has been central to population debates since the late eighteenth century. Alison Bashford, *Global Population: History, Geopolitics, and Life on Earth* (New York: Columbia University Press, 2014). While vegetarians argued that a meatless diet saved grain, and thus could be useful on a national level, they did not extend this argument globally until after the Second World War. One of the first books to make this argument was Frances Moore Lappé's *Diet for a Small Planet* (New York: Ballantine Books, 1971). Individual articles in vegetarian magazines, however, have discussed the problem since the 1950s. See, for instance, Peter Freeman, "Vegetarianism or World Famine," *The Vegetarian*, 10th ser., 3, no. 4 (1955): 92–94.

12. Rosinka Chaudhuri, *Freedom and Beef Steaks: Colonial Calcutta Culture* (Delhi: Orient Blackswan, 2012), 17–40.

13. See, for instance, Mohini Mohun Chatterji, "Vegetarianism and Christianity in India," *Almonds and Raisins* 4 (1885): 18–21; Byramji Dinshaji Pandey, *Vegetarian Cookery with Testimony of Eminent Physicians, Chemists, Scientists, Naturalists, Physiologists, &c., Showing the Evil Effects of Flesh Eating and the Natural Diet of Man* (Bombay: Imperial Standard Printing and Rajyabhakta Presses, 1890); *Essays on the Advantages of a Vegetarian Diet: Being a Collection of the Essays of Successful Candidates in Its Prize Essay Scheme No. IV* (Bombay: Sanj Vartaman Press, 1914); Bhavanidas Narandas Motivala and R. S. Gokhale, *Rationale of Vegetarianism: A First-Prize and Second Prize Essays of "Competitive Prize Essay Scheme No. 16"* (Bombay: Humanitarian League, 1919). While these authors used the term "vegetarianism," they infused it with a different meaning compared to their European and American counterparts. See chapter 2.

14. On Gandhi's agenda of vegetarianism and anticolonialism, see Leela Gandhi, *Affective Communities: Anticolonial Thought, Fin-De-Siècle Radicalism, and the Politics of Friendship* (Durham, NC: Duke University Press, 2006), 67–114; Parama Roy, *Alimentary Tracts: Appetites, Aversions, and the Postcolonial* (Durham, NC: Duke University Press, 2010), 75–115; Nico Slate, *Gandhi's Search for the Perfect Diet* (Seattle: University of Washington Press, 2019). On the links between violent anticolonial nationalism, see Hauser, "Körper, Moral, Gesellschaft," and chapter 2 of this study.

INTRODUCTION

15. Mary Douglas, *Purity and Danger: An Analysis of Concepts of Pollution and Taboo* (London: Routledge and Kegan Paul 1966); Pierre Bourdieu, *Distinction: A Social Critique of the Judgement of Taste* (London: Routledge and Kegan Paul, 1984); Jeffrey Miller and Jonathan Deutsch, eds., *Food Studies: An Introduction to Research Methods* (Oxford: Berg, 2009); David A. Davis, "A Recipe for Food Studies," *American Quarterly* 62, no. 2 (2010): 365–375; Warren Belasco, Amy Bentley, Charlotte Biltekoff, Psyche Williams-Forson, and Carolyn de La Peña, "The Frontiers of Food Studies," *Food, Culture & Society* 14, no. 3 (2011): 301–315; Richard Wilk, "The Limits of Discipline: Towards Interdisciplinary Food Studies," *Physiology & Behavior* 107, no. 4 (2012): 471–475; Ken Albala, ed., *Routledge International Handbook of Food Studies* (London: Routledge, 2014); Melissa L. Caldwell, *Why Food Matters: Critical Debates in Food Studies* (London: Bloomsbury, 2021).
16. See, for instance, Laura Wright, ed., *The Routledge Handbook of Vegan Studies* (London: Routledge, 2021); Andrew Linzey and Clair Linzey, eds., *Ethical Vegetarianism and Veganism* (London: Routledge, 2019); Carol Helstosky, "Food Studies and Animal Rights," in Albala, *Routledge International Handbook of Food Studies*, 322–333; Carol J. Adams, *The Sexual Politics of Meat: A Feminist-Vegetarian Critical Theory* (New York: Continuum, 1990); Adams, *The Pornography of Meat* (New York: Continuum, 2004).
17. For comparison, see Paul Waldau and Kimberley Patton, eds., *A Communion of Subjects: Animals in Religion, Science, and Ethics* (New York: Columbia University Press, 2006); Saurav Kumar, "Veganism, Hinduism, and Jainism in India," in Wright, *The Routledge Handbook of Vegan Studies*, 205–214.
18. Gurminder Bhambra, *Rethinking Modernity: Postcolonialism and the Sociological Imagination* (Basingstoke, UK: Palgrave Macmillan, 2007).
19. Ravindra S. Khare, ed., *The Hindu Hearth and Home: Culinary Systems Old and New in North India* (New Delhi: Vikas Publishing House, 1976); Khare, ed., *The Eternal Food: Gastronomic Ideas and Experiences of Hindus and Buddhists* (Albany: State University of New York Press, 1992); Chitrita Banerji, *Feeding the Gods: Memories of Food and Culture in Bengal* (Oxford: Seagull, 2006).
20. Utsa Ray, "Eating 'Modernity': Changing Dietary Practices in Colonial Bengal," *Modern Asian Studies* 46, no. 3 (2012): 703–729; Ray, *Culinary Culture in Colonial India: A Cosmopolitan Platter and the Middle-Class* (Delhi: Cambridge University Press, 2015). See also Rachel Berger, "Between Digestion and Desire: Genealogies of Food in Nationalist North India," *Modern Asian Studies* 47, no. 5 (2013): 1622–1643; Jayanta Sengupta, "Nation on a Platter: The Culture and Politics of Food and Cuisine in Colonial Bengal," *Modern Asian Studies* 44, no. 1 (2010): 81–98; Chaudhuri, *Freedom and Beef Steaks*.
21. Ray, "Eating 'Modernity.'"
22. Mrinalini Sinha, *Colonial Masculinity: The "Manly Englishman" and the "Effeminate Bengali" in the Late Nineteenth Century* (Manchester: Manchester University Press, 1995).
23. Joseph S. Alter, *Gandhi's Body: Sex, Diet, and the Politics of Nationalism* (Philadelphia: University of Pennsylvania Press, 2000); Gandhi, *Affective Communities*, 67–114; Roy, *Alimentary Tracts*, 75–115; Parama Roy, "Meat-Eating, Masculinity, and Renunciation in India: A Gandhian Grammar of Diet," *Gender & History* 14, no. 1 (2002): 62–91; Slate, *Gandhi's Search for the Perfect Diet*.

INTRODUCTION

24. For an exception, see Albert Wirz, *Die Moral auf dem Teller* (Zürich: Chronos, 1993), who compares the work of Maximilian Bircher-Benner in Switzerland and John Harvey Kellogg in the United States.
25. For Germany, see note 26 below. For Britain and the United States, see Richard W. Schwarz, "Dr. John Harvey Kellogg as a Social Gospel Practitioner," *Journal of the Illinois State Historical Society* 57, no. 1 (1964): 5–22; Janet Barkas, *The Vegetable Passion: A History of the Vegetarian State of Mind* (London: Routledge and Keegan Paul, 1975); Twigg, "The Vegetarian Movement in England, 1847–1981"; Barkas, "Food for Thought: Purity and Vegetarianism," *Religion* 9, no. 1 (1979): 13–35; Richard Francis, "Circumstances and Salvation: The Ideology of the Fruitlands Utopia," *American Quarterly* 25, no. 2 (1973): 202–234; Regina Morantz, "Making Women Modern: Middle Class Women and Health Reform in 19th Century America," *Journal of Social History* 10, no. 4 (1977): 490–507; James C. Whorton, "Muscular Vegetarianism: The Debate over Diet and Athletic Performance in the Progressive Era," *Journal of Sport History* 8, no. 2 (1981): 58–75; Alice Ross, "Health and Diet in 19th-Century America: A Food Historian's Point of View," *Historical Archaeology* 27, no. 2 (1993): 42–56; Wirz, *Die Moral auf dem Teller*; Colin Spencer, *The Heretic's Feast: A History of Vegetarianism* (Hanover, NH: University Press of New England, 1995); Ouédraogo, "De la secte religieuse à l'utopie philanthropique"; Karen Iacobbo and Michael Iacobbo, *Vegetarian America: A History* (Westport, CT: Praeger, 2004); Margaret Puskar-Pasewicz, "Kitchen Sisters and Disagreeable Boys: Debates over Meatless Diets in Nineteenth-Century Shaker Communities," in *Eating in Eden: Food and American Utopias*, ed. Etta M. Madden and Martha L. Finch (Lincoln: University of Nebraska Press, 2006), 109–124; Tristram Stuart, *The Bloodless Revolution: Radical Vegetarians and the Discovery of India* (London: Harper, 2006); Alan Pert, *Red Cactus: The Life of Anna Bonus Kingsford* (Watson's Bay, AU: Books & Writers, 2006); Gregory, *Of Victorians and Vegetarians*; Rosemary Dellar, *Josiah Oldfield: Eminent Fruitarian* (Rainham, UK: Rainmore, 2008); John M. Gilheany, *Familiar Strangers: The Church and the Vegetarian Movement in Britain (1809–2009)* (Cardiff: Ascendant Press, 2010); Ina Zweiniger-Bargielowska, *Managing the Body: Beauty, Health, and Fitness in Britain, 1880–1939* (Oxford: Oxford University Press, 2011); Adam D. Shprintzen, *The Vegetarian Crusade: The Rise of an American Reform Movement, 1817–1921* (Chapel Hill: University of North Carolina Press, 2013).
26. Krabbe, *Gesellschaftsveränderung durch Lebensreform*, 48–77; Ute Druvins, "Alternative Projekte um 1900. Utopie und Realität auf dem 'Monte Verità' und in der 'Neuen Gemeinschaft,'" in *Literarische Utopie-Entwürfe*, ed. Hiltrud Gnüg (Frankfurt/Main: Suhrkamp, 1982), 236–249; Ulrich Linse, *Barfüßige Propheten: Erlöser der zwanziger Jahre* (Berlin: Siedler, 1983); *Ökopax und Anarchie: Eine Geschichte der ökologischen Bewegungen in Deutschland* (Frankfurt/Main: Dt. Taschenbuch-Verl, 1986); Martin Green, *Mountain of Truth: The Counterculture Begins, Ascona, 1900–1920* (Hanover, NH: University Press of New England, 1986); Walter M. Sprondel, "Kulturelle Modernisierung durch antimodernistischen Protest: Der lebensreformerische Vegetarismus," *Kölner Zeitschrift für Soziologie* 27 (1986): 314–330; Judith Baumgartner, *Ernährungsreform—Antwort auf Industrialisierung und Ernährungswandel: Ernährungsreform als Teil der Lebensreformbewegung am Beispiel der Siedlung und des Unternehmens Eden seit*

*1893* (Frankfurt/Main: Lang, 1992); "Vegetarismus," in *Handbuch der deutschen Reformbewegungen 1880–1933*, ed. Diethart Kerbs (Wuppertal: Hammer, 1998), 127–140; Wirz, *Die Moral auf dem Teller*; Barlösius, *Naturgemäße Lebensführung*; Sabine Merta, "'Keep Fit and Slim!' Alternative Ways of Nutrition as Aspects of the German Health Movement, 1880–1930," in *Order and Disorder the Health Implications of Eating and Drinking in the Nineteenth and Twentieth Centuries*, ed. Alexander Fenton (East Linton, UK: Tuckwell Press, 2000), 170–202; Kai Buchholz, ed., *Die Lebensreform: Entwürfe zur Neugestaltung von Leben und Kunst um 1900* (Darmstadt: Häusser, 2001); Michael Hau, *The Cult of Health and Beauty in Germany: A Social History, 1890–1930* (Chicago: University of Chicago Press, 2003); Matthew Jefferies, "Lebensreform: A Middle-Class Antidote to Wilhelminism?," in *Wilhelminism and Its Legacies: German Modernities, Imperialism, and the Meanings of Reform, 1890–1930*, ed. Geoff Eley and James Retallack (New York: Berghahn, 2003), 91–106; Hermann Kaienburg, "Der Traum vom Garten Eden. Die Gartenbausiedlung 'Eden' in Oranienburg als alternative Wirtschafts- und Lebensgemeinschaft," *Zeitschrift für Geschichtswissenschaft* 52 (2004): 1077–1090; Florentine Fritzen, *Gesünder leben. Die Lebensreformbewegung im 20. Jahrhundert* (Stuttgart: Steiner, 2006); Andreas Schwab, *Monte Verità—Sanatorium der Sehnsucht* (Zürich: Orell Füssli, 2003); Uwe Puschner, "Mit Vollkornbrot und Nacktheit—Arbeit am völkischen Körper. Gustav Simons und Richard Ungewitter—Lebensreformer und völkische Weltanschauungsagenten," in *Avantgarden der Biopolitik. Jugendbewegung, Lebensreform und Strategien biologischer Aufrüstung*, ed. Uwe Puschner, Felix Linzner, and John Khairi-Taraki (Göttingen: V&R Unipress, 2017), 77–93; Treitel, *Eating Nature in Modern Germany*; Bernd Wedemeyer-Kolwe, *Aufbruch. Die Lebensreform in Deutschland* (Mainz: Philipp von Zabern, 2017), 45–69; *"Der Neue Mensch": Körperkultur Im Kaiserreich Und in Der Weimarer Republik* (Würzburg: Königshausen & Neumann, 2004).

27. The most important studies to have done so are Twigg, "The Vegetarian Movement in England, 1847–1981"; Gregory, *Of Victorians and Vegetarians*; Shprintzen, *The Vegetarian Crusade*; Barlösius, *Naturgemäße Lebensführung*; Fritzen, *Gesünder leben*; Treitel, *Eating Nature in Modern Germany*.

28. Krabbe, *Gesellschaftsveränderung durch Lebensreform*, 50–51; Ulrich Linse, "Mazdaznan—Die Rassenreligion vom arischen Friedensreich," in *Völkische Religion und Krisen der Moderne. Entwürfe "arteigener" Glaubenssysteme seit der Jahrhundertwende*, ed. Stefanie v. Schnurbein and Justus H. Ulbricht (Würzburg: Königshausen & Neumann, 2001), 268–291; Wedemeyer-Kolwe, *"Der neue Mensch,"* 129–189; Wedemeyer-Kolwe, "The Reception of Yoga in Alternative Cultures at the Beginning of the 20th Centuries," in *On the Paths of Englightenment: The Myth of India in Western Culture, 1808–2017*, ed. Elio Schenini (Geneva: Skira, 2017), 258–275; Suzanne Marchand, "Eastern Wisdom in an Age of Western Despair: Orientalism in 1920s Central Europe," in *Weimar Thought: A Contested Legacy*, ed. Peter Gordon and John McCormick (Princeton, NJ: Princeton University Press, 2013), 341–360; Heinz Mürmel, "'Die Religion liegt im Blut'—Sächsisch-arische Konzepte der Kaiserzeit. Kurze Bemerkungen zur 'arischen Lebensreform,'" in *Devianz und Dynamik. Festschrift für Hubert Seiwert zum 65. Geburtstag*, ed. Edith Franke, Christoph Kleine, and Heinz Mürmel (Göttingen:

INTRODUCTION

Vandenhoeck & Ruprecht, 2014), 97–121; Bernadett Bigalke, *Lebensreform und Esoterik um 1900. Die Leipziger alternativ-religiöse Szene am Beispiel der Internationalen Theosophischen Verbrüderung* (Würzburg: Ergon, 2016).

29. Elija Horn, "Indienmode und Tagore-Hype: Reformpädagogik in der Weimarer Republik in der Perspektive des Orientalismus," in *Reformpädagogik und Reformpädagogik-Rezeption in neuer Sicht: Perspektiven und Impulse*, ed. Wolfgang Keim, Ulrich Schwerdt, and Sabine Reh (Bad Heilbrunn: Julius Klinkhardt, 2016), 149–168; *Indien als Erzieher: Orientalismus in der deutschen Reformpädagogik und Jugendbewegung 1918-1933* (Bad Heilbrunn: Verlag Julius Klinkhardt, 2018); "New Education, Indophilia and Women's Activism," *South Asia Chronicle* 8 (2018): 79–109; "Sexuelle Befreiung aus Indien. Jugendkulturelle Verknüpfung von Östlicher Spiritualität und Sexualität um 1918 und um 1980," in *Lebensreform um 1900 und Alternativmilieu um 1980: Kontinuitäten und Brüche in Milieus der gesellschaftlichen Selbstreflexion im frühen und späten 20. Jahrhundert*, ed. Detlef Siegfried and David Templin (Göttingen: V&R Unipress, 2019), 195–211; "Jugendbewegung und Indien. Zur Herausbildung eines jugendkulturellen Topos um 1918," in *1918 in Bildung und Erziehung: Traditionen, Transitionen, Visionen*, ed. Andrea de Vincenti, Norbert Grube, and Andreas Hoffmann-Ocon (Bad Heilbrunn: Julius Klinkhardt, 2020), 87–105; Gerdien Jonker, "In Search of Religious Modernity: Conversion to Islam in Interwar Berlin," in *Muslims in Interwar Europe: A Transcultural Historical Perspective*, ed. Bekim Agai, Umar Ryad, and Mehdi Sajid (Leiden: Brill, 2016), 18–46; *The Ahmadiyya Quest for Religious Progress: Missionizing Europe 1900–1965* (Leiden: Brill, 2016); *On the Margins: Jews and Muslims in Interwar Berlin* (Leiden: Brill, 2020); Razak Khan, "Entanglements of Translation: Psychology, Pedagogy, and Youth Reform in German and Urdu," *Comparative Studies of South Asia, Africa and the Middle East* 40, no. 2 (2020): 295–308. Entangled perspectives are more established in research on the Theosophical Society. See, for instance, Hans Martin Krämer and Julian Strube, eds., *Theosophy across Boundaries: Transcultural and Interdisciplinary Perspectives on a Modern Esoteric Movement* (Albany: State University of New York Press, 2020); Mriganka Mukhopadhyay, "Mohini: A Case Study of a Transnational Spiritual Space in the History of the Theosophical Society," *Numen* 67, nos. 2–3 (2019): 165–190; "Occult's First Foot Soldier in Bengal: Peary Chand Mittra and the Early Theosophical Movement," in *The Occult Nineteenth Century*, ed. Lukas Pokorny and Franz Winter (Cham: Palgrave Macmillan, 2021), 269–286; Maria Moritz, "Globalizing 'Sacred Knowledge': South Asians and the Theosophical Society, 1879–1930" (PhD diss., Jacobs University Bremen, 2012).

30. While Julia Twigg and Joanna Bourke were the first scholars to examine this metaphor, it plays a role throughout this study. Julia Twigg, "Food for Thought"; Joanna Bourke, *What It Means to Be Human. Reflections from 1791 to the Present* (London: Virago, 2011), 286–294. See also Hauser, "A Frugal Crescent."

31. Kenneth Jones, *Arya Dharm: Hindu Consciousness in 19th-Century Punjab* (New Delhi: Ajay Kumar Jain, 1976); Jyortirmaya Sharma, *Hindutva: Exploring the Idea of Hindu Nationalism* (New Delhi: Penguin Books, 2011); C. S. Adcock, *The Limits of Tolerance: Indian Secularism and the Politics of Religious Freedom* (New York: Oxford University Press, 2014). However, recent research shows the influence of Western thought on Hindu nationalism. See, for instance, Maria Framke,

INTRODUCTION

*Delhi—Rom—Berlin. Die Indische Wahrnehmung von Faschismus und Nationalsozialismus 1922–1939* (Darmstadt: Wissenschaftliche Buchgesellschaft, 2013).
32. Parama Roy, "Vegetarianism," in *Keywords in South Asian Studies*, ed. Gita Dharampal-Frick, Monika Kirloskar-Steinbach, Rachel Dwyer, and Jahnavi Phalkey (New Delhi: Oxford University Press, 2015), 272–275. Neither had the cow always been sacrosanct in Hinduism, nor had Ayurvedic medicine ruled out the consumption of meat. Dwijendra Narayan Jha, *The Myth of the Holy Cow* (London: Verso, 2002); Francis Zimmermann, *The Jungle and the Aroma of Meats: An Ecological Theme in Indian Medicine* (Berkeley: University of California Press, 1987).
33. Cases in point discussed in this book are the Theosophical Society, Mazdaznan, and life reform appropriations of Buddhism, but also Christian communities like German Catholicism and Christian humanism, whose adherents included Gustav Struve and Eduard Baltzer, notable figures in early German vegetarianism. Peter Van der Veer, *Imperial Encounters: Religion and Modernity in India and Britain* (Princeton, NJ: Princeton University Press, 2001); Bigalke, *Lebensreform und Esoterik um 1900*. The emergence of new religious movements in Europe and the United States belies the narrative of secularization long embraced by the humanities and social sciences during the nineteenth and twentieth centuries. For recent criticisms of this narrative, see Rebekka Habermas, "Weibliche Religiösität, oder: Von der Fragilität bürgerlicher Identitäten," in *Wege zur Geschichte des Bürgertums*, ed. Klaus Tenfelde and Hans-Ulrich Wehler (Göttingen: Vandenhoeck & Ruprecht, 1994), 125–148; Talal Asad, *Formations of the Secular: Christianity, Islam, Modernity* (Stanford, CA: Stanford University Press, 2003); José Casanova, "Public Religions in the Modern World," in *Powers of the Secular Modern: Talal Asad and His Interlocutors*, ed. David Scott and Charles Hirschkind (Stanford, CA: Stanford University Press, 2006), 12–30.
34. Such an agenda was first proposed by Ann Laura Stoler and Frederick Cooper in their influential chapter "Between Metropole and Colony: Rethinking a Research Agenda," in *Tensions of Empire: Colonial Cultures in a Bourgeois World*, ed. Stoler and Cooper (Berkeley: University of California Press, 1997), 1–56. In Europe, it led to further methodological interventions, most importantly by Michael Werner and Bénédicte Zimmermann. See their "Beyond Comparison: Histoire Croisée and the Challenge of Reflexivity," *History and Theory* 41, no. 1 (2006): 30–50. Prior to Werner and Zimmermann's intervention, historians working beyond the nation-state had mainly engaged in comparative studies and studies of transfers. Werner and Zimmermann rejected the notion of simple transfers, arguing that cultural phenomena as well as the participants involved were always subject to transformations in the course of such processes, and that historians likewise interact with their objects of research, forcing them to also critically consider their own standpoints.
35. Sebastian Conrad and Shalini Randeria, "Einleitung. Geteilte Geschichten— Europa in einer postkolonialen Welt," in *Jenseits des Eurozentrismus*, ed. Conrad and Randeria (Frankfurt/Main: Campus-Verl, 2002), 18.
36. For introductions to the debates in this field in general, see Sebastian Conrad, Andreas Eckert, and Ulrike Freitag, eds., *Globalgeschichte. Theorien, Ansätze, Themen* (Frankfurt/Main: Campus, 2007); Sebastian Conrad, *What Is Global*

INTRODUCTION

*History?* (Princeton, NJ: Princeton University Press, 2016); Dominic Sachsenmaier, *Global Perspectives on Global History: Theories and Approaches in a Connected World* (Cambridge: Cambridge University Press, 2011); Lynn Hunt, *Writing History in the Global Era* (New York: Norton, 2014); Diego Olstein, *Thinking History Globally* (Houndmills, UK: Palgrave Macmillan, 2015); Jürgen Osterhammel, "Global History," in *Debating New Approaches to History*, ed. Marek Tamm and Peter Burke (London: Bloomsbury Academic, 2019), 21–48; Romain Bertrand and Guillaume Calafat, "La microhistoire globale: Affaire(s) à suivre," *Annales Histoire Sciences Sociales* 73, no. 1 (2019): 3–18.

37. Sanjay Subrahmanyam, "Connected Histories: Notes towards a Reconfiguration of Early Modern Eurasia," *Modern Asian Studies* 31 (1997): 735–762; Ulrike Freitag and Achim von Oepen, "Translocality: An Approach to Connection and Transfer in Area Studies," in *Translocality: The Study of Globalizing Processes from a Southern Perspective*, ed. Freitag and von Oepen (Leiden: Brill, 2010), 1–24.
38. Margrit Pernau, "Global History—Wegbereiter für einen neuen Kolonialismus?," *Connections: A Journal for Historians and Area Specialists*, December 17, 2004, https://www.connections.clio-online.net/debate/id/fddebate-132110; *Transnationale Geschichte* (Göttingen: Vandenhoeck & Ruprecht, 2011), 132–147. Vinay Lal criticized global history for similar reasons. See "Provincializing the West: World History from the Perspective of Indian History," in *Writing World History 1800–2000*, ed. Benedikt Stuchtey and Eckhardt Fuchs (Oxford: Oxford University Press, 2002), 271–290.
39. Jean-Paul Ghobrial, "The Secret Life of Elias of Babylon and the Uses of Global Microhistory," *Past & Present* 222, no. 1 (2014): 51–93.
40. Jeffrey Adelman, "What Is Global History Now?," *Aeon*, March 2, 2017, https://aeon.co/essays/is-global-history-still-possible-or-has-it-had-its-moment.
41. See, for instance, the research agenda of the global dis:connect project of the Munich-based Kate Hamburger Centre: https://www.globaldisconnect.org/forschung/diskonnektivitat/?lang=en (accessed October 20, 2022).
42. Shalini Randeria, "Geteilte Geschichte und verwobene Moderne," in *Zukunftsentwürfe. Ideen für eine Kultur der Veränderung*, ed. Jörn Rüsen (Frankfurt/Main: Campus, 1999), 87–96; Conrad and Randeria, "Einleitung," 9–49.
43. Robert Proctor, "Agnotology: A Missing Term to Describe the Cultural Production of Ignorance (and Its Study)," in *Agnotology: The Making and Unmaking of Ignorance*, ed. Robert Proctor and Londa Schiebinger (Stanford, CA: Stanford University Press, 2008), 1–35.
44. Benjamin Nicholas Lawrance, Emily Lynn Osborn, and Richard L. Roberts, eds., *Intermediaries, Interpreters, and Clerks: African Employees in the Making of Colonial Africa* (Madison: University of Wisconsin Press, 2006); David Lambert and Alan Lester, eds., *Colonial Lives across the British Empire: Imperial Careering in the Long Nineteenth Century* (Cambridge: Cambridge University Press, 2006); Desley Deacon and Angela Woollacott, eds., *Transnational Lives: Biographies of Global Modernity* (Basingstoke, UK: Palgrave Macmillan, 2010); Ghobrial, "The Secret Life of Elias of Babylon and the Uses of Global Microhistory"; Dominic Sachsenmaier, ed., *Global Entanglements of a Man Who Never Traveled: A Seventeenth-Century Chinese Christian and His Conflicted Worlds* (New York: Columbia University Press, 2018).

INTRODUCTION

45. Harald Fischer-Tiné, *Pidgin-Knowledge: Wissen und Kolonialismus* (Zürich: Diaphanes, 2013).
46. See, for instance, Linse, *Barfüßige Propheten*; Wirz, *Die Moral auf dem Teller*; Barlösius, *Naturgemäße Lebensführung*; Gregory, *Of Victorians and Vegetarians*.

## 1. IN SEARCH OF PURITY

1. "Nahrungsweise/Volksdichtigkeit," in *Physikalischer Atlas*, ed. Heinrich Berghaus (Gotha: Perthes, 1848), pt. 7.
2. Charles Forsdick, "Taste," in *Keywords for Travel Writing Studies: A Critical Glossary*, ed. Charles Forsdick, Zoë Kinsley, and Kathryn Walchester (London: Anthem, 2019), 244–246; Robert Launay, "Tasting the World: Food in Early European Travel Narratives," *Food and Foodways* 11, no. 1 (2003): 27–47. It was not just European authors who made these connections, as Christian Junge shows in his discussion of the nineteenth-century Arab writer Faris al-Shidyaq: Christian Junge, "Food, Body, Society: Al-Shidyāq's Somatic Critique of Nineteenth-Century Communities," in *Food as a Cultural Signifier: Perspectives on the Middle East and Beyond*, ed. Kirill Dmitriev and Bilal Orfali (Leiden: Brill, 2020), 142–161.
3. Charles Louis Secondat de Montesquieu, *The Spirit of the Laws*, ed. Anne M. Cohler, Basia C. Miller, and Harold S. Stone (Cambridge: Cambridge University Press, 1989), 102, 232, 354, 477. As Emma Spary shows, food was also central to the self-fashioning of eighteenth-century savants: Emma C. Spary, *Eating the Enlightenment: Food and the Sciences in Paris* (Chicago: University of Chicago Press, 2012).
4. See, for instance, "Meeting of the Committee of the Association for Promoting the Discovery of the Interior Parts of Africa, Held at the House of Sir Joseph Banks on Saturday, the 18th of December, 1790," in *Records of the African Association 1788–1831*, ed. Robin Hallett (London: Thomas Nelson, 1964), 125; Joseph-Marie Dégerando, *The Observation of Savage Peoples* (London: Routledge and Kegan Paul, 1969), 78–79.
5. Rebecca Earle, *The Body of the Conquistador: Food, Race and the Colonial Experience in Spanish America, 1492–1700* (Cambridge: Cambridge University Press, 2012).
6. Emma C. Spary, *Feeding France: New Sciences of Food, 1760–1815* (Cambridge: Cambridge University Press, 2014); Rebecca Earle, *Feeding the People: The Politics of the Potato* (Cambridge: Cambridge University Press, 2020).
7. Jeffery Sobal, "Food System Globalization, Eating Transformations, and Nutrition Transitions," in *Food in Global History*, ed. Raymond Grew (Boulder, CO: Westview Press, 1999), 186–213; Alexander Nützenadel and Frank Trentmann, "Introduction: Mapping Food and Globalization," in *Food and Globalization: Consumption, Markets and Politics in the Modern World*, ed. Nützenadel and Trentmann (Oxford: Berg, 2008), 1–15; Yves Segers, "Food Systems in the Nineteenth Century," in *A Cultural History of Food*, vol. 5, *In the Age of Empire*, ed. Martin Bruegel (London: Berg, 2012), 49–66; Boris Loheide, "Beef around the World. Die Globalisierung des Rindfleischhandels bis 1914," *Comparativ* 17, no. 3 (2007): 46–67.

## 1. IN SEARCH OF PURITY

8. Fabio Parasecoli, "World Food: The Age of Empire, c. 1800–1920," in Bruegel, *A Cultural History of Food*, 199–208.
9. Mike Davis, *Late Victorian Holocausts: El Niño Famines and the Making of the Third World* (London: Verso, 2001).
10. Alison K. Smith, "National Cuisines," in *The Oxford Handbook of Food History*, ed. Jeffrey M. Pilcher (Oxford: Oxford University Press, 2012), 444–460. This process paralleled the emergence of political nationalism during globalization, on which see, for instance, Sebastian Conrad, *Globalisierung und Nation im Deutschen Kaiserreich* (Munich: Beck, 2006).
11. See, for instance, Peter J. Atkins, Peter Lummel, and Derek J. Oddy, eds., *Food and the City in Europe since 1800* (Aldershot, UK: Ashgate, 2007); Jakob Tanner, *Fabrikmahlzeit: Ernährungswissenschaft, Industriearbeit und Volksernährung in der Schweiz 1890–1950* (Zürich: Chronos, 1999).
12. Nitin Varma, *Coolies of Capitalism: Assam Tea and the Making of Coolie Labour* (Berlin: De Gruyter Oldenburg, 2017), 43–103. For a contrary perspective arguing that plantation hospitals fed slaves particularly well to better exploit their labor force, see Ilaria Berti, "'Feeding the Sick upon Stewed Fish and Pork': Slave Health and Food in West Indian Sugar Plantation Hospitals," *Food & History* 14, nos. 1–3 (2016): 81–105.
13. Mrinalini Sinha, *Colonial Masculinity. The "Manly Englishman" and the "Effeminate Bengali" in the Late Nineteenth Century* (Manchester: Manchester University Press, 1995).
14. Sinha.
15. Tristram Stuart, *The Bloodless Revolution: Radical Vegetarians and the Discovery of India* (London: Harper, 2006), 180–251.
16. Detlef Briesen, *Das gesunde Leben. Ernährung und Gesundheit seit dem 18. Jahrhundert* (Frankfurt/Main: Campus, 2010), 28; Spary, *Eating the Enlightenment*, 23–28; E. M. Collingham, *Imperial Bodies: The Physical Experience of the Raj, c. 1800–1947* (Cambridge: Polity, 2001), 26–27.
17. Gurmindur Bhambra, *Rethinking Modernity: Postcolonialism and the Sociological Imagination* (Basingstoke, UK: Palgrave Macmillan, 2007), 124–144. Giorgio Riello put forward a similar argument in his analysis of the globalization of the cotton industry: Giorgio Riello, *Cotton: The Fabric that Made the Modern World* (Cambridge: Cambridge University Press, 2013).
18. Eric Hobsbawm, *The Age of Capital* (London: Weidenfeld and Nicolson, 1975), 245–269; Hugh Cunningham, *Children and Childhood in Western Society Since 1500*, 2nd ed. (Harlow: Longman, 2005), 89. More recent research, by contrast, is less concerned about the hardships of labor in early industrialization, stressing instead its economic benefits. See, for instance, Emma Griffin, *A Short History of the British Industrial Revolution* (London: Palgrave Macmillan, 2018), 81–82.
19. Stanley D. Chapman, ed., *The History of Working-Class Housing* (Newton Abbot, UK: David & Charles, 1971); Stuart Hylton, *A History of Manchester* (Chichester, UK: Phillimore, 2003), 122–133; Michael Nevell, "Living in the Industrial City: Housing Quality, Land Ownership and the Archaeological Evidence from Industrial Manchester, 1740–1850," *International Journal of Historical Archaeology* 15 (2011): 594–606.

1. IN SEARCH OF PURITY

20. Earle, *Feeding the People*; Christine Kinealy, ed., *The History of the Irish Famine* (London: Routledge, 2019); Cormac Ó Gráda, "Ireland's Great Famine: An Overview," in *When the Potato Failed: Causes and Effects of the "Last" European Subsistence Crisis, 1845–1850*, ed. Richard Paping, Eric Vanhaute, and Cormac Ó Gráda (Turnhout, BE: Brepols, 2007), 41–57.
21. Dominik Collet and Daniel Krämer, "Germany, Switzerland, and Austria," in *Famine in European History*, ed. Guido Alfani and Cormac Ó Gráda (Cambridge: Cambridge University Press, 2017), 101–118; Hans Bass, "The Crisis in Prussia," in Paping, Vanhaute, and Gráda, *When the Potato Failed*, 185–211.
22. Corinna Treitel, *Eating Nature in Modern Germany: Food, Agriculture, and Environment, c. 1870 to 2000* (Cambridge: Cambridge University Press, 2017), 19–52; Tobias Kaiser, "Eine etwas andere Mediengeschichte—Anmerkungen zur Entstehung der vegetarischen Publizistik des 19. Jahrhunderts im preußisch-thüringischen Nordhausen," in *Medien—Kommunikation—Öffentlichkeit. Vom Spätmittelalter bis zur Gegenwart. Festschrift für Werner Greiling zum 65. Geburtstag*, ed. Holger Böning et al. (Wien: Böhlau, 2019), 51–67.
23. John Marriott, *The Other Empire: Metropolis, India and Progress in the Colonial Imagination* (Manchester: Manchester University Press, 2004), 160–186; Rolf Lindner, *Walks on the Wild Side: Eine Geschichte der Stadtforschung* (Frankfurt/Main: Campus, 2004), 11–18, 43–95.
24. On the moral dimension of nineteenth-century charity, see, for instance, Peter Mandler, ed., *The Uses of Charity: The Poor on Relief in the Nineteenth-Century Metropolis* (Philadelphia: University of Pennsylvania Press, 1990); Jane Rendall, "Gender, Philanthropy, and Civic Identities in Edinburgh, 1795–1830," in *The Routledge History Handbook of Gender and the Urban Experience*, ed. Deborah Simonton (London: Routledge, 2017), 209–220.
25. "Vegetarianism and Temperance," *Vegetarian Messenger* 3 (1849): 14–16; "The Vegetarian and Temperance Principles," *Vegetarian Messenger* 4 (1854): 25–26; Eduard Baltzer, *Das Buch von der Arbeit oder die menschliche Arbeit in persönlicher und volkswirthschaftlicher Beziehung* (Nordhausen: Förstemann, 1870), 127.
26. Daniel Pick, *Faces of Degeneration: A European Disorder, c. 1848–1918* (Cambridge: Cambridge University Press, 1989); Alison Bashford, "Introduction," in *The Oxford Handbook of the History of Eugenics*, ed. Bashford (Oxford: Oxford University Press, 2010), 3–24.
27. See, for instance, Eduard Baltzer, *Die natürliche Lebensweise, der Weg zu Gesundheit und sozialem Heil* (Nordhausen: Förstemann, 1867), 65–66; T. S. Nichols, *How to Live on Six-Pence a Day: Vegetarian Meal Planning* (London: Nichols & Co., 1878), 45.
28. Mieke Roscher, *Ein Königreich für Tiere. Die Geschichte der britischen Tierrechtsbewegung* (Marburg: Tectum), 2009, 63–68.
29. Massimo Montanari, *The Culture of Food* (Oxford: Blackwell, 1994); Hans Jürgen Teuteberg, "The Birth of the Modern Consumer Age: Food Innovations from 1800," in *Food: The History of Taste*, ed. Paul H. Freedman (London: Thames & Hudson, 2007), 238–239.
30. William Cronon, *Nature's Metropolis: Chicago and the Great West* (New York: Norton, 1991); Joshua Specht, *Red Meat Republic: A Hoof-to-Table History of How Beef Changed America* (Princeton, NJ: Princeton University Press, 2019).

## 1. IN SEARCH OF PURITY

31. Eric Baratay and Elisabeth Hardouin-Fugier, *Zoo: A History of Zoological Gardens in the West* (London: Reaktion Books, 2002), 147–197, 386–392.
32. Roscher, *Ein Königreich für Tiere*, 63–64.
33. Hilda Kean, "The Moment of Greyfriars Bobby: The Changing Cultural Position of Animals, 1800–1920," in *A Cultural History of Animals*, vol. 5, *In the Age of Empire*, ed. Kathleen Kete (Oxford: Berg, 2007), 25–46, 175–184; Kathleen Kete, *The Beast in the Boudoir: Petkeeping in Nineteenth-Century Paris* (Berkeley: University of California Press, 2004).
34. Roscher, *Ein Königreich für Tiere*; Miriam Zerbel, *Tierschutz im Kaiserreich: Ein Beitrag zur Geschichte des Vereinswesens* (Frankfurt/Main: Lang, 1993).
35. Richard W. Bulliet, *Hunters, Herders, and Hamburgers: The Past and Future of Human-Animal Relationships* (New York: Columbia University Press, 2005), 15–19, 27–34.
36. Friedrich Engels, *The Condition of the Working Class in England in 1844* (New York: John W. Lovell, 1887), 32; Julia Twigg, "The Vegetarian Movement in England, 1847–1981" (PhD diss., London School of Economics, 1981), 83–88; James Gregory, *Of Victorians and Vegetarians: The Vegetarian Movement in Nineteenth-Century Britain* (London: Tauris Academic Studies, 2007), 30–50. In her analysis of the animal welfare movement in Britain, Mieke Roscher likewise underlines the urban character of the movement. Roscher, *Ein Königreich für Tiere*, 34.
37. Twigg, "The Vegetarian Movement in England, 1847–1981," 113. According to James Gregory, the Vegetarian Society had almost six thousand members and associates in 1899. Gregory, *Of Victorians and Vegetarians*, 3.
38. Gustav von Struve, *Mandaras Wanderungen*, 3rd ed. (Leipzig: Struve, 1906).
39. Eva Barlösius, *Naturgemäße Lebensführung. Zur Geschichte der Lebensreform um die Jahrhundertwende* (Frankfurt/Main: Campus, 1997), 104.
40. Ceri Crossley, *Consumable Metaphors: Attitudes towards Animals and Vegetarianism in Nineteenth-Century France* (Oxford: Lang, 2005); Arouna Ouédraogo, "De la secte religieuse à l'utopie philanthropique. Genèse sociale du végétarisme occidental," *Annales Histoire, Sciences Sociales* 55 (2000): 825–843; Peter Brang, *Ein unbekanntes Russland: Kulturgeschichte vegetarischer Lebensweisen von den Anfängen bis zur Gegenwart.* (Cologne: Böhlau, 2002).
41. Twigg, "The Vegetarian Movement in England, 1847–1981," 61–62, 177–178. Treitel, *Eating Nature in Modern Germany*, 22–29.
42. Barlösius, *Naturgemäße Lebensführung*, 164–171.
43. Treitel, *Eating Nature in Modern Germany*.
44. "The Vegetarian Principle. Lecture I: Introductory, Physical Advantages," *Vegetarian Messenger* 1 (1851): 26.
45. Gustav von Struve, *Pflanzenkost. Die Grundlage einer neuen Weltanschauung* (Stuttgart: Struve, 1869), 43–44; Eduard Baltzer, "Gefahren des Vegetarianismus," *Vereins-Blatt für Freunde der naturgemäßen Lebensweise (Vegetarianer)* 3 (1870): 356; E. Wallot, "Zeitbetrachtung," *Thalysia*, no. 5 (1885): 35–37, 74. For Britain, see Gregory, *Of Victorians and Vegetarians*, 163.
46. "The Banquet of the Seventh Annual Meeting of the Vegetarian Society," *Vegetarian Messenger* 5 (1859): 77; Struve, *Pflanzenkost*, 54–55.
47. "The Vegetarian Principle," 17; John Smith, "Fruit and Farinacea the Proper Food of Man," *Vegetarian Messenger* 1 (1851): 87–91; Struve, *Pflanzenkost*, 54–55.

1. IN SEARCH OF PURITY

48. "The Original Food of Man," *Vegetarian Messenger* 1 (1851): 43. Struve, *Mandaras Wanderungen*.
49. Sylvester Graham, *Lectures on the Science of Human Life: People's Edition* (London: Horsell, 1849), 214; "Jottings on Vegetarian Diet," *Vegetarian Messenger* 7 (1857): 7. On this motive, see also Julia Twigg, "Food for Thought: Purity and Vegetarianism," *Religion* 9, no. 1 (1979): 13–35.
50. Wilhelm Zimmermann, *Der Weg zum Paradies. Eine Beleuchtung der Hauptursachen des physisch-moralischen Verfalls der Culturvölker, sowie naturgemäße Vorschläge, diesen Verfall zu sühnen* (Quedlinburg: Basse, 1846), 17; "The Vegetarian Movement: Its Claims Upon Public Attention," *Vegetarian Messenger* 2 (1849): 3.
51. Reynolds, "Central Africans," *Vegetarian Messenger* 3 (1853): 2–3; "The Bushman and the Kaffir," *Vegetarian Messenger* 7 (1857): 82–83; Graham, "Vegetarian Diet in Africa," *Vegetarian Messenger* 9 (1859): 22–23; "The Hottentots and Bosjesmans," *Vegetarian Messenger* 8 (1858): 132–133; Eduard Baltzer, "Vom Kongo," *Vereins-Blatt für Freunde der natürlichen Lebensweise* 112 (1879): 1778–1782.
52. "The Japanese—Primeval Diet of Man," *Vegetarian Messenger* 4 (1854): 34–35; Chambers, "Abstinence of the Japanese from Flesh Meat," *Vegetarian Messenger* 7 (1857): 22–25.
53. S. Wells Williams, "Food of the Chinese," *Vegetarian Messenger* 7 (1857): 60–61; Eduard Baltzer, "China und Japan," *Vereins-Blatt für Freunde der natürlichen Lebensweise* 36 (1872): 567–568.
54. "Nahrung der Sclaven im Alterthum," *Vereins-Blatt für Freunde der natürlichen Lebensweise* 9 (1869): 142; Dr. Whitlaw, "Diet and Health of the Romans," *The Vegetarian Messenger* 5 (1855): 6–7.
55. L. Hahn, "Mexico, December 1869," *Vereins-Blatt für Freunde der natürlichen Lebensweise* 18 (1870): 286–287.
56. Anna Kingsford, *The Perfect Way in Diet: A Treatise Advocating a Return to the Natural and Ancient Food of Our Race* (London: Kegan Paul, Trench, Trübner & Co., 1881), 23.
57. Kris Manjapra, "Plantation Dispossessions: The Global Travel of Agricultural Racial Capitalism," in *American Capitalism: New Histories*, ed. Sven Beckert and Christine Desan (New York: Columbia University Press, 2018), 361–391. The term was first coined by Cedric J. Robinson in his book *Black Marxism* (London: Zed Press, 1983).
58. Stuart, *The Bloodless Revolution*.
59. Pedro Martins, "An Ontological Dispute in the Writings of Porphyry of Tyre: The Discussion of Meat Eating as a Battlefield for Competing Worldviews in Antiquity," in Dmitriev and Orfali, *Food as a Cultural Signifier*, 245–259; Ken Parry, "Vegetarianism in Late Antiquity and Early Byzantium," in *Feast, Fast or Famine: Food and Drink in Byzantium*, ed. Wendy Mayer and Silke Trzcionka (Brisbane: Australian Association for Byzantine Studies, 2005), 171–187; Richard Stoneman, "Who Are the Brahmans? Indian Lore and Cynic Doctrine in Palladius' De Bragmanibus and Its Models," *Classical Quarterly* 44, no. 2 (1994): 500–510. Some of these ancient authors also believed that Pythagoras, a Greek philosopher who would become a model to vegetarians in Europe during the nineteenth century, was inspired by India. Stoneman rejects this argument, stressing that Greek

## 1. IN SEARCH OF PURITY

and Brahmin motivations for vegetarianism differed considerably. "Who Are the Brahmans?," 507. He also emphasizes the vagueness of Greek knowledge of India. See Stoneman, "Naked Philosophers: The Brahmans in the Alexander Historians and the Alexander Romance," *Classical Quarterly* 44, no. 2 (1995): 500–510.

60. Stuart, *The Bloodless Revolution*, 42–57.
61. Stuart, 50–51, 56; Parama Roy, "Gothic Vegetarianism," in *Food and Literature*, ed. Gitanjali G. Shahani (Cambridge: Cambridge University Press, 2018), 75–96.
62. Jean Antoine Dubois, *Hindu Manners, Customs, and Ceremonies. Translated from the Author's Later French Ms. and Edited with Notes, Corrections, and Biography by Henry K. Beauchamp. With a Prefatory Note by the Right Hon. F. Max Müller* (Oxford: Clarendon Press, 1906), 52–53, 88–92, 105, 560–561. On the strategies of "blending in" generally pursued by Jesuit missionaries, see, inter alia, Williard J. Peterson, "What to Wear? Observation and Participation by Jesuit Missionaries in Late Ming Society," in *Implicit Understandings: Observing, Reporting, and Reflecting on the Encounters between Europeans and Other Peoples in the Early Modern Era*, ed. Stuart B. Schwartz (Cambridge: Cambridge University Press, 1994), 403–421.
63. Stuart, *The Bloodless Revolution*, xxv.
64. On Böhme, see Ariel Hessayon and Sarah Apetrei, eds., *An Introduction to Jacob Boehme: Four Centuries of Thought and Reception* (New York: Routledge, 2014).
65. Timothy Morton, "The Plantation of Wrath," in *Radicalism in British Literary Culture, 1650–1830: From Revolution to Revolution*, ed. Morton and Nigel Smith (Cambridge: Cambridge University Press, 2002), 64–85. On Tryon's opposition to slavery, see also Philippe Rosenberg, "Thomas Tryon and the Seventeenth-Century Dimensions of Antislavery," *William and Mary Quarterly*, 3rd ser., 61, no. 4 (2004): 609–642.
66. Thomas Tryon, *Some Memoirs of the Life of Mr. Tho. Tryon, Late of London, Merchant: Written by Himself. Together with Some Rules and Orders, Proper to Be Observed by All Such as Would Train up and Govern, Either Familes, or Societies, in Cleanness, Temperance, and Innocency* (London: T. Sowle, 1705), 27–30, 14, 41, 83–87. Tryon's autobiography is inconsistent in the numbering of pages: the numbering starts again three times across the volume.
67. Thomas Tryon, *Averroeana. Being a Transcript of Several Letters from Averroes an Arabian Philosopher at Corduba in Spain, to Metrodorus a Young Grecian Nobleman, Student at Athens in the Years 1149 and 1150* (London: T. Sowle, 1695), 66–67.
68. Tryon, 140–155.
69. Tryon, 66–67.
70. Morton, "The Plantation of Wrath."
71. Tryon, *Averroeana*, 5, 70–182.
72. For an introduction to Hindu notions of caste, see Louis Dumont, *Homo hierarchicus. Le système des castes et ses implications* (Paris: Gallimard, 1966).
73. André Lichtenberg, "John Oswald, écossais, jacobin et socialiste," *La Révolution française: Revue historique* 32 (1897): 482.
74. T. F. Henderson and Ralph A. Manogue, "Oswald, John (c. 1760–1793)," in *Oxford Dictionary of National Biography* (Oxford: Oxford University Press, 2004), http://www.oxforddnb.com.460264923.erf.sbb.spk-berlin.de/view/article/20922

## 1. IN SEARCH OF PURITY

(accessed March 23, 2016). On Oswald's life, see also David W. Erdman, *Commerce des Lumières: John Oswald and the British in Paris, 1790–1793* (Columbia: University of Missouri Press, 1986), which, however, hardly pays attention to Oswald's vegetarianism as part of his political agenda.

75. John Oswald, *The Cry of Nature, or, an Appeal to Mercy and to Justice on Behalf of the Persecuted Animals* (London: Johnson, 1791).
76. Oswald, 15.
77. Oswald, 15–16.
78. Oswald, 17–18.
79. Oswald, 5–10.
80. Oswald, 9.
81. Murdering animals for food, or so Oswald opined, was especially amoral when the name of God was invoked, as in Islamic ritual slaughter, as it made God an accomplice of murder. Oswald, *The Cry of Nature*, 50–51.
82. Oswald, 32.
83. George Nicholson, *On the Conduct of Man to Inferior Animals, &c.* (Manchester: Nicholson, 1797). This first edition, however, is no longer available. Accordingly, the following references are taken from this edition: *On the Conduct of Man to Inferior Animals, &c.* (Stourport, UK: Nicholson, 1819).
84. While David Erdman, in his biography of Oswald, admits that he could not find books influenced by *The Cry of Nature*, Nicholson's book is very much a case in point. Erdman, *Commerce des Lumières*, 90. In several passages of his book, Nicholson pilfered from Oswald without naming or citing him, most notably in the following passage, which was directly taken from Oswald's book. Nicholson, *On the Conduct of Man to Inferior Animals*, 9. This passage corresponds to the following one: Oswald, *The Cry of Nature*, 5–6.
85. Nicholson, *On the Conduct of Man to Inferior Animals*, 201.
86. Nicholson, 9–10.
87. Nicholson, 9–10.
88. Nicholson, 10.
89. Nicholson, 46, 143, 196, 180.
90. On perceptions of Islam among British radicals around 1800, particularly Byron and Percy Bysshe Shelley, as informed by their sympathies for Greek independence from Ottoman rule, see Nigel Leask, *British Romantic Writers and the East: Anxieties of Empire* (Cambridge: Cambridge University Press, 1992); Jeffrey Einboden, *Islam and Romanticism: Muslim Currents from Goethe to Emerson* (London: Oneworld, 2014), 133–144. As Florian Kerschbaumer and Korinna Schönhärl point out, the Vienna Congress of 1814–1815 played a pivotal role in shaping philhellenism as a political movement in Europe. Florian Kerschbaumer and Korinna Schönhärl, "Der Wiener Kongress als "Kinderstube" des Philhellenismus. Das Beispiel des Bankiers Jean-Gabriel Eynard," *Forum Vormärz Forschung* 18 (2013): 99–127.
91. William A. Alcott, *Vegetable Diet: As Sanctioned by Medical Men, and by Experience in All Ages* (Boston: Marsh, Capen & Lyon, 1838), 151. On the influence of Alcott's writing in Britain, which inspired a vegetarian community named after him, see Gregory, *Of Victorians and Vegetarians*, 21–26. The characterization of Muslim rulers as despots had a long tradition among European writers. Whereas

## 1. IN SEARCH OF PURITY

Edward Said stressed the connection between Orientalism and imperialism, more recent studies, while not calling into doubt either Said's argument or the stereotypical nature of European perceptions of "Oriental" rule, emphasize the concept's role in criticizing autocratic tendencies in Europe. Edward Said, *Orientalism* (London: Penguin, 1978); Joao-Pau Rubiés, "Oriental Despotism and European Orientalism: Botero to Montesquieu," *Journal of Early Modern History* 9, no. 1 (2005): 109–180. During the nineteenth century, the stereotype of the Muslim ruler as despot was picked up again by philhellenic writers like Shelley, whose poem "The Revolt of Islam" precisely expresses such views. Percy Bysshe Shelley, *The Revolt of Islam. A Poem, in Twelve Cantos* (London: C. and J. Oliver, 1818).

92. "The Vegetarian Treasury," *Vegetarian Messenger* 3 (1852): 11–12; "The Vegetarian Treasury," *Vegetarian Messenger* 3 (1853): 21–22; "Supplement to the Vegetarian Messenger," *Vegetarian Messenger* 4 (1853): 1–10.
93. "Cheering Words from India," *Dietetic Reformer*, n.s., 12 (1885): 173–175; William E. A. Axon, "Vegetarianism and the Land Question," *Dietetic Reformer*, n.s., 12 (1885): 126–128.
94. "The Banquet of the Fifth Annual Meeting of the Vegetarian Society," *Vegetarian Messenger* 3 (1852): 8–20; "On the Proper Food of Man," *Vegetarian Messenger* 5 (1855): 10–12; "The Natural Food of Man," *Dietetic Reformer and Vegetarian Messenger*, 3rd ser., 9 (1883): 362–363; William E. A. Axon, "The Rise of Vegetarianism in India. A Paper Contributed to the Annual Meeting of the Vegetarian Society, October 18, 1882," *Dietetic Reformer and Vegetarian Messenger*, 3rd ser., 9 (1883): 28–30.
95. "Fourth Annual Meeting of the Vegetarian Society," *Vegetarian Messenger* 2 (1851): 66–76. B. Lindsay, "The British Workman and the Hindoo," *Dietetic Reformer and Vegetarian Messenger* 12 (1885): 348–49.
96. "The Controversialist and Correspondent," *Vegetarian Messenger* 6 (1855): 38–22; "Diet in Hindustan," *Dietetic Reformer and Vegetarian Messenger*, 3rd ser. 8 (1881): 174.
97. John Smith, *Fruits and Farinacea the Proper Food of Man* (Boston: Fowler and Wells, 1854), 287.
98. Smith, 197.
99. Param Roy, "Vegetarianism," in *Keywords in South Asian Studies*, ed. Gita Dharampal-Frick et al. (New Delhi: Oxford University Press, 2015), 272.
100. On Kingsford, see her nearly hagiographic biography by Alan Pert, *Red Cactus: The Life of Anna Bonus Kingsford* (Watson's Bay, AU: Books & Writers, 2006).
101. Kingsford, *The Perfect Way in Diet*, 19–20.
102. Kingsford, 61–62. On the colonial connotations of the concept of "pariah," see Rupa Viswanath, *The Pariah Problem: Caste, Religion, and the Social in Modern India* (New York: Columbia University Press, 2014).
103. Sinha, *Colonial Masculinity*.
104. The stereotype of the hardy Hindu was not just found in vegetarian journals. Indeed, authors like Samuel Ball, member of the East India Company's establishment at Canton, had already evoked it in the late 1830s to show that Hindus, on account of their few alimentary and material needs and physical endurance, were as efficient and cheap tea plantation workers as Chinese coolies—if not more so.

1. IN SEARCH OF PURITY

Samuel Ball, *An Account of the Cultivation and Manufacture of Tea in China* (London: Longman, Brown, Green, and Longmans, 1838), 333–361.
105. Briesen, *Das gesunde Leben*, 28.
106. On the *Vormärz* and 1848 revolution, see David Blackbourn, *The Long Nineteenth Century: A History of Germany, 1780–1918* (Oxford: Oxford University Press, 1998), 120–137; Mark Hewitson, *Nationalism in Germany, 1848–1866: Revolutionary Nation* (Basingstoke, UK: Palgrave Macmillan, 2010), 29–63; Wolfram Siemann, *Die deutsche Revolution von 1848/49* (Frankfurt/Main: Suhrkamp, 1985); Rüdiger Hachtmann, ed., *Berlin 1848. Eine Politik- und Gesellschaftsgeschichte der Revolution* (Bonn: Dietz, 1997).
107. Peter Hank, "Einführung," in *Gustav und Amalie Struve. Freiheit und Menschlichkeit. Ausgewählte Programmschriften* (Eggingen: Edition Isele, 2003), 9–43; Jürgen Peiser, "Gustav Struve als politischer Schriftsteller und Revolutionär" (PhD diss., University of Frankfurt/Main, 1973); Ansgar Reiß, *Radikalismus und Exil. Gustav Struve und die Demokratie in Deutschland und Amerika* (Stuttgart: Franz Steiner, 2004).
108. Jürgen Osterhammel, *Die Entzauberung Asiens. Europa und die asiatischen Reiche im 18. Jahrhundert* (Munich: Beck, 1998).
109. On the "Aryan" connection in Indology, see Romila Thapar, "The Historiography of the Concept of 'Aryan,'" in *India: Historical Beginnings and the Concept of the Aryan*, ed. Thapar, Jonathan Mark Kenoyer, Madhav M. Deshpande, and Shereen Ratnagar (Delhi: National Book Trust, 2006), 1–40.
110. Struve, *Mandaras Wanderungen*, 6. On the use of the "Aryan" metaphor in German scholarship and science, see Léon Poliakov, *The Aryan Myth: A History of Racist and Nationalistic Ideas in Europe* (London: Chatto; Heinemann, 1974); Sheldon Pollock, "Deep Orientalism? Notes on Sanskrit and Power Beyond the Raj," in *Orientalism and the Post-Colonial Predicament: Perspectives on South Asia*, ed. Carol A. Breckenridge and Peter van der Veer (Philadelphia: University of Pennsylvania Press, 1993), 76–133; Dorothy M. Figueira, *Aryans, Jews, Brahmins: Theorizing Authority through Myths of Identity* (Albany: State University of New York Press, 2002); Douglas T. McGetchin, *Indology, Indomania, and Orientalism: Ancient India's Rebirth in Modern Germany* (Madison, NJ: Fairleigh Dickinson University Press, 2009); McGetchin, "The Rise of Ancient India in Modern Germany," in *On the Paths of Enlightenment: The Myth of India in Western Culture, 1808–2017*, ed. Elio Schenini (Geneva: Skira, 2017).
111. McGetchin, "The Rise of Ancient India in Modern Germany," 6–7.
112. McGetchin, 21. On the feathered hat as a symbolic garment of radical democrats in the German revolutions of 1848, see Hermann Bausinger, "Die Dinge der Macht," in *Die Macht der Dinge. Symbolische Kommunikation und kulturelles Handeln*, ed. Andreas Hartmann, Peter Höher, and Christiane Cantaw (Münster: Waxmann, 2011), 27–34.
113. Struve, *Mandaras Wanderungen*, 280–284.
114. Struve, 7–8, 54–58, 62–63, 73–74, 87–102, 280–284.
115. Struve, 7, 8, 24.
116. Struve, 7–8, 25–38.
117. Struve, 62–63.

## 1. IN SEARCH OF PURITY

118. Wolfgang R. Krabbe, *Gesellschaftsveränderung durch Lebensreform* (Göttingen: Vandenhoeck und Ruprecht, 1974), 55.
119. Marc Cluet, "Persische Briefe eines urtümlichen Himalaja-Inders: Mandaras Wanderungen von Gustav Struve," in *Akten des XI. internationalen Germanistenkongresses Paris 2005 "Germanistik im Konflikt der Kulturen." Band 9: Divergente Kulturräume in der Literatur*, ed. Jean-Marc Valentin (Bern: Peter Lang, 2007), 27–32. See also Cécile Vantard, "Le végétarisme 'occidental-oriental' de Gustav Struve," in *La fascination de l'Inde en Allemagne*, ed. Marc Cluet (Rennes: Presses universitaires de Rennes, 2004), 155–163.
120. Poliakov, *The Aryan Myth*, 183–254.
121. Thapar, "The Historiography of the Concept of 'Aryan,'" 1–40.
122. Brian A. Hatcher, "Brahmo Samaj and Keshub Chandra Sen," in *Brill's Encyclopedia of Hinduism, vol. 5, Religious Symbols, Hinduism and Migration, Contemporary Communities Outside South Asia, Some Modern Religious Groups and Teachers*, ed. Knut A. Jacobsen et al. (Leiden: Brill, 2012), 437–444; Nalini Bhushan and Jay L. Garfield, *Minds without Fear: Philosophy in the Indian Renaissance* (Oxford: Oxford University Press, 2017), 78–84.
123. Chitrita Banerji, *Bengali Cooking: Seasons & Festivals* (Delhi: Aleph, 2017), 27–28.
124. Struve, a convert to German Catholicism (*Deutschkatholizismus*), a Christian sect that aimed at reconciling Protestantism and Catholicism while also embracing radical social reform, was sympathetic to religious reform. Reiß, *Radikalismus und Exil. Gustav Struve und die Demokratie in Deutschland und Amerika*, 103–105. On German Catholicism, see Sylvia Paletschek, *Frauen und Dissens. Frauen im Deutschkatholizismus und in den freien Gemeinden 1841–1852* (Göttingen: Vandenhoeck & Ruprecht, 1990).
125. On bhakti, see Vasudha Narayanan, "Bhakti," in *Brill's Encyclopedia of Hinduism Online*, ed. Knut A. Jacobsen et al. (Leiden: Brill, 2018), http://dx.doi.org/10.1163/2212-5019_BEH_COM_2050060 (accessed April 1, 2021).
126. Jones's edition of the Code of Manu appeared in English in 1796, and in a German translation the following year. William Jones, *Institutes of Hindu Law or the Ordinances of Menu, According to the Gloss of Cullúca. Comprising the Indian System of Duties, Religious & Civil; Verbally Translated from the Original Sanscrit* (London: Sewell, 1796); *Hindu Gesetzbuch. Oder Menu's Verordnungen nach Cullucas Erläuterung* (Weimar: Verlag des Industrie-Comptoirs, 1797). Even if Struve did not know these works themselves, he might have encountered them in Friedrich Schlegel's *Sprache und Weisheit der Indier* (Language and wisdom of the Indians), which makes ample reference to Manu.
127. While Struve does not elaborate on the theme of gender equality in the novel, he does underline that the same moral code is valid for both men and women, and his male characters are just as emotional as their female counterparts. He is thus a late exponent of the "gentle masculinity" that Anne-Charlott Trepp describes as typical of the German middle class from the late eighteenth century to the 1840s. Anne-Charlott Trepp, *Sanfte Männlichkeit und selbständige Weiblichkeit: Frauen und Männer im Hamburger Bürgertum zwischen 1770 und 1840* (Göttingen: Vandenhoeck & Ruprecht, 1996). Moreover, his marriage to and explicit support of a feminist demonstrate that gender equality was central to his political vision,

## 1. IN SEARCH OF PURITY

as it was to that of other radical vegetarians in the early nineteenth century such as Percy Bysshe Shelley. Timothy Morton, "Nature and Culture," in *The Cambridge Companion to Shelley*, ed. Morton (Cambridge: Cambridge University Press, 2006), 185–207. Scholarship on Gustav Struve has paid little attention to his own gender politics so far, although his biographers admit that he supported his wife's political work. See, for instance, Peter Hank, "Einführung," 9–43; Reiß, *Radikalismus und Exil*, 230–235.

128. There is no reference to Oswald in *Mandaras Wanderungen*. In one of her political essays, however, Amalie Struve recommends a number of British and French authors to readers curious about vegetarianism, which suggests that Struve was acquainted with British vegetarian discourse to some extent. Amalie Struve, *Erinnerungen aus den badischen Freiheitskämpfen* (Hamburg: Hoffmann & Campe, 1850), 9. His biographer, Löwenfels, mentions that Struve spoke French and English fluently. M. W. Löwenfels, *Gustav Struve's Leben, nach authentischen Quellen und von ihm selbst mitgetheilten Notizen dargestellt* (Basel: Helbig und Scherb, 1848), 27.
129. Zimmermann, *Der Weg zum Paradies*.
130. Zimmermann, v–vi.
131. Zimmermann, 19–20.
132. Johannes Fabian, *Time and the Other: How Anthropology Makes Its Object* (New York: Columbia University Press, 1983), 25–35.
133. Zimmermann, *Der Weg zum Paradies*, 145–147, 153–158, 168, 170–72.
134. Contemporary scholars argue that the prohibition of wine in the Qur'an was subject to varying interpretations. A. J. Wensinck and J. Sadan, "Ḵẖamr," in *Encyclopaedia of Islam*, 2nd ed., ed. P. Bearman et al. (Leiden: Brill, 2012), http://dx-1doi-1org-10078da2907cd.erf.sbb.spk-berlin.de/10.1163/1573-3912_islam_COM_0490 (accessed April 12, 2021).
135. Zimmermann, *Der Weg zum Paradies*, 170–172.
136. Eduard Baltzer, "Erster Vereinsbericht," *Vereins-Blatt für Freunde der natürlichen Lebensweise* 1 (1868): 9–10.
137. Theodor Fliedner, *Reisen in das heilige Land, nach Smyrna, Beirut, Constantinopel, Alexandrien und Cairo, etc. Theil 1.* (Kaiserswerth: Verlag der Diakonissen-Anstalt, 1858), 52. On the context of Fliedner's trip to the Ottoman Empire, see Julia Hauser, *German Religious Women in Late Ottoman Beirut: Competing Missions* (Leiden: Brill, 2015), 31–33.
138. "Die Bektaschis," *Vereins-Blatt für Freunde der natürlichen Lebensweise* 13 (1869): 205–206; E. W., "Damaskus," *Vereins-Blatt für Freunde der natürlichen Lebensweise* 1 (1886): 14–15, Eduard Baltzer, "Aus Professor Brenneckes Reise: Die Länder an der unteren Donau und Konstantinopel," *Vereins-Blatt für Freunde der natürlichen Lebensweise* 22 (1870): 349–51; "Aus Arabien," *Vereins-Blatt für Freunde der natürlichen Lebensweise* 64 (1874): 1016–1018; "Aegypten," *Vereins-Blatt für Freunde der naturgemäßen Lebensweise (Vegetarianer)* 11 (1868): 171–172; "Von der türkischen Grenze," *Vereins-Blatt für Freunde der natürlichen Lebensweise* 29 (1871): 456–459; "Cypern," *Vereins-Blatt für Freunde der natürlichen Lebensweise* 111 (1879): 1766–1768. The *Vereins-Blatt* even featured reports by a German-speaking vegetarian who, attracted by the meat-free diet embraced by Greek Orthodox monks, converted to Greek Orthodox Christianity and entered

## 1. IN SEARCH OF PURITY

a monastic order. Slavibor Breüer, "Vom Athos," *Vereins-Blatt für Freunde der natürlichen Lebensweise* 155 (1883): 2471–2473; Monach Sava, "Vom Athos," *Vereins-Blatt für Freunde der natürlichen Lebensweise* 165 (1884): 2635–2636.

139. It was because of this inaccessibility of the private realm that the harem became a focus of desire for male travelers. For copious literature on the topic, see Reina Lewis, *Rethinking Orientalism: Women, Travel and the Ottoman Harem* (London: I. B. Tauris, 2004), 13; Ruth Bernhard Yeazell, *Harems of the Mind: Passages of Western Art and Literature* (New Haven, CT: Yale University Press, 2000), 17.

140. David Waines and Manuela Marín, "Muzawwar: Counterfeit Fare for Fasts and Fevers," in *Patterns of Everyday Life*, ed. Waines and Marín (Aldershot, UK: Ashgate Variorum, 2002), 303–315; Charles Perry, "The Description of Familiar Foods (Kitāb waṣf al-aṭʿima al-muʿtāda)," in *Medieval Arab Cookery*, trans. Maxime Rodinson, A. J. Arberry, and Charles Perry (Totnes, UK: Prospect Books, 2001), 443–450.

141. Hedda Reindl-Kiel, "The Chickens of Paradise: Official Meals in the Mid-seventeenth Century Ottoman Palace," in *The Illuminated Table, the Prosperous House: Food and Shelter in Ottoman Material Culture*, ed. Suraiya Faroqhi and Christoph K. Neumann (Würzburg: Ergon, 2003), 38; Özge Samanci, "Culinary Consumption Patterns of the Ottoman Elite During the First Half of the Nineteenth Century," in Faroqhi and Neumann, *The Illuminated Table*, 171–172; Paulina B. Lewicka, *Food and Foodways of Medieval Cairenes: Aspects of Life in an Islamic Metropolis of the Eastern Mediterranean* (Leiden: Brill, 2011), 256–257.

142. In eighteenth-century England, the central role of meat in Bedouin hospitality led George Sale, the editor of one of the first English translations of the Qurʾan, to suppose that the Bedouin themselves consumed large amounts of meat, to which he attributed their allegedly fiery temperament. George Sale, "Preliminary Discourse," in *The Koran: Commonly Called the Alcoran of Mohammed, Translated into English Immediately from the Original Arabic; with Explanatory Notes, Taken from the Most Approved Commentators. To Which Is Prefixed a Preliminary Discourse* (London: C. Ackers, 1734), 22. John Oswald based his generally negative views of the Arabs on this passage (51, 102–103). Present-day researchers, however, emphasize that occasions for slaughter among the Bedouin were rare—not surprising, as camels were a principal form of transport. Peter Heine, *Kulinarische Studien. Untersuchungen zur Kochkunst im arabisch-islamischen Mittelalter* (Wiesbaden: Harassowitz, 1988), 50.

143. *Über die guten Sitten beim Essen und Trinken. Das ist das 11. Buch von Al-Ghazzālī's Hauptwerk. Übersetzung und Bearbeitung als ein Beitrag zur Geschichte unserer Tischsitten von Hans Kindermann* (Leiden: Brill, 1964), 32.

144. Lewicka, *Food and Foodways of Medieval Cairenes*, 128. This argument is also put forward in an earlier study by Peter Heine, *Food Culture in the Near East, Middle East, and North Africa* (Westport, CT: Greenwood Press, 2004), 4.

145. Nawal Nasrallah, ed., *Annals of the Caliphs' Kitchens: Ibn Sayyār al-Warrāq's Tenth-Century Baghdadi Cookbook* (Leiden: Brill, 2007), 34–35.

146. Christian Saßmannshausen, "Eating Up: Food Consumption and Social Status in Late Ottoman Greater Syria," in Dmitriev and Orfali, *Food as a Cultural Signifier*, 27–49.

1. IN SEARCH OF PURITY

147. Alan Mikhail, *The Animal in Ottoman Egypt* (Oxford: Oxford University Press, 2014), 28–30, 46.
148. Amy Singer, *Charity in Islamic Societies* (Cambridge: Cambridge University Press, 2008), 74; Mai Yamani, "You Are What You Cook: Cuisine and Class in Mecca," in *A Taste of Thyme: Culinary Cultures of the Middle East*, ed. Sami Zubaida (London: Tauris Parke, 2000), 182.
149. Amy Singer, "The 'Michelin Guide' to Public Kitchens in the Ottoman Empire," in *Starting with Food: Culinary Approaches to Ottoman History*, ed. Amy Singer (Princeton, NJ: Markus Wiener Publishers, 2011), 49–68; Nina Ergin, Christoph K. Neumann, and Amy Singer, "Introduction," in *Feeding People, Feeding Power: Imarets in the Ottoman Empire*, ed. Ergin, Neumann, and Singer (Istanbul: Eren, 2007), 15.
150. Singer, "The 'Michelin Guide' to Public Kitchens in the Ottoman Empire"; Christoph K. Neumann, "Remarks on the Symbolism of Ottoman Imarets," in Ergin, Neumann, and Singer, *Feeding People, Feeding Power*, 285.
151. Alan Mikhail, "Unleashing the Beast: Animals, Energy, and the Economy of Labor in Ottoman Egypt," *American Historical Review* 118, no. 2 (2013): 317–348; Mikhail, *The Animal in Ottoman Egypt*, 28–29, 46.
152. Souad Slim and Hasan Abiad, *The Banquet of Old Times: Cuisine of Al-Kurah / Al-Ma'duba 'ayām Zamān. Al-Matbakh Al-Kūrānī* (Balamand, LB: University of Balamand, 2012), 29. Wild herbs were likewise resorted to during times of scarcity in the region during the First World War. Tylor Brand, "Some Eat to Remember, Some to Forget: Starving, Eating, and Coping in the Syrian Famine of World War I," in Dmitriev and Orfali, *Food as a Cultural Signifier*, 319–339. They also form a central part of present-day culinary identity in the Palestinian territories. Atsuko Ichijo and Ronald Ranta, eds., *The Emergence of National Food: The Dynamics of Food and Nationalism* (London: Palgrave Macmillan, 2016), 55.
153. Kevin Blankinship, "Missionary and Heretic: Debating Veganism in the Medieval Islamic World," in Dmitriev and Orfali, *Food as a Cultural Signifier*, 260–291.
154. Valerie Hoffman, "Eating and Fasting for God in Sufi Tradition," *Journal of the American Academy of Religion* 63 (1995): 465–484; Michael Cooperson, "Bishr Al-Hāfī," in *Encyclopaedia of Islam Three*, ed. Kate Fleet et al. (Leiden: Brill, 2011), http://dx.doi.org.encyclopaediaofislam.han.sub.uni-goettingen.de/10.1163/1573-3912_ei3_COM_24019 (accessed January 21, 2020); Richard C. Foltz, *Animals in Islamic Tradition and Muslim Cultures* (Oxford: Oneworld, 2006), 109; Ahmet T. Karamustafa, "Antinomian Sufis," in *The Cambridge Companion to Sufism*, ed. Lloyd Ridgeon (Cambridge: Cambridge University Press, 2014), 101.
155. Nicolas Trépanier, "Starting Without Food: Fasting and the Early Mawlawi Order," in Singer, *Starting with Food*, 1–22; Hoffman, "Eating and Fasting for God in Sufi Tradition."
156. Febe Armanios, *Coptic Christianity in Ottoman Egypt* (Oxford: Oxford University Press, 2011), 128, 34–35.
157. Costi Bendaly, *Jeûne et oralité. Aspects psychologiques, spirituels et pastoraux du jeûne orthodoxe* (Beirut: An-Nour, 2007); Athanasius N. J. Louvaris, "Fast and Abstinence in Byzantium," in *Feast, Fast or Famine: Food and Drink in*

## 1. IN SEARCH OF PURITY

*Byzantium*, ed. Wendy Mayer and Silke Trzcionka (Brisbane: Australian Association for Byzantine Studies, 2005), 189–198; Issa Khalil, "The Orthodox Fast and the Philosophy of Vegetarianism," *The Greek Orthodox Theological Review* 35, no. 3 (1990): 237–259; Alexander Schmemann, *Great Lent* (Crestwood, NY: St. Vladimir's Seminary Press, 1974); Archimandrite Akaios, *Fasting in the Orthodox Church: Its Theological, Pastoral, and Social Implications*, 2nd ed. (Etna, CA: Center for Traditionalist Orthodox Studies, 1996). While these studies examine fasting on a normative level, there are as yet no historical studies of Orthodox fasting as a lived cultural practice.

158. Antonia-Leda Matalas, Eleni Tourlouki, and Chrystalleni Lazarou, "Fasting and Food Habits in the Eastern Orthodox Church," in *Food & Faith in Christian Culture*, ed. Ken Albala (New York: Columbia University Press, 2011), 189–203.

159. *Nafs*, and hence the opposition between a carnal and a spiritual soul (*rūḥ*), is a motive employed in Sufi ascetic discourse as well. Trépanier, "Starting Without Food," 7; Gabriel Said Reynolds, "The Sufi Approach to Food: A Case Study of Ādāb," *Muslim World* 90, no. 1 (2000): 198; Mark J. Sedgwick, *Sufism: The Essentials* (Cairo: American University in Cairo Press, 2000), 9–10.

160. Gerāsīmūs Masarrah, "Al-Ṣawm Al-Arbaʿīnī," *Al-Hadīyya* 7, no. 174 (1889): 66.

161. On the strategy of Protestant missions regarding Orthodox Christians, see Heleen Murre-van den Berg, "The Middle East: Western Missions and the Eastern Churches, Islam and Judaism," in *Cambridge History of Christianity*, vol. 8, *World Christianities, c. 1800–1914*, ed. Sheridan Gilley (Cambridge: Cambridge University Press, 2006), 458–472; Habib Badr, "American Protestant Missionary Beginnings in Beirut and Istanbul: Policy, Politics, Practice and Response," in *New Faith in Ancient Lands: Western Missions in the Middle East in the Nineteenth and Early Twentieth Centuries*, ed. Heleen Murre-van den Berg (Leiden: Brill, 2006), 211–240. Rejecting the fast therefore became an important part of performing one's new religious affiliation. Christine Lindner, "'In This Religion I Will Live, and in This Religion I Will Die': Performativity and the Protestant Identity in Late Ottoman Syria," *Chronos* 22 (2010): 25–48. For one example of a convert's rejection of fasting, see Abraham Rihbany, *A Far Journey* (Boston: Houghton Mifflin, 1914), 189–190. Nonetheless, some converts remained ambivalent about what they saw as the meat-centeredness of Western foodways. Junge, "Food, Body, Society," 142–161.

162. In Egypt, Coptic Christians followed a similar fasting pattern. Armanios, *Coptic Christianity in Ottoman Egypt*, 127–135. Christian fasting practices were often respected by non-Christian social contacts. Saßmannshausen, "Eating Up," 27.

163. Eduard Baltzer, *Vegetarianisches Kochbuch für Freunde der natürlichen Lebensweise* (Rudolstadt: H. Hartung & Sohn, 1886), 11–12, 26. Several hadiths, too, condemn the cruel treatment of animals and recommend treating them with compassion. Richard C. Foltz, "'This She-Camel of God Is a Sign to You...': Dimensions of Animals in Islamic Tradition and Muslim Culture," in *A Communion of Subjects: Animals in Religion, Science, and Ethics*, ed. Paul Waldau and Kimberley Patton (New York: Columbia University Press, 2006), 152; Foltz, *Animals in Islamic Tradition and Muslim Cultures*, 19–21, 24.

164. On the other hand, race, including the "Aryan" one, was central to the worldview of the Theosophical Society, which influenced British vegetarians. Thapar, "The Historiography of the Concept of 'Aryan,'" 18–19.

## 2. EVOLUTION, COWS, AND COMMUNALISM

1. Dharampal and T. M. Mukundan, "Introduction," in *British Origin of Cow-Slaughter in India*, ed. Dharampal and Mukundan (Mussoorie: Society for Integrated Development of Himalayas, 2002), 1–83; "British Correspondence on the Agitation in Bihar," in Dharampal and Mukundan, *British Origin of Cow-Slaughter in India*, 291–428; "Narrative on the Agitation in the Punjab (Iol: L/P&J 298/1894). Note on the Agitation Regarding the Cow Question in the Punjab Compiled in the Office of the Assistant to the Inspector-General of the Police, Punjab, Special Branch," in Dharampal and Mukundan, *British Origin of Cow-Slaughter in India*, 123–289.
2. Theo Baness, *An Essay on Cows Protection by Mr. Theo. Baness, Contractor, Amritsar, Published by Lala Shambhu Nath by the Permission of Pandit Gosavak Jagat Narain of Benares* (Amritsar: National Press, 1893).
3. Associating Muslims with dirt and disease was common in Hindu nationalist discourse. See, for instance, Kashi Nath Khattri, *Go Pukar* [Call for help on behalf of the cow] (Allahabad: Sirsha Zilla; Benares: Bharat Jiwan Press, 1888); Dayānanda Sarasvatī, *The Light of Truth or an English Translation of the Satyarth Prakash* (New Delhi: Sarvadeshik Arya Pratinidhi Sabha, 1975), 325–326.
4. Baness, *An Essay on Cows Protection*.
5. Utsa Ray, *Culinary Culture in Colonial India: A Cosmopolitan Platter and the Middle-Class* (Delhi: Cambridge University Press, 2015), 56.
6. Kenneth Jones, *Arya Dharm: Hindu Consciousness in 19th-Century Punjab* (New Delhi: Ajay Kumar Jain, 1976).
7. Sandria B. Freitag, "Sacred Symbol as Mobilizing Ideology: The North Indian Search for a 'Hindu' Community," *Comparative Studies in Society and History* 22, no. 4 (1980): 597–625.
8. Gyanendra Pandey, "Rallying around the Cow: Sectarian Strife in the Bhojpuri Region, c. 1888–1917," in *Subaltern Studies II: Writings on South Asian History and Society*, ed. Ranajit Guha (New Delhi: Oxford University Press, 1983), 60–129.
9. Rohit De, "Cows and Constitutionalism," *Modern Asian Studies* 53, no. 1 (2019): 240–277.
10. Therese O'Toole, "Secularizing the Sacred Cow: The Relationship between Religious Reform and Hindu Nationalism," in *Hinduism in Public and Private: Reform, Hindutva, Gender, and Sampraday*, ed. Anthony Copley (New Delhi: Oxford University Press, 2003), 84–109; Cassie Adcock, "Sacred Cows and Secular History: Cow Protection Debates in Colonial North India," *Comparative Studies of South Asia, Africa and the Middle East* 30, no. 2 (2010): 297–311; Adcock, *The Limits of Tolerance: Indian Secularism and the Politics of Religious Freedom* (New York: Oxford University Press, 2014).
11. Samiparna Samanta, *Meat, Mercy, and Morality: Animals and Humanitarianism in Colonial Bengal, 1850–1920* (New Delhi: Oxford University Press, 2021), 133–205.

## 2. EVOLUTION, COWS, AND COMMUNALISM

12. Shabnum Tejani, "Cow Protection, Hindu Identity and the Politics of Hurt in India, c. 1890–2019," *Emotions: History, Culture, Society* 3, no. 1 (2019): 136–157.
13. Cassie Adcock, "'Preserving and Improving the Breeds': Cow Protection's Animal-Husbandry Connection," *South Asia: Journal of South Asian Studies* 42, no. 6 (2019): 1141–1155.
14. Parama Roy, "Vegetarianism," in *Keywords in South Asian Studies*, ed. Gita Dharampal-Frick et al. (New Delhi: Oxford University Press, 2015), 272.
15. Ludwig Alsdorf, *The History of Vegetarianism and Cow-Veneration in India* (London: Routledge, 2010).
16. Roy, "Vegetarianism"; Renate Syed, "Das heilige Essen—Das heilige Essen. Religiöse Aspekte des Speiseverhaltens im Hinduismus," in *Die Religionen und das Essen*, ed. Perry Schmidt-Leukel (Munich: Diederichs, 2000), 133–134.
17. Francis Zimmermann, *The Jungle and the Aroma of Meats: An Ecological Theme in Indian Medicine* (Berkeley: University of California Press, 1987); Dominik Wujastyk, *The Roots of Ayurveda* (London: Penguin, 2003), xx–xxi; "Caraka's Compendium," in Wujastyk, *The Roots of Ayurveda*, 16–17.
18. Peter Berger, "Food," in *Brill's Encyclopedia of Hinduism*, vol. 3, ed. Knut A. Jacobsen et al. (Leiden: Brill, 2011), 69.
19. Wendy Doniger, *On Hinduism* (Oxford: Oxford University Press, 2014), 415–417.
20. Doniger, 41–42. Individual cults, such as that of Kali in Bengal, however, continued to rely on animal sacrifice. Syed, "Das heilige Essen—Das heilige Essen," 102, 134.
21. Roy, "Vegetarianism," 273–274; P. S. Jaini, "Fear of Food: Jaina Attitudes on Eating," in *Collected Papers on Jaina Studies*, ed. Jaini (Delhi: Motilal Banarsidass, 2000), 284–285. As Paul Dundas emphasizes, early Jain ascetics did not reject meat when it was donated. Paul Dundas, *The Jains*, 2nd ed. (London: Routledge, 1992), 177.
22. Romila Thapar, *Early India: From the Origins to AD 1300* (London: Penguin, 2002), 381.
23. Alsdorf, *The History of Vegetarianism and Cow-Veneration in India*, 68. Dairy foods were a preserve of the upper castes and were either not available to lower-caste individuals or posed the risk of them being attacked for their consumption. Bhimrao Ramji Ambedkar, "Right and Might," in *The Past of the Outcaste: Readings in Dalit History*, ed. Sabyasachi Bhattacharya and Yagati Chinna Rao (Delhi: Orient Blackswan, 2017), 51.
24. Raj Gauthaman, *Dark Interiors: Essays on Caste and Dalit Culture* (New Delhi: SAGE Publications, 2021), 5.
25. According to Deryck Lodrick, asylums for cattle (*goshalas*) were only established beginning in the twelfth century CE. Most of the establishments he charted, however, were inaugurated during the 1830s, and were run chiefly by Jains and Banians in Gujarat. Lodrick, *Sacred Cows, Sacred Places: Origins and Survivals of Animal Homes in India* (Berkeley: University of California Press, 1981), 62–69. *Pinjrapoles*, on the other hand, housed all aged and sick animals. Lodrick, 14. As Dwijendra Narayan Jha argues, however, the veneration of the cow did not constitute an unbroken tradition in India. Jha, *The Myth of the Holy Cow* (London: Verso, 2002).
26. Peter van der Veer, *Religious Nationalism: Hindus and Muslims in India* (Berkeley: University of California Press, 1994), 90.

## 2. EVOLUTION, COWS, AND COMMUNALISM

27. Shaheed Amin, *Conquest and Community: The Afterlife of Warrior Saint Ghazi Miyan* (New Delhi: Orient Blackswan, 2015), 79–89.
28. Martha Alter Chen, "Satī and Widowhood," in Jacobson et al., *Brill's Encyclopedia of Hinduism*, 3:174–175; Lourens P. Van den Bosch, "The Ultimate Journey: Satī and Widowhood in India," in *Between Poverty and the Pyre: Moments in the History of Widowhood*, ed. Jan Bremmer and Lourens P. Van den Bosch (London: Routledge, 1995), 191–192; Henrike Donner, "New Vegetarianism: Food, Gender and Neo-liberal Regimes in Bengali Middle-Class Families," *South Asia: Journal of South Asian Studies* 31, no. 1 (2008): 148. From a popular perspective, see also Chitrita Banerji, *The Hour of the Goddess: Memories of Women, Food, and Ritual in Bengal* (New Delhi: Penguin, 2006), 95–105.
29. Syed, "Das heilige Essen—Das heilige Essen," 110.
30. Syed, 110–113; B. A. Holdrege, "Body Connections: Hindu Discourses of the Body and the Study of Religions," *Indian Journal of Hindu Studies* 2, no. 3 (1998): 368. Foods were considered unevenly susceptible to contamination. Water and food cooked in it were considered particularly vulnerable, while food fried in ghee was considered relatively immune to contamination. Louis Dumont, *Homo hierarchicus: Le Système Des Castes Et Ses Implications* (Paris: Gallimard, 1966), 182–183.
31. Aloka Parasher-Sen, "Foreigner (Mleccha)," in Jacobson et al., *Brill's Encyclopedia of Hinduism*, 3:76–81, expounds on notions of cultural alterity in the history of Hinduism, mentioning the ritual impurity ascribed to Muslims and lower-caste or casteless individuals only in passing but specifying that the word for "impure" was considered a synonym for "Muslim" in some Indian languages.
32. Peter van der Veer, *Imperial Encounters: Religion and Modernity in India and Britain* (Princeton, NJ: Princeton University Press, 2001), 134–144.
33. Ravindra S. Khare, "Food with Saints: An Aspect of Hindu Gastrosemantics," in *The Eternal Food: Gastronomic Ideas and Experiences of Hindus and Buddhists*, ed. Khare, (Albany: State University of New York Press, 1992), 29.
34. *Manu's Code of Law: A Critical Edition and Translation of the Mānava-Dharmásāstra*, ed. Patrick Olivelle and Suman Olivelle (New York: Oxford University Press, 2004), 92.
35. *Manu's Code of Law*, 113.
36. Manoranjan Byapari, *Interrogating My Chandal Life: An Autobiography of a Dalit* (New Delhi: SAGE Publications, 2017), 75–77. For further extracts of Dalit autobiographies that discuss food, see the anthology edited by Sharmila Rege, *Writing Caste/Writing Gender: Reading Dalit Women's Testimonios* (New Delhi: Zubaan, 2006).
37. So far there has been little research on Dalits and food from a historiographical perspective. What seems clear is that they had very limited access to the foods deemed the purest—namely, dairy products—and beef and pork, shunned by upper-caste Hindus, became their signature foods. Gauthaman, *Dark Interiors*, 5. Dalit autobiographies, a genre that emerged in the second half of the twentieth century, are vocal on food discrimination against Dalits. See, for instance, Byapari, *Interrogating My Chandal Life*, 29–33, 60, 75–77, 113, 131; Rege, *Writing Caste/Writing Gender*. Omprakash Valmiki even called his autobiography *Joothan* (leftovers), referring to the leftover food Dalits received from upper-caste tables.

## 2. EVOLUTION, COWS, AND COMMUNALISM

Omprakash Valmiki, *Joothan: A Dalit's Life* (New York: Columbia University Press, 2003).
38. This is also how Gandhi described his consumption of meat dishes in the company of a Muslim friend who held nationalist and anticolonial positions. M. K. Gandhi, *An Autobiography or the Story of My Experiments with Truth*, trans. Mahadev Desai (London: Penguin, 2001), 33–39.
39. Rosinka Chaudhuri, *Freedom and Beef Steaks: Colonial Calcutta Culture* (Delhi: Orient Blackswan, 2012), 17–40; Utsa Ray, "Eating 'Modernity': Changing Dietary Practices in Colonial Bengal," *Modern Asian Studies* 46, no. 3 (2012): 703–729.
40. M. N. Srinivas, *The Cohesive Role of Sanskritization and Other Essays* (New Delhi: Oxford University Press, 1989), 42. A case in point were the Chamars of Uttar Pradesh, in central India. From at least the 1920s, Chamar associations attempted to claim a higher caste status, that of the Kshatriya (warrior) caste. In this process, they cooperated with the Arya Samaj, a Hindu reform organization, and purified their lifestyle—a process to which meat abstention was generally deemed central, even though the Kshatriyas had traditionally consumed meat. Ramnarayan S. Rawat, "Colonial Archive vs. Colonial Sociology: Writing Dalit History," in *Dalit Studies*, ed. Rawat and K. Satyanarayana (Durham, NC: Duke University Press, 2016), 53–74.
41. Such as the Arya Samaj, on which see below.
42. Scholarship on the Theosophical Society includes Bruce F. Campbell, *Ancient Wisdom Revived: A History of the Theosophical Movement* (Berkeley: University of California Press, 1980); Joscelyn Godwin, *The Theosophical Enlightenment* (Albany: State University of New York Press, 1994); Olav Hammer and Mikael Rothstein, eds., *Handbook of the Theosophical Current* (Leiden: Brill, 2013); Gauri Viswanathan, "Theosophical Society," in *Brill's Encyclopedia of Hinduism*, vol. 5, *Religious Symbols, Hinduism and Migration, Contemporary Communities Outside South Asia, Some Modern Religious Groups and Teachers*, ed. Knut A. Jacobson (Leiden: Brill, 2013), 679–689; James A. Santucci, "Theosophy," in *The Cambridge Companion to New Religious Movements*, ed. Olav Hammer and Mikael Rothstein (Cambridge: Cambridge University Press, 2012), 231–246.
43. On Theosophy and Islam, see Mark J. Sedgwick, *Western Sufism: From the Abbasids to the New Age* (Oxford: Oxford University Press, 2017), 144–155.
44. Olav Hammer, *Claiming Knowledge: Strategies of Epistemology from Theosophy to the New Age* (Leiden: Brill, 2001), 256–258.
45. Joscelyn Godwin, "Blavatsky and the First Generation of Theosophy," in Hammer and Rothstein, *Handbook of the Theosophical Current*, 22–26.
46. On the Indian members of the Theosophical Society, see Regina Moritz, "Globalizing 'Sacred Knowledge': South Asians and the Theosophical Society, 1879–1930" (PhD diss., Jacobs University Bremen, 2012).
47. "Officers of the Theosophical Society and Universal Brotherhood," *The Theosophist* 13 (1891–1892): 62–72.
48. Alan Trevithick, "The Theosophical Society and Its Subaltern Acolytes (1880–1986)," *Marburg Journal of Religion* 13, no. 1 (2008): 1–32. While there is some

## 2. EVOLUTION, COWS, AND COMMUNALISM

research on the role of the Theosophical Society in Indian nationalism, as well as on some notable South Asian members such as the Anagharika Dharmapala, there are few studies on the role of less prominent local fellows. Tessa J. Bartholomeusz, "Dharmapala at Chicago: Mahayana Buddhist or Sinhala Chauvinist," in *Museum of Faiths: Histories and Legacies of the 1893 World's Parliament of Religions*, ed. Eric J. Ziolkowski (Atlanta, GA: Scholars Press, 1993), 235–250; Moritz, "Globalizing 'Sacred Knowledge'"; Moritz, " 'The Empire of Righteousness': Anagarika Dharmapala and His Vision of Buddhist Asianism," in *Asianisms: Regionalist Interactions and Asian Integration*, ed. Nicola Spakowski and Marc Frey (Singapore: National University of Singapore Press, 2016), 19–48; Mark Bevir, "Theosophy and the Origins of the Indian National Congress," *International Journal of Hindu Studies* 7, no. 1 (2003): 99–115; Mriganka Mukhopadhyay, "Mohini: A Case Study of a Transnational Spiritual Space in the History of the Theosophical Society," *Numen* 67, nos. 2–3 (2019): 165–190; Mukhopadhyay, "Occult's First Foot Soldier in Bengal: Peary Chand Mittra and the Early Theosophical Movement," in *The Occult Nineteenth Century*, ed. Lukas Pokorny and Franz Winter (London: Palgrave Macmillan, 2021), 269–287.

49. Dayanand's first name is also transcribed as Dayananda; it ends on a short vowel that is not necessarily pronounced.
50. Har Bilas Sarda, *Dayanand Sarasvati: World Teacher* (Ajmer: Vedic Yantralaya, 1946), 525–526; J. T. F. Jordens, *Dayananda Saraswati: His Life and Ideals* (New Delhi: Oxford University Press, 1960), 509–512. The letters exchanged between Dayananda, Olcott, and Blavatsky are reprinted in *Maharishi Dayanand Saraswati Ka Patra-Vayvahar, Vol. 9* (Ajmer: Vedic Pustakalay, 2015).
51. Hermann Kulke and Dietmar Rothermund, *A History of India*, 4th ed. (Oxon, UK: Routledge, 2010), 31–35. While the idea of an Indo-European relationship had occupied scholars since the discoveries of Sir William Jones, this argument was first expanded on by Max Müller. See Müller, *A History of Ancient Sanskrit Literature, So Far as It Illustrates the Primitive Religion of the Brahmins* (London: Williams and Norgate, 1860), 12–16, 25.
52. Jones, *Arya Dharm*; Harald Fischer-Tiné, "Arya Samaj," in Jacobsen, *Brill's Encyclopedia of Hinduism*, 5: 389–396.
53. Fischer-Tiné, "Arya Samaj," 391.
54. Harald Fischer-Tiné, *Der Gurukul-Kangri oder die Erfindung der Arya-Nation. Kolonialismus, Hindureform und "nationale Bildung" in Britisch-Indien (1897–1922)* (Würzburg: Ergon, 2003), 40.
55. Already in *Isis Unveiled*, Blavatsky was telling the history of humankind in terms of the history of civilizations. Helena Petrovna Blavatsky, *Isis Unveiled* (New York: J. W. Bouton, 1877). It was only in her *Secret Doctrine*, however, that she came up with a theory of races in which the "Aryan" race reigned supreme, although she emphasized that the occult doctrine did "not admit of any divisions" between races. Blavatsky, *The Secret Doctrine: The Synthesis of Science, Religion, and Philosophy* (London: Theosophical Publishing Company, 1888). There is no extensive research on whether her racial theory was influenced by her exchange with Swami Dayananda or vice versa. However, Romila Thapar shows that Dayananda was influenced by the Theosophical Society with regard to his views on the origin of the "Aryans," which he located in Tibet. Thapar, "The Historiography of the

## 2. EVOLUTION, COWS, AND COMMUNALISM

Concept of 'Aryan,'" in *India: Historical Beginnings and the Concept of the Aryan*, ed. Thapar et al. (Delhi: National Book Trust, 2006), 18. On the notion of race in the writing of Blavatsky and her successor, Annie Besant, see also Gauri Viswanathan, *Outside the Fold: Conversion, Modernity, and Belief* (Princeton, NJ: Princeton University Press, 1998), 177–207.

56. Romila Thapar, *Early India: From the Origins to AD 1300* (London: Penguin, 2002), 12–15.
57. Swami Dayananda Sarasvati, "The Killing of Cows and Other Useful Beasts," *The Theosophist* 2 (1880): 52. Dayananda's widely read treatise on cow protection would appear only two years later.
58. Veer, *Imperial Encounters*, 55–57.
59. Sarda, *Dayanand Sarasvati*, 522–592; Jordens, *Dayananda Saraswati*, 209–212.
60. Alsdorf, *The History of Vegetarianism and Cow-Veneration in India*.
61. Alsdorf; Jha, *The Myth of the Holy Cow*; Doniger, *On Hinduism*, 409–425.
62. *Vaidiki Himsa Himsa Na Bhavati* [Vedic rules regarding non-vegetarian consumption] (Ajmer: Mahadayanand Vaidik Pustakalaya, 1884). Similar ideas were evoked in a well-known print by the artist Raja Ravi Varma that represents the cow as mother of all deities. Such prints were distributed during public meetings for the cause of cow protection and occasionally censored by British authorities to maintain peace between Hindus and Muslims. Christopher Pinney, *Photos of the Gods: The Printed Image and Political Struggle in India* (New Delhi: Oxford University Press, 2004), 107–112.
63. E. M. Collingham, *Imperial Bodies: The Physical Experience of the Raj, c. 1800–1947* (Cambridge: Polity, 2001), 29–30.
64. E. Mittwoch, "'īd Al- Aḍḥā," in *Encyclopaedia of Islam*, 2nd ed., ed. P. Bearman et al. (Leiden: Brill, 2012), http://dx-1doi-1org-10078da9jo983.erf.sbb.spk-berlin.de/10.1163/1573-3912_islam_SIM_3472 (accessed March 26, 2019).
65. Samanta, *Meat, Mercy, and Morality*, 62–132.
66. Dayananda Sarasvati, "The Killing of Cows and Other Useful Beasts.;" Dayananda Sarasvati, *The Ocean of Mercy. An English Translation of Maharshi Swami Dayanand Saraswati's "Gocaruna Nidhi" by Durga Prasad* (Lahore: Virjanand Press, 1889). The original Hindi edition of Dayanand's treatise appears to be lost; all studies on cow protection cite this translation by a fellow member of the Arya Samaj.
67. In all likelihood, Dayananda borrowed this argument from European sources since it was not employed in classical Indic texts. I am indebted to Wendy Doniger and Cassie Adcock for an enlightening email exchange on this subject.
68. Anna Kingsford, *The Perfect Way in Diet: A Treatise Advocating a Return to the Natural and Ancient Food of Our Race* (London: Kegan Paul, Trench, Trübner & Co., 1881), 1–14. Kingsford had not been the first to employ the anatomy argument, which had already been put forward by John Oswald in *The Cry of Nature, or, an Appeal to Mercy and to Justice on Behalf of the Persecuted Animals* (London: Johnson, 1791), 12–14.
69. Sarda, *Dayanand Sarasvati: World Teacher*, 79, 89; Jordens, *Dayananda Saraswati: His Life and Ideals*, 56, 156.
70. O'Toole, "Secularizing the Sacred Cow"; Gita Dharampal-Frick and Sudha Sitharaman, "Cow Protection," in *Key Concepts in Modern Indian Studies*, ed.

Dharampal-Frick et al. (Oxford: Oxford University Press, 2015); Adcock, "Sacred Cows and Secular History."

71. Sarasvatī, *The Ocean of Mercy*, 28–37.
72. Freitag, "Sacred Symbol as Mobilizing Ideology," 11; Pandey, "Rallying around the Cow," 60; Dharampal and Mukundan, "Introduction," 23–24; O'Toole, "Secularizing the Sacred Cow," 86–91.
73. Alsdorf, *History of Vegetarianism*; Jones, *Arya Dharm*, 152–153; Freitag, "Sacred Symbol as Mobilizing Ideology," 597–627; Ikram Ali Malik, *Hindu Muslim Riots in the British Punjab, 1849–1900* (Lahore: Gosha-i-Adab, 1984); Pandey, "Rallying around the Cow," 60–129; O'Toole, "Secularizing the Sacred Cow," 84–109; Ian Copland, "What to Do About Cows? Princely versus British Approaches to a South Asian Dilemma," *Bulletin of the School of Oriental and African Studies* 68, no. 1 (2005): 59–76; Jyortirmaya Sharma, "Digesting the 'Other': Hindu Nationalism and the Muslims in India," in *Political Hinduism: The Religious Imagination in Public Spheres*, ed. Vinay Lal (New Delhi: Oxford University Press, 2009), 150–172; Adcock, "Sacred Cows and Secular History," 297–311; Adcock, *The Limits of Tolerance*; De, "Cows and Constitutionalism," 240–277; Shabnum Tejani, *Indian Secularism: A Social and Intellectual History 1890–1950* (Bloomington: Indiana University Press, 2008), 27–75.
74. Malik, *Hindu Muslim Riots in the British Punjab*, 1.
75. Allan Octavian Hume, *Agricultural Reform in India* (London: W. H. Allen, 1879), 1–11.
76. Hume, 33. In his previous capacity as a district officer in Etawah, Hume also took steps toward social reform, founding free elementary schools. William Wedderburn, *Allan Octavian Hume, C.B., "Father of the Indian National Congress," 1829 to 1912* (London: T. Fisher Unwin, 1913), 15–19.
77. Hume, *Agricultural Reform in India*, 41–59, 89; Adcock, "'Preserving and Improving the Breeds.'"
78. Edward C. Moulton, "Hume, Allan Octavian (1829–1912), Administrator in India, Founder of the Indian National Congress, and Ornithologist," in *Oxford Dictionary of National Biography* (Oxford: Oxford University Press, 2004), http://www.oxforddnb.com.007135ip0ad9.erf.sbb.spk-berlin.de/view/10.1093/ref:odnb/9780198614128.001.0001/odnb-9780198614128-e-34049 (accessed February 28, 2019); Hume, *Agricultural Reform in India*. Godwin, "Blavatsky and the First Generation of Theosophy," 23.
79. *Times of India*, October 6, 1882, 3.
80. *Times of India*, October 6, 1882, 3; "Editorial Article 1," *Times of India*, October 3, 1883, 2.
81. "Minutes of the Vegetarian Society 24 Jun 1884–28 Sep 1886," in *G 24 The Vegetarian Society* (Manchester County Record Office), 276. A regular Indian branch of the Vegetarian Society, however, never came into being.
82. Manchester County Record Office, G24 Minutes, 259–260. In the end, however, Hume's attempts seem to have been fruitless. Neither the official guide nor the official catalogue of the Colonial and Indian Exhibition featured the Manchester Vegetarian Society.
83. Manchester County Record Office, G24 Minutes, 276.
84. Manchester County Record Office, G24 Minutes, 79–84.

## 2. EVOLUTION, COWS, AND COMMUNALISM

85. Mark Bevir and S. R. Mehrotra stress the importance of Hume's efforts in the foundation of the Indian National Congress. Mehrotra, *A History of the Indian National Congress* (New Delhi: Vikas, 1995), 5–12; Bevir, "Theosophy and the Origins of the Indian National Congress." More recent studies question the centrality of his role. See, for instance, Amales Tripathi, *Indian National Congress and the Struggle for Freedom* (New Delhi: Oxford University Press, 2014), 21–24.
86. Wedderburn, *Allan Octavian Hume*, 60.
87. Chaudhuri, *Freedom and Beef Steaks*.
88. Samanta, *Meat, Mercy, and Morality*, 62–132.
89. Samanta, *Meat, Mercy, and Morality*; Pratik Chakrabarti, "Beasts of Burden: Animals and Laboratory Research in Colonial India," *History of Science* 48, no. 2 (2010): 125–152. On Peary Chand Mittra, see Mukhopadhyay, "Occult's First Foot Soldier in Bengal."
90. Samanta, *Meat, Mercy, and Morality*.
91. Peary Chand Mittra, *Life of Colesworthy Grant, Founder and Late Honorary Secretary of the Calcutta Society for the Prevention of Cruelty to Animals* (Calcutta: I. C. Bose, 1881), 29–30, xviii. It thus appears that the society began focusing on cows in the 1880s. In 1872, the only year for which I could retrieve a member list, members included not only Hindus, but also Parsis and Muslims. Colesworthy Grant, *To the Children of Calcutta. On Cruelty. By the Hon. Secretary Calcutta Society for the Prevention of Cruelty to Animals (C. G.)* (Calcutta: Calcutta Society for the Prevention of Cruelty to Animals, 1872), 30.
92. Mittra, *Life of Colesworthy Grant*, 96–97.
93. Forty-six cow protection riots took place in Bengal between 1886 and 1893. Malik, *Hindu Muslim Riots in the British Punjab*, 1.
94. G. H. Khandekar, *The Indian Companion: Being a Manual of Universal Statistics of All the Provinces in and the Countries Adjacent to India* (Poona: Law Printing Press, 1894), 285; *Catalogue of Books, Received during the Quarter Ending 31st December 1888-Continued* (Calcutta: Calcutta Gazette, 1889), 74–75. The journal could not be retrieved via from WorldCat, the National Library of India, or the Bengal Theosophical Society.
95. Leopold Salzer was born in Vienna to Jewish parents, Daniel and Barbara Salzer, in 1827. His father served as an employee of the Jewish community. I am indebted to Georg Gaugusch and Randy Schoenberg for this piece of information (email communication with author, August 25, 2015). *The British Homoeopathic Review* 40 (1896): 248. Salzer criticized the Theosophical Society's preoccupation with Buddhism and Hinduism, and stressed the merits of Christianity instead. Leopold Salzer, *Theosophical Christianity* (Calcutta: Thacker, Spink & Co., 1891).
96. Lal bazaars were established around the turn of the nineteenth century for British soldiers to control their access to prostitution. Anil Kumar, *Medicine and the Raj: British Medical Policy in India, 1835–1911* (London: SAGE Publications, 1998), 108. Calcutta's Lal Bazaar had the same function. Ashutosh Kumar, *Coolies of the Empire: Indentured Indians in the Sugar Colonies, 1830–1920* (Cambridge: Cambridge University Press, 2017), 43. The fact that Salzer's practice started out in a less reputable neighborhood may hint at homoeopathy's position in the medical market in India. Though it rejected academic medical practices like vivisection and vaccine and relied on herbal medicines, it still had the appeal of being of

## 2. EVOLUTION, COWS, AND COMMUNALISM

Western origin. It may also have been less costly than Western medicine. On the history of homoeopathy in colonial India, see Samuiel Vijaya Bhaskar Poldas, *Geschichte der Homöopathie in Indien von ihrer Einführung bis zur ersten offiziellen Anerkennung 1937* (Stuttgart: Haug, 2010); David Arnold and Sumit Sarkar, "In Search of Rational Remedies: Homoeopathy in Nineteenth-Century Bengal," in *Plural Medicine, Tradition, and Modernity, 1800–2000*, ed. Waltraud Ernst (London: Routledge, 2002), 40–57.

97. This is suggested by the detailed travel diary of Wilhelm Hübbe-Schleiden, a German theosophist who visited India from 1894 to 1896, spending ample time with Salzer. Hübbe-Schleiden, *Indisches Tagebuch 1894/96. Mit Anmerkungen und einer Einleitung herausgegeben von Norbert Klatt* (Göttingen: Norbert Klatt Verlag, 2009), 137, 139–140, 142, 144, 150, 154, 169.

98. Leopold Salzer, *The Psychic Aspect of Vegetarianism: A Lecture Delivered by L. Salzer at the Inaugural Meeting of the Calcutta Vegetarian Society, in March 1887* (Calcutta: C. Ringer & Co., 1888), 12.

99. Salzer, 17.

100. Code of Manu, Manu chapter 12, verse 40, cited in Lance Nelson, "Cows, Elephants, Dogs, and Other Lesser Embodiments of *Ātman*: Reflections on Hindu Attitudes towards Nonhuman Animals," in *A Communion of Subjects: Animals in Religion, Science, and Ethics*, ed. Paul Waldau and Kimberley Patton (New York: Columbia University Press, 2006), 185. On the three *guṇas*, see Angelika Malinar, "Guṇa," in *Brill's Encyclopedia of Hinduism*, vol. 2, *Sacred Texts, Ritual Traditions, Arts, Concepts*, ed. Knut A. Jacobsen et al. (Leiden: Brill, 2010), 758–762. The Code of Manu was one of the first Sanskrit texts to be translated into English and was used to help codify Hindu law at the onset of British rule in India. The Bhagavad Gita was also translated into English at the end of the eighteenth century. They came to be considered classical texts of Hinduism during the nineteenth century, with the Bhagavad Gita inspiring Romanticism in both Europe and the United States. See J. J. Clarke, *Oriental Enlightenment: The Encounter between Asian and Western Thought* (London: Routledge, 1997); Bernard S. Cohn, *Colonialism and Its Forms of Knowledge: The British in India* (Princeton, NJ: Princeton University Press, 1996), 57–75.

101. While connections between vegetarianism, scientific, and occult arguments and concerns for animal welfare cannot be proven with regard to Leopold Salzer, these motives did come together in the work of more prominent members of the Theosophical Society. Gauri Viswanathan, "'Have Animals Souls?': Theosophy and the Suffering Body," *Publications of the Modern Language Association of America* 126, no. 3 (2011): 440–447.

102. As Olav Hammer points out, evolutionary theory was also prominent in Blavatsky's work: Olav Hammer, *Claiming Knowledge: Strategies of Epistemology from Theosophy to the New Age* (Leiden: Brill, 2001), 256–258.

103. On the popularity of evolutionary theory in Hindu nationalist discourse, see Meena Nanda, "Madame Blavatsky's Children: Modern Hindu Encounters with Darwinism," in *Handbook of Religion and the Authority of Science*, ed. James R. Lewis and Olav Hammer (Leiden: Brill, 2012), 279–344; Harald Fischer-Tiné, "From Brahmacharya to 'Conscious Race Culture': Victorian Discourses of Science and Hindu Traditions in Early Indian Nationalism," in *Beyond*

## 2. EVOLUTION, COWS, AND COMMUNALISM

*Representation: Colonial and Post-Colonial Constructions of Indian Identity*, ed. Crispin Bates (New Delhi: Oxford University Press, 2006), 241–269.
104. Lodrick, *Sacred Cows, Sacred Places*, 39, 69–70.
105. Stephen Meredyth Edwardes, *The Rise of Bombay: A Retrospect* (Bombay: Times of India Press, 1902), 265.
106. Prashant Kidambi, *The Making of an Indian Metropolis: Colonial Governance and Public Culture in Bombay, 1890–1920* (Aldershot, UK: Ashgate, 2007), 202–233.
107. Kidambi, 25–26; Gyan Prakash, *Mumbai Fables: History of an Enchanted City* (Princeton, NJ: Princeton University Press, 2010), 43.
108. Michael Stausberg, *Die Religion Zarathushtras*, vol. 2 (Stuttgart: Kohlhammer, 2004), 118–120.
109. Lodrick, *Sacred Cows, Sacred Places*, 39, 69–70.
110. On the history of Parsis in India, see John R. Hinnells and Alan Williams, eds., *Parsis in India and the Diaspora* (London: Routledge, 2007); Stausberg, *Die Religion Zarathushtras*, 2:13–151; Jesse S. Palsetia, *The Parsis of India: Preservation of Identity in Bombay City* (Leiden: Brill, 2001).
111. Palsetia, *The Parsis of India*, 277–319.
112. "Minutes of the Vegetarian Society 24 Jun 1884–28 Sep 1886," in *G 24 The Vegetarian Society* (Manchester County Record Office), 110.
113. "Minutes of the Vegetarian Society 24 Jun 1884–28 Sep 1886," 348–349.
114. "Minutes of the Vegetarian Society 24 Jun 1884–28 Sep 1886," 356.
115. Pandey, *Vegetarian Cookery*.
116. On Malabari, see Dayaran Gidumal Shahani, *The Life and Life-Work of Behramji M. Malabari: Being a Biographical Sketch, with Selections from His Writings and Speeches on Infant Marriage and Enforced Widowhood, and Also His "Rambles of a Pilgrim Reformer"* (Byculla: Education Society, 1888), i–cxx; "Malabari, Behramji Merwanji," in British Biographical Archive I, 1234, 1–4. For Mehta, see "Mehta, Sir Ferozeshah Mervanji," in Indian Biographical Archive 137, 186–188. On the Gostlings, see Sarah Gostling's writings on economics, education, and diet: "Mr. David Gostling," *Bombay Gazette*, September 17, 1908, 7; Sarah Gostling, *The Poverty of India and the Land Question: Thoughts Evolved Out of the Late Mahometan Riots at Delhi and Etawah. Paper Read at a Special Meeting of the London Arya Samaj, 5th December 1886* (London: Commonweal Office, 1886); Sarah Gostling, "Vegetarianism. A Paper Read by Mrs. S. S. Gostling Written for the 4th Anniversary of the Panjab Vegetarian Society and Read on the 2nd December 1894," *The Harbinger* 4 (1894): 209–210; Sarah Gostling and Lakshmi Narayan, *India's Position: Social and Economic. A Paper Read at a Special Meeting Under the Auspices of the Indian Society, March 8th, 1887* (London: Charles Cordingley, 1887). On David and Sarah Gostling, see also James Gregory, "British Vegetarianism and the Raj" (unpublished manuscript, last revised 2023), https://www.academia.edu/3837521/British_Vegetarianism_and_the_Raj.
117. "Minutes of the Vegetarian Society 20 January 1891–20 January 1897," in *G 24 The Vegetarian Society* (Manchester County Record Office),
118. *The Natural Living Vegetarian Society (Established, 6th September 1891)* (Bombay: J. N. Petit Parsi Orphanage Captain Printing Press, 1891), 2.
119. *The Natural Living Vegetarian Society*, 3.
120. *The Natural Living Vegetarian Society*, 4.

## 2. EVOLUTION, COWS, AND COMMUNALISM

121. *The Natural Living Vegetarian Society*, 1–2.
122. *The Natural Living Vegetarian Society*, 2.
123. *The Natural Living Vegetarian Society*, 5.
124. Ray, *Culinary Culture in Colonial India*, 162–164.
125. Gauthaman, *Dark Interiors*, 70.
126. The communication of diseases through contaminated meat and fish had been the subject of intense discussion in British vegetarian magazines since the 1850s. See, for instance, "Poisonous Sausages," *Vegetarian Messenger* 3, no. 29 (1852): 6; "Poisonous Fishes," *Vegetarian Messenger* 3, no. 43 (1853): 16; "Vegetarian Diet as a Curative Agent Against Scrofula," *Vegetarian Messenger* 5, no. 65 (1855): 22–23; "Shall We Eat Pork?," *Vegetarian Messenger* 109 (1858): 195; "Leprosy," *Dietetic Reformer and Vegetarian Messenger*, 3rd ser., 4 (1877): 77–80; "Outbreak of Trichinosis," *Vegetarian Messenger* 40 (1883): 63; "Oysters and Typhoid," *Vegetarian Messenger* 48 (1896): 161–162; "Phtisis and Flesh Meat," *Vegetarian Messenger* 50 (1898): 482–483.
127. Michael Stausberg, "Hinduism and Zoroastrianism," in *Brill Encyclopedia of Hinduism*, ed. Knut A. Jacobsen, Angelika Malinar, and Helene Basu (Leiden: Brill, 2012), 607.
128. Stausberg, *Die Religion Zarathushtras*, 2:112–118.
129. Stausberg, 118–120.
130. Ervad Phiroze S. Masani, *Zoroastrianism Ancient and Modern: Comprising a Review of Dr. Dhalla's Book of Zoroastrian Theology* (Bombay: Parsi Vegetarian and Temperance Society, 1917), 198–204. According to Tooraj Daryaee, however, even early Parsi texts already show distinctions along the lines of "purity" and "impurity," with Muslims being considered impure because of their dietary norms, while Hindus were considered pure, particularly because of their appreciation of dairy products. Touraj Daryaee, "Food, Purity and Pollution: Zoroastrian Views on the Eating Habits of Others," *Iranian Studies* 45, no. 2 (2012): 229–242.
131. In 1890–1891 and 1909, sixteen treatises were published annually on cow protection and related issues in the Bombay Presidency. Books criticizing cow protection and vegetarianism, mostly but not exclusively by Muslims, were also published in the Bombay Presidency in that period. For publications against cow slaughter, see *Catalogue of Books Printed in the Bombay Presidency During the Quarter Ending 31st March 1890* (Bombay: Government Central Press, 1890), 32–33; *Catalogue of Books Printed in the Bombay Presidency During the Quarter Ending 30th June 1890* (Bombay: Government Central Press, 1890), 14–15, 66–67; *Catalogue of Books Printed in the Bombay Presidency During the Quarter Ending 31st December 1890* (Bombay: Government Central Press, 1890), 22–25; *Catalogue of Books Printed in the Bombay Presidency During the Quarter Ending 30th September 1909* (Bombay: Government Central Press, 1909), 18, 24–27. For publications opposing cow protection, see *Catalogue of Books Printed in the Bombay Presidency During the Quarter Ending 31st March 1890*, 32–33; *Catalogue of Books Printed in the Bombay Presidency During the Quarter Ending 30th June 1890*, 14–15.
132. "Narrative on the Agitation in the Punjab," 174.
133. "May Meetings of the Vegetarian Society," *Vegetarian Messenger*, 4th ser., 4 (1890): 157–165; "Annual Meetings of the Vegetarian Society," *Vegetarian Messenger*, 4th ser., 4 (1890): 321–332; Joseph Knight, "Spare the Cattle—a Voice from India,"

## 2. EVOLUTION, COWS, AND COMMUNALISM

*Vegetarian Messenger*, new ser., 4 (1890): 202–207, 228–233; "Spare the Cattle. A Voice from India," *Vegetarian Messenger*, 4th ser., 4 (1890): 228–233.

134. Meena Menon, *Riots and After in Mumbai: Chronicles of Truth and Reconciliation* (Los Angeles: SAGE Publications, 2012), 3; *Times of India*, April 20, 1887, 3; *The Mahomedan and Hindu Riots August 1893. From the Bombay Gazette* (Bombay: Bombay Gazette Steam Press, 1894).
135. Dharampal and Mukundan, "Introduction," 48–50; Menon, *Riots and After in Mumbai*, 24–25; Kidambi, *The Making of an Indian Metropolis*, 178–179.
136. Sher-Gil Sivasundaram Arts Foundation, Umrao Singh Sher-Gil, *After 15 Days of Fasting II*, black-and-white photograph, Paris, 1930.
137. Yashodhara Dalmia, *Amrita Sher-Gil: A Life* (Gurgaon: Penguin, 2006).
138. Michel Foucault, "Technologies of the Self," in *Technologies of the Self: A Seminar with Michel Foucault*, ed. Luther H. Martin, H. Gutman, and P. H. Hutton (Amherst: University of Massachusetts Press, 1982).
139. See, for instance, an earlier work: Sher-Gil Sivasundaram Arts Foundation, Umrao Singh Sher-Gil, *After a Bath*, black-and-white photograph, Lahore 1904. On Umrao Singh's photography and self-portraits, see Shanay Jhaveri, "The Journey in My Head: Cosmopolitanism and Indian Male Self-Portraiture in 20th Century India—Umrao Singh Sher-Gil, Bhupen Khakhar, Raghubir Singh" (PhD diss., Royal College of Art, 2016); Vivan Sundaram and Deepak Ananth, *Umrao Singh Sher-Gil: His Misery and His Manuscript* (New Delhi: Photoink, 2001).
140. Dalmia, *Amrita Sher-Gil*, 2.
141. According to Paul Smethurst, cycling helped Indian men counter the British argument of the feeble Indian male. Paul Smethurst, *The Bicycle: Towards a Global History* (Houndmills, UK: Palgrave Macmillan, 2015), 129–130. As a Sikh, however, Umrao Singh would have been considered a member of the so-called martial races that came to be held in high esteem by the British after the "Indian Mutiny" of 1857. Heather Streets, *Martial Races: The Military, Race, and Masculinity in British Imperial Culture, 1857–1914* (Manchester: Manchester University Press, 2004). Probably, then, Umrao Singh, as an adherent of Tolstoy and a member of the upper class, wished to underline his efforts at simple living.
142. Politisches Archiv des Auswärtigen Amtes, R 210.89/3 IA—Weltkrieg WK Nr. 11–12. Har Dayal to Baron von Wesendonk, Berlin, September 30, 1915. On Tolstoy's vegetarianism and his influence on the international vegetarian movement, see Charlotte Alston, *Tolstoy and His Disciples: The History of a Radical International Movement* (London: Tauris, 2014); Peter Brang, *Ein unbekanntes Russland: Kulturgeschichte vegetarischer Lebensweisen von den Anfängen bis zur Gegenwart* (Cologne: Böhlau, 2002), 59–113.
143. See the correspondence between Umrao Singh Sher-Gil, Har Dayal, and members of the German Foreign Office in Politisches Archiv des Auswärtigen Amtes, R 210.89/3 IA —Weltkrieg WK Nr. 11–12. On the Ghadar Party, see Seema Sohi, *Echoes of Mutiny: Race, Surveillance, and Anticolonialism in North America* (New York: Oxford University Press, 2014); Maia Ramnath, *Haj to Utopia: How the Ghadar Movement Charted Global Radicalism and Attempted to Overthrow the British Empire* (Berkeley: University of California Press, 2011).
144. At the same time, Umrao Singh's self-portraits in the nude in young age, such as his self-portrait *After a Bath* (shown in figure 2.4), suggest that his vision of

masculinity was not monolithic, but fluid. Sikhs—both men and women—were ritually forbidden from cutting their hair. Normally, men's long tresses were hidden under a turban, which, along with uncut hair, is a signifier of Sikh identity, and is exclusively worn by men. Doris Jakobsh, "Gender," in *Brill's Encyclopedia of Sikhism Online*, ed. Knut A. Jacobsen (Leiden: Brill, 2017), http://dx.doi.org/10.1163/2589-2118_BESO_COM_031684 (accessed April 2, 2021). It seems to me that in this picture, Sher-Gil both displays the marker of his Sikh strength and turns the Western gaze on himself. That gaze would see his long hair as feminine, and he appears to be both seducing and mocking the glance that seeks to ridicule him. In this way he subverts the clear-cut gender hierarchies the British sought to introduce in an India where both gender and sexuality had been far more fluid. On this, see (albeit from a popular perspective) Madhavi Menon, *Infinite Variety: A History of Desire in India* (New Delhi: Speaking Tiger, 2018). In other self-portraits, Umrao Singh also showed his hair, tying it in a topknot like a Hindu god, which gave his hair a more unambiguously male connotation.

145. "Annual Report," *The Harbinger* 4 (1894): 207–208; "Panjab Vegetarian Society. Established 1889," *The Harbinger* 5 (1895): 72; *The Harbinger* 5 (1895): 80; "Har Dayal to Baron Von Wesendonk, Berlin, 30.09.1915," Politisches Archiv des Auswärtigen Amtes, R 210.89/3 IA—Weltkrieg WK Nr. 11–12.
146. William J. Glover, *Making Lahore Modern: Constructing and Imagining a Colonial City* (Minneapolis: University of Minnesota Press, 2008), 1–26.
147. Glover, 19–25.
148. Glover; Jones, *Arya Dharm*, 169.
149. Gregory, *British Vegetarianism and the Raj*, 3; Bertram Keightley, "Indian Section Report," *The Theosophist* 14, no. 1 (1892): 27; "India," *The Theosophist* 15, no. 1 (1894): 462; "Correspondence," *The Harbinger* 5 (1895): 22.
150. "Panjab Vegetarian Society," 72.
151. *The Tribune*, November 12, 1893, 4.
152. *The Tribune*, November 12, 1893, 4; "Annual Report," *The Harbinger* 4 (1894): 207–208.
153. *The Harbinger* 5, no. 7 (1895): 80.
154. *Vegetarian Messenger*, December 1891, 375.
155. "Correspondence," *The Harbinger* 5 (1895): 71.
156. "Correspondence," 71.
157. "Advertisements," *The Harbinger* 5 (1895): 48; *The Harbinger* 5 (1895): 80; "Advertisements," *The Harbinger* 5 (1895): 107–108.
158. *The Harbinger* 4 (1894): 75.
159. *The Harbinger* 4 (1894): 158.
160. Like Durga Prasad, Pandit Khunnilal Shastri was a member of the Arya Samaj. Two years before, he had published a treatise with Virjanand Press, in which he argued against meat eating, using Ayurveda and evolutionary theory as evidence. Pandit Khunnilal Shastri, *Mans Bhakshan Nishedh* [Prohibition of meat eating] (Lahore: Virjananda Yantralaya, 1892). On Khunnilal Shastri, see also Jones, *Arya Dharm*, 169.
161. Parama Roy, *Alimentary Tracts: Appetites, Aversions, and the Postcolonial* (Durham, NC: Duke University Press, 2010), 46.

## 2. EVOLUTION, COWS, AND COMMUNALISM

162. Pandit Khuni Lal Shastri, "Doshkal Charya [Natural living]," *The Harbinger* 4 (1894): 81–82.
163. "Sacred Authorities for Vegetarianism," *The Harbinger* 4 (1894): 203, 228; "Sacred Authorities for Vegetarianism," *The Harbinger* 5 (1895): 9, 59.
164. "Panjab Vegetarian Society," 72.
165. *The Harbinger* 4 (1894): 168.
166. Angelika Malinar, "Kṛṣṇa," in *Brill's Encyclopedia of Hinduism*, vol. 1, *Regions, Pilgrimages, Deities*, ed. Knut A. Jacobsen et al. (Leiden: Brill, 2009), 605–619.
167. *The Harbinger* 4 (1894): 232–233.
168. Veer, *Religious Nationalism*, 104–105; O'Toole, "Secularizing the Sacred Cow."
169. *The Harbinger* 4 (1894): 80; *The Harbinger* 4 (1894): 150. Muslims were depicted negatively in other *Harbinger* articles as well. They were associated with the oppression and trafficking of women in Punjab, as well as with military aggression. This applied not just to the present, but to the Mughal past, and even to perceptions of Mughal rulers like Akbar, who, because of his interest in Sufism as well as Hinduism, was often portrayed in a relatively positive manner in later Indian texts on vegetarianism and cow protection. "Traffic in Women," *The Harbinger* 4 (1894): 78–79; *The Harbinger* 5 (1895): 20; *The Harbinger* 5 (1895): 81; *The Harbinger* 5 (1895): 69.
170. Leopold Salzer, *Vegetarianism, Pure and Simple* (Calcutta: I. C. Bose & Co., Stanhope Press, 1892).
171. *The Tribune*, November 12, 1893, 4.
172. "Punjab Vegetarian Society," *The Harbinger* 4 (1894): 207; "Narrative on the Agitation in the Punjab," 244.
173. *The Tribune*, September 16, 1891, 4.
174. Pestonji Sorabji Hormudji, "Vegetarianism Shall Never Fail," *The Harbinger* 4 (1894): 180.
175. On the communalist implications of music in front of mosques, see Julian Anthony Lynch, "Music and Communal Violence in Colonial South Asia," *Ethnomusicology Review* 17 (2012), http://ethnomusicologyreview.ucla.edu/journal/volume/17/piece/603.
176. "Annual Report," 207–208.
177. *The Harbinger* 4 (1894): 108; *The Harbinger* 5 (1895): 45.
178. "Narrative on the Agitation in the Punjab," 244.
179. John Heywood, "Punjab Vegetarian Society," *Vegetarian Messenger*, new ser., 6 (1892): 259.
180. *Vegetarian Messenger*, 4th ser., 10 (1896): 131.
181. Sidney H. Beard, *The Testimony of Science in Favour of a Natural and Humane Diet* (London: Order of the Golden Age, 1906). The first page of this publication contains the order's bylaws.
182. On the history of the Order of the Golden Age, see Jon M. Gilheany, *Familiar Strangers: The Church and the Vegetarian Movement in Britain (1809-2009)* (Cardiff: Ascendant Press, 2010), 100–122, and Rosemary Dellar, *Josiah Oldfield: Eminent Fruitarian* (Rainham, UK: Rainmore, 2008), 87–93. The names of the members of the board were listed regularly on the back of the title pages of the *Herald of the Golden Age*, the order's journal, which, however, has been preserved incompletely.

## 2. EVOLUTION, COWS, AND COMMUNALISM

183. See, for instance, Sidney H. Beard, *A Simple Guide to a Natural and Humane Diet* (Ilfracombe, UK: Order of the Golden Age, 1898); Robert H. Perks, *Why I Condemn Vivisection* (Paignton, UK: Order of the Golden Age, 1904); Robert Bell, *The Cancer Scourge and How to Destroy It* (n.p.: Order of the Golden Age, n.d., ca. 1903); Alexander Haig, *Uric Acid, an Epitome of the Subject* (London: Churchill, 1904); William Earnshaw Cooper, *The Blood-Guiltiness of Christendom (May We Slay for Food?)* (London: Order of the Golden Age, 1922).
184. Beard, *The Testimony of Science in Favour of a Natural and Humane Diet*, n.p.
185. Beard called the diet advocated by the order a "fruitarian" one, by which he meant a diet chiefly based on fruits and vegetables. As is evident from his publications, however, that diet included dairy and eggs. Beard, *A Comprehensive Guide-Book to Natural, Hygienic, and Humane Diet* (London: Order of the Golden Age, n.d., ca. 1922), 25.
186. "The Order of the Golden Age," *Vegetarian Messenger*, 5th ser., 1 (1898): 3.
187. John Todd-Ferrier, *Concerning Human Carnivorism* (Paignton: Order of the Golden Age, 1903), 112–115. Other publications of the Order of the Golden Age associated meat consumption with criminal propensities. Eustace Miles, *Avenues to Health* (London: Swan Sonnenschein; New York: Dutton, 1902), 326–337; Sidney H. Beard, "The Law of Reincarnation," *Herald of the Golden Age* 8, no. 6 (1903): 1–2. These far-reaching connections between food and morality recalled similar themes in Hindu discourses as well as British notions of "criminal castes" in India (generally castes known to be meat eaters). On the British construction of "criminal castes," see Kim A. Wagner, "Confessions of a Skull: Phrenology and Colonial Knowledge in Early Nineteenth-Century India," *History Workshop Journal* 69 (2010): 27–51.
188. Dellar, *Josiah Oldfield*, 112–113.
189. "Cooper, Sir William Earnshaw," in British Biographical Archive II, 1403, 076–078, 076–078.
190. *Herald of the Golden Age* 4, no. 10 (1899): half title.
191. "Dr. Oldfield's Indian Tour," *Herald of the Golden Age* 7, no. 1 (1902): 6. On Oldfield's trip, see also Dellar, *Josiah Oldfield*, 122–128.
192. Laxmidas cooperated with the Order of the Golden Age already in 1900, when the organization first published one of his treatises. Labshankar Laxmidas, *For Your Decision. Correspondence Appealing to the Metropolitan of Calcutta to Use His Influence in the Protection of Animals against Cruelty* (Paignton, UK: Order of the Golden Age, 1900). As Ian Copland outlines, Junagadh, though a Muslim state, had had a comparatively strict policy on cow slaughter since the mid-nineteenth century. Copland, "What to Do About Cows?"
193. "Our Indian Pioneer," *Herald of the Golden Age* 8, no. 3 (1903): 30. In addition, individual members of the Order of the Golden Age published articles in the *Times of India*. See, for instance, Robert H. Perks, "'On Vegetarianism.' To the Editor of the Times of India," *Times of India*, September 20, 1904, 5.
194. *The Indian Humanitarian. The Bombay Humanitarian League. Silver Jubilee Number, 1910–1934, Etc.* (Bombay: Bombay Humanitarian League, 1934), 1, 5. Despite its name, the Bombay Humanitarian League was not a branch of the British Humanitarian League, which is never mentioned in the former's publications.

## 2. EVOLUTION, COWS, AND COMMUNALISM

195. *The Indian Humanitarian*.
196. Horniman also acted as a chairman at the Third Humanitarian Conference in India in 1918. Chhanganlal Parmanandadas Nanavaty, ed., *Report of the Third Humanitarian Conference, Bombay. Held on 2nd and 3rd September, 1918* (Bombay: Bombay Humanitarian League, 1918), iii. Apparently, he did not just embrace vegetarianism, but occasionally wore Indian clothes. M. K. Azad, *Benjamin Guy Horniman, Editor "Bombay Chronicle," Deported on 26th April 1919* (Bombay: Lakhmidas Rawji Tairsee, 1920), 15–16; Joachim Alva, *Men and Supermen of Hindustan* (Bombay: Thacker, 1943), 189. After his return to India, he does not seem to have assumed a prominent role in the Bombay Humanitarian League. On Horniman, see also Ramachandra Guha, *Rebels Against the Raj: Western Fighters for Indian Freedom* (Dublin: Harper Collins, 2022), 54–81, 209–236.
197. *The Indian Humanitarian*, 6.
198. *The Indian Humanitarian*, 2.
199. *The Indian Humanitarian*, 7; "Preface," in *Essays on the Advantages of a Vegetarian Diet. Being a Collection of the Essays of Successful Candidates in Its Prize Essay Scheme No. IV* (Bombay: Rustom N. Vatchaghandy at the "Sanj Vartaman" Press, 1914). Up to 1934, the Bombay Humanitarian League organized 102 essay competitions. *The Indian Humanitarian*, 14.
200. Of the 41 members of the jury from 1902 to 1934, 14 were Europeans or Americans, of whom 4 were on the board of the Order of the Golden Age. *The Indian Humanitarian*, 9, 14.
201. *The Indian Humanitarian*, 12.
202. In the 1914 essays, collected in *Essays on the Advantages of a Vegetarian Diet*, five contributions referred to Bell, *The Cancer Scourge*: Pandit Bishen Das, "The Advantages of 'a Vegetarian Diet'"; Girish Chandra Deb, "The Advantages of 'a Vegetarian Diet'"; Mahadev Kanthariaker, "The Advantages of Vegetarian Diet"; Rao Bahadur Dullabhji Dharamshi Ved, "The Advantages of 'a Vegetarian Diet'"; and Yudhishthir Shridharram Mehta, "The Advantages of 'a Vegetarian Diet.' " Seven articles referred to Haig, *Uric Acid, an Epitome of the Subject*: Das, "The Advantages of 'a Vegetarian Diet'"; P. K. Mehta, "Vegetarian Diet"; and Sitaram M. Phadke, "The Advantages of 'a Vegetarian Diet.' " And five essays explicitly referred to the Code of Manu: Ved, "The Advantages of 'a Vegetarian Diet'"; Kanthariaker, "The Advantages of Vegetarian Diet"; Phadke, "The Advantages of 'a Vegetarian Diet'"; Deb, "The Advantages of 'a Vegetarian Diet'"; and Das, "The Advantages of 'a Vegetarian Diet.' "
203. See, for instance, Kanthariaker, "The Advantages of Vegetarian Diet"; S. C. Chatterji, "The Advantages of 'a Vegetarian Diet.' "
204. Chatterji, "The Advantages of 'a Vegetarian Diet,' " 7. Within the volume, page count begins again with each article.
205. Chatterji, 8.
206. Deb, "The Advantages of 'a Vegetarian Diet'"; Kathleen Gomes, "The Advantages of 'a Vegetarian Diet,' " in *Essays on the Advantages of a Vegetarian Diet*.
207. Dullabhji Dharamshi Ved, *Essay on the Advantages of Vegetarian Diet. With Special Reference to the Haig System and with Scriptural Quotations* (Bombay: Shri Jiva Daya Gnan Prasarak Fund, 1913), 8–9. The Order of the Golden Age, on the other hand, promoted raw foods for reasons of health, attributing Hindus' alleged

physical weakness to their consumption of cooked dishes. "A Brahminical Banquet," *Herald of the Golden Age* 16, no. 10 (1911): 202.
208. Shewantibai K. Dhurandhar, "The Advantages of 'a Vegetarian Diet,'" in *Essays on the Advantages of a Vegetarian Diet*, 14–16.
209. Ved, *Essay on the Advantages of Vegetarian Diet*, 15. The article claimed that Norway was beset with leprosy because of Norwegians' ingestion of meat. Contemporary European scientists considered bad fish the cause of these epidemics. Kajsa Katharina Wennberg-Hilger, "Das Seuchenhafte Auftreten von Lepra in Einigen Küstenregionen West-Norwegens im 19. Jahrhundert. Mit einem ergänzenden Bericht über die entsprechende Situation in Schweden" (medical dissertation, University of Bonn, 2011), 94. In India, leprosy had been attributed even earlier to the consumption of meat, particularly beef, with Muslims and lower-caste individuals—social groups that Hindus already saw as impure—considered the main victims of the disease. Khattri, *Go Pukar*, 25–26.
210. Kanthariaker, "The Advantages of Vegetarian Diet," 40.
211. Kanthariaker, 57.
212. Kanthariaker, 6; Burjor R. Doctor, "The Advantages of 'a Vegetarian Diet,'" in *Essays on the Advantages of a Vegetarian Diet*, 9.
213. Deb, "The Advantages of a Vegetarian Diet." Deb here paraphrases verse chapter 17, verse 10 of the Bhagavad Gita specifying the alleged alimentary preferences of the *tamasic*. *The Bhagavad Gītā*, 25th ann. ed., ed. Christopher Key Chapple, trans. Winthrop Sargeant (Albany: Excelsior Editions/State University Press of New York, 2009), 643.
214. Chatterji, "The Advantages of 'a Vegetarian Diet,'" 16–19.
215. Das, "The Advantages of 'a Vegetarian Diet,'" 15.
216. Das, 22–23.
217. Barbara N. Ramusack, "Gaikwar, Sayaji Rao, Maharaja of Baroda (1863–1939)," in *Oxford Dictionary of National Biography* (Oxford: Oxford University Press, 2004), https://doi.org/10.1093/ref:odnb/30613 (accessed April 3, 2019). Twenty-four years ago, interestingly enough, Sayaji Rao III funded the publication of a cookbook containing "preparations of meat used by the Hindus, made up according to the European, Mahomedan and Madrasi Hindu methods." *Supa Shastra* (Poona: Jagaddhitechchhu Press, 1890), quoted in *Catalogue of Books Printed in the Bombay Presidency During the Quarter Ending 31st December 1890*, 6–7.

# 3. THE CHICAGO EFFECT

1. Robert W. Rydell, "World's Columbian Exposition," Encyclopedia of Chicago, Chicago Historical Society, accessed March 1, 2021, http://encyclopedia.chicagohistory.org/pages/1386.html. On the World's Columbian Exposition, see also Rydell, "A Cultural Frankenstein? The Chicago World's Columbian Exposition of 1893," in *Grand Illusions: Chicago's World's Fair of 1893*, ed. Neil Harris et al. (Chicago: Chicago Historical Society, 1993), 143–170; Rydell, *All the World's a Fair: Visions of Empire at American International Expositions, 1876–1916* (Chicago: University of Chicago Press, 1984); Norman Bolotin and Christine Laing,

## 3. THE CHICAGO EFFECT

*The World's Columbian Exposition: The Chicago World's Fair of 1893* (Urbana: University of Illinois Press, 2002).
2. Burton Benedict, "The Anthropology of World's Fairs," in *The Anthropology of World's Fairs: San Francisco's Panama Pacific International Exposition of 1915*, ed. Benedict (Aldershot, UK: Scolar Press, 1983).
3. Neil Rosendorf, "Expositions," in *The Palgrave Dictionary of Transnational History*, ed. Akira Iriye and Pierre-Yves Saunier (Houndmills, UK: Palgrave Macmillan, 2009), 371.
4. Benjamin Cummings Truman, *History of the World's Fair: Being a Complete Description of the World's Columbian Exposition from Its Inception* (Chicago: Mammoth Publishing, 1893), 128–129.
5. Dominic A. Pacyga, *Chicago: A Biography* (Chicago: University of Chicago Press, 2009), 8–18.
6. Christopher Robert Reed, *Black Chicago's First Century*, vol. 1, *1833–1900* (Columbia: University of Missouri Press, 2005).
7. Joanna Merwood-Salisbury, *Chicago 1890: The Skyscraper and the Modern City* (Chicago: University of Chicago Press, 2009).
8. Wim de Wit, "Building an Illusion: The Design of the World's Columbian Exposition," in Haris et al., *Grand Illusions*, 43–98.
9. Frederick Douglass, "Introduction," in *The Reason Why the Colored American Is Not in the World's Columbian Exposition: The Afro-American's Contribution to Columbian Literature*, ed. Ida B. Wells (Urbana: University of Illinois Press, 1999), 3–7. On Ida B. Well's activism, see Alex Zamalin, *Struggle on Their Minds: The Political Thought of African American Resistance* (New York: Columbia University Press, 2017).
10. Henry Louis Gates Jr., *Stony the Road: Reconstruction, White Supremacy, and the Rise of Jim Crow* (New York: Penguin, 2019).
11. John P. Burris, *Exhibiting Religion: Colonialism and Spectacle at International Expositions, 1851–1893* (Charlottesville: University Press of Virginia, 2001), 156–166.
12. John J. Flinn, *Official Guide to the World's Columbian Exposition* (Chicago: Columbian Guide Company, 1893), 22–25; Paul Greenhalgh, *Ephemeral Vistas: The Expositions Universelles, Great Exhibitions, and World's Fairs, 1851–1939* (Manchester: Manchester University Press, 1988), 43.
13. Greenhalgh, *Ephemeral Vistas*, 98. At the same time, these parts of the exposition offered anthropologists occasion for research, as indeed did ethnic shows at the time: James Snead et al., eds., *Coming of Age in Chicago: The 1893 World's Fair and the Coalescence of American Anthropology* (Lincoln: University of Nebraska Press, 2016). On ethnic shows as sites of anthropological research, see Christopher Balme, "New Compatriots: Samoans on Display in Wilhelminian Germany," *Journal of Pacific History* 42 (2007): 331–344; Pascal Blanchard, ed., *Human Zoos: Science and Spectacle in the Age of Colonial Empires* (Liverpool: Liverpool University Press, 2008).
14. Nathan Cardon, *A Dream of the Future: Race, Empire, and Modernity at the Atlanta and Nashville World's Fairs* (Oxford: Oxford University Press, 2018), 5; Debra Hanson, "East Meets West: Re-presenting the Arab-Islamic World at the Nineteenth-Century World's Fairs," in *Expanding Nationalisms at World Fairs:*

*Identity, Diversity, and Exchange, 1851–1915,* ed. David Raizman and Ethan Robey (London: Routledge, 2018), 15–32.
15. Rosendorf, "Expositions," 371. For comparison, see Alexander C. T. Geppert, "World's Fairs," in *EGO: Europäische Geschichte Online,* January 15, 2018, para. 9, http://ieg-ego.eu/en/threads/crossroads/knowledge-spaces/alexander-c-t-geppert-worlds-fairs.
16. Timothy Mitchell, "The World as Exhibition," *Comparative Studies in Society and History* 31, no. 2 (1989): 217–236.
17. Greenhalgh, *Ephemeral Vistas*; Zeynep Çelik, *Displaying the Orient: Architecture of Islam at Nineteenth-Century World's Fairs* (Berkeley: University of California Press, 1992); Tessa J. Bartholomeusz, "Dharmapala at Chicago: Mahayana Buddhist or Sinhala Chauvinist," in *A Museum of Faiths: Histories and Legacies of the 1893 World's Parliament of Religions,* ed. Eric J. Ziolkowski (Atlanta, GA: Scholars Press, 1993), 235–250; Richard Hughes Seager, *The World's Parliament of Religions: The East/West Encounter, Chicago, 1893* (Bloomington: Indiana University Press, 2009).
18. Rossiter Johnson, *A History of the World's Columbian Exposition. Held in Chicago in 1893* (New York: Appleton, 1897), 6–7; Benedict, "The Anthropology of World's Fairs," 42.
19. William Cronon, *Nature's Metropolis: Chicago and the Great West* (New York: Norton, 1991), 207–260; Michael D. Wise, "Meat," in *The Routledge History of American Foodways,* ed. Wise and Jennifer Jensen Wallach (New York: Routledge, 2016), 97–112; Boris Loheide, "Beef Around the World. Die Globalisierung des Rindfleischhandels bis 1914," *Comparativ* 17, no. 3 (2007): 46–67.
20. Upton Sinclair, *The Jungle* (New York: Doubleday, Page & Co., 1906). On *The Jungle,* see also Kevin Mattson, *Upton Sinclair and the Other American Century* (Hoboken, NJ: Wiley, 2006), 57–67.
21. Adam D. Shprintzen, *The Vegetarian Crusade: The Rise of an American Reform Movement, 1817–1921* (Chapel Hill: University of North Carolina Press, 2013), 154.
22. Shprintzen, 10–58.
23. Shprintzen, 59–62.
24. Shprintzen, 115–155.
25. Förster, an author of an anti-Semitic petition addressed to Bismarck, was already known for his anti-Semitic take on animal welfare. Miriam Zerbel, "Tierschutzbewegung," in *Handbuch zur "völkischen Bewegung" 1871–1918,* ed. Uwe Puschner (Munich: De Gruyter, 1999), 546–557. Neither this nor his pronounced nationalism, however, prevented him from entertaining a wide-ranging international network. His association included members from Britain, France, Russia, and India. *Verzeichnis der Mitglieder des internationalen Vereins zur Bekämpfung der wissenschaftlichen Tierfolter* (Guben: Albert Koenig, 1889).
26. Ida B. Wells, ed., *The Reason Why the Colored American Is Not in the World's Columbian Exposition: The Afro-American's Contribution to Columbian Literature* (Urbana: University of Illinois Press, 1999). On the participation of Black Americans in the World's Columbian Exposition, see Reed, *Black Chicago's First Century,* 1:359–382.
27. "International Vegetarian Congress, Chicago, June, 1893," *Vegetarian Messenger* 7 (1893): 282–286; Karen Iacobbo and Michael Iacobbo, *Vegetarian America:*

## 3. THE CHICAGO EFFECT

*A History* (Westport, CT: Praeger, 2004), 116. Douglass had already been in contact with vegetarians as possible sympathizers with the Black American cause. During a trip to Ireland in the 1840s, he had been supported by abolitionists who embraced vegetarianism. "Frederick Douglass to William Lloyd Garrison, Dublin, 16 September 1845," in *The Frederick Douglass Papers*, ser. 3, *Correspondence*, vol. 1, *1842–1852*, ed. John McKivigan (New Haven, CT: Yale University Press, 2009), 52–56.

28. Catherine Albanese, *A Republic of Mind and Spirit: A Cultural History of American Metaphysical Religion* (New Haven, CT: Yale University Press, 2007), 346–350; Vijay Prashad, *The Karma of Brown Folk* (Minneapolis: University of Minnesota Press, 2001), 58–65; Arthur Christy, *The Orient in American Transcendentalism: A Study of Emerson, Thoreau, and Alcott* (New York: Columbia University Press, 1932), 199–222. India also played a role in the alternative religious movement known as New Thought, on which more below. Charles Samuel Braden, *Spirits in Rebellion: The Rise and Development of New Thought* (Dallas: Southern Methodist University Press, 1963), 102, 173–174, 289, 414.

29. Alice Bunker Stockham, "Food of the Orient," *Hygienic Review* 2 (1893): 315–322.

30. "International Vegetarian Congress, Chicago, June, 1893," *Hygienic Review* 2 (1893): 231–232; Satish K. Kapoor, *Cultural Contact and Fusion: Swami Vivekananda in the West, 1893–96* (Jalandhar: ABS, 1987), 46; Indra Chowdhury-Sengupta, "Reconstructing Hinduism on a World Platform: The World's First Parliament of Religions, Chicago 1892," in *SOAS Studies on South Asia*, ed. William Radice (Delhi: Oxford University Press, 1998), 22; *Lucifer. A Theosophical Magazine* 14 (March–August 1894): 174; Harold W. French, *The Swan's Wide Waters: Ramakrishna and Western Culture* (Port Washington, NY: Kenniket, 1974), 54.

31. John Henry Barrows, *The World's Parliament of Religions. An Illustrated and Popular Story of the World's First Parliament of Religions, Held in Chicago in Connection with the Columbian Exposition of 1893* (Chicago: Parliament Publishing Co., 1893), 64. On *shuddhi*, see Harald Fischer-Tiné, "Arya Samaj," in *Brill's Encyclopedia of Hinduism*, vol. 5, *Religious Symbols, Hinduism and Migration, Contemporary Communities Outside South Asia, Some Modern Religious Groups and Teachers*, ed. Knut A. Jacobsen (Leiden: Brill, 2012), 389–396; C. S. Adcock, *The Limits of Tolerance: Indian Secularism and the Politics of Religious Freedom* (New York: Oxford University Press, 2014), 116–142.

32. Seager, *The World's Parliament of Religions*, 296–313; Gwilym Beckerlegge, "The Early Spread of Vedanta Societies: An Example of 'Imported Localism,'" *Numen* 51, no. 3 (2004): 296–320. On this aspect, see also Maria Moritz, "Between 'Eastern Sacred Space' and Esoteric Capitals of 'the West': Indian Theosophists as Mediators Between India and Euro-America, 1882–1893," in *Capitales de l'ésotérisme européen et dialogue des cultures. Actes du IIe colloque international, European Society for the Study of Western Esotericism 2–4 Juillet 2009*, ed. European Society for the Study of Western Esotericism (Strasbourg, FR: Maison interuniversitaire des sciences de l'homme, 2009), 181–196.

33. However, both Anagarika Dharmapala and Virchand Gandhi argued that "taking life" was considered unlawful in Buddhism and Jainism. Anagharika Dharmapala, "The World's Debt to Buddha," in Barrows, *The World's Parliament of*

## 3. THE CHICAGO EFFECT

*Religions*, 868, 873; Virchand A. Gandhi, "The Philosophy and Ethics of the Jains," in Barrows, *The World's Parliament of Religions*, 1226.

34. Swami Vivekānanda, "Response to Welcome at the World's Parliament of Religions, Chicago 11th September, 1893," in *Complete Works of Swami Vivekananda*, vol. 1 (Calcutta: Ramakrishna Math, 2010), 324–326.
35. Vivekānanda, 326.
36. Meena Nanda, "Madame Blavatsky's Children: Modern Hindu Encounters with Darwinism," in *Handbook of Religion and the Authority of Science*, ed. James R. Lewis and Olav Hammer (Leiden: Brill, 2012), 279–344.
37. Parama Roy, "A Dietetics of Virile Emergency," *Women's Studies International Forum* 14, no. 4 (2014): 255–265. Karl Baier, in his history of yoga, also cites the autobiography of Paul Deussen, a German Indologist who, having met Vivekananda in Europe in 1896, later recalled his hearty appetite for meat and wine. Paul Deussen, *Mein Leben* (Leipzig: Brockhaus, 1922), 306–307, cited in Karl Baier, *Yoga auf dem Weg nach Westen. Beiträge zur Rezeptionsgeschichte* (Würzburg: Königshausen und Neumann, 1998), 174n326.
38. Roy, "A Dietetics of Virile Emergency."
39. While some Kayasths opted for vegetarianism during the nineteenth century to advance socially by adapting to Brahmin norms, as Lucy Carroll has shown, Vivekananda's case shows that this was not a uniform trend. Lucy Carroll, "Origins of the Kayastha Temperance Movement," *Indian Economic & Social History Review* 11, no. 4 (1974): 432–447.
40. On Ramakrishna's biography, see the contrasting books by Kripal and Sen, with Kripal stressing the physical aspects of tantrism, including the consumption of meat and alcohol, and Sen painting a bowdlerized picture of Ramakrishna's teaching. Jeffrey J. Kripal, *Kālī's Child: The Mystical and the Erotic in the Life and Teachings of Ramakrishna* (Chicago: University of Chicago Press, 1995); Amiya Prosad Sen, *Ramakrishna Paramahamsa: The Sadhaka of Dakshineswar* (Delhi: Penguin, 2010).
41. Sanjuka Gupta, "The Domestication of a Goddess: *Caraṇa-Tīrtha* Kālīghāt, the *Mahāpīṭha* of Kālī," in *Encountering Kālī: In the Margins, at the Center, in the West*, ed. Rachel Fell McDermott (Berkeley: University of California Press, 2003), 64; Suchitra Samanta, "The 'Self-Animal' and Divine Digestion: Goat Sacrifice to the Goddess Kali in Bengal," *Journal of Asian Studies* 53, no. 3 (1994): 779–803. In line with the generally negative colonial perspective on Kali worship, Indologist Max Müller considered Kali worship to be polluting the Vedic tradition. Hugh Urban, "'India's Darkest Heart': Kālī in the Colonial Imagination," in McDermott, *Encountering Kālī*, 169–195.
42. Sister Devamata, an American Vedanta follower who visited India in the 1920s, mentions having learned from elder members of the order that Ramakrishna tailored his followers' diets to their specific missions and possibly also their castes. Sister Devamata, *Days in an Indian Monastery* (La Crescenta, CA: Ananda Ashram, 1927), 31. On Devamata's remarks regarding the caste system, see Devamata, 301–314. On caste in Vivekananda's work, see Jyotirmaya Sharma, *Hindutva: Exploring the Idea of Hindu Nationalism* (New Delhi: Harper Collins, 2011), 109–114.

## 3. THE CHICAGO EFFECT

43. Swami Vivekānanda, *Vedânta Philosophy: Lectures on Jnâna-Yoga* (New York: Vedanta Society, 1902), 209.
44. Elizabeth de Michelis, "Modern Yoga: History and Forms," in *Yoga in the Modern World: Uses, Adaptations, Appropriations*, ed. Jean Byrne and Mark Singleton (London: Routledge, 2008), 150.
45. Michelis, 160; Dermot Killingley, "Manufacturing Yogis: Swami Vivekananda as a Yoga Teacher," in *Gurus of Modern Yoga*, ed. Mark Singleton and Ellen Goldberg (Oxford: Oxford University Press, 2014); Lola Williamson, *Transcendent in America: Hindu-Inspired Meditation Movements as New Religion* (New York: NYU Press, 2010), 26–40.
46. Mark Singleton, "Modern Yoga," in *Brill's Encyclopedia of Hinduism*, vol. 3, *Religious Specialists—Religious Traditions—Philosophy*, ed. Knut A. Jacobson et al. (Leiden: Brill, 2011), 782–788.
47. Singleton, 782–788.
48. Andrea Jain, *Selling Yoga: From Counterculture to Pop Culture* (Oxford: Oxford University Press, 2014), 1–19. As scholars like Carl Ernst and Nile Green have shown, Yoga and Sufism have a long and entangled history. According to Green, it was only in the late nineteenth century, with its increasing communalist climate, that Hindus and Muslims sought to purge their respective meditative traditions of the influence of the religious other. Carl W. Ernst, "Situating Sufism and Yoga," *Journal of the Royal Asiatic Society*, 3rd ser., 15, no. 1 (2005): 15–43; Nile Green, "Breathing in India, c. 1890," *Modern Asian Studies* 42, nos. 2–3 (2008): 281–315.
49. James Mallinson, "Haṭha Yoga," in Jacobson et al., *Brill's Encyclopedia of Hinduism*, 3:770–781. As Andrea Jain emphasizes, protagonists stressing the physical dimensions of yoga in the West often faced charges of indecency, which resulted in a "bifurcation between yogic meditative, philosophical, and ethical dimensions . . . and the physical techniques associated with hatha yoga." Jain, *Selling Yoga*, 27.
50. Mark Singleton, *Yoga Body: The Origins of Modern Posture Practice* (Oxford: Oxford Academic, 2010), 40.
51. Singleton, 71. Michelis, "Modern Yoga," 21–22.
52. Swami Vivekānanda, *Yoga Philosophy: Lectures . . . On Raja Yoga, or Conquering the Internal Nature: Also Patanjali's Yoga Aphorisms, with Commentaries, etc.*, 7th ed. (New York: Baker & Taylor, 1899), 211, 257–262. On the importance of concentration in Vivekananda's interpretation of yoga, see also Karl Baier, "Swami Vivekananda: Reform Hinduism, Nationalism and Scientistic Yoga," *Interdisciplinary Journal for Religion and Transformation in Contemporary Society* 5 (2019): 230–257.
53. Nanda, "Madame Blavatsky's Children," 279–344; C. Mackenzie Brown, "Vivekananda and the Scientific Legitimation of Advaita Vedānta," in *Handbook of Religion and the Authority of Science*, ed. James R. Lewis and Olav Hammer (Leiden: Brill, 2012), 207–248.
54. Ruth Harris, "Vivekananda, Sarah Farmer, and Global Spiritual Transformations in the Fin De Siècle," *Journal of Global History* 14, no. 2 (2019): 179–198.
55. *Patañjali's Yoga Sūtra*, trans. Shyam Ranganathan (Gurgaon: Penguin, 2008), 109–110, 169–182, 187–188, 191.

## 3. THE CHICAGO EFFECT

56. Vivekānanda, *Yoga Philosophy*, 15–16.
57. Harris, "Vivekananda, Sarah Farmer, and Global Spiritual Transformations in the Fin De Siècle," 179–198.
58. Sister Shivani, *An Apostle of Monism: An Authentic Account of the Activities of Swami Abhedananda in America* (Calcutta: Ramakrishna Vedanta Math, 1947), 91. On the further development of Vivekananda's mission in the United States (which continues to this day), see Carl T. Jackson, *Vedanta for the West: The Ramakrishna Movement in the United States* (Bloomington: Indiana University Press, 1994); Philippe Deslippe, "The Swami Circuit: Mapping the Terrain of Early American Yoga," *Journal of Yoga Studies* 1 (2018): 5–44.
59. Shivani, *An Apostle of Monism*.
60. "Swami Vivekananda to Swami Abhedananda, USA, November 1894," in *Complete Works of Swami Vivekananda*, vol. 7, 5th ed. (Calcutta: Advaita Ashrama, 1958), 1965.
61. Swami Abhedananda, *Why a Hindu Is a Vegetarian. Delivered Before the Vegetarian Society, New York, March 22, 1898* (New York: Vedanta Society, 1900).
62. The book was also published in Germany and reviewed in the *Vegetarische Warte*: Benno Buerdorff, "Review of Swami Abhedananda 1. Warum verwirft ein Hindu das moderne Kirchentum, obwohl er Christus anerkennt? . . . 2. Warum sind alle Hindus Vegetarier?," *Vegetarische Warte* 36 (1903): 137.
63. Buerdorff, 1.
64. Buerdorff, 2.
65. June McDaniel, *Offering Flowers, Feeding Skulls: Popular Goddess Worship in West Bengal* (Oxford: Oxford University Press, 2004), 34–38, 136.
66. Abhedananda, *Why a Hindu Is a Vegetarian*, 6.
67. Abhedananda, 6.
68. Abhedananda, 15.
69. Tithi Bhattacharya, "Tracking the Goddess: Religion, Community, and Identity in the Durga Puja Ceremonies of Nineteenth-Century Calcutta," *Journal of Asian Studies* 66, no. 4 (2007): 919–962; Hillary Rodrigues, "Durgā," in *Brill's Encyclopedia of Hinduism Online*, ed. Knut A. Jacobsen et al. (2018), http://dx.doi.org/10.1163/2212-5019_BEH_COM_1030180 (accessed April 12, 2021).
70. Swami Abhedananda, *Leaves from My Diary*, in *Complete Works of Swami Abhedananda*, vol. 10 (Calcutta: Ramakrishna Vedanta Math, 1970), 12.
71. "Sarada Devi to Swami Abhedananda, Calcutta, March 1899," in *Complete Works of Swami Abhedananda*, 10:111.
72. Swami Abhedananda, *Complete Works of Swami Abhedananda*, 10:322n5.
73. "How to Gain Self-Control," *Vedanta Monthly Bulletin* 2, no. 1 (1906-7): 19–29; "How to Be a Yogi," in *Complete Works of Swami Abhedananda*, 10:29; "Yoga, Its Theory and Practice," in *Complete Works of Swami Abhedananda*, 10:362–363, 420.
74. Several scholars have shown that Vedanta, with its emphasis on the female goddesses Kali and Durga and feminine spiritual energy, met with most resonance among white upper- and middle-class women—an aspect it shared with New Thought. Hiltrud Rüstau, "The Ramakrishna Mission: Its Female Aspect," in *Gurus and Their Followers: New Religious Reform Movements in Colonial India*, ed. Anthony Copley (New Delhi: Oxford University Press, 2000), 83–103; Elleke Boehmer, *Empire, the National, and the Postcolonial (1890–1920): Resistance in Interaction* (Oxford: Oxford University Press, 2005), 79–123.

## 3. THE CHICAGO EFFECT

75. See, for instance, "Sun Worshiper Is Back," *Chicago Daily Tribune*, April 30, 1906, 4. While research on Mazdaznan in Germany is copious, there is little research so far on its beginnings in the United States or its character as a transnational movement, although studies on the German branch generally briefly mention its origins in Chicago. Bernadett Bigalke, however, places the movement in the context of New Thought. Bigalke, *Lebensreform und Esoterik um 1900. Die Leipziger alternativ-religiöse Szene am Beispiel der Internationalen Theosophischen Verbrüderung* (Würzburg: Ergon, 2016), 188–215. For other studies focusing primarily on Mazdaznan in Germany, see Johannes Graul, *Nonkonforme Religionen im Visier der Polizei. Eine Untersuchung am Beispiel der Mazdaznan-Religion im deutschen Kaiserreich* (Würzburg: Ergon, 2013); Séverine Desponds, "Eugenik und die Konstruktion der weiblichen Übernatur. Eine Fallstudie über die Mazdaznan-Bewegung in den vierziger Jahren," in *Handbuch Gender und Religion*, ed. Anna-Katharina Höpflinger (Göttingen: Vandenhoeck & Ruprecht, 2008), 297–307; Ulrich Linse, "Mazdaznan," in *Lexikon neureligiöser Gruppen, Szenen und Weltanschauungen: Orientierungen im religiösen Pluralismus*, ed. Harald Baer and Thomas Becker (Freiburg/Breisgau: Herder, 2005), 776–777; Linse, "Mazdaznan—die Rassenreligion vom arischen Friedensreich," in *Völkische Religion und Krisen der Moderne. Entwürfe "arteigener" Glaubenssysteme seit der Jahrhundertwende*, ed. Stefanie V. Schnurbein and Justus H. Ulbricht (Würzburg: Königshausen & Neumann, 2001), 268–291; Bernd Wedemeyer-Kolwe, *"Der Neue Mensch": Körperkultur im Kaiserreich und in der Weimarer Republik* (Würzburg: Königshausen & Neumann, 2004), 153–163; Wolfgang R. Krabbe, *Gesellschaftsveränderung durch Lebensreform* (Göttingen: Vandenhoeck und Ruprecht, 1974), 73–77. Michael Stausberg analyzes Mazdaznan's appropriation of Zoroastrian elements: Stausberg, "Para-Zoroastrians: Memetic Traditions and Appropriations," in *Parsis in India and the Diaspora*, ed. John R. Hinnells and Alan Williams (London: Routledge, 2007), 236–254; Stausberg, *Die Religion Zarathushtras*, vol. 2 (Stuttgart: Kohlhammer, 2004), 378–401.
76. Linse, "Mazdaznan—die Rassenreligion vom arischen Friedensreich," 281.
77. Léon Poliakov, *The Aryan Myth: A History of Racist and Nationalistic Ideas in Europe* (London: Chatto & Windus Heinemann, 1974), 186.
78. Linse, "Mazdaznan—die Rassenreligion vom arischen Friedensreich"; Bigalke, *Lebensreform und Esoterik um 1900*, 215–235.
79. Lisa Joy Pruitt, *A Looking-Glass for Ladies: American Protestant Women and the Orient in the Nineteenth Century* (Macon, GA: Mercer University Press, 2005).
80. Susan Nance, *How the Arabian Nights Inspired the American Dream, 1790–1935* (Chapel Hill: University of North Carolina Press, 2009), 164–170.
81. "Chicago Followers of Strange Religions," *Chicago Daily Tribune*, April 6, 1899, 46. On the spread of the Baha'i faith in the United States, see Harris, "Vivekananda, Sarah Farmer, and Global Spiritual Transformations in the Fin De Siècle"; William Garlington, *The Baha'i Faith in America* (Westport, CT: Praeger, 2005). The U.S. branch of the Baha'i community emerged in the wake of the World's Columbian Exposition, where its teachings were first presented in the United States. Bruce W. Whitmore, *The Dawning Place: The Building of a Temple, the Forging of the North American Bahá'í Community* (Wilmette, IL: Bahá'í Publishing Trust, 1984), 7.

3. THE CHICAGO EFFECT

82. *As-salāmu alaykum*, Arabic for "May peace be with you." Hanisch transcribed the greeting as was common in German sources of the time. Wedemeyer-Kolwe, *"Der neue Mensch,"* 163.
83. Stausberg, *Die Religion Zarathushtras*, 2:378–379.
84. Friedrich Nietzsche, *Also sprach Zarathustra. Ein Buch für alle und keinen*, 4 vols. (Chemnitz: Schmeitzner, 1883–1891).
85. Stausberg, "Para-Zoroastrians," 240–241. Hanisch's insistence on a vegetarian Zoroastrianism was not entirely fictitious. As Patricia Crone explains, Zoroastrianism did have a vegetarian faction in the beginning. Crone, *The Nativist Prophets of Early Islamic Iran: Rural Revolt and Local Zoroastrianism* (Cambridge: Cambridge University Press, 2012), 13, 23, 257.
86. Upton Sinclair, *The Profits of Religion* (New York: Doubleday, Page & Co., 1918), 28–31.
87. *Portrait and Biographical Record of Waukesha County, Wisconsin, Containing Biographical Sketches of Old Settlers and Representative Citizens of the County* (Chicago: Excelsior, 1894), 464–467.
88. "Hanish in Jail; U.S. Ransacks Temple of Sun," *Chicago Daily Tribune*, March 3, 1912, 1; Sinclair, *The Profits of Religion*, 250–253.
89. *Portrait and Biographical Record of Waukesha County*, 467; *Typographical Journal* 4 (1892): 9.
90. In the American vegetarian press, Mazdaznan only appeared from 1910 on. "The Sun Worshippers," *Vegetarian Magazine* 13 (1909–1910): 20; "Review of Mazdaznan Encyclopedia of Dietetics," *Vegetarian Magazine* 14 (1910): 71. This renders dubious Mazdaznan's own assertion that the group was founded around 1890, a view shared, inter alia, in Wedemeyer-Kolwe, *"Der neue Mensch,"* 155; Stausberg, *Die Religion Zarathushtras*, 2: 393.
91. Bigalke, *Lebensreform und Esoterik um 1900*, 188–215.
92. Braden, *Spirits in Rebellion*, 48–66, 85–86; Albanese, *A Republic of Mind and Spirit*, 285–287.
93. Albanese, *A Republic of Mind and Spirit*, 322–326.
94. Braden, *Spirits in Rebellion*, 6–46; Carl T. Jackson, "The New Thought Movement and the Nineteenth Century Discovery of Oriental Philosophy," *Journal of Popular Culture* 9, no. 3 (1975): 523–548. However, New Thought was not only influenced by Asian spiritual knowledge, it was also met with a degree of resonance in South Asia. This is illustrated by the oeuvre of New Thought author Edward Earle Purinton, parts of which were reprinted in an Arya Samaj journal. Edward Earle Purinton, *The Triumph of the Man Who Acts and Other Papers* (New York: McBride, 1920); Purinton, *Personal Efficiency in Business* (New York: Robert M. McBride & Co., 1919); Purinton, *Lords of Ourselves* (1908); Purinton, *The Philosophy of Fasting: A Message for Sufferers and Sinners* (New York: Benedict Lust, 1906); Purinton, "Suggestive Thoughts," *Arya Patrika* (1911): 9–10.
95. Joy Dixon, *Divine Feminine: Theosophy and Feminism in England* (Baltimore: Johns Hopkins University Press, 2001).
96. Beryl Satter, *Each Mind a Kingdom: American Women, Sexual Purity, and the New Thought Movement, 1875–1920* (Berkeley: University of California Press, 1999), 134–139; Catherine Tumber, *American Feminism and the Birth of New Age*

## 3. THE CHICAGO EFFECT

*Spirituality: Searching for the Higher Self, 1875–1915* (Lanham, MD: Rowman & Littlefield, 2002), 161–163.

97. Jürgen Martschukat, "The Pursuit of Fitness: Von Freiheit und Leistungsfähigkeit in der Geschichte der USA," *Geschichte und Gesellschaft* 42, no. 3 (2016): 409–440; Martschukat, "'The Necessity for Better Bodies to Perpetuate Our Institutions, Insure a Higher Development of the Individual, and Advance the Conditions of the Race': Physical Culture and the Formation of the Self in the Late Nineteenth and Early Twentieth Century USA," *Journal of Historical Sociology* 24, no. 4 (2011): 472–493. On the emergence of physical culture as the predecessor of modern bodybuilding, with reference to, but also many examples from outside of, the United States, see Wedemeyer-Kolwe, *"Der neue Mensch,"* 290–388; Ina Zweiniger-Bargielowska, *Managing the Body: Beauty, Health, and Fitness in Britain, 1880–1939* (Oxford: Oxford University Press, 2011), 62–104.
98. Otoman Zar Adusht Hanish, *Mazdaznan Health and Breath Culture*, 2nd ed. (Chicago: Mazdaznan Publishing Company, 1914), v. The first edition of this book, published in 1902, could not be retrieved. Note that in citations, I employ the "Hanish" spelling (as opposed to "Hanisch," used in the main text), to reflect the name under which he published.
99. Hanish, 11.
100. Hanish.
101. Hanish, 10. On the centrality of the image of the body as God's temple to New Thought, see Braden, *Spirits in Rebellion*, 109, 195.
102. On the perception of neurasthenia as a threat to heterosexual middle-class masculinity, see Tom Lutz, *American Nervousness, 1903: An Anecdotal History* (Ithaca, NY: Cornell University Press, 1991); Gail Bederman, *Manliness and Civilization: A Cultural History of Gender and Race in the United States, 1880–1917* (Chicago: University of Chicago Press, 1995), 77–120; Joachim Radkau, *Das Zeitalter der Nervosität: Deutschland zwischen Bismarck und Hitler* (Munich: Hanser, 1998), 42–74; Marijke Gijswijt-Hofstra and Roy Porter, eds., *Cultures of Neurasthenia: From Beard to the First World War* (Leiden: Brill, 2001); David G. Schuster, *Neurasthenic Nation: America's Search for Health, Comfort, and Happiness, 1869–1920* (New Brunswick, NJ: Rutgers University Press, 2011), 85–112; Julian B. Carter, *The Heart of Whiteness: Normal Sexuality and Race in America, 1880–1940* (Durham, NC: Duke University Press, 2007).
103. Hanish, *Mazdaznan Health and Breath Culture*, 31, 88.
104. Hanish, 14, 72.
105. Hanish, 28, 65.
106. Hanish, *Mazdaznan Health and Breath Culture*. *Shusumna* and *kundalini*, introduced by Hindu members of the Theosophical Society, were also terms employed among Theosophists. See, for instance, C. R. Srinivasa Ayangar, "Occult Physiology," *Theosophical Siftings* 6 (1894): 1–19.
107. Hanish, *Mazdaznan Health and Breath Culture*, vii, 33–34, 146.
108. Hanish, 38.
109. Jain, *Selling Yoga*, 34–35.
110. Hanish, *Mazdaznan Health and Breath Culture*, 106–108.
111. Hanish, 134–135.

112. Hanish, 128–129.
113. Hanish, 126–127.
114. See, for instance, Norman Chevers, *A Commentary on the Diseases of India* (London: J. & A. Churchill, 1886), 23.
115. Hanish, *Mazdaznan Health and Breath Culture*, 199.
116. Otoman Zar Adusht Hanish, *Inner Studies: A Course of Twelve Lessons* (Chicago: Sun-Worshipper Publishing Company, 1902).
117. Hanish, *Inner Studies*, 130–139. Until well into the nineteenth century, middle-class morality encouraged leaving girls in the dark about sexuality, including their own anatomy, although it is difficult to know to what extent these moral precepts were followed. Alain Corbin, "Backstage," in *A History of Private Life*, vol. 4, *From the Fires of Revolution to the Great War*, ed. Michelle Perrot (Cambridge, MA: Belknap Press of Harvard University Press, 1990), 493-494. More recent research stresses discrepancies between norm and practice, emphasizing that even in the nineteenth century, at the height of the middle-class cult of maternity, women did seek and gain access to knowledge about sex: Tanya Evans, "Knowledge and Experience: From 1750 to the 1960s," in *The Routledge History of Sex and the Body: 1500 to the Present*, ed. Sarah Toulalan and Kate Fisher (London: Routledge, 2013), 256–276. Hanisch was not the first author in the United States to make sexual knowledge available to women. Indeed, one of the first such authors was a woman, gynecologist Alice Bunker Stockham. On Stockham, see below.
118. Hanish, *Inner Studies*, 130.
119. Hanish, 130–139.
120. Hanish, 141.
121. Hanish, 109–111. Hanish's notion of gender was probably indebted to contemporary sexologists like Richard Krafft-Ebing, Havelock Ellis, Magnus Hirschfeld, or authors like Otto Weininger, all of whom challenged the idea of an absolute polarity of gender. Anna Katharina Schaffner, *Modernism and Perversion: Sexual Deviance in Sexology and Literature, 1850–1930* (Houndmills, UK: Palgrave Macmillan, 2012), 112–121; Katie Sutton, "Representing the 'Third Sex': Cultural Translations of the Sexological Encounter in Early Twentieth-Century Germany," in *Sexology and Translation: Cultural and Scientific Encounters Across the Modern World*, ed. Heike Bauer (Philadelphia: Temple University Press, 2015), 53–71; Chandak Sengoopta, *Otto Weininger: Sex, Science, and Self in Imperial Vienna* (Chicago: University of Chicago Press, 2000), 69–86.
122. Hanish, *Inner Studies*, 58.
123. Carol Smith-Rosenberg, "A Richer and a Gentler Sex," *Social Research* 53, no. 2 (1986): 283–309; Satter, *Each Mind a Kingdom*, 134–138; Marsha Silberman, "The Perfect Storm: Late Nineteenth-Century Chicago Sex Radicals: Moses Harman, Ida Craddock, Alice Stockham and the Comstock Obscenity Laws," *Journal of the Illinois State Historical Society* 102, nos. 3–4 (2009): 324–357. Stockham was not the first to come up with the idea of continence as a means of both birth control and liberating female sexuality from the burden of pregnancy. An important predecessor was the utopian Christian community in Oneida, New York, founded in the 1840s, whose members attempted to "create ideal reproductive unions in a fully controlled way," using continence in the preparatory stage of this process. Alison Bashford, "Introduction: Eugenics and the Modern World," in *The Oxford*

## 3. THE CHICAGO EFFECT

*Handbook of the History of Eugenics*, ed. Bashford (Oxford: Oxford University Press, 2010), 5–6.
124. Mallinson, "Haṭha Yoga," 770. This was also the argument for chastity (*brahmacharya*) in contemporary Hindu discourses, represented by, among others, the Arya Samaj. Harald Fischer-Tiné, "From Brahmacharya to 'Conscious Race Culture': Victorian Discourses of Science and Hindu Traditions in Early Indian Nationalism," in *Beyond Representation: Colonial and Post-Colonial Constructions of Indian Identity*, ed. Crispin Bates (New Delhi: Oxford University Press, 2006), 241–269.
125. Hanish, *Inner Studies*, 97; Edward Said, *Orientalism* (London: Penguin, 1978), 6, 186–188.
126. Hanish, *Inner Studies*, 67–68. In sexualizing "Oriental" women, Hanisch drew on a classic trope of Orientalism and particularly Orientalist painting. Said, *Orientalism*, 186–188. On the "Harem" as a sexualized place in Orientalist painting, see Ruth Bernhard Yeazell, *Harems of the Mind: Passages of Western Art and Literature* (New Haven, CT: Yale University Press, 2000), 95–134; Mary Roberts, *Intimate Outsiders: The Harem in Ottoman and Orientalist Art and Travel Literature* (Durham, NC: Duke University Press, 2007), 19–56.
127. Hanish, *Inner Studies*, 77–78.
128. Ainsley Hawthorn, "La popularisation de la 'danse du ventre.' Origine et diffusion d'un nom vulgaire," *Recherches en danse* 9 (2020), https://doi.org/10.4000/danse.3287.
129. Hanish, *Inner Studies*, 28, 79, 190, 199.
130. For an example of these "outbreathings," see Hanish, *Mazdaznan Health and Breath Culture*, vii.
131. Otoman Zar Adusht Hanish, *Ainyahita in Pearls. From the Original* (Chicago: Mazdaznan, 1913); Hanish, *Yehoshua Nazir; Jesus the Nazarite; Life of Christ* (Los Angeles: Mazdaznan Press, 1917).
132. "'Dr.' Hanish on Trial," *Chicago Daily Tribune*, June 5, 1905, 7.
133. "Hanish Plea for Release Refused: Case Continued," *Chicago Daily Tribune*, May 27, 1904, 3; "Visits to Fire Worshipers Cause Woman to Burn Self," *Chicago Daily Tribune*, March 9, 1906, 2.
134. "Boy Disappears in Cult Mystery," *Chicago Daily Tribune*, January 5, 1912, 5.
135. National Archives Chicago, Records of the United States District Court for the Northern District of Illinois 4914, 4915, 4957, and 4984.
136. Bigalke, *Lebensreform und Esoterik um 1900*, 216.
137. While later celebrated for the fourteen-point agenda whose emphasis on self-determination gave rise to anticolonial nationalism (Erez Manela, *The Wilsonian Moment: Self-Determination and the International Origins of Anticolonial Nationalism* [New York: Oxford University Press, 2007]), President Wilson also reinforced racial segregation in the United States. Eric Stevens Yellin, *Racism in the Nation's Service: Government Workers and the Color Line in Woodrow Wilson's America* (Chapel Hill: University of North Carolina Press, 2013). On Christian-Jewish relations and the rise of anti-Semitism in turn-of-the-twentieth-century Germany, see Till van Rahden, *Juden und andere Breslauer. Die Beziehungen zwischen Juden, Protestanten und Katholiken in einer deutschen Großstadt von 1860 bis 1925* (Göttingen: Vandenhoeck & Ruprecht, 2000); Helmut Walser Smith,

## 3. THE CHICAGO EFFECT

ed., *Protestants, Catholics and Jews in Germany, 1800–1914* (Oxford: Berg, 2001); Uffa Jensen, *Gebildete Doppelgänger: Bürgerliche Juden und Protestanten im 19. Jahrhundert* (Göttingen: Wallstein, 2005).

138. Ernest Renan, *The Life of Jesus* (London: Trübner & Co., 1864); Virchand R. Gandhi, *The Unknown Life of Jesus Christ. From an Ancient Manuscript, Recently Discovered in a Buddhist Monastery in Thibet by Nicholas Notovitch, Translated from the French* (Chicago: Indo-American Book Co., 1907).

139. Renan, *The Life of Jesus*, 206–207; Hanish, *Yehoshua Nazir*, 151–165; Houston Stewart Chamberlain, *Foundations of the Nineteenth Century*, vol. 1 (London: Ballantyne, 1911), 174–251.

140. Hanish, *Yehoshua Nazir*, 151–165. On the attitude of Christian missions in the Middle East toward Jews, see Bruce Masters, *Christians and Jews in the Ottoman Arab World: The Roots of Sectarianism* (Cambridge: Cambridge University Press, 2001), 148; Gudrun Krämer, "Moving Out of Place: Minorities in Middle Eastern Urban Societies, 1800–1914," in *The Urban Social History of the Middle East, 1750–1950*, ed. Peter Slugglett (Syracuse, NY: Syracuse University Press, 2008), 210; Julia Hauser, *German Religious Women in Late Ottoman Beirut: Competing Missions* (Leiden: Brill, 2015), 29, 34, 43, 252–253.

141. Eric Arden Weed, *The Religion of White Supremacy in the United States* (Lanham, MD: Lexington, 2017), 21–35.

142. Hanish, *Yehoshua Nazir*, 34–41, 183–191.

143. Hanish, 34–41, 161. This "Hinduization" of Jesus may also have been influenced by the characterization of Jesus as a "Hindu holy man" offered by the proponents of yoga in the United States. As Carl Jackson explains, "several swamis promoted the theory that Jesus had spent the crucial period between his twelfth and twenty-eighth year in Asia, studying yoga and other Eastern religious practices." Jackson, *Vedanta for the West*, 84.

144. On Anahita, see Stausberg, *Die Religion Zarathushtras*, 2:379.

145. Hanish, *Ainyahita in Pearls*, 158, 191.

146. Hanish, *Ainyahita in Pearls*, 133.

147. Hanish, 135–136.

148. Hanish, 138–139.

149. Isaac Lubelsky, "Mythological and Real Race Issues in Theosophy," in *Handbook of the Theosophical Current*, ed., Olav Hammer and Mikael Rothstein (Leiden: Brill, 2013), 335–356.

150. David Ammann, "The Coming Race and Race Hygiene," *Mazdaznan* 13 (1914): 273–286, 304–312.

151. Johannes Graul, "Die Mazdaznan-Bewegung im deutschen Kaiserreich. Eine archivalienbasierte Spurensuche," in *Nonkonformismus und europäische Religionsgeschichten / Nonconformism and European Histories of Religions*, ed. Danny Schäfer (Berlin: Lit, 2012); Graul, *Nonkonforme Religionen im Visier der Polizei*; Bigalke, *Lebensreform und Esoterik um 1900*, 211.

152. Although blood was already central to concepts of heredity in early modern Europe, particularly *Reconquista*-era Spain, it had only been racialized from the late eighteenth century on: Neil MacMaster, *Racism in Europe 1870–2000* (Houndmills, UK: Palgrave Macmillan, 2001), 22–23.

153. Marius Turda, *Modernism and Eugenics* (New York: Palgrave Macmillan, 2010), 18.

## 3. THE CHICAGO EFFECT

154. In the international eugenicist movement dominated by European and American scientists, only Europeans, North Americans, and Australians of European origin were considered white. Stefan Kühl, *For the Betterment of the Race: The Rise and Fall of the International Movement for Eugenics and Racial Hygiene* (New York: Palgrave Macmillan, 2013), 48. As studies on Arab migration to the United States during the late nineteenth century show, Arab immigrants in the United States were not necessarily classified as white, and they frequently faced racism. Alixa Naff, *Becoming American: The Early Arab Immigrant Experience* (Carbondale: Southern Illinois Press, 1985), 252–258; Randa Kayyali, *The Arab Americans* (Westport, CT: Greenwood, 2006), 46–52.
155. See chapter 2.
156. There is no such passage in the Avesta, although the sacred texts of Zoroastrianism do associate darkness with evil. *Avesta: The Religious Books of the Parsees* (Hertford, UK: Muncherjee Hormusjee Cama, 1864), vol. 1, 24, 47, 59, 78, 108, 134, 143. If his elaborations were based on a textual reference at all, Ammann probably drew on the three temperaments (*guṇas*) associated with a difference in skin color in the Hindu Bhagavad Gita and Code of Manu. On the three *guṇas*, see chapter 2.
157. Ammann, "The Coming Race and Race Hygiene," 304.
158. "Zoroastrianism—Its History," *Mazdaznan* 15 (1916): 8–13.
159. For the United States, see Jennifer Lynn Ritterhouse, *Growing Up Jim Crow: How Black and White Southern Children Learned Race* (Chapel Hill: University of North California Press, 2006); Jane Dailey, *White Fright: The Sexual Panic at the Heart of America's Racist History* (New York: Basic Books, 2020). On women's role in German colonial racism, see Lora Wildenthal, *German Women for Empire, 1884–1945* (Durham, NC: Duke University Press, 2001); Birthe Kundrus, *Moderne Imperialisten. Das Kaiserreich im Spiegel seiner Kolonien* (Cologne: Böhlau, 2003).
160. Ardaser Sorabjee N. Wadia, *The Call of the World, Being Reminiscences of a Year's Tour Round the World* (London: J. M. Dent & Sons, 1918), 127, 131–186.
161. Peter Spohr, "Noch einmal Mazdaznan," *Vegetarische Warte* 43, no. 21 (1910): 210–211; "Einige Proben aus der Mazdaznanbibel," *Vegetarische Warte* 44, no. 3 (1911): 26–27; "Zum letzten Male Mazdaznan," *Vegetarische Warte* 44, no. 15 (1911): 143–144; Dr. Bracke, "Weiteres vom Mazdaznan-Meister," *Vegetarische Warte* 46, no. 24 (1913): 234–235; "Dr. Otoman Zar Adusht Hanish oder der Janus-Kopf," *Vegetarische Warte* 46, no. 12 (1913): 117–119; Werner Zimmermann, "Masdasnan," *Tao. Monatsblätter für Verinnerlichung und Selbstgestaltung* 32 (1927): n.p.
162. On anti-Asian racism in the United States around the turn of the twentieth century, see Charles McClain, *In Search of Equality: The Chinese Struggle Against Discrimination in Nineteenth-Century America* (Berkeley: University of California Press, 1994); Seema Sohi, *Echoes of Mutiny: Race, Surveillance, and Anticolonialism in North America* (New York: Oxford University Press, 2014). For Germany, see Lars Amenda, *Fremde—Hafen—Stadt. Chinesische Migration und ihre Wahrnehmung in Hamburg 1897–1972* (Munich: Dölling und Galitz, 2006).
163. In this spirit, Hanisch founded a "Society for the Promotion of the Federation of Nations" in 1918. While its name recalled early concepts for a league of nations such as that suggested by President Theodore Roosevelt before the First World War, the society aimed at "expounding the science of genealogical ties of the Twelve

Tribes of the Aryan, or White Race." It was a short-lived initiative and does not seem to have existed beyond 1918. "Federator. The Call of Every Land," *Federator* 1, no. 1 (1918): 2–3. While espousing internationalism, Mazdaznan publications—even in English—accorded Germans a special mission in history, although not all of its members were from the German-American community. See, for instance, Ammann, "The Coming Race and Race Hygiene," 308.

164. Kühl, *For the Betterment of the Race*; Kiran Klaus Patel, "Afterword: On the Chances and Challenges of Populating Internationalism," in *Internationalists in European History*, ed. Jessica Reinisch and David Brydan (London: Bloomsbury, 2022), 263–280.

165. For Germany, see Bernd Wedemeyer-Kolwe, "The Reception of Yoga in Alternative Cultures."

166. The following volumes of British vegetarian journals are no longer available in public libraries; they are therefore quoted from the International Vegetarian Union website, which, however, does not always include volume and page numbers. " 'International Congress' at Cologne," *The Vegetarian*, September 28, 1889, https://ivu.org/index.php/blogs/congress-vegfest-updates/336-1st-international-congress-1889-rpoert-on-the-congress (accessed April 12, 2021).

167. "'International Congress' at Cologne."

168. "The Vegetarian Federal Union," *The Vegetarian*, October 12, 1889, https://ivu.org/history/vfu/constitution.html (accessed April 12, 2021).

169. "The International Vegetarian Congress," *Vegetarian Messenger*, October 1890, https://ivu.org/congress/1890/report.html (accessed April 12, 2021); "The Federal Union Report (Secretary's Report Read at Portsmouth, May, 1891)," *The Vegetarian*, May 23, 1891, https://ivu.org/history/vfu/secretary.html (accessed April 12, 2021).

170. "2nd International Vegetarian Congress 1890—London, England" (May 1891), International Vegetarian Union, https://ivu.org/index.php/blogs/congress-vegfest-updates/192-2nd-international-vegetarian-congress-1890-london-england (accessed April 12, 2021).

171. "The Federal Union Report (Secretary's Report Read at Portsmouth, May, 1891)."

172. In fact, the cook was a retired Indian army officer, Edward Palmer, whose grandmother was from an Indian Muslim princely family. "The International Vegetarian Congress, September 13th to 18th, 1897," *Vegetarian Messenger*, October 1897, https://ivu.org/congress/1897/manchester.html (accessed April 12, 2021). See also Wikipedia, s.v. "Veeraswamy," last modified March 22, 2023, 23:38, https://en.wikipedia.org/wiki/Veeraswamy. Edward Palmer went on to open an Indian restaurant in Mayfair. As his posthumously published cookbook suggests, however, its menu included vegetarian as well as meat dishes. E. P. [Edward Palmer] Veerasawmy, *Indian Cookery for Use in All Countries* (Bombay: New Book Co., 1947).

173. "Vegetarian Federal Union," *The Vegetarian*, June 9, 1900, https://ivu.org/history/vfu/1900-paris1.html (accessed April 12, 2021).

174. "Paris Exhibition: The Coming Vegetarian Congress," *The Vegetarian*, May 5, 1900, https://ivu.org/history/vfu/1900-paris1.html (accessed April 12, 2021).

175. "International Vegetarian Congress 1904—St Louis, USA," *Vegetarian Messenger*, January 1905, https://ivu.org/index.php/blogs/congress-vegfest-updates/196-international-vegetarian-congress-1904-st-louis-usa (accessed April 12, 2021).

4. BETWEEN BUDDHA, GANDHI, SUFISM, AND MASCULINITY

176. Markus A. Denzel, "Messe- und Finanzplatz," in *Geschichte der Stadt Leipzig*, vol. 3, *Vom Wiener Kongress bis zum Ersten Weltkrieg*, ed. Susanne Schötz (Leipzig: Leipziger Universitätsverlag, 2017), 561–572; Thomas Keiderling, "Buchstadt auf dem Höhepunkt," in Schötz, *Geschichte der Stadt Leipzig*, 3:592–599; Jens Blecher, "Universität Leipzig," in Schötz, *Geschichte der Stadt Leipzig*, 3:703–711; Marion Recknagel, "Musikstadt Leizig—Die Silberne Zeit," in Schötz, *Geschichte der Stadt Leipzig*, 3:733–741.
177. Florentine Fritzen, *Gesünder leben. Die Lebensreformbewegung im 20. Jahrhundert* (Stuttgart: Steiner, 2006), 38.
178. Bigalke, *Lebensreform und Esoterik um 1900*; Mustafa Haikal, "Auf der Suche nach dem neuen Menschen," in Schötz, *Geschichte der Stadt Leipzig*, 3:880–892. Leipzig natural healing authorities like Louis Kuhne were popularized in the United States by Benedict Lust, a publisher of German origin specializing in life reform, who published translations of pertinent German works and a journal, *Naturopath* (later: *Nature's Path*), that brought together expertise from Germany, the United States, Britain, and India. It was through these channels that Gandhi became familiar with the work of German naturopaths like Kuhne and Adolf Just, to which he introduced his readers in his widely read *Guide to Health*. The guide was translated into German and reviewed in German-speaking periodicals, with reviewers criticizing his adoption of Western knowledge, but praising the supposedly authentic Indian knowledge presented in the book, thus ignoring the extent to which knowledge around nature cure and vegetarianism had become pidgin knowledge. Louis Kuhne, *Neo-naturopathy. New Science of Healing, or the Doctrine of the Unity of Diseases* (Butler, NJ: Benedict Lust, 1917); Kuhne, *The Naturopath and Herald of Health* (later: *Nature's Path*, 1902–1937 [?]); Joseph S. Alter, *Gandhi's Body: Sex, Diet, and the Politics of Nationalism* (Philadelphia: University of Philadelphia Press, 2000), 59–64; Mohandas Karamchand Gandhi, *A Guide to Health*, trans. A. Rama Iyer (Madras: S. Ganesan, 1921), 44–46, 90, 95–96; Gandhi, *Ein Wegweiser zur Gesundheit* (Erlenbach-Zürich: Rotapfel, 1925); S., "Mahatma Gandhi als Wegweiser zur Gesundheit," *Die weiße Fahne* 6, no. 5 (1925): 211–214; Werner Zimmermann, "Review of Mahatma Gandhi, Wegweiser zur Gesundheit (a Guide to Health), Zürich: Rotapfel, 1925," *Tao. Monatsblätter für Verinnerlichung und Selbstgestaltung*, no. 14 (1925): 30–31.
179. See "History of the International Vegetarian Union," International Vegetarian Union, https://ivu.org/history-legacy-pages/2013-02-17-21-29-31.html (accessed October 17, 2019).

## 4. BETWEEN BUDDHA, GANDHI, SUFISM, AND MILITANT MASCULINITY

1. In 1914, Esperanto vegetarians founded a journal and an organization of their own, the Vegetara Ligo Esperantista, later called the TEVA (Tutmondo Esperanta Vegetara Asocio). This organization published an Esperanto vegetarian periodical, *Vegetarano*, into the late 1950s, featuring articles on vegetarianism, pacifism, temperance, and the anticolonial struggle. See, for instance, "La Vegetarismo Post La Militio," *Vegetarano* 4, no. 1 (1920): 1–2; "Alkohola Veneno Kaj Nikotina

## 4. BETWEEN BUDDHA, GANDHI, SUFISM, AND MASCULINITY

Veneno En Rilato Kun La Seksa Edukado," *Vegetarano* 6, no. 3 (1922): 18–19; "Gandhi," *Vegetarano* 13, no. 4 (1930): 40. On the political dimensions and heterogeneity of the Esperanto movement, see Roberto Garvía, *Esperanto and Its Rivals: The Struggle for an International Language* (Philadelphia: University of Pennsylvania Press, 2015), 59–65, 103–116; Ulrich Lins, *Dangerous Language*, vol. 1, *Esperanto Under Hitler and Stalin* (London: Palgrave Macmillan, 2017).

2. From a wealth of articles, see, for instance, Werner Zimmermann, "Berichte. weltjugendtreffen 1927," *Tau*, no. 33 (1927): 125; "Internationales Jugendlager—Baumarcus Schweiz," *Vegetarische Presse* 10 (1927): 117; J., "Für einen weltbund der jugend," *Tau*, no. 51 (1928): 37; Josef Drahovsky, "Ungarischer Vegetarier-Verein," *Vegetarische Presse* 12 (1929): 4–5; James Hough, "England," *Vegetarische Presse* 12 (1929): 114–115; "Norwegen. Vegetarierkongreß in Oslo," *Vegetarische Presse* 13 (1930): 126; "Von der Tätigkeit des Vegetarier-Vereins zu Dorpat im Jahre 1932," *Vegetarische Presse* 16 (1933): 139–140.

3. This was, for instance, true for both Gandhi and Tolstoy: Werner Zimmermann, "Review of Mahatma Gandhi, Wegweiser zur Gesundheit (a Guide to Health), Zurich: Rotapfel, 1925," *Tao*, no. 14 (1925): 30–31; W. Schröter, "Leo Tolstoj zu seinem 100. Geburtstag," *Vegetarische Presse* 11 (1928): 118; "Review of Mahatma Gandhi: Mein Leben, Leipzig: Insel, 1931," *Vegetarische Presse* 14 (1931): 69.

4. See, for instance, "Esperanto-Vegetariertag in Leipzig," *Vegetarische Presse* 12, no. 8 (1928): 103. The Nazi government took a hostile attitude toward Esperanto, eventually abolishing its organizations in 1940. Lins, *Dangerous Language*, 1:97–118.

5. The Sanskrit inscription on the facade (*Griha Vidyaya Dadet Om*) means "This building is where education/knowledge is rightfully imparted."

6. See, for instance, Kris Manjapra, *Age of Entanglement: German and Indian Intellectuals Across Empire* (Cambridge, MA: Harvard University Press, 2014); Benjamin Zachariah, "Indian Political Activities in Germany, 1914–1945," in *Transcultural Encounters Between Germany and India*, ed. Joanne Miyang Cho, Eric Kurlander, and Douglas T. McGetchin (Abingdon, UK: Routledge, 2014), 141–154; Harald Fischer-Tiné, "The Other Side of Internationalism: Switzerland as a Hub of Militant Anti-colonialism (c. 1910–1920)," in *Colonial Switzerland: Rethinking Colonialism from the Margins*, ed. Patricia Purtschert and Harald Fischer-Tiné (Basingstoke, UK: Palgrave Macmillan, 2015), 221–258; Razak Khan, "Entanglements of Translation: Psychology, Pedagogy, and Youth Reform in German and Urdu," *Comparative Studies of South Asia, Africa and the Middle East* 40, no. 2 (2020): 295–308; Douglas T. McGetchin, *Indology, Indomania, and Orientalism: Ancient India's Rebirth in Modern Germany* (Madison, NJ: Fairleigh Dickinson University Press, 2009); McGetchin, "The Rise of Ancient India in Modern Germany," in *On the Paths of Enlightenment: The Myth of India in Western Culture, 1808–2017*, ed. Elio Schenini (Geneva: Skira, 2017), 40–55.

7. Paula Diehl, *Macht—Mythos—Utopie. Die Körperbilder der SS-Männer* (Berlin: Akademie-Verlag, 2005), 74–78.

8. On the German youth movement, see Ulrike Brunotte, *Zwischen Eros und Krieg. Männerbund und Ritual in der Moderne* (Berlin: Wagenbach, 2004); Birgit Dahlke, *Jünglinge der Moderne. Jugendkult und Männlichkeit in der Literatur um 1900* (Cologne: Böhlau, 2006); Ulrich Herrmann, ed., *"Mit uns zieht die neue Zeit..."*

## 4. BETWEEN BUDDHA, GANDHI, SUFISM, AND MASCULINITY

*Der Wandervogel in der deutschen Jugendbewegung* (Weinheim: Juventa, 2006); John Alexander Williams, *Turning to Nature in Germany: Hiking, Nudism, and Conservation, 1900–1940* (Stanford, CA: Stanford University Press, 2007); Christian Niemeyer, *Die dunklen Seiten der Jugendbewegung. Vom Wandervogel zur Hitlerjugend* (Tübingen: Francke, 2013); Karl Braun, Felix Linzner, and John Khairi-Taraki, eds., *Avantgarden der Biopolitik. Jugendbewegung, Lebensreform und Strategien biologischer, Aufrüstung,'* (Göttingen: V&R Unipress, 2017).

9. See, for instance, Wolfgang R. Krabbe, *Gesellschaftsveränderung durch Lebensreform* (Göttingen: Vandenhoeck und Ruprecht, 1974), 50–77; Ulrich Linse, ed., *Zurück o Mensch zur Mutter Erde: Landkommunen in Deutschland 1890–1933* (Frankfurt/Main: Deutscher Taschenbuch-Verlag, 1983); Linse, *Barfüßige Propheten: Erlöser der zwanziger Jahre* (Berlin: Siedler, 1983); Linse, *Ökopax und Anarchie: Eine Geschichte der ökologischen Bewegungen in Deutschland* (Frankfurt/Main: Dt. Taschenbuch-Verl, 1986); Eva Barlösius, *Naturgemäße Lebensführung. Zur Geschichte der Lebensreform um die Jahrhundertwende* (Frankfurt/Main: Campus, 1997), 24–25, 36–47; Kai Buchholz, ed., *Die Lebensreform: Entwürfe zur Neugestaltung von Leben und Kunst um 1900* (Darmstadt: Häusser, 2001); Florentine Fritzen, *Gesünder leben: Die Lebensreformbewegung im 20. Jahrhundert* (Stuttgart: Steiner, 2006); Corinna Treitel, *Eating Nature in Modern Germany: Food, Agriculture, and Environment, c. 1870 to 2000* (Cambridge: Cambridge University Press, 2017), 29–40.

10. Bernd Wedemeyer-Kolwe, *"Der Neue Mensch": Körperkultur im Kaiserreich und in der Weimarer Republik* (Würzburg: Königshausen & Neumann, 2004); Suzanne Marchand, "Eastern Wisdom in an Age of Western Despair: Orientalism in 1920s Central Europe," in *Weimar Thought: A Contested Legacy*, ed. Peter Gordon and John McCormick (Princeton, NJ: Princeton University Press, 2013), 341–360; Bernadett Bigalke, *Lebensreform und Esoterik um 1900. Die Leipziger alternativreligiöse Szene am Beispiel der Internationalen Theosophischen Verbrüderung* (Würzburg: Ergon, 2016).

11. In this, my research connects to recent studies on life reform more broadly, which have shown the same: Elija Horn, *Indien als Erzieher: Orientalismus in der deutschen Reformpädagogik und Jugendbewegung 1918–1933* (Bad Heilbrunn: Verlag Julius Klinkhardt, 2018); Khan, "Entanglements of Translation," 295–308.

12. On this, see also Julia Hauser, "The Birth of the Ascetic Leader. 'Die Botschaft des Mahatma Gandhi' in Troubled Weimar Germany," in *Nodes of Translation: Rethinking Modern Intellectual History Between South Asia and Germany*, ed. Martin Christof-Füchsle and Razak Khan (Berlin: De Gruyter, forthcoming).

13. Krabbe, *Gesellschaftsveränderung durch Lebensreform*, 459; Karl Eduard Rothschuh, *Naturheilbewegung, Reformbewegung, Alternativbewegung* (Stuttgart: Hippokrates-Verl., 1983), 126; Fritzen, *Gesünder leben*, 252–253.

14. Ludwig Ankenbrand, "Eine buddhistische Wallfahrt rund um die Welt," *Die Buddhistische Welt: Deutsche Monatsschrift für Buddhismus* 5 (1911–1912): 248; Ankenbrand, "Weltreise-Vorspiel (mit einem Bilde)," *Vegetarische Warte* 45, nos. 63–64 (1912): 63–64; "Eine Weltreise zu Fuß," *Mazdaznan* 4 (1911): 202.

15. Jörg Albrecht, "Ludwig Ankenbrand. Introduction," in *Religious Dynamics Under the Impact of Imperialism and Colonialism*, ed. Björn Bentlage et al. (Leiden: Brill, 2016), 186–191. Ankenbrand's publications on animal welfare are too numerous to

be mentioned in full. Interestingly, he wrote several books on birds, arguing that they preferred living in a cage to living in nature. Ludwig Ankenbrand, *Vogelschutz im Winter und Sommer* (Berlin: Berliner Tierschutz-Verein, 1909), 77.

16. On Hewavitharane's contribution to reformist Buddhism, see Richard F. Gombrich, *Theravāda Buddhism: A Social History from Ancient Benares to Modern Colombo*, 2nd ed. (London: Routledge, 2006), 186–194; Maria Moritz, "'The Empire of Righteousness': Anagarika Dharmapala and His Vision of Buddhist Asianism," in *Asianisms: Regionalist Interactions and Asian Integration*, ed. Nicola Spakowski and Marc Frey (Singapore: National University of Singapore Press, 2016), 19–48; David L. McMahan, *The Making of Buddhist Modernism* (New York: Oxford University Press, 2008), 19–48, 91–97, 110–113; Torkel Brekke, *Makers of Modern Indian Religion in the Late Nineteenth Century* (Oxford: Oxford University Press, 2002), 86–115; Tessa J. Bartholomeusz, "Dharmapala at Chicago: Mahayana Buddhist or Sinhala Chauvinist," *A Museum of Faiths: Histories and Legacies of the 1893 World's Parliament of Religions*, ed. Eric J. Ziolkowski (Atlanta, GA: Scholars Press, 1993), 235–250; G. V. Saroja, "The Contribution of Anagarika Devamitta Dharmapāla to the Revival of Buddhism in India," in *Buddhist Themes in Modern Indian Literature*, ed. J. Parthasarathi (Madras: Institute of Asian Studies, 1992), 27–38; Ria Kloppenborg, "The Anagarika Dharmapala (1864–1933) and the Puritan Pattern," *Nederlands Theologisch Tijdschrift* 46, no. 4 (1992): 277–283; Anne M. Blackburn, *Locations of Buddhism: Colonialism and Modernity in Sri Lanka* (Chicago: University of Chicago Press, 2010), 104–142.

17. On the Protestant influence on reformist Buddhism in Sri Lanka, see Kloppenborg, "The Anagarika Dharmapala (1864–1933) and the Puritan Pattern"; Gombrich, *Theravāda Buddhism*, 171–195.

18. Anagarika Dharmapala, "The Ethics of Buddha," in *Return to Righteousness: A Collection of Speeches, Essays and Letters of the Anagarika Dharmapala*, ed. Ananda Guruge (Colombo: Government Press, 1965), 199–210. As Ria Kloppenborg stresses, ethics and rules of conduct for both clergy and laity were central to Dharmapala's notion of Buddhism. The two hundred rules laid down in his Daily Code for the Laity regulated, among other things, eating. Kloppenborg, "The Anagarika Dharmapala (1864–1933) and the Puritan Pattern," 281. Indeed, Dharmapala stressed quite clearly that both laymen and members of the clergy must not consume meat. Dharmapala, "The Ethics of Buddha," 210. According to Alan Trevithick, Dharmapala himself never altogether rejected meat, but did take a stand against cow slaughter—an issue central also to emerging Sinhalese nationalism from the late nineteenth century on. Alan Trevithick, *The Revival of Buddhist Pilgrimage at Bodh Gaya (1811–1949): Anagarika Dharmapala and the Mahabodhi Temple* (Delhi: Motilal Banarsidass Publications, 2006), 181. On cow slaughter as an issue in nineteenth- and twentieth-century Sinhalese nationalism, see H. L. Seneviratne, "Food Essence and the Essence of Experience," in *The Eternal Food: Gastronomic Ideas and Experiences of Hindus and Buddhists*, ed. Ravindra S. Khare (Delhi: Sri Satguru Publications, 1992), 195–196.

19. Trevithick, *The Revival of Buddhist Pilgrimage at Bodh Gaya (1811–1949)*, 55.

20. McMahan, *The Making of Buddhist Modernism*, 95–97; Bartholomeusz, "Dharmapala at Chicago."

21. McGetchin, *Indology, Indomania, and Orientalism*, 128.

## 4. BETWEEN BUDDHA, GANDHI, SUFISM, AND MASCULINITY

22. Martin Baumann, "Buddhism in Europe: Past, Present, Prospects," in *Westwards Dharma: Buddhism Beyond Asia*, ed. C. S. Prebish and M. Baumann (Berkeley: University of California Press, 2002), 88; Heinz Mürmel, "Buddhismus und Theosophie in Leipzig vor dem Ersten Weltkrieg," in *Buddhisten und Hindus im deutschsprachigen Raum: Akten des zweiten Grazer religionswissenschaftlichen Symposiums (2.—3. März 2000)*, ed. Manfred Hutter (Frankfurt/Main: Peter Lang, 2000), 123-136. The decisive influence of Protestantism on reformist Buddhism in Germany is also stressed by Perry Myers, *German Visions of India, 1871-1918: Commandeering the Holy Ganges During the Kaiserreich* (New York: Palgrave Macmillan, 2013), 29-52, 92, 139-142.
23. After the American Maha Bodhi Society (1897), the German offshoot was the second branch founded after the initial establishment of the Maha Bodhi Society in Ceylon. A British equivalent was established in 1926. Baumann, "Buddhism in Europe: Past, Present, Prospects," 89.
24. Hellmuth Hecker, *Der erste deutsche Bhikkhu. Das bewegte Leben des ehrwürdigen Nyanatiloka (1878-1957) und seine Schüler* (Konstanz: Hecker, 1995), 18-29.
25. "Geschäftsbericht des B. F. B. L.," *Zeitschrift für Buddhismus. Herausgegeben vom Bund für buddhistisches Leben* 1 (1913): 29.
26. Volker Zotz, *Auf den glücklichen Inseln. Buddhismus in der deutschen Kultur* (Berlin: Theseus, 2000), 72-82; Myers, *German Visions of India, 1871-1918*, 93-103.
27. Marchand, "Eastern Wisdom in an Age of Western Despair." The anti-Semitic nexus is only stressed in recent research, most notably by Zotz, *Auf den glücklichen Inseln*, 341-360. See also Heinz Mürmel, "'Die Religion liegt im Blut'—Sächsisch-arische Konzepte der Kaiserzeit. Kurze Bemerkungen zur 'Arischen Lebensreform,'" in *Devianz und Dynamik. Festschrift für Hubert Seiwert zum 65. Geburtstag*, ed. Edith Franke, Christoph Kleine and Heinz Mürmel (Göttingen: Vandenhoeck & Ruprecht, 2014), 97-121.
28. It is interesting that German-speaking research on the *völkisch* movement has so far paid no attention to the cross-cultural entanglements involved in shaping the concept of Aryanness, instead pursuing a narrowly national focus even when analyzing phenomena such as Mazdaznan. Uwe Puschner, Walter Schmitz, and Justus H. Ulbricht, eds., *Handbuch zur "Völkischen Bewegung" 1871-1918* (Munich: K. G. Saur, 2012); Linse, *Zurück o Mensch zur Mutter Erde*; Linse, "Mazdaznan—Die Rassenreligion vom arischen Friedensreich," in *Völkische Religion und Krisen der Moderne. Entwürfe "arteigener" Glaubenssysteme seit der Jahrhundertwende*, ed. Stefanie V. Schnurbein and Justus H. Ulbricht (Würzburg: Königshausen & Neumann, 2001), 268-291.
29. McMahan, *The Making of Buddhist Modernism*, 96-97, 111-112.
30. Ludwig Ankenbrand, "Der Buddhismus und die modernen Reformbestrebungen," *Buddhistische Warte* 3 (1911): 56-61. Wolfgang Bohn also stressed the allegedly Semitic character of Christianity, but without sharing Ankenbrand's hope of a return to ancient glory. Wolfgang Bohn, *Buddhismus als Reformgedanke für unsere Zeit* (Breslau: Markgraf, 1910), 4-7.
31. As G. V. Saroja explains, Dharmapala (who by this stage had moved to Calcutta) viewed Islam and Christianity as a threat because they welcomed lower-caste Hindus and Dalits into their ranks. Dharmapala hoped to attract them to Buddhism so India would not be lost to either Islam or Christianity. Saroja, "The

Contribution of Anagarika Devamitta Dharmapāla to the Revival of Buddhism in India," 34; Dharmapala, "Christianity in Europe," in *Return to Righteousness: A Collection of Speeches, Essays and Letters of the Anagarika Dharmapala*, ed. Ananda Guruge (Colombo: Government Press, 1965), 451–458. For German Buddhist claims of Semitic religions as materialist, see, for instance, Bohn, *Buddhismus als Reformgedanke für unsere Zeit*, 4–7. By equating Christianity and "Semitic" culture, German Buddhists played on a classic anti-Semitic trope: that of Jews as supposedly economically greedy.

32. Bohn, *Buddhismus als Reformgedanke für unsere Zeit*, 4. On Bohn's positions, see also Mürmel, "'Die Religion liegt im Blut.'"
33. Mürmel, "Buddhismus und Thesophie in Leipzig vor dem Ersten Weltkrieg"; Bigalke, *Lebensreform und Esoterik um 1900*.
34. On Baltzer's attitude toward German Jews, see also Tobias Kaiser, "Eine etwas andere Mediengeschichte—Anmerkungen zur Entstehung der vegetarischen Publizistik des 19. Jahrhunderts im preußisch-thüringischen Nordhausen," in *Medien—Kommunikation—Öffentlichkeit. Vom Spätmittelalter bis zur Gegenwart. Festschrift für Werner Greiling zum 65. Geburtstag*, ed. Holger Böning et al. (Wien: Böhlau, 2019), 51–67.
35. G. Starker, "Zur Auswanderung nach Neu-Germanien," *Thalysia. Vereins-Blatt für Freunde der natürlichen Lebensweise* 21, no. 1 (1888): 6–11.
36. Daniela Kraus, "Förster, Bernhard," in *Handbuch des Antisemitismus*, vol. 2.1, *Personen: A-K*, ed. Wolfgang Benz (Berlin: de Gruyter Saur, 2009), 236–237; "(Dr. Bernhard Förster †)," *Deutsche Kolonialzeitung. Neue Folge* 2, no. 28 (1889): 232.
37. After coauthoring the so-called *Antisemitenpetition*, a petition against Jewish emancipation, with his brother and others in 1880, Förster founded the Antisemitische Deutschsoziale Partei in 1889. Daniela Kraus, "Förster, Paul," in *Handbuch des Antisemitismus*, 2.1: 238–239.
38. On the association, see also Miriam Zerbel, "Tierschutzbewegung," in *Handbuch zur "Völkischen Bewegung" 1871–1918*, ed. Uwe Puschner (Munich: De Gruyter, 1999), 550.
39. *Verzeichniss der Mitglieder des Internationalen Vereins zur Bekämpfung der wissenschaftlichen Tierfolter* (Guben: Albert Koenig, 1889).
40. "Ludwig Ankenbrand. Zu seinem 60. Geburtstag," *Vegetarische Presse* 21, no. 5 (1938): 56–57.
41. Ludwig Ankenbrand, "Von Genua nach Kairo," *Vegetarische Warte* 46, no. 2 (1913): 16–17. After being raped by the son-in-law of German painter Karl Wilhelm Diefenbach in Capri, Minna was sent home by Ankenbrand and his wife, who blamed Minna for the incident. On her return, she was immediately admitted to the psychiatric ward in Dalldorf, near Berlin, where she died on January 16, 1916. Landesarchiv Berlin, A Rep. 003-04-04-Wittenauer Heilstätten der Stadt Berlin No. 8293, Patientinnenakte Minna Symanzick.
42. A Rep. 003-04-04-Wittenauer Heilstätten der Stadt Berlin No. 8293, Patientinnenakte Minna Symanzick, 16.
43. IfA Stuttgart, "Aus Diatalawa," *Deutsche Kolonial- und Kriegsgefangenenzeitung Diyatalawa*, no. 2 (1914): 6.

## 4. BETWEEN BUDDHA, GANDHI, SUFISM, AND MASCULINITY

Since Ankenbrand could not correspond with German journals while interned, German Buddhists only learned of his wartime circumstances in an article he published after his return. Ludwig Ankenbrand, "Deutsche Buddhisten in Indien während der Kriegszeit," *Zeitschrift für Buddhismus* 2 (1920): 62–63. After his grand plan of a vegetarian journey around the world failed, Ankenbrand stopped publishing in vegetarian journals.

44. "Kaisertreu" means "loyal to the emperor."
45. "Vom Kriegsschauplatz," *Deutsche Kolonial- und Kriegsgefangenenzeitung Diyatalawa*, no. 1 (1914): 4; "Aus Diatalawa," *Deutsche Kolonial- und Kriegsgefangenenzeitung Diyatalawa*, no. 1 (1914): 6; "Ich habe keine Zeit, muede zu sein," *Deutsche Kolonial- und Kriegsgefangenenzeitung Diyatalawa*, no. 10 (1915): 5–6; "Aus Diatalawa" *Deutsche Kolonial- und Kriegsgefangenenzeitung Diyatalawa*, no. 10 (1915): 9. Importantly, Ankenbrand's criticism of the British was not accompanied by a view of Germany as a potentially superior colonial power in South Asia, a perspective frequently expressed by German observers of the late German Empire. On this, see Perry Myers, "German Travelers to India at the Fin-De-Siècle and Their Ambivalent Views of the Raj," in Cho, Kurlander, and McGetchin, *Transcultural Encounters Between Germany and India*, 84–98.
46. "Bilder aus Ceylon," *Deutsche Kolonial- und Kriegsgefangenenzeitung Diyatalawa*, no. 15 (1915): 2–6.
47. "Aus Diyatalawa," *Deutsche Kolonial- und Kriegsgefangenenzeitung Diyatalawa*, no. 5 (1914): 9.
48. Ludwig Lang and Ludwig Ankenbrand, *Buddha und Buddhismus* (Stuttgart: Franckh, 1923), 78.
49. Lang and Ankenbrand, 5. Ankenbrand was not alone in stressing the connection between caste and skin color. It was also embraced by early Hindu nationalists and, later, by German eugenicists like Hans F. K. Günther. Lucia Staiano-Daniels, "The Melancholy of the Thinking Racist: India and the Ambiguities of Race in the Work of Hans F.-K. Günther," in in Cho, Kurlander, and McGetchin, *Transcultural Encounters Between Germany and India*, 170–185.
50. Lang and Ankenbrand, *Buddha und Buddhismus*, 31–32.
51. Hermann Gradl and Ludwig Ankenbrand, *Der schöne deutsche Süden. Die Seele unserer Heimat in Bildern; Das Land der Franken, Bayern, Schwaben und Alemannen abseits der großen Verkehrswege* (Stuttgart: Hädecke, 1944). For Ankenbrand's membership, see BArch R 9361 IX Kartei 561311.
52. See, for instance, the following works by Lisbeth Ankenbrand: *Die Rohkostküche: Gesundheit durch vitaminreiche Nahrung; 308 erprobte u. bewährte Rezepte mit Speisenfolge; Anweisg zur Herstellg von Rohkost; neuzeitliche Gemüsezubereitg u. vegetar. Bratspeisen* (Stuttgart: Süddeutsches Verlagshaus, 1928); *Gesunde fleischlose Küche* (Stuttgart: Süddeutsches Verlagshaus, 1929); *Die tägliche Schönheitspflege der Frau: Rezepte und wirksame Mittel, die wenig Geld kosten* (Stuttgart: Süddeutsches Verlagshaus, 1930); *Die gesunde glückliche Frau* (Stuttgart: Süddeutsches Verlagshaus, 1932); *Schenk deinem Kinde Schönheit. Neuzeitliche praktische Gesundheits- und Schönheitspflege vom ersten Lebenstage bis zur Reife* (Stuttgart: Süddeutsches Verlagshaus, 1937); *Gesund und schön ins Alter* (Stuttgart: Süddeutsches Verlagshaus, 1938).

## 4. BETWEEN BUDDHA, GANDHI, SUFISM, AND MASCULINITY

53. While the first edition of Ankenbrand's *Will to Beauty*, with the title strikingly reminiscent of the (later) Leni Riefenstahl film, still stressed the "strong competition" of "Semitic" women in the alleged beauty contest of the races, this passage was taken from the second edition, which stressed that the "Aryan race" was the "most perfect race." Lisbeth Ankenbrand, *Der Wille zur Schönheit* (Stuttgart: Süddeutsches Verlagshaus, 1928), 9–10; *Der Wille zur Schönheit*, 2nd ed. (Stuttgart: Süddeutsches Verlagshaus, 1935), 11–12. The 1950 edition, otherwise nearly identical, was purged of references to the "Aryan" race. *Der Wille zur Schönheit*, 3rd ed. (Stuttgart: Süddeutsches Verlagshaus, 1950), 9.
54. Hauptstaatsarchiv Stuttgart. Sonderbestand 8600. Autographensammlung Ankenbrand. S. M. Abdullah to Ludwig Ankenbrand, Berlin-Wilmersdorf, 21. September 1929. H. Mazooruddin Ahmad to Ludwig Ankenbrand, Berlin-Friedenau, 24. September 1942. For Bose's mission to Germany, see Manjapra, *Age of Entanglement*, 105–107. On the Berlin Ahmadiyya community, see Jonker, *The Ahmadiyya Quest for Religious Progress: Missionizing Europe 1900–1965* (Leiden: Brill, 2016).
55. Already in the Diyatalawa camp journal, Ankenbrand had portrayed pan-Islamism and a support of Islam as the "lesser evil" in comparison with British colonialism and a British victory—a fairly standard German idea during the First World War. Ankenbrand, "Der Stand des Weltkrieges im November und Dezember," *Deutsche Kolonial- und Kriegsgefangenenzeitung Diyatalawa*, no. 16 (1915): 5. On German policy toward Islam during the war, see Heike Liebau, "Das deutsche Auswärtige Amt, indische Emigranten und propagandistische Bestrebungen unter den Südasiatischen Kriegsgefangenen im 'Halbmondlager,'" in *Soldat Ram Singh und der Kaiser. Indische Kriegsgefangene in deutschen Propagandalagern 1914–1918*, ed. Franziska Roy, Heike Liebau, and Ravi Ahuja (Heidelberg: Draupadi-Verlag, 2014), 109–143.
56. As Maria Framke shows, the Nazi government likewise did not believe in the idea of a common Aryan ancestry joining Germans and South Asians. Framke, *Delhi—Rom—Berlin. Die indische Wahrnehmung von Faschismus und Nationalsozialismus 1922–1939* (Darmstadt: Wissenschaftliche Buchgesellschaft, 2013), 126–128.
57. "Ludwig Ankenbrand siebzig," *Vegetarisches Universum* 11, no. 5 (1958): 8.
58. On the constitutional revolution in Iran, see Vanessa Martin, "Constitutional Revolution. II. Events," in *Encyclopedia Iranica*, vol. 6.2, ed. Ehsan Yarshater (Leiden: Brill, 1996), 176–187; Abbas Amanat, *Iran: A Modern History* (New Haven, CT: Yale University Press, 2017), 315–385.
59. Janet Afary, *The Iranian Constitutional Revolution, 1906–1911: Grassroots Democracy, Social Democracy, & the Origins of Feminism* (New York: Columbia University Press, 1996), particularly 177–208; Afsaneh Najmabadi, *Women with Mustaches and Men Without Beards: Gender and Sexual Anxieties of Iranian Modernity* (Berkeley: University of California Press, 2005), 181–231.
60. Sivan Balslev, "Dressed for Success: Hegemonic Masculinity, Elite Men and Westernisation in Iran, c. 1900–40," *Gender & History* 26, no. 3 (2014): 545–564; Balsley, "Population Crisis, Marriage Reform and the Regulation of Male Sexuality in Interwar Iran," *British Journal of Middle Eastern Studies* 45, no. 2 (2018): 121–37; Balsley, *Iranian Masculinities: Gender and Sexuality in Late Qajar and Early Pahlavi Iran* (Cambridge: Cambridge University Press, 2019). On polarized

## 4. BETWEEN BUDDHA, GANDHI, SUFISM, AND MASCULINITY

gender concepts as a unifying force of the global bourgeoisie, see Christof Dejung, David Motadel, and Jürgen Osterhammel, "Worlds of the Bourgeoisie," in *The Global Bourgeoisie: The Rise of the Middle Classes in the Age of Empire*, ed. Dejung, Motadel, and Osterhammel (Princeton, NJ: Princeton University Press, 2019), 11–12.

61. Farzin Vahdat, *God and Juggernaut: Iran's Intellectual Encounter with Modernity* (Syracuse, NY: Syracuse University Press, 2002), 83.
62. Jamshid Behnam, "Irānšahr, Ḥosayn Kāẓemẓāda," in Yarshater, *Encyclopedia Iranica*, 8.5: 537–539. On the National Committee, see also Amanat, *Iran*, 477–479.
63. Behnam, "Irānšahr, Ḥosayn Kāẓemẓāda."
64. Sending students abroad to draw on their knowledge for modernizing the country was practiced in Persia in the late nineteenth century, when, however, their main destination was France. From the First World War into the 1930s, Germany became more important as a place of study. While the German government initially funded Persian students, the Persian government established a funding scheme of its own in 1928. David Menashri, *Education and the Making of Modern Iran* (Ithaca, NY: Cornell University Press, 1992), 125–133.
65. PA AAB RZ 201/19017 Ausbildung von Persern in Deutschland.
66. On Kazemzadeh's biography, see Bahman Nirumand and Gabriele Yonan, *Iraner in Berlin* (Berlin: Ausländerbeauftrage des Senats, 1994), 72–78; Behnam, "Irānšahr, Ḥosayn Kāẓemẓāda," 537–539.
67. Hosein Kazemzadeh, "Aus dem Leben der Sufi-Meister des Islam," *Moslemische Revue* 9, nos. 3–4 (1933): 50–69; Kazemzadeh, "Meine Pilgerfahrt nach Mekka, der heiligen Stadt des Islams," *Moslemische Revue* 9, nos. 3–4 (1933): 75–87; Kazemzadeh, "Meine Pilgerfahrt nach Mekka, der heiligen Stadt des Islams," *Moslemische Revue* 9, no. 2 (1936): 36–46.
68. Universitätsbibliothek Kassel, Landesbibliothek und Murhardsche Bibliothek, Wilhelm Schwaner Papers, Signature: 2° Ms. Hist. Litt. 38, Hossein Kazemzadeh to Wilhelm Schwaner, Berlin, October 11, 1933.
69. Nirumand and Yonan, *Iraner in Berlin*, 75–78; Behnam, "Irānšahr, Ḥosayn Kāẓemẓāda," 537–539.
70. Behnam, "Irānšahr, Ḥosayn Kāẓemẓāda." Kazemzadeh's journal had a column called "Women's World," which featured articles on love, marriage, children's education, but also important historical figures such as Jeanne d'Arc, the status of women in early Iran, etc. "Zanān-e nāmvar: Žāndārk kīst?," *Iranshahr*, no. 5 (1924–1925): 301–309; "Jahān-e zanān: Zan dar jāme'e-ye Īrān-e bāstān," *Iranshahr*, no. 6 (1924–1925): 368–378. In this respect, his journal resembled the periodicals of the Arab *nahda*, in which debates on women's social status, education, and home lives, but also articles on famous historical female characters, were central—with many of these articles, however, written by women. Beth Baron, *The Women's Awakening in Egypt: Culture, Society, and the Press* (New Haven, CT: Yale University Press, 1994); Magda Nammour, "Perception de l'éducation dans la presse levantine de la fin du XIXème siècle," in *Entangled Education: Foreign and Local Schools in Ottoman Syria and Mandate Lebanon (19th–20th Centuries)*, ed. Julia Hauser, Christine Lindner, and Esther Möller (Würzburg: Ergon, 2015), 101–123; Marilyn Booth, *May Her Likes Be Multiplied: Biography and Gender Politics in Egypt* (Berkeley: University of California Press, 2001).

71. "Ta'līm va tarbiyat: (Yān) pedār-e varzesh dar almān," *Iranshahr*, no. 3 (1924–1925): 154–164; "Ma'āref dar Īrān: 'Aql-e salīm dar jesm-e sālem," *Iranshahr*, no. 9 (1924–1925): 544–556; "Qesmat-e ejtemā'ī: Ta'līm va tarbiyat dar madāres," *Iranshahr*, no. 3 (1924–1925): 449–458.

72. He reviewed, for instance, a book by the young Persian writer Sadeq Hedayagh on human-animal relations. "Maṭbū'āt-e vārede," *Iranshahr*, no. 3 (1924–1925): 510–511. On Sadeq Hedayat's vegetarianism, see Hushang Philsooph, "Hedayat, Vegetarianism and Modernity: Altruism, Leonardo da Vinci, and Sub-Humanization," in *Sadeq Hedayat: His Work and His Wondrous World*, ed. Homa Katouzian (London: Routledge, 2008), 153.

73. "Tajliyāt-e rūḥ-e Īrān: Jam'iyyat-e Mazdāsnān. Mazdaznan—Tempel Society," *Iranshahr* 4, no. 4 (1924–1925): 249. The misspelling ("Tempel") is in the original title. I thank Anne-Marie Brack, Stefan Popp, and Niusha Ramzani for translating from the Persian the *Iranshahr* articles quoted in this paragraph.

74. "Tajliyāt-e rūḥ-e Īrān: Jam'iyyat-e Mazdāsnān. Mazdaznan—Tempel Society," 438–444.

75. "Tajliyāt-e rūḥ-e Īrān: Jam'iyyat-e Mazdāsnān. Mazdaznan—Tempel Society," 312–319; "Tajliyāt-e rūḥ-e Īrān: Jam'iyyat-e Mazdāsnān. Mazdaznan—Tempel Society," 375–381.

76. Marc David Baer, *German, Jew, Muslim, Gay: The Life and Times of Hugo Marcus* (New York: Columbia University Press, 2020), 42–44.

77. H. K. Iranschähr, *Die Gathas von Zarathushtra* (Berlin-Steglitz: Iranschähr, 1930). As Mark Sedgwick stresses, however, the Gathas were also central to the Sufism propagated by Inayat Khan, on which see below. Sedgwick, *Western Sufism: From the Abbasids to the New Age* (Oxford: Oxford University Press, 2017), 168.

78. Johannes Itten, "Mahatma Gandhi," *Mazdaznan* 1, no. 10 (1925): 251–254. There is a possibility that Itten's baldness, read by Peter Wilson as a statement of being modern, was modeled on Gandhi's (a connection that Wilson does not draw). Peter Wilson, "Baldness and Modernism," *AA Files* 74 (2017): 3–16.

79. On Itten's relationship with Mazdaznan, see Paul Citroën, "Mazdaznan at the Bauhaus," in *Our Bauhaus: Memories of Bauhaus People*, ed. Magdalena Droste and Boris Friedewald (Munich: Prestel, 2019), 64–70; Christoph Wagner, "Johannes Itten. Leitmotive einer Künstlerbiographie," in *Johannes Itten. Alles in Einem—Alles im Sein*, ed. Ernest W. Uthemann and Christoph Wagner (Ostfildern-Ruit: Hatje Cantz, 2003), 46, 56–57, 68–69; "Zwischen Lebensreform und Esoterik: Johannes Ittens Weg ans Bauhaus in Weimar," in *Das Bauhaus und die Esoterik*, ed. Wagner (Bielefeld: Kerber, 2005), 65–77; Ulrich Linse, "Der spurenlose Mazdaznan-Vortrag von Otto Rauth," in *Bauhausvorträge. Gastredner am Weimarer Bauhaus 1919–1925*, ed. Peter Bernhard (Berlin: Gebrüder Mann, 2017), 217–232; Linn Burchert, "The Spiritual Enhancement of the Body: Johannes Itten, Gertrud Grunow, and Mazdaznan at the Early Bauhaus," in *Bauhaus Bodies: Gender, Sexuality, and Body Culture in Modernism's Legendary Art School*, ed. Elizabeth Otto and Patrick Rössler (New York: Bloomsbury Visual Arts, 2019), 49–72. Itten became interested in Mazdaznan around 1916. Wagner, "Johannes Itten und die Esoterik: Ein Schlüssel zum frühen Bauhaus?," in *Esoterik am Bauhaus. Eine Revision der Moderne?*, ed. Wagner (Regensburg: Schnell and

## 4. BETWEEN BUDDHA, GANDHI, SUFISM, AND MASCULINITY

Steiner, 2009), 120. Itten's wife became a member of the community in 1922. Bauhaus-Archiv Berlin, Johannes Itten Papers, Masdasnan-Bund to Frau H. Itten, Weimar, Leipzig, January 3, 1922. Christoph Wagner, appointed trustee of the Itten papers by Itten's daughter, generally downplays Itten's racism and implies that he distanced himself from Mazdaznan in the 1920s, but archival sources show that he was still a member of the organization in 1945. Wagner, "Johannes Itten. Leitmotive einer Künstlerbiographie," 68–69. Mazdaznan-Gesellschaft Bern to Herrn Böhm, Bern, 29 June 1945 (copy), in Bauhaus-Archiv Berlin, Johannes Itten Papers. Itten was also interested in Sufism and invited Inayat Khan to lecture at the Bauhaus in 1921. Peter Bernhard, "Ein Sufi am Bauhaus," in *Bauhausvorträge. Gastredner am Weimarer Bauhaus 1919–1925*, ed. Bernhard (Berlin: Gebrüder Mann, 2017), 233–236.

80. Johannes Itten, "Rassenlehre und Kunstentwicklung," *Mazdaznan* 16 (1923): 89–92
81. Peter Spohr, "Noch einmal Mazdaznan," *Vegetarische Warte* 43, no. 21 (1910): 210–211; Spohr, "Einige Proben aus der Mazdaznanbibel," *Vegetarische Warte* 44, no. 3 (1911): 26–27; Dr. Bracke, "Etwas von 'Meister' Hanisch," *Vegetarische Warte* 46, no. 1 (1913): 87–88; Bracke, "Dr. Otoman Zar Adusht Hanish oder der Janus-Kopf," *Vegetarische Warte* 46, no. 12 (1913): 117–119; Bracke, "Weiteres vom Mazdaznan-Meister," *Vegetarische Warte* 46, no. 24 (1913): 234–235; "Otto Hanisch," *Vegetarische Warte* 47, no. 5 (1914): 42.
82. Johannes Graul, "Die Mazdaznan-Bewegung Im deutschen Kaiserreich. Eine archivalienbasierte Spurensuche," in *Nonkonformismus und Europäische Religionsgeschichten = Nonconformism and European Histories of Religions*, ed. Danny Schäfer (Berlin: Lit, 2012), 376.
83. Wagner, "Johannes Itten,"53.
84. On the establishment of the *Deutsche Gesellschaft für Lebensreform*, see Fritzen, *Gesünder leben*, 71–76.
85. Martin Vogel, "Mazdaznan Ernährungs-Lehre von Dr. J. A. Hanish, Elektor der Mazdaznan-Bewegung," *Leib und Leben* 3 (1935): 58; "Mazdaznan und Lebensreform," *Leib und Leben* 3 (1935): 77, 137. On the importance of wholemeal bread in Nazi food politics, see Uwe Spiekermann, "Vollkorn für die Führer. Zur Geschichte der Vollkornbrotpolitik im 'Dritten Reich,'" *1999* (2001): 91–128.
86. "Mazdaznan und Lebensreform. Für und gegen Mazdaznan," *Leib und Leben* 6 (1935): 135.
87. G. Weber, "Verfälschung des Rassegedankens durch Geheimlehren," *Leib und Leben* 3 (1935): 293–399. This article was also published in the monthly periodical of the Nazi Party: "Verfälschung des Rassegedankens durch Geheimlehren," *Nationalsozialistische Monatshefte* 6 (1935): 770–779.
88. "Mazdaznan und Lebensreform," 75–76. On the Nazi notion of the *Volksgemeinschaft*, see Michael Wildt, *Volksgemeinschaft als Selbstermächtigung. Gewalt gegen Juden in der deutschen Provinz 1919 bis 1939* (Hamburg: Hamburger Edition, 2007); Frank Bajohr and Michael Wildt, *Volksgemeinschaft. Neue Forschungen zur Gesellschaft des Nationalsozialismus* (Frankfurt/Main: Fischer, 2009); Martina Steber and Bernhard Gotto, eds., *Visions of Community in Nazi Germany: Social Engineering and Private Lives* (Oxford: Oxford University Press, 2014); Lisa Pine,

## 4. BETWEEN BUDDHA, GANDHI, SUFISM, AND MASCULINITY

*Hitler's "National Community": Society and Culture in Nazi Germany*, 2nd ed. (London: Bloomsbury Academic, 2017).

89. Vogel, "Mazdaznan Ernährungs-Lehre von Dr. J. A. Hanish," 58. On Nazis' enthusiasm for South Asia-inspired forms of esotericism, see Nicholas Goodrick-Clarke, *The Occult Roots of Nazism: Secret Aryan Cults and Their Influence on Nazi Ideology: The Ariosophists of Austria and Germany, 1890–1935* (New York: New York University Press, 1992); Eric Kurlander, "The Orientalist Roots of National Socialism? Nazism, Occultism, and South Asian Spirituality, 1919–1945," in *Transcultural Encounters Between Germany and India*, ed. Joanne Miyang Cho, Eric Kurlander, and Douglas T. McGetchin (Abingdon, UK: Routledge, 2014), 155–169.

90. Soon afterward, Mazdaznan was abolished in Bavaria as well. BArch, R 187/267 a Religiöse Gemeinschaften, Bayerische Politische Polizei an alle Polizeidirektionen, Staatspolizeiämter, Bezirksämter, Bezirksaussensitze u. Stadtkommissäre. Nachr. an alle Kreisregierungen, den Herrn Reichsstatthalter in Bayern u. die Oberbürgermeister der kreisunmittelbaren Städte, Munich, October 23, 1935. On the abolition of Mazdaznan in Germany, see also Fritzen, *Gesünder leben*, 66–67.

91. "To Herr Adolph Hitler," *British Mazdaznan Magazine* 12 (1935): 231–232. Even after its abolition, authors in the British magazine continued to express hopes that the Nazi government would come to esteem Mazdaznan. "Mazdaznan in Germany. Nazis Worship the Sun," *British Mazdaznan Magazine* 12 (1936): 385.

92. Katherine Dashwood, "Gahanbar at Zurich," *British Mazdaznan Magazine* 13 (1936): 158–159.

93. Gerdien Jonker, *On the Margins: Jews and Muslims in Interwar Berlin* (Leiden: Brill, 2020), 101.

94. Wilhelm Warschatka, also known as Omar el-Geber (or sometimes even "Saint Omar"), was a Mazdaznan apostate based near Stuttgart who continued to publish books on what he claimed were Zoroastrian dietary ethics. See, for instance, Omar El Geber, *Praktische zarathuschtrische Heildiätetik* (Freiburg/Breisgau: Geber, 1925). It may have been lost on German readers that these books on seasonal fasting cures, rather than dietetics as such, were published by someone who possibly called himself a "giant" (*Jabbār* or *gebb[e]r*, in Egyptian pronunciation). Hans Wehr, *Arabisches Wörterbuch für die Schriftsprache der Gegenwart. Arabisch—Deutsch*, 5th ed. (Wiesbaden: Harassowitz, 1989), 111. At the same time, his eponym may hint at the agenda of a creation of a New Man of unprecedented strength and vigor by dietary regulation. For Kazemzadeh's emphasis on his Persian identity, see, for instance, the advertisements at the end of his books, such as H. K. Iranschähr, *Die Heilkraft des Schweigens. Eine Pilgerfahrt zum Tempel des Schweigens*, 2nd ed. (Berlin: Iranschähr, 1933), n.p.

95. Behnam, "Irānšahr."

96. Nirumand and Yonan, *Iraner in Berlin*, 76.

97. H. K. Iranschähr, *Der Meister und sein Jünger* (Berlin: Iranschähr, 1929); *Der Pfad der Jüngerschaft zur Erweckung der Seelen-Kräfte!* (Berlin: Iranschähr, 1934).

98. Linse, *Barfüßige Propheten*. Eva Barlösius observes the same for the early protagonists of the German vegetarian movement, to whom she refers, in the same caustic manner, as "prophets." Barlösius, *Naturgemäße Lebensführung*.

99. On Inayat Khan, see Sedgwick, *Western Sufism*, 157–171.

## 4. BETWEEN BUDDHA, GANDHI, SUFISM, AND MASCULINITY

100. Jonker, *On the Margins*, 56, 101; Younes Jalali, *Taghi Erani: A Polymath in Interwar Berlin: Fundamental Science, Psychology, Orientalism, and Political Philosophy* (Cham, CH: Springer, 2018), 143.
101. Inayat Khan, *Health* (Deventer, NL: Kluwer, 1938), 101–102.
102. Iranschähr, *Der Meister und sein Jünger*, 27. Emphasis added.
103. Iranschähr, 28; Iranschähr, *Die Heilkraft des Schweigens. Eine Pilgerfahrt zum Tempel des Schweigens*, 53; Iranschähr, *Das Mysterium der Seele* (Berlin: Iranschähr, 1936), 83–84. On the split between body and soul in Kazemzadeh's thought, see also Vahdat, *God and Juggernaut*, 83–85, who, however, does not explore his carnal soul vs. spiritual soul or his human vs. animal dichotomy and its relation to Sufism.
104. Ḥusain Kaẓim-Zāda, *Rahbar-I-Niẓād-I-Nau Dar Ġustūġūj-I-Ḥošbaḥtī* (Berlin-Wilmersdorf: Iranschähr, 1928), 65–71. As explained in chapter 1, Sufis differentiated between two types of soul, both present within the human body, *nafs* (the carnal soul) and *rūḥ* (the spiritual soul). An attribute frequently bestowed on *nafs* was *hayyawani*, which literally means "animal." To my knowledge, there is no research investigating the influence of this Sufi dichotomy on Hinduism or on Theosophy, although it seems to be patent.
105. Iranschähr, *Der Meister und sein Jünger*, 29.
106. Bigalke, *Lebensreform und Esoterik um 1900*, 229–235; Graul, "Die Mazdaznan-Bewegung im deutschen Kaiserreich."
107. H. K. Iranschähr, *Grundlagen der neuen Erziehung* (Olten, CH: Amadeo, 1947), 63–82.
108. After the Second World War, Kazemzadeh would embrace the idea of "prenatal education" also advocated by Mazdaznan, thus adopting the core aspect of their eugenics. In this context, Kazemzadeh stressed that pregnant women should adopt a vegetarian diet. Iranschähr, *Grundlagen der neuen Erziehung*, 63–70.
109. Behnam, "Irānšahr, Ḥosayn Kāẓemẓāda."
110. Behnam. Khan's Sufi movement had already moved its headquarters to Geneva in the mid-1920s, choosing, not coincidentally, the seat of the League of Nations for its universalist message. Sedgwick, *Western Sufism*, 170.
111. Bernd W. Ziegler, "Bad Liebenzell ist bereit zum "Kongreß der Ideale," *Vegetarisches Universum* 6, no. 4 (1953): 3; "6. 'Kongreß der Ideale' zu Freudenstadt im Schwarzwald," *Vegetarisches Universum* 9, no. 2 (1956): 1.
112. For the contemporary nuances and usage of the term, see Cornelia Schmitz-Berning, "Gleichschaltung," in *Vokabular des Nationalsozialismus*, ed. Schmitz-Berning (Berlin: De Gruyter, 2010), 277–280.
113. See the section on Magnus Schwantje in this chapter.
114. The journals in question are *Neuleben*, which fused with *Lebenskunst* (founded in 1906) in 1935, and the *Vegetarische Presse*, founded in 1923. The following analysis will focus on the latter. For reasons unknown, the first six volumes of this journal are no longer available. There is a possibility, therefore, that the journal started off as a pacifist or even socialist venture, and that its first issues were destroyed by its holders, the members of the Deutscher Vegetarierbund (German Vegetarian Union), in 1933 or earlier. As will become clear, by the late 1920s, it did not champion these views.
115. As Birgit Dahlke and others observe, heroic masculinity, understood as a masculinity ready to sacrifice itself for the sake of the nation, united otherwise opposed

4. BETWEEN BUDDHA, GANDHI, SUFISM, AND MASCULINITY

political factions after the First World War. However, the bulk of this research does not look at left-wing contexts. Dahlke, *Jünglinge der Moderne*, 198. On heroic masculinity as a trope in interwar Germany, see also Brunotte, *Zwischen Eros und Krieg*; Claudia Bruns, *Politik des Eros. Der Männerbund in Wissenschaft, Politik und Jugendkultur* (Cologne: Böhlau, 2008).

116. On the ISK, see Jan Foitzik, *Zwischen den Fronten. Zur Politik, Organisation und Funktion linker politischer Kleinorganisationen im Widerstand 1933 Bis 1939/40* (Bonn: Neue Gesellschaft, 1986); Sabine Lemke-Müller, *Ethik des Widerstands. Der Kampf des Internationalen sozialistischen Kampfbundes (ISK) gegen den Nationalsozialismus. Quellen und Texte zum Widerstand aus der Arbeiterbewegung 1933–1945* (Bonn: Dietz, 1996); Udo Vorholt, *Die politische Theorie Leonard Nelsons. Eine Fallstudie zum Verhältnis von philosophisch-politischer Theorie und konkret-politischer Praxis* (Baden-Baden: Nomos, 1998); Heiner Lindner, "*Um etwas zu erreichen, muss man sich etwas vornehmen, von dem man glaubt, dass es unmöglich sei.*" *Der Internationale sozialistische Kampf-Bund (ISK) und seine Publikationen* (Bonn: Friedrich-Ebert-Stiftung, 2006).

117. Members included a Bulgarian student of philosophy at Göttingen, Zeko Torbov, as well as Si-Luan Wei, a Chinese doctoral candidate in mathematics at Göttingen. Zeko Torbov, *Erinnerungen an Leonard Nelson 1925–1927* (Hildesheim: Olms, 2005); Nikolay Milkov, "Einleitung des Herausgebers," in Zorbov, *Erinnerungen an Leonard Nelson*, xlv.

118. Renate Brucker, "Für eine radikale Ethik—Die Tierrechtsbewegung in der ersten Hälfte des 20. Jahrhunderts," in *Das Mensch-Tier-Verhältnis. Eine sozialwissenschaftliche Einführung*, ed. Renate Brucker et al. (Wiesbaden: Springer, 2014), 211–268. Nelson argued that anyone who rejected equal rights for humans and animals ought not be protected by law. Leonard Nelson, "Das Recht der Tiere," *Mitteilungen des Bundes für radikale Ethik* 7 (1926): 8–9.

119. Vorholt, *Die politische Theorie Leonard Nelsons*, 199; Lindner, "*Um etwas zu erreichen, muss man sich etwas vornehmen, von dem man glaubt, dass es unmöglich sei*," 48–56.

120. Vorholt, *Die politische Theorie Leonard Nelsons*, 202–204. ISK members were asked to vote as left-wing as possible in the 1933 elections. Vorholt, 204.

121. "Zum Kampf gegen die NS," *ISK-Mitteilungen* 5, no. 4 (1930): 55–66. In his educational establishments, Nelson rejected any distinction along racial lines. Lindner, "*Um etwas zu erreichen, muss man sich etwas vornehmen, von dem man glaubt, dass es unmöglich sei*," 45.

122. Leonard Nelson, *Erziehung zum Führer. Vortrag, gehalten im Zentralinstitut für Erziehung und Unterricht in Berlin am 14. April 1920* (Leipzig: Der Neue Geist, 1920); Nelson, *Demokratie und Führerschaft. Vortrag, Gehalten im schweizer Ferien-Kurs des Internationalen Jugend-Bundes im Fextal am 27. Juni 1919* (Leipzig: Der Neue Geist, 1920). Nelson had previously founded a youth organization whose members were required to join the Social Democratic Party, which, however, ended the cooperation once it learnt of Nelson's rejection of democracy. Willi Eichler, "Der 'Internationale Jugend-Bund' (IJB) und der 'Internationale sozialistische Kampf-Bund' (ISK)," *Mitteilungen des Bundes für radikale Ethik* 7 (1926): 10.

## 4. BETWEEN BUDDHA, GANDHI, SUFISM, AND MASCULINITY

123. Eichler, "Der 'Internationale Jugend-Bund' "; Nelson, *Erziehung zum Führer*, 17. As testimonies of ISK members preserved in Nelson's papers show, many of them had difficulties accepting or following through with these principles. BArch, Leonard Nelson Papers, N 2210/258. On this aspect, see also Lindner, *"Um etwas zu erreichen, muss man sich etwas vornehmen, von dem man glaubt, dass es unmöglich sei,"* 30–36. Although Nelson disapproved of ISK members forming relationships, he was not sexually conservative, or so the presence of Max Hodann, a renowned sex educator, in his circle suggests. Karl Braun, "Jugendbewegung, Sexualaufklärung, Sozialhygiene. Das Beispiel Max Hodann (1894–1946)," in *Avantgarden der Biopolitik. Jugendbewegung, Lebensreform und Strategien biologischer, Aufrüstung*, ed. Braun, Felix Linzner, and John Khairi-Taraki (Göttingen: V&R Unipress, 2017), 33–60. Nelson violated the rule of celibacy he required of his followers, although he never formalized his relationship with Minna Specht. Vorholt, *Die politische Theorie Leonard Nelsons*, 46.
124. Susanne Miller, " 'Ich wollte ein anständiger Mensch bleiben.' " Frauen des Internationalen sozialistischen Kampfbundes (ISK) Im Widerstand (1995)," in *Ethik des Widerstandes. Der Kampf des Internationalen Sozialistischen Kampfbundes (ISK) gegen den Nationalsozialismus. Quellen und Texte zum Widerstand aus der Arbeiterbewegung 1933–1945*, ed. Sabine Lemke-Müller (Bonn: Dietz, 1996), 151; Ludwig Gehm, " 'Wir wollten zeigen: Es gibt noch andere.' Vier Jahre unentdeckt im Widerstandskampf (1989)," in Lemke-Müller, *Ethik des Widerstandes*, 178, 181; Helmut Kalbitzer, "Widerstehen oder mitmachen. eigensinnige Ansichten und sehr persönliche Erinnerungen (1987)," in Lemke-Müller, *Ethik des Widerstandes*, 244; Foitzik, *Zwischen den Fronten*, 87, 155–156.
125. Willi Eichler, "Sogar Vegetarier?," *ISK-Mitteilungen* 1, no. 12 (1926): 206–212; Erna Siem, "Vegetarische Praxis," *ISK-Mitteilungen* 2, no. 5 (1927): 91–92; "Höchstzulässige Strafe für einen Tierquäler," *ISK-Mitteilungen* 4, no. 7 (1929): 116; "Aussprache," *ISK-Mitteilungen* 2, no. 3 (1927): 57–60; Hans Lehnert, "Aberglauben, Tierquälerei und Politik in Bayern," *ISK-Mitteilungen* 5, no. 2 (1930): 40–44.
126. For ISK coverage of the Indian independence movement, see Minna Specht, "Indien in Aufruhr," *ISK-Mitteilungen* 5, no. 9 (1930): 169–179.
127. Robert N. Proctor, *The Nazi War on Cancer* (Princeton, NJ: Princeton University Press, 1999), 134–141; Boria Sax, *Animals in the Third Reich: Pets, Scapegoats, and the Holocaust* (New York: Continuum, 2000), 23; Treitel, *Eating Nature in Modern Germany*, 1–2.
128. Both Gandhi and Hitler were interested in what they considered to be the particularly energizing qualities of raw food. Proctor, *The Nazi War on Cancer*, 134–135; Nico Slate, *Gandhi's Search for the Perfect Diet* (Seattle: University of Washington Press, 2019), 74–99.
129. The one other non-state vegetarian journal at the time was *Neuleben*, founded in 1935, which had a more relaxed stance toward meat eating. The journal on food reform, *Leib und Leben*, was published by the Deutsche Gesellschaft für Lebensreform, a body founded by the Nazi government. Like *Neuleben*, *Leib und Leben* merely encouraged vegetarianism. Fritzen, *Gesünder Leben*, 126.
130. "Führer. George Bernhard Shaw," *Vegetarische Presse* 9 (1926): 92; "Führer. Leo Tolstoi als Vegetarier," *Vegetarische Presse* 15 (1932): 103–105; "Führer. Mikkel

## 4. BETWEEN BUDDHA, GANDHI, SUFISM, AND MASCULINITY

Hindhede," *Vegetarische Presse* 15 (1932): 19–20. While this column was dominated by male contemporaries, it also featured articles on women such as the celebrity pianist Elly Ney, a vegetarian and soon a prominent Nazi. Hugo Krannhals-Russell, "Führer. Elly Neys deutsche Sendung," *Vegetarische Presse* 16 (1933): 128–129. On Elly Ney's affinities with Nazism, see Martha Schad, *Sie liebten den Führer. Wie Frauen Hitler verehrten* (Munich: Herbig, 2009), 132–147.

131. "Der Mädchenhandel und die schwarze Schmach," *Vegetarische Presse* 9 (1926): 18. Germans' racist attitudes toward French colonial troops in the Rhineland have been the subject of recent research. See, for instance, Christian Koller, "Enemy Images: Race and Gender Stereotypes in the Discussion on Colonial Troops: A Franco-German Comparison, 1914–1923," in *Home/Front: The Military, War and Gender in Twentieth-Century Germany*, ed. Karen Hagemann and Stefanie Schüler-Springorum (Oxford: Berg, 2002), 139–157; Iris Wigger, *The "Black Horror on the Rhine": Intersections of Race, Nation, Gender and Class in 1920s Germany* (London: Palgrave Macmillan, 2017); Fatima El-Tayeb, ed., *Schwarze Deutsche. Der Diskurs um "Rasse" und nationale Identität 1890–1933* (Frankfurt/Main: Campus-Verlag, 2001), 158–177; Sandra Maß, *Weiße Helden, schwarze Krieger. Zur Geschichte kolonialer Männlichkeit in Deutschland 1918–1964* (Cologne: Böhlau, 2006), 71–119.

132. The *Vegetarische Presse* and other vegetarian journals evoked Mussolini (who, while not openly vegetarian, nevertheless promoted, like the Nazis, a diet high in plant components as the golden path toward autarky) as another example of the ascetic leader. "Mussolini gegen Tierquälerei," *Vegetarische Presse* 14 (1931): 4; M. Bircher-Benner, "Italien," *Vegetarische Presse* 15 (1932): 45; Werner Zimmermann, "Review of Emil Ludwig, Mussolinis Gespräche, Berlin: Paul Zsolnay, 1932," *Tau*, no. 102 (1932): 21–23. On Mussolini's agricultural politics, see Tiago Saraiva, *Fascist Pigs: Technoscientific Organisms and the History of Fascism* (Cambridge, MA: MIT Press, 2016), 21–42.

133. "Mahatma Gandhi," *Vegetarische Presse* 9 (1926): 127.

134. On Gandhi's critique of masculinity, see Parama Roy, "Meat-Eating, Masculinity, and Renunciation in India: A Gandhian Grammar of Diet," *Gender & History* 14, no. 1 (2002): 62–91.

135. Paul Albrecht, "Der Vegetarismus und die Politik," *Vegetarische Presse* 12 (1929): 65.

136. In the *Vegetarische Presse*, an article emphasizing the benefits of an alliance between socialism and vegetarianism unleashed a controversy in which most authors condemned communism both for its attitude toward private property and its purported use of violence against both humans and animals. Viktor Hinze, "Roter Vegetarismus," *Vegetarische Presse* 14 (1931): 1–2; Arthur Rothe, "Roter Vegetarismus!," *Vegetarische Presse* 14 (1931): 15–16; Paul Albrecht, "Noch einmal: "roter Vegetarismus"," *Vegetarische Presse* 14 (1931): 27–29; Josef Drahovsky, "Bemerkungen zum "roten" Vegetarismus," *Vegetarische Presse* 14 (1931): 16–17; Drahovsky, "Vegetarismus kann nur edlen Bestrebungen dienen," *Vegetarische Presse* 14 (1931): 39–41.

137. Paul Albrecht, "Gandhi," *Vegetarische Presse* 13 (1930): 37–38.

138. Georg Förster, "Indien kämpft," *Vegetarische Presse* 14 (1931): 134–135.

## 4. BETWEEN BUDDHA, GANDHI, SUFISM, AND MASCULINITY

139. Albrecht, "Der Vegetarismus und die Politik"; Josef Drahovsky, "Nur eine Einheitsfront aller Vegetarier und Lebensreformer kann zur Geltung kommen," *Vegetarische Presse* 14 (1931): 80.
140. Georg Förster, "Politik. Reichspräsidenten-Wahl," *Vegetarische Presse* 15 (1932): 34; "Adolf Hitler," *Vegetarische Presse* 15 (1932): 50.
141. Förster, "Adolf Hitler," *Vegetarische Presse* 15 (1932): 50; Arthur Rothe, "Lebensreformer und ihre Politik!," *Vegetarische Presse* 14 (1931): 5. Rothe, in the first article cited here, also alerted his readers to an illustrated volume on Hitler introduced by Baldur von Schirach, in which Hitler was presented as a vegetarian. Baldur von Schirach, "Zum Geleit," in *Hitler wie ihn keiner kennt. 100 Bild-Dokumente aus dem Leben des Führers*, ed. Heinrich Hoffmann (Berlin: Zeitgeschichte, 1932), xiii.
142. Georg Förster, "Wahlen," *Vegetarische Presse* 15 (1932): 40–41. As Jörg Melzer stresses, vegetarian communities like the Gemeinnützige Obstbausiedlung in Eden, Oranienburg (near Berlin), some of whose steering committee and advisory board members had already joined the Nazi Party, also welcomed Hitler's rise to power. Jörg Melzer, *Vollwerternährung. Diätetik, Naturheilkunde, Nationalsozialismus, sozialer Anspruch* (Stuttgart: Steiner, 2003), 145.
143. Georg Förster, "Vegetarier Hitler Reichskanzler," *Vegetarische Presse* 16 (1933): 13; Georg Förster and Karl Buck, "Aufruf zum vegetarischen Großkampf auf der ganzen Linie!," *Vegetarische Presse* 16 (1933): 133–134.
144. As Norman Ohler showed recently, Hitler, increasingly addicted to drugs, was far from being the ascetic leader he claimed to be. Corinna Treitel and others likewise stress that evidence of his vegetarianism is not conclusive. Norman Ohler, *Der totale Rausch: Drogen im Dritten Reich* (Cologne: Kiepenheuer und Witsch, 2015), 146–249.
145. Förster and Buck, "Aufruf zum vegetarischen Großkampf auf der ganzen Linie!," 134.
146. Eugen Dühring, "Internationale Vegetarier-Union," *Vegetarische Presse* 16 (1933): 127. Since Förster was unhappy with the IVU for some time, it is quite unlikely that his organization left the IVU merely because of pressure from the Nazi government and disbanded the German Vegetarian Union in 1936 out of protest, as Florentine Fritzen claims. Florentine Fritzen, "'Neuzeitlich leben': Reformhausbewegung und Moderne 1925–1933," in *Die "Krise" der Weimarer Republik*, ed. Moritz Föllmer (Frankfurt/Main: Campus, 2005), 73–74. The bone of contention at the IVU meeting of 1935 had been German members' opposition to the discrimination against Jews, Catholics, and Marxists under Nazi rule. Wolfgang R. Krabbe, "Biologismus und Lebensreform," in *Die Lebensreform. Entwürfe zur Neugestaltung von Leben und Kunst um 1900*, ed. Kai Buchholz (Häusser, 2001), 541–543.
147. H. Eßler, "Gedanken und Meinung zum 8. Internationalen Vegetarier-Kongreß in der Obstbausiedlung Eden bei Oranienburg/Berlin," *Vegetarische Presse* 15 (1932): 81–82; Georg Förster, "Abwehr. Deutschenhetze des niederländischen Vegetarierbundes," *Vegetarische Presse* 16 (1933): 93–94; Förster, "Abwehr. Unerhörte Beschimpfung der deutschen Vegetarier," *Vegetarische Presse* 16 (1933): 135–136.
148. Ernst Waag, "Zwölfter Weltkongreß der Internationalen Vegetarier Union (IVU)," *Sei Mensch* 1, no. 2 (1950): 15–18.

149. Treitel, *Eating Nature in Modern Germany*, 189-233. For more research on Nazi nutritional policy, see Gustavo Corni and Horst Gies, *Brot—Butter—Kanonen. Die Ernährungswirtschaft in Deutschland unter der Diktatur Hitlers* (Berlin: Akademie-Verlag, 1997); Werner Abelshauser, "Guns, Butter and Economic Miracles," in *The Economics of World War Two: Six Great Powers in International Comparison*, ed. Mark Harrison (Cambridge: Cambridge University Press, 1998), 122-176; Christian Gerlach, *Krieg, Ernährung, Völkermord. Forschungen zur deutschen Vernichtungspolitik im Zweiten Weltkrieg* (Hamburg: Hamburger Edition, 1998); Spiekermann, "Vollkorn für die Führer," 91-128; Susanne Heim, ed., *Autarkie und Ostexpansion. Pflanzenzucht und Agrarforschung im Nationalsozialismus* (Göttingen: Wallstein, 2002); Heim, *Kalorien, Kautschuk, Karrieren. Pflanzenzüchtung und landwirtschaftliche Forschung in Kaiser-Wilhelm-Instituten 1933-1945* (Göttingen: Wallstein-Verlag, 2003); Jörg Melzer, *Vollwerternährung. Diätetik, Naturheilkunde, Nationalsozialismus, sozialer Anspruch* (Stuttgart: Steiner, 2003), 143-259; Joachim Drews, *Die "Nazi-Bohne"* (Münster: LIT, 2004); Alexander Neumann, "Nutritional Physiology in the 'Third Reich' 1933-1945," in *Man, Medicine, and the State: The Human Body as an Object of Government Sponsored Medical Research in the 20th Century*, ed. W. U. Eckart (Stuttgart: Steiner, 2006), 49-59; Reinhold Reith, "'Hurrah die Butter ist alle!' 'Fettlücke' und 'Eiweißlücke' im Dritten Reich," in *Erfahrung der Moderne. Festschrift für Roman Sandgruber zum 60. Geburtstag*, ed. Michael Pammer and Hertha Neiß (Stuttgart: Steiner, 2007), 403-425; Birgit Pelzer-Reith and Reinhold Reith, "Fischkonsum und 'Eiweißlücke' im Nationalsozialismus," *Vierteljahrschrift für Sozial- und Wirtschaftsgeschichte* 96, no. 1 (2009): 4-26; Gine Elsner, ed., *Heilkräuter, "Volksernährung," Menschenversuche. Ernst Günther Schenck (1904-1998), Eine deutsche Arztkarriere* (Hamburg: VSA, 2010); "Die 'Eiweißlücke' und die biotechnologische Eiweißsynthese. Synthetische Nahrungsmittel in der nationalsozialistischen Autarkiepolitik," *Technikgeschichte* 79, no. 4 (2012): 303-340; Christine Stahl, *Sehnsucht Brot. Essen und hungern im KZ-Lagersystem Mauthausen* (Wien: Edition Mauthausen, 2010); Jürgen Finger, Sven Keller, and Andreas Wirsching, *Dr. Oetker und der Nationalsozialismus. Geschichte eines Familienunternehmens 1933-1945* (Munich: Beck, 2013); Gesine Gerhard, *Nazi Hunger Politics: A History of Food in the Third Reich* (Lanham, MD: Rowman & Littlefield, 2015); Alice Autumn Weinreb, *Modern Hungers: Food and Power in Twentieth-Century Germany* (New York: Oxford University Press, 2017); Uwe Spiekermann, *Künstliche Kost. Ernährung in Deutschland, 1840 bis Heute* (Göttingen: Vandenhoeck & Ruprecht, 2018), especially 235-622; Ulrich Schlie, "Das Reichsministerium für Ernährung und Landwirtschaft in der Zeit des Nationalsozialismus," in *Agrarpolitik im 20. Jahrhundert. Das Bundesministerium für Ernährung und Landwirtschaft und seine Vorgänger*, ed. Joachim Bitterlich et al. (Berlin: De Gruyter Oldenbourg, 2020), 103-262; Daniela Rüther, *Der "Fall Nährwert." Ein Wirtschaftskrimi aus der Zeit des Zweiten Weltkrieges* (Göttingen: Wallstein, 2020).

150. On the Nazi politics of autarky, see Corni and Gies, *Brot—Butter—Kanonen*; Gerhard, *Nazi Hunger Politics*, 34-82; Saraiva, *Fascist Pigs*, 71-141. Nazi officials supported a mixed diet not just to forestall discontent, but also for reasons of health. Melzer, *Vollwerternährung*, 164-165.

## 4. BETWEEN BUDDHA, GANDHI, SUFISM, AND MASCULINITY

151. Corni and Gies, *Brot—Butter—Kanonen*, 353–363; Drews, *Die "Nazi-Bohne"*; Ines Prodöhl, "'A Miracle Bean': How Soy Conquered the West, 1909–1950," *Bulletin of the German Historical Institute* 46 (2010): 111–129; Pelzer-Reith and Reith, "Fischkonsum und Eiweißlücke im Nationalsozialismus"; Birgit Pelzer and Reinhold Reith, *Margarine. Die Karriere der Kunstbutter* (Berlin: Klaus Wagenbach, 2001); Reith, "'Hurrah die Butter ist alle!'"; Pelzer-Reith and Reith, "Fischkonsum und Eiweißlücke im Nationalsozialismus"; "Die 'Eiweißlücke' und die biotechnologische Eiweißsynthese"; Spiekermann, *Künstliche Kost*, 504–548.
152. Melzer, *Vollwerternährung*, 183–198; Spiekermann, "Vollkorn für die Führer," 91–128. As Corinna Treitel points out, Nazi food policy began by stressing consumption of "natural foods," an aim increasingly at odds with the scarcity brought about by war and the racially coded distribution of food. Treitel, *Eating Nature in Modern Germany*, 189–233; Uwe Puschner, "Mit Vollkornbrot und Nacktheit."
153. Gerlach, *Krieg, Ernährung, Völkermord*, 167–257; Adam Tooze, *The Wages of Destruction: The Making and Breaking of the Nazi Economy* (London: Allen Lane, 2006), 461–486; Gerhard, *Nazi Hunger Politics*, 133–158; Weinreb, *Modern Hungers*, 65–84.
154. Melzer, *Vollwerternährung*, 198–204; Pelzer-Reith and Reith, "Die 'Eiweißlücke' und die biotechnologische Eiweißsynthese," 303–340; Weinreb, *Modern Hungers*, 65–84.
155. Fritzen, *Gesünder leben*, 71–77.
156. Erich Sperling, "So kämpfen wir für Frieden und Menschlichkeit," *Leib und Leben* 3 (1935): 293.
157. Elisabeth Hase, "Deutschlands Zukunft," *Vegetarische Presse* 23, no. 3 (1940): half title; E. Drewitz, "Zum Erntedankfest im Kriegsjahr 1940 (6. Oktober)," *Vegetarische Presse* 23, no. 10 (1940): n.p.; Rudi Seidel, "Kriegskameraden," *Vegetarische Presse*, no. 11 (1940): n.p. While scholars like Raewyn Connell stress that there were multiple male gender roles under Nazism, recent studies show that violence and emotional control were central to Nazi notions of masculinity. See, e.g., Raewyn Connell, "Masculinity and Nazism," in *Männlichkeitskonstruktionen im Nationalsozialismus. Formen, Funktionen und Wirkungsmacht von Geschlechterkonstruktionen im Nationalsozialismus und ihre Reflexion in der pädagogischen Praxis*, ed. Anette Dietrich and Ljiljana Heise (Frankfurt/Main: Peter Lang, 2013), 37–42; Frank Werner, "'Noch härter, noch kälter, noch mitleidloser.' Soldatische Männlichkeit im deutschen Vernichtungskrieg 1941–1944," in Dietrich and Heise, *Männlichkeitskonstruktionen im Nationalsozialismus*, 45–63; Diehl, *Macht—Mythos—Utopie*.
158. E. Drewig, "Zum Erntedankfest Im Kriegsjahr 1940 (6. Oktober)," *Vegetarische Presse* 23 (1940): title page.
159. Nathan Chavkin, "Palästina," *Vegetarische Presse* 9 (1926): 105; "Palästina. Vegetarier-Siedlung," *Vegetarische Presse* 11 (1928): 39; "Palästina," *Vegetarische Presse* 14 (1931): 76–77; "Palästina als Zukunftsland vegetarischer Siedelung," *Vegetarische Presse* 127–128; "Palästina als Zukunftsland vegetarischer Siedelung," *Vegetarische Presse* 15 (1932): 9–10, 20–21. Chavkin remained committed to both vegetarianism and Esperanto after migrating to Palestine. "Palestino," *Vegetarano* 17, no. 2 (1934): 27; *Jarlibro de la Internacia Esperanto-Ligo* (1943): 60. German vegetarian journals ceased mentioning him as of 1933, only reporting on his activities

again after the Second World War. See, for instance, Nathan Benzion Chavkin, "Schlachthaus-Gedanken," *Vegetarisches Universum* 7, no. 2 (1954): 3. On Chavkin's biography and activities in Palestine/Israel, see "Hebrew Vegetarian Association," Central Zionist Archives, World Zionist Organization, accessed 18 December 2020, http://www.zionistarchives.org.il/en/AttheCZA/AdditionalArticles/Pages/vegetarianism.aspx.

160. "Vivisektion in Preußen verboten," *Vegetarische Presse* 16 (1933): 105; "Nationalsozialisten gegen Vivisektion," *Vegetarische Presse* 16 (1933): 3–4; "Schächtverbote in Deutschland," *Vegetarische Presse* 16 (1933): 3; H. W. Knuest, "Tierschutz. Unser Besuch im Schlachthof," *Vegetarische Presse* 16 (1933): 75–76. As Francesco Buscemi justly remarks, the Nazis' restrictive attitude toward vivisection and slaughter protected animals from a degree of cruelty that humans excluded from the *Volksgemeinschaft* routinely suffered. Francesco Buscemi, "Edible Lies: How Nazi Propaganda Represented Meat to Demonise the Jews," *Media, War and Conflict* 9, no. 2 (2016): 180–197.

161. Eugen Dühring, "Absolute Herrschaft über die Tiere—Eine Hebräersatzung," *Vegetarische Presse* 23 (1940): 28. One of the paradigmatic Nazi texts stressing the alleged link between Jewishness and cruelty to animals was published by the then minister of agriculture. It blamed Jews for "Aryan" Germans' hunger during the First World War, claiming they had slaughtered all the pigs. Richard Walther Darré, *Der Schweinemord* (Munich: Eher, 1937). Even though openly anti-Semitic, however, the *Vegetarische Presse* was superseded in this respect by another journal, *Lichtheilgrüße*, edited by Walter Sommer, a life reformer and youth movement leader from Hamburg. Sommer's journal stood out not only for its recommending a diet of only raw fruit and vegetables; it was also the most unabashedly pro-Nazi, anti-Semitic, and most racist of the German vegetarian journals. See, for instance, Walter Sommer, "Blut und Boden. Das deutsche Bodenrecht," *Lichtheilgrüße* 9 (1933): 98–103; Ernst Waag, "Rasse und Nahrung," *Lichtheilgrüße* 12 (1933): 222–225; "Zur Kolonialfrage," *Lichtheilgrüße* 14 (1938): 371–372; Robert Breske, "Der Frischköstler ein Fürst und Führer," *Lichtheilgrüße* 4 (1928): 326–328. After the Second World War, Walter Sommer continued to publish and was a much-appreciated speaker at vegetarian congresses in Germany. Obscure present-day websites praise him as a "super hero" and the earliest protagonist of lifelong raw veganism in Germany. Walter Sommer (1887–1985), https://germanygoesraw.de/superheroes/walter-sommer/ (accessed 12 January 2021).

162. Gerhard Härtel, "Als Vegetarier im Polenfeldzug," *Vegetarische Presse* 23 (1940): 44–45; E. M., "Krieg und Vegetarismus," *Vegetarische Presse* 23 (1940): 81–82. Several articles in the *Vegetarische Presse* also tied in with Nazi debates on autarky, arguing that it could best be achieved by giving preference to agriculture rather than livestock keeping, and moving to organic methods. Kühl, "Die volkswirtschaftliche Bedeutung der fleischlosen Ernährung," *Vegetarische Presse* 23 (1940): 23; "Der einfachste und natürlichste Weg zu Deutschlands Nahrungsfreiheit," *Vegetarische Presse* 23 (1940): 41–43, 51–52, 59, 67–68, 83; "Die Eiweißfrage und ihre Lösung," *Vegetarische Presse* 23 (1940), 13–14, 19–20; D. V., "Die Ernährung des deutschen Volkes sichergestellt," *Vegetarische Presse* 23 (1940), 23.

163. Fritzen, *Gesünder leben*, 75.

## 4. BETWEEN BUDDHA, GANDHI, SUFISM, AND MASCULINITY

164. Julius Groß, "Werner Zimmermann, stehend und Gestikulierend, mit nacktem Oberkörper während einer Rede," in *8. Internationaler Vegetarierkongress in der Obstbaukolonie Eden in Berlin*, Archiv der deutschen Jugendbewegung, AdJb B, 1932.
165. Groß, "Werner Zimmermann"; B. Hinze, "Politik und Ernährungsweise," *Vegetarische Presse* 16 (1933): 37–38.
166. "Tagungen. 8. Internationaler Vegetarier-Tag," *Vegetarische Presse* 15 (1932): 89–91.
167. In 1932, Zimmermann gave a whole series of talks on Gandhi in Switzerland, Germany, and central Europe. Later, he came back to this topic repeatedly. Werner Zimmermann, "Berichte. gandhi," *Tau*, no. 93 (1932): 27; "Vorträge von Dr. h. c. Werner Zimmermann," *Vegetarisches Universum* 4, no. 10 (1951): 3; "Werner-Zimmermann Vorträge," *Vegetarisches Universum* 7, no. 5 (1954): 4; "Werner-Zimmermann Vorträge," *Vegetarisches Universum* 7, no. 10 (1954): 3; "Werner-Zimmermann Vorträge," *Vegetarisches Universum* 7, no. 11 (1954): 5; "Werner-Zimmermann Vorträge," *Vegetarisches Universum* 7, no. 12 (1954): 4; "Werner-Zimmermann-Vorträge," *Vegetarisches Universum*, no. 11 (1955): 4. For Zimmermann as a connecting figure, see Wedemeyer-Kolwe, *"Der neue Mensch,"* 232.
168. On German reform educators' connections with India, see Horn, *Indien als Erzieher*.
169. Studies on German-speaking nudism generally focus exclusively on Germany. Marc Cluet, *La "libre culture." Le mouvement nudiste en Allemagne depuis ses origines au seuil du XXe siècle jusq'à l'arrivée de Hitler au pouvoir (1905–1933). Présupposés, développements et enjeux historiques* (Villeneuve d'Ascq: Presses Universitaires du Septentrion, 2002); Wedemeyer-Kolwe, *"Der neue Mensch"*; Maren Möhring, *Marmorleiber: Körperbildung in der deutschen Nacktkultur, 1890–1930* (Cologne: Böhlau, 2004); Chad Ross, *Naked Germany: Health, Race and the Nation* (Oxford: Berg, 2005); Williams, *Turning to Nature in Germany*. Zimmermann's contribution to life reform is only starting to be researched. Toshiko Ito, "Transzendenz und Orientalismus in der Reformpädagogik: Eine Fallstudie zur Kooperation zwischen Werner Zimmermann und Kuniyoshi Obara," *International Journal for the History of Education* 2 (2012): 36–50; Stefan Rindlisbacher, "Popularisierung und Etablierung der Freikörperkultur in der Schweiz (1900–1930)," *Schweizerische Zeitschrift für Geschichte* 65, no. 3 (2015): 393–413; Rindlisbacher, "Jugendzeitschriften zwischen Wandervogel und Lebensreform (1904–1924)," in *Let's Historize It! Jugendmedien im 20. Jahrhundert*, ed. Aline Maldener and Clemens Zimmermann (Wien: Böhlau, 2018), 37–60.
170. The first edition of Zimmermann's work can no longer be retrieved in German or Swiss libraries. Werner Zimmermann, *Weltvagant. Erlebnisse und Gedanken* (Lauf/Pegnitz: Rudolf Zitzmann, 1921). Citations are thus from a later edition: *Weltvagant. Erlebnisse und Gedanken* (Lauf/Nuremberg: Die Neue Zeit, 1927), 7.
171. Zimmermann, *Weltvagant. Erlebnisse und Gedanken*, 94–95n. On Gandhi's nutritional experiments, see, inter alia, Joseph S. Alter, *Gandhi's Body: Sex, Diet, and the Politics of Nationalism* (Philadelphia: University of Philadelphia Press, 2000); Parama Roy, *Alimentary Tracts: Appetites, Aversions, and the Postcolonial* (Durham, NC: Duke University Press, 2010), 75–115; Slate, *Gandhi's Search for the Perfect Diet*.

## 4. BETWEEN BUDDHA, GANDHI, SUFISM, AND MASCULINITY

172. Werner Zimmermann, *Tropenheimat* (Lauf/Nuremberg: Die Neue Zeit, 1930); *Weltheimat* (Lauf/Nuremberg: Rudolf Zitzmann, 1937).
173. Zimmermann, *Zu freien Ufern* (Munich: Drei Eichen, 1950).
174. Zimmermann, *Weltheimat*, 245. On Madeleine Slade, see Thomas Weber, *Going Native: Gandhi's Relationship with Western Women* (New Delhi: Lotus, 2011), 190–218.
175. Instead, Zimmermann encountered Nehru, and was not impressed by his open anti-vegetarianism and smoking. Zimmermann, *Zu freien Ufern*, 234–235.
176. Stefan Rindlisbacher, "Jugendzeitschriften zwischen Wandervogel und Lebensreform (1904–1924)," in Maldener and Zimmermann, *Let's Historize It!*, 37–60.
177. Brunotte, *Zwischen Eros und Krieg*, 70–118; Dahlke, *Jünglinge der Moderne*, 180–197; Herrmann, *"Mit uns zieht die neue Zeit...,"* 107–145; Niemeyer, *Die dunklen Seiten der Jugendbewegung*; Susanne Rappe-Weber, "'Hoch das Wandern!' Neue Gemeinschaftsformen im Wandervogel," in *Wanderland. Eine Reise durch die Geschichte des Wanderns*, ed. Claudia Selheim, Frank Matthias Kammel, and Thomas Brehm (Nürnberg: Verlag des Germanischen Nationalmuseums, 2018), 134–141.
178. Williams, *Turning to Nature in Germany*, 69–99.
179. On the topos of the heroic explorer, see Beau Riffenburgh, *The Myth of the Explorer: The Press, Sensationalism, and Geographical Discovery* (London: Belhaven Press, 1993).
180. Stefan Rindlisbacher, *Lebensreform in der Schweiz (1850–1950). Vegetarisch essen, nackt baden und Im Grünen wohnen* (Berlin: Peter Lang, 2022), 305–317.
181. See, for instance, Werner Zimmermann, "Kuniyoshi obara," *Tau*, no. 73 (1930): 27–31; "Bücher. china- und japan-bücher," *Tau*, no. 82 (1931): 22–25; "Die dukhoborzen und die frage wirtschaftlicher gemeinschaft," *Tau*, no. 78 (1930): 1–16; "Berichte. indien," *Tau*, no. 66 (1929): 22–25.
182. Indeed, Zimmermann was highly critical of Mazdaznan, associating it not with Zoroastrianism, but with intellectual dishonesty: Zimmermann, "Masdasnan," *Tao. Monatsblätter für Verinnerlichung und Selbstgestaltung*, no. 32 (1927).
183. The book was first published in Dutch as Henri Borel, *Wijsheid en schoonheid uit China* (Amsterdam: P. N. Van Kampen & Zoon, 1895). English and French translations appeared in the following decades: Borel, *Wu Wei: A Phantasy Based on the Philosophy of Lao-Tse*, trans. Meredith Ianson (London: Luzac, 1903); *Wu Wei: Fiction basée sur la philosophie de Lao Tse* (Paris: Fischbacher, 1913). There is no research so far on either Borel's life or book, although both would be highly interesting in the context of Dutch colonialism in the East Indies, given that Borel served as a colonial official. "Borel, Henri Jean François," in *De Nederlandse en Vlaamse auteurs van middeleeuwen tot heden met inbegrip van de Friese auteurs* (Weesp, NL: De Haan, 1985), cited in *Biografisch Archief Van De Benelux*, vol. 1, microfiche 83, 315, and vol. 2, microfiche 29, 212.
184. Werner Zimmermann, "Vorwort," in *Wu-Wei. Eine Auslegung der Lehren Laotses. Deutsch von Werner Zimmermann*, ed. Henri Borel (Lauf/Nuremberg: Rudolf Zitzmann, 1933), 10.
185. Borel, *Wu-Wei. Eine Auslegung der Lehren Laotses. Deutsch von Werner Zimmermann*, 24–31.
186. Zimmermann, "Vorwort," 10.

## 4. BETWEEN BUDDHA, GANDHI, SUFISM, AND MASCULINITY

187. Samir Banerjee, *Tracing Gandhi: Satyarthi to Satyagrahi* (Abingdon, UK: Routledge, 2020), 68–76; Slate, *Gandhi's Search for the Perfect Diet*, 55.
188. Werner Zimmermann, "Recht-shreibung," *Tao. Monatsblätter für Verinnerlichung und Selbstgestaltung*, no. 15 (1925): 2–21; "Rechtshreibung," *Tao. Monatsblätter für Verinnerlichung und Selbstgestaltung*, no. 17 (1925): 29–35; "Preisausschreiben. zur formfindung fom einheitszeichen für ch und sch," *Tao. Monatsblätter für Verinnerlichung und Selbstgestaltung*, no. 25 (1926): 32–33. Ironically, it was when Zimmermann abandoned these ideas in 1927 without further discussion that the title of the journal changed from *Tao* to *Tau*.
189. Gösta Erdling, "Rudolf von laban, der freiwirtshaftliche tänzer," *Tao*, no. 17 (1925): 26–28; Werner Zimmermann, "Fysiokratie," *Tau*, no. 52 (1928): 1–11; "Silvio Gesell. Ausschnitte aus seinem Leben," *Tau*, no. 72 (1930): 4–11; Philibert Hundertpfund, "'Freie friedlandsiedlungen' (Fr. Fr. S.)," *Tau*, no. 94 (1932): 7–10.
190. R. M., "Ein jahr siedlung schatzacker," *Tau*, no. 110 (1933): 1–6; Werner Zimmermann, "Wir. wirtschaftsring," *Tau*, 11, no. 123 (1934): 1–13; *Wir schaffen freies Land! Tatsachen und Pläne* (Lauf/Nuremberg: Rudolf Zitzmann, 1937), 12–19.
191. "Rohkost und wirtshaftsreform," *Tao* 1, no. 6 (1924): 43–46; Erwin Hof, "Rohkost," *Tao*, no. 6 (1924): 2–39; Walter Rudolf, "Der gehalt macht's. Gedanken über herkunft und wertigkeit der paradieskost," *Tao*, no. 6 (1924): 2–39; "Fasten," *Tao*, no. 7 (1925): 14–15.
192. Godwin Rall, "Fasten," *Tao*, no. 14 (1925): 2–11.
193. Roy, *Alimentary Tracts*, 97–99.
194. Mohandas Karamchand Gandhi, "Speech on Cow Protection, Bettiah (about 9 October 1917)," in *The Collected Works of Mohandas Karamchand Gandhi*, vol. 16, *1 September, 1917–23 April, 1918* (New Delhi: Publications Division Government of India, 1999), 55–56; "Presidential Address at Cow-Protection Conference Belgaum (28 December 1924)," in *The Collected Works of Mohandas Karamchand Gandhi*, vol. 38, *2 January, 1927–3 June, 1927* (New Delhi: Publications Division Government of India, 1999), 457–459; "The Khilafat Against Cow-Protection," in *The Collected Works of Mohandas Karamchand Gandhi*, vol. 44, *16 January, 1929–3 February, 1929* (New Delhi: Publications Division Government of India, 1999), 447–451.
195. Higginbottom, an American missionary, had lived in India since 1903, soon turning from direct mission to agriculture as a means of "uplifting" India. In 1919, he founded the Allahabad Institute of Agriculture. Higginbottom was in contact with many anticolonial activists, most importantly Gandhi, many of whose views on cow protection were shaped by Higginbottom's ideas, including the need for improving Indian cattle breeds and increasing their milk yield. Sam Higginbottom, "More and Better Milk," *Allahabad Farmer* 11, no. 2 (1937): 65–71; Prakash Kumar, "American Modernisers and the Cow Question in Colonial and Nationalist India," *South Asia: Journal of South Asian Studies* 44, no. 1 (2021): 185–200.
196. Only articles in the 1933 and 1934 volumes discussed animal welfare. See, e.g., Richard Feldhaus, "Giftgas-experimente an tieren," *Tau* 10, no. 114 (1933): 19–22; Hans Much, "Vivisektion. Anatomische Zerstückelung eines lebenden Wesens," *Tau* 11, no. 118 (1934): 1–11.
197. It would be interesting to explore Gandhi's and other vegetarians' opposition to vaccination (which, for much of the twentieth century, involved animal experiments, if not actually using animals as a vehicle for creating the vaccine; vaccines

often led to direct contact between human and animal blood more directly than meat consumption). Since most of these vegetarians stressed the necessity of abstaining from meat to suppress what they characterized as the "animal drives" of human nature, their argument was very much about purity and self-control—and neatly dividing human from nonhuman bodies.

198. For his books on love and sexuality, see Werner Zimmermann, *Liebe. Von ihrem dreifachen Sinn*, 2nd ed. (Erfurt: Steiger, 1923); Alice B. Stockham, *Ethik der Ehe: Karezza. Berechtigt übersetzt aus dem Amerikanischen von Werner Zimmermann* (Jena: Die neue Zeit, 1925); Werner Zimmermann, *Liebes-Klarheit: Eine Frucht aus Erlebnis, Erkenntnis und Tat* (Lauf/Nuremberg: Rudolf Zitzmann, 1938).
199. Hof, "Rohkost," 2–39.
200. Zimmermann, *Liebes-Klarheit*, 27, 55–58.
201. Werner Zimmerman, "Liebe und ehe," *Tao. Monatsblätter für Verinnerlichung und selbstgestaltung*, no. 13 (1925): 28; "Form und inhalt der ehe," *Tao. Monatsblätter für Verinnerlichung und Selbstgestaltung*, no. 21 (1925): 4–14. On divorce in Switzerland, see Caroline Arni, *Entzweiungen. Die Krise der Ehe um 1900* (Cologne: Böhlau, 2004).
202. F. Landmann, "Das geshlechtliche empfinden der frau," *Tao. Monatsblätter für Verinnerlichung und Selbstgestaltung*, no. 13 (1925): 15–24; Zimmermann, "Form und inhalt der ehe," 4–14; Hanna Blumenthal, "Der weg zur freude. Die frauenbewegung und die fysiokratie," *Tau*, no. 33 (1927): 18–22.
203. Werner Zimmermann, "Review of Miroslav Schlesinger, Die Onanie im Lichte der modernen Seelenkunde, Radeburg: Madaus, 1925," *Tau. Monatsblätter für Verinnerlichung und Selbstgestaltung*, no. 41 (1927): 25–26. During the 1930s, Zimmermann's position became more restrictive again. Zimmermann, *Heimatkräfte persönlicher Gesundung* (Lauf/Nuremberg: Zitzmann, 1938), 12–13. Throughout, his comments referred to male masturbation. Women had long been considered less sexually driven, although from the late eighteenth century on, women's novel reading had caused concern. Moreover, male masturbation, because of the "waste" of sperm, seemed to cause the greater loss of energy. Thomas Laqueur, *Solitary Sex: A Cultural History of Masturbation* (New York: Zone Books, 2008), 340–358; Philipp Sarasin, *Reizbare Maschinen. Eine Geschichte des Körpers 1765–1914* (Frankfurt/Main: Suhrkamp, 2001), 404–417.
204. Werner Zimmermnn, "Verhütungsmittel," *Tao. Monatsblätter für Verinnerlichung und Selbstgestaltung*, no. 4 (1924): 21–24.
205. Stockham, *Ethik der Ehe*.
206. "Lichtkleid," *Tao. Monatsblätter für Verinnerlichung und Selbstgestaltung*, no. 13 (1925): 2–12. Maren Möhring locates the same argument in German nudist discourse: Möhring, *Marmorleiber*, 124–125.
207. See, for instance, Werner Zimmermann, "Ferienlager 1925," *Tao. Monatsblätter für Verinnerlichung und Selbstgestaltung*, nos. 18–19 (1925): 13–23.
208. Stefan Rindlisbacher comes to much the same conclusion about Zimmermann's attitude to eugenics: Rindlisbacher, "Popularisierung und Etablierung der Freikörperkultur in der Schweiz (1900–1930)," 403. On the eugenic dimension of German-speaking nudism, see Arnd Krüger, "There Goes This Art of Manliness: Naturism and Racial Hygiene in Germany," *Journal of Sport History* 18, no. 1 (1991): 135–158; Uwe Schneider, "Nacktkultur im Kaiserreich," in *Handbuch*

## 4. BETWEEN BUDDHA, GANDHI, SUFISM, AND MASCULINITY

zur "Völkischen Bewegung" 1871–1918, ed. Uwe Puschner, Walter Schmitz, and Justus H. Ulbricht (Munich: K. G. Saur, 1996), 411–435; Ulrich Linse, "Völkisch-Rassische Siedlungen der Lebensreform," in Handbuch zur "Völkischen Bewegung," ed. Uwe Puschner (Munich: Saur, 1996), 397–410; Ross, Naked Germany, 235–260.

209. Gandhi had read the writings of Adolf Just, the founder of the Jungborn sanatorium in the Harz Mountains, who cured his patients' bodies by exposing them to light and sun and feeding them raw fruits, as well as those of Louis Kuehne, who, convinced that the genitals were the locus of health, recommended the so-called friction sitz bath. Alter, Gandhi's Body, 14, 38, 59–64, 69, 79.
210. Mohandas Karamchand Gandhi, A Guide to Health, trans. A. Rama Iyer (Madras: S. Ganesan, 1921), 67–68.
211. As Douglas Haynes argues, Gandhi's concept of brahmacharya was also inspired by contemporary debates on eugenics in Europe. According to Harald Fischer-Tiné, the Arya Samaj also followed debates on eugenics in Europe. Douglas E. Haynes, "Gandhi, Brahmacharya and Global Sexual Science, 1919–1938," South Asia: Journal of South Asian Studies 43, no. 6 (2020): 1163–1178; Harald Fischer-Tiné, "From Brahmacharya to 'Conscious Race Culture': Victorian Discourses of Science and Hindu Traditions in Early Indian Nationalism," in Beyond Representation: Colonial and Post-Colonial Constructions of Indian Identity, ed. Crispin Bates (New Delhi: Oxford University Press, 2006), 241–269.
212. Gandhi, A Guide to Health, 74–75.
213. Roy, Alimentary Tracts, 97–99.
214. Gandhi, A Guide to Health, 78–79.
215. Gandhi, 71.
216. Gandhi, 72.
217. Werner Zimmermann, "Hass oder libe," Tao, no. 24 (1926): 8–17.
218. Werner Zimmermann, "Berichte. Gandhi," Tau, no. 91 (1931): 25. On Gandhi's meeting with Rolland, see R. A. Francis, Romain Rolland (Oxford: Berg, 1999), 136–139.
219. Zimmermann, "Berichte. Gandhi," 25.
220. Zimmermann, 27.
221. Rindlisbacher, Lebensreform in der Schweiz (1850–1950), 374–382.
222. "Werner-Zimmermann-Vorträge für Truppen," Vegetarische Presse 23 (1940): 6.
223. Zimmermann was a popular speaker at German vegetarian congresses in the 1950s: "Vorträge von Dr. h. c. Werner Zimmermann," 3; "Werner Zimmermann-Obara-Vorträge," Vegetarisches Universum 8, no. 5 (1955): 4; "Werner-Zimmermann-Vorträge," 4.
224. Magnus Schwantje, Ram Chandra Sharma's Kampf gegen die religiösen Tieropfer in Indien. Sonder-Abdruck aus der Zeitschrift "Der Vivisektionsgegner" (Bern: Vegetarierbund, 1937).
225. Renate Brucker, "Tierrechte und Friedensbewegung: 'Radikale Ethik' und gesellschaftlicher Fortschritt in der deutschen Geschichte," in Tierische Geschichte. Die Beziehung von Mensch und Tier in der Kultur der Moderne, ed. Dorothee Brantz and Christof Mauch (Paderborn: Schöningh, 2010), 268–285.
226. On his pacifist positions, see, for instance, Magnus Schwantje, "Sozialismus und Pazifismus," Mitteilungen des Bundes für radikale Ethik 1 (1920): 2–5; "Schenkt den

## 4. BETWEEN BUDDHA, GANDHI, SUFISM, AND MASCULINITY

Kindern kein Kriegsspielzeug und keine Peitschen," *Mitteilungen des Bundes für radikale Ethik* 7 (1926): 21; "Radikaler Tierschutz und Kriegsbekämpfung," *Mitteilungen des Bundes für radikale Ethik* 11 (1930): 20–23; "Gegen die Wiedereinführung der allgemeinen Wehrpflicht," *Mitteilungen des Bundes für radikale Ethik* 12 (1931): 12–13.

227. Afas, Magnus Schwantje Papers, Magnus Schwantje to Gesellschaft für christlich-jüdische Zusammenarbeit, Berlin-Wilmersdorf, July 25, 1950.
228. This is not just evident from Schwantje's journal, the *Ethische Rundschau*, renamed *Mitteilungen des Bundes für radikale Ethik* in 1920, but also from his papers, hitherto uncataloged, at the Archiv für alternatives schrifttum (Afas), Duisburg. On the Schwantje Papers, see Jürgen Bacia, "Unsere Geschichte gehört uns! Die Archive der neuen sozialen Bewegungen," in *Logik und Lücke. Die Konstruktion des authentischen in Archiven und Sammlungen*, ed. Michael Farrenkopf, Andreas Ludwig, and Achim Saupe (Göttingen: Wallstein, 2021), 263–266. I am indebted to Jürgen Bacia for his assistance during my research at the archive.
229. Afas, Magnus Schwantje Papers, Magnus Schwantje, Berlin (?), to Jules Stiber, Würzburg, May 29, 1917. Schwantje, Berlin (?), to Isidor Trötschler, Radolfzell, February 6, 1920. Since few passages in his letters hint at romantic interest in women, but his correspondence with Ram Chandra carries overtones of romantic love, there is a possibility that Schwantje was homosexual. He was in close contact with Magnus Hirschfeld, probably because of Hirschfeld's support for pacifism. "Bericht über das erste Tätigkeitsjahr (1. Juli 1919 bis 30. Juli 1920) des Instituts für Sexualwissenschaft," *Jahrbuch für sexuelle Zwischenstufen* 20 (1920): 71–72. I thank Ma Ralf Dose of the Magnus Hirschfeld Society for sending me this source. Schwantje's journal never discussed tolerance toward all sexual orientations as a humanitarian issue, but he supported Anita Augspurg and Lida Gustava Heymann, two important queer pacifists and feminists, who published there. Brucker, "Für eine radikale Ethik," 235.
230. Schwantje, "Tierrechte und Friedensbewegung," 282–283.
231. His associate Ria Scheib founded a charity for animals in Abyssinia when the country was shaken by the Italian invasion. Afas, Magnus Schwantje Papers, Magnus Schwantje to Mrs. Falk, Zurich, April 6, 1936.
232. Brucker, "Tierrechte und Friedensbewegung," 272.
233. Afas, Magnus Schwantje Papers, Magnus Schwantje to Pandit Ram Chandra Sharma, c/o Dr. K. N. Palit, Secretary of the All-India Adarsh Hindu Sangh, Gaya (Bihar), India, Zurich, June 9, 1937. During the 1920s and early 1930s, Schwantje regularly attended and reported from international animal welfare, pacifist, and youth congresses. Magnus Schwantje, "Tagung des Internationalen Jugendbundes," *Mitteilungen des Bundes für radikale Ethik* 3 (1922): 4–5; "Resolutionen des XI. deutschen Pazifisten-Kongresses," *Mitteilungen des Bundes für radikale Ethik* 3 (1922): 6–8; "Internationaler Tierschutz-Kongreß in Paris," *Mitteilungen des Bundes für radikale Ethik* 6 (1925): 1–3; "Internationaler Tierschutz- und Antivivisektions-Kongreß in London," *Mitteilungen des Bundes für radikale Ethik* 8 (1927): 3–8.
234. "The Bombay Humanitarian League. Its Why and What," in *The Indian Humanitarian. The Bombay Humanitarian League. Silver Jubilee Number, 1910–1934, Etc.* (Bombay: Bombay Humanitarian League, 1934), 7–11.

## 4. BETWEEN BUDDHA, GANDHI, SUFISM, AND MASCULINITY

235. Dahyabhai H. Jani, *Romance of the Cow* (Bombay: Bombay Humanitarian League, 1938), 118–121.
236. Labhshankar Laxmidas, "Hitler Has Become Vegetarian. Appeal to Rulers for Mercy to Millions of Human Beings and Millions of Animals," in *The Indian Humanitarian*, 84.
237. Bishamber Dayal Yadav, "Introduction," in *M. P. T. Acharya. Reminiscences of an Indian Revolutionary*, ed. Yadav (New Delhi: Anmol, 1991), 9–15. The India House, a home to "radical Indian nationalism," was created by Shyamji Krishnavarma, a Hindu scholar then living in Britain, in 1907. It soon came to be associated with revolutionary activities against British rule in India. Harald Fischer-Tiné, *Shyamji Krishnavarma: Sanskrit, Sociology and Anti-Imperialism* (New Delhi: Routledge, 2014), 62–68.
238. Ole Birk Laursen, "Introduction: M. P. T. Acharya: A Revolutionary, an Agitator, a Writer," in *Acharya, M. P. T.: We Are Anarchists. Essays on Anarchism, Pacifism, and the Indian Independence Movement, 1923–1953*, ed. Laursen (Edinburgh: Chico, 2019), 6; Yadav, "Introduction," 34–43.
239. "Anarchist" was a term Acharya used to describe his political positions: M. P. T. Acharya, "Anarchist Manifesto" in Laursen, *We Are Anarchists*, 45–49.
240. Laursen, "Introduction: M. P. T. Acharya," 13–17.
241. Acharya, "Gandhi and Non-Violence," in Laursen, *We Are Anarchists*, 103–106.
242. Acharya, "On the Question of Race," in Laursen, *We Are Anarchists*, 137–139.
243. Afas, Magnus Schwantje Papers, Magnus Schwantje, Oberhausen (?) to Helene Haas, Wuppertal-Elberfeld, August 10, 1952; Schwantje, Oberhausen (?) to Erika Krüche, Jena, September 4, 1956; M. P. T. Acharya, Bombay, to Magnus Schwantje, July 29, 1950. Acharya's biographies do not mention Theosophy, perhaps because he is generally studied as an anarchist/critical leftist, and research on these political movements has long overlooked religion except for Christian readings of anarchism. It is possible that he contacted German Theosophists since the Theosophical Society in India was known as a supporter of Indian nationalism, and, despite the prominent position of Europeans within the organization, a critic of colonial rule. Acharya may have hoped to find political allies against British rule among German Theosophists, even though German Theosophist lodges had no anticolonial leanings.
244. Scheib evidently was not aware that the Theosophical Society in India, most notably under the aegis of Annie Besant in Madras, had indeed promoted animal welfare from the early twentieth century on, and that Theosophists were equally prominent in the British antivivisection movement. Annie Besant, *On the Protection of Animals: An Address at the Calcutta Town Hall* (Madras: Theosophist Office, 1910); Mieke Roscher, *Ein Königreich für Tiere. Die Geschichte der britischen Tierrechtsbewegung* (Marburg: Tectum, 2009), 162, 171.
245. "Über Vegetarismus und Gewaltbekämpfung (aus der "Vegetarischen Presse")," *Mitteilungen des Bundes für radkale Ethik* 12 (1931): 23–24.
246. Magnus Schwantje, *Ram Chandra Sharma's Kampf gegen die religiösen Tieropfer in Indien; Lutte de Ram Chandra Sharma contre les sacrifices religieux d'animaux aux Indes. Reproduction spéciale du bulletin de la ligue antivivisectionniste "L'antivivisection"* (Geneva: Ligue Antivivisectionniste, 1937). For contemporary Indian accounts of Ram Chandra's fast, see "Fast to Stop Animal Sacrifice,"

## 4. BETWEEN BUDDHA, GANDHI, SUFISM, AND MASCULINITY

*Times of India*, September 26, 1935, 3; "Pandit Ram Chandra Sharma's Fast for Stopping Animal Sacrifice," *Modern Review* 58, no. 4 (1935): 482–483; "Rabindranath Tagore and Pandit Ram Chandra Sharma's Fast," *Modern Review* 58, no. 4 (1935): 484. Schwantje attempted unsuccessfully to publish his essay in the *Vegetarische Warte*. Most likely, Georg Förster was no longer willing to publish anything remotely pacifist. Afas, Magnus Schwantje Papers, Schwantje to Georg Förster, Zurich, July 5, 1937.

247. Schwantje, *Ram Chandra Sharma's Kampf gegen die religiösen Tieropfer in Indien*.
248. Afas, Magnus Schwantje Papers, Magnus Schwantje to Pandit Ram Chandra Sharma, c/o Dr. K. N. Palit, Secretary of the All India Adarsh Hindu Sangh, Gaya (Bihar), India, Zurich, June 9, 1937.
249. Afas, Magnus Schwantje Papers, Magnus Schwantje to Ram Chandra Sharma, Zurich, after January 26, 1938.
250. Afas, Magnus Schwantje Papers, Ram Chandra Sharma to Magnus Schwantje, Gaya, August 5, 1937.
251. Afas, Magnus Schwantje Papers, Magnus Schwantje to Pandit Ram Chandra Sharma, Zurich, June 9, 1937.
252. Afas, Magnus Schwantje Papers, Magnus Schwantje to Ram Chandra Sharma, Zurich, after January 26, 1938.
253. As there is no research on him so far, and contemporary biographies could not be retrieved as of September 2020, the most extensive information on Ram Chandra's life may be found at Wikipedia, s.v. "Maharishi Ram Chandra Vir," last modified May 4, 2023, 20:39, https://hi.wikipedia.org/wiki/महात्मा_रामचन्द्र_वीर. On the Gurukul Kangri, see Harald Fischer-Tiné, *Der Gurukul-Kangri oder die Erfindung der Arya-Nation. Kolonialismus, Hindureform und "Nationale Bildung" in Britisch-Indien (1897–1922)* (Würzburg: Ergon, 2003).
254. Wikipedia, s.v. "Maharishi Ram Chandra Vir," last modified May 4, 2023, 20:39, https://hi.wikipedia.org/wiki/महात्मा_रामचन्द्र_वीर.
255. For a rather ironic coverage of the Kalyan protest, see "Satyagraha Against Animal Sacrifice. Pandit's Unsuccessful Attempts," *Times of India*, April 22, 1935, 4.
256. Wikipedia, s.v. "Maharishi Ram Chandra Vir," last modified May 4, 2023, 20:39, https://hi.wikipedia.org/wiki/महात्मा_रामचन्द्र_वीर. This treatise could not be retrieved so far.
257. Afas, Magnus Schwantje Papers, Ram Chandra Sharma to Magnus Schwantje, Gaya, August 5, 1937.
258. Faisal Devji, *The Impossible Indian: Gandhi and the Temptation of Violence* (London: Hurst, 2012).
259. Savitri Devi, *L'étang aux lotus* (Brabant, BE: Thule Sodalitas, 1998), 41–42, 50. On Savarkar's notion of Hindutva and the "Hindian" nation, which included Hindus, Jains, and Sikhs, but not Muslims, Christians, or Jews, see Vinayak Damodar Savarkar, "Extract from Hindutva: Who Is a Hindu?," in *Hindu Nationalism: A Reader*, ed. Christophe Jaffrelot (Princeton, NJ: Princeton University Press, 2007), 94–95; Jyortirmaya Sharma, *Hindutva: Exploring the Idea of Hindu Nationalism* (New Delhi: Harper Collins, 2011), 193–203.

## 4. BETWEEN BUDDHA, GANDHI, SUFISM, AND MASCULINITY

260. In his support of the Nazi government, Ram Chandra was not a singular case among Hindu nationalists. As Maria Framke and others have shown, Hitler and the Nazis were widely admired and even read in Hindu nationalist circles. Framke, *Delhi—Rom—Berlin*.
261. Nathuram Godse, *May It Please Your Honour*, 3rd ed. (Delhi: Surya Prakashan, 1987), 78–109.
262. Pandit Rāmacandra Śarmā Vīra, *Vijaya-Patākā* (1943; Sāgara: Akhila Bhāratīya Ādarśa Hindū-Saṅgha Madhyaprāntīya Śākhā, 2000), 170–187. I thank Sarover Zaidi for translating this source.
263. "Pandit Ram Chandra Sharma's Fast for Stopping Animal Sacrifice," 482–483. This position was shared by other Congress leaders: "Mr. Sarat Bose on Animal Sacrifice," *Times of India*, September 27, 1935, 16.
264. "Mohandas Karamchand Gandhi to Purushottamdas Bujna, 02.10.1935," in *The Collected Works of Mahatma Gandhi*, vol. 68, Sep 23, 1935–May 15, 1936 (New Delhi: Publications Division Government of India, 1999), 33.
265. Afas, Magnus Schwantje Papers, K. G. Mashruwala to M. P. T. Acharya, Bajajwadi, Wardha, August 1, 1950.
266. Afas, Magnus Schwantje Papers, Magnus Schwantje to M. P. T. Acharya, Stade, n.d. (after June 1950).
267. Walter Sommer, "Ex Oriente Lux," *Lichtheilgrüße* 9 (1933): 337–339.
268. Sommer, "Blut und Boden. Das deutsche Bodenrecht," 98–103.
269. Nicholas Goodrick-Clarke examined Savitri Devi's fascination with Nazism, related in part to Hitler's vegetarianism. Nicholas Goodrick-Clarke, *Hitler's Priestess: Savitri Devi, the Hindu-Aryan Myth, and Neo-Nazism* (New York: New York University Press, 1998), especially 64–76. What his research does not clearly point out is Savitri Devi's hostile attitude toward Indian Muslims. For her, India was a genuinely Hindu country where Muslims would always be a foreign element—the very attitude embraced by V. D. Savarkar, the founding father of Hindutva. While vegetarianism was not the center of Savitri Devi's work, she published a book on animal welfare in the 1950s—in which, however, she stressed the charity of individual Muslims toward animals. For Labshankar Laxmias's appreciation of Hitler's vegetarianism, see Laxmidas, "Hitler Has Become Vegetarian," 84. V. D. Savarkar himself corresponded with the Nazi government asking Hitler to stop cow slaughter in Germany, as is evident from Hitler's response to the Sanathan Dharam Pratinidhi Sabha. "Adolf Hitler, Berlin, to Sanathan Dharam Pratinidhi Sabha, Punjab, Office Note, Office of Hony. Foreign Publicity Secretary S. D. Pratinidhi Sabha Pj, Dina Nath Building, Pahaganj, New Delhi, 28.11.," Nehru Memorial Archives and Library, D. V. Savarkar Papers. Some leaders of the independence movement, such as B. S. Moonje, the president of the Hindu Mahasabha, recommended meat consumption. K. Vishwanatham, "Flesh Diet and Alcoholism in Relation to Life and the Community," in *The Indian Humanitarian*, 101. So did M. Cholkar, a member of the Indian National Congress: "Through Indian Eyes: Noble Exploits," *Times of India*, October 3, 1925, 17; "Beef and Spirituality in India: Were Ancient Hindus Vegetarians?," *Times of India*, March 23, 1926, 8. I would like to thank Maria Framke (Erfurt) for these references.

## 5. RACE, NATION, AND PEACE

1. Glenda Sluga, *Internationalism in the Age of Nationalism* (Philadelphia: University of Pennsylvania Press, 2013).
2. Bradley G. Shope, *American Popular Music in Britain's Raj* (Rochester, NY: University of Rochester Press, 2016). 22.
3. Due to the custom of referring to married women by their husband's name, Gasque was often referred to as "Mrs. Clarence Gasque" in official reports.
4. Caroline van Hasselt, *High Wire Act: Ted Rogers and the Empire that Debt Built* (New York: Wiley, 2007), 85; Sam Tonkin, "'Phantom of Love' Vintage Rolls-Royce Built in 1926 as a Gift for a Woolworths Boss's Wife and Kitted Out with Fine Art and Tapestries 'Resembling the Throne Room at Versailles' Sells for £561,000," *Daily Mail*, December 5, 2016, https://www.dailymail.co.uk/news/article-4000854/Phantom-Love-vintage-Rolls-Royce-built-1926-gift-Woolworths-boss-s-wife-kitted-fine-art-tapestries-resembling-throne-room-Versailles-sells-561-000.html.
5. "London House of Mrs. Gasque Concert Scene. Former Winnetkan Loans Home for First of Three Grand Chamber Events," *Chicago Tribune*, April 25, 1936, part 8, page 3.
6. O. Z. A. Hanish, "Unsere Reise 1929," *Mazdaznan*, no. 1 (1930): 8–10; "Mother Gloria's Visit to the Halifax Fortress," *British Mazdaznan Magazine* 12 (1936): 627; Katherine Dashwood, "Gahanbar at Zurich," *British Mazdaznan Magazine* 12 (1936): 13.
7. Gasque's presence is mentioned in passing by Michael Stausberg, who does not, however, draw on the *British Mazdaznan Magazine*. Michael Stausberg, *Die Religion Zarathushtras*, vol. 2 (Stuttgart: Kohlhammer, 2004), 400–401.
8. In 1911, two Parsi priests allegedly praised Hanisch's understanding of Zoroastrianism: Cawas Pestonji Sirkaris, "Gutachten eines Zendgelehrten," *Mazdaznan* 4 (1911): 54; Jamshid Jaranmard Shirmad, "Anerkennung aus Persien," *Mazdaznan* 4 (1911): 55.
9. "Gault, Lieut.-Col. Arthur Fitzroy," in *Who's Who and Why: A Biographical Dictionary of Men and Women of Canada and Newfoundland*, vol. 5 (Vancouver, BC: International Press, 1914), cited in *American Biographical Archive*, 1:600, 336. Gault (who hailed from a family of real-estate brokers) was nominated to be one of the five trustees of Mazdaznan in 1917. Los Angeles Museum of Natural History, Seaver Center for Western History Research, "The Reorganized Mazdaznan Temple Association of Associates of God" (1917).
10. See, for instance, Ardaser Sorabjee N. Wadia, "From India," *British Mazdaznan Magazine* 1 (1925): 248; "From India," *British Mazdaznan Magazine* 17 (1940): 53. On Wadia's first contact with Mazdaznan, see Wadia, *The Call of the World, Being Reminiscences of a Year's Tour Round the World* (London: J. M. Dent & Sons, 1918), 126–203. Wadia wrote several esoteric books on Buddha, Moses, and Jesus. The Wadias were a prominent, politically influential, wealthy, and widespread Parsi merchant family of Bombay, members of which had been active in the Theosophical Society since the 1880s, as well as in the Bombay Natural Living and Vegetarian Society. Khursedji J. B. Wadia, "Humanitarianism and Vegetarianism Among the Parsis," in *The Indian Humanitarian. The Bombay Humanitarian*

## 5. RACE, NATION, AND PEACE

*League Silver Jubilee Number 1910–1934, etc.* (Bombay: Bombay Humanitarian League, 1934), 65–66; Regina Moritz, "Globalizing 'Sacred Knowledge': South Asians and the Theosophical Society, 1879–1930" (PhD diss., Jacobs University Bremen, 2012), 93–137; Jesse S. Palsetia, *The Parsis of India: Preservation of Identity in Bombay City* (Leiden: Brill, 2001), 41–42, 58–59.

11. See chapter 3.
12. Stausberg, *Die Religion Zarathushtras*, 2: 378. Gasque also intended to visit the Tower of Silence, where the body of Hanisch's mother had allegedly been disposed according to Parsi custom, in Surat: "From India," *British Mazdaznan Magazine* 15 (1938): 301–302. Since in the first half of the twentieth century, non-Parsis were generally prohibited from visiting Parsi temples and towers of silence or even seeing photographs of their interiors, it is unlikely that she succeeded in doing so—which the report in the *British Mazdaznan Magazine* conveniently omits.
13. "From India," *British Mazdaznan Magazine* 15 (1938).
14. Banu Bam, "To My Mazdaznan Sisters and Brothers," *Mazdaznan India* (1942): 144–145; "From India," *British Mazdaznan Magazine* 15 (1939): 621–622; "From Bombay," *British Mazdaznan Magazine* 16 (1939): 192–193. On Gasque's Swiss associates, see also Jean-François Meyer, *Les nouvelles voies spirituelles. Enquête sur la religiosité parallèle en Suisse* (Lausanne: L'age de l'homme, 1993), 153–154.
15. "From India," *British Mazdaznan Magazine* 15 (1938): 621–622; "From Bombay," 192–193.
16. Nanabhoy F. Mama, "From India," *British Mazdaznan Magazine* 16 (1940): 358–359; Wadia, "From India," 53.
17. "Mazdaznan Magazine in India," *British Mazdaznan Magazine* 18 (1941): 100.
18. "The Six Races," *Mazdaznan India* (1943): 16–30.
19. Lora Wildenthal, *German Women for Empire, 1884–1945* (Durham, NC: Duke University Press, 2001); Ann Laura Stoler, *Carnal Knowledge and Imperial Power: Race and the Intimate in Colonial Rule* (Berkeley: University of California Press, 2002); Antoinette Burton, *Burdens of History: British Feminists, Indian Women, and Imperial Culture, 1865–1914* (Chapel Hill: University of North Carolina Press, 2010).
20. Gloria Gasque, "Our Loving Remembrance," *Mazdaznan India* 2, no. 4 (1942): 171.
21. "From Mother Superior Gloria," *British Mazdaznan Magazine* 15 (1939): 546–548; Gloria Gasque, "'Equality of Opportunity,'" *British Mazdaznan Magazine* 17 (1940): 88–89.
22. Joscelyn Godwin, "Blavatsky and the First Generation of Theosophy," in *Handbook of the Theosophical Current*, ed. Olav Hammer and Mikael Rothstein (Leiden: Brill, 2013), 16; Stausberg, "Para-Zoroastrians," 242.
23. Mriganka Mukhopadhyay, "Mohini: A Case Study of a Transnational Spiritual Space in the History of the Theosophical Society," *Numen* 67, nos. 2–3 (2019): 165–190.
24. While the cow was central to Zoroastrian texts, animal sacrifice was nonetheless practiced well into the nineteenth century. Jenny Rose, *Zoroastrianism: An Introduction* (London: I. B. Tauris, 2011), 11–25, 55, 199; Albert De Jong, "Animal Sacrifice in Ancient Zoroastrianism: A Ritual and Its Interpretation," in *Sacrifice in Religious Experience*, ed. A. I. Baumgarten (Leiden: Brill, 2002), 127–148. As Saul Shaked stresses, however, there was a tendency to minimize animal suffering in

5. RACE, NATION, AND PEACE

Zoroastrianism: slaughter was preceded by suffocating, just as it would be preceded by bleeding in Muslim and Jewish practices of slaughter. Shaul Shaked, "The Yasna Ritual in Pahlavi Literature," in *Zoroastrian Rituals in Context*, ed. Michael Stausberg (Leiden: Brill, 2004), 342.

25. Ervad Phiroze S. Masani, *Zoroastrianism Ancient and Modern. Comprising a Review of Dr. Dhalla's Book of Zoroastrian Theology* (Bombay: Parsi Vegetarian and Temperance Society, 1917), 2, 206-209.

26. Rose, *Zoroastrianism*, 199, 212. On the Mazdakites and vegetarianism in early Zoroastrianism, see Patricia Crone, *The Nativist Prophets of Early Islamic Iran: Rural Revolt and Local Zoroastrianism* (Cambridge: Cambridge University Press, 2012), 257-260, 303-316.

27. John R. Hinnells, "The Parsis," in *The Wiley Blackwell Companion to Zoroastrianism*, ed. Michael Stausberg, Yuhan Sohrab-Dinshaw Vevaina, and Anna Tessmann (Chichester, UK: Wiley Blackwell, 2015), 170.

28. Sanjam Ahluwalia and Anshu Malhotra stressed the role of class/caste in Indian eugenics, a project they argue was largely driven by middle-class Indian women. According to Sarah Hodges, by contrast, enthusiasm for eugenics in late colonial India transcended class, being advocated by both Brahmins with a paternalist agenda toward the lower castes and by lower-caste activists with emancipatory objectives. Anshu Malhotra, "Of Dais and Midwives: 'Middle-Class' Interventions in the Management of Women's Reproductive Health," *Indian Journal of Gender Studies* 10, no. 2 (2003): 229-259; Sarah Hodges, *Reproductive Health in India: History, Politics, Controversies* (New Delhi: Orient Longman, 2006); "South Asia's Eugenic Past," in *The Oxford Handbook of the History of Eugenics*, ed. Alison Bashford (Oxford: Oxford University Press, 2006), 228-242; Sanjam Ahluwalia, *Reproductive Restraints: Birth Control in India, 1877-1947* (Urbana: University of Illinois Press, 2008).

29. Sapur Faredun Desai, *Parsis and Eugenics* (Bombay: Mody Printing Press, 1940), 3, 14, 19. On Laughlin, who advocated the sterilization of criminals and those he termed "feeble-minded," see Edward J. Larson, *Sex, Race and Science: Eugenics in the Deep South* (Baltimore: Johns Hopkins University Press, 1995; Mark A. Largent, *Breeding Contempt: The History of Coerced Sterilization in the United States* (New Brunswick, NJ: Rutgers University Press, 2008), 56-58, 61-63, 99-100, 118-119, 136-137; Paul A. Lombardo, *Three Generations, No Imbeciles: Eugenics, the Supreme Court, and Buck V. Bell* (Baltimore: Johns Hopkins University Press, 2008).

30. Desai, *Parsis and Eugenics*, 68-79.

31. Desai, 83-103.

32. Desai, 106-119. While it is not clear whether Mazdaznan cooking demonstrations were held in schools, Gasque gave papers on the inclusion of cookery and household management in the curricula of girls' schools. Gloria Gasque, "Place of Cookery in the Curricula of Girls' and Women's Education," *Mazdaznan India* (1942): 596-601.

33. Desai, *Parsis and Eugenics*, 17.

34. In a biography of one of the founders of *ilm-e khshnoom* published in 1944 and serialized in the *British Mazdaznan Magazine* before publication, Mama referred to Otto Hanisch as a notable exponent of Zoroastrian esotericism. He also

## 5. RACE, NATION, AND PEACE

stressed the value of vegetarianism to this esotericism and the development of Shroff's spiritual path. Nanabhoy F. Mama, *A Mazdaznan Mystic. Life-Sketch of the Late Behramshah Navroji Shroff, the 20th Century Exponent of Zarthosthi Elm-E-Khshnoom (i.e. Esotericism of Zoroastrianism)* (Bombay: Parsi Vegetarian and Temperance Society/Zarthoshti Radih Society of Bombay, 1944), 18, 24, 30–31. For the preprint of the book, see Mama, "A Mazdaznan Mystic. The Mysteries and the Marvels of Khshoom," *British Mazdaznan Magazine* 16 (1939): 33–34, 79–80, 116–117; "A Mazdaznan Mystic. The Mysteries and the Marvels of Khshoom," *British Mazdaznan Magazine* 16 (1940): 279–281; "A Mazdaznan Mystic. The Mysteries and the Marvels of Khshoom," *British Mazdaznan Magazine* 17 (1941): 174–175; "A Mazdaznan Mystic," *British Mazdaznan Magazine* 18 (1942): 242–243.

35. *The Jamshedji Nusserwanji Petit Parsi Orphanage Golden Jubilee Memorial Volume, 1888–1938* (Bombay: J. N. Petit Parsi Orphanage, 1939), 98–99. On Bode's reformist leanings, see S. Dabu, "Foreword," in *Man Soul Immortality in Zoroastrianism*, ed. Dastur Framroze Ardeshir Bode (Bombay: K. B. Cama Oriental Institute, 1960), i–v. The Parsi Petit Orphanage was a nucleus of Parsi social reform and was most likely connected to attempts to reinvent vegetarianism as a Parsi tradition. The bylaws of the Natural Living and Vegetarian Society were printed in its press (see chapter 2), and it seems to have served vegetarian fare to its charges. *The Jamshedji Nusserwanji Petit Parsi Orphanage Golden Jubilee Memorial Volume*, 60.
36. Sapur Faredun Desai, *History of the Bombay Parsi Punchayet (1860–1960)* (Bombay: R. M. D. C., 1977), 159–161.
37. Palsetia, *The Parsis of India*, 321.
38. Gloria Gasque, "Mazdaznan in India," *British Mazdaznan Magazine* 16 (1940): 393; "Third Birthday Celebration," *Mazdaznan India* 2 (1942): 61–63.
39. "Requisition of Premises: Rule Issued Against Collector of Bombay," *Times of India*, September 26, 1944, 3. In the photos of Mazdaznan ceremonies in Bombay, however, Gasque and Bode were rarely shown with more than ten supporters.
40. Ardaser Sorabjee N. Wadia, "From India," *British Mazdaznan Magazine* 16 (1940): 395–396.
41. Stausberg, *Die Religion Zarathushtras*, 2:398–401; Desai, *History of the Bombay Parsi Punchayet (1860–1960)*, 161, 340–344; "Requisitioning of Parsi Temple: Petition Dismissed," *Times of India*, December 4, 1944, 7.
42. Robert V. Hine, *California's Utopian Colonies* (New Haven, CT: Yale University Press, 1966); Emmett A. Greenwalt, *City of Glass: The Theosophical Invasion of Point Loma* (San Diego: Cabrillo Historical Association, 1981); Tim Rudbøg, "Point Loma, Theosophy, and Katherine Tingley," in *Handbook of the Theosophical Current*, ed. Olav Hammer and Mikael Rothstein (Leiden: Brill, 2013), 51–73.
43. "Gloria (Maude) Gasque. IVU President, 1953–59," International vegetarian Union, accessed April 14, 2021, https://ivu.org/members/council/maude-gasque.html. At this congress, the acting general secretary, Kaj Dessau (Denmark), criticized the lack of organization within the IVU, referring to it as "a dream that never came true" and calling for a unification of the agendas of its national member associations. For a German translation of his speech (the original text is unavailable), see Kaj Dessau, "Die Zukunft der Internationalen Vegetarischen Bewegung," *Vegetarisches Universum* 3 (1950): 7.

5. RACE, NATION, AND PEACE

44. Elisabeth Ecker-Lauer, "Nachruf auf Mrs. Clarence Gasque," *Sontraer Gesundheits-Bote* 14, no. 1 (1959): 7.
45. "Dastur F. Bode. IVU Executive Committee 1957–60," International Vegetarian Union, accessed April 14, 2021, https://ivu.org/members/council/dastur-bode.html.
46. "An Alle Vegetarier!," *Der Wendepunkt im Leben und im Leiden* 21, no. 6 (1944): n.p. Briest's very short appeal appeared among the classified ads, which were not paginated. The short text read, "To all vegetarians! Those interested in a settlement of true vegetarians in Germany are asked to send their address to nordbron, Süttorf near Dahlenberg." Five additional advertisements appeared in the following issues.
47. Adolf Briest and Helmut Gringmann, *Die Ernährung des denkenden Menschen*, 2nd ed. (Hamburg: Verlag der Rohkost-Förderung, 1933), 5.
48. Briest and Gringmann, 6.
49. Briest and Gringmann, 21–28.
50. Briest and Gringmann, 35. Mazdaznan made the same claim (see chapter 3).
51. Briest and Gringmann, 35. This is distantly reminiscent of Hindu notions of diet as specified in the concept of the three *gunas*. It is unclear whether Briest knew texts such as the Bhagavad Gita or the Code of Manu. Some of his correspondents, however, quoted from the former.
52. Briest and Gringmann, 77–78. Briest explicitly opposed the women's movement and claimed that women's roles were confined to running the household and having children.
53. Briest's enthusiasm for Gandhi may have been increased by the fact that he was critical of Christianity and established religion. See below.
54. "Vegetarier. Bis es nicht mehr schmeckt," *Spiegel*, no. 28 (1950): 33–34.
55. On Fidus, see Jost Hermand, "Meister Fidus: Jugendstil-Hippie to Aryan Faddist," *Comparative Literature Studies* 12, no. 3 (1975): 288–307; Marina Schuster, "Fidus—ein Gesinnungskünstler der völkischen Kulturbewegung," in *Handbuch zur "Völkischen Bewegung" 1871–1918*, ed. Uwe Puschner, Walter Schmitz, and Justus H. Ulbricht (Munich: K. G. Saur, 1996), 634–650; "Lichtgebet. Die Ikone der Lebensreform- und Jugendbewegung," in *Das Jahrhundert der Bilder (1900–1949)*, ed. Gerhard Paul (Göttingen: Vandenhoeck & Ruprecht, 2009), 140–147; Ulrich Alexander Goetz, "Hugo Höppener," in *Handbuch der völkischen Wissenschaften. Akteure, Netzwerke, Forschungsprogramme*, ed. Michael Fahlbusch, Ingo Haar, and Alexander Pinwinkler (Berlin: Saur, 2017), 302–305.
56. Afas, AMA 1944–46 DEROG/VUD correspondence E–F, Briest to Fidus (Hugo Höppener), Süttorf, October 12, 1944.
57. Justus Liebig Universität Gießen, Universitätsbibliothek, FH Eden Z, *nordbron-rundbrief* 3 (1944): 2.
58. *nordbron-rundbrief* 2 (1944): 1.
59. *nordbron-rundbrief* 6 (1944); Adolf Briest, "Die richtige Ernährung," 1; *nordbron-rundbrief* 2, no. 1 (1945). Not all issues of the circular were paginated.
60. *nordbron-rundbrief* 3, no. 2 (1946): 4.
61. While the concept of the "Age of Aquarius" is now generally associated with the New Age movement of the 1960s, it existed in the 1920s, when it was discussed by groups like the Theosophical Society and the Rosicrucians and authors

sympathetic to them. "The Lord's Passover," *Herald of the Cross* 7 (1911): 83; *The Theosophist* 43 (1922): 1–6, 61. It was also evoked by prominent Black leaders such as Marcus Garvey. *Black Man* (1933), 17. To Briest, however, it clearly had white supremacist implications.

62. Justus Liebig Universität Gießen, Universitätsbibliothek, FH Eden Z, *nordbron-rundbrief* 3, nos. 6–7 (1946): 1; *nordbron-rundbrief* 3, nos. 8–9 (1946): 1.
63. Justus Liebig Universität Gießen, Universitätsbibliothek, FH Eden Z. Niederschrift über die erste Arbeitstagung der Vegetarier Union (VU) Deutschland (1946).
64. Rudolf Simek, *Lexikon der Germanischen Mythologie*, 3rd ed. (Stuttgart: Krömer, 2006), 278.
65. Ulrich Linse, "Völkisch-Rassische Siedlungen der Lebensreform," in *Handbuch zur "Völkischen Bewegung,"* ed. Uwe Puschner (Munich: Saur, 1996), 407–408. Linse also implies that Donnershagians were influenced in their concept of marriage by the sexual reform concepts advocated by Werner Zimmermann, who, however, did not explicitly stress race. Literature on Donnershag is scarce, and so are unpublished primary sources. On Donnershag, see also Anne Quinchon-Caudal, "Les haras humains, ou comment arracher la vraie vie à l'abîme de la décadence," in *"Lebensreform." Die soziale Dynamik der politischen Ohnmacht / La dynamique sociale de l'impuissance politique*, ed. Marc Cluet and Catherine Repussard (Tübingen: Narr Francke, 2013), 283–316; Ulrich Linse, ed., *Zurück o Mensch zur Mutter Erde: Landkommunen in Deutschland 1890–1933* (Frankfurt/Main: Deutscher Taschenbuch-Verlag, 1983), 188–199.
66. The concept of *Mittgart* or *Midgart* marriage was first developed by Willibald Hentschel, a Saxon physician. Hentschel suggested establishing settlements where one thousand men lived with one hundred women; all residents were to be blond and blue-eyed, of supposedly pure "Aryan" stock, and without hereditary or sexually transmissible diseases. Men were to maintain relationships with women until they got pregnant, then move on to the next partner. Hentschel later entered the Nazi Party, receiving felicitations on his seventieth birthday from Hitler even though he was no longer a party member. Willibald Hentschel, *Mittgart. Ein Weg zur Erneuerung der germanischen Rasse. Programmschrift*, 3rd ed. (Dresden: Mittgartbund, 1911). On Hentschel, see also Günter Hartung, "Völkische Ideologie," in *Handbuch zur "Völkischen Bewegung" 1871–1918*, ed. Uwe Puschner, Walter Schmitz, and Justus H. Ulbricht (Munich: K. G. Saur, 1996), 22–42.
67. Venus Bivar, *Organic Resistance: The Struggle Over Industrial Farming in Postwar France* (Chapel Hill: University of North Carolina Press, 2018), 51–70.
68. Afas, VUD-Vorläufer 1947 DEROG Briefwechsel 48/49 VUD, Dritte Arbeitstagung der Vegetarier Union (VU) Deutschland 15–17 Mai 1947 in Hann.-Münden, Hotel Andreesberg.
69. *Bild*'s use of soft pornography would be attacked by the German student movement of the 1960s, leading members of which criticized the right-wing leanings of its publisher, Springer. Frank Biess, *German Angst: Fear and Democracy in the Federal Republic of Germany* (Oxford: Oxford University Press, 2020), 207–208. The layout of *Vegetarisches Universum* calls into doubt Carol J. Adams's argument that the representation of women as consumable matter was limited to carnivorous contexts—and suggests that sexuality was being moved center stage within the vegetarian movement, albeit with a double standard for men and women.

## 5. RACE, NATION, AND PEACE

Adams, *The Sexual Politics of Meat: A Feminist-Vegetarian Critical Theory* (New York: Continuum, 1990), and *The Pornography of Meat* (New York: Continuum, 2004). To some extent, this ties in with Dagmar Herzog's argument of both a "lingering traditionalism" and increasingly liberal attitudes regarding sexuality in the Cold War era. Herzog, *Sexuality in Europe: A Twentieth-Century History* (Cambridge: Cambridge University Press, 2011), 106–111.

70. On the *Fresswelle*, see Michael Wildt, "Promise of More: The Rhetorik of (Food) Consumption in a Society Searching for Itself: West Germany in the 1950s," in *Food, Drink and Identity*, ed. Peter Scholliers (Oxford: Berg, 2001), 63–80; *Am Beginn der "Konsumgesellschaft." Mangelerfahrung, Lebenshaltung, Wohlstandshoffnung in Westdeutschland in den fünfziger Jahren* (Hamburg: Ergebnisse, 1994).
71. Wildt, *Am Beginn der "Konsumgesellschaft,"* 20–37; Paul Steege, *Black Market, Cold War: Everyday Life in Berlin, 1946–1949* (Cambridge: Cambridge University Press, 2007).
72. Benjamin Ziemann, "German Angst? Debating Cold War Anxieties in West Germany, 1945–90," in *Understanding the Imaginary War: Culture, Thought and Nuclear Conflict, 1945–90*, ed. Matthew Grant and Benjamin Ziemann (Manchester: Manchester University Press, 2016), 133–134; Frank Biess, "'Jeder hat eine Chance.' Die Zivilschutzkampagnen der 1960er Jahre und die Angstgeschichte der Bundesrepublik," in *Angst im Kalten Krieg*, ed. Bernd Greiner, Christian Th. Müller, and Dierk Walter (Hamburg: Hamburger Edition, 2009), 61–93.
73. East Germany does not seem to have had any vegetarian organizations, and there were no vegetarian journals in the GDR, although Leipzig and Dresden had been important centers before. The GDR did not promote vegetarianism, perhaps conforming to Russian politics toward the vegetarian movement since the rise of the Bolsheviki. On vegetarianism in Russia after 1917, see Peter Brang, *Ein unbekanntes Russland: Kulturgeschichte vegetarischer Lebensweisen von den Anfängen bis zur Gegenwart* (Cologne: Böhlau, 2002), 275–290.
74. Arthur Rothe, "Weltfrieden auf neuer Grundlage. Sozialwirtschaft auf Basis wissenschaftlicher Lebensform," *Vegetarisches Universum* 2, nos. 2–3 (1949): 2; Johannes Ude, "Weltfriede, Lebensreform und Arzt," *Vegetarisches Universum* no. 8 (1949): 3; "Vegetarismus gegen Atombombe!," *Vegetarisches Universum* no. 3 (1950): 1.
75. "Molenaar, Heinrich," *Deutsches Biographisches Archiv* 2: 906, 207–208.
76. Heinrich Molenaar, "Magna Charta Humanitatis. Die zehn Grundgesetze der Menschheit," *Vegetarisches Universum* 2, no. 6 (1949): 4.
77. Wido H. Moormann, "War Hitler Vegetarier?," *Vegetarisches Universum* 3, no. 3 (1950): 2.
78. Friedrich Vogtherr, "Atlantropa," *Vegetarisches Universum* 4, no. 2 (1951): 5. I could not find out much about Vogtherr, except that he was an architect who participated at least once in one of Rall's vegetarian meetings. *Vegetarisches Universum* 9 (1956), 2.
79. On Sörgel's plan, see Dirk van Laak, *Weiße Elefanten. Anspruch und Scheitern technischer Großprojekte* (Stuttgart: DVA, 1999), 166–173; Alexander Gall, *Das Atlantropa-Projekt: Die Geschichte einer gescheiterten Vision. Herman Sörgel und die Absenkung des Mittelmeers* (Frankfurt/Main: Campus, 1998), 99–128; "Atlantropa: A Technological Vision of a United Europe," in *Networking Europe: Transnational Infrastructures and the Shaping of Europe, 1850–2000*, ed. Erik van

## 5. RACE, NATION, AND PEACE

der Vleuten and Arne Kaijser (Sagamore Beach, MA: Science History Publications, 2006). Van Laak portrays Sörgel as a cosmopolitan pacifist, whereas Gall stresses the colonialist aspects of his plan.

80. Peo Hansen and Stefan Jonsson, "Another Colonialism: Africa in the History of European Integration," *Journal of Historical Sociology* 27 (2014): 442–461; *Eurafrica: The Untold History of European Integration and Colonialism* (London: Bloomsbury, 2015).
81. Vogtherr, "Atlantropa," 5.
82. See, for instance, Hossein Kazemzadeh Iranschähr, "Wie segensreich könnte die Weihnacht gefeiert werden!," *Vegetarisches Universum* 10, no. 12 (1957): 12; Schweizerisches Bundesarchiv E2001E#1976/17#665* Iranschär, H. K., Flawil (Dossier), Hossein Kazemzadeh to the Eidgenössisches Politisches Department, Flawil, December 7, 1961. In the journal *Welt-Harmonie*, however, which Kazemzadeh founded in 1950, he referred occasionally to Sufism—for example, the aim of many Sufi saints to avoid animal suffering. H. K. Iranschähr, "Aus dem Leben der islamischen Mystikerin Râbi'äh," *Welt-Harmonie* 9 (1957): 23–24, 39–40.
83. H. K. Iranschähr, "Die Menschheit steht vor drei Möglichkeiten," *Vegetarisches Universum* 3, no. 8 (1950): 2.
84. In *Welt-Harmonie* as well as in his correspondence with the Swiss government, by contrast, he repeatedly stressed Switzerland's role as a global arbiter of peace. "Das Neue Zeitalter und die Mission der Schweiz," *Welt-Harmonie* 9 (1957): 49–52. Audiences of *Vegetarisches Universum* and *Welt-Harmonie* may have overlapped to some extent. Kazemzadeh, at any rate, warmly recommended *Vegetarisches Universum* to his readers. "Vegetarisches Universum," *Welt-Harmonie* 12 (1952): 9.
85. Werner Zimmermann, "Atom-Entwicklung zwingt zum Weltfrieden," *Vegetarisches Universum* 10, no. 8 (1957): 1–2.
86. Martin Brecht, "Der Württembergische Pietismus," in *Der Pietismus iim cahtzehnten Jahrhundert*, ed. Martin Brecht and Friedhelm Ackva (Göttingen: Vandenhoeck & Ruprecht, 1995), 225–293; Eberhard Fritz, ed., *Radikaler Pietismus in Württemberg. Religiöse Ideale im Konflikt mit gesellschaftlichen Realitäten* (Epfendorf/Neckar: bibliotheca academica, 2003); Ulrike Gleixner, *Pietismus und Bürgertum. Eine historische Anthropologie der Frömmigkeit (Württemberg 17.–19. Jahrhundert)* (Göttingen: Vandenhoeck & Ruprecht, 2005).
87. The conventions organized by Rall took place in spas, stays in which were generally paid for by German health insurance in the postwar era: David Clay Large, *The Grand Spas of Central Europe: A History of Intrigue, Politics, Art, and Healing* (Lanham, MD: Rowman & Littlefield, 2015), 811–812.
88. "Kongreß der Ideale. Bad Liebenzell," *Vegetarisches Universum* 5, no. 4; 5 (1952): 1; Bernd W. Ziegler, "Bad Liebenzell ist bereit zum 'Kongreß der Ideale,'" *Vegetarisches Universum* 6, no. 4 (1953): 3; "Bildbericht vom vierten "Kongreß der Ideale" zu Bad Liebenzell," *Vegetarisches Universum* 7, no. 7 (1954): 8; "Bilderbericht vom 5. 'Kongreß der Ideale' zu Freudenstadt," *Vegetarisches Universum* 8, no. 7 (1955): 8; "6. 'Kongreß der Ideale' zu Freudenstadt im Schwarzwald," *Vegetarisches Universum* 9, no. 2 (1956): 1; "Das Fest der Freude zu Freudenstadt 1957," *Vegetarisches Universum* 10, no. 7 (1957): 10. On Freudenstadt's and Bad Liebenzell's career as health resorts, see *Radio-Thermal-Bad und Luftkurort Liebenzell und*

## 5. RACE, NATION, AND PEACE

*seine Umgebung* (Liebenzell: Städtische Kurverwaltung, 1922); Gerhard Hertel, "Chronologie des Wiederaufbauprozesses von Freudenstadt 1945–1956 mit einem vorangestellten Abriß der Entstehungsgeschichte Freudenstadts 1597 bis 1945," in *Stadtgestalt und Heimatgefühl. Der Wiederaufbau von Freudenstadt 1945–1954. Analysen, Vergleich und Dokumente*, ed. Hans-Günther Burkhardt et al. (Hamburg: Christians, 1988), 245–246.

89. Arnd Krüger and Wiliiam Murray, eds., *The Nazi Olympics: Sport, Politics, and Appeasement in the 1930s* (Urbana: University of Illinois Press, 2003); Barbara Keys, *Globalizing Sport: National Rivalry and International Community in the 1930s* (Cambridge, MA: Harvard University Press, 2013), 115–157.

90. Bernd W. Ziegler, "Und nach dem Kongreß an den Lago Maggiore. Freudenstadt rüstet zum 7. Kongreß der Ideale," *Vegetarisches Universum* 10, no. 3 (1957): 3; "Von Freudenstadt ans blaue Mittelmeer," *Vegetarisches Universum* 11, no. 12 (1958): 12. On German postwar tourism to Italy, see Till Manning, *Die Italiengeneration. Stilbildung durch Massentourismus in den 1950er und 1960er Jahren* (Göttingen: Wallstein, 2011).

91. On trips to Schoenenberger's factory, see, for instance, Ziegler, "Bad Liebenzell ist bereit zum 'Kongreß der Ideale,' " 3. Schoenenberger was also felicitated in *Vegetarisches Universum* on the occasion of his company's twenty-fifth anniversary (without reference to his political past). "Frische Kräfte-Pflanzensäfte," *Vegetarisches Universum* 5, no. 6 (1952): 8. Beginning in 1950, Schoenenberger served as the chairman of the Arbeitsgemeinschaft der Reformwarenhersteller, the German union of natural food producers. During the Nazi period, Schoeneberger was a member of the Nazi German Society of Life Reform and in 1933 had joined the Nazi Party as well as the SA, where he had had a leading position. After being dismissed from the party in 1941, perhaps because of his Swiss nationality, Schoeneberger became one of the most prolific lobbyists of the health food sector in postwar Germany. Florentine Fritzen, *Gesünder leben. Die Lebensreformbewegung im 20. Jahrhundert* (Stuttgart: Steiner, 2006), 110–113, 153–160. His biography, therefore, is a prime example of the personal continuities between Nazi and postwar Germany as highlighted in Norbert Frei, *Karrieren im Zwielicht. Hitlers Eliten nach 1945* (Frankfurt/Main: Campus, 2001).

92. "Vegetarisches Universum wählt der Welt schönste Vegetarierin 1956," *Vegetarisches Universum* 8 (1955): 8; " 'VU' wählt der Welt schönste Vegetarierin 1956," *Vegetarisches Universum* 9, no. 1 (1956): 8.

93. "Bad Liebenzell," *Vegetarisches Universum* 5, no. 4 (1952): 1; "Eine Olympiade der guten Herzen," *Vegetarisches Universum* 7, no. 7 (1954): 2; "6. 'Kongreß der Ideale' zu Freudenstadt im Schwarzwald," 1. On these stars' Nazi pasts, see Martha Schad, *Sie liebten den Führer. Wie Frauen Hitler verehrten* (Munich: Herbig, 2009); Gerte Muurmann, *Komödianten für den Krieg. Deutsches und alliiertes Fronttheater* (Düsseldorf: Droste, 1992), 122, 149; Lu Seegers, "Filmstars und Reichtum im 'Dritten Reich.' (Auto-)biografische Repräsentationen und Narrativ," in *Reichtum in Deutschland: Akteure, Räume und Lebenswelten im 20. Jahrhundert*, ed. Eva Maria Gajek, Anne Kurr, and Lu Seegers (Göttingen: Wallstein, 2019), 201–225; Elise Petit, *Musique et politique en Allemagne. Du IIIe reich à l'aube de la guerre froide* (Paris: Presses de l'Université Paris-Sorbonne, 2018), 54–56.

## 5. RACE, NATION, AND PEACE

94. "Kongreß der Ideale. Bad Liebenzell," *Vegetarisches Universum* 5, no. 4 (1952): 1; "Kongreß der Ideale. Bad Liebenzell," *Vegetarisches Universum* 5, no. 5 (1952): 1; "Kongreß der Ideale Bad Liebenzell, 12.-18. Mai," *Vegetarisches Universum* 6, no. 3 (1953): 1.
95. *Vegetarisches Universum* 6, no. 3 (1953): 1.
96. "Kongreß der Ideale 1954 Bad Liebenzell," *Vegetarisches Universum* 7, no. 2 (1954): 2; *Vegetarisches Universum* 7, no. 3 (1954): 1.
97. Ziegler, "Bad Liebenzell ist bereit zum 'Kongreß der Ideale.'"
98. Ziegler, "Bad Liebenzell ist bereit zum 'Kongreß der Ideale.'" As Pascal Germann points out, Ganz carried out anthropological measurements on his plantation workers in Kenya in the late 1930s. I could not find out if he was a Mazdaznan member by then. It would certainly fit in with Mazdaznan's racist outlook. Pascal Germann, *Laboratorien der Vererbung: Rassenforschung und Humangenetik in der Schweiz, 1900–1970* (Göttingen: Wallstein, 2016), 118–119.
99. "Expert Claims Esperanto Can Serve World Peace," *Fresno Bee. The Republican from Fresno, California*, May 4, 1969, 40; Esther Schor, *Bridge of Words: Esperanto and the Dream of a Universal Language* (New York: Metropolitan Books, 2016), 205-206.
100. Megalli is first mentioned in *Jarlibro de la Internacia Esperanto-Ligo* (1943): 56.
101. Schor, *Bridge of Words*, 205-206.
102. Ch. A., "La langue de l'avenir?," *Images. L'hebdomadaire de l'actualité*, no. 821 (June 4, 1945): 8. The only more extensive source on Megalli's biography is the obituary published by his son in a German vegetarian journal: Theo Megalli, "Zur Erinnerung an Tadros Megalli: Vegetarisch und natürlich Esperanto," *Natürlich vegetarisch* 53, no. 1 (2003): 12.
103. In 1949, Megalli participated in an Esperanto congress in Australia. "One Tongue," *The Examiner*, September 18, 1949, 5. During the 1950s and 1960s, when living in Germany, he visited Bulgaria several times, publishing his observations in an Esperanto periodical. "Impresoj Pri Bulgario," *Internacia Jurnalisto. Organo de Tutmonda Esperantista Jurnalista Asocio (TEJA)* 8, no. 1 (1965): 3.
104. Tadros Megalli, "Ein ägyptischer Vegetarier erzählt," *Vegetarisches Universum* 4, no. 11 (1951): 3.
105. On the introduction of the tarboosh in the Ottoman Empire, see Donald Quataert, "Clothing Laws, State, and Society in the Ottoman Empire, 1720–1829," *International Journal of Middle East Studies* 29, no. 3 (1997): 403-425. For its connotations in Egypt, see for comparison Wilson Chacko Jacob, "The Turban, the Tarbush, and the Top Hat: Masculinity, Modernity, and National Identity in Interwar Egypt," *Al-Raida* 21, nos. 104–105 (2004): 23-37. In the West, by contrast, the tarboosh, or the fez, as it was known in Europe and North America, represented the very essence of "Orientalness," and esoteric communities like the Shriners had turned it into a sign of spiritism (of which Megalli was likewise an adherent). On the Shriners, see chapter 3. On the tarboosh as a signifier of Orientalness in the West, see also Julia Phillips Cohen, "Oriental by Design: Ottoman Jews, Imperial Style, and the Performance of Heritage," *American Historical Review* 119, no. 2 (2014): 364-398.
106. Tadros Megalli, "Ein ägyptischer Vegetarier reist als Globetrotter um die Welt," *Vegetarisches Universum* 6, no. 9 (1953): 6.

## 5. RACE, NATION, AND PEACE

107. "Vorträge Dr. Tadros Megalli (Kairo)," *Vegetarisches Universum* 6, no. 7 (1954): 3; Megalli, "Ein äyptischer Vegetarier reist als Globetrotter um die Welt."
108. Megalli, "Ein ägyptischer Vegetarier erzählt."
109. Megalli, "Zur Erinnerung an Tadros Megalli: Vegetarisch und natürlich Esperanto."
110. Dieter Ertel, *Zeichen der Zeit. Kongreß der Ideale. Beobachtungen bei einem Vegetariertreffen* (Stuttgart: Süddeutscher Rundfunk, 1959). I would like to thank Südwestrundfunk for providing me with a copy of the film.
111. "German Societies and IVU in the 1940s & 50s," International Vegetarian Union, accessed April 15, 2021, https://ivu.org/history/societies/vbd-ivucouncil.html.
112. "Grüße von Mrs. Gloria Gasque," *Vegetarisches Universum* 4, no. 10 (1951): 2.
113. "Elizabeth Ecker-Lauer. IVU Executive Committee 1953–57," International Vegetarian Union, accessed April 15, 2021, https://ivu.org/members/council/Elizabeth-Ecker-Lauer.html.
114. British vegetarianism, by contrast, already had many connections to feminism in the late nineteenth century. James Gregory, *Of Victorians and Vegetarians: The Vegetarian Movement in Nineteenth-Century Britain* (London: Tauris Academic Studies, 2007), 165–173. Mieke Roscher observes the same for the British animal welfare movement: *Ein Königreich für Tiere. Die Geschichte der britischen Tierrechtsbewegung* (Marburg: Tectum, 2009), 166–173.
115. "Ruf an die Frauen der Welt. Ein Aufruf der neugegründeten Föderation der Mazdaznan-Frauen an alle Frauen der Welt." *Vegetarisches Universum* 4, no. 10 (1951): 3; "Nationale und Internationale Frauen-Weltaktion," *Vegetarisches Universum* 7, no. 3 (1954): 4; "Frauen in die UN!," *Vegetarisches Universum* 7, no. 10 (1954): 4.
116. "Nationale und Internationale Frauen-Weltaktion," 4.
117. Otoman Zar Adusht Hanish, *Inner Studies: A Course of Twelve Lessons* (Chicago: Sun-Worshipper Publishing Company, 1902), 148–154; Hossein Kazemzadeh Iranschähr, *Grundlagen der neuen Erziehung* (Olten, CH: Amadeo, 1947), 63–82.
118. Barbara Welter, "The Cult of True Womanhood: 1820–1860," *American Quarterly* 18, no. 2 (1966): 151–174; Karin Hausen, "'Eine Ulme für das schwankende Efeu.' Ehepaare im deutschen Bildungsbürgertum," in *Bürgerinnen und Bürger. Geschlechterverhältnisse im 19. Jahrhundert*, ed. Ute Frevert (Göttingen: Vandenhoeck & Ruprecht, 1988), 85–117; "Öffentlichkeit und Privatheit. Gesellschaftspolitische Konstruktionen und die Geschichte der Geschlechterbeziehungen," in *Frauengeschichte—Geschlechtergeschichte*, ed. Karin Hausen and Heide Wunder (Frankfurt/Main: Campus 1992), 81–88.
119. Patricia Hill, *The World Their Household: The American Women's Foreign Mission Movement and Cultural Transformation, 1870–1920* (Ann Arbor: University of Michigan Press, 1985); Leonore Davidoff and Catherine Hall, *Family Fortunes: Men and Women of the English Middle Class, 1780–1850* (Chicago: University of Chicago Press, 1987); Leonore Davidoff, "Gender and the 'Great Divide': Public and Private in British Gender History," *Journal of Women's History* 15, no. 1 (2003): 11–27; Clare Midgley, *Feminism and Empire: Women Activists in Imperial Britain, 1790–1865* (London: Routledge, 2007); Julia Hauser, *German Religious Women in Late Ottoman Beirut: Competing Missions* (Leiden: Brill, 2015); "Mothers of a Future Generation: The Journey of an Argument for Female Education," in *Entangled*

## 5. RACE, NATION, AND PEACE

*Education: Foreign and Local Schools in Ottoman Syria and Mandate Lebanon (19th–20th Centuries)*, ed. Julia Hauser, Christine Lindner, and Esther Möller (Würzburg: Ergon, 2016), 143–161.
120. "Nationale und Internationale Frauen-Weltaktion."
121. A slightly extended version of this chapter section was first published as Julia Hauser, "Internationalism and Nationalism: Indian Protagonists and Their Political Agendas at the 15th World Vegetarian Congress in India (1957)," *South Asia: Journal of South Asian Studies* 44 (2021): 152–166.
122. "P. R. Lele Surveys the Indian Scene. Diwali—1957 Was Festival of Famine," *Blitz*, November 1, 1957, 4. Emphasis in the original.
123. Benjamin Robert Siegel, *Hungry Nation: Food, Famine, and the Making of Modern India* (Cambridge: Cambridge University Press, 2018).
124. Johanna Simonow, "The Rise and Demise of Multi-Purpose Food in India: Food Technology, Population Control and Nutritional Development in the Post-War Era, C. 1944–66," *South Asia: Journal of South Asian Studies* 44 (2021): 167–184.
125. Ministry of Food and Agriculture, *Report on the Marketing of Cattle in India* (Delhi: Government of India Press, 1956).
126. "World Vegetarian Congress in City: 16 Countries to Participate," *Times of India*, November 2, 1957, 8.
127. Lilavati Munshi, "Opening of the Food Exhibition," *World Forum* 9, no. 4 (1957–1958): 25–26.
128. Photo Division/Government of India, Raj Bhavan/November, 1957, 5/A22a(v), *The President, Dr. Rajendra Prasad, photographed with the delegates of World vegetarian Congress at a "At Home" at Rashtrapati Bhavan, New Delhi on November 16, 1957*. Photo Number:-64882, http://photodivision.gov.in/writereaddata/webimages/thumbnails/64882.jpg (accessed October 12, 2016; no longer accessible). At the National Archives, the original could not be retrieved.
129. Geoffrey L. Rudd, "Editorial. 15th World Vegetarian Congress in India," *Vegetarian and Humanitarian World Forum* 11, no. 4 (1957–1958): 14. The Nāmdhārī Sikhs, who emerged around the middle of the nineteenth century, rejected meat, alcohol, and tobacco. During the 1870s, they were involved in violent confrontations with the British over the issue of cow protection. Joginder Singh, "Nāmdhārī," in *Brill's Encyclopedia of Sikhism*, vol. 1, *History Literature Society Beyond Punjab*, ed. Knut A. Jacobsen et al. (Leiden: Brill, 2017), 359–367.
130. Both the *Times of India* and the *Free Press Journal* covered the congress in several articles from November 6 to 13, 1957, with the *Times of India* running advertisements for it as early as September. The British vegetarian journal *World Forum* devoted an entire issue to the congress. *World Forum* 11, no. 4 (1957–1958).
131. "Congress Resolutions," *World Forum* 11, no. 4 (1957–1958): 2.
132. Framroze Ardeshir Bode, "Vegetarianism: A Message for the New Age," in *Souvenir of the XV World Vegetarian Congress 1957* (Bombay: All-India Reception Committee, 1957), 1–5.
133. Jake Hodder, "Conferencing the International at the World Pacifist Meeting, 1949," *Political Geography* 49 (2015): 42.
134. Rajendra Prasad, "Inaugural Address at Bombay by the President of India," *Vegetarian and Humanitarian World Forum* 11, no. 4 (1957–1958): 16–19. The speech is also reprinted as "Moral Aspect of Eating," in *Dr Rajendra Prasad: Correspondence*

## 5. RACE, NATION, AND PEACE

*and Select Documents*, ed. Valmiki Choudhary (New Delhi: Allied Publishers, 1992), 447–451.
135. On Indian Multi-Purpose Food, see Simonow, "The Rise and Demise of Multi-Purpose Food in India."
136. Siegel, *Hungry Nation*, 87. On Lilavati Munshi's activities, see Siegel, *Hungry Nation*, 110–111; Lilavati Munshi, "Cafeteria Training. To the Editor, Times of India," *Times of India*, May 26, 1952, 6; "College of Catering at Andheri. U.N. Donates Equipment," *Times of India*, April 17, 1954, 5; Manmohini Zutshi Sahgal, *An Indian Freedom Fighter Recalls Her Life* (Armond: M. E. Sharp, 1994), 150–151; *Annapurna Recipes of Supplementary Foods*, 2 vols. (New Delhi: All India Women's Food Council, 1952). Despite Munshi's conservative positions, her catering college taught students how to prepare meat dishes.
137. Munshi, "Opening of the Food Exhibition." The fact that Munshi insisted on the unifying potential of vegetarian food is particularly interesting since her husband was one of the main exponents of the "Hindutva underground" in the Indian National Congress and, unlike Gandhi, approved of the use of violence. K. M. Munshi was the main figure behind the destruction of a mosque and its replacement with a Hindu temple at Somnath, Gujarat, an effort to address the temple destruction that Hindu nationalists ascribed to the Mughal ruler Aurangzeb in the seventeenth century. Munshi was thus instrumental in efforts to erase Islam from Indian history to shape a new, "Hindian" nation. In many ways, the destruction of the mosque at Somnath prefigured that of the Babri Masjid in 1992. Manu Bhagavan, "The Hindutva Underground: Hindu Nationalism and the Indian National Congress in Late Colonial and Early Post-Colonial India," *Economic and Political Weekly* 43, no. 37 (2008): 39–48. For Munshi's agenda in Somnath, see Romila Thapar, *Somanatha: The Many Voices of a History* (London: Verso, 2005), 180–194. On K. M. Munshi, see also Beatrix Martinez Saavedra, "Shaping the Community: Hindu Nationalist Imagination in Gujarat, 1800–1950" (PhD diss., University of Warwick, Department of History, 2013).
138. Considering that slaughter was integral to Id al-Adha, a major Muslim holiday, this was clearly an infringement on the Indian constitution ensures religious liberty in part 3, article 15. See "The Constitution of India 1949," Indian Kanoon, accessed April 14, 2021, https://indiankanoon.org/doc/237570/.
139. "Congress Resolutions." This rhetoric was not wholly new, having been employed in the late nineteenth century by such Hindu reformers as Swami Vivekananda, who had imagined India as the "spiritual teacher of mankind." Harald Fischer-Tiné, "'Deep Occidentalism?' Europa und der Westen in der Wahrnehmung hinduistischer Intellektueller und Reformer (ca. 1890–1930)," *Journal of Modern European History* 4, no. 2 (2006): 171–203.
140. Avanthi Meduri, "Bharatanatyam as a Global Dance: Some Issues in Research, Teaching, and Practice," *Dance Research Journal* 36, no. 2 (2004): 11–29; Sreebitha P. V., "Sanskritization or Appropriation: Caste and Gender in 'Indian' Music and Dance," *Savari: Adivasi Bahujan and Dalit Women Conversing*, April 6, 2014, http://www.dalitweb.org/?p=2499; *Women Members of the Rajya Sabha* (New Delhi: Rajya Sabha, 2003), 14; Lela Samson, *Rukmini Devi: A Life* (New Delhi: Penguin, 2010); Cornelia Haas, "Jagadamba tanzt. Rukmini Devi und das World-Mother-Movement," in *Frauenkörper/Frauenbilder. Inszenierungen des Weiblichen in den*

## 5. RACE, NATION, AND PEACE

*Gesellschaften Süd- und Ostasiens*, ed. Stephan Koehn and Heike Moser (Wiesbaden: Harassowitz, 2013), 161–177.

141. Rukmini Devi Arundale, "Address of Welcome," *World Forum* 11, no. 4 (1958): 20–23.
142. Geoffrey L. Rudd, "The 15th World Vegetarian Congress, India," *The Vegetarian* 6, no. 1 (1958): 6.
143. For this conflict in agricultural policy, see Benjamin Siegel, *Hungry Nation*, 174–179, whose analysis, however, does not include animal husbandry.
144. On the Hindu Code Bill, see Ramachandra Guha, *India After Gandhi: The History of the World's Largest Democracy* (London: Picador, 2007), 226–241. Although intended as a law fostering secularism, the Hindu Code Bill relied on Savarkar's notion of Hindutva. On definitions of the nation according to Hindutva, see Vinayak Damodar Savarkar, *Hindutva. Who Is a Hindu?* (Bombay: Veer Savarkar Prakashan, 1923).
145. Bhimrao Ramji Ambedkar, "The Untouchables," in *Dr. Babasaheb Ambedkar: Writings and Speeches*, ed. Vasant Moon (Mumbai: Education Department Government of Maharashtra, 1990), 223–379; E. V. R. Periyar, "March Towards Peace, Prosperity, and Progress," in *Collected Works of Periyar E. V. R.* (Chennai: Periyar Self-Respect Propaganda Institution, 1992), 285–310; Christophe Jaffrelot, *Dr Ambedkar and Untouchability: Analysing and Fighting Caste* (London: Hurst, 2005), 31–42; Shraddha Chigateri, "'Glory to the Cow': Cultural Difference and Social Justice in the Food Hierarchy in India," *Journal of South Asian Studies* 31, no. 1 (2008): 10–35.
146. Christophe Jaffrelot, *Religion, Caste, and Politics in India* (Delhi: Primus Books, 2010), 47–48.
147. Benjamin Zachariah, *Developing India: An Intellectual and Social History, c. 1930–50* (New Delhi: Oxford University Press, 2005); Michael Philipp Brunner, "Teaching Development: Debates on 'Scientific Agriculture' and 'Rural Reconstruction' at Khalsa College, Amritsar, c. 1915–47," *Indian Economic and Social History Revie*, 55, no. 1 (2018): 77–132. I would like to thank the author for a copy of this article.
148. Nikhil Menon, "'Help the Plan—Help Yourself': Making Indians Plan-Conscious," in *The Postcolonial Moment in South and Southeast Asia*, ed. Gyan Prakash, Nikhil Menon, and Michael Laffan (London: Bloomsbury, 2014), 221–242.
149. Government of India, Planning Commission, 2nd Five-Year Plan, chap. 25, "Health," accessed April 12, 2023, http://164.100.161.239/plans/planrel/fiveyr/2nd/2planch25.html. For the notion of "protective foods" as coined by the noted nutritionist Robert McCarrison, see Ashok Malhotra, "Cutting Edge Research in the Contact Zone? The Establishment of the Nutritional Research Laboratories in Coonoor (1925–27)," *South Asia: Journal of South Asian Studies* 44, no. 1 (2021): 117–134.
150. Government of India, Planning Commission, 1st Five-Year Plan, chap. 19, "Animal Husbandry," accessed April 12, 2023, http://164.100.161.239/plans/planrel/fiveyr/2nd/2planch14.html. On the history of *goshalas*, see Deryck O. Lodrick, *Sacred Cows, Sacred Places: Origins and Survivals of Animal Homes in India* (Berkeley: University of California Press, 1981).

5. RACE, NATION, AND PEACE

151. All-India Animal Welfare Association. For Prasad's positions on *goshala* reform, see Rajendra Prasad, "Improving the Cattle. Free Translation of Address in Hindi at the Distribution of Prizes at the All-India Cattle Show, Hissar, March 3, 1951," in *Speeches of President Rajendra Prasad*, vol. 1, *January 1950–May 1952* (Bombay: Ministry of Information and Broadcasting, 1973), 227–231.
152. As explained in chapter 2, many Kayathas in the second half of the nineteenth century became vegetarians.
153. Rajendra Prasad, *Autobiography* (Bombay: Asia Publishing House, 1957), 271.
154. Consequently, the bill met with severe criticism both from state governments and Nehru, with the result that it was not passed. For discussion of Arundale's proposal, see National Archives of India (henceforth: NAI), Ministry of Food and Agriculture, Policy Coordination File No. 2–44/53 PC II (1953–1954), *Prevention of Cruelty to Animals Bill 1953 of Shrimati Rukmini Devi Arundale*. Seth Govind Das had already introduced in 1952 a bill demanding a complete ban on cattle slaughter. As Akshaya Mukul stresses, Govind had collaborated with M. S. Gowalkar, leader of the Rashtriya Swayamsevak Sangh, in the draft. Akshaya Mukul, *Gita Press and the Making of Hindu India* (Noida: Harper Collins, 2015), 301. This bill was rejected by the Lok Sabha in 1955 and was criticized by Nehru, who could not "accept that animals are more important than economics," and considered "human beings . . . more important than cows." NAI, Ministry of Food and Agriculture, Policy Coordination File No. 2–33/52 PC II, 124. On the 1890 act, see Pratik Chakrabarti, "Beasts of Burden: Animals and Laboratory Research in Colonial India," *History of Science* 48, no. 2 (2010): 125–152.
155. Gauri Viswanathan, "'Have Animals Souls?' Theosophy and the Suffering Body," *Publications of the Modern Language Association of America* 126, no. 3 (2011): 440–447. On antivivisectionist discourses in Britain, see Roscher, *Ein Königreich für Tiere*, 145–157; Hilda Kean, *Animal Rights: Political and Social Change in Britain Since 1800* (London: Penguin, 1998), 96–112.
156. NAI, Ministry of Food and Agriculture, Policy Coordination File No. 2–44/53-PC II (1953–1954), Rukmini Devi Arundale to the Secretary, the Council of States, Parliament House, New Delhi, Kalakshetra, Madras, March 7, 1953 (copy).
157. "The Prevention of Cruelty to Animals Bill, 1953—Withdrawn," in *Parliamentary Debates Council of States Official Report* (1954), VI/15, 1785–1809.
158. Government of India, The Prevention of Cruelty to Animals Act, 1960 (59 of 1960). As amended by Central Act 26 of 1926 (1960), https://www.indiacode.nic.in/bitstream/123456789/11237/1/the_prevention_of_cruelty_to_animals_act%2C_1960.pdf (accessed December 16, 2018).
159. Rukmini Devi was a member of the Animal Welfare Board at least until 1968. Sunil Kothari, *Photo Biography of Rukmini Devi* (Chennai: Kalakshetra Foundation, 2004), 159.
160. This trope had also been cultivated at the Asian Relations Conference in Delhi in 1947. Vineet Thakur, "An Asian Drama: The Asian Relations Conference, 1947," *International History Review* 41, no. 3 (2019): 673–695; Carolien Stolte, "'The Asiatic Hour': New Perspectives on the Asian Relations Conference, New Delhi, 1947," in *The Non-Aligned Movement and the Cold War: Delhi—Bandung—Belgrade*, ed. Natasa Miskovic, Harald Fischer-Tine, and Nada Boskovska (London: Routledge, 2014), 57–75.

## 5. RACE, NATION, AND PEACE

161. Joseph Regenstein Library, University of Chicago, Special Archives and Collections, International Association for Cultural Freedom, Box 173, Folder 7; Box 184, Folder 2, "Indian Congress for Cultural Freedom" (1951). Rukmini Devi continued to be on the executive board of the ICCF well into the 1960s. "Indian Committee for Cultural Freedom. A Brief Report of Activities," in *International Association for Cultural Freedom* (Bombay: Joseph Regenstein Library University of Chicago, 1957), 2; "I.C.C.F. Conference: A Report," *Freedom First*, no. 68 (1958): 9–10; *Indian Committee for Cultural Freedom* (Calcutta: Congress for Cultural Freedom, 1962–1963); *Indian Committee for Cultural Freedom. Report of Work January 1963 to June 1964* (Bombay: Committee for Cultural Freedom, 1964); *Indian Committee for Cultural Freedom, Calcutta Centre (October 1962–May 1965)* (Calcutta: Congress for Cultural Freedom, 1965). There is no mention of the World Vegetarian Congress in the files of the ICCF. Lilavati and K. M. Munshi were close to Frank Buchman's Moral Re-Armament, an evangelical movement in the United States and Britain that sought to spread conservative values as an antidote to the supposed global threat of communism. The Munshis visited one of its centers during a trip to the United States, meeting Gandhi's grandson, whom they referred to as a "rising star" in the movement. K. M. Munshi and Lilavati Munshi, *The World We Saw. Letters by K. M. Munshi and Lilavati Munshi Written During a Tour in America, Europe and Asia. Reprinted from the "Bhavan's Journal"* (Bombay: Bharatiya Vidya Bhavan, 1960), 90–92. Some German vegetarians were also close to this movement. Gertrud Schmidt, "Die 'Moralische Aufrüstung' und wir," *Der Vegetarier* 7 (1956): 2–3
162. Manchester County Record Office, G24 Manchester Vegetarian Society, Register of Members. The members concerned, all residing with "Brother Yogesh" in Lahore, most likely a guru, at the time of application, were Dev Kumar Chopra, Madan Lal Lucker, Giom Chandra Mody, Surendra Mohan Mehra, Nand Lal Nandi, Tilak Raj Yogesh, and Mrs. Umesh Kumari Yogesh. Their names are rendered here as spelled in the membership roster.
163. Sukhdev Pershed Bhatia, Mexboro, United States (medical doctor); D. D. Desai, Jesmond; B. Gopalan, Ashton on Mersey, United Kingdom; Vasandkumar Narsislal, London (student); Kumar Sudhanshu Jain, Meerut, India (technical assistant); N. Jeapudoori, Lagos, Nigeria; Russy Pesholan Mistry, Bombay, India (electrical engineer); Suroyder Prasad, Burdwan, India; S. S. Rao, Bombay, India (radio engineer), M. Kar Sharma, Burdwan, India.
164. Hiller, a natural foods trader from Hanover who, following his father, the senior company director, had joined the Nazi Party in 1931, and wore a Hitler moustache even in the 1950s, is another example of continuity between the Nazi and the postwar eras in German organized vegetarianism. Bundesarchiv Berlin, NSDAP-Zentralkartei BArch R 9361-VIII KARTEI 11071233. Bundesarchiv Berlin, BArch R 9361-VIII KARTEI / 11071200.
165. Geo Hiller, "Aus meinem indischen Tagebuch," *Der Vegetarier* 9, no. 2 (1958): 5–7; *Der Vegetarier* 9, no. 5 (1958): 1–5; *Der Vegetarier* 9, no. 5 (1958): 9; *Der Vegetarier* 9, no. 6 (1958): 6–9; *Der Vegetarier* 9, no. 9 (1958): 6–9; *Der Vegetarier* 9, no. 10 (1958): 2–5; *Der Vegetarier* 9, no. 10 (1958): 4–7; *Der Vegetarier* 9, no. 11 (1958): 3–7; *Der Vegetarier* 10, no. 1 (1959): 4–9; *Der Vegetarier* 10, no. 3 (1959): 7–14; *Der Vegetarier* 10, no. 5 (1959): 15–20; *Der Vegetarier* 10, no. 9 (1959): 3–6; *Der Vegetarier* 10, no. 11 (1959): 25–27; *Der Vegetarier* 10, no. 12 (1959): 10–12.

## 5. RACE, NATION, AND PEACE

166. H. Buys, "Ahimsa und der Vegetarismus," *Der Vegetarier* 7 (1956): 1–2; "15. Weltkongreß in Indien," *Der Vegetarier* 8 (1957): 12; "Yoga," *Der Vegetarier* 8 (1957): 24–25; S. Radhakrishnan, "Indische Philosophie," *Der Vegetarier* 8 (1957), 30; Karl Kriemer, "Bericht über das Yogiturnen im Vegetarier-Jugend-Ferienlager," *Der Vegetarier* 9 (1958): 10; Vegetarier-Union Deutschland, "'Indische Heilige verändern die Welt,'" *Der Vegetarier* 10 (1959): 31–32.
167. D. V. Gokhale, "Weihnachtsbotschaft aus dem Fernen Osten," *Sontraer Gesundheitsbote* 11 (1957): 5–7; Oswald Kiehne, "Unsere Botschaft an den Fernen Osten," *Sontraer Gesundheitsbote* 11 (1957): 7–8; D. V. Gokhale, "Für den indisch-deutschen Weltfrieden, Brüderlichkeit, Verstehen unter den Völkern und gewaltlosen Frieden!," *Sontraer Gesundheitsbote* 12 (1958): 10–11; "Hiroshima-Tag—Weltfriedenstag!," *Sontraer Gesundheitsbote* 12 (1958): 3–4; Oswald Kiehne, "Indien und wir," *Sontraer Gesundheitsbote* 12, no. 3 (1958): 5–7; D. V. Gokhale, "Unsere indischen Freunde grüßen an der Schwelle des neuen Jahres," *Sontraer Gesundheitsbote* 13 (1959): 4–9; "Osterbotschaft aus Indien," *Sontraer Gesundheitsbote* 13 (1959): 4–7; "Der Schlüssel zum Frieden," *Sontraer Gesundheitsbote* 13 (1959): 3–6; Oswald Kiehne, "Achtzehn Bilder aus Indien als Weihnachtsgruß," *Sontraer Gesundheitsbote* 13 (1959): 21. Kiehne (who did not participate in the 1957 IVU congress in India) first mentioned Gokhale as an alleged correspondent of the *Sontraer Gesundheitsbote*: "Weltkongreß der Internationalen Vegetarier-Union," *Sontraer Gesundheits-Bote* 11, no. 11 (1957): half title.
168. Stefan Tetzlaff, "'A New Passage to India?' Westdeutsche Außenwirtschaftspolitik und Wirtschaftsbeziehungen mit Indien, ca. 1950–72," in *Dekolonisierungsgewinner. Deutsche Außenpolitik und Außenwirtschaftsbeziehungen im Zeitalter des Kalten Krieges*, ed. Christian Kleinschmidt and Dieter Ziegler (Berlin: De Gruyter Oldenbourg, 2018), 191–209.
169. Without using the term "Aryan," former National Socialist functionaries like Otto-Albrecht Isbert became yoga experts in the 1950s. Isbert, a geographer and linguist of Hungarian descent, worked for the Volksdeutsche Mittelstelle of the SS, investigating the alleged German blood percentage among members of the Hungarian elite. Having participated in the Nazi politics of expansion and ethnic cleansing in eastern Europe, he was dismissed from his research position at Tübingen University after the war. In the 1950s, Isbert published handbooks and articles on yoga. On his career, see Mario Daniels, *Geschichtswissenschaft im 20. Jahrhundert. Institutionalisierungsprozesse und Entwicklung des Personenverbandes an der Universität Tübingen 1918–1964* (Stuttgart: Steiner, 2009), 63–64, 244–246; Michael Fahlbusch, *Wissenschaft im Dienst der nationalsozialistischen Politik? Die "Volksdeutschen Forschungsgemeinschaften" von 1931–1945* (Baden-Baden: Nomos, 1999), 132–133, 159, 269, 651. His publications include Otto Albrecht Isbert, ed., *Volksboden und Nachbarschaft der Deutschen in Europa: Ein Taschenbuch* (Langensalza: Beltz, 1936); Otto Albrecht Isbert and Heinz Kloß, eds., *Völker und Grenzen* (Stuttgart: Kohlhammer, 1942); Otto-Albrecht Isbert, *Yoga und der Weg des Westens. Der geistige Pfad des modernen Menschen* (Stuttgart: Günther, 1955); *Indien und wir. Die deutsch-indische Begegnung* (Bad-Godesberg: Verlag des Instituts für Geosoziologie und Politik, 1957). Isbert also lectured on the "Age of Aquarius" and "Spiritual India" at vegetarian meetings in southwest Germany in the 1950s: "Mitteilungen," *Der Neue Mensch* 6, no. 12 (1955): 185–186.

EPILOGUE

170. "Mitteilungen," *Friede. Deutsch-indische Monatsschrift für Yoga—Mystik—Lebensreform* 2, no. 10 (1954): 46–47, introduced a new "Aryan" universal language in the name of world peace; Mönch Ram, "Weltreligion," *Friede. Deutsch-indische Monatsschrift für Yoga—Mystik—Lebensreform* 3, no. 10 (1955): 408–413, invoked an "Indo-Aryan religion of the sun."

## EPILOGUE

1. While some of the vegetarians introduced in this book were vegans in practice, occasionally referring to themselves as "strict vegetarians" to set themselves apart from those vegetarians who consumed dairy products and eggs, the term itself was only coined in 1942. Florentine Fritzen, *Gemüseheilige: Eine Geschichte des veganen Lebens* (Stuttgart: Fritz Steiner, 2016).
2. Tom Regan, *The Case for Animal Rights* (Berkeley: University of California Press, 1983).
3. Andy Howell and Zoë Eisenberg, *The Lusty Vegan: A Cookbook and Relationship Manifesto for Vegans and the People Who Love Them* (Woodstock, NY: Vegan Heritage Press, 2014).
4. Yogi Tea, https://www.yogitea.com (accessed April 17, 2021). Yogi Tea's most recent rival in German health and organic food stores is a UK-based brand, Pukka Herbs. "Pukka Herbs. Organic Teas and Supplements," https://uk.pukkaherbs.com (accessed April 17, 2021). The term "pukka" means pure, or more precisely, pure food not touched, gazed on, or overshadowed by lower-caste or non-Hindu individuals. One may assume that this meaning is unknown to the company's British directors despite their close ties to partners in India.
5. The company's website does not give the full history of Arya Laya. It merely states that the brand (whose name is rendered, in a somewhat bowdlerized translation, as "carrier of beauty") was bought by Diaderma, another German organic cosmetics company, in 1970. "Arya Laya Shop. Der offizielle Arya Laya Onlineshop," https://www.aryalaya-shop.de (accessed April 17, 2021). For an early ad that reveals that the company's seat was Hanover, see *Vegetarische Presse* 13, no. 11 (1930): n.p.
6. "Corona-Demos in Berlin: 'Unglaubliches Unbehagen gegen unsere Regierungsform'. Mely Kiyak im Gespräch mit Vladimir Balzer,'" Deutschlandfunk Kultur, August 29, 2020, https://www.deutschlandfunkkultur.de/corona-demos-in-berlin-unglaubliches-unbehagen-gegen-unsere.1013.de.html?dram:article_id=483277.
7. See chapter 4.
8. Ananya Bhardwaj, "Muslim Boy Stabbed to Death on Train After Argument Turns Into Religious Slurs," *Hindustan Times*, June 27, 2017, http://www.hindustantimes.com/india-news/man-stabbed-to-death-2-injured-on-mathura-train-after-fight-with-passengers-for-allegedly-carrying-beef/story-BiJyILYlUloErWASvKQ51M.html. See also the documentary by Shirley Abraham and Amit Madheshiya, *The Hour of Lynching: The Killing of Muslim Cow Farmers in India*, prod. *The Guardian* (UK), May 2019, video, 19:11 min., https://www.theguardian.com/news/ng

-interactive/2019/may/24/the-hour-of-lynching-vigilante-violence-against-muslims-in-india-video.

9. Sindhu Ajay, "India State Government Pushes Ahead with Law Banning Cow Slaughter," *Jurist: Legal News and Commentary*, January 21, 2021, https://www.jurist.org/news/2021/01/india-state-government-pushes-ahead-with-law-banning-cow-slaughter/. For an earlier overview, see "Cow Slaughter Prevention Laws in India: How the Law not Just Protects Cow Vigilantes, but Sanctifies Lynchings," Citizens for Justice and Peace, July 2, 2018, https://cjp.org.in/cow-slaughter-prevention-laws-in-india/.
10. Madeeha Mudjawar, "Muslims Not Allowed—the Stereotypes of Mumbai's Rental Property Market," CNBCTV18, September 21, 2020, https://www.cnbctv18.com/views/muslims-not-allowed-the-stereotypes-of-mumbais-rental-property-market-6970051.htm.
11. "Ram Navami: Sale of Raw Meat Banned in Bengaluru, Parts of Delhi Today," India.com, April 10, 2022, https://www.india.com/news/india/ram-navami-sale-of-raw-meat-banned-in-bengaluru-parts-of-delhi-today-5329549/; "Several JNU Students Hurt in Scuffle Allegedly Over Meat in Hostel Mess on Ram Navami," Scroll.in, April 11, 2022, https://scroll.in/latest/1021553/several-students-injured-at-delhis-jnu-in-scuffle-allegedly-over-serving-meat-on-ram-navami.
12. Kalyani Devaki Menon, *Making Place for Muslims in Contemporary India* (Ithaca, NY: Cornell University Press, 2022), 33.
13. Michel Foucault, "Nietzsche, Genealogy, History," in *Language, Counter-Memory, Practice: Selected Essays and Interviews*, ed. D. F. Bouchard (Ithaca, NY: Cornell University Press, 1977), 154.
14. Robert Proctor, "Agnotology: A Missing Term to Describe the Cultural Production of Ignorance (and Its Study)," in *Agnotology: The Making and Unmaking of Ignorance*, ed. Proctor and Londa Schiebinger (Stanford, CA: Stanford University Press, 2008), 1–35.
15. Jakob A. Klein, "Afterword: Comparing Vegetarianisms," *Journal of South Asian Studies* 31, no. 1 (2008): 199–212.
16. Jennifer Jensen Wallach, *Every Nation Has Its Dish: Black Bodies and Black Food in Twentieth-Century America* (Chapel Hill: University of North Carolina Press, 2019), 138, 80–88; Elijah Muhammad, *How to Eat to Live* (Los Gatos, CA: Secretarius MEMPS, 1972).

# BIBLIOGRAPHY

## ARCHIVAL PRIMARY SOURCES

Archiv der deutschen Jugendbewegung, Burg Ludwigstein, Witzenhausen
  AdJb Bestand F 1 Nr. 475
Archiv für alternatives Schrifttum (afas)
  AMA 1944–46 DEROG/VUD Schriftwechsel E–F. Briest to Fidus (Hugo Höppener)
  Magnus Schwantje Papers
  VUD-Vorläufer 1947 DEROG Briefwechsel 48/49 VUD
Bauhaus-Archiv Berlin
  Johannes Itten Papers
Bundesarchiv Berlin-Lichterfelde (BArch)
  NSDAP-Zentralkartei
  N 2210/258: Leonard Nelson Papers
  R 187/267 a: Religiöse Gemeinschaften. Bayerische politische Polizei an alle Polizeidirektionen, Staatspolizeiämter, Bezirksämter, Bezirksaussensitze u. Stadtkommissäre.
Hauptstaatsarchiv Stuttgart
  Sonderbestand 8600: Autographensammlung Ankenbrand
Institut für Auslandsbeziehungen Stuttgart
  Deutsche Kolonial- und Kriegsgefangenenzeitung Diyatalawa
Joseph Regenstein Library, University of Chicago. Special Archives and Collections.
  International Association for Cultural Freedom, Box 173, Folder 7; Box 184, Folder 2. "Indian Congress for Cultural Freedom" (1951)
Justus Liebig Universität Gießen, Universitätsbibliothek

BIBLIOGRAPHY

FH Eden Z: Journals and unpublished documents from the library of the vegetarian community at Eden, Oranienburg
Landesarchiv Berlin
  A Rep. 003-04-04-Wittenauer Heilstätten der Stadt Berlin: No. 8293
Manchester County Record Office
  G24 Manchester Vegetarian Society
National Archives Chicago
  Records of the United States District Court for the Northern District of Illinois 4914, 4915, 4957, and 4984
National Archives of India
  Ministry of Food and Agriculture, Policy Coordination File No. 2–33/52 PC II, 124
  Ministry of Food and Agriculture, Policy Coordination File No. 2–44/53-PC II (1953–1954)
Nehru Memorial Archives and Library
  D. V. Savarkar Papers
Politisches Archiv des Auswärtigen Amtes, Berlin (PA AAB RZ)
  RZ 201/19017 Ausbildung von Persern in Deutschland
  R 210.89/3 IA—Weltkrieg WK Nr. 11 f. R 210.89/3za
Schweizerisches Bundesarchiv, Berne
  E2001E#1976/17#665* Iranschär, H. K., Flawil (Dossier)
Seaver Center for Western History Research, Los Angeles Museum of Natural History
  The Reorganized Mazdaznan Temple Association of Associates of God
Universitätsbibliothek Kassel, Landesbibliothek und Murhardsche Bibliothek
  2° Ms. Hist. Litt. 38: Wilhelm Schwaner papers
Vegetarian Society, Altrincham
  Register of Members

## PUBLISHED PRIMARY SOURCES

A., Ch. "La langue de l'avenir?" *Images. L'hebdomadaire de l'actualité*, no. 821 (June 4, 1945): 8.
Abhedananda, Swami. *Complete Works of Swami Abhedananda*. Vol. 10. Calcutta: Ramakrishna Vedanta Math, 1970.
——. "How to Be a Yogi." In *Complete Works of Swami Abhedananda*, vol. 3, 3–81. Calcutta: Ramakrishna Vedanta Math, 1958.
——. "How to Gain Self-Control." *Vedanta Monthly Bulletin* 2, no. 1 (1906–1907): 19–29.
——. *Leaves from My Diary*. In *Complete Works of Swami Abhedananda*, vol. 10. Calcutta: Ramakrishna Vedanta Math, 1970.
——. *Why a Hindu Is a Vegetarian. Delivered Before the Vegetarian Society, New York, March 22, 1898*. New York: Vedanta Society, 1900.
——. "Yoga, Its Theory and Practice." In *Complete Works of Swami Abhedananda*, vol. 3, 323–433. Calcutta: Ramakrishna Vedanta Math, 1958.
Acharya, M. P. T. "'Anarchist Manifesto' (Originally Published in the Road to Freedom 3, 1 (September 1, 1926), 5–6." In *Acharya, M. P. T.: We Are Anarchists: Essays on Anarchism, Pacifism, and the Indian Independence Movement, 1923–1953*, edited by Ole Birk Laursen, 45–49. Edinburgh: Chico, 2019.

## BIBLIOGRAPHY

———. "Gandhi and Non-Violence." In *Acharya, M. P. T.: We Are Anarchists: Essays on Anarchism, Pacifism, and the Indian Independence Movement, 1923–1953*, edited by Ole Birk Laursen, 103–106. Edinburgh: Chico, 2019.
———. "On the Question of Race." In *Acharya, M. P. T.: We Are Anarchists: Essays on Anarchism, Pacifism, and the Indian Independence Movement, 1923–1953*, edited by Ole Birk Laursen, 137–139. Edinburgh: Chico, 2019.
"Advertisements." *The Harbinger* 5 (1895): 107–108.
"Advertisements." *The Harbinger* 5 (1895): 48.
"Aegypten." *Vereins-Blatt für Freunde der naturgemäßen Lebensweise (Vegetarianer)* 11, no. (1868): 171–172.
Albrecht, Paul. "Der Vegetarismus und die Politik." *Vegetarische Presse* 12 (1929): 65.
———. "Gandhi." *Vegetarische Presse* 13 (1930): 37–38.
———. "Noch einmal: 'Roter Vegetarismus.'" *Vegetarische Presse* 14 (1931): 27–29.
Alcott, William A. *Vegetable Diet: As Sanctioned by Medical Men, and by Experience in All Ages*. Boston: Marsh, Capen & Lyon, 1838.
"Alkohola Veneno Kaj Nikotina Veneno En Rilato Kun La Seksa Edukado." *Vegetarano* 6, no. 3 (1922): 18–19.
"All India Gahanbar Bombay—Gahanbar Reports." *Mazdaznan India* 2 (1942): 425–444.
Alva, Joachim. *Men and Supermen of Hindustan*. Bombay: Thacker, 1943.
Ambedkar, Bhimrao Ramji. "Right and Might." In *The Past of the Outcaste: Readings in Dalit History*, edited by Sabyasachi Bhattacharya and Yagati Chinna Rao, 49–54. Delhi: Orient Blackswan, 2017.
———. "The Untouchables." In *Dr. Babasaheb Ambedkar: Writings and Speeches*, edited by Vasant Moon, 223–379. Bombay: Education Department Government of Maharashtra, 1990.
Ammann, David. "The Coming Race and Race Hygiene." *Mazdaznan* 13 (1914): 273–286, 304–312.
"An alle Vegetarier!" *Der Wendepunkt im Leben und im Leiden* 21, no. 6 (1944): n.p.
Ankenbrand, Lisbeth. *Der Wille zur Schönheit*. Stuttgart: Süddeutsches Verlagshaus, 1928.
———. *Der Wille zur Schönheit*. 2nd ed. Stuttgart: Süddeutsches Verlagshaus, 1935.
———. *Der Wille zur Schönheit*. 3rd ed. Stuttgart: Süddeutsches Verlagshaus, 1950.
———. *Die gesunde glückliche Frau*. Stuttgart: Süddeutsches Verlagshaus, 1932.
———. *Die Rohkostküche: Gesundheit durch vitaminreiche Nahrung*. Stuttgart: Süddeutsches Verlagshaus, 1928.
———. *Die tägliche Schönheitspflege der Frau: Rezepte und wirksame Mittel, die wenig Geld kosten*. Stuttgart: Süddeutsches Verlagshaus, 1930.
———. *Gesund und schön ins Alter*. Stuttgart: Süddeutsches Verlagshaus, 1938.
———. *Gesunde fleischlose Küche*. Stuttgart: Süddeutsches Verlagshaus, 1929.
———. *Schenk deinem Kinde Schönheit. Neuzeitliche praktische Gesundheits- und Schönheitspflege vom ersten Lebenstage bis zur Reife*. Stuttgart: Süddeutsches Verlagshaus, 1937.
Ankenbrand, Ludwig. "Buddhism and the Modern Reform Efforts (Germany, 1911)." In *Religious Dynamics Under the Impact of Imperialism and Colonialism*, edited by Björn Bentlage, Marion Eggert, Hans Martin Krämer, and Stefan Reichmuth, 191–196. Leiden: Brill, 2017.

———. "Der Buddhismus und die modernen Reformbestrebungen." *Zeitschrift für Buddhismus* (1911–1912): 56–61.
———. "Deutsche Buddhisten in Indien während der Kriegszeit." *Zeitschrift für Buddhismus* 2 (1920): 62–63.
———. "Eine buddhistische Wallfahrt rund um die Welt." *Die Buddhistische Welt: Deutsche Monatsschrift für Buddhismus* 5 (1911–1912): 248.
———. *Vogelschutz im Winter und Sommer*. Berlin: Berliner Tierschutz-Verein, 1909.
———. "Von Genua nach Kairo." *Vegetarische Warte* 46, no. 2 (1913): 16–17, 46–47.
———. "Weltreise-Vorspiel (mit einem Bilde)." *Vegetarische Warte* 45, nos. 63–64 (1912): 63–64.
*Annapurna Recipes of Supplementary Foods*. 2 vols. New Delhi: All India Women's Food Council, 1952.
"Annual Meetings of the Vegetarian Society." *Vegetarian Messenger*, 4th ser., 4 (1890): 321–322.
"Annual Report." *The Harbinger* 4 (1894): 207–208.
Arundale, Rukmini Devi. "Address of Welcome." *World Forum* 11, no. 4 (1958): 20–24.
"Aus Arabien." *Vereins-Blatt für Freunde der natürlichen Lebensweise* 64 (1874): 1016–1018.
"Aussprache." *ISK-Mitteilungen* 2, no. 3 (1927): 57–60.
*Avesta: The Religious Books of the Parsees; from Professor Spiegel's German Translation of the Original Manuscripts by Arthur Henry Bleeck [. . . ] in Three Volumes*. Hertford, UK: Muncherjee Hormusjee Cama, 1864.
Axon, William E. A. "The Rise of Vegetarianism in India. A Paper Contributed to the Annual Meeting of the Vegetarian Society, October 18, 1882." *Dietetic Reformer and Vegetarian Messenger*, 3rd ser., 9 (1883): 28–30.
———. "Vegetarianism and the Land Question." *Dietetic Reformer*, n.s., 12 (1885): 126–128.
Ayangar, C. R. Srinivasa. "Occult Physiology." *Theosophical Siftings* 6 (1894): 1–19.
"Bad Liebenzell." *Vegetarisches Universum* 5, no. 4 (1952): 1.
Ball, Samuel. *An Account of the Cultivation and Manufacture of Tea in China*. London: Longman, Brown, Green, and Longmans, 1838.
Baltzer, Eduard. "Aus Professor Brenneckes Reise: Die Länder an der Unteren Donau und Konstantinopel." *Vereins-Blatt für Freunde der natürlichen Lebensweise* 22 (1870): 349–51.
———. "China und Japan." *Vereins-Blatt für Freunde der natürlichen Lebensweise* 36 (1872): 567–568.
———. *Das Buch von der Arbeit oder die menschliche Arbeit in persönlicher und volkswirthschaftlicher Beziehung*. Nordhausen: Förstemann, 1870.
———. *Die natürliche Lebensweise, der Weg zu Gesundheit und sozialem Heil*. Nordhausen: Förstemann, 1867.
———. "Erster Vereinsbericht." *Vereins-Blatt für Freunde der natürlichen Lebensweise* 1 (1868): 3–16.
———. "Gefahren des Vegetarianismus." *Vereins-Blatt für Freunde der naturgemäßen Lebensweise (Vegetarianer)* 3 (1870): 353–358.
———. "Nahrung der Sclaven im Alterthum." *Vereins-Blatt für Freunde der natürlichen Lebensweise* 9 (1869): 142.

## BIBLIOGRAPHY

———. "Vom Kongo." *Vereins-Blatt für Freunde der natürlichen Lebensweise* 112 (1879): 1778–1782.
———. "Von der türkischen Grenze." *Vereins-Blatt für Freunde der natürlichen Lebensweise* 29 (1871): 456–459.
———. *Vegetarianisches Kochbuch für Freunde der natürlichen Lebensweise.* Rudolstadt in Thüringen: H. Hartung & Sohn, 1886.
Bam, Banu. "To My Mazdaznan Sisters and Brothers." *Mazdaznan India* 2 (1942): 144–145.
Baness, Theo. *An Essay on Cows Protection by Mr. Theo. Baness, Contractor, Amritsar, Published by Lala Shambhu Nath by the Permission of Pandit Gosavak Jagat Narain of Benares.* Amritsar: National Press, 1893.
"The Banquet of the Fifth Annual Meeting of the Vegetarian Society." *Vegetarian Messenger* 3 (1852): 8–20.
"The Banquet of the Seventh Annual Meeting of the Vegetarian Society." *Vegetarian Messenger* 5 (1859): 65–78.
Barrows, John Henry. "The World's Parliament of Religions. An Illustrated and Popular Story of the World's First Parliament of Religions, Held in Chicago in Connection with the Columbian Exposition of 1893." Chicago: Parliament Publishing Co., 1893.
Beard, Sidney H. *A Comprehensive Guide-Book to Natural, Hygienic, and Humane Diet.* London: Order of the Golden Age, n.d. [ca. 1922].
———. "The Law of Reincarnation." *Herald of the Golden Age* 8, no. 6 (1903): 1–2.
———. *A Simple Guide to a Natural and Humane Diet.* Ilfracombe, UK: Order of the Golden Age, 1898.
———. *The Testimony of Science in Favour of a Natural and Humane Diet.* London: Order of the Golden Age, 1906.
———. *Why I Condemn Vivisection.* Paignton, UK: Order of the Golden Age, 1904.
"Beef and Spirituality in India: Were Ancient Hindus Vegetarians?" *Times of India*, March 23, 1926, 8.
Bell, Robert. *The Cancer Scourge and How to Destroy It.* N.p.: Order of the Golden Age, n.d. [ca. 1903].
"Bericht über das erste Tätigkeitsjahr (1. Juli 1919 bis 30. Juli 1920) des Instituts für Sexualwissenschaft." *Jahrbuch für sexuelle Zwischenstufen* 20 (1920): 54–74.
Besant, Annie. *On the Protection of Animals: An Address at the Calcutta Town Hall.* Madras: Theosophist Office, 1910.
*The Bhagavad Gītā.* Translated by Winthrop Sargeant. Edited and with a preface by Christopher Key Chapple. Albany, NY: Excelsior Editions, 2009.
"Bilderbericht vom 5. 'Kongreß der Ideale' zu Freudenstadt." *Vegetarisches Universum* 8, no. 7 (1955): 8.
"Bildbericht vom vierten 'Kongreß der Ideale' zu Bad Liebenzell." *Vegetarisches Universum* 7, no. 7 (1954): 8.
Bircher-Benner, M. "Italien." *Vegetarische Presse* 15 (1932): 45.
Blavatsky, Helena Petrovna. *Isis Unveiled.* New York: J. W. Bouton, 1877.
Blavatsky, Helena. *The Secret Doctrine. The Synthesis of Science, Religion, and Philosophy.* London: Theosophical Publishing Company, 1888.
Blumenthal, Hanna. "Der Weg zur Freude. Die Frauenbewegung und die Fysiokratie." *Tau*, no. 33 (1927): 18–22.

## BIBLIOGRAPHY

Bode, Framroze Ardeshir. "Vegetarianism: A Message for the New Age." In *Souvenir of the XV World Vegetarian Congress 1957*, 1–5. Bombay: All-India Reception Committee, 1957.

"The Bombay Humanitarian League. Its Why and What." In *The Indian Humanitarian. The Bombay Humanitarian League. Silver Jubilee Number, 1910–1934, Etc.*, 5–24. Bombay: Bombay Humanitarian League, 1934.

Borel, Henri. *Wijsheid en schoonheid uit China*. Amsterdam: P. N. Van Kampen & Zoon, 1895.

———. *Wu Wei. A Phantasy Based on the Philosophy of Lao-Tse*. London: Luzac, 1903.

———. *Wu-Wei. Eine Auslegung der Lehren Laotses. Deutsch von Werner Zimmermann*. Lauf/Nuremberg: Rudolf Zitzmann, 1933.

———. *Wu Wei: Fiction basée sur la philosophie de Lao Tse*. Paris: Fischbacher, 1913.

Bracke, Dr. "Dr. Otoman Zar Adusht Hanish oder der Janus-Kopf." *Vegetarische Warte* 46, no. 12 (1913): 117–119.

———. "Etwas von 'Meister' Hanisch." *Vegetarische Warte* 46, no. 1 (1913): 87–88.

———. "Weiteres vom Mazdaznan-Meister." *Vegetarische Warte* 46, no. 24 (1913): 234–235.

"A Brahminical Banquet." *Herald of the Golden Age* 16, no. 10 (1911): 202.

Breske, Robert. "Der Frischköstler ein Fürst und Führer." *Lichtheilgrüße* 4 (1928): 326–328.

Breüer, Slavibor. "Vom Athos." *Vereins-Blatt für Freunde der natürlichen Lebensweise* 155 (1883): 2471–2473.

Briest, Adolf, and Helmut Gringmann. *Die Ernährung des denkenden Menschen*. 2nd ed. Hamburg: Verlag der Rohkost-Förderung, 1933.

"British Correspondence on the Agitation in Bihar." In *British Origin of Cow-Slaughter in India*, edited by Dharampal and T. M. Mukundan, 291–428. Mussoorie: Society for Integrated Development of Himalayas, 2002.

"The Bushman and the Kaffir." *Vegetarian Messenger* 7 (1857): 82–83.

Buys, H. "Ahimsa und der Vegetarismus." *Der Vegetarier* 7 (1956): 1–2.

Byapari, Manoranjan. *Interrogating My Chandal Life: An Autobiography of a Dalit*. New Delhi: SAGE Publications, 2017.

*Caraka Samhita*. Translated by A. Chandra Kaviratna and P. Sharma. Preface by Dr. Jan Erik Sidgell. 2nd rev. ed. 3 vols. Delhi: Sri Satguru Publications, 1996.

"Caraka's Compendium." In *The Roots of Ayurveda*, edited by Dominik Wujastyk, 1–60. London: Penguin, 2003.

*Catalogue of Books Printed in the Bombay Presidency During the Quarter Ending 31st March 1890*. Bombay: Government Central Press, 1890.

*Catalogue of Books Printed in the Bombay Presidency During the Quarter Ending 30th June 1890*. Bombay: Government Central Press, 1890.

*Catalogue of Books Printed in the Bombay Presidency During the Quarter Ending 31st December 1890*. Bombay: Government Central Press, 1891.

*Catalogue of Books Printed in the Bombay Presidency During the Quarter Ending 30st September 1909*. Bombay: Government Central Press, 1909.

*Catalogue of Books, Received During the Quarter Ending 31st December 1888–Continued*. Calcutta: Calcutta Gazette, 1889.

Chamberlain, Houston Stewart. *Foundations of the Nineteenth Century*. London: Ballantyne, 1911.

## BIBLIOGRAPHY

Chambers. "Abstinence of the Japanese from Flesh Meat." *Vegetarian Messenger* 7 (1857): 22–25.
Chatterji, Mohini Mohun. "Vegetarianism and Christianity in India." *Almonds and Raisins* 4 (1885): 18–21.
Chatterji, S. C. "The Advantages of 'a Vegetarian Diet.'" In *Essays on the Advantages of a Vegetarian Diet. Being a Collection of the Essays of Successful Candidates in Its Prize Essay Scheme No. IV*, 1–26. Bombay: Sanj Vartaman Press, 1914.
Chavkin, Nathan Benzion. "Palästina." *Vegetarische Presse* 9 (1926): 105.
———. "Palästina als Zukunftsland vegetarischer Siedelung." *Vegetarische Presse* 14 (1931): 127–128.
———. "Palästina als Zukunftsland vegetarischer Siedelung." *Vegetarische Presse* 15 (1932): 9–10, 20–21.
———. "Schlachthaus-Gedanken." *Vegetarisches Universum* 7, no. 2 (1954): 3.
———. "Stimmen aus Jerusalem. Ein jüdischer Vegetarier über die Schächtungsfrage." *Vegetarisches Universum* 5, no. 5 (1952): 3.
"Cheering Words from India." *Dietetic Reformer*, n.s., 12 (1885): 173–175.
Chevers, Norman. *A Commentary on the Diseases of India*. London: J. & A. Churchill, 1886.
"Chicago Followers of Strange Religions." *Chicago Daily Tribune*, April 6, 1899, 46.
Citroën, Paul. "Mazdaznan at the Bauhaus." In *Our Bauhaus: Memories of Bauhaus People*, edited by Magdalena Droste and Boris Friedewald, 64–70. Munich: Prestel, 2019.
"College of Catering at Andheri. U.N. Donates Equipment." *Times of India*, April 17, 1954, 5.
"Congress Resolutions." *World Forum* 11, no. 4 (1957–1958): 2.
"The Controversialist and Correspondent." *Vegetarian Messenger* 3 (1853): 13–14.
"The Controversialist and Correspondent." *Vegetarian Messenger* 6 (1855): 38–42.
Cooper, William Earnshaw. *The Blood-Guiltiness of Christendom. (May We Slay for Food?)*. London: Order of the Golden Age, 1922.
"Correspondence." *The Harbinger* 5 (1895): 22.
"Correspondence." *The Harbinger* 5 (1895): 71.
"Cypern." *Vereins-Blatt für Freunde der natürlichen Lebensweise* 111 (1879): 1766–1768.
Dabu, S. "Foreword." In *Man Soul Immortality in Zoroastrianism*, edited by Dastur Framroze Ardeshir Bode, i–v. Bombay: K. B. Cama Oriental Institute, 1960.
Darré, Richard Walther. *Der Schweinemord*. Munich: Eher, 1937.
"Das Fest der Freude zu Freudenstadt 1957." *Vegetarisches Universum* 10, no. 7 (1957): 10.
Das, Pandit Bishen. "The Advantages of 'a Vegetarian Diet.'" In *Essays on the Advantages of a Vegetarian Diet. Being a Collection of the Essays of Successful Candidates in Its Prize Essay Scheme No. IV*, 1–30. Bombay: Sanj Vartaman Press, 1914.
Dashwood, Katherine. "Gahanbar at Zurich." *British Mazdaznan Magazine* 13 (1936): 158–159.
Dayananda Sarasvati, Swami. "The Killing of Cows and Other Useful Beasts." *The Theosophist* 2 (1880): 52.
Deb, Girish Chandra. "The Advantages of 'a Vegetarian Diet.'" In *Essays on the Advantages of a Vegetarian Diet. Being a Collection of the Essays of Successful Candidates in Its Prize Essay Scheme No. IV*, 1–29. Bombay: Sanj Vartaman Press, 1914.

BIBLIOGRAPHY

Dégerando, Joseph-Marie. *The Observation of Savage Peoples*. London: Routledge and Kegan Paul, 1969.
"Der Mädchenhandel und die schwarze Schmach." *Vegetarische Presse* 9 (1926): 18.
Desai, Sapur Faredun. *History of the Bombay Parsi Punchayet (1860–1960)*. Bombay: R. M. D. C., 1977.
———. *Parsis and Eugenics*. Bombay: Mody Printing Press, 1940.
Dessau, Kaj. "Die Zukunft der internationalen vegetarischen Bewegung." *Vegetarisches Universum* 3 (1950): 7.
Deussen, Paul. *Mein Leben*. Leipzig: Brockhaus, 1922.
Devamata, Sister. *Days in an Indian Monastery*. La Crescenta, CA: Ananda Ashram 1927.
Dharmapala, Anagarika. "Christianity in Europe." In *Return to Righteousness: A Collection of Speeches, Essays and Letters of the Anagarika Dharmapala*, edited by Ananda Guruge, 451–458. Colombo: Government Press, 1965.
———. "The Ethics of Buddha." In *Return to Righteousness: A Collection of Speeches, Essays and Letters of the Anagarika Dharmapala*, edited by Ananda Guruge, 199–210. Colombo: Government Press, 1965.
———. "The World's Debt to Buddha." In *The World's Parliament of Religions. An Illustrated and Popular Story of the World's First Parliament of Religions, Held in Chicago in Connection with the Columbian Exposition of 1893*, edited by John Henry Barrows, 862–880. Chicago: Parliament Publishing Co., 1893.
Dhurandhar, Shewantibai K. "The Advantages of 'a Vegetarian Diet.'" In *Essays on the Advantages of a Vegetarian Diet. Being a Collection of the Essays of Successful Candidates in Its Prize Essay Scheme No. IV*, 1–16. Bombay: Sanj Vartaman Press, 1914.
"Die Bektaschis." *Vereins-Blatt für Freunde der natürlichen Lebensweise* 13 (1869): 205–206.
"Die Dukhoborzen und die Frage wirtschaftlicher Gemeinschaft." *Tau*, no. 78 (1930): 1–16.
"Diet in Hindustan." *Dietetic Reformer and Vegetarian Messenger*, 3rd ser., 8 (1881): 174.
Doctor, Burjor R. "The Advantages of 'a Vegetarian Diet.'" In *Essays on the Advantages of a Vegetarian Diet. Being a Collection of the Essays of Successful Candidates in Its Prize Essay Scheme No. IV*, 1–24. Bombay: Sanj Vartaman Press, 1914.
Douglass, Frederick. "Introduction." In *The Reason Why the Colored American Is Not in the World's Columbian Exposition. The Afro-American's Contribution to Columbian Literature*, edited by Ida B. Wells, 3–7. Urbana: University of Illinois Press, 1999.
"Dr. Bernhard Förster †." *Deutsche Kolonialzeitung. Neue Folge* 2, no. 28 (1889): 232.
"Dr. Oldfield's Indian Tour." *Herald of the Golden Age* 7, no. 1 (1902): 6.
"Dr." Hanish on Trial." *Chicago Daily Tribune*, June 5, 1905, 7.
Drahovsky, Josef. "Bemerkungen zum 'roten' Vegetarismus." *Vegetarische Presse* 14 (1931): 16–17.
———. "Nur eine Einheitsfront aller Vegetarier und Lebensreformer kann zur Geltung kommen." *Vegetarische Presse* 14 (1931): 80.
———. "Ungarischer Vegetarier-Verein." *Vegetarische Presse* 12 (1929): 4–5.
———. "Vegetarismus kann nur edlen Bestrebungen dienen." *Vegetarische Presse* 14 (1931): 39–41.

BIBLIOGRAPHY

Dubois, Jean Antoine. *Hindu Manners, Customs, and Ceremonies*. Translated by Henry K. Beauchamp. Oxford: Clarendon Press, 1906.
Dühring, Eugen. "Absolute Herrschaft über die Tiere—eine Hebräersatzung." *Vegetarische Presse* 23 (1940): 28.
———. "Internationale Vegetarier-Union." *Vegetarische Presse* 16 (1933): 127.
Ecker-Lauer, Elisabeth. "Nachruf auf Mrs. Clarence Gasque." *Sontraer Gesundheits-Bote* 14, no. 1 (1959): 7.
"Editorial Article 1." *Times of India*, October 3, 1883, 2.
Edwardes, Stephen Meredyth. *The Rise of Bombay: A Retrospect*. Bombay: Times of India Press, 1902.
Eichler, Willi. "Der 'Internationale Jugend-Bund' (IJB) und der 'Internationale sozialistische Kampf-Bund' (ISK)." *Mitteilungen des Bundes für radikale Ethik* 7 (1926): 9–11.
———. "Sogar Vegetarier?" *ISK-Mitteilungen* 1, no. 12 (1926): 206–212.
"Eine Olympiade der guten Herzen." *Vegetarisches Universum* 7, no. 7 (1954): 2.
"Eine Weltreise zu Fuß." *Mazdaznan* 4 (1911): 202.
El Geber, Omar. *Praktische zarathuschtrische Heildiätetik*. Freiburg/Breisgau: Geber, 1925.
Engels, Friedrich. *The Condition of the Working Class in England in 1844*. New York: John W. Lovell, 1887.
Erdling, Gösta. "Rudolf von laban, der freiwirtshaftliche tänzer." *Tao. Monatsblätter für Verinnerlichung und Selbstgestaltung*, no. 17 (1925): 26–28.
Ertel, Dieter. *Zeichen der Zeit. Kongreß der Ideale. Beobachtungen bei einem Vegetariertreffen*. Stuttgart: Süddeutscher Rundfunk, 1959.
Eßler, H. "Gedanken und Meinungen zum 8. internationalen Vegetarier-Kongreß in der Obstbausiedlung Eden bei Dranienburg/Berlin." *Vegetarische Presse* 15 (1932): 91–92.
"Esperanto-Vegetariertag in Leipzig." *Vegetarische Presse* 12, no. 8 (1928): 103.
*Essays on the Advantages of a Vegetarian Diet. Being a Collection of the Essays of Successful Candidates in Its Prize Essay Scheme No. IV*. Bombay: Sanj Vartaman Press, 1914.
"Expert Claims Esperanto Can Serve World Peace." *Fresno Bee. The Republican from Fresno, California*, May 4, 1969, 40.
"Fast to Stop Animal Sacrifice." *Times of India*, September 26, 1935, 3.
"Fasten." *Tao. Monatsblätter für Verinnerlichung und Selbstgestaltung* 1, no. 7 (1925): 14–15.
"The Federal Union Report (Secretary's Report Read at Portsmouth, May 1891)." *The Vegetarian*, May 23, 1891, https://ivu.org/history/vfu/secretary.html.
"Federator. The Call of Every Land." *The Federator* 1, no. 1 (1918): 2–3.
Feldhaus, Richard. "Giftgas-experimente an tieren." *Tau* 10, no. 114 (1933): 19–22.
Fliedner, Theodor. *Reisen in das heilige Land, nach Smyrna, Beirut, Constantinopel, Alexandrien und Cairo, etc. Theil 1*. Kaiserswerth: Verlag der Diakonissen-Anstalt, 1858.
Flinn, John J. *Official Guide to the World's Columbian Exposition*. Chicago: Columbian Guide Company, 1893.
"Food Per Acre." *Dietetic Reformer and Vegetarian Messenger*, 3rd ser. 9 (1883): 57.
Förster, Georg. "Abwehr. Deutschenhetze des niederländischen Vegetarierbundes." *Vegetarische Presse* 16 (1933): 93–94.

BIBLIOGRAPHY

———. "Adolf Hitler." *Vegetarische Presse* 15 (1932): 50.
———. "Indien kämpft." *Vegetarische Presse* 14 (1931): 134–135.
———. "Politik. Reichspräsidenten-Wahl." *Vegetarische Presse* 15 (1932): 34.
———. "Vegetarier Hitler Reichskanzler." *Vegetarische Presse* 16 (1933): 13.
———. "Wahlen." *Vegetarische Presse* 15 (1932): 40–41.
Förster, Georg, and Karl Buck. "Abwehr. Unerhörte Beschimpfung der deutschen Vegetarier." *Vegetarische Presse* 16 (1933): 135–136.
———. "Aufruf zum vegetarischen Großkampf auf der ganzen Linie!" *Vegetarische Presse* 16 (1933): 133–134.
"Fourth Annual Meeting of the Vegetarian Society." *Vegetarian Messenger* 2 (1851): 66–76.
"Frauen in die UN!" *Vegetarisches Universum* 7, no. 10 (1954): 4.
"Frederick Douglass to William Lloyd Garrison, Dublin, 16 September 1845." In *The Frederick Douglass Papers*. Ser. 3, *Correspondence*. Vol. 1, *1842–1852*, edited by John McKivigan, 52–56. New Haven, CT: Yale University Press, 2009.
Freeman, Peter. "Vegetarianism or World Famine." *The Vegetarian*, 10th ser., 3, no. 4 (1955): 92–94.
"Frische Kräfte—Pflanzensäfte." *Vegetarisches Universum* 5, no. 6 (1952): 8.
"From Bombay." *British Mazdaznan Magazine* 16 (1939): 192–193.
"From India." *British Mazdaznan Magazine* 15 (1938): 301–302.
"From India." *British Mazdaznan Magazine* 15 (1939): 621–622.
"From Mother Gloria." *British Mazdaznan Magazine* 15 (1939): 664–667.
"From Mother Superior Gloria." *British Mazdaznan Magazine* 15 (1939): 546–548.
"Führer. George Bernhard Shaw." *Vegetarische Presse* 9 (1926): 92.
"Führer. Leo Tolstoi als Vegetarier." *Vegetarische Presse* 15 (1932): 103–105.
"Führer. Mikkel Hindhede." *Vegetarische Presse* 15 (1932): 19–20.
"Fünfzehnter Weltkongreß in Indien." *Der Vegetarier* 8 (1957): 12.
"Gandhi." *Vegetarano* 13, no. 4 (1930): 40.
Gandhi, Mohandas Karamchand. *An Autobiography or the Story of My Experiments with Truth*. Translated by Mahadev Desai. Introduction by Sunil Khilnani. London: Penguin, 2001.
———. *Ein Wegweiser zur Gesundheit*. Erlenbach-Zurich: Rotapfel, 1925.
———. *A Guide to Health*. Translated by A. Rama Iyer. Madras: S. Ganesan, 1921.
———. "Indian Vegetarians." In *The Collected Works of Mahatma Gandhi*, vol. 1, 19–29. New Delhi: Publications Division/Ministry of Information and Broadcasting, Government of India, 1958.
———. "The Khilafat Against Cow-Protection." In *The Collected Works of Mohandas Karamchand Gandhi*. Vol. 44, *16 January, 1929–3 February, 1929*, 447–451. New Delhi: Publications Division Government of India, 1999.
———. "Presidential Address at Cow-Protection Conference Belgaum [December 28, 1924]." In *The Collected Works of Mohandas Karamchand Gandhi (Electronic Book)*. Vol. 38, *2 January, 1927–3 June, 1927*, 457–459. New Delhi: Publications Division Government of India, 1999.
———. "Speech on Cow Protection, Bettiah [ca. October 9, 1917]." In *The Collected Works of Mohandas Karamchand Gandhi (Electronic Book)*. Vol. 16, *1 September, 1917–23 April, 1918*, 55–56. New Delhi: Publications Division Government of India, 1999.

———. *Village Swaraj*. Ahmedabad: Navajivan, 1963; repr., Delhi: Prabhat Prakashan, 2015.
Gandhi, Virchand A. "The Philosophy and Ethics of the Jains." In *The World's Parliament of Religions. An Illustrated and Popular Story of the World's First Parliament of Religions, Held in Chicago in Connection with the Columbian Exposition of 1893*, edited by John Henry Barrows, 1222–1226. Chicago: Parliament Publishing Co., 1893.
———. *The Unknown Life of Jesus Christ. From an Ancient Manuscript, Recently Discovered in a Buddhist Monastery in Thibet by Nicholas Notovitch, Translated from the French*. Chicago: Indo-American Book Co., 1907.
Gasque, Gloria. "'Equality of Opportunity.'" *British Mazdaznan Magazine* 17 (1940): 88–89.
———. "Mazdaznan in India." *British Mazdaznan Magazine* 16 (1940): 393.
———. "Our Loving Remembrance." *Mazdaznan India* 2 (1942): 171.
———. "Place of Cookery in the Curricula of Girls' and Women's Education." *Mazdaznan India* 2 (1942): 596–601.
———. "Third Birthday Celebration." *Mazdaznan India* 2 (1942): 61–63.
"Gegen die Wiedereinführung der allgemeinen Wehrpflicht." *Mitteilungen des Bundes für radikale Ethik* 12 (1931): 12–13.
"Geschäftsbericht des B. F. B. L." *Zeitschrift für Buddhismus. Herausgegeben vom Bund für buddhistisches Leben* 1 (1913): 29.
Godse, Nathuram. *May It Please Your Honour*. 3rd ed. Delhi: Surya Prakashan, 1987.
Gokhale, D. V. "Der Schlüssel zum Frieden." *Sontraer Gesundheitsbote* 13, no. 9 (1959): 3–6.
———. "Für den indisch-deutschen Weltfrieden, Brüderlichkeit, verstehen unter den Völkern und gewaltlosen Frieden!." *Sontraer Gesundheitsbote* 12, nos. 7–8 (1958): 10–11.
———. "Hiroshima-Tag—Weltfriedenstag!." *Sontraer Gesundheitsbote* 12, no. 9 (1958): 3–4.
———. "Osterbotschaft aus Indien." *Sontraer Gesundheitsbote* 13, no. 4 (1959): 4–7.
———. "Unsere indischen Freunde grüßen an der Schwelle des neuen Jahres." *Sontraer Gesundheitsbote* 13, no. 1 (1959): 4–9.
———. "Weihnachtsbotschaft aus dem fernen Osten." *Sontraer Gesundheitsbote* 11, no. 12 (1957): 5–7.
Gomes, Kathleen. "The Advantages of 'a Vegetarian Diet.'" In *Essays on the Advantages of a Vegetarian Diet. Being a Collection of the Essays of Successful Candidates in Its Prize Essay Scheme No. IV*, 1–32. Bombay: Sanj Vartaman Press, 1914.
Gostling, Sarah. *The Poverty of India and the Land Question: Thoughts Evolved Out of the Late Mahometan Riots at Delhi and Etawah. Paper Read at a Special Meeting of the London Arya Samaj, 5th December 1886*. London: Commonweal Office, 1886.
———. "Vegetarianism. A Paper Read by Mrs. S. S. Gostling Written for the 4th Anniversary of the Panjab Vegetarian Society and Read on the 2nd December 1894." *The Harbinger* 4 (1894): 209–210.
Gostling, Sarah, and Lakshmi Narayan. *India's Position: Social and Economic. A Paper Read at a Special Meeting Under the Auspices of the Indian Society, March 8th, 1887*. London: Charles Cordingley, 1887.
Government of India. The Prevention of Cruelty to Animals Act, 1960 (59 of 1960). As amended by Central Act 26 of 1926 (1960). Accessed December 16, 2018. https://www

.indiacode.nic.in/bitstream/123456789/11237/1/the_prevention_of_cruelty_to _animals_act%2C_1960.pdf.

———. Planning Commission. 2nd Five-Year Plan. Accessed April 12, 2023. http://164.100.161.239/plans/planrel/fiveyr/2nd/2ndindex.htm.

Gradl, Hermann, and Ludwig Ankenbrand. *Der schöne deutsche Süden. Die Seele unserer Heimat in Bildern; Das Land der Franken, Bayern, Schwaben und Alemannen abseits der goßen Verkehrswege.* Stuttgart: Hädecke, 1944.

Graham, Sylvester. *Lectures on the Science of Human Life.* People's Edition. London: Horsell, 1849.

Graham. "Vegetarian Diet in Africa." *Vegetarian Messenger* 9 (1859): 22–23.

Grant, Colesworthy. *To the Children of Calcutta. On Cruelty. By the Hon. Secretary Calcutta Society for the Prevention of Cruelty to Animals (C. G.).* Calcutta: Calcutta Society for the Prevention of Cruelty to Animals, 1872.

"Grüße von Mrs. Gloria Gasque." *Vegetarisches Universum* 4, no. 10 (1951): 2.

Hahn, L. "Mexico, December 1869." *Vereins-Blatt für Freunde der natürlichen Lebensweise* 18 (1870): 286–287.

Haig, Alexander. *Uric Acid, an Epitome of the Subject.* London: Churchill, 1904.

Hammer, Walter, ed. *Dokumente des Vegetarismus. Als Privatdruck herausgegeben von Walter Hammer in Elberfeld-Sonnborn.* 6th ed. Leipzig: Dr. Hugo Vollrath, 1914.

"Hanish in Jail; U.S. Ransacks Temple of Sun." *Chicago Daily Tribune*, March 5, 1912, 1.

Hanish, Otoman Zar Adusht. *Ainyahita in Pearls. From the Original.* Chicago: Mazdaznan, 1913.

———. *Inner Studies: A Course of Twelve Lessons.* Chicago: Sun-Worshipper Publishing Company, 1902.

———. *Mazdaznan Health and Breath Culture.* Chicago: Sun-Worshiper Publishing Company, 1902; repr., Chicago: Mazdaznan Publishing Company, 1914.

———. "Unsere Reise 1929." *Mazdaznan*, no. 1 (1930): 8–10.

———. *Yehoshua Nazir; Jesus the Nazarite; Life of Christ.* Los Angeles: Mazdaznan Press, 1917.

Härtel, Gerhard. "Als Vegetarier im Polenfeldzug." *Vegetarische Presse* 23 (1940): 36, 44–45.

Hase, Elisabeth. "Deutschlands Zukunft." *Vegetarische Presse* 23, no. 3 (1940): title page.

Hentschel, Willibald. *Mittgart. Ein Weg zur Erneuerung der germanischen Rasse. Programmschrift.* 3rd ed. Dresden: Mittgartbund, 1911.

Heywood, John. "Punjab Vegetarian Society." *Vegetarian Messenger*, n.s. 6 (1892): 258–259.

Higginbottom, Sam. "More and Better Milk." *Allahabad Farmer* 11, no. 2 (1937): 65–71.

Hiller, Geo. "Aus meinem indischen Tagebuch" [regular column]. *Der Vegetarier* 9, no. 2 (1958): 5–7; no. 5: 1–5; no. 6: 6–9; no. 9: 6–9; no. 10: 2–7; no. 11: 3–7; 10, no. 1 (1959): 4–9; no. 3: 7–14; no. 5: 15–20; no. 9: 3–6; no. 11: 25–27; no. 12: 10–12.

*Hindu Gesetzbuch. Oder Menu's Verordnungen nach Cullucas Erläuterung.* Weimar: Verlag des Industrie-Comptoirs, 1797.

Hinze, B. "Politik und Ernährungsweise." *Vegetarische Presse* 16 (1933): 37–38.

Hinze, Viktor. "Roter Vegetarismus." *Vegetarische Presse* 14 (1931): 1–2.

"Höchstzulässige Strafe für einen Tierquäler." *ISK-Mitteilungen* 4, no. 7 (1929): 116.

Hof, Erwin. "Rohkost." *Tao. Monatsblätter für Verinnerlichung und Selbstgestaltung* 1, no. 6 (October–November 1924): 2–39.

# BIBLIOGRAPHY

Hormudji, Pestonji Sorabji. "Vegetarianism Shall Never Fail." *The Harbinger* 4 (1894): 180.
"The Hottentots and Bosjesmans." *Vegetarian Messenger* 8 (1858): 132–133.
Howell, Andy, and Zoë Eisenberg. *The Lusty Vegan: A Cookbook and Relationship Manifesto for Vegans and the People Who Love Them.* Woodstock, NY: Vegan Heritage Press, 2014.
Hübbe-Schleiden, Wilhelm. *Indisches Tagebuch 1894/96. Mit Anmerkungen und einer Einleitung herausgegeben von Norbert Klatt.* Göttingen: Norbert Klatt Verlag, 2009.
Hume, Allan Octavian. *Agricultural Reform in India.* London: W. H. Allen, 1879.
Hundertpfund, Philibert. "'Freie Friedlandsiedlungen' (Fr. Fr. S.)." *Tau*, no. 94 (1932): 7–10.
"I.C.C.F. Conference: A Report." *Freedom First*, no. 68 (1958): 9–10.
"Impresoj Pri Bulgario." *Internacia Jurnalisto. Organo de Tutmonda Esperantista Jurnalista Asocio (TEJA)* 8, no. 1 (1965): 3.
"India." *The Theosophist* 15, no. 1 (1894): 462–463.
*The Indian Humanitarian. The Bombay Humanitarian League. Silver Jubilee Number, 1910–1934, Etc.* Bombay: Bombay Humanitarian League, 1934.
"Indische Heilige verändern die Welt." *Der Vegetarier* 10 (1959): 31–32.
"International Vegetarian Congress, Chicago, June, 1893." *Hygienic Review* 7 (1893): 230–233.
"International Vegetarian Congress, Chicago, June, 1893." *Vegetarian Messenger* 7 (1893): 282–286.
"The International Vegetarian Congress, September 13th to 17th." *Vegetarian Messenger*, October 1897. Retrieved from International Vegetarian Union, accessed April 12, 2021. https://ivu.org/congress/1897/manchester.html.
"International Vegetarian Congress 1904—St Louis, USA." *Vegetarian Messenger*, January 1905 (also reproduced in *The Vegetarian*, February 1905). Possibly abridged version, retrieved from International Vegetarian Union, accessed April 12, 2021. https://ivu.org/index.php/blogs/congress-vegfest-updates/196-international-vegetarian-congress-1904-st-louis-usa.
"Internationales Jugendlager—Baumarcus Schweiz." *Vegetarische Presse* 10 (1927): 117.
Iranschähr, Hossein Kazemzadeh (see also Kazemzadeh, Hossein). "Aus dem Leben der islamischen Mystikerin Râbi'äh." *Welt-Harmonie* 9 (1957): 23–24, 39–40.
———. *Das Mysterium der Seele.* Berlin: Iranschähr, 1936.
———. "Das neue Zeitalter und die Mission der Schweiz." *Welt-Harmonie* 9 (1957): 49–52.
———. *Der Meister und sein Jünger.* Berlin: Iranschähr, 1929.
———. *Der Pfad der Jüngerschaft zur Erweckung der Seelen-Kräfte!* Berlin: Iranschähr, 1934.
———. *Die Gathas von Zarathushtra.* Berlin-Steglitz: Iranschähr, 1930.
———. *Die Heilkraft des Schweigens. Eine Pilgerfahrt zum Tempel des Schweigens.* 2nd ed. Berlin: Iranschähr, 1933.
———. "Die Menschheit steht vor drei Möglichkeiten." *Vegetarisches Universum* 3, no. 8 (1950): 2.
———. *Grundlagen der neuen Erziehung.* Olten, CH: Amadeo, 1947.
———. "Vegetarisches Universum." *Welt-Harmonie* 12 (1952): 9.
———. "Wie segensreich könnte die Weihnacht gefeiert werden!" *Vegetarisches Universum* 10, no. 12 (1957): 12.

BIBLIOGRAPHY

Isbert, Otto Albrecht' *Indien und wir. Die deutsch-indische Begegnung.* Bad-Godesberg: Verlag des Instituts für Geosoziologie und Politik, 1957.
———, ed. *Volksboden und Nachbarschaft der Deutschen in Europa: Ein Taschenbuch.* Langensalza: Beltz, 1936.
———. *Yoga und der Weg des Westens. Der geistige Pfad des modernen Menschen.* Stuttgart: Günther, 1955.
Isbert, Otto Albrecht, and Heinz Kloß, eds. *Völker und Grenzen.* Stuttgart: Kohlhammer, 1942.
Itten, Johannes. "Mahatma Gandhi." *Mazdaznan* 1, no. 10 (1925): 251–254.
———. "Rassenlehre und Kunstentwicklung." *Mazdaznan* 16 (1923): 89–92.
J. "Für einen Weltbund der Jugend." *Tau*, no. 51 (1928): 37.
"Jahān-e Zanān: Zan dar jāme'e-ye Īrān-e bāstān." *Iranshahr*, no. 6 (1924–1925): 368–378.
*The Jamshedji Nusserwanji Petit Parsi Orphanage Golden Jubilee Memorial Volume, 1888–1938.* Bombay: J. N. Petit Parsi Orphanage, 1939.
Jani, Dahyabhai H. *Romance of the Cow.* Bombay: Bombay Humanitarian League, 1938.
"The Japanese—Primeval Diet of Man." *Vegetarian Messenger* 4 (1854): 34–35.
Johnson, Rossiter. *A History of the World's Columbian Exposition. Held in Chicago in 1893.* New York: Appleton, 1897.
Jones, William. *Institutes of Hindu Law or the Ordinances of Menu, According to the Gloss of Cullúca. Comprising the Indian System of Duties, Religious & Civil; Verbally Translated from the Original Sanscrit.* London: Sewell, 1796.
"Jottings on Vegetarian Diet." *Vegetarian Messenger* 7 (1857): 58–59.
Kanthariaker, Mahadev. "The Advantages of Vegetarian Diet." In *Essays on the Advantages of a Vegetarian Diet. Being a Collection of the Essays of Successful Candidates in Its Prize Essay Scheme No. IV*, 1–63. Bombay: Sanj Vartaman Press, 1914.
Kazemzadeh, Hossein (see also Iranschähr, Hossein Kazemzadeh). "Aus dem Leben der Sufi-Meister des Islam." *Moslemische Revue* 9, nos. 3–4 (1933): 50–69.
———. "Meine Pilgerfahrt nach Mekka, der heiligen Stadt des Islams." *Moslemische Revue* 9, nos. 3–4 (1935): 75–87.
———. "Meine Pilgerfahrt nach Mekka, der heiligen Stadt des Islams." *Moslemische Revue* 9, no. 2 (1936): 36–46.
———. *Rahbar-i-nižād-i-nau dar gustūġūj-i-ḫošbaḫtī.* Berlin-Wilmersdorf: Iranschähr, 1928.
———. "Tajliyāt-e rūḥ-e Īrān: Jam'iyyat-e Mazdāsnān. Mazdaznan—Tempel Society." *Iranshahr* 4, no. 4 (1924–1925): 248–253.
———. "Tajliyāt-e rūḥ-e Īrān. Jam'iyyat-e mazdāsnān. Mazdaznan—Tempel Society." *Iranshahr* 4, no. 5 (1924–1925): 312–319.
———. "Tajliyāt-e rūḥ-e Īrān. Jam'iyyat-e mazdāsnān. Mazdaznan—Tempel Society." *Iranshahr* 4, no. 5 (1924–1925): 375–381.
———. "Tajliyāt-e rūḥ-e Īrān. Jam'iyyat-e mazdāsnān. Mazdaznan—Tempel Society." *Iranshahr* 4, no. 5 (1924–1925): 438–444.
———. "Ta'līm va tarbiyat: (Yān) pedār-e varzesh dar Ālmān." *Iranshahr*, no. 3 (1924–1925): 154–164.
Keightley, Bertram. "Indian Section Report." *The Theosophist* 14, no. 1 (1892): 20–33.
Khan, Inayat. *Health.* Deventer, NL: Kluwer, 1938.

BIBLIOGRAPHY

Khandekar, G. H. *The Indian Companion: Being a Manual of Universal Statistics of All the Provinces in and the Countries Adjacent to India.* Poona: Law Printing Press, 1894.
Khattri, Kashi Nath. *Go Pukar.* Allahabad: Sirsha Zilla; Benares: Bharat Jiwan Press, 1888.
Kiehne, Oswald. "Achtzehn Bilder aus Indien als Weihnachtsgruß." *Sontraer Gesundheitsbote* 13 (1959): 21.
———. "Indien und wir." *Sontraer Gesundheits-Bote* 12, no. 3 (1958): 5–7.
———. "Unsere Botschaft an den fernen Osten." *Sontraer Gesundheitsbote* 11 (1957): 7–8.
Kingsford, Anna. *The Perfect Way in Diet. A Treatise Advocating a Return to the Natural and Ancient Food of Our Race.* London: Kegan Paul, Trench, Trübner & Co., 1881.
Knight, Joseph. "Spare the Cattle—a Voice from India." *Vegetarian Messenger*, 4th ser., 4 (1890): 202–207, 228–233.
Knuest, H. W. "Tierschutz. Unser Besuch im Schlachthof." *Vegetarische Presse* 16 (1933): 75–76.
"Kongreß der Ideale 1954 Bad Liebenzell" [regular column]. *Vegetarisches Universum* 7, no. 2 (1954): 2; 7, no. 3 (1954): 1.
"Kongreß der Ideale Bad Liebenzell 10.–17. Mai." *Vegetarisches Universum* 7, no. 4 (1954): 1.
"Kongreß der Ideale Bad Liebenzell, 12.–18. Mai." *Vegetarisches Universum* 6, no. 3 (1953): 1.
"Kongreß der Ideale. Bad Liebenzell" [regular column]. *Vegetarisches Universum* 5, no. 4 (1952): 1; 5, no. 5 (1952): 1.
Krannhals-Russell, Hugo. "Führer. Elly Neys deutsche Sendung." *Vegetarische Presse* 16 (1933): 128–129.
"Kreuz." In *Meyers Großes Konversations-Lexikon*, 645–647. Leipzig: Bibliographisches Institut, 1907.
Kriemer, Karl. "Bericht über das Yogiturnen im Vegetarier-Jugend-Ferienlager." *Der Vegetarier* 9 (1958): 10.
Kühl. "Der einfachste und natürlichste Weg zu Deutschlands Nahrungsfreiheit." *Vegetarische Presse* 23 (1940): 41–43, 51–52, 59, 67–68, 83.
———. "Die Eiweißfrage und ihre Lösung." *Vegetarische Presse* 23 (1940): 13–14, 19–20.
———. "Die volkswirtschaftliche Bedeutung der fleischlosen Ernährung." *Vegetarische Presse* 23 (1940): 23.
"La Vegetarismo Post La Militio." *Vegetarano* 4, no. 1 (1920): 1–2.
Landmann, F. "Das geschlechtliche Empfinden der Frau." *Tao. Monatsblätter für Verinnerlichung und Selbstgestaltung*, no. 13 (1925): 15–24.
Lang, Ludwig, and Ludwig Ankenbrand. *Buddha und Buddhismus.* Stuttgart: Franckh, 1923.
Lappé, Frances Moore. *Diet for a Small Planet.* New York: Ballantine Books, 1971.
Laxmidas, Labhshankar. *For Your Decision. Correspondence Appealing to the Metropolitan of Calcutta to Use His Influence in the Protection of Animals Against Cruelty.* Paignton, UK: Order of the Golden Age, 1900.
———. "Hitler Has Become Vegetarian. Appeal to Rulers for Mercy to Millions of Human Beings and Millions of Animals." In *The Indian Humanitarian. The Bombay Humanitarian League. Silver Jubilee Number, 1910–1934, Etc.*, 84. Bombay: Bombay Humanitarian League, 1934.

"Lichtkleid." *Tao. Monatsblätter für Verinnerlichung und Selbstgestaltung*, no. 13 (1925): 2–12.
Lindsay, B. "The British Workman and the Hindoo." *Dietetic Reformer and Vegetarian Messenger* 12 (1885): 348–349.
"London House of Mrs. Gasque Concert Scene. Former Winnetkan Loans Home for First of Three Grand Chamber Events." *Chicago Tribune*, April 25, 1936, pt. 8, p. 3.
"The Lord's Passover." *Herald of the Cross* 7 (1911): 83.
"Ludwig Ankenbrand siebzig." *Vegetarisches Universum* 11, no. 5 (1958): 8.
"Ludwig Ankenbrand. Zu seinem 60. Geburtstag." *Vegetarische Presse* 21, no. 5 (1938): 56–57.
M., E. "Krieg und Vegetarismus." *Vegetarische Presse* 23 (1940): 81–82.
M., R. "Ein Jahr Siedlung Schatzacker." *Tau*, no. 110 (1933): 1–6.
"Ma'āref dar Īrān: 'Aql-e salīm dar jesm-e sālem." *Iranshahr*, no. 9 (1924–1925): 544–556.
*Maharishi Dayanand Saraswati Ka Patra-Vayvahar*. Vol. 9. Ajmer: Vedic Pustakalay, 2015.
"Mahatma Gandhi." *Vegetarische Presse* 9 (1926): 127.
*The Mahomedan and Hindu Riots August 1893. From the Bombay Gazette*. Bombay: Bombay Gazette Steam Press, 1894.
Mama, Nanabhoy F. "From India." *British Mazdaznan Magazine* 16 (1940): 358–359.
———. "A Mazdaznan Mystic." *British Mazdaznan Magazine* 18 (1942): 242–243.
———. *A Mazdaznan Mystic. Life-Sketch of the Late Behramshah Navroji Shroff, the 20th Century Exponent of Zarthosthi Elm-E-Khshnoom (i.e. Esotericism of Zoroastrianism)*. Bombay: Parsi Vegetarian and Temperance Society/Zarthoshti Radih Society of Bombay, 1944.
———. "A Mazdaznan Mystic. The Mysteries and the Marvels of Khshoom." *British Mazdaznan Magazine* 16 (1940): 279–281.
———. "A Mazdaznan Mystic. The Mysteries and the Marvels of Khshoom." *British Mazdaznan Magazine* 17 (1941): 174–175.
Masani, Ervad Phiroze S. *Zoroastrianism Ancient and Modern. Comprising a Review of Dr. Dhalla's Book of Zoroastrian Theology*. Bombay: Parsi Vegetarian and Temperance Society, 1917.
Masarrah, Gerāsīmūs. "Al-ṣawm al-arba'īnī." *Al-Hadīyya* 7, no. 174 (1889): 65–67.
"Maṭbū'āt-e vārede." *Iranshahr*, no. 3 (1924–1925): 510–513.
"May Meetings of the Vegetarian Society." *Vegetarian Messenger*, 4th ser., 4 (1890): 157–165.
"Mazdaznan in Germany. Nazis Worship the Sun." *British Mazdaznan Magazine* 12 (1936): 385.
"Mazdaznan Magazine in India." *British Mazdaznan Magazine* 18 (1941): 100.
"A Mazdaznan Mystic. The Mysteries and the Marvels of Khshoom." *British Mazdaznan Magazine* 16 (1939): 33–34, 79–80, 116–117.
"Mazdaznan und Lebensreform. Für und gegen Mazdaznan." *Leib und Leben* 3 (1935): 134–137.
"Mazdaznan und Lebensreform." *Leib und Leben* 3 (1935): 74–75.
"Meeting of the Committee of the Association for Promoting the Discovery of the Interior Parts of Africa, Held at the House of Sir Joseph Banks on Saturday, the 18th of December, 1790." In *Records of the African Association 1788–1831*, edited by Robin Hallett, 121–129. London: Thomas Nelson, 1964.

## BIBLIOGRAPHY

Megalli, Tadros. "Ein ägyptischer Vegetarier erzählt." *Vegetarisches Universum* 4, no. 11 (1951): 3.

———. "Ein ägyptischer Vegetarier reist als Globetrotter um die Welt." *Vegetarisches Universum* 6, no. 9 (1953): 6.

Megalli, Theo. "Zur Erinnerung an Tadros Megalli: Vegetarisch und natürlich Esperanto." *Natürlich vegetarisch* 53, no. 1 (2003): 12.

Mehta, P. K. "Vegetarian Diet." In *Essays on the Advantages of a Vegetarian Diet. Being a Collection of the Essays of Successful Candidates in Its Prize Essay Scheme No. IV*, 1–34. Bombay: Sanj Vartaman Press, 1914.

Mehta, Yudhishthir Shridharram. "The Advantages of 'a Vegetarian Diet.'" In *Essays on the Advantages of a Vegetarian Diet. Being a Collection of the Essays of Successful Candidates in Its Prize Essay Scheme No. IV*, 1–54. Bombay: Sanj Vartaman Press, 1914.

Miles, Eustace. *Avenues to Health*. London: Swan Sonnenschein; New York: Dutton, 1902.

"Mitteilungen." *Der Neue Mensch* 6, no. 12 (1955): 185–186.

"Mitteilungen." *Friede. Deutsch-indische Monatsschrift für Yoga—Mystik—Lebensreform* 2, no. 10 (1954): 46–47.

Mittra, Peary Chand. *Life of Colesworthy Grant, Founder and Late Honorary Secretary of the Calcutta Society for the Prevention of Cruelty to Animals*. Calcutta: I. C. Bose, 1881.

"Mohandas Karamchand Gandhi to Purushottamdas Bujna, 02.10.1935." In *The Collected Works of Mahatma Gandhi (Electronic Book)*, vol. 68, *September 23, 1935–May 15, 1936)*, 33. New Delhi: Publications Division Government of India, 1999.

Molenaar, Heinrich. "Magna Charta Humanitatis. Die zehn Grundgesetze der Menschheit." *Vegetarisches Universum* 2, no. 6 (1949): 4.

Montesquieu, Charles Louis Secondat de. *The Spirit of the Laws*. Edited by Anne M. Cohler, Basia C. Miller, and Harold S. Stone. Cambridge: Cambridge University Press, 1989.

Moormann, Wido H. "War Hitler Vegetarier?" *Vegetarisches Universum* 3, no. 3 (1950): 2.

"Mother Gloria's Visit to the Halifax Fortress." *British Mazdaznan Magazine* 12 (1936): 627.

Motivala, Bhavanidas Narandas, and R. S. Gokhale. *Rationale of Vegetarianism. A First-Prize and Second Prize Essays of "Competitive Prize Essay Scheme No. 16."* Bombay: Humanitarian League, 1919.

"Mr. Sarat Bose on Animal Sacrifice." *Times of India*, September 27, 1935, 16.

Much, Hans. "Vivisektion. Anatomische Zerstückelung eines lebenden Wesens." *Tau* 11, no. 118 (1934): 1–11.

Muhammad, Elijah. *How to Eat to Live*. Vol. 2. Los Gatos, CA: Secretarius MEMPS, 1972.

Müller, Max. *A History of Ancient Sanskrit Literature, So Far as It Illustrates the Primitive Religion of the Brahmins*. London: Williams and Norgate, 1860.

Munshi, K. M., and Lilavati Munshi. *The World We Saw. Letters by K. M. Munshi and Lilavati Munshi Written During a Tour in America, Europe and Asia. Reprinted from the "Bhavan's Journal."* Bombay: Bharatiya Vidya Bhavan, 1960.

Munshi, Lilavati. "Cafeteria Training. To the Editor, Times of India." *Times of India*, May 26, 1952, 6.

———. "Opening of the Food Exhibition." *World Forum* 9, no. 4 (1957–1958): 25–26.

"Mussolini gegen Tierquälerei." *Vegetarische Presse* 14 (1931): 4.

"Nahrungsweise/Volksdichtigkeit." In *Physikalischer Atlas*, vol. 7, edited by Heinrich Berghaus. Gotha: Perthes, 1848.

Nanavaty, Chhanganlal Parmanandadas. *Report of the Third Humanitarian Conference, Bombay. Held on 2nd and 3rd September, 1918*. Bombay: Bombay Humanitarian League, 1918.

"Narrative on the Agitation in the Punjab (IOL L/P&J 298/1894). Note on the Agitation Regarding the Cow Question in the Punjab Compiled in the Office of the Assistant to the Inspector-General of the Police, Punjab, Special Branch." In *British Origin of Cow-Slaughter in India*, edited by Dharampal and T. M. Mukundan, 124–259. Mussoorie: Society for Integrated Development of Himalayas, 2002.

"Nationale und internationale Frauen-Weltaktion." *Vegetarisches Universum* 7, no. 3 (1954): 4.

"Nationalsozialisten gegen Vivisektion." *Vegetarische Presse* 16 (1933): 3–4.

"The Natural Food of Man." *Dietetic Reformer and Vegetarian Messenger* 3rd ser., 9 (1883): 362–363.

*The Natural Living Vegetarian Society (Established, 6th September 1891)*. Bombay: J. N. Petit Parsi Orphanage Captain Printing Press, 1891.

Nelson, Leonard. "Das Recht der Tiere." *Mitteilungen des Bundes für radikale Ethik* 7 (1926): 8–9.

———. *Demokratie und Führerschaft. Vortrag, gehalten im Schweizer Ferien-Kurs des Internationalen Jugend-Bundes im Fextal am 27. Juni 1919*. Leipzig: Der Neue Geist, 1920.

———. *Erziehung zum Führer. Vortrag, gehalten im Zentralinstitut für Erziehung und Unterricht in Berlin am 14. April 1920*. Leipzig: Der Neue Geist, 1920.

Nichols, T. S. *How to Live on Six-Pence a Day: Vegetarian Meal Planning*. London: Nichols & Co., 1878.

Nicholson, George. *On the Conduct of Man to Inferior Animals, &c*. Manchester: Nicholson, 1797.

———. *On the Conduct of Man to Inferior Animals, &c*. Stourport, UK: Nicholson, 1819.

Nietzsche, Friedrich. *Also sprach Zarathustra. Ein Buch für alle und keinen*. 4 vols. Chemnitz: Schmeitzner, 1883–1891.

"Norwegen. Vegetarierkongreß in Oslo." *Vegetarische Presse* 13 (1930): 126.

"Officers of the Theosophical Society and Universal Brotherhood." *Theosophist* 13 (1891–1892): 61–80.

"Officials Elected at the Congress." *World Forum* 9, no. 3 (1955): 49.

Olivelle, Patrick, and Suman Olivelle. *Manu's Code of Law. A Critical Edition and Translation of the Mānava-Dharmáśāstra*. New York: Oxford University Press, 2004.

"On the Proper Food of Man." *Vegetarian Messenger* 5 (1855): 10–12.

"One Tongue." *The Examiner*, September 18, 1949.

"The Order of the Golden Age." *Vegetarian Messenger*, 5th ser., 1 (1898): 504.

"The Original Food of Man." *Vegetarian Messenger* 1 (1851): 40–45.

Oswald, John. *The Cry of Nature, or, an Appeal to Mercy and to Justice on Behalf of the Persecuted Animals*. London: Johnson, 1791.

BIBLIOGRAPHY

"Otto Hanisch." *Vegetarische Warte* 47, no. 5 (1914): 42.
"Our Indian Pioneer." *Herald of the Golden Age* 8, no. 3 (1903): 30.
"Outbreak of Trichinosis." *Vegetarian Messenger* 40 (1883): 63.
"Oysters and Typhoid." *Vegetarian Messenger* 48 (1896): 161–162.
"P. R. Lele Surveys the Indian Scene. Diwali—1957 Was Festival of Famine." *Blitz*, November 1, 1957, 4.
"Palästina." *Vegetarische Presse* 14 (1931): 76–77.
"Palästina. Vegetarier-Siedlung." *Vegetarische Presse* 11 (1928): 39.
"Palestino." *Vegetarano* 17, no. 2 (1934): 27.
Pandey, Byramji Dinshaji. *Vegetarian Cookery with Testimony of Eminent Physicians, Chemists, Scientists, Naturalists, Physiologists, &c., Showing the Evil Effects of Flesh Eating and the Natural Diet of Man*. Bombay: Imperial Standard Printing and Rajyabhakta Presses, 1890.
"Pandit Ram Chandra Sharma's Fast for Stopping Animal Sacrifice." *Modern Review* 58, no. 4 (1935): 482–483.
"Panjab Vegetarian Society. Established 1889." *The Harbinger* 5 (1895): 72.
*Patañjali's Yoga Sūtra*. Translated with introduction and commentary by Shyam Ranganathan. Gurgaon: Penguin, 2008.
"Paris Exhibition. The Coming Vegetarian Congress." *The Vegetarian*, May 5, 1900. Retrieved from International Vegetarian Union, accessed April 12, 2021. https://ivu.org/history/vfu/1900-paris1.html.
Periyar, E. V. R. "March Towards Peace, Prosperity, and Progress." In *Collected Works of Periyar E. V. R.*, 285–310. Chennai: Periyar Self-Respect Propaganda Institution, 1992.
Perks, Robert H. "'On Vegetarianism.' To the Editor of the Times of India." *Times of India*, September 20, 1904, 5.
———. *Why I Condemn Vivisection*. Paignton, UK: Order of the Golden Age, 1904.
Pestonji Sirkaris, Cawas. "Gutachten eines Zendgelehrten." *Mazdaznan* 4 (1911): 54.
Phadke, Sitaram M. "The Advantages of 'a Vegetarian Diet.'" In *Essays on the Advantages of a Vegetarian Diet. Being a Collection of the Essays of Successful Candidates in Its Prize Essay Scheme No. IV*, 1–35. Bombay: Sanj Vartaman Press, 1914.
"Phtisis and Flesh Meat." *Vegetarian Messenger* 50 (1898): 482–483.
"Poisonous Fishes." *Vegetarian Messenger* 3, no. 43 (1853): 16.
"Poisonous Sausages." *Vegetarian Messenger* 3, no. 29 (1852): 6.
*Portrait and Biographical Record of Waukesha County, Wisconsin, Containing Biographical Sketches of Old Settlers and Representative Citizens of the County*. Chicago: Excelsior, 1894.
Prasad, Rajendra. *Autobiography*. Bombay: Asia Publishing House, 1957.
———. "Improving the Cattle. Free Translation of Address in Hindi at the Distribution of Prizes at the All-India Cattle Show, Hissar, March 3, 1951." In *Speeches of President Rajendra Prasad*, vol. 1, *January 1950–May 1952*, 227–231. Bombay: Ministry of Information and Broadcasting, 1973.
———. "Inaugural Address at Bombay by the President of India." *Vegetarian and Humanitarian World Forum* 11, no. 4 (1957–1958): 16–19.
———. "Moral Aspect of Eating." In *Dr. Rajendra Prasad: Correspondence and Select Documents*, edited by Valmiki Choudhary, 447–451. New Delhi: Allied Publishers, 1992.

"Preface." In *Essays on the Advantages of a Vegetarian Diet. Being a Collection of the Essays of Successful Candidates in Its Prize Essay Scheme No. IV*, 3. Bombay: Sanj Vartaman Press, 1914.
"Preisausschreiben. Zur formfindung fom einheitszeichen für ch und sch." *Tao. Monatsblätter für Verinnerlichung und Selbstgestaltung*, no. 25 (1926): 32–33.
"The Prevention of Cruelty to Animals Bill, 1953—Withdrawn." In *Parliamentary Debates Council of States Official Report*, 1785–1809. New Delhi: Government of India Press, 1954.
"Psychanalyse." *Tao. Monatsblätter für Verinnerlichung und Selbstgestaltung* 1, no. 9 (1925): 9–19.
"Punjab Vegetarian Society." *The Harbinger* 4 (1894): 207.
Purinton, Edward Earle. *Lords of Ourselves*. New York: Benedict Lust, 1908.
———. *Personal Efficiency in Business*. New York: Robert M. McBride & Co., 1919.
———. *The Philosophy of Fasting. A Message for Sufferers and Sinners*. New York: Benedict Lust, 1906.
———. "Suggestive Thoughts." *Arya Patrika* 28, no. 16 (1911): 9–10.
———. *The Triumph of the Man Who Acts and Other Papers*. New York: McBride, 1920.
"Qesmat-e ejtemā'ī: Ta'līm va tarbiyat dar madāres." *Iranshahr*, no. 3 (1924–1925): 449–458.
"Rabindranath Tagore and Pandit Ramchandra Sharma's Fast." *Modern Review* 58, no. 4 (1935): 484.
Radhakrishnan, S. "Indische Philosophie." *Der Vegetarier* 8 (1957): 30.
*Radio-Thermal-Bad und Luftkurort Liebenzell und seine Umgebung*. Liebenzell: Städt, Kurverwaltung, 1922.
Rall, Godwin. "Fasten." *Tao. Monatsblätter für Verinnerlichung und Selbstgestaltung*, no. 14 (1925): 2–11.
Ram, Mönch. "Weltreligion." *Friede. Deutsch-indische Monatsschrift für Yoga—Mystik—Lebensreform* 3, no. 10 (1955): 408–413.
Rāmacandra Śarmā Vīra, Pandit. *Vijaya-Patākā*. 1943; Sāgara: Akhila Bhāratīya Ādarśa Hindū-Saṅgha Madhyaprāntīya Śākhā, 2000.
Regan, Tom. *The Case for Animal Rights*. Berkeley: University of California Press, 1983.
Rege, Sharmila, ed. *Writing Caste/Writing Gender: Reading Dalit Women's Testimonios*. New Delhi: Zubaan, 2006.
Renan, Ernest. *The Life of Jesus*. London: Trübner & Co., 1864.
"Requisition of Premises: Rule Issued against Collector of Bombay." *Times of India*, September 26, 1944, 3.
"Requisitioning of Parsi Temple: Petition Dismissed." *Times of India*, December 4, 1944, 7.
"[Review of] Carl Gustav Jung, Zur Psychologie der unbewussten Prozesse, Zurich: Rascher, 1917." *Tao. Monatsblätter für Verinnerlichung und Selbstgestaltung* 1, no. 9 (1925): 26.
"[Review of] Mahatma Gandhi: Mein Leben, Leipzig: Insel, 1931." *Vegetarische Presse* 14 (1931): 69.
"Review of Mazdaznan Encyclopedia of Dietetics." *Vegetarian Magazine* 14 (1910): 71.
"[Review of] Sigmund Freud, Vorlesungen zur Einführung in die Psychanalyse, Wien: Psychoanalytischer Verlag,[4]1922." *Tao. Monatsblätter für Verinnerlichung und Selbstgestaltung* 1, no. 9 (1925): 25.

## BIBLIOGRAPHY

Reynolds. "Central Africans." *Vegetarian Messenger* 3 (1853): 2–3.
Rihbany, Abraham. *A Far Journey*. Boston: Houghton Mifflin/Riverside Press Cambridge, 1914.
"Rohkost und wirtshaftsreform." *Tao. Monatsblätter für Verinnerlichung und Selbstgestaltung* 1, no. 6 (1924): 43–46.
Rothe, Arthur. "Lebensreformer und ihre Politik!" *Vegetarische Presse* 14 (1931): 5.
———. "Roter Vegetarismus!" *Vegetarische Presse* 14 (1931): 15–16.
———. "Weltfrieden auf neuer Grundlage. Sozialwirtschaft auf Basis wissenschaftlicher Lebensform." *Vegetarisches Universum* 2, nos. 2–3 (1949): 2.
Rudd, Geoffrey L. "Editorial. 15th World Vegetarian Congress in India." *Vegetarian and Humanitarian World Forum* 11, no. 4 (1957–1958): 13–15.
———. "The 15th World Vegetarian Congress, India." *The Vegetarian* 6, no. 1 (1958): 2–6.
Rudolf, Walter. "Der gehalt macht's. Gedanken über herkunft und wertigkeit der paradieskost." *Tao. Monatsblätter für Verinnerlichung und Selbstgestaltung* 1, no. 6 (1924): 2–39.
"Ruf an die Frauen der Welt. Ein Aufruf der neugegründeten Föderation der Mazdaznan-Frauen an alle Frauen der Welt." *Vegetarisches Universum* 4, no. 10 (1951): 3.
S. "Mahatma Gandhi als Wegweiser zur Gesundheit." *Die weiße Fahne* 6, no. 5 (1925): 211–214.
"Sacred Authorities for Vegetarianism." *The Harbinger* 4 (1894): 203.
"Sacred Authorities for Vegetarianism." *The Harbinger* 4 (1894): 228.
"Sacred Authorities for Vegetarianism." *The Harbinger* 5 (1895): 9.
"Sacred Authorities for Vegetarianism." *The Harbinger* 5 (1895): 59.
Sahgal, Manmohini Zutshi. *An Indian Freedom Fighter Recalls Her Life*. Armonk, NY: M. E. Sharp, 1994.
Sale, George. "Preliminary Discourse." In *The Koran: Commonly Called the Alcoran of Mohammed, Translated into English Immediately from the Original Arabic; with Explanatory Notes, Taken from the Most Approved Commentators. To Which Is Prefixed a Preliminary Discourse. By George Sale, Gent*, 1–132. London: C. Ackers, 1734.
Salzer, Leopold. *The Psychic Aspect of Vegetarianism: A Lecture Delivered by L. Salzer at the Inaugural Meeting of the Calcutta Vegetarian Society, in March 1887*. Calcutta: C. Ringer & Co., 1888.
———. *Theosophical Christianity*. Calcutta: Thacker, Spink & Co., 1891.
———. *Vegetarianism, Pure and Simple*. Calcutta: I. C. Bose & Co./Stanhope Press, 1892.
Sandweg, Adolf. "Tropensiedlung." *Tau*, no. 54 (1928): 27.
"Sarada Devi to Swami Abhedananda, Calcutta, March 1899." In *Complete Works of Swami Abhedananda*, vol. 10. Calcutta: Ramakrishna Vedanta Math, 1970.
Sarasvati, Dayananda. *The Light of Truth or an English Translation of the Satyarth Prakash*. New Delhi: Sarvadeshik Arya Pratinidhi Sabha, 1975.
———. *The Ocean of Mercy. An English Translation of Maharshi Swami Dayanand Saraswati's "Gocaruna Nidhi" by Durga Prasad*. Lahore: Virjanand Press, 1889.
"Satyagraha Against Animal Sacrifice. Pandit's Unsuccessful Attempts." *Times of India*, April 22, 1935, 4.
Sava, Monach. "Vom Athos." *Vereins-Blatt für Freunde der natürlichen Lebensweise* 165 (1884): 2635–36.

Savarkar, Vinayak Damodar. "Extract from *Hindutva: Who Is a Hindu?*" In *Hindu Nationalism: A Reader*, edited by Christophe Jaffrelot, 85–96. Princeton, NJ: Princeton University Press, 2007.
———. *Hindutva. Who Is a Hindu?* Bombay: Veer Savarkar Prakashan, 1923.
Savitri Devi. *L'étang aux lotus*. Calcutta: Hindu Mission Press, 1940; repr., Brabant, BE: Thule Sodalitas, 1998.
"Schächtverbote in Deutschland." *Vegetarische Presse* 16 (1933): 3.
Schirach, Baldur von. "Zum Geleit." In *Hitler wie ihn keiner kennt. 100 Bild-Dokumente aus dem Leben des Führers*, edited by Heinrich Hoffmann, ix–xiv. Berlin: Zeitgeschichte, 1932.
Schmidt, Gertrud. "Die 'moralische Aufrüstung' und wir." *Der Vegetarier* 7 (1956): 2–3.
Schröter, W. "Leo Tolstoj zu seinem 100. Geburtstag." *Vegetarische Presse* 11 (1928): 118.
Schwantje, Magnus. "Internationaler Tierschutz- und Antivivisektions-Kongreß in London." *Mitteilungen des Bundes für radikale Ethik* (1927): 3–8.
———. "Internationaler Tierschutz-Kongreß in Paris." *Mitteilungen des Bundes für radikale Ethik* (1925): 1–3.
———. *Lutte de Ram Chandra Sharma contre les Sacrifices religieux d'animaux aux Indes. Reproduction spéciale du Bulletin De La Ligue Antivivisectionniste "L'antivivisection."* Geneva: Ligue Antivivisectionniste, 1937.
———. "Radikaler Tierschutz und Kriegsbekämpfung." *Mitteilungen des Bundes für radikale Ethik* 11 (1930): 20–23.
———. *Ram Chandra Sharma's Kampf gegen die religiösen Tieropfer in Indien. Sonder-Abdruck aus der Zeitschrift "Der Vivisektionsgegner."* Bern: Vegetarierbund, 1937.
———. "Resolutionen des XI. deutschen Pazifisten-Kongresses." *Mitteilungen des Bundes für radikale Ethik* (1922): 6–8.
———. "Schenkt den Kindern kein Kriegsspielzeug und keine Peitschen." *Mitteilungen des Bundes für radikale Ethik* 7 (1926): 21.
———. "Sozialismus und Pazifismus." *Mitteilungen des Bundes für radikale Ethik* 1 (1920): 2–5.
———. "Tagung des Internationalen Jugendbundes." *Mitteilungen des Bundes für radikale Ethik* (1922): 4–5.
"Sechster 'Kongreß der Ideale' zu Freudenstadt im Schwarzwald." *Vegetarisches Universum* 9, no. 2 (1956): 1.
"Second International Vegetarian Congress 1890—London, England." International Vegetarian Union, accessed April 12, 2021. https://ivu.org/index.php/blogs/congress-vegfest-updates/192-2nd-international-vegetarian-congress-1890-london-england.
Shahani, Dayaran Gidumal. *The Life and Life-Work of Behramji M. Malabari: Being a Biographical Sketch, with Selections from His Writings and Speeches on Infant Marriage and Enforced Widowhood, and Also His "Rambles of a Pilgrim Reformer."* Byculla: Education Society, 1888.
"Shall We Eat Pork?" *Vegetarian Messenger*, no. 109 (1858): 195.
Shastri, Pandit Khunni Lal. "Doshkal Charya." *The Harbinger* 4 (1894): 81–82.
———. *Mans Bhakshan Nishedh*. Lahore: Virjananda Yantralaya, 1892.
Shelley, Percy Bysshe. *The Revolt of Islam. A Poem, in Twelve Cantos*. London: C. and J. Oliver, 1818.
Shirmad, Jamshid Jaranmard. "Anerkennung aus Persien." *Mazdaznan* 4 (1911): 55.

Shivani, Sister. *An Apostle of Monism. An Authentic Account of the Activities of Swami Abhedananda in America.* Calcutta: Ramakrishna Vedanta Math, 1947.
Siem, Erna. "Vegetarische Praxis." *ISK-Mitteilungen* 2, no. 5 (1927): 91–92.
"Silvio Gesell. Ausschnitte aus seinem Leben." *Tau,* no. 72 (1930): 4–11.
Sinclair, Upton. *The Jungle.* New York: Doubleday, Page & Co., 1906.
———. *The Profits of Religion.* New York: Doubleday, Page & Co., 1918.
"The Six Races." *Mazdaznan India* 3 (1943): 16–30.
Smith, John. "Fruit and Farinacea the Proper Food of Man." *Vegetarian Messenger* 1 (1851): 87–91.
———. *Fruits and Farinacea the Proper Food of Man.* Boston: Fowler and Wells, 1854.
Sommer, Walter. "Blut und Boden. Das deutsche Bodenrecht." *Lichtheilgrüße* 9 (1933): 98–103.
———. "Ex Oriente Lux." *Lichtheilgrüße* 9 (1933): 337–339.
Specht, Minna. "Indien in Aufruhr." *ISK-Mitteilungen* 5, no. 9 (1930): 169–179.
Spohr, Peter. "Einige Proben aus der Mazdaznanbibel." *Vegetarische Warte* 44, no. 3 (1911): 26–27.
———. "Noch einmal Mazdaznan." *Vegetarische Warte* 43, no. 21 (1910): 210–211.
———. "Zum letzten Male Mazdaznan." *Vegetarische Warte* 44, no. 15 (1911): 143–144.
Starker, G. "Zur Auswanderung nach Neu-Germanien." *Thalysia. Vereins-Blatt für Freunde der natürlichen Lebensweise* 21, no. 1 (1888): 6–11.
Stockham, Alice Bunker. *Ethik der Ehe: Karezza. Berechtigt übersetzt aus dem Amerikanischen von Werner Zimmermann.* Jena: Die neue Zeit, 1925.
———. "Food of the Orient." *Hygienic Review* 2 (1893): 315–322.
———. *Tokology. A Book for Every Woman.* Chicago: Alice B. Stockham, 1883.
Struve, Amalie. *Erinnerungen aus den badischen Freiheitskämpfen.* Hamburg: Hoffmann & Campe, 1850.
Struve, Gustav von. *Mandaras Wanderungen.* 3rd ed. Leipzig: Struve, 1906.
———. *Pflanzenkost. Die Grundlage einer neuen Weltanschauung.* Stuttgart: Struve, 1869.
"Sun Worshiper Is Back." *Chicago Daily Tribune,* April 30, 1906, 4.
"The Sun Worshippers." *Vegetarian Magazine* 13 (1909–1910): 20.
*Supa Shastra.* Poona: Jagaddhitechchhu Press, 1890.
"Supplement to the Vegetarian Messenger." *Vegetarian Messenger* 4, no. 50 (1853): 1–10.
"Swami Vivekananda to Swami Abhedananda, USA, November 1894." In *Complete Works of Swami Vivekananda.* Mayavati Memorial Edition. Vol. 7, 1965. 5th ed. Calcutta: Advaita Ashrama, 1958.
"Tagungen. 8. Internationaler Vegetarier-Tag." *Vegetarische Presse* 15 (1932): 89–91.
"The Theosophical Society and Swami Dayanand." *Supplement to the Theosophist* 3 (1882): 8.
"Through Indian Eyes: Noble Exploits." *Times of India,* October 3, 1925, 17.
"To Herr Adolph Hitler." *British Mazdaznan Magazine* 12 (1935): 231–232.
Todd-Ferrier, John. *Concerning Human Carnivorism.* Paignton, UK: Order of the Golden Age, 1903.
Torbov, Zeko. *Erinnerungen an Leonard Nelson 1925–1927.* Hildesheim: Olms, 2005.
"Traffic in Women." *The Harbinger* 4 (1894): 78–79.
Truman, Benjamin Cummings. *History of the World's Fair: Being a Complete Description of the World's Columbian Exposition from Its Inception.* Chicago: Mammoth Publishing, 1893.

Tryon, Thomas. *Averroeana. Being a Transcript of Several Letters from Averroes an Arabian Philosopher at Corduba in Spain, to Metrodorus a Young Grecian Nobleman, Student at Athens in the Years 1149 and 1150.* London: Printed and sold by T. Sowle, 1695.

———. *Some Memoirs of the Life of Mr. Tho. Tryon, Late of London, Merchant: Written by Himself. Together with Some Rules and Orders, Proper to Be Observed by All Such as Would Train Up and Govern, Either Familes, or Societies, in Cleanness, Temperance, and Innocency.* London: T. Sowle, 1705.

*Über die guten Sitten beim Essen und Trinken. Das ist das 11. Buch von Al-Ghazzālī's Hauptwerk. Übersetzung und Bearbeitung als ein Beitrag zur Geschichte unserer Tischsitten von Hans Kindermann.* Leiden: Brill, 1964.

"Über Vegetarismus und Gewaltbekämpfung (aus der 'Vegetarischen Presse')." *Mitteilungen des Bundes für radkale Ethik*, nos. 23–24 (1931): 23–24.

Ude, Johannes. "Weltfriede, Lebensreform und Arzt." *Vegetarisches Universum* 2, no. 8 (1949): 3.

V., D. "Die Ernährung des deutschen Volkes sichergestellt." *Vegetarische Presse* 23 (1940): 23.

*Vaidiki Himsa Himsa Na Bhavati.* Ajmer: Mahadayanand Vaidik Pustakalaya, 1884.

Valmiki, Omprakash. *Joothan: A Dalit's Life.* New York: Columbia University Press, 2003.

Ved, Dullabhji Dharamshi. *Essay on the Advantages of Vegetarian Diet. With Special Reference to the Haig System and with Scriptural Quotations.* Bombay: Shri Jiva Daya Gnan Prasarak Fund, 1913.

Ved, Rao Bahadur Dullabhji Dharamshi. "The Advantages of 'a Vegetarian Diet.'" In *Essays on the Advantages of a Vegetarian Diet. Being a Collection of the Essays of Successful Candidates in Its Prize Essay Scheme No. IV.* Bombay: Sanj Vartaman Press, 1914.

Veerasawmy, E. P. [Edward Palmer]. *Indian Cookery for Use in All Countries.* London: Herbert Joseph, 1936; repr., Bombay: New Book Co., 1947.

"The Vegetarian and Temperance Principles." *Vegetarian Messenger* 4 (1854): 25–26.

"Vegetarian Diet as a Curative Agent Against Scrofula." *Vegetarian Messenger* 5, no. 65 (1855): 22–23.

Vegetarian Federal Union. *The Vegetarian*, June 9, 1900. Retrieved from International Vegetarian Union, accessed April 12, 2021. https://ivu.org/history/vfu/1900-paris1.html.

"The Vegetarian Movement. Its Claims Upon Public Attention." *Vegetarian Messenger* 2 (1849): 1–4.

"The Vegetarian Principle. Lecture I: Introductory, Physical Advantages." *Vegetarian Messenger* 1 (1851): 17–26.

"The Vegetarian Treasury." *Vegetarian Messenger* 3, no. 32 (1852): 11–12.

"The Vegetarian Treasury." *Vegetarian Messenger* 3, no. 45 (1853): 21–22.

"Vegetarianism and Temperance." *Vegetarian Messenger* 3 (1849): 14–16.

"Vegetarier. Bis es nicht mehr schmeckt." *Spiegel*, no. 28 (July 13, 1950): 33–34.

"Vegetarisches Universum wählt der Welt schönste Vegetarierin 1956." *Vegetarisches Universum* 8 (1955): 8.

"Vegetarismus gegen Atombombe!" *Vegetarisches Universum* 3, no. 8 (1950): 1.

*Verzeichnis der Mitglieder des internationalen Vereins zur Bekämpfung der wissenschaftlichen Tierfolter.* Guben: Albert Koenig, 1889.

## BIBLIOGRAPHY

Vishwanatham, K. "Flesh Diet and Alcoholism in Relation to Life and the Community." *The Indian Humanitarian. The Bombay Humanitarian League. Silver Jubilee Number, 1910-1934, Etc.*, 93-106. Bombay: Bombay Humanitarian League, 1934.
"Visits to Fire Worshipers Cause Woman to Burn Self." *Chicago Daily Tribune*, March 9, 1906, 2.
Vivekānanda, Swami. *Vedânta Philosophy. Lectures on Jnâna-Yoga*. New York: Vedanta Society, 1902.
———. *Yoga Philosophy: Lectures . . . On Râja Yoga, or Conquering the Internal Nature: Also Patanjali's Yoga Aphorisms, with Commentaries, Etc.* 7th ed. New York: Baker & Taylor, 1899.
"Vivisektion in Preußen verboten." *Vegetarische Presse* 16 (1933): 105.
Vogel, Martin. "Mazdaznan Ernährungs-Lehre von Dr. J. A. Hanish, Elektor der Mazdaznan-Bewegung." *Leib und Leben* 3 (1935): 58.
Vogtherr, Friedrich. "Atlantropa." *Vegetarisches Universum* 4, no. 2 (1951): 5.
"Von der Tätigkeit des Vegetarier-Vereins zu Dorpat im Jahre 1932." *Vegetarische Presse* 16 (1933): 139-140.
"Von Freudenstadt ans blaue Mittelmeer." *Vegetarisches Universum* 11, no. 12 (1958): 12.
"Vorbericht vom VU-Kongress." *Vegetarisches Universum* 3, no. 10 (1950): 7.
"Vorträge Dr. Tadros Megalli (Kairo)." *Vegetarisches Universum*, no. 7 (1954): 3.
"Vorträge von Dr. h. c. Werner Zimmermann." *Vegetarisches Universum* 4, no. 10 (1951): 3.
"'VU' wählt der Welt schönste Vegetarierin 1956." *Vegetarisches Universum* 9, no. 1 (1956): 8.
W., E. "Damaskus." *Vereins-Blatt für Freunde der natürlichen Lebensweise* 1 (January 1886): 14-15.
Waag, Ernst. "Rasse und Nahrung." *Lichtheilgrüße* 12 (1933): 222-225.
———. "Zwölfter Weltkongreß der Internationalen Vegetarier Union (IVU)." *Sei Mensch* 1, no. 2 (1950): 15-18.
Wadia, Ardaser Sorabjee N. *The Call of the World, Being Reminiscences of a Year's Tour Round the World*. London: J. M. Dent & Sons, 1918.
———. "From India." *British Mazdaznan Magazine* 1 (1925): 248.
———. "From India." *British Mazdaznan Magazine* 16 (1940): 395-396.
———. "From India." *British Mazdaznan Magazine* 17 (1940): 53.
———. "Humanitarianism and Vegetarianism Among the Parsis." In *The Indian Humanitarian. The Bombay Humanitarian League. Silver Jubilee Number, 1910-1934, Etc.*, 64-65. Bombay: Bombay Humanitarian League, 1934.
Wallot, E. "Zeitbetrachtung." *Thalysia*, no. 5 (1885): 35-37.
Weber, G. "Verfälschung des Rassegedankens durch Geheimlehren." *Leib und Leben* 3 (1935): 293-229.
———. "Verfälschung des Rassegedankens durch Geheimlehren." *Nationalsozialistische Monatshefte* 6 (1935): 770-779.
Wells, Ida B., ed. *The Reason Why the Colored American Is Not in the World's Columbian Exposition: The Afro-American's Contribution to Columbian Literature*. Urbana: University of Illinois Press, 1999.
"Weltkongreß der Internationalen Vegetarier-Union." *Sontraer Gesundheits-Bote* 11, no. 11 (1957).

"Werner Zimmermann- Obara-Vorträge." *Vegetarisches Universum* 8, no. 5 (1955): 4.
"Werner-Zimmermann Vorträge" [regular column]. *Vegetarisches Universum* 7, no. 5 (1954): 4; no. 10: 3; no. 11: 5; no. 12: 4.
"Werner-Zimmermann-Vorträge." *Vegetarisches Universum*, no. 11 (1955): 4.
"Werner-Zimmermann-Vorträge für Truppen." *Vegetarische Presse* 23 (1940): 6.
Whitlaw, Dr. "Diet and Health of the Romans." *Vegetarian Messenger* 5 (1855): 6–7.
Williams, S. Wells. "Food of the Chinese." *Vegetarian Messenger* 7 (1857): 60–61.
"World Vegetarian Congress in City: 16 Countries to Participate." *Times of India*, November 2, 1957.
"Yoga." *Der Vegetarier* 8 (1957): 24–25.
"Zanān-e nāmvar: Žāndārk kīst?" *Iranshahr*, no. 5 (1924–1925): 301–309.
Ziegler, Bernd W. "Bad Liebenzell ist bereit zum 'Kongreß der Ideale.'" *Vegetarisches Universum* 6, no. 4 (1953): 3.
———. "Und nach dem Kongreß an den Lago Maggiore. Freudenstadt rüstet zum 7. Kongreß der Ideale." *Vegetarisches Universum* 10, no. 3 (1957): 3.
Zimmermann, Werner. "Atom-Entwicklung zwingt zum Weltfrieden." *Vegetarisches Universum* 10, no. 8 (1957): 1–2.
———. "Berichte. Gandhi." *Tau*, no. 91 (1931): 25.
———. "Berichte. Gandhi." *Tau*, no. 93 (1932): 27.
———. "Berichte. Indien." *Tau*, no. 66 (1929): 22–25.
———. "Berichte. Weltjugendtreffen 1927." *Tau*, no. 33 (1927): 25.
———. "Bücher. China- und Japan-Bücher." *Tau*, no. 82 (1931): 22–25.
———. "Ferienlager 1925." *Tao. Monatsblätter für Verinnerlichung und Selbstgestaltung*, nos. 18–19 (1925): 13–23.
———. "Form und Inhalt der Ehe." *Tao. Monatsblätter für Verinnerlichung und Selbstgestaltung*, no. 21 (1925): 4–14.
———. "Fysiokratie." *Tau*, no. 52 (1928): 1–11.
———. "Grundgesetze des Liebeslebens." *Tao. Monatsblätter für Verinnerlichung und Selbstgestaltung*, no. 3 (1924): 14–19.
———. "Hass oder Libe." *Tao. Monatsblätter für Verinnerlichung und Selbstgestaltung*, no. 24 (1926): 8–17.
———. *Heimatkräfte persönlicher Gesundung*. Lauf/Nuremberg: Zitzmann, 1938.
———. "Kuniyoshi Obara." *Tau*, no. 73 (1930): 27–31.
———. "Liebe und Ehe." *Tao. Monatsblätter für Verinnerlichung und Selbstgestaltung*, no. 13 (1925): 28.
———. *Liebe. Von ihrem dreifachen Sinn*. 2nd ed. Erfurt: Steiger, 1923.
———. *Liebes-Klarheit: Eine Frucht aus Erlebnis, Erkenntnis und Tat*. Lauf/Nuremberg: Rudolf Zitzmann, 1938.
———. "Masdasnan." *Tao. Monatsblätter für Verinnerlichung und Selbstgestaltung*, no. 32 (1927): n.p.
———. "Recht-Shreibung." *Tao. Monatsblätter für Verinnerlichung und Selbstgestaltung*, no. 15 (1925): 2–21.
———. "Rechtshreibung." *Tao. Monatsblätter für Verinnerlichung und Selbstgestaltung*, no. 17 (1925): 29–35.
———. "Review of Emil Ludwig, Mussolinis Gespräche, Berlin: Paul Zsolnay, 1932." *Tau*, no. 102 (1932): 21–23.

———. "Review of Mahatma Gandhi, Wegweiser zur Gesundheit (a Guide to Health), Zurich: Rotapfel, 1925." *Tao. Monatsblätter für Verinnerlichung und Selbstgestaltung*, no. 14 (1925): 30–31.
———. "Review of Max Hodann, Geschlecht und Liebe, Rudolstadt: Greifenverlag, 1927." *Tau*, no. 41 (1927): 24–25.
———. "Review of Miroslav Schlesinger, Die Onanie im Lichte der modernen Seelenkunde, Radeburg: Madaus, 1925." *Tau. Monatsblätter für Verinnerlichung und Selbstgestaltung*, no. 41 (1927): 25–26.
———. *Tropenheimat*. Lauf/Nuremberg: Die neue Zeit, 1930.
———. "Verhütungsmittel." *Tao. Monatsblätter für Verinnerlichung und Selbstgestaltung*, no. 4 (1924): 21–24.
———. "Vorwort." In *Wu-Wei. Eine Auslegung der Lehren Laotses. Deutsch von Werner Zimmermann*, edited by Henri Borel, 7–10. Lauf/Nuremberg: Rudolf Zitzmann, 1933.
———. *Weltheimat*. Lauf/Nuremberg: Rudolf Zitzmann, 1937.
———. *Weltvagant. Erlebnisse und Gedanken*. Erfurt: Steigerverlag, 1922.
———. *Weltvagant. Erlebnisse und Gedanken*. Lauf/Nuremberg: Die Neue Zeit, 1927.
———. *Wir schaffen freies Land! Tatsachen und Pläne*. Lauf/Nuremberg: Rudolf Zitzmann, 1937.
———. "Wir. wirtschaftsring." *Tau* 11, no. 123 (1934): 1–13.
———. *Zu freien Ufern*. Munich: Drei Eichen, 1950.
Zimmermann, Wilhelm. *Der Weg zum Paradies. Eine Beleuchtung der Hauptursachen des physisch-moralischen Verfalls der Culturvölker, so wie naturgemäße Vorschläge, diesen Verfall zu sühnen*. Quedlinburg: Basse, 1846.
"Zoroastrianism—Its History." *Mazdaznan* 15 (1916): 8–13.
"Zum Kampf gegen die NS." *ISK-Mitteilungen* 5, no. 4 (1930): 55–66.
"Zur Kolonialfrage." *Lichtheilgrüße* 14 (1938): 371–372.
"Zur Schlachtfrage." *Tier- und Menschenfreund* 33, no. 4 (1913): 53–54.

## SECONDARY SOURCES

Abelshauser, Werner. "Guns, Butter and Economic Miracles." In *The Economics of World War Two: Six Great Powers in International Comparison*, edited by Mark Harrison, 122–176. Cambridge: Cambridge University Press, 1998.
Abraham, Shirley, and Amit Madheshiya. *The Hour of Lynching: The Killing of Muslim Cow Farmers in India*. Produced by *The Guardian* (UK), May 2019. Video, 19:11, https://www.theguardian.com/news/ng-interactive/2019/may/24/the-hour-of-lynching-vigilante-violence-against-muslims-in-india-video.
Adams, Carol J. *The Pornography of Meat*. New York: Continuum, 2004.
———. *The Sexual Politics of Meat: A Feminist-Vegetarian Critical Theory*. New York: Continuum, 1990.
Adcock, C. S. *The Limits of Tolerance: Indian Secularism and the Politics of Religious Freedom*. New York: Oxford University Press, 2014.
———. "'Preserving and Improving the Breeds': Cow Protection's Animal-Husbandry Connection." *South Asia: Journal of South Asian Studies* 42, no. 6 (2019): 1141–1155.

## BIBLIOGRAPHY

———. "Sacred Cows and Secular History: Cow Protection Debates in Colonial North India." *Comparative Studies of South Asia, Africa and the Middle East* 30, no. 2 (2010): 297–311.
Adelman, Jeffrey. "What Is Global History Now?" *Aeon*, March 2, 2017. https://aeon.co/essays/is-global-history-still-possible-or-has-it-had-its-moment.
Afary, Janet. *The Iranian Constitutional Revolution, 1906–1911: Grassroots Democracy, Social Democracy, and the Origins of Feminism*. New York: Columbia University Press, 1996.
Ahluwalia, Sanjam. *Reproductive Restraints: Birth Control in India, 1877–1947*. Urbana: University of Illinois Press, 2008.
Ajay, Sindhu. "India State Government Pushes Ahead with Law Banning Cow Slaughter." *Jurist. Legal News and Commentary*, January 1, 2021. https://www.jurist.org/news/2021/01/india-state-government-pushes-ahead-with-law-banning-cow-slaughter/.
Akaios, Archimandrite. *Fasting in the Orthodox Church: Its Theological, Pastoral, and Social Implications*. 2nd ed. Etna, CA: Center for Traditionalist Orthodox Studies, 1996.
Albala, Ken, ed. *Routledge International Handbook of Food Studies*. London: Routledge, 2014.
Albanese, Catherine. *A Republic of Mind and Spirit: A Cultural History of American Metaphysical Religion*. New Haven, CT: Yale University Press, 2007.
Albrecht, Jörg. "Ludwig Ankenbrand. Introduction." In *Religious Dynamics Under the Impact of Imperialism and Colonialism*, edited by Björn Bentlage, Marion Eggert, Hans Martin Krämer, and Stefan Reichmuth, 186–191. Leiden: Brill, 2016.
Alsdorf, Ludwig. *The History of Vegetarianism and Cow-Veneration in India*. London: Routledge, 2010.
Alston, Charlotte. *Tolstoy and His Disciples: The History of a Radical International Movement*. London: Tauris, 2014.
Alter, Joseph S. *Gandhi's Body: Sex, Diet, and the Politics of Nationalism*. Philadelphia: University of Philadelphia Press, 2000.
Amanat, Abbas. *Iran: A Modern History*. New Haven, CT: Yale University Press, 2017.
Amenda, Lars. *Fremde—Hafen—Stadt. Chinesische Migration und ihre Wahrnehmung in Hamburg 1897–1972*. Munich: Dölling und Galitz, 2006.
Amin, Shaheed. *Conquest and Community: The Afterlife of Warrior Saint Ghazi Miyan*. New Delhi: Orient Blackswan, 2015.
Antic, Ana, Johanna Conterio, and Dora Vargha. "Conclusion: Beyond Liberal Internationalism." *Contemporary European History* 25, no. 2 (2016): 359–371.
Appadurai, Arjun. "Comparing Race to Caste Is an Interesting Idea, but There Are Crucial Differences Between Both." *The Wire*, September 12, 2020. https://thewire.in/books/book-review-isabel-wilkerson-caste-racism-america.
Armanios, Febe. *Coptic Christianity in Ottoman Egypt*. Oxford: Oxford University Press, 2011.
Arni, Caroline. *Entzweiungen. Die Krise der Ehe um 1900*. Cologne: Böhlau, 2004.
Arnold, David, and Sumit Sarkar. "In Search of Rational Remedies: Homoeopathy in Nineteenth-Century Bengal." In *Plural Medicine, Tradition, and Modernity, 1800–2000*, edited by Waltraud Ernst, 40–57. London: Routledge, 2002.

# BIBLIOGRAPHY

Asad, Talal. *Formations of the Secular: Christianity, Islam, Modernity*. Stanford, CA: Stanford University Press, 2003.
Atkins, Peter J., Peter Lummel, and Derek J. Oddy, eds. *Food and the City in Europe Since 1800*. Aldershot, UK: Ashgate, 2007.
Azad, M. K. *Benjamin Guy Horniman, Editor "Bombay Chronicle," Deported on 26th April 1919*. Bombay: Lakhmidas Rawji Tairsee, 1920.
Bacia, Jürgen. "Unsere Geschichte gehört uns! Die Archive der neuen Sozialen Bewegungen." In *Logik und Lücke. Die Konstruktion des authentischen in Archiven und Sammlungen*, edited by Michael Farrenkopf, Andreas Ludwig, and Achim Saupe, 257–268. Göttingen: Wallstein, 2021.
Badr, Habib. "American Protestant Missionary Beginnings in Beirut and Istanbul: Policy, Politics, Practice and Response." In *New Faith in Ancient Lands: Western Missions in the Middle East in the Nineteenth and Early Twentieth Centuries*, edited by Heleen Murre-van den Berg, 211–40. Leiden: Brill, 2006.
Baer, Marc David. *German, Jew, Muslim, Gay: The Life and Times of Hugo Marcus*. New York: Columbia University Press, 2020.
Baier, Karl. "Swami Vivekananda. Reform Hinduism, Nationalism and Scientistic Yoga." *Interdisciplinary Journal for Religion and Transformation in Contemporary Society* 5 (2019): 230–257.
———. *Yoga auf dem Weg nach Westen. Beiträge zur Rezeptionsgeschichte*. Würzburg: Königshausen und Neumann, 1998.
Bajohr, Frank, and Michael Wildt. *Volksgemeinschaft. Neue Forschungen zur Gesellschaft des Nationalsozialismus*. Frankfurt/Main: Fischer, 2009.
Balme, Christopher. "New Compatriots: Samoans on Display in Wilhelminian Germany." *Journal of Pacific History* 42 (2007): 331–344.
Balslev, Sivan. "Dressed for Success: Hegemonic Masculinity, Elite Men and Westernisation in Iran, c. 1900–40." *Gender & History* 26, no. 3 (2014): 545–564.
———. *Iranian Masculinities: Gender and Sexuality in Late Qajar and Early Pahlavi Iran*. Cambridge: Cambridge University Press, 2019.
———. "Population Crisis, Marriage Reform and the Regulation of Male Sexuality in Interwar Iran." *British Journal of Middle Eastern Studies* 45, no. 2 (2018): 121–137.
Banerjee, Samir. *Tracing Gandhi: Satyarthi to Satyagrahi*. Abingdon, UK: Routledge, 2020.
Banerji, Chitrita. *Bengali Cooking: Seasons & Festivals*. Delhi: Aleph, 2017.
———. *Feeding the Gods: Memories of Food and Culture in Bengal*. Oxford: Seagull, 2006.
———. *The Hour of the Goddess: Memories of Women, Food, and Ritual in Bengal*. New Delhi: Penguin, 2006.
Baratay, Eric, and Elisabeth Hardouin-Fugier. *Zoo: A History of Zoological Gardens in the West*. London: Reaktion Books, 2002.
Barkas, Janet. *The Vegetable Passion: A History of the Vegetarian State of Mind*. London: Routledge and Keegan Paul, 1975.
Barlösius, Eva. *Naturgemäße Lebensführung. Zur Geschichte der Lebensreform um die Jahrhundertwende*. Frankfurt/Main: Campus, 1997.
Baron, Beth. *The Women's Awakening in Egypt: Culture, Society, and the Press*. New Haven, CT: Yale University Press, 1994.

BIBLIOGRAPHY

Barstow, Geoffrey. *Food of Sinful Demons: Meat, Vegetarianism, and the Limits of Buddhism in Tibet*. New York: Columbia University Press, 2017.
Bartholomeusz, Tessa J. "Dharmapala at Chicago: Mahayana Buddhist or Sinhala Chauvinist." In *A Museum of Faiths: Histories and Legacies of the 1893 World's Parliament of Religions*, edited by Eric J. Ziolkowski, 235–250. Atlanta, GA: Scholars Press, 1993.
Bashford, Alison. *Global Population: History, Geopolitics, and Life on Earth*. New York: Columbia University Press, 2014.
———. "Introduction." In *The Oxford Handbook of the History of Eugenics*, edited by Alison Bashford, 3–24. Oxford: Oxford University Press, 2010.
———, ed. *The Oxford Handbook of the History of Eugenics*. Oxford: Oxford University Press, 2010.
Bass, Hans. "The Crisis in Prussia." In *When the Potato Failed: Causes and Effects of the "Last" European Subsistence Crisis, 1845–1850*, edited by Cormac Ó Gráda, Richard Paping, and Eric Vanhaute, 185–211. Turnhout, BE: Brepols, 2007.
Baumann, Martin. "Buddhism in Europe: Past, Present, Prospects." In *Westwards Dharma: Buddhism Beyond Asia*, edited by C. S. Prebish and M. Baumann, 85–105. Berkeley: University of California Press, 2002.
Baumgartner, Judith. *Ernährungsreform—Antwort auf Industrialisierung und Ernährungswandel: Ernährungsreform als Teil der Lebensreformbewegung am Beispiel der Siedlung und des Unternehmens Eden seit 1893*. Frankfurt/Main: Lang, 1992.
———. "Vegetarismus." In *Handbuch der deutschen Reformbewegungen 1880–1933*, edited by Diethart Kerbs, 127–140. Wuppertal: Hammer, 1998.
Bausinger, Hermann. "Die Dinge der Macht." In *die Macht der Dinge. Symbolische Kommunikation und kulturelles Handeln*, edited by Andreas Hartmann, Peter Höher, and Christiane Cantaw, 27–34. Münster: Waxmann, 2011.
Beckerlegge, Gwilym. "The Early Spread of Vedanta Societies: An Example of 'Imported Localism.'" *Numen* (2004): 296–320.
Bederman, Gail. *Manliness and Civilization: A Cultural History of Gender and Race in the United States, 1880–1917*. Chicago: University of Chicago Press, 1995.
Behnam, Jamshid. "Irānšahr." In *Encyclopedia Iranica*, edited by Ehsan Yarshater, 533–536. Leiden: Brill, 2006.
———. "Irānšahr, Ḥosayn Kāẓemzāda." In *Encyclopedia Iranica*, edited by Ehsan Yarshater, 537–539. Leiden: Brill, 2006.
Belasco, Warren, Amy Bentley, Charlotte Biltekoff, Psyche Williams-Forson, and Carolyn de La Peña. "The Frontiers of Food Studies." *Food, Culture & Society* 14, no. 3 (2011): 301–315.
Bendaly, Costi. *Jeûne et oralité. Aspects psychologiques, spirituels et pastoraux du jeûne orthodoxe*. Beirut: An-Nour, 2007.
Benedict, Burton. "The Anthropology of World's Fairs." In *The Anthropology of World's Fairs: San Francisco's Panama Pacific International Exposition of 1915*, edited by Benedict Burton, 1–65. Aldershot, UK: Scolar Press, 1983.
Berger, Peter. "Food." In *Brill's Encyclopedia of Hinduism*. Vol. 3, edited by Knut A. Jacobsen, Helene Basu, Angelika Malinar, and Vasudha Narayanan, 68–75. Leiden: Brill, 2011.
Berger, Rachel. "Alimentary Affairs: Historicizing Food in Modern India." *History Compass* 16, no. 2 (2018): e12438. https://doi.org/10.1111/hic3.12438.

# BIBLIOGRAPHY

———. "Between Digestion and Desire: Genealogies of Food in Nationalist North India." *Modern Asian Studies* 47, no. 5 (2013): 1622–1643.

———. "Clarified Commodities: Managing Ghee in Interwar India." *Technology and Culture* 60, no. 4 (2019): 1004–1026.

Bernal, Martin. *Black Athena: The Afroasiatic Roots of Classical Civilization.* London: Free Association Books, 1987.

Bernhard, Peter. "Ein Sufi am Bauhaus." In *Bauhausvorträge. Gastredner am Weimarer Bauhaus 1919–1925,* edited by Peter Bernhard, 233–236. Berlin: Gebrüder Mann, 2017.

Berti, Ilaria. "'Feeding the Sick Upon Stewed Fish and Pork': Slave Health and Food in West Indian Sugar Plantation Hospitals." *Food & History* 14, nos. 1–3 (2016): 81–105.

Bertrand, Romain, and Guillaume Calafat. "La microhistoire globale: Affaire(s) à suivre." *Annales histoire sciences sociales* 73, no. 1 (2019): 3–18.

Bevir, Mark. "Theosophy and the Origins of the Indian National Congress." *International Journal of Hindu Studies* 7, no. 1 (2003): 99–115.

Bhagavan, Manu. "The Hindutva Underground: Hindu Nationalism and the Indian National Congress in Late Colonial and Early Post-Colonial India." *Economic and Political Weekly* 43, no. 37 (2008): 39–48.

Bhambra, Gurminder. *Rethinking Modernity: Postcolonialism and the Sociological Imagination.* Basingstoke, UK: Palgrave Macmillan, 2007.

Bhardwaj, Ananya. "Muslim Boy Stabbed to Death on Train After Argument Turns Into Religious Slurs." *Hindustan Times,* June 27, 2017. http://www.hindustantimes.com/india-news/man-stabbed-to-death-2-injured-on-mathura-train-after-fight-with-passengers-for-allegedly-carrying-beef/story-BiJyILYlUloErWASvKQ51M.html.

Bhattacharya, Tithi. "Tracking the Goddess: Religion, Community, and Identity in the Durga Puja Ceremonies of Nineteenth-Century Calcutta." *Journal of Asian Studies* 66, no. 4 (2007): 919–962.

Bhushan, Nalini, and Jay L. Garfield. *Minds Without Fear: Philosophy in the Indian Renaissance.* Oxford: Oxford University Press, 2017.

Biess, Frank. *German Angst: Fear and Democracy in the Federal Republic of Germany.* Oxford: Oxford University Press, 2020.

———. "'Jeder hat eine Chance.' Die Zivilschutzkampagnen der 1960er Jahre und die Angstgeschichte der Bundesrepublik." In *Angst im Kalten Krieg,* edited by Bernd Greiner, Christian Th. Müller, and Dierk Walter, 61–93. Hamburg: Hamburger Edition, 2009.

Bigalke, Bernadett. *Lebensreform und Esoterik um 1900. Die Leipziger alternativ-religiöse Szene am Beispiel der Internationalen Theosophischen Verbrüderung.* Würzburg: Ergon, 2016.

Bivar, Venus. *Organic Resistance: The Struggle Over Industrial Farming in Postwar France.* Chapel Hill: University of North Carolina Press, 2018.

Blackbourn, David. *The Long Nineteenth Century: A History of Germany, 1780–1918.* Oxford: Oxford University Press, 1998.

Blackburn, Anne M. *Locations of Buddhism: Colonialism and Modernity in Sri Lanka.* Chicago: University of Chicago Press, 2010.

Blanchard, Pascal, ed. *Human Zoos: Science and Spectacle in the Age of Colonial Empires.* Liverpool: Liverpool University Press, 2008.

BIBLIOGRAPHY

Blankinship, Kevin. "Missionary and Heretic: Debating Veganism in the Medieval Islamic World." In *Food as a Cultural Signifier: Perspectives on the Middle East and Beyond*, edited by Kevin Blankinship, Kirill Dmitriev, and Bilal Orfali, 260–291. Leiden: Brill, 2020.

Blecher, Jens. "Universität Leipzig." In *Geschichte der Stadt Leipzig*. Vol. 3, *Vom Wiener Kongress bis zum Ersten Weltkrieg*, edited by Susanne Schötz, 703–711. Leipzig: Leipziger Universitätsverlag, 2017.

Boehmer, Elleke. *Empire, the National, and the Postcolonial (1890–1920): Resistance in Interaction*. Oxford: Oxford University Press, 2005.

Bohn, Wolfgang. *Buddhismus als Reformgedanke für unsere Zeit*. Breslau: Markgraf, 1910.

Bolotin, Norman, and Christine Laing. *The World's Columbian Exposition: The Chicago World's Fair of 1893*. Urbana: University of Illinois Press, 2002.

Booth, Marilyn. *May Her Likes Be Multiplied: Biography and Gender Politics in Egypt*. Berkeley: University of California Press, 2001.

"Borel, Henri Jean François." In *De Nederlandse en Vlaamse auteurs van middeleeuwen tot heden met inbegrip van de Friese auteurs*. Weesp, NL: De Haan, 1985. Cited in *Biografisch Archief Van De Benelux*, vol. 1, microfiche 83,315, and vol. 2, microfiche 29, 212.

Bourdieu, Pierre. *Distinction: A Social Critique of the Judgement of Taste*. London: Routledge and Kegan Paul, 1984.

Bourke, Joanna. *What It Means to Be Human: Reflections from 1791 to the Present*. London: Virago, 2011.

Braden, Charles Samuel. *Spirits in Rebellion: The Rise and Development of New Thought*. Dallas, TX: Southern Methodist University Press, 1963.

Brand, Tylor. "Some Eat to Remember, Some to Forget: Starving, Eating, and Coping in the Syrian Famine of World War I." In *Food as a Cultural Signifier: Perspectives on the Middle East and Beyond*, edited by Kirill Dmitriev, Julia Hauser, and Bilal Orfali, 319–339. Leiden: Brill, 2020.

Brang, Peter. *Ein unbekanntes Russland: Kulturgeschichte vegetarischer Lebensweisen von den Anfängen bis zur Gegenwart*. Cologne: Böhlau, 2002.

Braun, Karl. "Jugendbewegung, Sexualaufklärung, Sozialhygiene. Das Beispiel Max Hodann (1894–1946)." In *Avantgarden der Biopolitik. Jugendbewegung, Lebensreform und Strategien biologischer, Aufrüstung*, edited by Karl Braun, Felix Linzner, and John Khairi-Taraki, 33–60. Göttingen: V&R Unipress, 2017.

Braun, Karl, Felix Linzner, and John Khairi-Taraki, eds. *Avantgarden der Biopolitik. Jugendbewegung, Lebensreform und Strategien biologischer, Aufrüstung*. Göttingen: V&R Unipress, 2017.

Brecht, Martin. "Der württembergische Pietismus." In *Der Pietismus im achtzehnten Jahrhundert*, edited by Martin Brecht and Friedhelm Ackva, 225–293. Göttingen: Vandenhoeck & Ruprecht, 1995.

Brekke, Torkel. *Makers of Modern Indian Religion in the Late Nineteenth Century*. Oxford: Oxford University Press, 2002.

Briesen, Detlef. *Das gesunde Leben. Ernährung und Gesundheit seit dem 18. Jahrhundert*. Frankfurt/Main: Campus, 2010.

Brock, William H. *Justus von Liebig: The Chemical Gatekeeper*. Cambridge: Cambridge University Press, 1997.

BIBLIOGRAPHY

Brucker, Renate. "Für eine radikale Ethik—Die Tierrechtsbewegung in der ersten Hälfte des 20. Jahrhunderts." In *das Mensch-Tier-Verhältnis. Eine sozialwissenschaftliche Einführung*, edited by Renate Brucker, Melanie Bujok, Birgit Mütherich, Martin Seeliger, and Frank Thieme, 211–268. Wiesbaden: Springer, 2014.

———. "Tierrechte und Friedensbewegung: 'Radikale Ethik' und gesellschaftlicher Fortschritt in der deutschen Geschichte." In *Tierische Geschichte. Die Beziehung von Mensch und Tier in der Kultur der Moderne*, edited by Dorothee Brantz and Christof Mauch, 268–285. Paderborn: Schöningh, 2010.

Brunner, Michael Philipp. "Teaching Development: Debates on 'Scientific Agriculture' and 'Rural Reconstruction' at Khalsa College, Amritsar, c. 1915–47." *Indian Economic and Social History Review* 55, no. 1 (2018): 77–132.

Brunotte, Ulrike. *Zwischen Eros und Krieg. Männerbund und Ritual in der Moderne*. Berlin: Wagenbach, 2004.

Bruns, Claudia. *Politik des Eros. Der Männerbund in Wissenschaft, Politik und Jugendkultur*. Cologne: Böhlau, 2008.

Buchholz, Kai, ed. *Die Lebensreform: Entwürfe zur Neugestaltung von Leben und Kunst um 1900*. Darmstadt: Häusser, 2001.

Buerdorff, Benno. "Review of Swami Abhedananda 1. Warum verwirft ein Hindu das moderne Kirchentum, obwohl er Christus anerkennt? [. . .] 2. Warum sind alle Hindus Vegetarier?" *Vegetarische Warte* 36 (1903): 137.

Bulliet, Richard W. *Hunters, Herders, and Hamburgers: The Past and Future of Human-Animal Relationships*. New York: Columbia University Press, 2005.

Burchert, Linn. "The Spiritual Enhancement of the Body: Johannes Itten, Gertrud Grunow, and Mazdaznan at the Early Bauhaus." In *Bauhaus Bodies: Gender, Sexuality, and Body Culture in Modernism's Legendary Art School*, edited by Elizabeth Otto and Patrick Rössler, 49–72. New York: Bloomsbury Visual Arts, 2019.

Burris, John P. *Exhibiting Religion: Colonialism and Spectacle at International Expositions, 1851–1893*. Charlottesville: University Press of Virginia, 2001.

Burton, Antoinette. *Burdens of History: British Feminists, Indian Women, and Imperial Culture, 1865–1914*. Chapel Hill: University of North Carolina Press, 2010.

Buscemi, Francesco. "Edible Lies: How Nazi Propaganda Represented Meat to Demonise the Jews." *Media, War and Conflict* 9, no. 2 (2016): 180–197.

Caldwell, Melissa L. *Why Food Matters: Critical Debates in Food Studies*. London: Bloomsbury, 2021.

Campbell, Bruce F. *Ancient Wisdom Revived: A History of the Theosophical Movement*. Berkeley: University of California Press, 1980.

Cardon, Nathan. *A Dream of the Future: Race, Empire, and Modernity at the Atlanta and Nashville World's Fairs*. Oxford: Oxford University Press, 2018.

Carroll, Lucy. "Origins of the Kayastha Temperance Movement." *Indian Economic and Social History Review* 11, no. 4 (1974): 432–447.

Carter, Julian B. *The Heart of Whiteness: Normal Sexuality and Race in America, 1880–1940*. Durham, NC: Duke University Press, 2007.

Casanova, José. "Public Religions in the Modern World." In *Powers of the Secular Modern: Talal Asad and His Interlocutors*, edited by David Scott and Charles Hirschkind, 12–30. Stanford, CA: Stanford University Press, 2006.

Çelik, Zeynep. *Displaying the Orient: Architecture of Islam at Nineteenth-Century World's Fairs*. Berkeley: University of California Press, 1992.

BIBLIOGRAPHY

Chakrabarti, Pratik. "Beasts of Burden: Animals and Laboratory Research in Colonial India." *History of Science* 48, no. 2 (2010): 125–152.

Chapman, Stanley D., ed. *The History of Working-Class Housing*. Newton Abbot, UK: David & Charles, 1971.

Chaudhuri, Rosinka. *Freedom and Beef Steaks: Colonial Calcutta Culture*. Delhi: Orient Blackswan, 2012.

Chen, Martha Alter. "Satī and Widowhood." In *Brill's Encyclopedia of Hinduism*. Vol. 3, edited by Knut A. Jacobson, Helene Basu, Angelika Malinar, and Vasudha Narayanan, 164–176. Leiden: Brill, 2011.

Chigateri, Shraddha. "'Glory to the Cow': Cultural Difference and Social Justice in the Food Hierarchy in India." *Journal of South Asian Studies* 31, no. 1 (2008): 10–35.

Chowdhury-Sengupta, Indra. "Reconstructing Hinduism on a World Platform: The World's First Parliament of Religions, Chicago 1892." In *SOAS Studies on South Asia*, edited by William Radice, 17–35. Delhi: Oxford University Press, 1998.

Christy, Arthur. *The Orient in American Transcendentalism: A Study of Emerson, Thoreau, and Alcott*. New York: Columbia University Press, 1932.

Clarke, J. J. *Oriental Enlightenment: The Encounter Between Asian and Western Thought*. London: Routledge, 1997.

Cluet, Marc. *La "libre culture." Le mouvement nudiste en Allemagne depuis ses origines au seuil du Xxe siècle jusq'à l'arrivée de Hitler au pouvoir (1905–1933). Présupposés, développements et enjeux historiques*. Villeneuve d'Ascq: Presses Universitaires du Septentrion, 2002.

———. "Persische Briefe eines urtümlichen Himalaja-Inders: Mandaras' Wanderungen von Gustav Struve." In *Akten des XI. internationalen Germanistenkongresses Paris 2005 "Germanistik im Konflikt der Kulturen." Band 9: Diergente Kulturräume in der Literatur*, edited by Jean-Marc Valentin, 27–32. Bern: Peter Lang, 2007.

Cohen, Julia Phillips. "Oriental by Design: Ottoman Jews, Imperial Style, and the Performance of Heritage." *American Historical Review* 119, no. 2 (2014): 364–398.

Cohn, Bernard S. *Colonialism and Its Forms of Knowledge: The British in India*. Princeton, NJ: Princeton University Press, 1996.

Collet, Dominik, and Daniel Krämer. "Germany, Switzerland, and Austria." In *Famine in European History*, edited by Guido Alfani and Cormac Ó Gráda, 101–118. Cambridge: Cambridge University Press, 2017.

Collingham, E. M. *Imperial Bodies: The Physical Experience of the Raj, c. 1800–1947*. Cambridge: Polity, 2001.

Connell, Raewyn. "Masculinity and Nazism." In *Männlichkeitskonstruktionen im Nationalsozialismus. Formen, Funktionen und Wirkungsmacht von Geschlechterkonstruktionen im Nationalsozialismus und ihre Reflexion in der pädagogischen Praxis*, edited by Anette Dietrich and Ljiljana Heise, 37–42. Frankfurt/Main: Peter Lang, 2013.

Conrad, Sebastian. *Globalisierung und Nation im Deutschen Kaiserreich*. Munich: Beck, 2006.

———. *What Is Global History?* Princeton, NJ: Princeton University Press, 2016.

Conrad, Sebastian, Andreas Eckert, and Ulrike Freitag, eds. *Globalgeschichte. Theorien, Ansätze, Themen*. Frankfurt/Main: Campus, 2007.

# BIBLIOGRAPHY

Conrad, Sebastian, and Shalini Randeria. "Einleitung. Geteilte Geschichten—Europa in einer postkolonialen Welt." In *Jenseits des Eurozentrismus*, edited by Sebastian Conrad and Shalini Randeria, 9–49. Frankfurt/Main: Campus-Verl, 2002.

Cooperson, Michael. "Bishr al-Ḥāfī." In *Encyclopaedia of Islam Three*, edited by Kate Fleet, Gudrun Krämer, Denis Matringe, John Nawas, and Everett Rowson. Leiden: Brill, 2011. http://dx.doi.org.encyclopaediaofislam.han.sub.uni-goettingen.de/10.1163/1573-3912_ei3_COM_24019.

Copland, Ian. "What to Do About Cows? Princely Versus British Approaches to a South Asian Dilemma." *Bulletin of the School of Oriental and African Studies* 68, no. 1 (2005): 59–76.

Corbin, Alain. "Backstage." In *A History of Private Life*. Vol. 4, *From the Fires of Revolution to the Great War*, edited by Michelle Perrot, 451–667. Cambridge, MA: Belknap Press of Harvard University Press, 1990.

Corni, Gustavo, and Horst Gies. *Brot—Butter—Kanonen. Die Ernährungswirtschaft in Deutschland unter der Diktatur Hitlers*. Berlin: Akademie-Verlag, 1997.

"Cow Slaughter Prevention Laws in India. How the Law Not Just Protects Cow Vigilantes, but Sanctifies Lynchings." Citizens for Justice and Peace, July 2, 2018. https://cjp.org.in/cow-slaughter-prevention-laws-in-india/.

Crone, Patricia. *The Nativist Prophets of Early Islamic Iran: Rural Revolt and Local Zoroastrianism*. Cambridge: Cambridge University Press, 2012.

Cronon, William. *Nature's Metropolis: Chicago and the Great West*. New York: Norton, 1991.

Crossley, Ceri. *Consumable Metaphors: Attitudes Towards Animals and Vegetarianism in Nineteenth-Century France*. Oxford: Lang, 2005.

Cunningham, Hugh. *Children and Childhood in Western Society since 1500*. 2nd ed. Harlow, UK: Longman, 2005.

Cwiertka, Katarzyna J. *Modern Japanese Cuisine: Food, Power and National Identity*. London: Reaktion Books, 2006.

Dahlke, Birgit. *Jünglinge der Moderne. Jugendkult und Männlichkeit in der Literatur um 1900*. Cologne: Böhlau, 2006.

Dailey, Jane. *White Fright: The Sexual Panic at the Heart of America's Racist History*. New York: Basic Books, 2020.

Dalmia, Yashodhara. *Amrita Sher-Gil: A Life*. Gurgaon: Penguin, 2006.

Daniels, Mario. *Geschichtswissenschaft im 20. Jahrhundert. Institutionalisierungsprozesse und Entwicklung des Personenverbandes an der Universität Tübingen 1918–1964*. Stuttgart: Steiner, 2009.

Daryaee, Touraj. "Food, Purity and Pollution: Zoroastrian Views on the Eating Habits of Others." *Iranian Studies* 45, no. 2 (2012): 229–242.

Dastur F. Bode. "IVU Executive Committee 1957–60." Retrieved from International Vegetarian Union, accessed April 14, 2021. https://ivu.org/members/council/dastur-bode.html.

Davidoff, Leonore. "Gender and the 'Great Divide': Public and Private in British Gender History." *Journal of Women's History* 15, no. 1 (2003): 11–27.

Davidoff, Leonore, and Catherine Hall. *Family Fortunes: Men and Women of the English Middle Class, 1780–1850*. Chicago: University of Chicago Press, 1987.

Davis, David A. "A Recipe for Food Studies." *American Quarterly* 62, no. 2 (2010): 365–375.

Davis, Mike. *Late Victorian Holocausts: El Niño Famines and the Making of the Third World*. London: Verso, 2001.
De, Rohit. "Cows and Constitutionalism." *Modern Asian Studies* 53, no. 1 (2019): 240–277.
De Jong, Albert. "Animal Sacrifice in Ancient Zoroastrianism: A Ritual and Its Interpretation." In *Sacrifice in Religious Experience*, edited by A. I. Baumgarten, 127–148. Leiden: Brill, 2002.
Deacon, Desley, and Angela Woollacott, eds. *Transnational Lives: Biographies of Global Modernity*. Basingstoke, UK: Palgrave Macmillan, 2010.
Dejung, Christof, David Motadel, and Jürgen Osterhammel. "Worlds of the Bourgeoisie." In *The Global Bourgeoisie: The Rise of the Middle Classes in the Age of Empire*, edited by Christof Dejung, David Motadel, and Jürgen Osterhammel, 1–39. Princeton, NJ: Princeton University Press, 2019.
Dellar, Rosemary. *Josiah Oldfield: Eminent Fruitarian*. Rainham, UK: Rainmore, 2008.
Denzel, Markus A. "Messe- und Finanzplatz." In *Geschichte der Stadt Leipzig*. Vol. 3, *Vom Wiener Kongress bis zum Ersten Weltkrieg*, edited by Susanne Schötz, 561–572. Leipzig: Leipziger Universitätsverlag, 2017.
Deslippe, Philippe. "The Swami Circuit: Mapping the Terrain of Early American Yoga." *Journal of Yoga Studies* 1 (2018): 5–44.
Desponds, Séverine. "Eugenik und die Konstruktion der weiblichen Übernatur. Eine Fallstudie über die Mazdaznan-Bewegung in den vierziger Jahren." In *Handbuch Gender Und Religion*, edited by Anna-Katharina Höpflinger, 297–307. Göttingen: Vandenhoeck & Ruprecht, 2008.
Devji, Faisal. *The Impossible Indian: Gandhi and the Temptation of Violence*. London: Hurst, 2012.
Dharampal, and T. M. Mukundan. "Introduction." In *British Origin of Cow-Slaughter in India*, edited by Dharampal and T. M. Mukundan, 1–83. Mussoorie: Society for Integrated Development of Himalayas, 2002.
Dharampal-Frick, Gita, and Sudha Sitharaman. "Cow Protection." In *Key Concepts in Modern Indian Studies*, edited by Gita Dharampal-Frick, Monika Kirloskar-Steinbach, Rachel M. Dwyer, and Jahnavi Phalkey, 49–51. Oxford: Oxford University Press, 2015.
Diehl, Paula. *Macht—Mythos—Utopie. Die Körperbilder der SS-Männer*. Berlin: Akademie-Verlag, 2005.
Dixon, Joy. *Divine Feminine: Theosophy and Feminism in England*. Baltimore: Johns Hopkins University Press, 2001.
Doniger, Wendy. *On Hinduism*. Oxford: Oxford University Press, 2014.
Donner, Henrike. "New Vegetarianism: Food, Gender and Neo-liberal Regimes in Bengali Middle-Class Families." *South Asia: Journal of South Asian Studies* 31, no. 1 (2008): 143–169.
Douglas, Mary. *Purity and Danger: An Analysis of Concepts of Pollution and Taboo*. London: Routledge and Kegan Paul 1966.
Drews, Joachim. *Die "Nazi-Bohne."* Münster: LIT, 2004.
Druvins, Ute. "Alternative Projekte um 1900. Utopie und Realität auf dem 'Monte Verità' und in der 'Neuen Gemeinschaft.'" In *Literarische Utopie-Entwürfe*, edited by Hiltrud Gnüg, 236–249. Frankfurt/Main: Suhrkamp, 1982.

BIBLIOGRAPHY

DuBois, Thomas David. "Many Roads from Pasture to Plate: A Commodity Chain Approach to China's Beef Trade, 1732–1931." *Journal of Global History* 14, no. 1 (2019): 22–43.
Dumont, Louis. *Homo Hierarchicus. Le Système Des Castes Et Ses Implications*. Paris: Gallimard, 1966.
Dundas, Paul. *The Jains*. 2nd ed. London: Routledge, 1992.
Earle, Rebecca. *The Body of the Conquistador: Food, Race and the Colonial Experience in Spanish America, 1492–1700*. Cambridge: Cambridge University Press, 2012.
———. *Feeding the People: The Politics of the Potato*. Cambridge: Cambridge University Press, 2020.
Einboden, Jeffrey. *Islam and Romanticism: Muslim Currents from Goethe to Emerson*. London: Oneworld, 2014.
"Elizabeth Ecker-Lauer. IVU Executive Committee 1953–57." Retrieved from International Vegetarian Union, accessed April 15, 2021. https://ivu.org/members/council/Elizabeth-Ecker-Lauer.html.
Elsner, Gine, ed. *Heilkräuter, "Volksernährung," Menschenversuche. Ernst Günther Schenck (1904–1998), eine deutsche Arztkarriere*. Hamburg: VSA, 2010.
El-Tayeb, Fatima, ed. *Schwarze Deutsche. Der Diskurs um "Rasse" und nationale Identität 1890–1933*. Frankfurt/Main: Campus-Verl., 2001.
Erdman, David W. *Commerce des Lumières: John Oswald and the British in Paris, 1790–1793*. Columbia: University of Missouri Press, 1986.
Ergin, Nina, Christoph K. Neumann, and Amy Singer. "Introduction." In *Feeding People, Feeding Power: Imarets in the Ottoman Empire*, edited by Nina Ergin, Christoph K. Neumann, and Amy Singer, 13–40. Istanbul: Eren, 2007.
Ernst, Carl W. "Situating Sufism and Yoga." *Journal of the Royal Asiatic Society*, 3rd ser., 15, no. 1 (2005): 15–43.
Evans, Tanya. "Knowledge and Experience: From 1750 to the 1960s." In *The Routledge History of Sex and the Body: 1500 to the Present*, edited by Sarah Toulalan and Kate Fisher, 256–276. London: Routledge, 2013.
Fabian, Johannes. *Time and the Other: How Anthropology Makes Its Object*. New York: Columbia University Press, 1983.
Figueira, Dorothy M. *Aryans, Jews, Brahmins: Theorizing Authority Through Myths of Identity*. Albany: State University of New York Press, 2002.
Finger, Jürgen, Sven Keller, and Andreas Wirsching. *Dr. Oetker und der Nationalsozialismus. Geschichte eines Familienunternehmens 1933–1945*. Munich: Beck, 2013.
Finlay, Mark R. "Early Marketing of the Theory of Nutrition: The Science and Culture of Liebig's Extract of Meat." In *The Science and Culture of Nutrition, 1840–1940*, edited by Harmke Kamminga, 48–74. Amsterdam: Rodopi, 1995.
Fischer-Tiné, Harald. "Arya Samaj." In *Brill's Encyclopedia of Hinduism. Vol. 5, Religious Symbols, Hinduism and Migration, Contemporary Communities Outside South Asia, Some Modern Religious Groups and Teachers*, edited by Knut A. Jacobsen, 389–396. Leiden: Brill, 2012.
———. "'Deep Occidentalism?' Europa und der Westen in der Wahrnehmung hinduistischer Intellektueller und Reformer (ca. 1890–1930)." *Journal of Modern European History* 4, no. 2 (2006): 171–203.

———. *Der Gurukul-Kangri oder die Erfindung der Arya-Nation. Kolonialismus, Hindu-reform und "Nationale Bildung" in Britisch-Indien (1897–1922)*. Würzburg: Ergon, 2003.

———. "Fitness for Modernity? The YMCA and Physical-Education Schemes in Late-Colonial South Asia (circa 1900–40)." *Modern Asian Studies* 53, no. 2 (2018): 512–559.

———. "From Brahmacharya to 'Conscious Race Culture': Victorian Discourses of Science and Hindu Traditions in Early Indian Nationalism." In *Beyond Representation: Colonial and Post-Colonial Constructions of Indian Identity*, edited by Crispin Bates, 241–269. New Delhi: Oxford University Press, 2006.

———. *Pidgin-Knowledge: Wissen und Kolonialismus*. Zurich: Diaphanes, 2013.

———. *Shyamji Krishnavarma: Sanskrit, Sociology and Anti-imperialism*. New Delhi: Routledge, 2014.

———. "The Other Side of Internationalism: Switzerland as a Hub of Militant Anti-colonialism (c. 1910–1920)." In *Colonial Switzerland: Rethinking Colonialism from the Margins*, edited by Patricia Purtschert and Harald Fischer-Tiné, 221–258. Basingstoke, UK: Palgrave Macmillan, 2015.

Fischer-Tiné, Harald, Stefan Huebner, and Ian Tyrrell, eds. *Spreading Protestant Modernity: Global Perspectives on the Work of the YMCA and the YWCA, 1889–1970*. Honolulu: University of Hawaii Press, 2021.

Foitzik, Jan. *Zwischen den Fronten. Zur Politik, Organisation und Funktion linker politischer Kleinorganisationen im Widerstand 1933 Bis 1939/40*. Bonn: Neue Gesellschaft, 1986.

Foltz, Richard C. *Animals in Islamic Tradition and Muslim Cultures*. Oxford: Oneworld, 2006.

———. "'This She-Camel of God Is a Sign to You . . .': Dimensions of Animals in Islamic Tradition and Muslim Culture." In *A Communion of Subjects: Animals in Religion, Science, and Ethics*, edited by Paul Waldau and Kimberley Patton, 149–159. New York: Columbia University Press, 2006.

Forsdick, Charles. "Taste." In *Keywords for Travel Writing Studies: A Critical Glossary*, edited by Charles Forsdick, Zoë Kinsley, and Kathryn Walchester, 244–246. London: Anthem, 2019.

Foucault, Michel. "Nietzsche, Genealogy, History." In *Language, Counter-Memory, Practice: Selected Essays and Interviews*, edited by D. F. Bouchard, 139–164. Ithaca, NY: Cornell University Press, 1977.

———. "Technologies of the Self." In *Technologies of the Self: A Seminar with Michel Foucault*, edited by Luther H. Martin, H. Gutman, and P. H. Hutton, 16–49. Amherst: University of Massachusetts Press, 1982.

Framke, Maria. *Delhi—Rom—Berlin. Die indische Wahrnehmung von Faschismus und Nationalsozialismus 1922–1939*. Darmstadt: Wissenschaftliche Buchgesellschaft, 2013.

Francis, R. A. *Romain Rolland*. Oxford: Berg, 1999.

Francis, Richard. "Circumstances and Salvation: The Ideology of the Fruitlands Utopia." *American Quarterly* 25, no. 2 (1973): 202–234.

Frei, Norbert. *Karrieren im Zwielicht. Hitlers Eliten nach 1945*. Frankfurt/Main: Campus, 2001.

## BIBLIOGRAPHY

Freitag, Sandria B. "Sacred Symbol as Mobilizing Ideology: The North Indian Search for a 'Hindu' Community." *Comparative Studies in Society and History* 22, no. 4 (1980): 597–625.

Freitag, Ulrike, and Achim von Oepen. "Translocality: An Approach to Connection and Transfer in Area Studies." In *Translocality: The Study of Globalizing Processes from a Southern Perspective*, edited by Ulrike Freitag and Achim von Oepen, 1–24. Leiden: Brill, 2010.

French, Harold W. *The Swan's Wide Waters: Ramakrishna and Western Culture*. Port Washington, NY: Kenniket, 1974.

Fritz, Eberhard, ed. *Radikaler Pietismus in Württemberg. Religiöse Ideale im Konflikt mit gesellschaftlichen Realitäten*. Epfendorf/Neckar: Bibliotheca academica, 2003.

Fritzen, Florentine. *Gemüseheilige: Eine Geschichte des veganen Lebens*. Stuttgart: Fritz Steiner, 2016.

———. *Gesünder leben. Die Lebensreformbewegung im 20. Jahrhundert*. Stuttgart: Steiner, 2006.

———. "'Neuzeitlich leben': Reformhausbewegung und Moderne 1925–1933." In *Die "Krise" der Weimarer Republik*, edited by Moritz Föllmer, 165–186. Frankfurt/Main: Campus, 2005.

Gall, Alexander. "Atlantropa: A Technological Vision of a United Europe." In *Networking Europe: Transnational Infrastructures and the Shaping of Europe, 1850–2000*, edited by Erik van der Vleuten and Arne Kaijser, 99–128. Sagamore Beach, MA: Science History Publications, 2006.

———. *Das Atlantropa-Projekt: Die Geschichte einer gescheiterten Vision. Herman Sörgel und die Absenkung des Mittelmeers*. Frankfurt/Main: Campus, 1998.

Gandhi, Leela. *Affective Communities: Anticolonial Thought, Fin-de-Siècle Radicalism, and the Politics of Friendship*. Durham, NC: Duke University Press, 2006.

Garlington, William. *The Baha'i Faith in America*. Westport, CT: Praeger, 2005.

Garvía, Roberto. *Esperanto and Its Rivals: The Struggle for an International Language*. Philadelphia: University of Pennsylvania Press, 2015.

Gates, Henry Louis Jr. *Stony the Road: Reconstruction, White Supremacy, and the Rise of Jim Crow*. New York: Penguin, 2019.

"Gault, Lieut.-Col. Arthur Fitzroy." In *Who's Who and Why: A Biographical Dictionary of Men and Women of Canada and Newfoundland*. Vol. 5. Vancouver: International Press, 1914. Cited in *American Biographical Archive*, vol. 1: 600, 336.

Gauthaman, Raj. *Dark Interiors: Essays on Caste and Dalit Culture*. New Delhi: SAGE, 2021.

Gehm, Ludwig. " 'Wir wollten zeigen: Es gibt noch Andere.' Vier Jahre unentdeckt im Widerstandskampf (1989)." In *Ethik des Widerstandes. Der Kampf des Internationalen sozialistischen Kampfbundes (ISK) gegen den Nationalsozialismus. Quellen und Texte zum Widerstand aus der Arbeiterbewegung 1933–1945*, edited by Sabine Lemke-Müller, 174–235. Bonn: Dietz, 1996.

Geppert, Alexander C. T. "World's Fairs." In *EGO: Europäische Geschichte Online*, January 15, 2018. http://ieg-ego.eu/en/threads/crossroads/knowledge-spaces/alexander-c-t-geppert-worlds-fairs.

Gerhard, Gesine. *Nazi Hunger Politics: A History of Food in the Third Reich*. Lanham, MD: Rowman and Littlefield, 2015.

BIBLIOGRAPHY

Gerlach, Christian. *Krieg, Ernährung, Völkermord. Forschungen zur deutschen Vernichtungspolitik im Zweiten Weltkrieg*. Hamburg: Hamburger Edition, 1998.
"German Societies and IVU in the 1940s & 50s." Retrieved from International Vegetarian Union, accessed April 15, 2021. https://ivu.org/history/societies/vbd-ivucouncil.html.
Germann, Pascal. *Laboratorien der Vererbung: Rassenforschung und Humangenetik in der Schweiz, 1900–1970*. Göttingen: Wallstein, 2016.
Ghobrial, Jean-Paul. "The Secret Life of Elias of Babylon and the Uses of Global Microhistory." *Past & Present* 222, no. 1 (2014): 51–93.
Gijswijt-Hofstra, Marijke, and Roy Porter, eds. *Cultures of Neurasthenia: From Beard to the First World War*. Leiden: Brill, 2001.
Gilheany, John M. *Familiar Strangers: The Church and the Vegetarian Movement in Britain (1809–2009)*. Cardiff, UK: Ascendant Press, 2010.
Gleixner, Ulrike, ed. *Pietismus und Bürgertum. Eine historische Anthropologie der Frömmigkeit (Württemberg 17.–19. Jahrhundert)*. Göttingen: Vandenhoeck & Ruprecht, 2005.
"Gloria (Maude) Gasque. IVU President, 1953–59." Retrieved from International Vegetarian Union, accessed April 15, 2021. https://ivu.org/members/council/maude-gasque.html.
Glover, William J. *Making Lahore Modern: Constructing and Imagining a Colonial City*. Minneapolis: University of Minnesota Press, 2008.
Godwin, Joscelyn. "Blavatsky and the First Generation of Theosophy." In *Handbook of the Theosophical Current*, edited by Olav Hammer and Mikael Rothstein, 15–32. Leiden: Brill, 2013.
———. *The Theosophical Enlightenment*. Albany: State University of New York Press, 1994.
Goetz, Ulrich Alexander. "Hugo Höppener." In *Handbuch der völkischen Wissenschaften. Akteure, Netzwerke, Forschungsprogramme*, edited by Michael Fahlbusch, Ingo Haar, and Alexander Pinwinkler, 302–305. Berlin: Saur, 2017.
Gombrich, Richard F. *Theravāda Buddhism: A Social History from Ancient Benares to Modern Colombo*. 2nd ed. London: Routledge, 2006.
Goodrick-Clarke, Nicholas. *Hitler's Priestess: Savitri Devi, the Hindu-Aryan Myth, and Neo-Nazism*. New York: New York University Press, 1998.
———. *The Occult Roots of Nazism: Secret Aryan Cults and Their Influence on Nazi Ideology: The Ariosophists of Austria and Germany, 1890–1935*. New York: New York University Press, 1992.
Graul, Johannes. "Die Mazdaznan-Bewegung im deutschen Kaiserreich. Eine archivalienbasierte Spurensuche." In *Nonkonformismus und europäische Religionsgeschichten = Nonconformism and European Histories of Religions*, edited by Danny Schäfer, 369–386. Berlin: Lit, 2012.
———. *Nonkonforme Religionen im Visier der Polizei. Eine Untersuchung am Beispiel der Mazdaznan-Religion im Deutschen Kaiserreich*. Würzburg: Ergon, 2013.
Green, Martin. *Mountain of Truth: The Counterculture Begins, Ascona, 1900–1920*. Hanover, NH: University Press of New England, 1986.
Green, Nile. "Breathing in India, C. 1890." *Modern Asian Studies* 42, nos. 2–3 (2008): 281–315.
Greenhalgh, Paul. *Ephemeral Vistas: The Expositions Universelles, Great Exhibitions, and World's Fairs, 1851–1939*. Manchester: Manchester University Press, 1988.

## BIBLIOGRAPHY

Greenwalt, Emmett A. *City of Glass: The Theosophical Invasion of Point Loma*. San Diego, CA: Cabrillo Historical Association, 1981.
Gregory, James. "British Vegetarianism and the Raj." Unpublished manuscript, last revised 2013. https://www.academia.edu/3837521/British_Vegetarianism_and_the_Raj.
———. *Of Victorians and Vegetarians: The Vegetarian Movement in Nineteenth-Century Britain*. London: Tauris Academic Studies, 2007.
Griffin, Emma. *A Short History of the British Industrial Revolution*. London: Palgrave Macmillan, 2018.
Guha, Ramachandra. *India After Gandhi: The History of the World's Largest Democracy*. London: Picador, 2007.
———. *Rebels Against the Ra: Western Fighters for Indian Freedom*. Dublin: Harper Collins, 2022.
Gupta, Charu. *The Gender of Caste: Representing Dalits in Print*. Delhi: Orient Black Swan, 2015.
Gupta, Sanjuka. "The Domestication of a Goddess: *Caraṇa-Tīrtha* Kālīghāt, the *Māhāpīṭha* of Kālī." In *Encountering Kālī: In the Margins, at the Center, in the West*, edited by Rachel Fell McDermott, 60–71. Berkeley: University of California Press, 2003.
Gutmann, Rachel. "Wie Zarathustra in die Lebensreform kam. Eine Untersuchung der Rezeption der Mazdaznan-Bewegung im deutschsprachigen Raum mit Fokus auf die Aryana-Siedlung in Herrliberg, Ca. 1910–1930." Master's thesis, ETH Zurich, 2021.
Haas, Cornelia. "Jagadamba tanzt. Rukmini Devi und das World-Mother-Movement." In *Frauenkörper/Frauenbilder. Inszenierungen des Weiblichen in den Gesellschaften Süd- und Ostasiens*, edited by Stephan Koehn and Heike Moser, 161–177. Wiesbaden: Harassowitz, 2013.
Habermas, Rebekka. "Piety, Power, and Powerlessness: Religion and Religious Groups in Germany, 1870–1945." In *The Oxford Handbook of Modern German History*, edited by Helmut Walser Smith, 453–480. Oxford: Oxford University Press, 2011.
———. "Weibliche Religiösität, oder: von der Fragilität bürgerlicher Identitäten." In *Wege zur Geschichte des Bürgertums*, edited by Klaus Tenfelde and Hans-Ulrich Wehler, 125–148. Göttingen: Vandenhoeck & Ruprecht, 1994.
Hachtmann, Rüdiger, ed. *Berlin 1848. Eine Politik- und Gesellschaftsgeschichte der Revolution*. Bonn: Dietz, 1997.
Haikal, Mustafa. "Auf der Suche nach dem neuen Menschen." In *Geschichte der Stadt Leipzig*. Vol. 3, *Vom Wiener Kongress bis zum Ersten Weltkrieg*, edited by Susanne Schötz, 880–892. Leipzig: Leipziger Universitätsverlag, 2017.
Hall, Donald E., ed. *Muscular Christianity: Embodying the Victorian Age*. Cambridge: Cambridge University Press, 1994.
Hammer, Olav. *Claiming Knowledge: Strategies of Epistemology from Theosophy to the New Age*. Leiden: Brill, 2001.
Hammer, Olav, and Mikael Rothstein, eds. *Handbook of the Theosophical Current*. Leiden: Brill, 2013.
Hank, Peter. "Einführung." In *Gustav und Amalie Struve. Freiheit und Menschlichkeit. Ausgewählte Programmschriften*, edited by Peter Hank, 9–43. Eggingen: Edition Isele, 2003.

Hansen, Peo, and Stefan Jonsson. "Another Colonialism: Africa in the History of European Integration." *Journal of Historical Sociology* 27 (2014): 442–461.

———. *Eurafrica: The Untold History of European Integration and Colonialism*. London: Bloomsbury, 2015.

Hanson, Debra. "East Meets West: Re-presenting the Arab-Islamic World at the Nineteenth-Century World's Fairs." In *Expanding Nationalisms at World Fairs: Identity, Diversity, and Exchange, 1851–1915*, edited by David Raizman and Ethan Robey, 15–32. London: Routledge, 2018.

Harris, Ruth. "Vivekananda, Sarah Farmer, and Global Spiritual Transformations in the Fin De Siècle." *Journal of Global History* 14, no. 2 (2019): 179–198.

Hartung, Günter. "Völkische Ideologie." In *Handbuch zur "Völkischen Bewegung" 1871–1918*, edited by Uwe Puschner, Walter Schmitz, and Justus H. Ulbricht, 22–42. Munich: K. G. Saur, 1996.

Hasselt, Caroline van. *High Wire Act: Ted Rogers and the Empire that Debt Built*. New York: Wiley, 2007.

Hatcher, Brian A. "Brahmo Samaj and Keshub Chandra Sen." In *Brill's Encyclopedia of Hinduism*. Vol. 5, *Religious Symbols, Hinduism and Migration, Contemporary Communities Outside South Asia, Some Modern Religious Groups and Teachers*, edited by Knut A. Jacobsen, Helene Basu, Angelika Malinar, and Vasudha Narayanan, 437–444. Leiden: Brill, 2012.

Hau, Michael. *The Cult of Health and Beauty in Germany: A Social History, 1890–1930*. Chicago: University of Chicago Press, 2003.

Hausen, Karin. "'Eine Ulme für das schwankende Efeu.' Ehepaare im deutschen Bildungsbürgertum." In *Bürgerinnen und Bürger. Geschlechterverhältnisse im 19. Jahrhundert*, edited by Ute Frevert, 85–117. Göttingen: Vandenhoeck & Ruprecht, 1988.

———. "Öffentlichkeit und Privatheit. Gesellschaftspolitische Konstruktionen und die Geschichte der Geschlechterbeziehungen." In *Frauengeschichte—Geschlechtergeschichte*, edited by Karin Hausen and Heide Wunder, 81–88. Frankfurt/Main: Campus, 1992.

Hauser, Julia. "The Birth of the Ascetic Leader: 'Die Botschaft des Mahatma Gandhi' in Troubled Weimar Germany." In *Nodes of Translation: Rethinking Modern Intellectual History Between South Asia and Germany*, edited by Martin Christof-Füchsle and Razak Khan. Berlin: De Gruyter, forthcoming.

———. "A Frugal Crescent: Perceptions of Foodways in the Ottoman Empire and Egypt in Nineteenth-Century Vegetarian Discourse." In *Food as a Cultural Signifier: Perspectives on the Middle East and Beyond*, edited by Julia Hauser, Kirill Dmitriev, and Bilal Orfali, 292–316. Leiden: Brill, 2020.

———. *German Religious Women in Late Ottoman Beirut. Competing Missions*. Leiden: Brill, 2015.

———. "Internationalism and Nationalism: Indian Protagonists and Their Political Agendas at the 15th World Vegetarian Congress in India (1957)." *South Asia: Journal of South Asian Studies* 40 (2021): 152–166.

———. "Körper, Moral, Gesellschaft: Debatten über Vegetarismus zwischen Europa und Indien, 1850–1914." In *Geschichte des Nicht-Essens: Verzicht, Vermeidung und Verweigerung in der Moderne*, edited by Norman Aselmeyer and Veronika Settele, 265–294. Munich: Oldenbourg, 2018.

BIBLIOGRAPHY

———. "Mothers of a Future Generation: The Journey of an Argument for Female Education." In *Entangled Education: Foreign and Local Schools in Ottoman Syria and Mandate Lebanon (19th–20th Centuries)*, edited by Julia Hauser, Christine Lindner, and Esther Möller, 143–161. Würzburg: Ergon, 2016.

Hawthorn, Ainsley. "La popularisation de la 'danse du ventre.' Origine et diffusion d'un nom vulgaire." *Recherches en danse* 9 (2020). https://doi.org/10.4000/danse.3287.

Hay, Stephen. "The Making of a Late-Victorian Hindu: M. K. Gandhi in London, 1888–1891." *Victorian Studies* 33, no. 1 (1989): 75–98.

Haynes, Douglas E. "Gandhi, Brahmacharya and Global Sexual Science, 1919–38." *South Asia: Journal of South Asian Studies* 43, no. 6 (2020): 1163–1178.

"Hebrew Vegetarian Association." Central Zionist Archives, World Zionist Organization, accessed 18 December 2020. http://www.zionistarchives.org.il/en/AttheCZA/AdditionalArticles/Pages/vegetarianism.aspx.

Hecker, Hellmuth. *Der erste deutsche Bhikkhu. Das bewegte Leben des ehrwürdigen Nyanatiloka (1878–1957) und seine Schüler*. Konstanz: Hecker, 1995.

Heim, Susanne, ed. *Autarkie und Ostexpansion. Pflanzenzucht und Agrarforschung im Nationalsozialismus*. Göttingen: Wallstein, 2002.

———. *Kalorien, Kautschuk, Karrieren. Pflanzenzüchtung und Landwirtschaftliche Forschung in Kaiser-Wilhelm-Instituten 1933–1945*. Göttingen: Wallstein-Verlag, 2003.

Heine, Peter. *Food Culture in the Near East, Middle East, and North Africa*. Westport, CT: Greenwood Press, 2004.

———. *Kulinarische Studien. Untersuchungen zur Kochkunst im arabisch-islamischen Mittelalter*. Wiesbaden: Harassowitz, 1988.

Helstosky, Carol. "Food Studies and Animal Rights." In *Routledge International Handbook of Food Studies*, edited by Ken Albala, 322–333. London: Routledge, 2013.

Henderson, T. F., and Ralph A. Manogue. "Oswald, John (c. 1760–1793)." In *Oxford Dictionary of National Biography*. Oxford: Oxford University Press, 2004.

Hermand, Jost. "Meister Fidus: Jugendstil-Hippie to Aryan Faddist." *Comparative Literature Studies* 12, no. 3 (1975): 288–307.

Herrmann, Ulrich, ed. *"Mit uns zieht die neue Zeit..." Der Wandervogel in der deutschen Jugendbewegung*. Weinheim; Munich: Juventa, 2006.

Hertel, Gerhard. "Chronologie des Wiederaufbauprozesses von Freudenstadt 1945–1956 mit einem vorangestellten Abriß der Entstehungsgeschichte Freudenstadts 1597 bis 1945." In *Stadtgestalt und Heimatgefühl. Der Wiederaufbau von Freudenstadt 1945–1954. Analysen, Vergleich und Dokumente*, edited by Hans-Günther Burkhardt, Hartmut Frank, Ulrich Höhns, and Klaus Stieghorst, 198–256. Hamburg: Christians, 1988.

Herzog, Dagmar. *Sexuality in Europe: A Twentieth-Century History*. Cambridge: Cambridge University Press, 2011.

Hessayon, Ariel, and Sarah Apetrei, eds. *An Introduction to Jacob Boehme: Four Centuries of Thought and Reception*. New York: Routledge, 2014.

Hewitson, Mark. *Nationalism in Germany, 1848–1866: Revolutionary Nation*. Basingstoke, UK: Palgrave Macmillan, 2010.

Hill, Patricia. *The World Their Household: The American Women's Foreign Mission Movement and Cultural Transformation, 1870–1920*. Ann Arbor: University of Michigan Press, 1985.

BIBLIOGRAPHY

Hine, Robert V. *California's Utopian Colonies.* New Haven, CT: Yale University Press, 1966.

Hinnells, John R. "The Parsis." In *The Wiley Blackwell Companion to Zoroastrianism,* edited by Michael Stausberg, Yuhan Sohrab-Dinshaw Vevaina, and Anna Tessmann, 157–172. Chichester, UK: Wiley Blackwell, 2015.

Hinnells, John R., and Alan Williams, eds. *Parsis in India and the Diaspora.* London: Routledge, 2007.

"History of the International Vegetarian Union." International Vegetarian Union, accessed October 17, 2019. https://ivu.org/history-legacy-pages/2013-02-17-21-29-31.html.

Hobsbawm, Eric. *The Age of Capital, 1845–1875.* London: Weidenfeld and Nicolson, 1975.

Hodder, Jake. "Conferencing the International at the World Pacifist Meeting, 1949." *Political Geography* 49 (2015): 40–50.

Hodges, Sarah. *Reproductive Health in India: History, Politics, Controversies.* New Delhi: Orient Longman, 2006.

———. "South Asia's Eugenic Past." In *The Oxford Handbook of the History of Eugenics,* edited by Alison Bashford, 228–242. Oxford: Oxford University Press, 2006.

Hoffman, Valerie. "Eating and Fasting for God in Sufi Tradition." *Journal of the American Academy of Religion* 63 (1995): 465–84.

Holdrege, B. A. "Body Connections: Hindu Discourses of the Body and the Study of Religions." *Indian Journal of Hindu Studies* 2, no. 3 (1998): 341–386.

Horn, Elija. *Indien als Erzieher: Orientalismus in der deutschen Reformpädagogik und Jugendbewegung 1918–1933.* Bad Heilbrunn: Verlag Julius Klinkhardt, 2018.

———. "Indienmode und Tagore-Hype: Reformpädagogik in der Weimarer Republik in der Perspektive des Orientalismus." In *Reformpädagogik und Reformpädagogik-Rezeption in neuer Sicht: Perspektiven und Impulse,* edited by Wolfgang Keim, Ulrich Schwerdt, and Sabine Reh, 149–168. Bad Heilbrunn: Julius Klinkhardt, 2016.

———. "Jugendbewegung und Indien. Zur Herausbildung eines jugendkulturellen Topos um 1918." In *1918 in Bildung und Erziehung: Traditionen, Transitionen, Visionen,* edited by Andrea de Vincenti, Norbert Grube, and Andreas Hoffmann-Ocon, 87–105. Bad Heilbrunn: Julius Klinkhardt, 2020.

———. "New Education, Indophilia and Women's Activism." *South Asia Chronicle* 8 (2018): 79–109.

———. "Sexuelle Befreiung aus Indien. Jugendkulturelle Verknüpfung von Östlicher Spiritualität und Sexualität um 1918 und um 1980." In *Lebensreform um 1900 und Alternativmilieu um 1980: Kontinuitäten und Brüche in Milieus der gesellschaftlichen Selbstreflexion im frühen und späten 20. Jahrhundert,* edited by Detlef Siegfried and David Templin, 195–211. Göttingen: V&R Unipress, 2019.

Hunt, Lynn. *Writing History in the Global Era.* New York: Norton, 2014.

Hylton, Stuart. *A History of Manchester.* Chichester, UK: Phillimore, 2003.

Iacobbo, Karen, and Michael Iacobbo. *Vegetarian America: A History.* Westport, CT: Praeger, 2004.

Ichijo, Atsuko, and Ronald Ranta, eds. *The Emergence of National Food: The Dynamics of Food and Nationalism.* London: Palgrave Macmillan, 2016.

Ito, Toshiko. "Transzendenz und Orientalismus in der Reformpädagogik: Eine Fallstudie zur Kooperation zwischen Werner Zimmermann und Kuniyoshi Obara." *International Journal for the History of Education* 2 (2012): 36–50.

## BIBLIOGRAPHY

Jackson, Carl T. "The New Thought Movement and the Nineteenth Century Discovery of Oriental Philosophy." *Journal of Popular Culture* 9, no. 3 (1975): 523–548.
———. *Vedanta for the West: The Ramakrishna Movement in the United States.* Bloomington: Indiana University Press, 1994.
Jacob, Wilson Chacko. "The Turban, the Tarbush, and the Top Hat: Masculinity, Modernity, and National Identity in Interwar Egypt." *Al-Raida* 21, no. 104–105 (2004): 23–37.
———. *Working Out Egypt: Effendi Masculinity and Subject Formation in Colonial Modernity (1870–1940).* Durham, NC: Duke University Press, 2011.
Jacobs, Marc, ed. *Eating Out in Europe: Picnics, Gourmet Dining and Snacks Since the Late Eighteenth Century.* Oxford: Berg, 2003.
Jaffrelot, Christophe. *Dr. Ambedkar and Untouchability: Analysing and Fighting Caste.* London: Hurst, 2005.
———. *Religion, Caste, and Politics in India.* Delhi: Primus Books, 2010.
Jain, Andrea. *Selling Yoga: From Counterculture to Pop Culture.* Oxford: Oxford University Press, 2014.
Jaini, P. S. "Fear of Food: Jaina Attitudes on Eating." In *Collected Papers on Jaina Studies*, edited by P. S. Jaini, 281–296. Delhi: Motilal Banarsidass, 2000.
Jakobsh, Doris. "Gender." In *Brill's Encyclopedia of Sikhism Online*, ed. Knut A. Jacobsen. Leiden: Brill, 2017. http://dx.doi.org/10.1163/2589-2118_BESO_COM_031 684.
Jalali, Younes. *Taghi Erani, A Polymath in Interwar Berlin: Fundamental Science, Psychology, Orientalism, and Political Philosophy.* Cham, CH: Springer, 2018.
Jefferies, Matthew. "Lebensreform: A Middle-Class Antidote to Wilhelminism?" In *Wilhelminism and Its Legacies: German Modernities, Imperialism, and the Meanings of Reform, 1890–1930*, edited by Geoff Eley and James Retallack, 91–106. New York: Berghahn, 2003.
Jensen, Uffa. *Gebildete Doppelgänger: Bürgerliche Juden und Protestanten im 19. Jahrhundert.* Göttingen: Wallstein, 2005.
Jha, Dwijendra Narayan. *The Myth of the Holy Cow.* London: Verso, 2002.
Jhaveri, Shanay. "The Journey in My Head: Cosmopolitanism and Indian Male Self-Portraiture in 20th Century India—Umrao Singh Sher-Gil, Bhupen Khakhar, Raghubir Singh." PhD diss., Royal College of Art, 2016.
Jones, Kenneth. *Arya Dharm: Hindu Consciousness in 19th-Century Punjab.* New Delhi: Ajay Kumar Jain, 1976.
Jonker, Gerdien. *The Ahmadiyya Quest for Religious Progress: Missionizing Europe 1900–1965.* Leiden: Brill, 2016.
———. "In Search of Religious Modernity: Conversion to Islam in Interwar Berlin." In *Muslims in Interwar Europe: A Transcultural Historical Perspective*, edited by Bekim Agai, Umar Ryad, and Mehdi Sajid, 18–46. Leiden: Brill, 2016.
———. *On the Margins: Jews and Muslims in Interwar Berlin.* Leiden: Brill, 2020.
Jordens, J. T. F. *Dayananda Saraswati: His Life and Ideals.* Delhi: Oxford University Press, 1960.
Junge, Christian. "Food, Body, Society: Al-Shidyāq's Somatic Critique of Nineteenth-Century Communities." In *Food as a Cultural Signifier: Perspectives on the Middle East and Beyond*, edited by Julia Hauser, Kirill Dmitriev, and Bilal Orfali, 142–161. Leiden: Brill, 2020.

Kaienburg, Hermann. "Der Traum vom Garten Eden. Die Gartenbausiedlung 'Eden' in Oranienburg als alternative Wirtschafts- und Lebensgemeinschaft." *Zeitschrift für Geschichtswissenschaft* 52 (2004): 1077–1090.
Kaiser, Tobias. "Eine etwas andere Mediengeschichte—Anmerkungen zur Entstehung der vegetarischen Publizistik des 19. Jahrhunderts im preußisch-thüringischen Nordhausen." In *Medien—Kommunikation—Öffentlichkeit. Vom Spätmittelalter bis zur Gegenwart. Festschrift für Werner Greiling zum 65. Geburtstag*, edited by Holger Böning, Hans-Werner Hahn, Alexander Krünes, and Uwe Schirmer, 51–67. Wien: Böhlau, 2019.
Kalbitzer, Helmut. "Widerstehen oder mitmachen. Eigensinnige Ansichten und sehr persönliche Erinnerungen (1987)." In *Ethik des Widerstandes. Der Kampf des Internationalen sozialistischen Kampfbundes (ISK) gegen den Nationalsozialismus. Quellen und Texte zum Widerstand aus der Arbeiterbewegung 1933–1945*, edited by Sabine Lemke-Müller, 236–277. Bonn: Dietz, 1996.
Kapoor, Satish K. *Cultural Contact and Fusion: Swami Vivekananda in the West, 1893–96*. Jalandhar: ABS, 1987.
Kayyali, Randa. *The Arab Americans*. Westport, CT: Greenwood, 2006.
Kean, Hilda. *Animal Rights: Political and Social Change in Britain Since 1800*. London: Penguin, 1998.
———. "The Moment of Greyfriars Bobby: The Changing Cultural Position of Animals, 1800–1920." In *A Cultural History of Animals*. Vol. 5, *In the Age of Empire*, edited by Kathleen Kete, 25–46. Oxford: Berg, 2007.
Keiderling, Thomas. "Buchstadt auf dem Höhepunkt." In *Geschichte der Stadt Leipzig*. Vol. 3, *Vom Wiener Kongress bis zum Ersten Weltkrieg*, edited by Susanne Schötz, 592–599. Leipzig: Leipziger Universitätsverlag, 2017.
Kerschbaumer, Florian, and Korinna Schönhärl. "Der Wiener Kongress als 'Kinderstube' des Philhellenismus. Das Beispiel des Bankiers Jean-Gabriel Eynard." In "Vormärz und Philhellenismus," special issue, *Forum Vormärz Forschung* 18 (2013): 99–127.
Kete, Kathleen. *The Beast in the Boudoir: Petkeeping in Nineteenth-Century Paris*. Berkeley: University of California Press, 2004.
Keys, Barbara. *Globalizing Sport: National Rivalry and International Community in the 1930s*. Cambridge, MA: Harvard University Press, 2013.
Khalil, Issa. "The Orthodox Fast and the Philosophy of Vegetarianism." *Greek Orthodox Theological Review* 35, no. 3 (1990): 237–259.
Khan, Razak. "Entanglements of Translation: Psychology, Pedagogy, and Youth Reform in German and Urdu." *Comparative Studies of South Asia, Africa and the Middle East* 40, no. 2 (2020): 295–308.
Khare, Ravindra S., ed. *The Eternal Food: Gastronomic Ideas and Experiences of Hindus and Buddhists*. Albany: State University of New York Press, 1992.
———. "Food with Saints. An Aspect of Hindu Gastrosemantics." In *The Eternal Food: Gastronomic Ideas and Experiences of Hindus and Buddhists*, edited by Ravindra S. Khare, 27–52. Albany: State University of New York Press, 1992.
———, ed. *The Hindu Hearth and Home: Culinary Systems Old and New in North India*. New Delhi: Vikas Publishing House, 1976.
Kidambi, Prashant. *The Making of an Indian Metropolis: Colonial Governance and Public Culture in Bombay, 1890–1920*. Aldershot, UK: Ashgate, 2007.

## BIBLIOGRAPHY

Kidd, Alan J., and Terry Wyke, eds. *Manchester: Making the Modern City*. Liverpool: Liverpool University Press, 2016.

Killingley, Dermot. "Manufacturing Yogis: Swami Vivekananda as a Yoga Teacher." In *Gurus of Modern Yoga*, edited by Mark Singleton and Ellen Goldberg, 17–37. Oxford: Oxford University Press, 2014.

Kinealy, Christine, ed. *The History of the Irish Famine*. London: Routledge, 2019.

Kiyak, Mely. "Corona-Demos in Berlin: Unglaubliches Unbehagen gegen unsere Regierungsform." Deutschlandfunk Kultur, August 29, 2020. https://www.deutschland funkkultur.de/corona-demos-in-berlin-unglaubliches-unbehagen-gegen-unsere .1013.de.html?dram:article_id=483277.

Klein, Jakob A. "Afterword: Comparing Vegetarianisms." *Journal of South Asian Studies* 31, no. 1 (2008): 199–212.

Kloppenborg, Ria. "The Anagarika Dharmapala (1864–1933) and the Puritan Pattern." *Nederlands Theologisch Tijdschrift* 46, no. 4 (1992): 277–283.

Koller, Christian. "Enemy Images: Race and Gender Stereotypes in the Discussion on Colonial Troops. A Franco-German Comparison, 1914–1923." In *Home/Front: The Military, War and Gender in Twentieth-Century Germany*, edited by Karen Hagemann and Stefanie Schüler-Springorum, 139–157. Oxford: Berg, 2002.

Kothari, Sunil. *Photo Biography of Rukmini Devi*. Chennai: Kalakshetra Foundation, 2004.

Krabbe, Wolfgang R. "Biologismus und Lebensreform." In *Die Lebensreform. Entwürfe zur Neugestaltung von Leben und Kunst um 1900*, edited by Kai Buchholz, 179–181. Darmstadt: Häusser, 2001.

———. *Gesellschaftsveränderung durch Lebensreform*. Göttingen: Vandenhoeck und Ruprecht, 1974.

Krämer, Gudrun. "Moving Out of Place: Minorities in Middle Eastern Urban Societies, 1800–1914." In *The Urban Social History of the Middle East, 1750–1950*, edited by Peter Sluggett, 182–223. Syracuse, NY: Syracuse University Press, 2008.

Krämer, Hans Martin. "'Not Befitting Our Divine Country': Eating Meat in Japanese Discourses of Self and Other from the Seventeenth Century to the Present." *Food and Foodways* 16, no. 1 (2008): 33–62.

———, and Julian Strube, eds. *Theosophy Across Boundaries: Transcultural and Interdisciplinary Perspectives on a Modern Esoteric Movement*. Albany: State University of New York Press, 2020.

Kraus, Daniela. "Förster, Bernhard." In *Handbuch des Antisemitismus*. Vol. 2.1, *Personen: A–K*, edited by Wolfgang Benz, 236–237. Berlin: de Gruyter Saur, 2009.

———. "Förster, Paul." In *Handbuch des Antisemitismus*. Vol. 2.1, *Personen: A–K*, edited by Wolfgang Benz, 238–239. Berlin: de Gruyter Saur, 2009.

Kripal, Jeffrey J. *Kālī's Child: The Mystical and the Erotic in the Life and Teachings of Ramakrishna*. Chicago: University of Chicago Press, 1995.

Krüger, Arnd. "There Goes This Art of Manliness: Naturism and Racial Hygiene in Germany." *Journal of Sport History* 18, no. 1 (1991): 135–158.

Krüger, Arnd, and Wiliiam Murray, eds. *The Nazi Olympics. Sport, Politics, and Appeasement in the 1930s*. Urbana: University of Illinois Press, 2003.

Kühl, Stefan. *For the Betterment of the Race: The Rise and Fall of the International Movement for Eugenics and Racial Hygiene*. New York: Palgrave Macmillan, 2013.

Kuhne, Louis. *Neo-naturopathy: New Science of Healing, or the Doctrine of the Unity of the Unity of Diseases.* Butler, NJ: Benedict Lust, 1917.

Kulke, Hermann, and Dietmar Rothermund. *A History of India.* 4th ed. Oxon: Routledge, 2010.

Kumar, Anil. *Medicine and the Raj: British Medical Policy in India, 1835–1911.* London: Sage, 1998.

Kumar, Ashutosh. *Coolies of the Empire: Indentured Indians in the Sugar Colonies, 1830–1920.* Cambridge: Cambridge University Press, 2017.

Kumar, Prakash. "American Modernisers and the Cow Question in Colonial and Nationalist India." *South Asia: Journal of South Asian Studies* 44, no. 1 (2021): 185–200.

Kumar, Saurav. "Veganism, Hinduism, and Jainism in India." In *The Routledge Handbook of Vegan Studies*, edited by Laura Wright, 205–214. London: Routledge, 2021.

Kundrus, Birthe. *Moderne Imperialisten. Das Kaiserreich jm Spiegel seiner Kolonien.* Cologne: Böhlau, 2003.

Kurlander, Eric. "The Orientalist Roots of National Socialism? Nazism, Occultism, and South Asian Spirituality, 1919–1945." In *Transcultural Encounters Between Germany and India*, edited by Joanne Miyang Cho, Eric Kurlander, and Douglas T. McGetchin, 155–169. Abingdon, UK: Routledge, 2014.

Laak, Dirk van. *Weiße Elefanten. Anspruch und Scheitern technischer Großprojekte.* Stuttgart: DVA, 1999.

Lal, Vinay. "Provincializing the West: World History from the Perspective of Indian History." In *Writing World History 1800–2000*, edited by Benedikt Stuchtey and Eckhardt Fuchs, 271–290. Oxford: Oxford University Press, 2002.

Lambert, David, and Alan Lester, eds. *Colonial Lives Across the British Empire: Imperial Careering in the Long Nineteenth Century.* Cambridge: Cambridge University Press, 2006.

Laqueur, Thomas. *Solitary Sex: A Cultural History of Masturbation.* New York: Zone Books, 2008.

Large, David Clay. *The Grand Spas of Central Europe: A History of Intrigue, Politics, Art, and Healing.* Lanham, MD: Rowman and Littlefield, 2015.

Largent, Mark A. *Breeding Contempt: The History of Coerced Sterilization in the United States.* New Brunswick, NJ: Rutgers University Press, 2008.

Larson, Edward J. *Sex, Race and Science: Eugenics in the Deep South.* Baltimore: Johns Hopkins University Press, 1995.

Launay, Robert. "Tasting the World: Food in Early European Travel Narratives." *Food and Foodways* 11, no. 1 (2003): 27–47.

Laursen, Ole Birk. "Introduction: M. P. T. Acharya: A Revolutionary, an Agitator, a Writer." In *Acharya, M. P. T.: We Are Anarchists. Essays on Anarchism, Pacifism, and the Indian Independence Movement, 1923–1953*, edited by Ole Birk Laursen, 1–34. Edinburgh: Chico, 2019.

Lawrance, Benjamin Nicholas, Emily Lynn Osborn, and Richard L. Roberts, eds. *Intermediaries, Interpreters, and Clerks: African Employees in the Making of Colonial Africa.* Madison: University of Wisconsin Press, 2006.

Leask, Nigel. *British Romantic Writers and the East: Anxieties of Empire.* Cambridge: Cambridge University Press, 1992.

BIBLIOGRAPHY

Lee, Paula Young, ed. *Meat, Modernity, and the Rise of the Slaughterhouse*. Durham: University of New Hampshire Press, 2008.
Lemke-Müller, Sabine. *Ethik des Widerstands. Der Kampf des Internationalen sozialistischen Kampfbundes (ISK) gegen den Nationalsozialismus. Quellen und Texte zum Widerstand aus der Arbeiterbewegung 1933–1945*. Bonn: Dietz, 1996.
Leong-Salobir, Cecilia. *Food Culture in Colonial Asia: A Taste of Empire*. London: Routledge, 2011.
Lévi-Strauss, Claude. *Introduction to a Science of Mythology*. Vol. 1, *The Raw and the Cooked*. New York: Harper and Row, 1970.
Lewicka, Paulina B. *Food and Foodways of Medieval Cairenes: Aspects of Life in an Islamic Metropolis of the Eastern Mediterranean*. Leiden: Brill, 2011.
Lewis, Reina. *Rethinking Orientalism: Women, Travel and the Ottoman Harem*. London: I. B. Tauris, 2004.
Lichtenberg, André. "John Oswald, écossais, jacobin et socialiste." *La Révolution française: Revue historique* 32 (1897): 481–95.
Liebau, Heike. "Das deutsche Auswärtige Amt, indische Emigranten und propagandistische Bestrebungen unter den südasiatischen Kriegsgefangenen im 'Halbmondlager.'" In *Soldat Ram Singh und der Kaiser. Indische Kriegsgefangene in deutschen Propagandalagern 1914–1918*, edited by Franziska Roy, Heike Liebau, and Ravi Ahuja, 109–143. Heidelberg: Draupadi, 2014.
Lindner, Christine. "'In This Religion I Will Live, and in This Religion I Will Die.' Performativity and the Protestant Identity in Late Ottoman Syria." *Chronos* 22 (2010): 25–48.
Lindner, Heiner. "*Um etwas zu erreichen, muss man sich etwas vornehmen, von dem man glaubt, dass es unmöglich sei.*" *Der Internationale sozialistische Kampf-Bund (Isk) und seine Publikationen*. Bonn: Friedrich-Ebert-Stiftung, 2006.
Lindner, Rolf. *Walks on the Wild Side: Eine Geschichte der Stadtforschung* Frankfurt/Main: Campus, 2004.
Lins, Ulrich. *Dangerous Language*. Vol. 1, *Esperanto Under Hitler and Stalin*. London: Palgrave Macmillan, 2017.
Linse, Ulrich, ed. *Barfüßige Propheten: Erlöser der zwanziger Jahre*. Berlin: Siedler, 1983.
———. "Der spurenlose Mazdaznan-Vortrag von Otto Rauth." In *Bauhausvorträge. Gastredner am Weimarer Bauhaus 1919–1925*, edited by Peter Bernhard, 217–232. Berlin: Gebrüder Mann, 2017.
———. "Mazdaznan." In *Lexikon neureligiöser Gruppen, Szenen und Weltanschauungen: Orientierungen im religiösen Pluralismus*, edited by Harald Baer and Thomas Becker, 776–777. Freiburg/Breisgau: Herder, 2005.
———. "Mazdaznan – Die Rassenreligion vom arischen Friedensreich." In *Völkische Religion und Krisen der Moderne. Entwürfe "arteigener" Glaubenssysteme seit der Jahrhundertwende*, edited by Stefanie V. Schnurbein and Justus H. Ulbricht, 268–291. Würzburg: Königshausen & Neumann, 2001.
———. *Ökopax und Anarchie: eine Geschichte der ökologischen Bewegungen in Deutschland*. Frankfurt/Main: Dt. Taschenbuch-Verl, 1986.
———. "Völkisch-Rassische Siedlungen der Lebensreform." In *Handbuch zur "Völkischen Bewegung*," edited by Uwe Puschner, 397–410. Munich: Saur, 1996.

———. *Zurück o Mensch zur Mutter Erde: Landkommunen in Deutschland 1890–1933*. Frankfurt/Main: Deutscher Taschenbuch-Verlag, 1983.
Linzey, Andrew, and Clair Linzey, eds. *Ethical Vegetarianism and Veganism*. London: Routledge, 2019.
Lodrick, Deryck O. *Sacred Cows, Sacred Places: Origins and Survivals of Animal Homes in India*. Berkeley: University of California Press, 1981.
Loheide, Boris. "Beef Around the World. Die Globalisierung des Rindfleischhandels bis 1914." *Comparativ* 17, no. 3 (2007): 46–67.
Lombardo, Paul A. *Three Generations, No Imbeciles: Eugenics, the Supreme Court, and Buck V. Bell*. Baltimore: Johns Hopkins University Press, 2008.
Louvaris, Athanasius N. J. "Fast and Abstinence in Byzantium." In *Feast, Fast or Famine: Food and Drink in Byzantium*, edited by Wendy Mayer and Silke Trzcionka, 189–98. Brisbane: Australian Association for Byzantine Studies, 2005.
Löwenfels, M. W. *Gustav Struve's Leben, nach authentischen Quellen und von ihm selbst mitgetheilten Notizen dargestellt*. Basel: Helbig und Scherb, 1848.
Lubelsky, Isaac. "Mythological and Real Race Issues in Theosophy." In *Handbook of the Theosophical Current*, edited by Olav Hammer and Mikael Rothstein, 335–356. Leiden: Brill, 2013.
Lutz, Tom. *American Nervousness, 1903: An Anecdotal History*. Ithaca, NY: Cornell University Press, 1991.
Lynch, Julian Anthony. "Music and Communal Violence in Colonial South Asia." *Ethnomusicology Review* 17 (2012). http://ethnomusicologyreview.ucla.edu/journal/volume/17/piece/603.
MacAloon, John, ed. "Muscular Christianity in Colonial and Post-Colonial Worlds." Special issue, *International Journal of the History of Sport* 23, no. 5 (2006).
MacClintock, Anne. *Imperial Leather: Race, Gender and Sexuality in the Colonial Contest*. New York: Routledge, 1995.
Mackenzie Brown, C. "Vivekananda and the Scientific Legitimation of Advaita Vedānta." In *Handbook of Religion and the Authority of Science*, edited by James R. Lewis and Olav Hammer, 207–248. Leiden: Brill, 2012.
MacMaster, Neil. *Racism in Europe 1870–2000*. Houndmills, UK: Palgrave, 2001.
Majima, Ayu. "Eating Meat, Seeking Modernity: Food and Imperialism in Late Nineteenth and Early Twentieth Century Japan." In *Critical Readings on Food in East Asia*, edited by Katarzyna J. Cwiertka, 111–133. Leiden: Brill, 2013.
Malhotra, Anshu. "Of Dais and Midwives: 'Middle-Class' Interventions in the Management of Women's Reproductive Health." *Indian Journal of Gender Studies* 10, no. 2 (2003): 229–259.
Malhotra, Ashok. "Cutting Edge Research in the Contact Zone? The Establishment of the Nutritional Research Laboratories in Coonoor (1925–27)." *South Asia: Journal of South Asian Studies* 44, no. 1 (2021): 117–134.
Malik, Ikram Ali. *Hindu Muslim Riots in the British Punjab, 1849–1900*. Lahore: Gosha-i-Adab, 1984.
Malinar, Angelika. "Guṇa." In *Brill's Encyclopedia of Hinduism*. Vol. 2, edited by Knut A. Jacobsen, Helene Basu, Angelika Malinar, and Vasudha Narayanan, 758–762. Leiden: Brill, 2010.

## BIBLIOGRAPHY

———. "Kṛṣṇa." In *Brill's Encyclopedia of Hinduism*. Vol. 1, *Regions, Pilgrimages, Deities*, edited by Knut A. Jacobsen, Helene Basu, Angelika Malinar, and Vasudha Narayanan, 605–619. Leiden: Brill, 2009.

Mallinson, James. "Haṭha Yoga." In *Brill's Encyclopedia of Hinduism*. Volume 3, *Religious Specialists—Religious Traditions—Philosophy*, edited by Knut A. Jacobson, Helene Basu, Angelika Malinar, and Vasudha Narayanan, 770–781. Leiden: Brill, 2011.

Mandler, Peter, ed. *The Uses of Charity: The Poor on Relief in the Nineteenth-Century Metropolis*. Philadelphia: University of Pennsylvania Press, 1990.

Manela, Erez. *The Wilsonian Moment: Self-Determination and the International Origins of Anticolonial Nationalism*. New York: Oxford University Press, 2007.

Manela, Erez, and Callum C. McKenzie, eds. *Militarism, Hunting, Imperialism: "Blooding" the Martial Male*. London: Routledge, 2010.

Mangan, J. A., ed., *Making European Masculinities. Sport, Europe, Gender*. London: Cass, 2000.

Manjapra, Kris. *Age of Entanglement: German and Indian Intellectuals Across Empire*. Cambridge, MA: Harvard University Press, 2014.

———. "Plantation Dispossessions: The Global Travel of Agricultural Racial Capitalism." In *American Capitalism: New Histories*, edited by Sven Beckert and Christine Desan, 361–391. New York: Columbia University Press, 2018.

Manning, Till, *Die Italiengeneration. Stilbildung durch Massentourismus in den 1950er und 1960er Jahren*. Göttingen: Wallstein, 2011.

Marchand, Suzanne. "Eastern Wisdom in an Age of Western Despair. Orientalism in 1920s Central Europe." In *Weimar Thought: A Contested Legacy*, edited by Peter Gordon and John McCormick, 341–360. Princeton, NJ: Princeton University Press, 2013.

Marriott, John. *The Other Empire: Metropolis, India and Progress in the Colonial Imagination*. Manchester: Manchester University Press, 2004.

Martin, Vanessa. "Constitutional Revolution. III. Events." In *Encyclopedia Iranica*, edited by Ehsan Yarshater, 176–187. Leiden: Brill, 1996.

Martins, Pedro. "An Ontological Dispute in the Writings of Porphyry of Tyre: The Discussion of Meat Eating as a Battlefield for Competing Worldviews in Antiquity." In *Food as a Cultural Signifier: Perspectives on the Middle East and Beyond*, edited by Julia Hauser, Kirill Dmitriev, and Bilal Orfali, 245–259. Leiden: Brill, 2020.

Martschukat, Jürgen. "'The Necessity for Better Bodies to Perpetuate Our Institutions, Insure a Higher Development of the Individual, and Advance the Conditions of the Race': Physical Culture and the Formation of the Self in the Late Nineteenth and Early Twentieth Century USA." *Journal of Historical Sociology* 24, no. 4 (2011): 472–493.

———. "The Pursuit of Fitness: Von Freiheit und Leistungsfähigkeit in der Geschichte der USA." *Geschichte und Gesellschaft* 42, no. 3 (2016): 409–440.

Maß, Sandra. *Weiße Helden, schwarze Krieger. Zur Geschichte kolonialer Männlichkeit in Deutschland 1918–1964*. Cologne: Böhlau, 2006.

Masters, Bruce. *Christians and Jews in the Ottoman Arab World: The Roots of Sectarianism*. Cambridge: Cambridge University Press, 2001.

Matalas, Antonia-Leda, Eleni Tourlouki, and Chrystalleni Lazarou. "Fasting and Food Habits in the Eastern Orthodox Church." In *Food & Faith in Christian Culture*, edited by Ken Albala, 189–203. New York: Columbia University Press, 2011.

Mattson, Kevin. *Upton Sinclair and the Other American Century.* Hoboken, NJ: Wiley, 2006.

McClain, Charles. *In Search of Equality: The Chinese Struggle Against Discrimination in Nineteenth-Century America.* Berkeley: University of California Press, 1994.

McDaniel, June. *Offering Flowers, Feeding Skulls: Popular Goddess Worship in West Bengal.* Oxford: Oxford University Press, 2004.

McGetchin, Douglas T. *Indology, Indomania, and Orientalism: Ancient India's Rebirth in Modern Germany.* Madison, NJ: Fairleigh Dickinson University Press, 2009.

———. "The Rise of Ancient India in Modern Germany." In *On the Paths of Enlightenment: The Myth of India in Western Culture, 1808–2017,* edited by Elio Schenini, 40–55. Geneva: Skira, 2017.

McMahan, David L. *The Making of Buddhist Modernism.* New York: Oxford University Press, 2008.

Meduri, Avanthi. "Bharatanatyam as a Global Dance: Some Issues in Research, Teaching, and Practice." *Dance Research Journal* 36, no. 2 (2004): 11–29.

———, ed. *Rukmini Devi Arundale (1904–1986): A Visionary Architect of Indian Culture and the Performing Arts.* Delhi: Motilal Banarsidass, 2005.

Mehrotra, S. R. *A History of the Indian National Congress.* New Delhi: Vikas, 1995.

Melzer, Jörg. *Vollwerternährung. Diätetik, Naturheilkunde, Nationalsozialismus, sozialer Anspruch.* Stuttgart: Steiner, 2003.

Menashri, David. *Education and the Making of Modern Iran.* Ithaca, NY: Cornell University Press, 1992.

Menon, Kalyani Devaki. *Making Place for Muslims in Contemporary India.* Ithaca, NY: Cornell University Press, 2022.

Menon, Madhavi. *Infinite Variety: A History of Desire in India.* New Delhi: Speaking Tiger, 2018.

Menon, Meena. *Riots and After in Mumbai: Chronicles of Truth and Reconciliation.* Los Angeles: SAGE, 2012.

Menon, Nikhil. "'Help the Plan—Help Yourself': Making Indians Plan-Conscious." In *The Postcolonial Moment in South and Southeast Asia,* edited by Gyan Prakash, Nikhil Menon, and Michael Laffan, 221–242. London: Bloomsbury, 2014.

Merta, Sabine. "'Keep Fit and Slim!' Alternative Ways of Nutrition as Aspects of the German Health Movement, 1880–1930." In *Order and Disorder the Health Implications of Eating and Drinking in the Nineteenth and Twentieth Centuries,* edited by Alexander Fenton, 170–202. East Linton, UK: Tuckwell Press, 2000.

Merwood-Salisbury, Joanna. *Chicago 1890: The Skyscraper and the Modern City.* Chicago: University of Chicago Press, 2009.

Meyer, Jean-François. *Les nouvelles voies spirituelles. Enquête sur la religiosité parallèle en Suisse.* Lausanne: L'age de l'homme, 1993.

Michelis, Elizabeth de. "Modern Yoga: History and Forms." In *Yoga in the Modern World: Uses, Adaptations, Appropriations,* edited by Jean Byrne and Mark Singleton, 17–35. London: Routledge, 2008.

Midgley, Clare. *Feminism and Empire: Women Activists in Imperial Britain, 1790–1865.* London: Routledge, 2007.

Mikhail, Alan. *The Animal in Ottoman Egypt.* Oxford: Oxford University Press, 2014.

———. "Unleashing the Beast: Animals, Energy, and the Economy of Labor in Ottoman Egypt." *American Historical Review* 118, no. 2 (2013): 317–348.

BIBLIOGRAPHY

Milkov, Nikolay. "Einleitung des Herausgebers." In Zeko Torbov, *Erinnerungen an Leonard Nelson 1925–1927*, xix–lviii. Hildesheim: Olms, 2005.
Miller, Jeffrey, and Jonathan Deutsch, eds. *Food Studies: An Introduction to Research Methods*. Oxford: Berg, 2009.
Miller, Susanne. "'Ich wollte ein anständiger Mensch bleiben.' Frauen des Internationalen sozialistischen Kampfbundes (ISK) im Widerstand (1995)." In *Ethik des Widerstandes. Der Kampf des Internationalen sozialistischen Kampfbundes (ISK) gegen den Nationalsozialismus. Quellen und Texte zum Widerstand aus der Arbeiterbewegung 1933–1945*, edited by Sabine Lemke-Müller, 143–157. Bonn: Dietz, 1996.
Mitchell, Timothy. "The World as Exhibition." *Comparative Studies in Society and History* 31, no. 2 (1989): 217–236.
Mitsuda, Tatsuya. "'Vegetarian' Nationalism: Critiques of Meat Eating for Japanese Bodies, 1880–1938." In *Culinary Nationalism in Asia*, edited by Michelle T. King, 23–40. London: Bloomsbury Academic, 2019.
Mittwoch, E. "'īd Al- Aḍḥā." In *Encyclopaedia of Islam*, 2nd ed., edited by P. Bearman, Th. Bianquis, C. E. Bosworth, E. Van Donzel, and W. P. Heinrichs. Leiden: Brill, 2012. http://dx-1doi-1org-10078da9jo983.erf.sbb.spk-berlin.de/10.1163/1573-3912_islam_SIM_3472.
Möhring, Maren. *Marmorleiber: Körperbildung in der deutschen Nacktkultur, 1890–1930*. Cologne: Böhlau, 2004.
Möhring, Maren, and Alexander Nützenadel, eds. "Ernährung im Zeitalter der Globalisierung." Special issue, *Comparativ* 17, no. 3 (2007).
"Molenaar, Heinrich." In *Degeners Wer ist's?* Berlin: Degener, 1935. Cited in *Deutsches Biographisches Archiv* II: 906, 207–208.
Montanari, Massimo. *The Culture of Food*. Oxford: Blackwell, 1994.
———. *Food Is Culture*. New York: Columbia University Press, 2006.
———. *Der Hunger und der Überfluß. Kulturgeschichte der Ernährung in Europa*. Munich: Beck, 1993.
Morantz, Regina. "Between 'Eastern Sacred Space' and Esoteric Capitals of 'the West': Indian Theosophists as Mediators Between India and Euro-America, 1882–1893." In *Capitales de l'ésotérisme européen et dialogue des cultures. Actes du IIe colloque international, European Society for the Study of Western Esotericism 2–4 Juillet 2009*, edited by European Society for the Study of Western Esotericism, 181–196. Strasbourg: Maison interuniversitaire des sciences de l'homme, 2009.
———. "Globalizing 'Sacred Knowledge': South Asians and the Theosophical Society, 1879–1930." PhD diss., Jacobs University Bremen, 2012.
———. "Making Women Modern: Middle Class Women and Health Reform in 19th Century America." *Journal of Social History* 10, no. 4 (1977): 490–507.
Moritz, Maria. "'The Empire of Righteousness': Anagarika Dharmapala and His Vision of Buddhist Asianism." In *Asianisms: Regionalist Interactions and Asian Integration*, edited by Nicola Spakowski and Marc Frey, 19–48. Singapore: National University of Singapore Press, 2016.
Morton, Timothy. "Nature and Culture." In *The Cambridge Companion to Shelley*, edited by Timothy Morton, 185–207. Cambridge: Cambridge University Press, 2006.
———. "The Plantation of Wrath." In *Radicalism in British Literary Culture, 1650–1830: From Revolution to Revolution*, edited by Timothy Morton and Nigel Smith, 64–85. Cambridge: Cambridge University Press, 2002.

Motadel, David. "The Global Authoritarian Moment and the Revolt Against Empire." *American Historical Review* 124, no. 3 (2019): 843–877.

Moulton, Edward C. "Hume, Allan Octavian (1829–1912), Administrator in India, Founder of the Indian National Congress, and Ornithologist." In *Oxford Dictionary of National Biography*. Online edition: Oxford University Press, 2004. http://www.oxforddnb.com.007135ip0ad9.erf.sbb.spk-berlin.de/view/10.1093/ref:odnb/9780198614128.001.0001/odnb-9780198614128-e-34049.

Mudjawar, Madeeha. "Muslims Not Allowed—the Stereotypes of Mumbai's Rental Property Market." CNBCTV18, September 21, 2020. https://www.cnbctv18.com/views/muslims-not-allowed-the-stereotypes-of-mumbais-rental-property-market-6970051.htm.

Mukhopadhyay, Mriganka. "Mohini: A Case Study of a Transnational Spiritual Space in the History of the Theosophical Society." *Numen* 67, nos. 2–3 (2019): 165–190.

———. "Occult's First Foot Soldier in Bengal: Peary Chand Mittra and the Early Theosophical Movement." In *The Occult Nineteenth Century*, edited by Lukas Pokorny and Franz Winter, 269–287. London: Palgrave Macmillan, 2021.

Mukul, Akshaya. *Gita Press and the Making of Hindu India*. Noida: Harper Collins, 2015.

Mürmel, Heinz. "Buddhismus und Theosophie in Leipzig vor dem Ersten Weltkrieg." In *Buddhisten und Hindus im deutschsprachigen Raum: Akten des zweiten Grazer religionswissenschaftlichen Symposiums (2.–3. März 2000)*, edited by Manfred Hutter, 123–136. Frankfurt/Main: Peter Lang, 2000.

———. "'Die Religion liegt im Blut'—Sächsisch-arische Konzepte der Kaiserzeit. Kurze Bemerkungen zur 'Arischen Lebensreform.'" In *Devianz und Dynamik. Festschrift für Hubert Seiwert zum 65. Geburtstag*, edited by Edith Franke, Christoph Kleine, and Heinz Mürmel, 97–121. Göttingen: Vandenhoeck & Ruprecht, 2014.

Murre-van den Berg, Heleen. "The Middle East: Western Missions and the Eastern Churches, Islam and Judaism. Vol. 8: World Christianities, c. 1800–1914." In *Cambridge History of Christianity*, 458–472. Cambridge: Cambridge University Press, 2006.

Muurmann, Gerte. *Komödianten für den Krieg. Deutsches und alliiertes Fronttheater*. Düsseldorf: Droste, 1992.

Myers, Perry. "German Travelers to India at the Fin-de-Siècle and Their Ambivalent Views of the Raj." In *Transcultural Encounters Between Germany and India*, edited by Joanne Miyang Cho, Eric Kurlander, and Douglas T. McGetchin, 84–98. Abingdon, UK: Routledge, 2014.

———. *German Visions of India, 1971–1918: Commandeering the Holy Ganges During the Kaiserreich*. New York: Palgrave Macmillan, 2013.

Naff, Alixa. *Becoming American: The Early Arab Immigrant Experience*. Carbondale: Southern Illinois Press, 1985.

Najmabadi, Afsaneh. *Women with Mustaches and Men Without Beards: Gender and Sexual Anxieties of Iranian Modernity*. Berkeley: University of California Press, 2005.

Nammour, Magda. "Perception de l'éducation dans la presse levantine de la fin du XIXème siècle." In *Entangled Education: Foreign and Local Schools in Ottoman Syria and Mandate Lebanon (19th–20th Centuries)*, edited by Julia Hauser, Christine Lindner, and Esther Möller, 101–123. Würzburg: Ergon, 2015.

# BIBLIOGRAPHY

Nance, Susan. *How the Arabian Nights Inspired the American Dream, 1790–1935*. Chapel Hill: University of North Carolina Press, 2009.
Nanda, Meena. "Madame Blavatsky's Children: Modern Hindu Encounters with Darwinism." In *Handbook of Religion and the Authority of Science*, edited by James R. Lewis and Olav Hammer, 279–344. Leiden: Brill, 2012.
Narayanan, Vasudha. "Bhakti." In *Brill's Encyclopedia of Hinduism Online*, edited by Knut A. Jacobsen, Helene Basu, Angelika Malinar, and Vasudha Narayanan. Leiden: Brill, 2018. https://doi.org/10.1163/2212-5019_BEH_COM_2050060.
Nasrallah, Nawal, ed. *Annals of the Caliphs' Kitchens: Ibn Sayyār al-Warrāq's Tenth-Century Baghdadi Cookbook*. Leiden: Brill, 2007.
Nehring, Holger, ed. *Politics of Security: British and West German Protest Movements and the Early Cold War, 1945–1970*. 1st ed. Oxford: Oxford University Press, 2013.
Nelson, Lance. "Cows, Elephants, Dogs, and Other Lesser Embodiments of *Ātman*: Reflections on Hindu Attitudes Towards Nonhuman Animals." In *A Communion of Subjects: Animals in Religion, Science, and Ethics*, edited by Paul Waldau and Kimberley Patton, 179–193. New York: Columbia University Press, 2006.
Nentwig, Theresa. *Hinrich Wilhelm Kopf (1893–1961). Ein konservativer Sozialdemokrat*. Hanover: Hahnsche Buchhandlung, 2013.
Neumann, Alexander. "Nutritional Physiology in the 'Third Reich' 1933–1945." In *Man, Medicine, and the State: The Human Body as an Object of Government: Sponsored Medical Research in the 20th Century*, edited by W. U. Eckart, 49–59. Stuttgart: Steiner, 2006.
Neumann, Christoph K. "Remarks on the Symbolism of Ottoman Imarets." In *Feeding People, Feeding Power: Imarets in the Ottoman Empire*, edited by Nina Ergin, Christoph K. Neumann, and Amy Singer, 275–286. Istanbul: Eren, 2007.
Nevell, Michael. "Living in the Industrial City: Housing Quality, Land Ownership and the Archaeological Evidence from Industrial Manchester, 1740–1850." *International Journal of Historical Archaeology* 15 (2011): 594–606.
Niemeyer, Christian. *Die dunklen Seiten der Jugendbewegung. Vom Wandervogel zur Hitlerjugend*. Tübingen: Francke, 2013.
Nirumand, Bahman, and Gabriele Yonan. *Iraner in Berlin*. Berlin: Ausländerbeauftrage des Senats, 1994.
Nützenadel, Alexander, and Frank Trentmann, eds. *Food and Globalization: Consumption, Markets and Politics in the Modern World*. Oxford; New York: Berg, 2008.
———. "Introduction. Mapping Food and Globalization." In *Food and Globalization: Consumption, Markets and Politics in the Modern World*, edited by Alexander Nützenadel and Frank Trentmann, 1–15. Oxford: Berg, 2008.
Ó Gráda, Cormac. "Ireland's Great Famine. An Overview." In *When the Potato Failed: Causes and Effects of the "Last" European Subsistence Crisis, 1845–1850*, edited by Cormac Ó Gráda, Richard Paping, and Eric Vanhaute, 41–57. Turnhout, BE: Brepols, 2007.
O'Toole, Therese. "Secularizing the Sacred Cow: The Relationship Between Religious Reform and Hindu Nationalism." In *Hinduism in Public and Private: Reform, Hindutva, Gender, and Sampraday*, edited by Anthony Copley, 84–109. New Delhi: Oxford University Press, 2003.
Ohler, Norman. *Der totale Rausch: Drogen im Dritten Reich*. Cologne: Kiepenheuer und Witsch, 2015.

Olstein, Diego. *Thinking History Globally*. Houndmills, UK: Palgrave Macmillan, 2015.
Omvedt, Gail. *Dalits and the Democratic Revolution: Dr. Ambedkar and the Dalit Movement in Colonial India*. New Delhi: SAGE, 1994.
———. *Understanding Caste: From Buddha to Ambedkar and Beyond*. Hyderabad: Orient Black Swan, 2011.
Osterhammel, Jürgen. *Die Entzauberung Asiens. Europa und die asiatischen Reiche im 18. Jahrhundert*. Munich: Beck, 1998.
———. "Global History." In *Debating New Approaches to History*, edited by Marek Tamm and Peter Burke, 21–48. London: Bloomsbury Academic, 2019.
Otter, Chris. "Civilizing Slaughter: The Development of the British Public Abattoir, 1850–1910." *Food and History* 3, no. 2 (2005): 29–51.
———. *Diet for a Large Planet: Industrial Britain, Food Systems, and World Ecology*. Chicago: University of Chicago Press, 2020.
———. "Planet of Meat: A Biological History." In *Challenging (the) Humanities*, edited by Tony Bennett, 33–49. Canberra: Australian Academy of the Humanities, 2013.
Ouédraogo, Arouna. "De la secte religieuse à l'utopie philanthropique. Genèse sociale du végétarisme occidental." *Annales Histoire, Sciences Sociales* 55 (2000): 825–843.
Pacyga, Dominic A. *Chicago: A Biography*. Chicago: University of Chicago Press, 2009.
Paletschek, Sylvia, *Frauen und Dissens. Frauen im Deutschkatholizismus und in den freien Gemeinden 1841–1852*. Göttingen: Vandenhoeck & Ruprecht, 1990.
Palsetia, Jesse S. *The Parsis of India: Preservation of Identity in Bombay City*. Leiden: Brill, 2001.
Pandey, Gyanendra. *A History of Prejudice: Race, Caste, and Difference in India and the United States*. Cambridge: Cambridge University Press, 2013.
———. "Rallying Around the Cow: Sectarian Strife in the Bhojpuri Region, c. 1888–1917." In *Subaltern Studies II: Writings on South Asian History and Society*, edited by Ranajit Guha, 60–129. Delhi: Oxford University Press, 1983.
Parasecoli, Fabio. "World Food: The Age of Empire, c. 1800–1920." In *A Cultural History of Food*. Vol. 5, *In the Age of Empire*, edited by Martin Bruegel, 199–208. London: Berg, 2012.
Parasher-Sen, Aloka. "Foreigner (Mleccha)." In *Brill's Encyclopedia of Hinduism*. Vol. 3, edited by Knut A. Jacobsen, Helene Basu, Angelika Malinar, and Vasudha Narayanan, 76–81. Leiden: Brill, 2011.
Parry, Ken. "Vegetarianism in Late Antiquity and Early Byzantium." In *Feast, Fast or Famine: Food and Drink in Byzantium*, edited by Wendy Mayer and Silke Trzcionka, 171–187. Brisbane: Australian Association for Byzantine Studies, 2005.
Patel, Kiran Klaus. "Afterword: On the Chances and Challenges of Populating Internationalism." In *Internationalists in European History*, edited by Jessica Reinisch and David Brydan, 263–280. London: Bloomsbury, 2022.
Peiser, Juergen. "Gustav Struve als politischer Schriftsteller und Revolutionär." PhD diss., University of Frankfurt/Main, 1973.
Pelzer-Reith, Birgit, and Reinhold Reith. "Die 'Eiweißlücke' und die biotechnologische Eiweißsynthese. Synthetische Nahrungsmittel in der nationalsozialistischen Autarkiepolitik." *Technikgeschichte* 79, no. 4 (2012): 303–340.
———. "Fischkonsum und 'Eiweißlücke' im Nationalsozialismus." *Vierteljahrschrift für Sozial- und Wirtschaftsgeschichte* 96, no. 1 (2009): 4–26.
———. *Margarine. Die Karriere der Kunstbutter*. Berlin: Klaus Wagenbach, 2001.

BIBLIOGRAPHY

Pernau, Margrit. "Global History—Wegbereiter für einen neuen Kolonialismus?." *Connections: A Journal for Historians and Area Specialists*, December 17, 2004. https://www.connections.clio-online.net/debate/id/fddebate-132110.

———. *Transnationale Geschichte*. Göttingen: Vandenhoeck & Ruprecht, 2011.

Perry, Charles. "The Description of Familiar Foods (Kitāb waṣf al-aṭʻima al-muʻtāda)." In *Medieval Arab Cookery*, 273–465. Translated by Maxime Rodinson, A. J. Arberry, and Charles Perry. Totnes, UK: Prospect Books, 2001.

Pert, Alan. *Red Cactus: The Life of Anna Bonus Kingsford*. Watson's Bay, AU: Books & Writers, 2006.

Peterson, Williard J. "What to Wear? Observation and Participation by Jesuit Missionaries in Late Ming Society." In *Implicit Understandings: Observing, Reporting, and Reflecting on the Encounters Between Europeans and Other Peoples in the Early Modern Era*, edited by Stuart B. Schwartz, 403–421. Cambridge: Cambridge University Press, 1994.

Petit, Elise. *Musique et politique en Allemagne. Du IIIe Reich à l'aube de la guerre froide*. Paris: Presses de l'Université Paris-Sorbonne, 2018.

Philsooph, Hushang. *Hedayat, Vegetarianism and Modernity: Altruism, Leonardo da Vinci, and Sub-humanization*. London: Routledge, 2008.

Pick, Daniel. *Faces of Degeneration: A European Disorder, c. 1848–1918*. Cambridge: Cambridge University Press, 1989.

Pine, Lisa. *Hitler's "National Community": Society and Culture in Nazi Germany*. 2nd ed. London: Bloomsbury Academic, 2017.

Pinney, Christopher. *Photos of the Gods: The Printed Image and Political Struggle in India*. New Delhi: Oxford University Press, 2004.

Poldas, Samuiel Vijaya Bhaskar. *Geschichte der Homöopathie in Indien von ihrer Einführung bis zur ersten offiziellen Anerkennung 1937*. Stuttgart: Haug, 2010.

Poliakov, Léon. *The Aryan Myth: A History of Racist and Nationalistic Ideas in Europe*. London: Chatto & Windus Heinemann, 1974.

Pollock, Sheldon. "Deep Orientalism? Notes on Sanskrit and Power Beyond the Raj." In *Orientalism and the Post-Colonial Predicament: Perspectives on South Asia*, edited by Carol A. Breckenridge and Peter van der Veer, 76–133. Philadelphia: University of Pennsylvania Press, 1993.

Prakash, Gyan. *Mumbai Fables: History of an Enchanted City*. Princeton, NJ: Princeton University Press, 2010.

Prashad, Vijay. *The Karma of Brown Folk*. Minneapolis: University of Minnesota Press 2001.

———. *Untouchable Freedom: A Social History of a Dalit Community*. New Delhi: Oxford University Press, 2001.

Proctor, Robert. "Agnotology: A Missing Term to Describe the Cultural Production of Ignorance (and Its Study)." In *Agnotology: The Making and Unmaking of Ignorance*, edited by Robert Proctor and Londa Schiebinger, 1–35. Stanford, CA: Stanford University Press, 2008.

———. *The Nazi War on Cancer*. Princeton, NJ: Princeton University Press, 1999.

Prodöhl, Ines. "'A Miracle Bean': How Soy Conquered the West, 1909–1950." *Bulletin of the German Historical Institute* 46 (2010): 111–129.

Pruitt, Lisa Joy. *A Looking-Glass for Ladies: American Protestant Women and the Orient in the Nineteenth Century*. Macon, GA: Mercer University Press, 2005.

Puschner, Uwe, Walter Schmitz, and Justus H. Ulbricht, eds. *Handbuch zur "Völkischen Bewegung" 1871–1918*. Munich: K. G. Saur, 1996.

———. "Vorwort." In *Handbuch zur "Völkischen Bewegung" 1871–1918*, edited by Uwe Puschner, Walter Schmitz, and Justus H. Ulbricht, ix–xxvii. Munich: K. G. Saur, 1996.

———. "Mit Vollkornbrot und Nacktheit—Arbeit am völkischen Körper. Gustav Simons und Richard Ungewitter—Lebensreformer und völkische Weltanschauungsagenten." In *Avantgarden der Biopolitik. Jugendbewegung, Lebensreform und Strategien biologischer, Aufrüstung,'* edited by Karl Braun, Felix Linzner, and John Khairi-Taraki, 77–93. Göttingen: V&R Unipress, 2017.

Puskar-Pasewicz, Margaret. "Kitchen Sisters and Disagreeable Boys: Debates Over Meatless Diets in Nineteenth-Century Shaker Communities." In *Eating in Eden: Food and American Utopias*, edited by Etta M. Madden and Martha L. Finch, 109–124. Lincoln: University of Nebraska Press, 2006.

Putney, Clifford. *Muscular Christianity: Manhood and Sports in Protestant America, 1880–1920*. Cambridge, MA: Harvard University Press, 2001.

P. V., Sreebitha. "Sanskritization or Appropriation: Caste and Gender in 'Indian' Music and Dance." *Savari: Adivasi Bahujan and Dalit Women Conversing*, April 6, 2014. http://www.dalitweb.org/?p=2499.

Quataert, Donald. "Clothing Laws, State, and Society in the Ottoman Empire, 1720–1829." *International Journal of Middle East Studies* 29, no. 3 (1997): 403–425.

Quinchon-Caudal, Anne. "Les haras humains, ou comment arracher la vraie vie à l'abîme de la décadence." In *"Lebensreform." Die soziale Dynamik der politischen Ohnmacht / La dynamique sociale de l'impuissance politique*, edited by Marc Cluet and Catherine Repussard, 283–316. Tübingen: Narr Francke, 2013.

Radkau, Joachim. *Das Zeitalter der Nervosität: Deutschland zwischen Bismarck und Hitler*. Munich: Hanser, 1998.

Rahden, Till van. *Juden und andere Breslauer. Die Beziehungen zwischen Juden, Protestanten und Katholiken in einer deutschen Großstadt von 1860 bis 1925*. Göttingen: Vandenhoeck & Ruprecht, 2000.

"Ram Navami Sale of Raw Meat Banned in Bengaluru and Parts of Delhi Today." India .com, April 10, 2022. https://www.india.com/news/india/ram-navami-sale-of-raw-meat-banned-in-bengaluru-parts-of-delhi-today-5329549/.

Ramnath, Maia. *Haj to Utopia: How the Ghadar Movement Charted Global Radicalism and Attempted to Overthrow the British Empire*. Berkeley: University of California Press, 2011.

Ramusack, Barbara N. "Gaikwar, Sayaji Rao, Maharaja of Baroda (1863–1939)." In *Oxford Dictionary of National Biography*. Online edition: Oxford University Press, 2004. https://doi.org/10.1093/ref:odnb/30613.

Randeria, Shalini. "Geteilte Geschichte und verwobene Moderne." In *Zukunftsentwürfe. Ideen für eine Kultur der Veränderung*, edited by Jörn Rüsen, 87–96. Frankfurt/Main: Campus, 1999.

Rappe-Weber, Susanne. "'Hoch das Wandern!' Neue Gemeinschaftsformen im Wandervogel." In *Wanderland. Eine Reise durch die Geschichte des Wanderns*, edited by Claudia Selheim, Frank Matthias Kammel, and Thomas Brehm, 134–141. Nuremberg: Verlag des Germanischen Nationalmuseums, 2018.

# BIBLIOGRAPHY

Rawat, Ramnarayan S. "Colonial Archive vs. Colonial Sociology: Writing Dalit History." In *Dalit Studies*, edited by Ramnarayan Rawat and K. Satyanarayana, 53–74. Durham, NC: Duke University Press, 2016.

Ray, Utsa. *Culinary Culture in Colonial India: A Cosmopolitan Platter and the Middle-Class*. Delhi: Cambridge University Press, 2015.

———. "Eating 'Modernity': Changing Dietary Practices in Colonial Bengal." *Modern Asian Studies* 46, no. 3 (2012): 703–729.

Recknagel, Marion. "Musikstadt Leizig—die Silberne Zeit." In *Geschichte Der Stadt Leipzig*. Vol. 3, *Vom Wiener Kongress Bis Zum Ersten Weltkrieg*, edited by Susanne Schötz, 733–741. Leipzig: Leipziger Universitätsverlag, 2017.

Reed, Christopher Robert. *Black Chicago's First Century*. Vol. 1, *1833–1900*. Columbia: University of Missouri Press, 2005.

Reindl-Kiel, Hedda. "The Chickens of Paradise: Official Meals in the Mid-Seventeenth Century Ottoman Palace." In *The Illuminated Table, the Prosperous House: Food and Shelter in Ottoman Material Culture*, edited by Suraiya Faroqhi and Christoph K. Neumann, 59–88. Würzburg: Ergon, 2003.

Reiß, Ansgar. *Radikalismus und Exil. Gustav Struve und die Demokratie in Deutschland und Amerika*. Stuttgart: Franz Steiner, 2004.

Reith, Reinhold. "'Hurrah die Butter ist alle!' 'Fettlücke' und 'Eiweißlücke' im Dritten Reich." In *Erfahrung der Moderne. Festschrift für Roman Sandgruber zum 60. Geburtstag*, edited by Michael Pammer and Hertha Neiß, 403–425. Stuttgart: Steiner, 2007.

Rendall, Jane. "Gender, Philanthropy, and Civic Identities in Edinburgh, 1795–1830." In *The Routledge History Handbook of Gender and the Urban Experience*, edited by Deborah Simonton, 209–220. London: Routledge, 2017.

Reynolds, Gabriel Said. "The Sufi Approach to Food: A Case Study of Ādāb." *Muslim World* 90, no. 1 (2000): 198–217.

Riello, Giorgio. *Cotton: The Fabric that Made the Modern World*. Cambridge: Cambridge University Press, 2013.

Riffenburgh, Beau. *The Myth of the Explorer: The Press, Sensationalism, and Geographical Discovery*. London: Belhaven Press, 1993.

Rindlisbacher, Stefan. "Jugendzeitschriften zwischen Wandervogel und Lebensreform (1904–1924)." In *Let's Historize It! Jugendmedien im 20. Jahrhundert*, edited by Aline Maldener and Clemens Zimmermann, 37–60. Wien: Böhlau, 2018.

———. *Lebensreform in der Schweiz (1850–1950). Vegetarisch essen, nackt baden und Im Grünen wohnen*. Berlin: Peter Lang, 2022.

———. "Popularisierung und Etablierung der Freikörperkultur in der Schweiz (1900–1930)." *Schweizerische Zeitschrift für Geschichte* 65, no. 3 (2015): 393–413.

Ritterhouse, Jennifer Lynn. *Growing Up Jim Crow: How Black and White Southern Children Learned Race*. Chapel Hill: University of North California Press, 2006.

Robb, Peter. "The Challenge of Gau Mata: British Policy and Religious Change in India, 1880–1916." *Modern Asian Studies* 20, no. 2 (1986): 285–319.

Roberts, Mary. *Intimate Outsiders: The Harem in Ottoman and Orientalist Art and Travel Literature* Durham, NC: Duke University Press, 2007.

Robinson, Cedric J. *Black Marxism*. London: Zed Press, 1983.

Rodrigues, Hillary. "Durgā." In *Brill's Encyclopedia of Hinduism Online*, edited by Knut A. Jacobsen, Helene Basu, Angelika Malinar, and Vasudha Narayanan, 2018. http://dx.doi.org/10.1163/2212-5019_BEH_COM_1030180.

Roscher, Mieke. *Ein Königreich für Tiere. Die Geschichte der britischen Tierrechtsbewegung*. Marburg: Tectum, 2009.

Rose, Jenny. *Zoroastrianism. An Introduction*. London: Tauris, 2011.

Rosenberg, Philippe. "Thomas Tryon and the Seventeenth-Century Dimensions of Antislavery." *William and Mary Quarterly*, 3rd ser., 61, no. 4 (2004): 609–642.

Rosendorf, Neil. "Expositions." In *The Palgrave Dictionary of Transnational History*, edited by Akira Iriye and Pierre-Yves Saunier, 370–376. Houndmills, UK: Palgrave Macmillan, 2009.

Ross, Alice. "Health and Diet in 19th-Century America: A Food Historian's Point of View." *Historical Archaeology* 27, no. 2 (1993): 42–56.

Ross, Chad. *Naked Germany: Health, Race and the Nation*. Oxford: Berg, 2005.

Röther, Christian. "Warum Verschwörungsideologien die Demokratie gefährden." *Deutschlandfunk*, April 25, 2020. https://www.deutschlandfunk.de/proteste-gegen-corona-massnahmen-warum.724.de.html?dram:article_id=482935.

Rothschuh, Karl Eduard. *Naturheilbewegung, Reformbewegung, Alternativbewegung*. Stuttgart: Hippokrates-Verl., 1983.

Roy, Parama. *Alimentary Tracts: Appetites, Aversions, and the Postcolonial*. Durham, NC: Duke University Press, 2010.

———. "A Dietetics of Virile Emergency." *Women's Studies International Forum* 14, no. 4 (2014): 255–265.

———. "Gothic Vegetarianism." In *Food and Literature*, edited by Gitanjali G. Shahani, 75–96. Cambridge: Cambridge University Press, 2018.

———. "Meat-Eating, Masculinity, and Renunciation in India: A Gandhian Grammar of Diet." *Gender & History* 14, no. 1 (2002): 62–91.

———. "Vegetarianism." In *Keywords in South Asian Studies*, edited by Gita Dharampal-Frick, Monika Kirloskar-Steinbach, Rachel Dwyer, and Jahnavi Phalkey, 272–275. New Delhi: Oxford University Press, 2015.

Rubiés, Joao-Pau. "Oriental Despotism and European Orientalism: Botero to Montesquieu." *Journal of Early Modern History* 9, no. 1 (2005): 109–180.

Rudbøg, Tim. "Point Loma, Theosophy, and Katherine Tingley." In *Handbook of the Theosophical Current*, edited by Olav Hammer and Mikael Rothstein, 51–73. Leiden: Brill, 2013.

Rüstau, Hiltrud. "The Ramakrishna Mission: Its Female Aspect." In *Gurus and Their Followers: New Religious Reform Movements in Colonial India*, edited by Anthony Copley, 83–103. New Delhi: Oxford University Press, 2000.

Rydell, Robert W. *All the World's a Fair: Visions of Empire at American International Expositions, 1876–1916*. Chicago: University of Chicago Press, 1984.

———. "A Cultural Frankenstein? The Chicago World's Columbian Exposition of 1893." In *Grand Illusions: Chicago's World's Fair of 1893*, edited by Neil Harris, Wim de Wit, James Gilbert, and Robert W. Rydell, 143–170. Chicago: Chicago Historical Society, 1993.

———. "World's Columbian Exposition." In Encyclopedia of Chicago, Chicago Historical Society, accessed March 1, 2021. http://encyclopedia.chicagohistory.org/pages/1386.html.

BIBLIOGRAPHY

Saavedra, Beatrix Martinez. "Shaping the Community: Hindu Nationalist Imagination in Gujarat, 1800–1950." PhD diss., University of Warwick, 2013.
Sachsenmaier, Dominic, ed. *Global Entanglements of a Man Who Never Traveled: A Seventeenth-Century Chinese Christian and His Conflicted Worlds*. New York: Columbia University Press, 2018.
——. *Global Perspectives on Global History: Theories and Approaches in a Connected World*. Cambridge: Cambridge University Press, 2011.
Said, Edward. *Orientalism*. London: Penguin, 1978.
Samancı, Özge. "Culinary Consumption Patterns of the Ottoman Elite During the First Half of the Nineteenth Century." In *The Illuminated Table, the Prosperous House: Food and Shelter in Ottoman Material Culture*, edited by Suraiya Faroqhi and Christoph K. Neumann, 161–184. Würzburg: Ergon, 2003.
Samanta, Samiparna. *Meat, Mercy, and Morality: Animals and Humanitarianism in Colonial Bengal, 1850–1920*. New Delhi: Oxford University Press, 2021.
Samanta, Suchitra. "The 'Self-Animal' and Divine Digestion: Goat Sacrifice to the Goddess Kali in Bengal." *Journal of Asian Studies* 53, no. 3 (1994): 779–803.
Samson, Lela. *Rukmini Devi: A Life*. New Delhi: Penguin, 2010.
Santucci, James A. "Theosophy." In *The Cambridge Companion to New Religious Movements*, edited by Olav Hammer and Mikael Rothstein, 231–246. Cambridge: Cambridge University Press, 2012.
Saraiva, Tiago. *Fascist Pigs: Technoscientific Organisms and the History of Fascism*. Cambridge, MA: MIT Press, 2018.
Sarasin, Philipp. *Reizbare Maschinen. Eine Geschichte des Körpers 1765–1914*. Frankfurt/Main: Suhrkamp, 2001.
Sarda, Har Bilas. *Dayanand Sarasvati: World Teacher*. Ajmer: Vedic Yantralaya, 1946.
Saroja, G. V. "The Contribution of Anagarika Devamitta Dharmapāla to the Revival of Buddhism in India." In *Buddhist Themes in Modern Indian Literature*, edited by J. Parthasarathi, 27–38. Madras: Institute of Asian Studies, 1992.
Saßmannshausen, Christian. "Eating Up: Food Consumption and Social Status in Late Ottoman Greater Syria." In *Food as a Cultural Signifier: Perspectives on the Middle East and Beyond*, edited by Kirill Dmitriev, Julia Hauser, and Bilal Orfali, 27–49. Leiden: Brill, 2020.
Satter, Beryl. *Each Mind a Kingdom: American Women, Sexual Purity, and the New Thought Movement, 1875–1920*. Berkeley: University of California Press, 1999.
Sax, Boria. *Animals in the Third Reich: Pets, Scapegoats, and the Holocaust*. New York: Continuum, 2000.
Schad, Martha. *Sie liebten den Führer. Wie Frauen Hitler verehrten*. Munich: Herbig, 2009.
Schaffner, Anna Katharina. *Modernism and Perversion: Sexual Deviance in Sexology and Literature, 1850–1930*. Houndmills, UK: Palgrave Macmillan, 2012.
Schayegh, Cyrus. "Eugenics in Interwar Iran." In *The Oxford Handbook of the History of Eugenics*, edited by Philippa Levine and Alison Bashford, 449–461. Oxford: Oxford University Press, 2010.
Schlie, Ulrich. "Das Reichsministerium für Ernährung und Landwirtschaft in der Zeit des Nationalsozialismus." In *Agrarpolitik im 20. Jahrhundert. Das Bundesministerium für Ernährung und Landwirtschaft und seine Vorgänger*, edited by Joachim Bitterlich, Gustavo Corni, Andreas Dornheim, Friedrich Kießling, Daniela Münkel, and Horst Möller, 105–261. Berlin: De Gruyter Oldenbourg, 2020.

Schmemann, Alexander. *Great Lent*. Crestwood, NY: St. Vladimir's Seminary Press, 1974.

Schmitz-Berning, Cornelia. "Gleichschaltung." In *Vokabular des Nationalsozialismus*, edited by Cornelia Schmitz-Berning, 277–280. Berlin: De Gruyter, 2010.

Schmitz, Walter, and Uwe Schneider. "Völkische Semantik im George-Kreis." In *Handbuch zur "Völkischen Bewegung" 1871–1918*, edited by Uwe Puschner, Walter Schmitz, and Justus H. Ulbricht, 711–746. Munich: K. G. Saur, 1996.

Schneider, Uwe. "Nacktkultur im Kaiserreich." In *Handbuch zur "Völkischen Bewegung" 1871–1918*, edited by Uwe Puschner, Walter Schmitz, and Justus H. Ulbricht, 411–435. Munich: K. G. Saur, 1996.

Schor, Esther. *Bridge of Words: Esperanto and the Dream of a Universal Language*. New York: Metropolitan Books, 2016.

Schuster, David G. *Neurasthenic Nation: America's Search for Health, Comfort, and Happiness, 1869–1920*. New Brunswick, NJ: Rutgers University Press, 2011.

Schuster, Marina. "Fidus—ein Gesinnungskünstler der völkischen Kulturbewegung." In *Handbuch zur "Völkischen Bewegung" 1871–1918*, edited by Uwe Puschner, Walter Schmitz, and Justus H. Ulbricht, 634–650. Munich: K. G. Saur, 1996.

———. "Lichtgebet. Die Ikone der Lebensreform- und Jugendbewegung." In *Das Jahrhundert der Bilder (1900–1949)*, edited by Gerhard Paul, 140–147. Göttingen: Vandenhoeck & Ruprecht, 2009.

Schwab, Andreas. *Monte Verità—Sanatorium der Sehnsucht*. Zurich: Orell Füssli, 2003.

Schwarz, Richard W. "Dr. John Harvey Kellogg as a Social Gospel Practitioner." *Journal of the Illinois State Historical Society* 57, no. 1 (1964): 5–22.

Seager, Richard Hughes. *The World's Parliament of Religions: The East/West Encounter, Chicago, 1893*. Bloomington: Indiana University Press, 2009.

Sedgwick, Mark J. *Sufism: The Essentials*. Cairo: American University in Cairo Press, 2000.

———. *Western Sufism: From the Abbasids to the New Age*. Oxford: Oxford University Press, 2017.

Seegers, Lu. "Filmstars und Reichtum im 'Dritten Reich.' (Auto-)Biografische Repräsentationen und Narrativ." In *Reichtum in Deutschland: Akteure, Räume und Lebenswelten im 20. Jahrhundert*, edited by Eva Maria Gajek, Anne Kurr, and Lu Seegers, 201–225. Göttingen: Wallstein, 2019.

Segers, Yves, Jan Bieleman, and Erik Buyst, eds. *Exploring the Food Chain: Food Production and Food Processing in Western Europe, 1850–1990*. Turnhout, BE: Brepols, 2009.

———. "Food Systems in the Nineteenth Century." In *A Cultural History of Food*. Vol. 5, *In the Age of Empire*, edited by Martin Bruegel, 49–66. London: Berg, 2012.

Sen, Amiya Prosad. *Ramakrishna Paramahamsa: The Sadhaka of Dakshineswar*. Delhi: Penguin, 2010.

Seneviratne, H. L. "Food Essence and the Essence of Experience." In *The Eternal Food: Gastronomic Ideas and Experiences of Hindus and Buddhists*, edited by Ravindra S. Khare, 179–200. Delhi: Sri Satguru Publications, 1992.

Sengoopta, Chandak. *Otto Weininger: Sex, Science, and Self in Imperial Vienna*. Chicago: University of Chicago Press, 2000.

Sengupta, Jayanta. "Nation on a Platter: The Culture and Politics of Food and Cuisine in Colonial Bengal." *Modern Asian Studies* 44, no. 1 (2010): 81–98.

"Several Students Injured at Delhi's JNU in Scuffle Allegedly Over Serving Meat on Ram Navami." Scroll.in, April 11, 2022. https://scroll.in/latest/1021553/several-students-injured-at-delhis-jnu-in-scuffle-allegedly-over-serving-meat-on-ram-navami.
Shaked, Shaul. "The Yasna Ritual in Pahlavi Literature." In *Zoroastrian Rituals in Context*, edited by Michael Stausberg, 333–344. Leiden: Brill, 2004.
Sharma, Jyortirmaya. "Digesting the 'Other': Hindu Nationalism and the Muslims in India." In *Political Hinduism: The Religious Imagination in Public Spheres*, edited by Vinay Lal, 150–72. New Delhi: Oxford University Press, 2009.
———. *Hindutva: Exploring the Idea of Hindu Nationalism*. New Delhi: Harper Collins, 2011.
Shope, Bradley G. *American Popular Music in Britain's Raj*. Rochester, NY: University of Rochester Press, 2016.
Shprintzen, Adam D. *The Vegetarian Crusade: The Rise of an American Reform Movement, 1817–1921*. Chapel Hill: University of North Carolina Press, 2013.
Siegel, Benjamin Robert. *Hungry Nation: Food, Famine, and the Making of Modern India*. Cambridge: Cambridge University Press, 2018.
Siemann, Wolfram. *Die deutsche Revolution von 1848/49*. Frankfurt/Main: Suhrkamp, 1985.
Silberman, Marsha. "The Perfect Storm: Late Nineteenth-Century Chicago Sex Radicals: Moses Harman, Ida Craddock, Alice Stockham and the Comstock Obscenity Laws." *Journal of the Illinois State Historical Society* 102, nos. 3–4 (2009): 324–367.
Simek, Rudolf. *Lexikon der Germanischen Mythologie*. 3rd ed. Stuttgart: Krömer, 2006.
Simonow, Joanna. "The Rise and Demise of Multi-Purpose Food in India: Food Technology, Population Control and Nutritional Development in the Post-War Era, c. 1944–66." *South Asia: Journal of South Asian Studies* 40 (2021): 167–184.
Singer, Amy. *Charity in Islamic Societies*. Cambridge: Cambridge University Press, 2008.
———. "The 'Michelin Guide' to Public Kitchens in the Ottoman Empire." In *Starting with Food: Culinary Approaches to Ottoman History*, edited by Amy Singer, 49–68. Princeton, NJ: Wiener, 2011.
Singh, Joginder. "Nāmdhārī." In *Brill's Encyclopedia of Sikhism*. Vol. 1, *History Literature Society Beyond Punjab*, edited by Knut A. Jacobsen, Gurinder Singh Mann, Kristina Myrvold, and Eleanor Nesbitt, 359–367. Leiden: Brill, 2017.
Singleton, Mark. "Modern Yoga." In *Brill's Encyclopedia of Hinduism*. Vol. 3, *Religious Specialists—Religious Traditions—Philosophy*, edited by Knut A. Jacobson, Helene Basu, Angelika Malinar, and Vasudha Narayanan, 782–188. Leiden: Brill, 2011.
———. *Yoga Body: The Origins of Modern Posture Practice*. Oxford: Oxford Academic, 2010.
Sinha, Mrinalini. *Colonial Masculinity: The "Manly Englishman" and the "Effeminate Bengali" in the Late Nineteenth Century*. Manchester: Manchester University Press, 1995.
Slate, Nico. *Gandhi's Search for the Perfect Diet*. Seattle: University of Washington Press, 2019.
Slim, Souad, and Hasan Abiad. *The Banquet of Old Times: Cuisine of Al-Kurah / Al-Ma'duba 'ayām Zamān. Al-Matbakh Al-Kūrānī*. Balamand, LB: University of Balamand, 2012.

Sluga, Glenda. *Internationalism in the Age of Nationalism.* Philadelphia: University of Pennsylvania Press, 2013.

Sluga, Glenda, and Patricia Clavin, eds. *Internationalisms: A Twentieth-Century History.* Cambridge: Cambridge University Press, 2017.

Smethurst, Paul. *The Bicycle: Towards a Global History.* Houndmills, UK: Palgrave Macmillan, 2015.

Smith, Alison K. "National Cuisines." In *The Oxford Handbook of Food History,* edited by Jeffrey M. Pilcher, 444–460. Oxford: Oxford University Press, 2012.

Smith, Helmut W. *German Nationalism and Religious Conflict: Culture, Ideology, Politics, 1870–1914.* Princeton, NJ: Princeton University Press, 1995.

———, ed. *Protestants, Catholics and Jews in Germany, 1800–1914.* Oxford: Berg, 2001.

Smith-Rosenberg, Carol. "A Richer and a Gentler Sex." *Social Research* 53, no. 2 (1986): 283–309.

Snead, James, Donald McVicker, Curtis M. Hinsley, and David R. Wilcox, eds. *Coming of Age in Chicago: The 1893 World's Fair and the Coalescence of American Anthropology.* Lincoln: University of Nebraska Press, 2016.

Sobal, Jeffery. "Food System Globalization, Eating Transformations, and Nutrition Transitions." In *Food in Global History,* edited by Raymond Grew, 186–213. Boulder, CO: Westview Press, 1999.

Sohi, Seema. *Echoes of Mutiny: Race, Surveillance, and Anticolonialism in North America.* New York: Oxford University Press, 2014.

Spang, Rebecca L. *The Invention of the Restaurant: Paris and Modern Gastronomic Culture.* Cambridge, MA: Harvard University Press, 2001.

Spary, Emma C. *Eating the Enlightenment: Food and the Sciences in Paris.* Chicago: University of Chicago Press, 2012.

———. *Feeding France: New Sciences of Food, 1760–1815.* Cambridge: Cambridge University Press, 2014.

Specht, Joshua. *Red Meat Republic: A Hoof-to-Table History of How Beef Changed America.* Princeton, NJ: Princeton University Press, 2019.

Spencer, Colin. *The Heretic's Feast: A History of Vegetarianism.* Hanover, ME: University Press of New England, 1995.

Spiekermann, Uwe. "Dangerous Meat? German-American Quarrels Over Pork and Beef, 1870–1900." *Bulletin of the German Historical Institute* 46 (2010): 93–110.

———. *Künstliche Kost. Ernährung in Deutschland, 1840 bis Heute.* Göttingen: Vandenhoeck & Ruprecht, 2018.

———. "Vollkorn für die Führer. Zur Geschichte der Vollkornbrotpolitik im 'Dritten Reich.'" *Zeitschrift für Sozialgeschichte des 20. und 21. Jahrhunderts* 16, no. 1 (2001): 91–128.

Sprondel, Walter M. "Kulturelle Modernisierung durch antimodernistischen Protest: Der lebensreformerische Vegetarismus." *Kölner Zeitschrift für Soziologie* 27 (1986): 314–330.

Srinivas, M. N. *The Cohesive Role of Sanskritization and Other Essays.* Delhi: Oxford University Press, 1989.

Stahl, Christine. *Sehnsucht Brot. Essen und Hungern im Kz-Lagersystem Mauthausen.* Wien: Edition Mauthausen, 2010.

Staiano-Daniels, Lucia. "The Melancholy of the Thinking Racist: India and the Ambiguities of Race in the Work of Hans F.-K. Günther." In *Transcultural Encounters*

BIBLIOGRAPHY

*Between Germany and India*, edited by Joanne Miyang Cho, Eric Kurlander, and Douglas T. McGetchin, 170–185. Abingdon, UK: Routledge, 2014.
Staples, James. *Sacred Cows and Chicken Manchurian: The Everyday Politics of Eating Meat in India*. Seattle: University of Washington Press, 2020.
Stausberg, Michael. *Die Religion Zarathushtras*. Vol. 2. Stuttgart: Kohlhammer, 2004.
———. "Hinduism and Zoroastrianism." In *Brill Encyclopedia of Hinduism*, edited by Knut A. Jacobsen, Angelika Malinar, and Helene Basu, 605–615. Leiden: Brill, 2012.
———. "Para-Zoroastrians: Memetic Traditions and Appropriations." In *Parsis in India and the Diaspora*, edited by John R. Hinnells and Alan Williams, 236–254. London: Routledge, 2007.
Steege, Paul. *Black Market, Cold War: Everyday Life in Berlin, 1946–1949*. Cambridge: Cambridge University Press, 2007.
Stolte, Carolien. "'The Asiatic Hour': New Perspectives on the Asian Relations Conference, New Delhi, 1947." In *The Non-Aligned Movement and the Cold War: Delhi—Bandung—Belgrade*, edited by Natasa Miskovic, Harald Fischer-Tiné, and Nada Boskovska, 57–75. London: Routledge, 2014.
Stoler, Ann Laura. *Carnal Knowledge and Imperial Power: Race and the Intimate in Colonial Rule*. Berkeley: University of California Press, 2002.
Stoler, Ann Laura, and Frederick Cooper. "Between Metropole and Colony: Rethinking a Research Agenda." In *Tensions of Empire*, edited by Anna Laura Stoler and Frederick Cooper, 1–56. Berkeley: University of California Press, 1997.
Stoneman, Richard. "Naked Philosophers: The Brahmans in the Alexander Historians and the Alexander Romance." *Classical Quarterly* 44, no. 2 (1995): 94–114.
———. "Who Are the Brahmans? Indian Lore and Cynic Doctrine in Palladius' De Bragmanibus and Its Models." *Classical Quarterly* 44, no. 2 (1994): 500–510.
Streets, Heather. *Martial Races: The Military, Race, and Masculinity in British Imperial Culture, 1857–1914*. Manchester: Manchester University Press, 2004.
Stuart, Tristram. *The Bloodless Revolution: Radical Vegetarians and the Discovery of India*. London: Harper, 2006.
Subrahmanyam, Sanjay. "Connected Histories: Notes Towards a Reconfiguration of Early Modern Eurasia." *Modern Asian Studies* 31 (1997): 735–762.
Sundaram, Vivan, and Deepak Ananth. *Umrao Singh Sher-Gil: His Misery and His Manuscript*. New Delhi: Photoink, 2001.
Sutton, Katie. "Representing the 'Third Sex': Cultural Translations of the Sexological Encounter in Early Twentieth-Century Germany." In *Sexology and Translation: Cultural and Scientific Encounters across the Modern World*, edited by Heike Bauer, 53–71. Philadelphia: Temple University Press, 2015.
Syed, Renate. "Das heilige Essen—Das heilige Essen. Religiöse Aspekte des Speiseverhaltens im Hinduismus." In *Die Religionen und das Essen*, edited by Perry Schmidt-Leukel, 97–144. Munich: Diederichs, 2000.
Tanner, Jakob. *Fabrikmahlzeit: Ernährungswissenschaft, Industriearbeit und Volksernährung in der Schweiz 1890–1950*. Zurich: Chronos, 1999.
Tejani, Shabnum. "Cow Protection, Hindu Identity and the Politics of Hurt in India, c. 1890–2019." *Emotions: History, Culture, Society* 3, no. 1 (2019): 136–157.
———. *Indian Secularism: A Social and Intellectual History 1890–1950*. Bloomington: Indiana University Press, 2008.

Tetzlaff, Stefan. "'A New Passage to India?' Westdeutsche Außenwirtschaftspolitik und Wirtschaftsbeziehungen mit Indien, ca. 1950–72." In *Dekolonisierungsgewinner. Deutsche Außenpolitik und Außenwirtschaftsbeziehungen im Zeitalter des Kalten Krieges*, edited by Christian Kleinschmidt and Dieter Ziegler, 191–209. Berlin: De Gruyter Oldenbourg, 2018.

Teuteberg, Hans Jürgen. "The Birth of the Modern Consumer Age: Food Innovations from 1800." In *Food: The History of Taste*, edited by Paul H. Freedman, 233–262. London: Thames & Hudson, 2007.

———. *Die Rolle des Fleischextrakts für die Ernährungswissenschaften und den Aufstieg der Suppenindustrie. Kleine Geschichte der Fleischbrühe*. Stuttgart: Steiner, 1990.

Thakur, Vineet. "An Asian Drama: The Asian Relations Conference, 1947." *International History Review* 41, no. 3 (2019): 673–695.

Thapar, Romila. *Early India: From the Origins to AD 1300*. London: Penguin, 2002.

———. "The Historiography of the Concept of 'Aryan.'" In *India: Historical Beginnings and the Concept of the Aryan*, edited by Romila Thapar, Jonathan Mark Kenoyer, Madhav M. Deshpande, and Shereen Ratnagar, 1–40. Delhi: National Book Trust, 2006.

———. *Somanatha: The Many Voices of a History*. London: Verso, 2005.

Thomas, Elizabeth. "Communities in Conflict: Fighting for the 'Sacred Cow.'" *International Journal of Social Sciences and Humanities* 2, no. 1 (2013): 131–147.

Tooze, Adam. *The Wages of Destruction: The Making and Breaking of the Nazi Economy*. London: Allen Lane, 2006.

Treitel, Corinna. *Eating Nature in Modern Germany: Food, Agriculture, and Environment, c. 1870 to 2000*. Cambridge: Cambridge University Press, 2017.

Trépanier, Nicolas. "Starting Without Food: Fasting and the Early Mawlawi Order." In *Starting with Food: Culinary Approaches to Ottoman History*, edited by Amy Singer, 1–22. Princeton, NJ: Wiener, 2011.

Trepp, Anne-Charlott. *Sanfte Männlichkeit und selbständige Weiblichkeit: Frauen und Männer im Hamburger Bürgertum zwischen 1770 und 1840*. Göttingen: Vandenhoeck & Ruprecht, 1996.

Trevithick, Alan. *The Revival of Buddhist Pilgrimage at Bodh Gaya (1811–1949): Anagarika Dharmapala and the Mahabodhi Temple*. Delhi: Motilal Banarsidass Publ., 2006.

———. "The Theosophical Society and Its Subaltern Acolytes (1880–1986)." *Marburg Journal of Religion* 13, no. 1 (2008): 1–32.

Tripathi, Amales. *Indian National Congress and the Struggle for Freedom*. New Delhi: Oxford University Press, 2014.

Tumber, Catherine. *American Feminism and the Birth of New Age Spirituality: Searching for the Higher Self, 1875–1915*. Lanham, MD: Rowman and Littlefield, 2002.

Turda, Marius. *Modernism and Eugenics*. New York: Palgrave Macmillan, 2010.

Twigg, Julia. "Food for Thought: Purity and Vegetarianism." *Religion* 9, no. 1 (1979): 13–35.

———. "The Vegetarian Movement in England, 1847–1981." PhD diss., London School of Economics, 1981.

Urban, Hugh B. "'India's Darkest Heart': Kālī in the Colonial Imagination." In *Encountering Kālī: In the Margins, at the Center, in the West*, edited by Rachel Fell McDermott, 169–195. Berkeley: University of California Press, 2003.

BIBLIOGRAPHY

Vahdat, Farzin. *God and Juggernaut: Iran's Intellectual Encounter with Modernity*. Syracuse, NY: Syracuse University Press, 2002.
Van den Bosch, Lourens P. "The Ultimate Journey: Satī and Widowhood in India." In *Between Poverty and the Pyre: Moments in the History of Widowhood*, edited by Jan Bremmer and Lourens P. Van den Bosch, 171–203. London: Routledge, 1995.
Vantard, Cécile. "Le végétarisme 'occidental-oriental' de Gustav Struve." In *La fascination de l'Inde en Allemagne*, edited by Marc Cluet, 155–163. Rennes, FR: Presses universitaires de Rennes, 2004.
Varma, Nitin. *Coolies of Capitalism: Assam Tea and the Making of Coolie Labour*. Berlin: De Gruyter Oldenburg, 2017.
Veer, Peter van der. *Imperial Encounters: Religion and Modernity in India and Britain*. Princeton, NJ: Princeton University Press, 2001.
———. *Religious Nationalism: Hindus and Muslims in India*. Berkeley: University of California Press, 1994.
Venters, Louis. *No Jim Crow Church: The Origins of South Carolina's Bahá'í Community*. Gainesville: University Press of Florida, 2015.
Viswanath, Rupa. "Caste and Untouchability." In *Hinduism in the Modern World*, edited by Brian Hatcher, 257–274. London: Routledge, 2016.
———. "Dalits/Ex-Untouchables." In *Brill's Encyclopedia of Hinduism Online*, edited by Knut A. Jacobson, Helene Basu, Angelika Malinar, and Vasudha Narayanan. Leiden: Brill, 2018. http://dx.doi.org/10.1163/2212-5019_BEH_COM_9000000009.
———. *The Pariah Problem: Caste, Religion, and the Social in Modern India*. New York: Columbia University Press, 2014.
Viswanathan, Gauri. "'Have Animals Souls?' Theosophy and the Suffering Body." *Publications of the Modern Language Association of America* 126, no. 3 (2011): 440–447.
———. *Outside the Fold: Conversion, Modernity, and Belief*. Princeton, NJ: Princeton University Press, 1998.
———. "Theosophical Society." In *Brill's Encyclopedia of Hinduism*. Vol. 5, *Religious Symbols, Hinduism and Migration, Contemporary Communities Outside South Asia, Some Modern Religious Groups and Teachers*, edited by Knut A. Jacobson, 679–689. Leiden: Brill, 2013.
Vorholt, Udo. *Die politische Theorie Leonard Nelsons. Eine Fallstudie zum Verhältnis von philosophisch-politischer Theorie und konkret-politischer Praxis*. Baden-Baden: Nomos, 1998.
Wagner, Christoph. "Johannes Itten. Leitmotive einer Künstlerbiographie." In *Johannes Itten. Alles in Einem—Alles im Sein*, edited by Ernest W. Uthemann and Christoph Wagner, 11–79. Ostfildern-Ruit: Hatje Cantz, 2003.
———. "Johannes Itten und die Esoterik: Ein Schlüssel zum frühen Bauhaus?" In *Esoterik am Bauhaus. Eine Revision der Moderne?*, edited by Christoph Wagner, 108–149. Regensburg: Schnell & Steiner, 2009.
———. "Zwischen Lebensreform und Esoterik: Johannes Ittens Weg ans Bauhaus in Weimar." In *Das Bauhaus und die Esoterik*, edited by Christoph Wagner, 65–77. Bielefeld: Hatje Cantz, 2005.
Wagner, Kim A. "Confessions of a Skull: Phrenology and Colonial Knowledge in Early Nineteenth-Century India." *History Workshop Journal* 69 (2010): 27–51.

Waines, David, and Manuela Marín. "Muzawwar: Counterfeit Fare for Fasts and Fevers." In *Patterns of Everyday Life*, edited by David Waines, 303–15. Aldershot, UK: Ashgate Variorum, 2002.

Waldau, Paul, and Kimberley Patton, eds. *A Communion of Subjects: Animals in Religion, Science, and Ethics*. New York: Columbia University Press, 2006.

Wallach, Jennifer Jensen. *Every Nation Has Its Dish: Black Bodies and Black Food in Twentieth-Century America*. Chapel Hill: University of North Carolina Press, 2019.

Warren, Wilson J. *Meat Makes People Powerful: A Global History of the Modern Era*. Iowa City: University of Iowa Press, 2018.

Weber, Thomas. *Going Native: Gandhi's Relationship with Western Women*. New Delhi: Lotus, 2011.

Wedderburn, William. *Allan Octavian Hume, C.B., "Father of the Indian National Congress," 1829 to 1912*. London: T. Fisher Unwin, 1913.

Wedemeyer-Kolwe, Bernd. *Aufbruch. Die Lebensreform in Deutschland*. Mainz: Philipp von Zabern, 2017.

———. *"Der Neue Mensch": Körperkultur im Kaiserreich und in der Weimarer Republik*. Würzburg: Königshausen & Neumann, 2004.

———. "The Reception of Yoga in Alternative Cultures at the Beginning of the 20th Centuries." In *On the Paths of Enlightenment: The Myth of India in Western Culture, 1808–2017*, edited by Elio Schenini, 258–275. Geneva: Skira, 2017.

Weed, Eric Arden. *The Religion of White Supremacy in the United States*. Lanham, MD: Lexington, 2017.

Wehr, Hans. *Arabisches Wörterbuch für die Schriftsprache der Gegenwart. Arabisch—Deutsch*. 5th ed. Wiesbaden: Harassowitz, 1989.

Weinreb, Alice Autumn. *Modern Hungers: Food and Power in Twentieth-Century Germany*. New York: Oxford University Press, 2017.

Welter, Barbara. "The Cult of True Womanhood: 1820–1860." *American Quarterly* 18, no. 2 (1966): 151–174.

Wennberg-Hilger, Kajsa Katharina. "Das seuchenhafte Auftreten von Lepra in einigen Küstenregionen West-Norwegens im 19. Jahrhundert mit einem ergänzenden Bericht über die entsprechende Situation in Schweden." PhD diss., University of Bonn, medical thesis, 2011.

Wensinck, A. J., and J. Sadan. "Khamr." In *Encyclopaedia of Islam*, 2nd ed., edited by P. Bearman, Th. Bianquis, C. E. Bosworth, E. van Donzel, and W. P. Heinrichs. Leiden: Brill, 2012. http://dx-1doi-1org-10078da2907cd.erf.sbb.spk-berlin.de/10.1163/1573-3912_islam_COM_0490.

Werner, Frank. "'Noch härter, noch kälter, noch mitleidloser.' Soldatische Männlichkeit im Deutschen Vernichtungskrieg 1941–1944." In *Männlichkeitskonstruktionen im Nationalsozialismus. Formen, Funktionen und Wirkungsmacht von Geschlechterkonstruktionen im Nationalsozialismus und ihre Reflexion in der pädagogischen Praxis*, edited by Anette Dietrich and Ljiljana Heise, 45–63. Frankfurt/Main: Peter Lang, 2013.

Werner, Michael, and Bénédicte Zimmermann. "Beyond Comparison: Histoire Croisée and the Challenge of Reflexivity." *History and Theory* 41, no. 1 (2006): 30–50.

Wessinger, Catherine. "Hinduism Arrives in America: The Vedanta Movement and the Self-Realization Fellowship." In *America's Alternative Religions*, edited by Timothy MIller, 173–190. Albany: State University of New York Press, 1995.

## BIBLIOGRAPHY

Whitmore, Bruce W. *The Dawning Place: The Building of a Temple, the Forging of the North American Bahá'i Community.* Wilmette, IL: Bahá'i Publishing Trust, 1984.

Whorton, James C. "Muscular Vegetarianism: The Debate Over Diet and Athletic Performance in the Progressive Era." *Journal of Sport History* 8, no. 2 (1981): 58–75.

Wigger, Iris. *The "Black Horror on the Rhine": Intersections of Race, Nation, Gender and Class in 1920s Germany.* London: Palgrave Macmillan, 2017.

Wildenthal, Lora. *German Women for Empire, 1884–1945.* Durham, NC: Duke University Press, 2001.

Wildt, Michael. *Am Beginn der "Konsumgesellschaft." Mangelerfahrung, Lebenshaltung, Wohlstandshoffnung in Westdeutschland in den fünfziger Jahren.* Hamburg: Ergebnisse, 1994.

———. "Promise of More: The Rhetorik of (Food) Consumption in a Society Searching for Itself: West Germany in the 1950s." In *Food, Drink and Identity,* edited by Peter Scholliers, 63–80. Oxford: Berg, 2001.

———. *Volksgemeinschaft als Selbstermächtigung. Gewalt gegen Juden in der deutschen Provinz 1919 bis 1939.* Hamburg: Hamburger Edition, 2007.

Wilk, Richard. "The Limits of Discipline: Towards Interdisciplinary Food Studies." *Physiology & Behavior* 107, no. 4 (2012): 471–475.

Williams, John Alexander. *Turning to Nature in Germany: Hiking, Nudism, and Conservation, 1900–1940.* Stanford, CA: Stanford University Press, 2007.

Williamson, Lola. *Transcendent in America: Hindu-Inspired Meditation Movements as New Religion.* New York: New York University Press, 2010.

Wilson, Peter. "Baldness and Modernism." *AA Files* 74 (2017): 3–16.

Wirz, Albert. *Die Moral auf dem Teller.* Zurich: Chronos, 1993.

Wise, Michael D. "Meat." In *The Routledge History of American Foodways,* edited by Michael D. Wise and Jennifer Jensen Wallach, 97–112. New York: Routledge, 2016.

Wit, Wim de. "Building an Illusion: The Design of the World's Columbian Exposition." In *Grand Illusions: Chicago's World's Fair of 1893,* edited by Neil Harris, Wim de Wit, James Gilbert, and Robert W. Rydell, 43–98. Chicago: Chicago Historical Society, 1993.

*Women Members of the Rajya Sabha.* New Delhi: Rajya Sabha, 2003.

Wright, Laura, ed. *The Routledge Handbook of Vegan Studies.* London: Routledge, 2021.

Wujastyk, Dominik. *The Roots of Ayurveda.* London: Penguin, 2003.

Yadav, Bishamber Dayal. "Introduction." In *M. P. T. Acharya: Reminiscences of an Indian Revolutionary,* edited by Bishamber Dayal Yadav, 1–59. New Delhi: Anmol, 1991.

Yamani, Mai. "You Are What You Cook: Cuisine and Class in Mecca." In *A Taste of Thyme: Culinary Cultures of the Middle East,* edited by Sami Zubaida, 173–184. London: Tauris Parke, 2000.

Yeazell, Ruth Bernhard. *Harems of the Mind: Passages of Western Art and Literature.* New Haven, CT: Yale University Press, 2000.

Yellin, Eric Stevens. *Racism in the Nation's Service: Government Workers and the Color Line in Woodrow Wilson's America.* Chapel Hill: University of North Carolina Press, 2013.

Zachariah, Benjamin. *Developing India: An Intellectual and Social History, c. 1930–50.* New Delhi: Oxford University Press, 2005.

———. "Indian Political Activities in Germany, 1914–1945." In *Transcultural Encounters Between Germany and India*, edited by Joanne Miyang Cho, Eric Kurlander, and Douglas T. McGetchin, 141–154. Abingdon, UK: Routledge, 2014.

Zamalin, Alex. *Struggle on Their Minds: The Political Thought of African American Resistance*. New York: Columbia University Press, 2017.

Zerbel, Miriam. *Tierschutz im Kaiserreich: Ein Beitrag zur Geschichte des Vereinswesens*. Frankfurt/Main: Lang, 1993.

———. "Tierschutzbewegung." In *Handbuch zur "Völkischen Bewegung" 1871–1918*, edited by Uwe Puschner, 546–557. Munich: De Gruyter, 1999.

Ziemann, Benjamin. "German Angst? Debating Cold War Anxieties in West Germany, 1945–90." In *Understanding the Imaginary War: Culture, Thought and Nuclear Conflict, 1945–90*, edited by Matthew Grant and Benjamin Ziemann, 116–139. Manchester: Manchester University Press, 2016.

———. "Situating Peace Movements in the Political Culture of the Cold War: Introduction." In *Peace Movements in Western Europe, Japan and the USA During the Cold War*, edited by Benjamin Ziemann, 11–37. Essen: Klartext, 2008.

Zimmermann, Francis. *The Jungle and the Aroma of Meats: An Ecological Theme in Indian Medicine*. Berkeley: University of California Press, 1987.

Zotz, Volker. *Auf den glücklichen Inseln. Buddhismus in der deutschen Kultur*. Berlin: Theseus, 2000.

Zweiniger-Bargielowska, Ina. *Managing the Body: Beauty, Health, and Fitness in Britain, 1880–1939*. Oxford: Oxford University Press, 2011.

# INDEX

Abdullah, Muhammad: 106
Abhedananda (Kaliprasad Chandra), Swami, 81–84; book reviewed in *Vegetarische Warte*, 222n62; perception of "Semitic" religions, 83; West in need of civilizing mission, 83; yoga as linked to vegetarianism, 82–84
Abyssinia, Italian invasion of, 255n211
Acharya, M. P. T., 127, 128, 131
Adams, Carol J., 265–266n69
Adcock, C. S., 40
Adelman, Jeffrey, 9
Age of Aquarius, 143, 264–265n61, 276n169
Agra, 67
Ahmad, H. Mazooruddin, 106
Ahluwalia, Sanjam, 262n8
Ahmadiyya, 111; in Berlin, 108; 111
Ahmedabad, 67
Akbar (Mughal emperor), 42, 213n169
Albrecht, Paul, 115
Alcott, William, 27; founder of Fruitlands, 76
All-India Animal Welfare Association: 158
Alter, Joseph, 6

Ambedkar, Bhimrao Ramji, 157
American Humane Association, 68
American Vegetarian Society, 76, 141
Ammann, David, 94–95, 109
Anagharika Dharmapala (Don David Hewavitarane), 102–103
Anahita, 93
Ankenbrand, Lisbeth, 2, 105–106
Ankenbrand, Ludwig, 2, 3, 13, 102–107, 133, 166; anti-Semitism, 104–107; contacts to South Asians in Germany, 106; member of the Nazi party, 106
Arab Americans, 229n154
Arab-Ottoman foodways: Abbasid food culture, 34; Arab Christians, 35; Bedouin, 34; lower classes, 34; Ottoman palace cuisine, 34; Sufism, 35
Arundale, George Sydney, 156
Arundale, Rukmini Devi, 152, 156–157, 158–159, 160; election into Rajya Sabha, 156–157; honorary patron of All-India Animal Welfare Association, 158; member of Congress for Cultural Freedom, 159; Prevention of Cruelty Against Animals Bill, 158–159

# INDEX

Arya Samaj, 59–66; appropriation of Western science, 47–48, 50, 52–53, 62–63, 65–66, 255n211; Aryanism, 45–46; cooperation of members with Theosophical Society, 39, 44–53, 57–66; eugenics, 255n211; Gurukul Kangri, 130; participation of members in World's Columbian Exposition: 77–78, 96; politics of caste, 203n40; split, 59, 66; stance on Muslims, 47–48, 63–65, 111. *See also* cow protection movement; Dayananda Saraswati; Durga Prasad; Punjab Vegetarian Society
Ashoka, 41, 159
Atlantropa, 146
Aurangzeb, 272n137
Augspurg, Anita, 255n211
Ayurveda, 212n160

Bad Liebenzell, 147–148
Baha'i, 85
Bakr-Id. *See* Id al-Aḍḥa
Ball, Samuel, 193n104
Baltzer, Eduard, 20, 21–22, 98, 104, 184n33
Baness, Theo, 38–39
Barlösius, Eva, 21, 242n98
Barnum, P. T., 74
Bauhaus, 109
Beard, Sidney H., 66, 68
Berghaus, Heinrich, 15–16
Besant, Annie: animal welfare, 257n244; espousal of Hinduism, 138; proclaiming Rukmini Devi World Mother, 154
Bhambra, Gurminder, 18
Bharatiya Jana Sangh, 157–158
Bible, the, 63
Bigalke, Bernadett, 100, 223n75
Bircher-Benner, Maximilian, 181n24
Bivar, Venus, 144
Black Americans, 74, 76–77, 95
Bode, Dastur Framroze Ardeshir, 140; IVU secretary, 141, 154–155
Bose, Subhas Chandra, 106

Blavatsky, Helena Petronvna, 44–46, 47, 208n102; concept of root races, 96, 204n55; conversion to Buddhism, 138; fictitious autobiography, 84–85, 138; position on vivisection, 76, 104
Bodh Gaya, 102
Bombay (Mumbai), 53–57, 67, 154; anti-Muslim violence, 57; cow protection societies, 57; Industrial Assurance Building, 137, 140; Institute of Hotel Management and Catering Technology, 156; J. N. Petit Parsi Orphanage, 54, 55, 140, 263n35; Taj Mahal Hotel, 135, 136; textile industry, 53. *See also* Vegetarian and Natural Living Society
Bombay Humanitarian Fund/League, 66, 67–70, 77, 126–127, 133, 152, 158
Borel, Henri, 121
Brahmo Samaj, 31
Briest, Adolf, 142–144, 150, 161; as admirer of Gandhi, 142–143; appeal for founding vegetarian settlement, 142–143; Aryanism, 143; interest in Mazdaznan, 144; promotion of raw foods, 142
Britain, vegetarianism in, 1, 2, 4–5, 12, 15–29, 66–67; Aryanism, 12, 70–71, 165; attitude toward Muslims, 27; class, 12, 19, 21, 23, 23, 26, 29; emergence, 4–5, 18–23; evangelicalism, 18; Greek antiquity as model, 26; human anatomy, 25–26; "India"/Hinduism as model, 3, 5, 8, 12, 23–29, 36, 52–53, 66, 71, 165, 169, 214n187; industrialization, 18–20; meat provoking "animal instincts" in humans, 7, 21, 22, 66–67; racism, 23; raw foods, 215–216n207; use of caste, 28; vegetarian settlement colonies, 23. *See also* Order of the Golden Age; *Vegetarian Messenger*; Vegetarian Society
British colonialism in India, and purported non-involvement in religious matters, 47

# INDEX

Buchman, Frank, 275n161
Buddhism, 3, 28, 41, 44, 126
Buddhist reform movement, 11, 78, 98, 102–107; Aryanism/anti-Semitism, 3, 13, 37, 101, 102–107; cow protection, 234n18; influenced by Theosophy and Protestantism, 102, 235n22; vegetarianism, 102, 184n33
Bulgaria, 116, 244n117, 269n103
Burton, Antoinette, 137
Byron, George Gordon (Lord Byron), 192n90

Calcutta, 50–53, 130; Kalighat temple, 129, 131; Lal Bazaar: 52
Calcutta Society for the Prevention of Cruelty Against Animals (CSPCA), 51; stereotyping of *goalas* (cowherds and milkmen), 51
Calcutta Vegetarian Society, 51–53
Cambridge, University of, 107
Canton, 193n104
Capri, 236n41
Carter, Julian B., 86
Ceylon: as central to the Buddhist revival, 3, 102–106; as destination of the Ankenbrand travel group, 3
Chamars, cooperation with Arya Samaj, 203n40
Chamberlain, Houston Stewart, 93
Chatterji, S. C., 69
Chavkin, Nathan, 118
Chicago, 72–81, 84–97, 135; Union Stockyards, 74
China, 244n117
Cholkar, M., 259n269
Christian Science, 81
Coptic Christians, 149
Christians, Indian, 68
Christians, Orthodox, 35, 149, 196–197n138, 199n162
Church of Latter-Day Saints (Mormons), 86
Cold War, 145, 153–162
Cologne, 97, 144
Congress for Cultural Freedom, 159

Conrad, Sebastian, 9–10
Cooper, William Earnshaw, 67
cow protection movement, 38–40, 44, 46–48, 164, 166; anti-British, 44, 47, 50; anti-Muslim, 1–3, 12, 38, 40, 47–48, 50, 57, 64; appropriation of Western science, 47–48, 50, 169, 170; cow shelters (*goshalas/gosadans*), 42, 48, 158; expression of secularism, 40; indigenous phenomenon, 40, publications of, 1, 38–39; societies, 3, 38; suggestions for improving cattle breeds, 49; women as role models, 63–64. *See also* Arya Samaj; Indian vegetarianism

Dagover, Lil, 148
Dailey, Jane, 96
Darré, Richard Walther, 250n161
Datta, Narendranath. *See* Swami Vivekananda
Davidoff, Leonore, 152
Degersheim, 112
Desai, Sapur Faredun, 139–140
Desai, Trimbakrai, 67
Dessau, Kaj, 263n43
Deutsche Gesellschaft für Lebensreform, 109, 116, 117
Deutscher Orden, 143–144
Deutscher Vegetarierbund (German Vegetarian Union), 243n114
Dieffenbach, Karl Wilhelm, 236n41
Doniger, Wendy, 46
Donnershag, 143–144
Douglass, Frederick, 74, 76
Doukhobors, 120
Durga, 83–84, 222n74
Durga Prasad, 59–66, 78, 97

East India Company, 193n104
Ecker-Lauer, Elisabeth, 151–152
Egypt: Esperanto movement in, 149; foodways in, 34–35, 149–150, 199n162; as model to German vegetarians, 18, 23, 32, 33–36, 149–50, 165
Ellis, Havelock, 226n121

Engels, Friedrich, 20
entangled history: and disconnections, 10–11, 168–169; as methodological approach, 9–11
Ertel, Dieter, 150
Esperanto, 99, 149; vegetarianism: 231–232n1, 249–250n159
Europeans in India, as sympathetic towards vegetarianism in India, 3

fasting, 57–58, 87, 91, 93, 108, 112, 117, 122, 124, 130; in Coptic and Orthodox Churches, 35
Fidus (Hugo Höppener), 143; membership in Nazi party, 143
Fischer-Tiné, Harald, 100
First World War, 39, 49, 98, 100, 105, 127, 198n152, 229–230n163, 239n64, 250n161
Fliedner, Theodor, 33
Förster, Bernhard, 104
Förster, Georg, 114–118, 125, 133
Förster, Paul, 104; at World's Columbian Exposition, 76
Foucault, Michel, 169
French Revolution, 25–26
Franklin, Benjamin, 25
Frantzen, Heinrich, 144
Freitag, Sandria, 40
Freudenstadt, 148
Frick, Wilhelm, 110
Fritzen, Florentine, 100

Gandhi, Leela, 7
Gandhi, Mohandas Karamchand, 6, 7, 9, 13, 37, 97, 98, 99, 100, 101, 119–123, 125, 128, 130, 131, 142–143, 156, 159, 170, 231n178, 232n3; concept of (triple) swaraj, 121; considered the ideal ascetic leader in Weimar Germany, 109, 114, 115, 116, 118, 132, 165, 240n78; eugenics, 255n211; meat consumption, 203n38; vaccination, 164; views on sexuality, 123–124, 255n211
Ganz, Ernst, 149
Garvey, Marcus, 264–265n61
Gasque, Gloria (Maude), 91, 134, 148, 150–152; activities in India, 13, 134–142, 167; classes on food in India, 136–137; motherly role as racist, 137, 138, 141; move to California, 141; president of International Vegetarian Union, 13, 85, 141–142, 152, 154; views on eugenics, 137, 167
Gault, Arthur Fitzroy, 136
German Catholicism, 184n33, 195n24
German Democratic Republic (GDR), 266n73
Germany, vegetarianism in, 3, 6, 8, 9, 11, 12, 13, 23, 98; 1848 revolution, 19, 29–30; anti-Semitism/Aryanism, 31, 101–107, 117, 132, 135, 142–144, 145–146, 159, 165, 167, 170; Buddhism rather than Hinduism as model, 37; class, 12, 19, 21, 23; connections to British and U.S. vegetarian movement, 98; contacts to vegetarians from/in India: 101, 125–132, 161; emergence, 4–5, 18–23; human anatomy, 30; image of Muslims, 33; meat provoking "animal instincts" in humans, 7, 21, 22, 32, 112; organic farming, 144; "Orient" as model, 12, 29–34, 36, 73, 85, 111, 165; pacifism, 13, 99, 104, 113, 114, 115, 117–118, 125–132, 145–147; perception of "India," 3, 29–32, 37, 99–100, 101, 114–118, 165, 169; relations with International Vegetarian Union, 116, 118, 133, 141, 144, 150, 151; role of Esperanto movement, 99; theories of climate, 15–17; vegetarian settlement colonies, 23, 104, 142–144
Ghadar Party, 58
Ghazali, al-, 34
Ghobrial, Jean-Paul, 9
Glover, William, 58
Godse, Nathuram, 130
Gokhale, D. V., 161
Golwalkar, M. S., 274n154
Gostling, David, 54; vice-president of the Punjab Vegetarian Society, 61
Gostling, Sarah: 54; vice-president of the Punjab Vegetarian Society, 61
Göttingen, University of, 113
Graham, Sylvester, 76

INDEX

Greece, 33, 165
Günther, Hans F. K., 237n49
Gujarat, 53, 54

hadith, 199n163
Hall, Catherine, 152
Hanisch, Otto (Otto Hanish, Otoman Zar Adusht Ha'nish), 73, 84–96, 108, 136, 137, 138, 151, 165, 262–263n34; birth in Silesia, 86; membership in Church of Latter-Day Saints, 86. *See also* Mazdaznan
*Harbinger, The* (newspaper), 62–66
Haynes, Douglas, 255n211
Hedayat, Sadeq, 240n73
Hentschel, Willibald, 265n66
Herzog, Dagmar, 265–266n69
Heymann, Lida Gustava, 255n211
Hiller, Geo, 161
Hirschfeld, Magnus, 226n121, 256n229
Hitler, Adolf, 110, 114, 116, 118, 165, 265n66; perception in India, 116, 127, 133
Hodann, Max, 245n123
Hodges, Sarah, 262n28
Hormudji, Pestonji Sorabji, 64
Horniman, Benjamin Guy, 67
Hübbe-Schleiden, Wilhelm, 209n97
Hufeland, Christoph Wilhelm, 18, 29
Hume, Allan Octavian, 39, 48–50, contact with Vegetarian Society, 49; membership in Theosophical Society, 49; suggestions for improving cattle breeds, 49; vegetarianism, 49; vice-president of the Punjab Vegetarian Society: 61

Id al-Aḍha (Muslim feast of sacrifice), 47, 64, 272n138
Inayat Khan, 111, 240–241n79
India: dependence on foreign food aid after independence, 153; Five-Year Plans, 158; Hindu Code Bill, 157; marketing of meat, 153; Prevention of Cruelty Against Animals Bill, 158–159
India, vegetarianism in: *ahiṃsa* (non-violence), 41, 81, 154, 155, 157, 160; animal sacrifice: 26, 79, 83, 84, 128–131, 167, 201n20; anti-colonialism, 5, 6, 12, 39, 40, 44, 47, 65, 69–70, 156–157; Aryanism, 12, 42, 50, 70–71, 165, 170; Bhagavad Gita, 43, 52, 69, 71, 94; caste, 1, 5, 12, 14, 39, 41–44, 45, 51, 56, 66–69, 71, 76, 81–84, 125–132, 154–157, 165, 201n23, 202n37, 214n187, 216n209, 229n156; Code of Manu, 41, 52, 63, 69, 71, 94, 229n156; cow/dairy products, 1, 38, 42, 43, 44, 56, 201n23; eggs, 42, 60, 130; garlic and onions, 42, 43, 109; meat provoking "animal instincts" in humans, 1–3, 43, 52–53, 83; perception of Muslims, 5, 8, 14, 38, 40, 41, 42–43, 44, 45, 47–48, 50, 57, 63, 64–65, 69, 70–71, 127, 130–131, 135, 139, 154, 156–157, 158–159, 170, 171, 202n31, 216n209; stereotyping of *goalas* (cowherds and milkmen), 51, 56; three *guṇas* (temperaments), 52, 69, 111, 208n100, 229n156, 264n51; use of Western science, 8, 12, 39, 40, 47–48, 50, 52, 56; 63–64, 68–70, 83, 155. *See also* Arya Samaj; Bombay Humanitarian Fund/League; Calcutta Vegetarian Society; cow protection movement; Punjab Vegetarian Society; Vegetarian and Natural Living Society; vegetarianism
Indian Independence Committee, Berlin, 127
Indian Multipurpose Food, 155
Indian National Congress, 38, 49, 54, 130, 153
International Vegetarian Union (IVU), 10, 85, 117–118, 134, 135; Fifteenth World Vegetarian Congress in India, 3, 14, 135, 141, 152–162, 167–168; foundation of in Leipzig, 13, 98, 104; German exit during Nazi rule, 117, 135; German re-entry, 135; India's membership, 15; Mazdaznan's role, 87, 91; pacifism, 150–152; women's role, 134, 150–159

INDEX

Internationaler Sozialistischer Kampfbund (ISK), 113–114; anti-colonialism, 114; promotion of vegetarianism, 113–114. *See also* Nelson, Leonard; Specht, Minna

Internationaler Verein zur Bekämpfung der wissenschaftlichen Tierfolter, 76, 104

Iran: 1906 revolution in, 107; and new masculinity, 107

Iranschähr, Hossein Kazemzadeh. *See* Kazemzadeh, Hossein

Irish potato famine, 19

Isbert, Otto Albrecht, 276n169

Itten, Johannes, 109

Jacobins, 25

Jains, 39, 41–42, 44, 50, 51, 53, 67, 68, 70, 71, 89, 123, 154, 155, 160, 165, 169, 170, 171; non-rejection of donated meat by ascetics, 201n21

Japan, beef consumption and nationalism in, 5

Jazairi, Abd al-Qadir al-, 85

Jesus, 93

Jha, Dwijendra Narayan, 46

Jones, Kenneth, 40

Jones, William, 31

Jonker, Gerdien, 110

Junagadh, 67, 214n192

Just, Adolf, 231n178, 255n209

Kali, 222n74; and animal sacrifice, 79, 129, 201n20

Kalighat temple. *See* Calcutta

Kalyan, 129, 130

Kazemzadeh, Hossein, 13, 101, 107–112, 133, 146–147, 149, 151, 166; Berlin Ahmadiyya community, 108; Berlin Sufi Lodge, 111; Ecole Mystique Esotérique, 112; Iranschähr journal, 108; National Committee for the Liberation of Iran, 107–108; notion of eugenics, 243n110; pacifism, 147; perception of Mazdaznan, 108–112, 151, 166–167; Theosophical Society, 111; translation of Gathas, 109; views on sexuality, 112. *See also* Iranschähr, Hossein Kazemzadeh

Kayastahs, 41, 59, 79, 158

Kayastha Temperance Society, 59

Kellogg, John Harvey, 62, 76; vice-president of the Punjab Vegetarian Society, 61, 181n24

Khairallah, Ibrāhīm Jirjis, 85

Khan, Razak, 100

Khunni Lal Shastri, 63

Kidwai, Rafi Ahmad, 159

Kiehne, Oswald, 143–144, 161

Killingley, Dermot, 80

Kingsford, Anna, 23, 47; image of Buddhism, 28; views on caste, 28

Klein, Jacob, 5

Koura, al-, 35

Krafft-Ebing, Richard, 226n121

Krishna, 64

Kshatriyas, 41, 203n40

Kuehne, Louis, 231n178, 255n209

Kühl, Stefan, 96

Lago Maggiore, 148

Lahore, 58–66, 67, 130, 161

Lala Jinda Ram, 77–78

Laughlin, H. H., 139

Laxmidas, Labshankar, 67, 133

*Leib und Leben* (journal), 109–110, 117

Leipzig: center of "international" organized vegetarianism, 13, 75–76, 98; hub of natural healing, 231n178; role in Buddhist revival, 98, 103–104

Lele, P. R., 153

Lewicka, Paulina, 34

Liebau, Heike, 100

London, 57, 67, 74, 80, 81, 97, 124, 126, 127, 135, 136

London Vegetarian Society, 61, 66, 67, 68

Lust, Benedict, 231n178

Maarri, Abu al-Ala al-, 35

Mahabharata, 41, 63

Maha Bodhi Society, 102

Malabari, Behramji, 54

Malhotra, Anshu, 262n28

Mama, Nanabhoy F., 140

# INDEX

Manchester: Bombay compared to, 53; as hub of industrialization, 20
*Mandaras Wanderungen* (novel), 20, 30–34;
Mankar, Jayantilal N., 152, 158
Manjapra, Kris, 23, 100
Marchand, Suzanne, 100
martial races, 211n141
Mary, Virgin, 93
Masani, Ervad Phiroze Shahpuri, 56
Masarrah, Gerasimos, 35
Mashruwala, K. G., 131
Mazdaznan, 13, 73, 84–96, 97, 98, 108–112, 133, 134, 144, 148, 149, 166, 184n33; Aryanism, notion of, 73, 85, 89, 92–96, 110, 136, 137, 166, 229–230n163; claim to restore Zoroastrianism, 85, 92–96, 140; contacts to Bombay Parsis, 13, 96, 134–142; connections to International Vegetarian Union, 85; Germany, 85, 87; in India, 134–142; influenced by Brahmin dietetics, 152; influenced by Friedrich Nietzsche, 85–86; influenced by Jain dietetics, 89; influenced by New Thought, 86–88; influenced by Theosophical Society, 84–85, 89, 97, 138, 140; influenced by World's Columbian Exposition, 86–87; influenced by yoga, 13, 87–89, 90–91, 140, influenced by Zoroastrianism, 85–86, 92–96; influence on vegetarianism, 87; Mazdaznan Women's Federation, 151–152; "Orient" as model, 13, 85, 87–89, 91, 92–96, 165; pacifism, 150–152; perception of Buddhism, 93, 95, 96; propagation of nudism, 91; protests against ban in Germany, 136; racial/spiritual evolution, 86–96, 109–110, 138, 155; role of women, 91, 134–142, 150–152; scandals, 89, 90, 91, 112; sexuality, 89–91; in Switzerland, 85, 87, 109, 110; teachings on breathing, 87–89. *See also* Ammann, David; Bode, Dastur Framroze Ardehir; Gasque, Gloria; Hanisch, Otto; Itten, Johannes; Mama, Nanabhoy F.; Wadia, A. S.

meat: consumption in India, 39, 41–44, 47, 50–51, 184n32, 202n37, 220n42; deemed healthy, 4, 184n32; growing importance of in diets, 4; halal slaughter, 158–159; *shehita* (Jewish ritual slaughter), 104, 118, 170; signifier of alleged racial superiority, 4; signifier of masculinity, 4, 39, 43; signifier of progress, 17, 43
meatpacking: Chicago as center, 4, 74, 75–76; conditions of workers, 4; food adulteration, 4; livestock diseases, 4
Megalli, Tadros, 149–150
Mehta, Phirozeshah: 54
Menon, Kalyani Devaki, 164
Midgley, Clare, 152
Miles, Eustace, 66
Mittra, Peary Chand, 51
Molenaar, Heinrich, 145–146, 147
Montesquieu, Charles Baron de la Brède et de: influence of climate on alimentary patterns, 16; Lettres Persanes, 31
Moonje, B. S., 259n269
Moral Re-Armament, 275n161
Mughals, 27, 42, 58–59; Hindu nationalist perceptions of, 1, 5, 213n169
Muhammad, Elijah, 170
Mukhul, Akshaya, 274n154
Muller, Henrietta, 61
Müller, Max, 31, 46
Munshi, K. M., 155–156
Munshi, Lilavati, 154, 155–156, 157; member of Congress for Cultural Freedom, 159; perception of British colonialism, 156–157; perception of Islam, 156–157
Mussolini, Benito, 125, 167, 246n132

*nahda* (Arab awakening), 239n70
Narain, Pandit Gosavak Jagat, 38
Naturfreunde, 120
Nazi regime: abolition of Mazdaznan, 109–110; alimentary politics, 109, 116–117, 132–133; Berlin Olympics, 148; persecution of vegetarians, 113, 133; re-organization of life reform movement, 109, 113, 116, 117

Nehru, Jawaharlal, 153, 274n154
Nelson, Leonard, 113–114; commitment to animal rights and vegetarianism, 113; notion of leadership, 113–114; rejection of Nazism, 113; views on democracy, 113; views on sexuality, 113–114. *See also* Internationaler Sozialistischer Kampfbund
*Neuleben* (journal), 114, 245n129
Neumann, Christoph, 34
neurasthenia, 88
Ney, Elly, 148, 245–246n130
New Thought, 81, 85, 219n28, 222n74; resonance in South Asia, 224n94
Nicholson, George, 26–27
Nietzsche, Friedrich, 85–86, 169
Norway, 216n209
Notovitch, Nicolai Alexandrovitch, 93
Nueva Germania, 104
Nyanatiloka (Anton Floris Gueth), 103

Olcott, Henry Steel: 44–46
Oldfield, Josiah, 62; member of the Order of the Golden Age, 66–67; vice-president of the Punjab Vegetarian Society, 61; visitor to the World's Columbian Exposition, 76
Oneida, New York, 226–227n123
Order of the Golden Age, 66–70
Oswald, John, 25–26, 27, 28, 205n68
O'Toole, Therese, 40
Otter, Chris, 4

Palestine, 149, 249–250n159
Palladius, 23–24
Palmer, Edward (Veeraswamy), 230n172
Pandey, Byramji, 54, 57; Pure Food and Temperance Society, 54
Pandey, Gyanendra, 40
Paraguay, 104
Paris, 57
Parsis: 1, 13, 39, 41, 44, 50, 51, 53–57, 68, 70; Aryanism, 139; cow protection, 138–139; esotericism (Ilm-e Khshnoom), 140; eugenics, 139–140; Navjote ceremony, 140; Parsi reform, 53, 56–57, 138–139;

proselytizing, 140, 141; vegetarianism, 56–57, 139, 263n35, 224n85. *See also* Zoroastrianism
Parsi Vegetarian and Temperance Society, 56, 139
Patāñjali, 80–81
Patel, Kiran Klaus, 96
Periyar, 157
Pernau, Margit, 169
Petit, Sir Dinshaw, 57
Philhellenism, 192n90
Poona, 161
Porphyry, 23–24
Prasad, Rajendra, 154, 155, 157, 158; honorary patron of All-India Animal Welfare Association, 158; perception of Islam, 158; vegetarianism as a means of preventing nuclear war, 158
Purinton, Edward Earle, 224n94
Prussia, vegetarianism in. *See* Germany, vegetarianism in
Punjab Vegetarian Society, 57–66, 77, 78, 97; *The Harbinger*, 62–66. *See also* Arya Samaj; Durga Prasad
Pythagoras, 190–191n59

Rajas, 41
Rall, Hellmuth Th. K., 144–145; 147–150; vegetarian conventions, 147–150
Ravi Varma Press, 1, 2
Ray, Utsa, 6
Roy, Parama, 6, 41, 79
Ramakrishna, 79
Ramakrishna Mission, 80, 81–84, 141
Ramayana, 41
Randeria, Shalini, 9–10
Rashtriya Swayamsevak Sangh, 157–158, 274n154
Reill, Wilhelm, 33
Renan, Ernest, 93
Rinderpest, 47, 51
Rindlisbacher, Stefan, 125
Ritter, Carl, 31
Robinson, Cedric, 23
Rolland, Romain, 124
Rosicrucians, 264–265n61
Roy, Parama, 6, 41, 79

# INDEX

Roy, Ram Mohun, 31
Rudd, Geoffrey, 157
Russia, 98, 107, 120, 153, 170

Said, Edward, 91, 192–193n91
Sale, George, 197n142
Salt Lake City, 86
Salzer, Leopold, 51–53, 61, 64, 83, 88–89, 138
Samanta, Samiparna, 40, 51
Sarada Devi, 83–84
Saraswati, Swami Dayananda, 45–46, 47–48, 50, 52, 53. *See also* Arya Samaj, cow protection
Savarkar, Vinayak Damodar, 130
Sayaji Rao Gaekwad III, 70
Savitri Devi (Maximiani Julia Portas), 133; attitude towards Muslims, 259n269
Scheib, Ria, 126, 127–128, 256n231
Schlegel, August Wilhelm and Friedrich, 31
Schoenenberger, Walter, 148
Schopenhauer, Artur, 103, 126
Schwantje, Magnus, 13, 125–132, 133, 167; anti-racism, 127; anti-speciecism, 126; exile in Switzerland, 126–132; interest in Buddhism, 126; pacifism, 125–126; views on sexuality, 126
Seager, Richard, 78
Second World War, 116–118, 120, 125, 126, 133, 140, 147, 167, 243n108, 250n161
Sen, Keshub Chandra (founder of Naya Vidhan), 79, 80
Shah, Mohan K., 126
Shaked, Saul, 261–262n24
Shaktism, 83
Sharma, Ram Chandra, 125, 126, 167; perception of Buddhism, 131; protests against animal sacrifice, 128–131; views on Muslims, 130–131; views on Nazi Germany, 131
Shelley, Percy Bysshe, 25, 192n90, 192–193n91, 195–196n127
Shidyaq, Faris al-, 186n2
Shraddhanand, Swami, 130
Shriners, 85, 269n105

Siddhu Ram, 77–78
Siegel, Benjamin, 153
Sinclair, Upton, 86
Singleton, Mark, 80
Sinha, Mrinalini, 6
Slate, Nico, 6, 7
slavery, and nutrition, 23, 29, 187n12
Smith, John, 28
Sommer, Walter, 132, 250n161
Somnath, 272n137
Sontraer Gesundheitsbote, 161
Sörgel, Hermann, 146
Sozialistische Partei Deutschlands (German Social Democratic Party), 244n122
Specht, Minna, 113–114
Sperling, Erich, 117
Srinivas, M. N., 44
Stockham, Alice Bunker: author of Karezza, 90–91, 112, 123, 226n117; first female gynecologist in the United States, 77; member of Theosophical Society and vegetarian, 77; participation in International Vegetarian Congress at World's Columbian Exposition, 77
Stoler, Ann-Laura, 137
Struve, Amalie, 20–21
Struve, Gustav, 20, 29–34, 37, 165; British vegetarianism, 196n128. *See also Mandaras Wanderungen* (Struve)
Stuart, Tristram, 24
Südwestdeutscher Rundfunk, 150
Sufism, 165; "animal"/carnal soul (*nafs hayyawanī*) vs. spiritual soul (*rūḥ*), 35, 199n159, 243n104; attitude toward animals, 267n82; fasting, 35; influence on yoga, 221n48; vegetarianism, 35. *See also* Inayat Khan; Kazemzadeh, Hossein
swastika: as symbol of Buddhism, 3; as symbol of the German *völkisch* movement, 3
Switzerland, 6, 9, 11, 13, 30, 76, 85, 87, 90, 96, 98, 100, 110, 112, 113, 118–132, 136, 149, 166

Symanzick, Minna, 105
Syria, 165

tantra, left-hand path (*vamachara*), 31, 220n42
Tarboush, 85, 149
Theosophical Society, 37, 39, 44–57, 59, 77, 78, 83, 84–85, 98, 102, 104, 127, 137–138, 156, 165, 184n33, 264–265n61; animal welfare, 158–159, 208n101, 257n244; California, 141; concept of "root races," 138, 199–200n164; evolutionary theory, 44, 138, 155; Indian members, 44–45, 51, 59; shared message of "World Religions," 44. *See also* Arundale, Rukmini Devi; Besant, Annie; Blavatsky, Helena Petrovna; Hume, Allan Octavian; Olcott, Henry Steel; Salzer, Leopold
Thoreau, Henry David, 77
Todd-Ferrier, John, 67
Tolstoy, Leo, 57, 98, 170, 211n141, 232n3
Torbov, Zeko, 244n117
transcendentalism, American, 80
Treitel, Corinna, 21, 100, 116
Tryon, Thomas, 24–25
Turkey, 165

Umrao Singh Sher-Gil of Majithia, 57–62
United Nations, 152
United States of America, 15; food aid to India after independence, 153; vegetarianism in, 3, 4, 5, 6, 8, 9, 10, 11, 13, 15, 20, 30, 50, 61, 63, 71, 72, 73, 76–98, 181n24

vaccination, 54, 104, 116, 145, 146, 164, 253–254n197
Vaishnavism, 83
Vedas, 1, 31, 41, 45, 46, 62, 63
veganism, as term, 277n1
Vegetarian and Natural Living Society (Bombay), 54–57, 61, 139, 263n35
Vegetarian Federal Union, 54, 66, 97, 98

*Vegetarian Messenger* (journal): attitude towards Hindus, 27–28; on foodways in North Africa and West Asia, 33
Vegetarian Society (Britain), 20, 21, 22, 27, 37, 49, 54, 57, 61, 62, 66, 67, 68, 75, 76, 157, 161
vegetarians, European: anti-Semitism, 8, 12; and purity, 12; sympathy toward vegetarianism in India, 3, 5, 8, 12
*Vegetarische Presse* (journal), 113, 114–118; pacifist tendencies, 114; perception of Nazism, 115–118; positions on military service and the Second World War, 117–118; racism, 116, 118; views on political leadership, 114–118;
*Vegetarisches Universum* (journal), 145–150
*Vegetarische Warte* (journal), 109, 114
Versailles Treaty, 116; and racism in Germany, 116
Vienna Congress of 1814–1815, 192n90
Vivekananda, Swami (Narendranath Datta), 79–81, 82, 84, 88, 89, 96, 102, 137; authority on yoga in the United States, 80–81; dietary recommendations, 79–81; as founder of Ramakrishna Mission, 80; influenced by American transcendentalism, 80; influenced by Social Darwinism, 80; use of evolutionary theory, 81; West in need of civilizing mission, 79
Vogtherr, Heinrich, 146, 147
Völkisch movement (Völkische Bewegung), 3, 108, 132, 142–144

Wadia, A. S., 136, 141
Wagner, Richard, 103
Wandervogel, 120
Washington, Booker T., 170
Wedderburn, William, 49
Wedemeyer-Kolwe, Bernd, 100
Wei, Si-Luan, 244n117
Weininger, Otto, 226n121
*Weltharmonie* (journal), 112

## INDEX

Wells, Ida B., 74
Wildenthal, Lora, 96, 137
Williamson, Lola, 80
Wilson, Woodrow, 227n137
World's Columbian Exposition: Orientalism, 74–75; Parliament of Religions, 72, 78–79, 102, 166; racism, 74–75; vegetarianism, 13, 50, 62, 71, 72–81
world wars. *See* First World War; Second World War

Yashodha, 64
yoga: Aryanism in German postwar yoga scene, 161–162; entanglement with Sufism, 221n48; hatha Yoga, 80, 221n49; hatha yogis as ostracized, 80; linked to vegetarianism in the West, 13, 72, 80–84; sexual abstinence, 80; subordinate role of the body in Vivekananda's yoga in the United States, 80
Young Bengal, 51

Zend-Avesta, 63, 95
Zimmermann, Werner, 13, 133, 147, 167; championing of Gandhi, 13, 118–125; fasting, 121–122; international travel, 119–120; nudism, 123; perception of fascism, 125, 167; perception of Taoism, 121; translation of Stockham's Karezza, 123; views on sexuality, 121, 122–124, 265n65
Zimmermann, Wilhelm, 32
Zoroastrianism, 108, 109; Anahita, 93; animal sacrifice, 261–262n24; cows, 261n24; influence on Mazdaznan, 85–86; perception of Muslims, 210n130; slaughter, 261–262n24. *See also* Parsis

GPSR Authorized Representative: Easy Access System Europe, Mustamäe tee 50, 10621 Tallinn, Estonia, gpsr.requests@easproject.com

www.ingramcontent.com/pod-product-compliance
Lightning Source LLC
Chambersburg PA
CBHW022028290426
44109CB00014B/785